Consumer Behaviour

Buying, Having, and Being

Michael R. Solomon
Auburn University

Judith L. Zaichkowsky
Simon Fraser University

Rosemary Polegato
Mount Allison University

Prentice Hall Canada Inc.
Scarborough, Ontario

Canadian Cataloguing in Publication Data

Soloman, Michael R.,
    Consumer behaviour: buying, having, and being

Canadian ed.
Includes index.
ISBN 0-13-758707-4

1. Consumer behaviour. I. Polegato, Rosemary. II. Title.
III. Title.

HF5415.32.S64 1999   658.8''342   C97-932750-4

 © 1999 Prentice-Hall Canada Inc., Scarborough, Ontario
A Division of Simon & Schuster/A Viacom Company

Prentice-Hall, Inc., Upper Saddle River, New Jersey
Prentice-Hall International (UK) Limited, London
Prentice-Hall of Australia, Pty. Limited, Sydney
Prentice-Hall Hispanoamericana, S.A., Mexico City
Prentice-Hall of India Private Limited, New Delhi
Prentice-Hall of Japan, Inc., Tokyo
Simon & Schuster Southeast Asia Private Limited, Singapore
Editora Prentice-Hall do Brasil, Ltda., Rio de Janeiro

ISBN: 0-13-758707-4

Publisher: Pat Ferrier
Acquisitions Editor: Mike Ryan
Developmental Editor: Amber Wallace
Senior Marketing Manager: Ann Byford
Production Editor: Andrew Winton
Copy Editor: John Sweet

Production Coordinator: Jane Schell
Permissions/Photo Research: Susan Wallace-Cox
Cover Design: Julia Hall
Cover Image: Masterfile/G. Biss
Page Layout: Phyllis Seto

Original English Language edition published by Prentice-Hall, Inc., Upper Saddle River, New Jersey
Copyright ©1996, 1994, 1992.

1 2 3 4 5   02 01 00 99 98

Printed and bound in the United States of America

Visit the Prentice Hall Canada Web site! Send us your comments, browse our catalogues, and more at
www.phcanada.com. Or reach us through e-mail at **phcinfo_pubcanada@prenhall.com**.

All cases in the book were prepared as a basis for class discussion rather than to illustrate either
effective or ineffective handling of an administrative situation.

Chapter Opening Photo Credits: p. 4, Courtesy of Tony Freeman/PhotoEdit; p. 46, Oliverio Toscani for BENETTON; p. 76, Agence France Presse/Corbis-Bettman; p. 112, Adidas Canada Limited; p. 142, Reproduced by Special Permission of *Playboy* magazine. Copyright © 1994 by Playboy; p. 176, © Laima Druska/Stock Boston; p. 216, Courtesy of Judy Zaichkowsky; p. 246, Courtesy of PETA; p. 284, Dick Hemingway; p. 320, Courtesy of Michael Newman/PhotoEdit; p. 356, Courtesy of Harley-Davidson Motor Company; p. 390, Courtesy of Hublein, Inc.; p. 428, Courtesy of Jaguar Cars Inc.; p. 462, Courtesy of Canadian Airlines and Gee, Jeffery & Partners; p. 498, Copyright © 1991 by General Media Inc.; p. 526, Dick Hemingway; p. 550, Agence France Presse/Corbis-Bettman.

Brief Contents

Contents

Michael R. Solomon is Human Sciences Professor of Consumer Behaviour in The Department of Consumer Affairs at Auburn University. Before joining Auburn in 1995, Professor Solomon was Chairman of the Department of Marketing in the School of Business at Rutgers University, New Brunswick, New Jersey. Prior to that appointment, he was a member of the faculty of the Graduate School of Business Administration at New York University. Professor Solomon earned B.A. degrees in Psychology and Sociology at Brandeis University and an M.A. and a Ph.D. in Sociology at Brandeis University and an M.A. Social Psychology at The University of North Carolina at Chapel Hill.

Professor Solomon's primary research interests include consumer behaviour and lifestyle issues, the symbolic aspects of products, the psychology of fashion and image, and services marketing. He has published many articles on these and related topics in academic journals. He is an Editorial Board Member of the *Journal of Consumer Research*, the *Journal of Retailing*, and *Psychology & Marketing*.

Professor Solomon received the first Cutty Sark Men's Fashion Award in 1981 for his research on the psychological aspects of clothing. He is the editor of *The Psychology of Fashion* and coeditor of *The Service Encounter: Managing Employee/Customer Interaction in Services Businesses*, both published in 1985 by Lexington Books.

Professor Solomon is also a frequent contributor to mass media. His feature articles have appeared in *Psychology Today, Gentleman's Quarterly*, and *Savvy*. He has been quoted in numerous national magazines and newspapers, including *Allure, Elle, Glamour, Mademoiselle, Mirabella, Newsweek, The New York Times Magazine, Self, USA Today*, and *The Wall Street Journal*. He has been a guest on "The Today Show," "Good Morning America," CNBC, Whittle Communications' Channel One, "Newsweek on the Air," "Inside Edition," and National Public Radio.

Professor Solomon has provided input to a variety of organizations on issues related to consumer behaviour. He has been a consultant to such companies as the Celanese Corporation, Levi Strauss & Company, Johnson & Johnson, Kayser-Roth, United Airlines, and Hakuhodo Advertising (Tokyo). He is also in demand as a speaker to many business groups on consumer behaviour and marketing topics. He lives with his wife, Gail; their three children, Amanda, Zachary, and Alexandra; and Chloe, their golden retriever, in Auburn, Alabama.

Judy Zaichkowsky is a Professor of Marketing at the Faculty of Business Administration at Simon Fraser University. Before joining SFU, Professor Zaichkowsky was at the American University in Washington, D.C. Professor Zaichkowsky started her career studying consumers while doing a Bachelor of Home Economics at the University of British Columbia. She then went on to earn a Master of Science in Consumer Studies at the University of Guelph. There she met her co-author Rosemary Polegato and they have been fast friends ever since. In 1979, Professor Zaichkowsky left Canada to earn a Ph.D. in Management at the University of California, Los Angeles. There she majored in Marketing, with minor concentrations in Psychology and Statistics.

Professor Zaichkowsky is widely known for her research on consumer involvement. Her articles dealing with the conceptualization and measurement of involvement are globally cited and are used as benchmark reading in many doctoral seminars. More recently she has authored a book on "Brand Imitation" which deals with the consumer and trademark infringement issues. She continues to do research and publish in the brand imitation area.

Professor Zaichkowsky is on the editorial review board for the *Journal of Advertising* and the *Journal of Promotion Management*. She is listed in *Who's Who of Canada* and *Canadian Women*. She lives in Vancouver and enjoys playing golf with her finance colleagues, although she rarely gets in a game.

Rosemary Polegato is Associate Professor of Commerce in the Faculty of Social Sciences at Mount Allison University. Before joining Mount Allison in 1994, Professor Polegato taught at St. Francis Xavier University, University of Guelph, University of Toronto, and The University of Western Ontario. She has taught numerous courses in the areas of Business Administration and Consumer Studies, including consumer behaviour (since 1976), marketing research, services and non-profit marketing, marketing management, international marketing, and policy. Professor Polegato earned a B.Sc. (H.E.) from St. Francis Xavier University, an M.Sc. from the University of Guelph, and an M.B.A. and Ph.D. from the Ivey Business School at The University of Western Ontario.

Professor Polegato is particularly interested in family decision making, diffusion of innovations (including information technology), non-profit marketing, and the effective use of computer technology in teaching. She has published academic articles in these areas, and presents workshops to various audiences. Her publications appear in *The Journal of Consumer Affairs*, *Business Quarterly*, and *Journal of Food Products Marketing*, as well as textbooks and published proceedings of several associations. She lives in Sackville, New Brunswick with her spouse Richard; their teenaged son, Mathieu; and their tabby cat, Swirls.

Preface

Michael Solomon wrote one of the most up-beat and interesting Consumer Behaviour texts ever to hit the market. We readily adopted it to our consumer behaviour classes in Canada. Jeff Collier, Prentice Hall Canada sales representative and also an ex-consumer behaviour student of mine, seemed to be after me for years to do a Canadian version of a consumer behaviour text. Only after extensive convincing and inclusion of Rosemary Polegato did this project take hold. It was an exhaustive, but personally rewarding experience for us.

The textbook is still a Solomon book. It carries his trademark of vastly interesting examples and issues. We have tried not to interfere with his winning style, but have definitely added our own "twist." Chapters 12, 13, 14, and 15 have been completely rewritten with a Canadian focus. They can now be used in the classroom, without telling students to skip over pages. Throughout the chapters we have tried to integrate successful Canadian stories. For example, the section on Opinion Leadership uses the M.A.C. cosmetics case to bring practise to theory.

We have also put our own personal twist on characters and examples of consumption. Role reversals are common. In addition, we realize that many students reading our book will be balancing jobs, families, and perhaps even seeking second careers. So the Marlboro Man has ridden off into the sunset and the "career woman" has taken his place.

We are all consumers. As a result, many of the topics dealt with in this book are of both professional and personal relevance to the reader, whether he or she is a student, professor, or marketing practitioner. Nearly everyone can relate to the trials and tribulations associated with last-minute shopping, primping for a big night out, agonizing over an expensive purchase decision, fantasizing about a week in the Caribbean, celebrating a holiday, or commemorating a landmark event, such as a graduation, getting a driver's license, or (dreaming about) winning the lottery.

APPROACH AND OBJECTIVE TO BUYING, HAVING, AND BEING

As the book's subtitle suggests, our version of this field goes beyond looking at the act of buying to having and being as well. Consumer behaviour is more than buying things, such as a can of peas; it also embraces the study of how having (or not having) things affects our lives and how our possessions influence the way we feel about ourselves and about each other—our state of being.

In addition to understanding why people buy things, we also try to appreciate how products, services, and consumption activities contribute to the broader social world we experience. Whether shopping, cooking, cleaning, playing basketball, hanging out at the beach, or even looking at ourselves in the mirror, our lives are touched by the marketing system. And, as if these experiences were not complex enough, the task of understanding the consumer multiplies geometrically when a multicultural perspective is taken. In addition to the numerous examples of marketing and consumer practices relating to consumers and companies, chapters contain boxes (easily identifiable by the icon in the margin) called "Multicultural Dimensions" that highlight cultural differences in consumer behaviour.

The book also emphasizes the importance of understanding consumers in formulating marketing strategy. Many (if not most) of the fundamental concepts in marketing are based on the practitioner's ability to know people. After all, if we don't understand why people behave as they do, how can we identify their needs? If we can't identify their needs, how can we satisfy those needs? If we can't satisfy people's needs, we don't have a marketing concept, so we might as well fold our tents and go home! To illustrate the potential of consumer research to inform marketing strategy, the text contains numerous examples of specific applications of consumer behaviour concepts by marketing practitioners as well as of windows of opportunity where such concepts could be used (perhaps by alert strategists after taking this course!). Many of these possibilities are highlighted in special features called "Marketing Opportunities."

This strategic focus is, however, tempered by an important qualification: Unlike some contemporary treatments of consumer behaviour, this book does not assume that everything marketers do is in the best interests of consumers or of their environment. Likewise, as consumers, we do many things that are not positive either. People are plagued by addictions, status envy, ethnocentrism, racism, sexism, and other "isms," and, regrettably, there are times when marketing activities—deliberately or not—encourage or exploit these human flaws. This book deals with the totality of consumer behaviour, warts and all. Marketing mistakes or ethically suspect activities are also highlighted in special features labeled "Marketing Pitfalls."

NEW TO THE CANADIAN EDITION

The Canadian edition of *Consumer Behaviour* contains some exciting new features.

CBC Video Vignettes: Sixteen written video cases are provided at key points in the text, supported by exciting videos from CBC news programs. These videos and cases help to bring key concepts and issues to life in the classroom.

Canadian/Regional Dimensions: Chapter 14 features several examples of consumer behaviour from a specifically Canadian perspective.

Case appendix: Six written cases have been added in an appendix at the end of the book. Some of these cases cross various chapters and instructors should find them useful.

Weblinks: To encourage students to learn about the Internet, we have included Weblinks (useful Internet addresses) throughout each chapter (easily identifiable by the Weblinks icon show here in the margin). Our Companion Website will provide regular updates to these Internet resources.

ADDITIONAL LEARNING AIDS

Chapter-opening example: Each chapter starts with an interesting vignette that introduces the chapter material and helps spark student interest.

Full-colour figures, photographs, advertisements and illustrations: Throughout each chapter, key concepts and applications are illustrated with strong, full-colour visual materials.

Key Terms: Key terms are highlighted within the text, defined in page margins, and listed at the end of each chapter with page references. All of the key terms are collected together in the Glossary.

Chapter Summary: Provides a concise review of the chapter's key topics.

Consumer Behaviour Challenge: Each chapter contains a set of questions that challenge the student to apply the key issues covered. Many new questions have been added to the Canadian Edition.

Indexes: A subject index, a product, corporate and celebrity index, and an author index reference all information and examples in the book.

SUPPLEMENTS

Consumer Behaviour, Canadian Edition, is accompanied by a complete supplements package.

Instructor's Resource Manual with Video Guide (013-096115-9) The Instructor's Resource Manual with Video Guide contains lecture notes, field project ideas, answers to the Consumer Behaviour challenge and informative case notes for the CBC Video Vignettes and case appendix.

Test Item File (013-096109-4) The Test Item File contains over 1,700 multiple-choice, true/false, and short essay questions. Each question is rated by level of difficulty and includes a text page reference. It is available in both printed and electronic formats.

Prentice Hall Custom Test (013-096100-0) The Prentice Hall Custom Test merges the Test Item File with a powerful software package in the Windows platform. With the Prentice Hall Custom Test's user-friendly test-creating abilities, you can create tailor-made, error-free tests quickly and easily. The Custom Test allows you to create an exam, administer it traditionally or online, and evaluate and track student's results—all with the click of the mouse.

Transparency Resource Package (013-096112-4) Over 150 transparency masters highlighting key concepts featured in the text are available in printed format and electronically in PowerPoint 4.0.

Prentice Hall Canada/CBC Video Library (013-096111-6) Prentice Hall Canada and the CBC have worked together to bring you sixteen segments from the CBC series *Venture, The National, Marketplace* and *Undercurrents.* Designed specifically to complement the text, this case collection is an excellent tool for bringing students in con-

tact with the world outside the classroom. These programs have extremely high production quality and have been chosen to relate directly to chapter content. Please contact your Prentice Hall Canada sales representative for details.

Companion Website For a multitude of practice questions, key terms and concepts, Weblinks to related sites, Newsgroups, CBC video updates and more, check out the *Consumer Behaviour*, C/e, Companion Website at **www.prenticehall.ca/solomon**.

Acknowledgements

The Canadian authors would like to thank Michael Solomon for writing a great textbook in the first place. The reviews we received were extensive and contained valuable comments. We were not able to integrate all the good suggestions this time. We will definitely be adding the reviewers total input to the next edition. We thank our reviewers: Malcolm Howe, Niagara College; Steven M. Kates, University of Northern British Columbia; John P. Liefeld, University of Guelph; Jo-Anne Procter, Mohawk College; M. Louise Ripley, York University; and Sheila Winder, Douglas College. Then we owe much to our colleagues who wrote many interesting articles that were incorporated to this text. We know we missed many additional important papers and hope our colleagues will point out to us where these can be added to the text for future editions. Work from many colleagues were a help in preparing this edition: Doug Olsen, University of Calgary; Rhonda Watson, University of Regina; Peter Darke, University of British Columbia; Tammi Feltham, Wilfrid Laurier University; Carmen Cullen, Brock University; Karen Finlay, University of Guelph; Brenda Gainer, York University; Larita Carter, Memorial University; Eileen Fisher, York University; Deirdre Grondin, University of New Brunswick; Rick Pollay, University of British Columbia; Ann Lavack, Concordia University; Louise Heslop, Carleton University; Nick Papadolous, Carleton University; Gad Saad, Concordia University; John Liefeld, University of Guelph; Shirley Taylor, Peggy Cunningham, Stephen Arnold, and Ida Berger, all of Queen's University.

Perhaps the most important input to this text came from John Sweet, the copy editor. His attention to detail was invaluable. In addition I would like to thank John Gomes for preparing the tables in chapter one; my MBA student Rosanna Mau for her help doing my other jobs, so I could work on the text; and Julianna Mewes for her extensive help in preparing the PowerPoint slides. We appreciate the work of the staff at Prentice Hall, including Andrew Winton, Amber Wallace, Mike Ryan, Ann Byford, Jane Schell, Susan Wallace-Cox, Phyllis Seto and Julia Hall. Lastly we would like to thank Pat Ferrier and Lesley Mann for their devotion to this project.

Michael R. Solomon
Judith L. Zaichkowsky
Rosemary Polegato

The Prentice Hall Canada

companion Website...

Your Internet companion to the most exciting, state-of-the-art educational tools on the Web!

The Prentice Hall Canada Companion Website is easy to navigate and is organized to correspond to the chapters in this textbook. The Companion Website is comprised of four distinct, functional features:

1) **Customized Online Resources**

2) **Online Study Guide**

3) **Reference Material**

4) **Communication**

Explore the four areas in this Companion Website. Students and distance learners will discover resources for indepth study, research and communication, empowering them in their quest for greater knowledge and maximizing their potential for success in the course.

A NEW WAY TO DELIVER EDUCATIONAL CONTENT

1) Customized Online Resources

Our Companion Websites provide instructors and students with a range of options to access, view, and exchange content.

- **Syllabus Builder** provides *instructors* with the option to create online classes and construct an online syllabus linked to specific modules in the Companion Website.

- **Mailing lists** enable *instructors* and *students* to receive customized promotional literature.

- **Preferences** enable *students* to customize the sending of results to various recipients, and also to customize how the material is sent, e.g., as HTML, text, or as an attachment.

- **Help** includes an evaluation of the user's system and a tune-up area that makes updating browsers and plug-ins easier. This new feature will enhance the user's experience with Companion Websites.

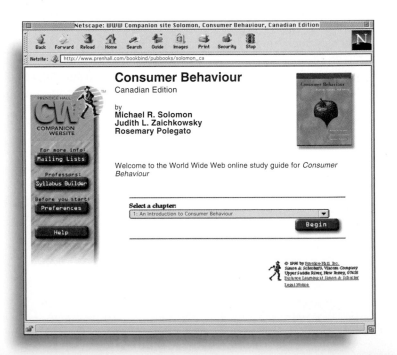

www.prenticehall.ca/solomon

2) Online Study Guide

Interactive Study Guide modules form the core of the student learning experience in the Companion Website. These modules are categorized according to their functionality:

- True-False
- Multiple Choice

The True-False and Multiple Choice modules provide students with the ability to send answers to our grader and receive instant feedback on their progress through our Results Reporter. Coaching comments and references back to the textbook ensure that students take advantage of all resources available to enhance their learning experience.

3) Reference Material

Reference material broadens text coverage with up-to-date resources for learning. **Web Destinations** provides a directory of Web sites relevant to the subject matter in each chapter. **NetNews (Internet Newsgroups)** are a fundamental source of information about a discipline, containing a wealth of brief, opinionated postings. **NetSearch** simplifies key term search using Internet search engines.

4) Communication

Companion Websites contain the communication tools necessary to deliver courses in a **Distance Learning** environment. **Message Board** allows users to post messages and check back periodically for responses. **Live Chat** allows users to discuss course topics in real time, and enables professors to host online classes.

Communication facilities of Companion Websites provide a key element for distributed learning environments. There are two types of communication facilities currently in use in Companion Websites:

- **Message Board** – this module takes advantage of browser technology providing the users of each Companion Website with a national newsgroup to post and reply to relevant course topics.

- **Live Chat** – enables instructor-led group activities in real time. Using our chat client, instructors can display Website content while students participate in the discussion.

Companion Websites are currently available for:
- Starke: Contemporary Management in Canada
- Kotler: Principles of Marketing
- Evans: Marketing Essentials
- Robbins: Fundamentals of Management
- Horngren: Introduction to Financial Accounting

Note: CW '99 content will vary slightly from site to site depending on discipline requirements.

The Companion Website can be found at:

www.prenticehall.ca/solomon

PRENTICE HALL CANADA

1870 Birchmount Road
Scarborough, Ontario M1P 2J7

To order:
Call: 1-800-567-3800
Fax: 1-800-263-7733

For samples:
Call: 1-800-850-5813
Fax: (416) 299-2539
E-mail: phcinfo_pubcanada@prenhall.com

I

Consumers in the Marketplace

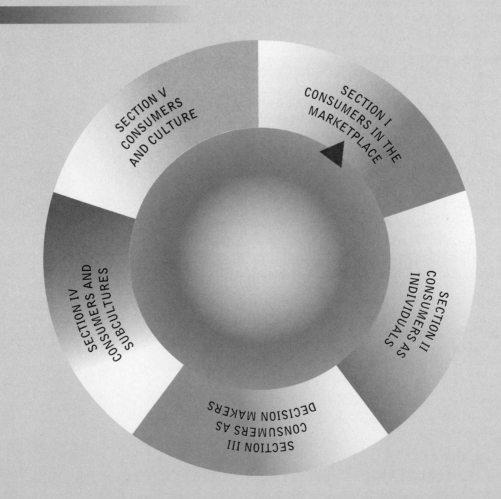

SECTION V
CONSUMERS
AND CULTURE

SECTION I
CONSUMERS IN THE
MARKETPLACE

SECTION II
CONSUMERS AS
INDIVIDUALS

SECTION IV
CONSUMERS AND
SUBCULTURES

SECTION III
CONSUMERS AS
DECISION MAKERS

This introductory section provides an overview of the field of consumer behaviour. Chapter 1 looks at how the field of marketing is influenced by the actions of consumers and also at how we as consumers are influenced by marketers. It describes the discipline of consumer behaviour and some of the different approaches to understanding what makes consumers tick.

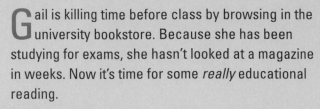

Gail is killing time before class by browsing in the university bookstore. Because she has been studying for exams, she hasn't looked at a magazine in weeks. Now it's time for some *really* educational reading.

The magazine section is filled with dozens of selections, from *Motor Trend* to *Mother Jones*. Gail is a dedicated *Seventeen* reader, but as she scans the racks, she is struck by the glamorous models on the covers of other women's magazines. She thinks it's time to expand her horizons and remake her old high-school image. She considers *Vogue*, but it seems a bit too old and stodgy. *Cosmopolitan* features slightly older working women in revealing dresses, and *Chatelaine* and *McCall's* look like magazines her mother would read. She sees *Family Circle* and *Ladies' Home Journal* when she visits her Aunt Ellen in the suburbs—as if she cared about endless diets and home decorating ideas.

Finally, Gail is intrigued by a magazine, *Marie Claire*. The cover model has a new, short hairstyle that she's been wanting to try. *Marie Claire* publishes in 22 countries and has been a major fashion magazine in Europe for years (**www.hearstcorp.com/mag8.html**).[1] As Gail scans the pages, her attention is caught by the many clothes ads and a whiff of the new perfume her friend Lisa just bought. This magazine is just what she needs to help update her look from high school to university.

An Introduction to Consumer Behaviour

INTRODUCTION

Consumer Behaviour: People in the Marketplace

This book is about people like Gail. It concerns the products and services they buy and use and the ways these fit into their lives. This introductory chapter briefly describes some important aspects of the field of consumer behaviour, including the topics studied, who studies them and some different ways these issues are approached by consumer researchers.

For now, though, let's return to one "typical" consumer: Gail, the business major. This brief story allows us to highlight some aspects of consumer behaviour that will be covered in the rest of the book.

* As a consumer, Gail can be described and compared to other individuals in a number of ways. For some purposes, marketers might find it useful to categorize Gail in terms of her age, sex, income or occupation. These are some examples of descriptive characteristics of a population, or *demographics*. In other cases, marketers would rather know something about Gail's interests in clothing or music,

or the way she spends her leisure time. This sort of information comes under the category of *psychographics,* which refers to aspects of a person's lifestyle and personality. Knowledge of consumer characteristics plays an extremely important role in many marketing applications, such as defining the market for a product or deciding upon the appropriate techniques to employ when targeting a certain group of consumers.

- Gail's purchase decisions are heavily influenced by the opinions and behaviours of her friends. A lot of product information, as well as recommendations to use or avoid particular brands, is transmitted by conversations among real people, rather than by way of television commercials, magazines or billboards. The bonds among Gail's group are cemented by the common products they use. There is also pressure on each group member to buy things that will meet with the group's approval and often a price to pay in the form of group rejection or embarrassment when one does not conform to others' conceptions of what is good or bad, "in" or "out."

- As members of a large society, people share certain cultural values or strongly held beliefs about the way the world should be structured. Other values are shared by members of *subcultures,* or smaller groups within the culture, such as French Canadians, teens, "prairie people" or even "Hell's Angels." The people who matter to Gail—her *reference group*—value the idea that women in their early twenties should be innovative, style-conscious, independent and daring (at least a little). While many marketers focus on aging "baby boomers" (consumers between 35 and 50 years old), some are recognizing that "twentysomethings" are a valuable, overlooked market. For example, women in their twenties are more likely to splurge on make-up and seek out brand names such as M.A.C., and they tend to regard shopping as entertainment.[2]

- When examining magazines, Gail was exposed to many competing "brands." Many magazines did not capture her attention at all, while others were noticed and rejected because they did not fit the "image" with which she identified or to which she aspired. The use of *market segmentation strategies* means targeting a brand only to a specific group of consumers rather than to everybody—even if it means that other consumers will not be interested or may even deliberately avoid that brand. See *mediafinder.com/magazines* to determine which magazines you would be interested in.

- Brands often have clearly defined images or "personalities" created by product advertising, packaging, branding and other marketing strategies that focus on positioning a product a certain way. The purchase of a magazine in particular is very much a lifestyle statement: it says a lot about what a person is interested in, as well as something about the type of person he or she would like to be. People often choose a product because they like its image or because they feel its "personality" somehow corresponds to their own. Moreover, a consumer may believe that when he or she buys and uses the product or service, its desirable qualities will magically "rub off" onto him or her.

- When a product succeeds in satisfying a consumer's specific needs or desires, as *Marie Claire* did for Gail, it may be rewarded with many years of *brand loyalty,* a bond between product and consumer that is very difficult for competitors to break. Often a change in one's life situation or self-concept is required to weaken this bond and thus create opportunities for competitors. Brand loyalty can also be affected when a brand's image is altered or repositioned, as *Vogue* is now attempting to do. For example, *Vogue* recently devoted an entire issue to fashion items that could be bought for under $500. Although these clothes are still very expensive by many women's standards, they still are a radical departure from the magazine's usual emphasis on *haute couture* apparel with price tags that could cover tuition at many universities.

• Consumers' evaluations of products are affected by their appearance, taste, texture or smell. We may be swayed by the shape and colour of a package, as well

MULTICULTURAL DIMENSIONS

The "Cosmo Girl" is an image that is carefully cultivated by the editors of *Cosmopolitan*. The Cosmo Girl, as described by editor Bonnie Fuller, expects to get married but is not in any hurry. She may wait until her late thirties to have children. Sex is "... very important, but not on the first date." She owns at least one long black skirt with a slit, possesses many pairs of shoes and wears big jewellery. The most recent edition can be found at ***cosmomag.com.month/index.html***.

Here is a sample of the various covers of *Cosmopolitan* published worldwide.
Courtesy of Hearst Magazine International.

While the Cosmo Girl is well defined, the magazine also publishes 25 international editions, most of which are separate entities with their own editorial staffs. In some cases, local cultures conflict with the Cosmo Girl's liberated image. Latin American editors, for instance, face problems created by a more macho society that often has a double sexual standard for men and women. Advertisers are sometimes reluctant to buy into a magazine they see as "perverted," and some parts of the magazine are censored. In other places, such as Hong Kong, the Cosmo image fits well, since women are expected to be more independent and ambitious. New Cosmo Girls are on the drawing board for Russia, Poland, Hungary and India.[3]

as by more subtle factors such as the symbolism used in a brand name, in an advertisement or even in the choice of a cover model for a magazine. These judgments are affected by—and often reflect—how a society feels that people should define themselves at that point in time. For example, Gail's choice of a new hairstyle says something about the type of image women like her want to project in the year 2000. If asked, Gail might not even be able to say exactly why she considered some magazines and rejected others. Many product meanings are hidden below the surface of the packaging and advertising, and this book will discuss some of the methods used by marketers and social scientists to discover or apply these meanings.

- *Marie Claire* has an international image that appealed to Gail. A product's image often is influenced by its *country of origin,* which helps to determine its "brand personality." In addition, our opinions and desires increasingly are shaped by input from around the world, which is becoming a much smaller place due to rapid advancements in communications and transportation systems. In today's global culture, consumers often prize products and services that "transport" them to different places and allow them to experience the diversity of other cultures.

What Is Consumer Behaviour?

consumer behaviour the processes involved when individuals or groups select, purchase, use or dispose of products, services, ideas or experiences to satisfy needs and desires

The field of **consumer behaviour** covers a lot of ground: it is the study of the processes involved when individuals or groups select, purchase, use or dispose of products, services, ideas or experiences to satisfy needs and desires. Consumers take many forms, ranging from an eight-year-old child begging her mother for Gummi Bears candy to an executive in a large corporation deciding on a multimillion-dollar computer system. The items that are consumed can include anything from canned peas to a massage, democracy or rap music, and even other people (the images of rock stars, for example). Needs and desires to be satisfied range from hunger and thirst to love, status or even spiritual fulfilment.

CONSUMERS ARE ACTORS ON THE MARKETPLACE STAGE

role theory the perspective that much of consumer behaviour resembles actions in a play

The perspective of **role theory** takes the view that much of consumer behaviour resembles actions in a play.[4] As in a play, each consumer has lines, props and costumes that are necessary for a good performance. Since people act out many different roles, they sometimes alter their consumption decisions depending on the particular "play" they are in at the time. The criteria that they use to evaluate products and services in one of their roles may be quite different from those used in another role. In the Carrier Furnaces ad shown here, the consumer is shown in two of his roles: engineer by day and homeowner by night.

CONSUMER BEHAVIOUR IS A PROCESS

In its early stages of development, the field was often referred to as *buyer behaviour,* reflecting an emphasis on the interaction between consumers and producers at the time of purchase. Marketers now recognize that consumer behaviour is an ongoing *process,* not merely what happens at the moment a consumer hands over money or a credit card and in turn receives some good or service.

This ad for Carrier Furnaces highlights the fact that consumers use different criteria to evaluate products, depending on the role they are playing at the time.
Courtesy of Carrier Corporation, subsidiary of United Technologies Corporation.

The **exchange,** in which two or more organizations or people give and receive something of value, is an integral part of marketing.[5] While exchange remains an important part of consumer behaviour, the expanded view emphasizes the entire consumption process, which includes the issues that influence the consumer before, during and after a purchase. Figure 1–1 illustrates some of the issues that are addressed during each stage of the consumption process.

exchange the process whereby two or more organizations or people give and receive something of value

FIGURE 1–1 • Some Issues That Arise during Stages in the Consumption Process

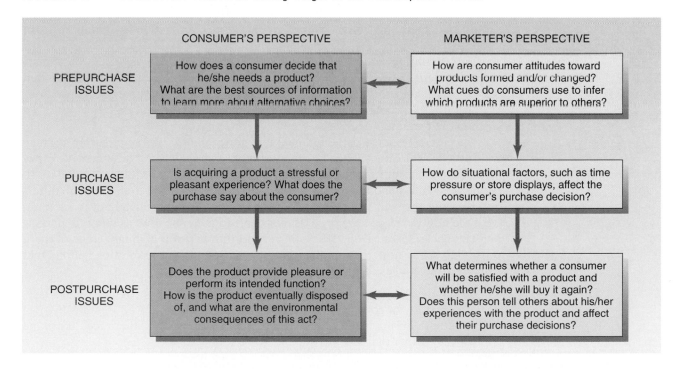

	CONSUMER'S PERSPECTIVE	MARKETER'S PERSPECTIVE
PREPURCHASE ISSUES	How does a consumer decide that he/she needs a product? What are the best sources of information to learn more about alternative choices?	How are consumer attitudes toward products formed and/or changed? What cues do consumers use to infer which products are superior to others?
PURCHASE ISSUES	Is acquiring a product a stressful or pleasant experience? What does the purchase say about the consumer?	How do situational factors, such as time pressure or store displays, affect the consumer's purchase decision?
POSTPURCHASE ISSUES	Does the product provide pleasure or perform its intended function? How is the product eventually disposed of, and what are the environmental consequences of this act?	What determines whether a consumer will be satisfied with a product and whether he/she will buy it again? Does this person tell others about his/her experiences with the product and affect their purchase decisions?

CONSUMER BEHAVIOUR INVOLVES MANY DIFFERENT ACTORS

A consumer is generally thought of as a person who identifies a need or desire, makes a purchase, and then disposes of the product during the three stages in the consumption process. In many cases, however, different people may be involved in the process. The *purchaser* and *user* of a product might not be the same person, as when a parent picks out clothes for a teenager (and makes selections that can result in "fashion suicide" in the view of the teen). In other cases, another person may act as an *influencer,* providing recommendations for or against certain products without actually buying or using them. For example, a friend accompanying a teen on a shopping trip, rather than a parent, might actually pick out the clothes that the teen decides to purchase.

Finally, consumers may be organizations or groups, in which one person may make the decisions involved in purchasing products that will be used by many, as when a purchasing agent orders the company's office supplies. In other organizational situations, purchase decisions may be made by a large group of people—for example, company accountants, designers, engineers, sales personnel and others—all of whom will have a say in the various stages of the consumption process. As we'll see in a later chapter, one type of important organization is the family, where different family members play pivotal roles in decision making regarding products and services used by all.

CONSUMERS' IMPACT ON MARKETING STRATEGY

Talking about buying magazines or other products can be a lot of fun (almost as much fun as actually making the purchases!). But, on the more serious side, why should managers, advertisers and other marketing professionals bother to learn about this field?

Very simply, understanding consumer behaviour is good business. A basic marketing concept states that firms exist to satisfy consumers' needs. These needs can only be satisfied to the extent that marketers understand the people or organizations that will use the products and services they are trying to sell and that they do so *better* than their competitors.

Consumer response is the ultimate test of whether or not a marketing strategy will succeed. Thus, knowledge about consumers is incorporated into virtually every facet of a successful marketing plan. Data about consumers helps marketers to define the market and to identify threats and opportunities in their own and different countries that will affect consumers' receptivity to the product. In every chapter, we'll see how developments in consumer behaviour can be used as input to marketing strategies. Boxes called "Marketing Opportunities" will highlight some of these possibilities. For now, though, here are a few examples of marketing actions that resulted from studies focused on understanding consumers:

- Schick devised an ad for its razors with a woman gently stroking a man's face, after a study of consumer perceptions of rival brands showed that ads by rival Gillette featuring men in rugged, outdoor situations made them feel like "lone wolves" rather than people who like to be touched.[6]

- A woman in a group of consumers who were gathered to talk about tooth care observed that tartar felt "like a wall" on her teeth. This imagery was used in ads for Colgate Tartar Control, in which room-sized teeth were shown covered by walls of tartar.[7]

- American Express redirected its advertising emphasis away from overachievers after its consumer research indicated that people were intimidated by this approach. One subject, asked to pretend that he was an American Express card come to life, sneered, "You're not really my type—you can't keep up." Later ads featured people in laid-back situations, such as spontaneous vacations.[8]

- Researchers for a manufacturer of Swiss chocolate found that many chocolate lovers hide secret "stashes" around their houses. One respondent confessed to hiding candy bars inside her lingerie drawer. The result was an ad campaign theme of "The True Confessions of Chocaholics."[9]

Segmenting Consumers

The process of *marketing segmentation* identifies groups of consumers who are similar to one another in one or more ways, and then devises marketing strategies that appeal to one or more groups—even at the expense of excluding other segments from the firm's target market. There are many dimensions that can be used to slice up a larger market.

Demographics are statistics that measure observable aspects of a population, such as birth rate, age distribution and income. Statistics Canada is a major source of demographic data on families. This information is available on the Internet at ***www. statcan.ca***. The changes and trends revealed in demographic studies are of great interest to marketers, because the data can be used to locate and predict the size of markets for many products, ranging from home mortgages to brooms and can openers. Imagine trying to sell baby food to a single male, or an around-the-world vacation to a couple making $15 000 a year!

Table 1–1 provides a statistical snapshot of the "typical" Canadian consumer, based on data compiled from Statistics Canada. As you go down this list, you will quickly see that many characteristics do not apply directly to you. How different are you from this mythical consumer?

In this book, we'll explore many of the important demographic variables that make consumers the same as or different from others. We'll also consider other important characteristics that are not so easy to measure, such as *psychographics*—differences in consumers' personalities and tastes that can't be objectively measured. For now, let's summarize a few of the most important demographic dimensions, each of which will be developed in more detail in later chapters.

AGE

Consumers of different age groups obviously have very different needs and wants. While people who belong to the same age group differ in many other ways, they do tend to share a set of values and common cultural experiences that they carry throughout life.[10] Levi Strauss, for example, has been successful in developing the idea that it is a "brand for life" by introducing products such as Dockers to meet the needs of their consumers as they age. As a Levi's marketing executive explained, "In

demographics the observable measurements of a population's characteristics, such as birth rate, age distribution and income

TABLE 1–1 A Statistical Picture of the Average or Typical Canadian Consumer

- The typical Canadian is a woman who is 36.7 years old.
- The average Canadian worked 37.8 hours per week in 1996.
- The average income of a Canadian was $585 per week in 1996.
- In 1992 the average Canadian household spent $6668 on shelter.
- In 1992 the typical Canadian household spent $60.91 per week at the supermarket.
- During 1992 this average house also spent $33.30 on restaurant meals per week.
- In 1990 the average household spent $887 on personal care.
- The average household spent $2596 on clothing purchases in 1990.
- During 1990 the typical household spent $289 on child-care expenses.
- The average household spent $1610 on entertainment and sports activities in 1990.
- The amount spent on air travel in 1990 by the typical household was $312.
- During 1990 the typical Canadian household owned 1.7 television sets.
- The average Canadian watched 22.8 hours of television per week during 1993.
- The typical Canadian exercised at least twice a week in 1995.

Sources: Statistics Canada, *Employment Earnings and Hours, 1997,* Cat. no. 72-002-XPB; Statistics Canada, *Family Expenditures in Canada, 1990,* Cat. no. 62-555; Statistics Canada, *Television Viewing 1993,* Cat. no. 87-208; Statistics Canada, *Annual Demographic Studies, 1994,* Cat. no. 91213; Statistics Canada, Cat. no. 82-221-XDB; www.statcan.ca

the 1960s, growth [in the jeans market] was due to adoption of jeans by 15- to 18-year-olds. . . . Now these people are 25–49 and Dockers meshes perfectly with what the Levi brand image is about for them."[11]

GENDER

Many products, from fragrances to footwear, are targeted to either men or women. Differentiating by sex starts at a very early age—even diapers are sold in pink versions for girls and blue for boys. As proof that consumers take these differences seriously, consider that market research has revealed that most parents refuse to put male infants in pink diapers![12]

One dimension that makes segmenting by gender so interesting is that the behaviours and tastes of men and women are constantly evolving. For example, in the past most marketers assumed that men were the primary decision makers for automobile purchases, but this perspective is changing with the times: more than six out of ten new-car buyers under the age of 50 now are women.[13]

FAMILY STRUCTURE

A person's family and marital status is yet another important demographic variable, since this has such a big effect on consumers' spending priorities. Young singles and newlyweds are the most likely to exercise; to go to bars, concerts and movies; and to consume alcohol. Families with young children are big purchasers of health foods and fruit juices, while single-parent households and those with older children buy

Marketers like Saturn are starting to recognize women's buying power in the 1990s.
Courtesy of Saturn Corporation.

more junk food. Home maintenance services are most likely to be used by older couples and dual career couples.

The Club Med Organization has highly segmented their clubs and marketing strategy around changing demographics of their guests. Club Med has had the same loyal customers for 20 to 30 years. As their customers changed from "swinging singles" to families in the 1980s, Club Med changed as well. Some clubs even have a staff to warm bottles and take care of babies as young as four months old.[14] Single people in their twenties would feel very disappointed at Club Med Sandpiper in Florida, where one-third of the guests are under six years old. The company has changed its advertising slogan from "The antidote to civilization" to "Take home a Club Med vacation," and is even airing television commercials during Saturday morning children's programming.[15]

There are special offers for seniors, allowing three generations to vacation at once. Club Med has one loyal customer, a retired single judge in his seventies, who travels to a different Club for one week each month. He has what we would call high "customer equity" for Club Med.

Budget-minded vacationers now can go to Club Aquarius, the same Club Med concept, with less included. Thus, there is a different type of Club for the different needs and wants of each type of "family." However, Club Med is facing a very severe identity crisis because it is now trying to be all things to all people. Consumers are confused as to which Club Med destination will guarantee a vacation that matches their needs and wants.[16] Club Med is trying to remedy all this confusion with their detailed Web site at *www.clubmed.com*.

SOCIAL CLASS AND INCOME

People who are grouped within the same social class are approximately equal in terms of their incomes and social standing in the community. They work in roughly similar occupations, and they tend to have similar tastes in music, clothing, art and so on. They also tend to socialize with one another and share many ideas and values regarding the way one's life should be lived.[17] The distribution of wealth is of great

This ad for an exclusive airline is clearly targeted to high-income travellers.
Courtesy of MGM Grand, Inc.

interest to marketers, since it determines what groups have the greatest buying power and market potential.

ETHNICITY

Multiculturalism and Canada go hand in hand. We are a country composed of immigrants from all over the globe. Canada accepts nearly one million immigrants and refugees every four years, by far the highest per capita rate of immigration in the world.[18] We are diverse in our languages and in our cultural consumption that stems from our ethnicity. Since Canadians blend together from many different racial and cultural backgrounds, we also blend together our consumption heritage signified by food.

For example, English is now a minority language in Vancouver. The growth of the Asian market in Canada has led to trilingual labelling of some products. As a culture we are just as likely to enjoy eating sushi as pyrohy or lasagna. It is a rich experience to be a Canadian.

GEOGRAPHY

The climate changes drastically from region to region in Canada, which makes segmenting by region for some products very obvious. For example, more snow blowers and fur coats are sold east of the Rocky Mountains, more umbrellas and rain coats to the west. Humidifiers and dehumidifiers are a must in regions around the Great Lakes. On the Prairies, it is not unusual for people to have two or more deep freezers in their basements. Many people who live in farming regions preserve the food they produce for winter and year-round consumption.

Within the regions also, there are some different cultural pockets and hence differences in food tastes. New Brunswick has the highest consumption of sliced white bread, while Alberta leads in bubble-gum sales. More corn flakes are sold on the Prairies, and linguini has its highest sales in Toronto. The Québécois are the lowest consumers of frozen french fries, preferring the real thing.[19]

Cosmetics lines developed specifically for black consumers have done well. Their skin can have 35 distinct undertones (as compared to 7 for whites), so possibilities for different product formulations are much larger. In a first for a major cosmetics company, Maybelline has introduced a line of makeup products called "Shades of You." Until this introduction, major companies included shade ranges for darker skin as part of their regular lines. Maybelline has devised a display that allows customers to select the shade that best matches their own skin tone.

Photo courtesy of Maybelline, Inc. (Nejet Delener, "Cosmetics & HBAs for Black Consumers: A Growing, Profitable but Ignored Market," Marketing News [March 15, 1985]: 32; Pat Sloan, "New Maybelline Line Targets Blacks," Advertising Age [December 17, 1990]: 1; Cyndee Miller, "Cosmetics Firms Finally Discover the Ethnic Market," Marketing News [August 30, 1992]: 2.)

Many firms, like Air Canada, are recognizing racial diversity in their advertising.
Courtesy of Air Canada and Marketel.

RELATIONSHIP MARKETING: BUILDING BONDS WITH CONSUMERS

relationship marketing the process of creating, maintaining and enhancing strong, value-laden relationships with customers

Marketers are carefully defining customer segments and listening to people in their markets as never before. Many of them have realized that a key to success is building relationships between brands and customers that will last a lifetime. Marketers who believe in this philosophy, called **relationship marketing**, are making an effort to interact with customers on a regular basis, giving them reasons to maintain a bond with the company over time.

Some companies build these ties by providing valuable services that are appreciated by customers. Hanna Andersson, a company that sells children's clothing, runs a program called Hannadowns, which gives a 20 percent credit toward new purchases when customers return used clothes that were bought from the company; the returned clothing is then distributed to charities. The company also donates 5 percent of its pretax profits to charities and shelters benefiting women and children.[20] This return of value to the community cements the relationship by giving customers an additional reason to continue buying the company's products year after year.

database marketing the process of creating a database of consumers and their purchases through tracking programs, and then customizing marketing appeals to suit these different customers

Another revolution in relationship building is being brought to us courtesy of the computer. **Database marketing** involves tracking consumers' buying habits very closely and crafting products and messages tailored precisely to people's wants and needs, based on this information. Sophisticated companies such as American Express, General Motors and Kraft General Foods are combining and constantly updating information from public records and marketing research surveys with data volunteered by consumers themselves when they return warranty cards, enter sweepstakes or purchase from catalogues to build complex databases that fine-tune their knowledge of what people are buying and how often.

Keeping close tabs on their customers allows database marketers to monitor people's preferences and communicate with those who show an interest in their products or services. For example, General Motors regularly surveys holders of its GM Card (a credit card offered in conjunction with MasterCard) to learn what they are driving and when they expect to be in the market for a new car. This information is passed along to the appropriate division for follow-up contacts. Blockbuster Entertainment Corp. is testing a system that makes movie recommendations based on a consumer's prior rentals and offers special promotions based on these choices.[21]

Here are just a few examples of the ways marketers have found to stay in touch with their customers:

- Revenues from legal gambling top $30 billion a year—more than the combined take for movies, books, recorded music, and park and arcade attractions.[22] To further encourage the droves of people flocking to casinos to become regular customers and even bigger bettors, sophisticated "player-tracking systems" are being developed.[23] Although casinos have always tried to keep track of the action among heavy bettors at the roulette or blackjack tables, now they are even monitoring the behaviour of the nickel-and-dime set. Slots players can join clubs that reward them with free dinners and shows based on how much change they throw into the "one-armed bandits." When club members insert a membership card in a machine, the casino knows their favourite drink and how much they typically spend on a casino outing. In addition, machines that are getting a lot of use can flag managers, who then send someone to greet the gambler with the offer of a free drink and a club membership.

- Levi Strauss is compiling a customer database by asking jeans buyers to register each new pair of pants. The company used a similar tactic when it launched its newer Slates line, including asking whether a girlfriend or wife was involved in the buying decision.[24]

- When Johnson & Johnson prepared to launch its Acuvue disposable contact lenses, the marketing strategy was based on the belief that no patient would switch to disposables without the encouragement of an optometrist. So, the program was driven by two linked databases: registered eye-care professionals who carried Acuvue and contact lens wearers who had earlier responded to disposable lens advertising. The database tracked customers as they moved from expressions of interest, through an appointment with an optometrist, and on to successive purchases. J&J actually coordinated the appointment process for the optometrists, as well as communicating with lens users by delivering incentive coupons and other material.[25]

Market Segmentation Strategies

Effective market segmentation creates segments whose members are similar to one another in one or more characteristics and different from members of other segments. Depending upon its goals and resources, a company may choose to focus on only one segment or on several, or it may ignore differences among segments by pursuing a mass-market strategy.

In many cases, it makes a lot of sense to target different market segments. Although Table 1–1 described the "typical" Canadian consumer based on available statistical information, it is likely that no one fits into that mold exactly; the issue is whether or not consumers differ from our profile in ways that will affect their likelihood of adopting the products that companies offer to meet their needs.

Many segmentation variables form the basis for slicing up a larger market, and a great deal of this book is devoted to exploring the ways marketers describe and

This Whittle Communications ad demonstrates the diversity of market segmentation.
Courtesy of Whittle Communications.

TABLE 1–2 Variables for Market Segmentation

CATEGORY	VARIABLES	LOCATION OF DISCUSSION
Demographics	Age	Chapter 15
	Gender	Chapter 5
	Social class, occupation, income	Chapter 13
	Ethnic group, religion	Chapter 14
	Stage in life	Chapter 12
	Purchaser versus user	Chapter 12
Geographic	Region	Chapter 14
	Country differences	Chapter 17
Psychographic	Self-concept	Chapter 5
	Lifestyle, personality	Chapter 6
Behavioural	Brand loyalty, extent of usage	Chapter 4
	Usage situation	Chapter 9
	Benefits desired	Chapter 4

characterize different segments. The segmentation variables listed in Table 1–2 are grouped into four categories, and the table indicates where in the book these categories are considered in more depth.

While consumers can be described in many ways, the segmentation process is valid only when the following criteria are met:

- Consumers within the segment are similar to one another in terms of product needs, and these needs are different from those of consumers in other segments.
- Important differences among segments can be identified.
- The segment is large enough to be profitable.
- Consumers in the segment can be reached by an appropriate marketing mix.
- The consumers in the segment will respond in the desired way to the marketing mix designed for them.

MARKETING'S IMPACT ON CONSUMERS

For better or for worse, we all live in a world that is significantly influenced by the actions of marketers. We are surrounded by marketing stimuli in the form of advertisements, stores and products competing for our attention and our dollars. Much of what we learn about the world is filtered by marketers, whether through the affluence depicted in glamorous magazine advertising or via the roles played by family members in commercials. Ads show us how we should act with regard to recycling, alcohol consumption and even the types of houses and cars we wish to own. In many ways we are also "at the mercy" of marketers, since we rely on them to sell us products that are safe and perform as promised, to tell us the truth about what they are selling, and to price and distribute these products fairly.

Marketing and Culture

Popular culture, consisting of the music, movies, sports, books, celebrities and other forms of entertainment consumed by the mass market, is both a product of and inspiration for marketers. Our lives are also affected in more far-reaching ways, ranging from how we acknowledge cultural events such as marriage, death or holidays to how we view social issues such as air pollution, gambling and addictions. The Stanley Cup, Christmas shopping, federal elections, newspaper recycling and Barbie dolls are all examples of products and activities that touch many lives.

popular culture the music, movies, sports, books, celebrities and other forms of entertainment consumed by the mass market

This cultural influence is hard to overlook, although many people do not seem to realize how much their views of the world around them—their movie and musical heroes, the latest fashions in clothing, food and decorating choices, and even the physical features that they find attractive or ugly in men and women—are affected by marketers.

For example, consider the product icons that marketers use to create an identity for their products. Various mythical creatures and personalities—from the Pillsbury Doughboy to the Sasquatch have been at one time or another central figures in popular culture. In fact, it is likely that more consumers could recognize such characters than could identify past prime ministers, business leaders or artists. Although these figures never really existed, many of us feel as if we "know" them, and they certainly are effective *spokescharacters* for the products they represent.

The Meaning of Consumption

One of the fundamental premises of the modern field of consumer behaviour is that people often buy products not for what they do, but for what they *mean*. This principle does not imply that a product's basic function is unimportant, but rather that the roles products play in our lives go well beyond the tasks they perform. And the deeper meanings of a product may help it to stand out from other, similar goods and services: all things being equal, a person will choose the brand that has an image (or even a personality!) consistent with his or her underlying needs.

For example, while most people probably couldn't run faster or jump higher if they were wearing Nikes versus Adidas, many die-hard loyalists swear by their favourite brand. These archrivals are largely marketed in terms of their images—meanings that have been carefully crafted with the help of legions of rock stars, athletes and slickly produced commercials—and many millions of dollars. So, when you buy a Nike "swoosh," you may be doing more than choosing footwear for the mall; you may also be making a lifestyle statement about the type of person you are or want to be. For a relatively simple item made of leather and laces, that's quite a feat!

Our allegiances to particular sneakers, musicians or soft drinks help us to define our place in modern society, and these choices also help each of us to form bonds with others who share similar preferences. This comment by a participant in a focus group captures the curious bonding that can be caused by consumption choices: "I was at a Stanley Cup party, and I picked up an obscure drink. Somebody else across the room went 'yo!' because he had the same thing. People feel a connection when you're drinking the same thing."[26]

As we have already seen, a trademark of marketing strategies in the late 1990s is an emphasis on building relationships with customers. The nature of these relationships can vary, and these bonds help us to understand some of the possible meanings products have for us. Here are some of the types of relationships a person may have with a product:[27]

self-concept attachment—The product helps to establish the user's identity.

nostalgic attachment—The product serves as a link with a past self.

interdependence—The product is a part of the user's daily routine.

love—The product elicits emotional bonds of warmth, passion or another strong emotion.

One consumer researcher recently developed a classification scheme in an attempt to explore the different ways that products and experiences can provide meaning to people. This perspective views consumption as a type of action where people make use of consumption objects in a variety of ways. Focusing on a professional sporting event like a ball game is a useful reminder that, when we refer to consumption, we are talking about *intangible* experiences, ideas and services (like the thrill of a home run hit out of the park or the antics of a team mascot) in addition to *tangible* objects (like the hot dogs eaten at the ball park). This analysis identified four distinct types of consumption activities:

consuming as experience—an emotional or aesthetic reaction to consumption objects. This would include activities like the pleasure derived from learning how to mark a scorecard, or appreciating the athletic ability of a favourite player.

consuming as integration—learning and manipulating consumption objects to express aspects of the self or society. For example, some fans wear club jerseys to express their solidarity with the team. Attending professional sporting events in person rather than watching them on TV allows the fan to more completely integrate her experience with that of the team.

consuming as classification—the activities that consumers engage in to communicate their association with objects, both to self and to others. For example, spectators might buy souvenirs to demonstrate to others that they are die-hard fans, or the more hard-core might throw the opposition team's home-run ball back onto the field as a gesture of contempt.

consuming as play—consumers use objects to participate in a mutual experience and merge their identities with that of a group. For example, happy fans might scream in unison and engage in an orgy of "high-fives" when one of their team's players hits a home run or scores a goal. This is a different dimension of shared experience than watching the game at home by oneself.

Semiotics: The Symbols Around Us

When we try to "make sense" of a marketing stimulus, whether a distinctive package, an elaborately staged television commercial or perhaps a model on the cover of a magazine, we do so by interpreting its meaning in light of associations we have with these images. For this reason, much of the meaning we take away is influenced by what we make of the symbolism we perceive. After all, on the surface many marketing images have virtually no literal connection to actual products. What does a cowboy have to do with a bit of tobacco rolled into a paper tube? How can a celebrity like basketball star Michael Jordan enhance the image of a soft drink or a fast-food restaurant?

For assistance in understanding how consumers interpret the meanings of symbols, some marketers are turning to a field of study known as **semiotics,** which examines the correspondence between signs and symbols and their role in the assignment of meaning.[28] Semiotics is important to the understanding of consumer behaviour since consumers use products to express their social identities. Products have learned meanings, and we rely on advertising to help us figure out what those meanings are. As one set of researchers put it, ". . . advertising serves as a kind of culture/consumption dictionary; its entries are products, and their definitions are cultural meanings."[29]

semiotics a field of study that examines the correspondence between a sign and the meaning or meanings it conveys

From a semiotic perspective, every marketing message has three basic components: an object, a sign or symbol, and an interpretant. The **object** is the product that is the focus of the message (Marlboro cigarettes). The **sign** is the sensory imagery that represents the intended meanings of the object (the Marlboro cowboy). The **interpretant** is the meaning derived (rugged, individualistic, American). This relationship is diagrammed in Figure 1–2.

object in semiotic terms, the product that is the focus of a message

sign the sensory imagery that represents the intended meanings of the object

According to semiotician Charles Sanders Peirce, signs are related to objects in one of three ways: they can resemble objects, be connected to them or be conventionally tied to them.[30] An *icon* is a sign that resembles the product in some way (for example, Bell Telephone uses an image of a bell to represent itself). An *index* is a

interpretant the meaning derived from a symbol

FIGURE 1–2 • Relationships of Components in Semiotic Analysis of Meaning

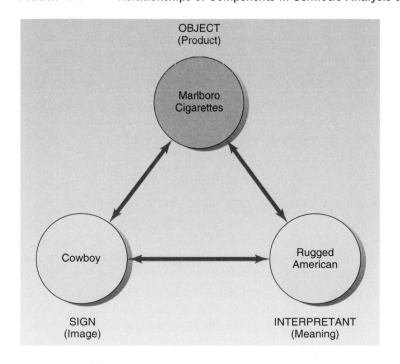

sign that is connected to a product because they share some property (the pine tree on some of Procter & Gamble's Spic and Span cleanser products conveys the shared property of fresh scent). A *symbol* is a sign that is related to a product through either conventional or agreed-upon associations (the lion in Dreyfus Fund ads provides the conventional association with fearlessness that is carried over to the company's approach to investments).

As we shall see in later chapters, these relationships often are culturally bound; that is, they only make sense to a person who is a member of a particular culture.[31] Marketers who forget that meanings do not automatically transfer from one cultural context to another do so at their peril.

THE GLOBAL CONSUMER

One highly visible—and controversial—by-product of sophisticated marketing strategies is the movement towards a *global consumer culture*, where people around the world are united by their common devotion to brand-name consumer goods, movie stars and musical celebrities. Some products in particular are associated with a coveted North American lifestyle. Levi's jeans, for example, are a status symbol among upwardly mobile Asian and European consumers, who snap them up even though they retail at over $100 in many countries.[32] The company sells its jeans in such far-flung places as India, Hungary, Poland, Korea and Turkey. This book will pay special attention to the good and bad aspects of this cultural homogenization. Each chapter features a box called "Multicultural Dimensions" that spotlights some international aspect of consumer behaviour, and this issue will also be explored in depth in Chapter 17.

Blurred Boundaries: Marketing and Reality

Marketers and consumers coexist in a complicated, two-way relationship. On the one hand, businesspeople try to anticipate buyers' tastes by monitoring evolving preferences and activities and then shaping their actions to "ride the wave" of consumer behaviour. When Spelling Entertainment Group found out about spontaneous Melrose Place parties happening in bars, the company alleged trademark infringement and sent cease-and-desist letters to bar owners. Then the firm licensed Hiram Walker & Sons' Kahlúa Royal Cream to develop an official Melrose Place promotion. Bar owners were sent a marketing kit for a sanctioned party, complete with life-size cutouts of the cast and Kahlúa knickknacks.[33]

To what degree is the world of popular culture—and even consumers' perceptions of reality—shaped by the efforts of marketers? More than many of us believe, and this influence is increasing dramatically in recent times.[34] Consider the following examples of this blurring of boundaries between marketing and culture:[35]

* During the O.J. Simpson murder trial, a computer monitor in the courtroom featured a large Sony logo. The company eventually had to replace this with a more discreet design after objections were raised about the free exposure Sony was receiving on news coverage of the proceedings.
* The pink Energizer bunny is being portrayed in documentary-style commercials where "Bunny Spotters" track his movements. According to an agency account director, "The bunny has sort of crossed the line from Hollywood and gone into the real world."[36]

Dale color a tu vida con **Levi's** 517 COLLECTION BOOT CUT

Levi's jeans are a status symbol among upwardly mobile Asian and European consumers, who snap them up even though they retail at over $100 in many countries. The company is beginning to sell the jeans in India, Hungary, Poland, Korea and Turkey.
Courtesy of Levi Strauss & Co.

- The Continental Indoor Soccer League includes a team called the Detroit Neon, named after Chrysler's successful compact car. Similarly, the Hooters restaurant chain now sponsors both an arena football team (the Miami Hooters) and the Jacksonville Hooters of the United States Basketball League.[37]

- In the United Kingdom, Unilever's Van den Bergh Foods Ltd. distributes a video game starring its snack sausage, Peperami. The character battles evil snack-food foes Carlos the Carrot and the Terminutter.[38]

- Some of the most popular episodes of the comedy hit "Seinfeld" are built around products, including Jerry's car (a Saab), Elaine's favourite candy (JuJuBees), Kenny Rogers's Roasters restaurant, Snapple, Junior Mints and Colombo frozen yogurt. Kramer drinks Diet Coke even though he has appeared in Pepsi commercials. On the other hand, George can be seen snacking on Rold Gold Pretzels, which he has also been paid to endorse.[39]

Marketing Ethics and Public Policy

In business, conflicts often arise between the goal of succeeding in the marketplace and the desire to conduct business honestly and to maximize the well-being of consumers by providing them with safe and effective products and services. Some argue that by the time people reach university or graduate school, or are employed by companies, it is a little late to start teaching ethics! Still, many universities and corporations are now focusing very intently on teaching and reinforcing ethical behaviour.

BUSINESS ETHICS

Business ethics essentially are rules of conduct that guide actions in the marketplace—the standards against which most people in a culture judge what is right and what is wrong, good or bad. These universal values include honesty, trustworthiness, fairness, respect, justice, integrity, concern for others, accountability and loyalty. The ethical conduct of some retailers involved in the wedding industry is examined in the video "Wedding Bills" that is attached to this chapter.

Sometimes, ethical decisions can be costly—in the short term—when they result in lost business. For example, despite robust sales of a video game called Night Trap made by Sega, executives at Toys 'R' Us decided to pull the product from store shelves.[40] This action came after they received complaints from parents about the game, in which players defend a group of barely dressed sorority sisters against zombies, who suck out the students' blood with a giant syringe if they win.

Notions of right and wrong do differ among people, organizations and cultures. Some businesses, for example, believe it is all right for salespeople to persuade customers to buy even if it means giving them false information, while other firms feel that anything less than total honesty with customers is terribly wrong. Because each culture has its own set of values, beliefs and customs, ethical business behaviours are defined quite differently around the world. For example, giving "gifts" in exchange for getting business from suppliers or customers is a way of life in many countries, even though this may be considered bribery or extortion in Canada.

PRESCRIBING ETHICAL STANDARDS OF CONDUCT

Professional organizations often devise a code of ethics for their members. For example, the American Marketing Association's Code of Ethics (see ***www.ama.org***) provides guidelines for conduct in many areas of marketing practice, some of which are as follows:[41]

- disclosure of all substantial risks associated with a product or service
- identification of added features that will increase the cost
- avoidance of false or misleading advertising
- rejection of high-pressure or misleading sales tactics
- prohibition of selling or fund raising under the guise of conducting market research.

Whether intentionally or not, some marketers do violate their bond of trust with consumers. In some cases these actions are actually illegal, as when a manufacturer deliberately mislabels the contents of a package or when a retailer adopts a bait and switch selling strategy whereby consumers are lured into the store with promises of inexpensive products with the sole intent of getting them to switch to higher-priced goods. In other cases, marketing practices have detrimental effects on society even though they are not explicitly illegal. Some companies erect billboards for alcohol and tobacco products in low-income neighbourhoods characterized by excessive abuse of these products, while others sponsor commercials depicting groups of people in an unfavourable light in order to get the attention of a target market.

Some time ago Labatt's withdrew their original Fox ad, which depicted the stereotypical "blonde babe" female, after complaints from the public. They changed the images to be more congruent with the attitudes and lifestyles of the new beer-drinking generation. Labatt's seems right on line now with their hip Web site *www.labatt.com*, which allows them to interact daily with their customers.

A crucial barometer of ethical behaviour is what actions a marketer takes once a company is made aware of a problem with its advertising or its products. To what extent will the company try to address the problem rather than attempt to sweep it under the carpet? Corporate marketing documents subpoenaed from Imperial Tobacco Ltd. and RJR–MacDonald Inc. present an inside look at how these competitors carefully craft their brand images to capture the youth market.[42] The tobacco industry as a whole has vehemently denied that it targets adolescents, but the corporate documents of these companies say otherwise. Excerpts from product positioning goals indicate Player's is positioned as "the brand with greatest relevant appeal to younger modern smokers, i.e., those people ranging from starters on up." Other strategy documents state "very young started smokers choose Export 'A' because it provides them with an instant badge of masculinity." The cigarette industry seems to say one thing in public while adopting another strategy in private.

In 1987 the Chrysler Corporation was involved in a scandal when the company was accused of resetting the odometers of supposedly new cars that had actually been driven by managers prior to sale. The company only admitted the practice after some managers tried to get out of paying speeding tickets by claiming that their speedometers didn't work because the cable was disconnected![43]

In contrast, Safeway stores in Vancouver withdrew all their frozen turkeys from their Christmas market shelves in 1995 after receiving a letter, from a radical group, which claimed some turkeys were injected with poison. Tests by Health Canada showed there was no possible way a needle could be injected into the rock-hard turkeys. Hundreds of turkeys were thawed and tested negatively for poison. Nevertheless, to retain customer confidence, Safeway destroyed all their frozen turkeys rather than sell them to the public. This action went a long way to instil the belief that Safeway always has their customers' best interests at heart.

Industry is increasingly coming to realize that ethical behaviour is also good business in the long run, since the trust and satisfaction of consumers translates into years of loyalty from customers whose needs have been met. However, many problems remain. Throughout this book, ethical issues related to the practice of marketing are highlighted. Special boxes called "Marketing Pitfalls" feature questionable practices by marketers or the possible adverse effects on consumers of certain marketing strategies.

NEEDS AND WANTS: DO MARKETERS MANIPULATE CONSUMERS?

One of the most common and stinging criticisms of marketing is that marketing techniques (especially advertising) are responsible for convincing consumers that they "need" many material things and that they will be unhappy and somehow inferior people if they do not have these "necessities." The issue is a complex one and is certainly worth considering: do marketers give people what they want, or do they tell people what they *should* want?

Do Marketers Create Artificial Needs?

The marketing system has come under fire from both ends of the political spectrum. On the one hand, some believe that advertising contributes to the moral breakdown of society by presenting images of hedonistic pleasure, thus encouraging the pursuit of secular humanism. On the other hand, some leftists argue that the same deceitful promises of material pleasure function to buy off people who would otherwise be revolutionaries working to change the system.[44] Through advertising, the system creates demand that only its products can satisfy.

MARKETING PITFALL

The charge that businesses create artificial needs is relevant in the case of gasoline marketing. Oil companies have attempted to convince consumers of the need for premium gasolines, even though this need has been questioned by many people. As one automotive engineer noted, "'Oil company advertising has led people to the conclusion that more expensive fuels will make their car [sic] start easier, get more gas mileage, and last longer, ...' But in most cases this is untrue.... Your engine has to be designed to use that extra octane.... Otherwise,... the extra cost is just lining the pockets of the oil companies." An oil industry executive wrote, "When prices go up a bit, people will come to their senses and premium volumes will diminish... ." But for now, people buy higher-octane fuel for reasons that have nothing to do with car engines; one, he theorized, is "the use of premium as an expression of self-worth."[45] Is the need for higher octane a genuine one or something manufactured by the oil companies through the association of premium gasoline with power, status, manliness and so on?

This ad was created by the American Association of Advertising Agencies to counter charges that ads create artificial needs.
Courtesy of American Association of Advertising Agencies.

Often a bridesmaid but never a bride

This ad from the early 1920s for Listerine mouth-wash is an example of a marketing strategy that highlights a need and then offers a solution. In this case, Edna's failure to get married is blamed on "halitosis" (bad breath). The answer is Listerine.
Courtesy of Warner Lambert, Inc.

A Response: A *need* is a basic biological motive, while a *want* represents one way that society has taught us that the need can be satisfied. For example, while thirst is biologically based, we are taught to want Coca-Cola (*www.cocacola.com*) to satisfy that thirst rather than, say, goat's milk. Thus, the need is already there; marketers simply recommend ways to satisfy it. A basic objective of advertising is to create awareness that these needs exist, rather than to create them.

Are Advertising and Marketing Necessary?

As social critic Vance Packard wrote over 30 years ago, "Large-scale efforts are being made, often with impressive success, to channel our unthinking habits, our purchasing decisions, and our thought processes by the use of insights gleaned from psychiatry and the social sciences."[46] The economist John Kenneth Galbraith feels that radio and television are important tools to accomplish this manipulation of the masses. Since virtually no literacy is required to use these media, they allow repetitive and compelling communications to reach almost everyone.

Goods are arbitrarily linked to desirable social attributes. One influential critic even argued that the problem is that we are not materialistic enough; that is, we do not sufficiently value goods for the utilitarian functions they deliver but instead focus on the irrational value of goods for what they symbolize. According to this view, for example, "Beer would be enough for us, without the additional promise that in drinking it we show ourselves to be manly, young at heart, or neighbourly."[47]

A Response: Products are designed to meet existing needs, and advertising merely helps to communicate their availability. Marketing overcomes some of the disadvantages of labour specialization, whereby most consumers are unfamiliar with the characteristics of mass-produced goods.[48] According to the economics-of-information perspective, advertising is an important source of consumer information.[49] This view emphasizes the economic cost of the time spent searching for products. Accordingly, advertising is a service for which consumers are willing to pay since the information it provides reduces search time.

Do Marketers Promise Miracles?

Consumers are led to believe through advertising that products have magical properties; that is, products will do special and mysterious things for them that will transform their lives. They will be beautiful, have power over others' feelings, be successful, be relieved of all ills, and so on. In this respect, advertising functions as mythology does in primitive societies: it provides simple, anxiety-reducing answers to complex problems.

A Response: Advertisers simply do not know enough about people to manipulate them. Consider that the failure rate for new products ranges from 40 to 80 percent. In testimony, one advertising executive observed that, while people think advertisers have an endless source of magical tricks and/or scientific techniques to manipulate them, in reality the industry is successful when it tries to sell good products and unsuccessful when it sells poor ones.[50]

Public Policy and Consumerism

The welfare of the consumer is protected by many laws at the federal, provincial and municipal levels. Regulations put forth by these governmental agencies sometimes overlap and are constantly changing. The main thrust of regulation is to protect the consumer from unfair business practices and to protect the broad interests of society. Laws involving "cooling off" periods for signing purchase agreements try to protect average consumers from getting into things they later regret. Other laws, such as the labelling of harmful products (e.g., cigarettes) and the prohibition of sales of cer-

This cartoon lampoons the widely held belief that marketers manipulate consumers by making us feel inadequate about ourselves. Then they bombard us with products and services we don't really want or need with the promise that we will be better people, more attractive, more successful and so on if only we will buy them. How valid is this criticism?
Copyright © 1994 by Bill Watterston.
Courtesy of Universal Press Syndicate.

tain substances (e.g., melatonin), are meant to protect the health of Canadians. Some of the various laws are outlined in Table 1–3.

The field of consumer behaviour can play an important role in improving our lives as consumers.[51] Many researchers assist in formulating or evaluating public policies such as those that ensure that products are labelled accurately, that people can comprehend important information presented in advertising, or that children are not exploited by program-length toy commercials masquerading as television shows.

Of course, to a large degree consumers are dependent on their governments to regulate and police safety and environmental standards. The extent of supervision may depend on such factors as the political climate in a country.

TABLE 1–3 Examples of Federal Government Legislation Intended to Enhance Consumers' Welfare		
YEAR	ACT	PURPOSE
1949	National Trademark and True Labelling Act	Sets out who is authorized to use the national trademark "Canada Standards" and how it is to be used. The Act also empowers the Governor in Council to regulate how the content and quality of goods are required to be labelled or described when advertised.
1953	Food and Drugs Act	Protects consumers from purchasing food, cosmetic, drug and therapeutic devices that are passed off in a deceptive or misleading manner or pose a risk to human health.
1969	Hazardous Products Act	Fosters consumer safety through the banning of products that pose unacceptable hazards to the consumer. Products that have a limited potential to harm individuals due to improper care or use are required to be affixed with labels warning consumers of the nature of the danger.
1970	Motor Vehicle Safety Act	Establishes minimum safety standards for motor vehicles and their components through the setting of specific design and performance requirements.
1970	Consumer Packaging and Labelling Act	Sets out regulations for the packaging, labelling and sale of prepackaged goods to consumers.
1970	The Textile Labelling Act	Requires all textile products that are offered for sale to consumers to bear labels attesting to the amount and types of generic fibres contained within the product. The Act also places conditions on the, importation, advertising and sale of these types of products.
1971	Weights and Measures Act	Establishes standardized forms of measurement for use in trade in Canada and assures the accuracy and correct use of all equipment used for this purpose.
1973	Precious Metals Marketing Act	Sets the quality and grading standards to be followed in the identification and marking of precious-metal items.
1986	Competition Act	Prohibits misleading advertising and deceptive marketing practices in promoting the supply or use of a product or service or any business interest.

Sources: *Revised Statutes of Canada, 1985* © Queen's Printer for Canada, Ottawa, 1985; Department of Consumer and Corporate Affairs, *Federal Legislation and Programs relating to Consumer Protection,* March 1973, revised February 1975.

THE DARK SIDE OF CONSUMER BEHAVIOUR

Despite the best efforts of researchers, government regulators and concerned industry people, consumers' worst enemies are sometimes themselves. Individuals often are depicted as rational decision makers, calmly doing their best to obtain products and services that will maximize the health and well-being of themselves, their families and their society. In reality, however, consumers' desires, choices and actions often result in negative consequences to the individual and/or the society in which he or she lives.

Some consumer activities stem from social pressures, such as excessive drinking or cigarette smoking, and the cultural value placed upon money can encourage such activities as shoplifting or insurance fraud. Exposure to unattainable media ideals of beauty and success can create dissatisfaction with the self. Many of these issues will be touched upon later in the book, but for now let's review some dimensions of what has been called the "dark side" of consumer behaviour.

Addictive Consumption

consumer addiction the physiological and/or psychological dependency on products or services

Consumer addiction is a physiological and/or psychological dependency on products or services. While most people equate addiction with drugs, virtually any product or service can be seen as relieving some problem or satisfying some need to the point where reliance on it becomes extreme. Indeed, some psychologists are even raising concerns about "Internet addiction," where people (particularly university students) become obsessed by online chat rooms to the point that their "virtual" lives take priority over their real ones.[52]

Compulsive Consumption

compulsive consumption the process of repetitive, often excessive, shopping used to relieve tension, anxiety, depression or boredom

For some consumers, the expression "born to shop" is taken quite literally. These consumers shop because they are compelled to do so, rather than because shopping is a pleasurable or functional task. **Compulsive consumption** refers to repetitive shopping, often excessive, done as an antidote to tension, anxiety, depression or boredom. "Shopaholics" turn to shopping much the way addicted people turn to drugs or alcohol.[53]

Compulsive consumption is distinctly different from impulse buying, which will be discussed in Chapter 10. The impulse to buy a specific item is temporary, and it centres on a specific product at a particular moment. In contrast, compulsive buying is an enduring behaviour that centres on the process of buying, not the purchases themselves. As one woman who spent $20 000 per year on clothing confessed, "I was possessed when I went into a store. I bought clothes that didn't fit, that I didn't like, and that I certainly didn't need."[54]

In some cases it is fairly safe to say that the consumer, not unlike a drug addict, has little or no control over consumption. The products, whether alcohol, cigarettes, chocolate or diet colas, control the consumer. Even the act of shopping itself is an addicting experience for some consumers. Much negative or destructive consumer behaviour can be characterized by the following three common elements:[55]

1. The behaviour is not done by choice.
2. The gratification derived from the behaviour is short-lived.
3. The person experiences strong feelings of regret or guilt afterwards.

While gambling may be a now-and-again recreational activity for most consumers, it is destructive behaviour for consumers who become addicted, whether it be to casino gambling or to wagering on sports events.
© Brad Bower/Picture Group.

Gambling is an example of a consumption addiction that touches every segment of consumer society. Whether it takes the form of casino gambling, playing the slots, betting on sports events with friends or through a bookie, or buying lottery tickets, excessive gambling can be quite destructive. Taken to extremes, gambling can result in lowered self-esteem, debt, divorce and neglected children. According to one psychologist, gamblers exhibit a classic addictive cycle: they experience a high while in action and depression when they stop gambling, which leads them back to the thrill of the action. Unlike drug addicts, however, money is the substance that hard-core gamblers abuse.[56] The Ontario government's Ministry of Health recently committed one million dollars to combat problem gambling;[57] this is eight times the amount budgeted to treat eating disorders.

Illegal Activities

Many consumer behaviours are not only self-destructive or socially damaging, they are illegal as well. Crimes committed by consumers against businesses have been estimated to total more than $40 billion per year. These include shoplifting, employee pilferage, arson and insurance fraud. Arson alone causes $2 billion per year in damages and is growing by 25 percent annually.[58]

A retail theft is committed every five seconds. **Shrinkage** is the industry term for inventory and cash losses due to shoplifting and employee theft. This is a massive problem for businesses, which is passed on to consumers in the form of higher prices (about 40 percent of the losses can be attributed to employees rather than shoppers). A family of four spends about $300 extra per year because of mark-ups to cover shrinkage.[59] The problem is not unique to North America. For example, shrinkage losses in Great Britain are estimated at more than £1 million per day.[60]

Shoplifting increased by a third in a period of only four years. The large majority of shoplifting is *not* done by professional thieves or by people who genuinely need the stolen items.[61] About three-quarters of those caught are middle- or high-

shrinkage the loss of money or inventory due to shoplifting and/or employee theft

This ad for the Colortag system promotes one technique that has been used in Europe and North America to deter shoplifters. A plastic tag squirts ink on a garment when a thief breaks it open, rendering the item worthless. *Courtesy of Colortag, Inc.*

income people who shoplift for the thrill of it or as a substitute for affection. Shoplifting is common among adolescents. Research evidence indicates that teen shoplifting is influenced by such factors as having friends who shoplift. It is also more likely to occur if the adolescent does not believe that this behaviour is morally wrong.[62]

ANTICONSUMPTION

anticonsumption the actions taken by consumers that involve the deliberate defacement or mutilation of products

culture jamming the defacement or alterations of advertising materials as a form of political expression

cultural resistance the process where subcultures of consumers who are alienated from mainstream society single out objects that represent the values of the larger group and modify them as an act of rebellion or self-expression

Some types of destructive consumer behaviour can be thought of as **anticonsumption,** whereby products and services are deliberately defaced or mutilated. Anticonsumption can range from product tampering, where innocent consumers are hurt or killed, to graffiti on buildings and subways. Anticonsumption can also take the form of political protest, in which activists alter or destroy billboards and other advertisements that promote what they feel to be unhealthy or unethical acts—a practice that has been termed **culture jamming.** For example, some members of the clergy in areas heavily populated by minorities have organized rallies to protest the proliferation of cigarette and alcohol advertising in their neighbourhoods.

In some cases these acts are a form of **cultural resistance,** whereby those in consumer subcultures that are alienated from mainstream society (juvenile delinquents, for example) single out objects that represent the values of the larger group and modify them as an act of rebellion or self-expression.[63]

CONSUMER BEHAVIOUR AS A FIELD OF STUDY

Hopefully by now it's clear that the field of consumer behaviour encompasses many things, from the simple purchase of a carton of milk to the selection of a complex

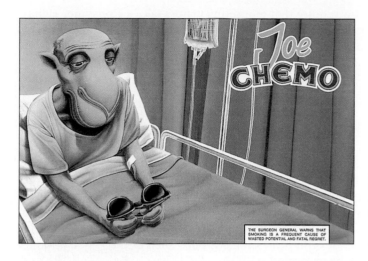

Adbusters Quarterly
(***www.adbusters.org***) is a
Canadian magazine devoted
to culture jamming.
Courtesy of Adbusters Quarterly 1-800-663-1243.

networked computer system, from the decision to donate money to a charity to devious plans to rip off a company or store. There's an awful lot to understand, and many ways to go about doing so.

Although people have certainly been consumers for a long time, it is only recently that consumption *per se* has been the object of formal study. In fact, while

Health Canada's approach to
curb smoking among the young
is to limit the distribution system.
Courtesy of Health Canada.

many business schools now require that marketing majors take a Consumer Behaviour course, most universities did not even offer such a course until the 1970s. Much of the impetus for the attention now being given to consumer behaviour was the realization by many business people that the consumer really *is* the boss.

Interdisciplinary Influences on the Study of Consumer Behaviour

Consumer behaviour is a very young field, and, as it grows, it is being influenced by many different perspectives. Indeed, it is hard to think of a field that is more interdisciplinary. People with training in a very wide range of fields—from psycho-physiology to literature—can now be found doing consumer research. Consumer researchers are employed by universities, manufacturers, museums, advertising agencies and governments. Several professional groups, such as the Association for Consumer Research, have been formed since the mid-1970s.

To gain an idea of the diversity of interests of people who do consumer research, consider the list of professional associations that sponsor the field's major journal, the *Journal of Consumer Research*. They are the American Home Economics Association, the American Statistical Association, the Association for Consumer Research, the Society for Consumer Psychology, the International Communication Association, the American Sociological Association, the Institute of Management Sciences, the American Anthropological Association, the American Marketing Association, the Society for Personality and Social Psychology, the American Asso-

FIGURE 1–3 • The Pyramid of Consumer Behaviour

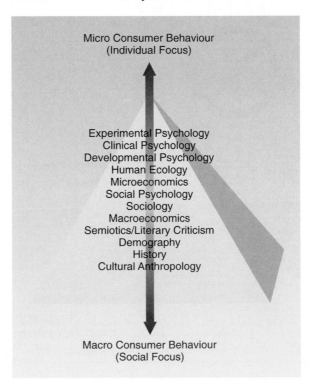

ciation for Public Opinion Research, and the American Economic Association.

These diverse researchers approach consumer issues from different perspectives. You might remember a children's story about the blind men and the elephant. The gist of the story is that each man touched a different part of the animal and, as a result, the descriptions each gave of the elephant were quite different. This analogy applies to consumer research as well. A similar consumer phenomenon can be studied in different ways and at different levels, depending on the training and interests of the researchers studying it.

Figure 1–3 provides a glimpse at some of the disciplines working in the field and the level at which each approaches research issues. These diverse disciplines can be roughly characterized in terms of their focus on micro versus macro consumer behaviour topics. The fields closer to the top of the pyramid concentrate upon the individual consumer (micro issues), while those towards the base are more interested in the aggregate activities that occur among larger groups of people (macro issues), such as consumption patterns shared by members of a culture or subculture.

To demonstrate that the same marketing issue can be explored at different levels, we return to the choice faced by Gail when she was selecting a magazine to buy. Table 1–4 lists research issues that might be of interest to each contributing disci-

TABLE 1–4 Interdisciplinary Research Issues in Consumer Behaviour

DISCIPLINARY FOCUS	MAGAZINE USAGE SAMPLE RESEARCH ISSUES
Experimental Psychology: product role in perception, learning, and memory processes	How specific aspects of magazines, such as their design or layout, are recognized and interpreted; which parts of a magazine are most likely to be read
Clinical Psychology: product role in psychological adjustment	How magazines affect readers' body images (e.g., do thin models make the average woman feel overweight?)
Microeconomics/Human Ecology: product role in allocation of individual or family resources	Factors influencing the amount of money spent on magazines in a household
Social Psychology: product role in the behaviour of individuals as members of social groups	Ways that ads in a magazine affect readers' attitudes towards the products depicted; how peer pressure influences a person's readership decisions
Sociology: product role in social institutions and group relationships	Pattern by which magazine preferences spread through a social group
Macroeconomics: product role in consumers' relations with the marketplace	Effects of the price of fashion magazines and expense of items advertised during periods of high unemployment
Semiotics/Literary Criticism: product role in the verbal and visual communication of meaning	Ways in which underlying messages communicated by models and ads in a magazine are interpreted
Demography: product role in the measurable characteristics of a population	Effects of age, income and marital status of a magazine's readers
History: product role in societal changes over time	Ways in which our culture's depictions of "femininity" in magazines have changed over time
Cultural Anthropology: product role in a society's beliefs and practices	Ways in which fashions and models in a magazine affect readers' definitions of masculine versus feminine behaviour

pline and provides examples of how these might be applied in the marketing of women's magazines.

The Issue of Strategic Focus

Many people regard the field of consumer behaviour as an applied social science. Accordingly, the value of the knowledge generated should be evaluated in terms of its ability to improve the effectiveness of marketing practice. Recently, though, some researchers have argued that consumer behaviour should not have a strategic focus at all; that is, the field should not be a "handmaiden to business." It should instead focus on the understanding of consumption for its own sake, rather than because the knowledge can be applied by marketers.[64] This rather extreme view is probably not held by most consumer researchers, but it has encouraged many to expand the scope of their work beyond the field's traditional focus on the purchase of consumer goods such as food, appliances, cars, and so on. And it has certainly led to some fiery debates among people working in the field!

The Issue of Two Perspectives on Consumer Research

paradigm a widely accepted view or model of phenomena being studied

positivism a research perspective that relies on principles of the "scientific method" and assumes that a single reality exists; events in the world can be objectively measured; and the causes of behaviour can be identified, manipulated and predicted

interpretivism a research perspective that produces a "thick description" of consumers' subjective experiences and stresses the importance of the individual's social construction of reality

One general way to classify consumer research is in terms of the fundamental assumptions the researchers make about what they are studying and how to study it. This set of beliefs is known as a **paradigm.** Like other fields of study, consumer behaviour is dominated by a paradigm, but some believe it is in the middle of a *paradigm shift,* which occurs when a competing paradigm challenges the dominant set of assumptions.

The basic set of assumptions underlying the dominant paradigm at this point in time is called **positivism** (or sometimes *modernism*). This perspective has significantly influenced Western art and science since the late sixteenth century. It emphasizes that human reason is supreme and that there is a single, objective truth that can be discovered by science. Positivism encourages us to stress the function of objects, to celebrate technology, and to regard the world as a rational, ordered place with a clearly defined past, present and future.

The emerging paradigm of **interpretivism** (or *postmodernism*) questions these assumptions. Proponents of this perspective argue that there is too much emphasis on science and technology in our society and that this ordered, rational view of consumers denies the complex social and cultural world in which we live. Others feel that positivism puts too much emphasis on material well-being and that its logical outlook is dominated by an ideology that stresses the homogeneous views of a culture dominated by white males.

Interpretivists instead stress the importance of symbolic, subjective experience and the idea that meaning is in the mind of the person—that is, we each construct our own meanings based on our unique and shared cultural experiences, so that there are no single right or wrong answers. In this view, the world in which we live is composed of a *pastiche,* or mixture of images.[65] The value placed on products because they help us to create order in our lives is replaced by an appreciation of consumption as a set of diverse experiences.

The major differences between these two perspectives on consumer research are summarized in Table 1–5.

TABLE 1–5 Positivist versus Interpretivist Approaches to Consumer Behaviour

ASSUMPTIONS	POSITIVIST APPROACH	INTERPRETIVIST APPROACH
Nature of reality	Objective, tangible Single	Socially constructed Multiple
Goal	Prediction	Understanding
Knowledge generated	Time free Context independent	Time bound Context dependent
View of causality	Existence of real causes	Multiple, simultaneous shaping events
Research relationship	Separation between researcher and subject	Interactive, cooperative with researcher being part of phenomenon under study

Source: Adapted from Laurel A. Hudson and Julie L. Ozanne, "Alternative Ways of Seeking Knowledge in Consumer Research," *Journal of Consumer Research* 14 (March 1988): 508–21. Reprinted with the permission of The University of Chicago Press.

TAKING IT FROM HERE: THE PLAN OF THE BOOK

This book covers many facets of consumer behaviour, and many of the research perspectives briefly described in this chapter will be highlighted in later chapters. The plan of the book is simple: it goes from micro to macro. Think of the book as a sort of photograph album of consumer behaviour: each chapter provides a "snapshot" of consumers, but the lens used to take each picture gets successively wider.

The book begins with issues related to the individual consumer and expands its focus until it eventually considers the behaviours of large groups of people in their social settings. The topics to be covered correspond to the wheel of consumer behaviour presented in Figure 1–4.

Section II, "Consumers as Individuals," considers the consumer at his or her most micro level. It examines how the individual receives information from his or her immediate environment and how this material is learned, stored in memory, and used to form and modify individual attitudes—both about products and about oneself. Section III, "Consumers as Decision Makers," explores the ways in which consumers use the information they have acquired to make decisions about consumption activities, both as individuals and as group members. Section IV, "Consumers and Subcultures," further expands the focus by considering how the consumer functions as a part of a larger social structure. This structure includes the influence of different social groups to which the consumer belongs and with which he or she identifies, including social class, ethnic groups and age groups. Finally, Section V, "Consumers and Culture," completes the picture as it examines marketing's impact on mass culture. These effects include the relationship of marketing to the expression of cultural values and lifestyles, how products and services are related to rituals and cultural myths, and the interface between marketing efforts and the creation of art, music and other forms of popular culture that are so much a part of our daily lives.

FIGURE 1–4   •   The Wheel of Consumer Behaviour

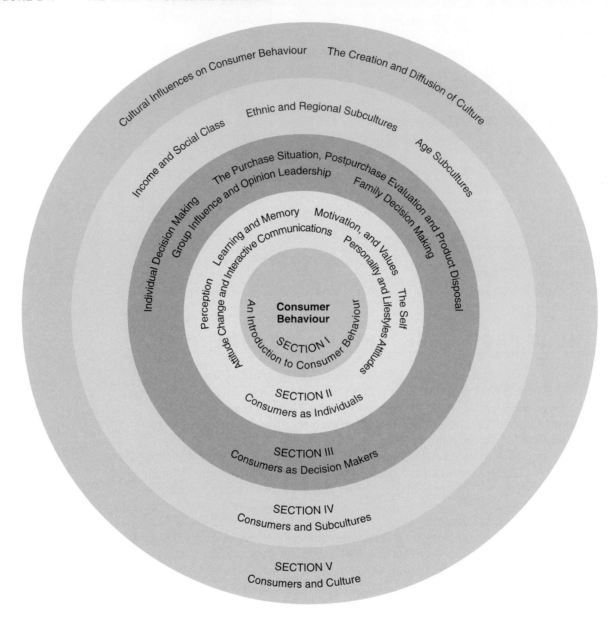

- Consumer behaviour is the study of the processes involved when individuals or groups select, purchase, use or dispose of products, services, ideas or experiences to satisfy needs and desires.

- A consumer may purchase, use and/or dispose of a product, but these functions may be performed by different people. In addition, consumers may be thought of as role players who need different products to help them play their various parts.

- Market segmentation is an important aspect of consumer behaviour. Consumers can be segmented along many dimensions, including product usage, demographics (the objective aspects of a population, such as age and sex) and psychographics (psychological and lifestyle characteristics). Emerging developments, such as the new emphasis on relationship marketing and the practice of database marketing, mean that marketers are much more attuned to the wants and needs of different consumer groups.

- Marketing activities exert an enormous impact on individuals. Consumer behaviour is relevant to our understanding of both public policy issues (for example, ethical marketing practices) and the dynamics of popular culture.

- Marketers try to communicate with consumers by creating relationships between their products or services and desired attributes. A semiotic analysis involves the correspondence between stimuli and the meaning of signs. The intended meaning may be literal (an icon like a street sign with a picture of children playing). The meaning may be indexical: it relies on shared characteristics (the red in a stop sign means danger). Finally, meaning can be conveyed by a symbol, where an image is given meaning by convention or by agreement by members of a society (stop signs are octagonal, while yield signs are triangular).

- While textbooks often paint a picture of the consumer as a rational, informed decision maker, in reality many consumer activities are harmful to individuals or to society. The dark side of consumer behaviour includes addiction, the use of people as products (consumed consumers) and theft or vandalism (anticonsumption).

- The field of consumer behaviour is interdisciplinary; it is composed of researchers from many different fields who share an interest in how people interact with the marketplace. These disciplines can be categorized by the degree to which their focus is micro (the individual consumer) versus macro (the consumer as a member of groups or of the larger society).

- There are many perspectives on consumer behaviour, but research orientations can roughly be divided into two approaches. The positivist perspective, which currently dominates the field, emphasizes the objectivity of science and the consumer as a rational decision maker. The interpretivist perspective, in contrast, stresses the subjective meaning of the consumer's individual experience and the idea that any behaviour is subject to multiple interpretations rather than a single explanation.

CHAPTER SUMMARY

KEY TERMS

Anticonsumption p. 32

Business ethics p. 24

Compulsive consumption p. 30

Consumer addiction p. 30

Consumer behaviour p. 8

Cultural resistance p.32

Culture jamming p. 32

Database marketing p. 16

Demographics p. 11

Exchange p. 9

Interpretant p. 21

Interpretivism p. 36

Object p. 21

Paradigm p. 36

Popular culture p. 19

Positivism p. 36

Relationship marketing p. 16

Role theory p. 8

Semiotics p. 21

Shrinkage p. 31

Sign p. 21

CONSUMER BEHAVIOUR CHALLENGE

1. This chapter states that people play different roles, and that their consumption behaviours may differ depending on the particular role they are playing. State whether you agree or disagree with this perspective, giving examples from your personal life.

2. Some researchers believe that the field of consumer behaviour should be a pure, rather than an applied, science; that is, research issues should be framed in terms of their scientific interest rather than their applicability to immediate marketing problems. Give your views on this issue.

3. Name some products or services that are widely used by your social group. State whether you agree or disagree with the notion that these products help to form the group bonds, supporting your argument with examples from your list of products used by the group.

4. Although demographic information on large numbers of consumers is used in many marketing contexts, some people believe that the sale of data on customers' incomes, buying habits and so on constitutes an invasion of privacy and should be stopped. Comment on this issue from both a consumer's and a marketer's point of view.

5. List the three stages in the consumption process. Describe the issues that you considered in each of these stages when you made a recent important purchase.

6. State the differences between the positivist and interpretivist approaches to consumer research. For each type of inquiry, give examples of product dimensions that would be more usefully explored using that type of research over the other.

7. What aspects of consumer behaviour are likely to be of interest to a financial planner? To a university administrator? To a graphic arts designer? To a social worker in a government agency? To a nursing instructor?

8. Do marketers have the ability to control our desires or the power to create needs?

9. Find an ad that is rich in symbolism and perform a semiotic analysis of it. Identify each type of sign used in the ad and the product qualities being communicated by each. Comment on the effectiveness of the signs that are used to communicate the intended message.

CBC VIDEO VIGNETTES

Concepts at Work for Wedding Bills

Some groups of consumers, such as children, the elderly, the physically and mentally challenged, and the poor, are recognized as vulnerable to "rip-offs" in the marketplace. Laws regarding consumer protection and competitive practices, and codes of ethics for various marketing activities, are in place to protect these consumers. However, even consumers with considerable savvy can be misled and overwhelmed by business tactics in certain situations, such as when making purchases for a wedding.

With a trend towards bigger and more formal weddings, couples are faced with an expensive and emotional event. Allen and Denise Fields documented some of the unscrupulous practices of retailers who take unfair advantage of the couple's situation. Retailers selling wedding merchandise can train their salespeople carefully to orchestrate the buying situation so that couples overspend on individual items, buy items they do not want, make

unwarranted penalty payments, limit their comparison shopping and misunderstand price tags. Newlyweds are left feeling resentful and burdened with bills that they did not expect and that may take years to pay.

QUESTIONS

1. Why are couples vulnerable when in the marketplace for wedding merchandise?

2. What kinds of unscrupulous practices might a couple encounter?

3. What can a couple do to protect themselves when planning a wedding?

4. Who, or what organization, should be responsible for consumer protection?

Video Resource: "Wedding Bills," *Marketplace* #24 (April 2, 1996).

NOTES

1. Deirdre Carmody, "Hearst Finds Unexpected Success in a Magazine for Dreamers," *New York Times* (September 12, 1994): D6.

2. Joanne Lipman, "Women in Their 20s Seem to Be Ignored," *Wall Street Journal* (June 9, 1992): B8.

3. Suzanne Cassidy, "Defining the Cosmo Girl: Check Out the Passport," *New York Times* (October 12, 1992): D8.

4. Erving Goffman, *The Presentation of Self in Everyday Life* (Garden City, NY: Doubleday, 1959); George H. Mead, *Mind, Self, and Society* (Chicago: University of Chicago Press, 1934); Michael R. Solomon, "The Role of Products as Social Stimuli: A Symbolic Interactionism Perspective," *Journal of Consumer Research* 10 (December 1983): 319–29.

5. William F. Schoell and Joseph P. Guiltinan, *Marketing: Contemporary Concepts and Practices*, 4th ed. (Boston: Allyn & Bacon, 1990).

6. Ronald Alsop, "Agencies Scrutinize Their Ads for Psychological Symbolism," *Wall Street Journal* (June 11, 1987): 27.

7. Jeffrey F. Durgee, "On Cezanne, Hot Buttons, and Interpreting Consumer Storytelling," *Journal of Consumer Marketing* 5 (Fall 1988): 47–51.

8. Bernice Kanner, "Mind Games," *Marketing Insights* 9 (Spring 1989): 50.

9. Annetta Miller, "You Are What You Buy," *Newsweek* (June 4, 1990): 59.

10. Natalie Perkins, "Zeroing in on Consumer Values," *Advertising Age* (March 22, 1993): 23.

11. Quoted in March Magiera, "Levi's Broadens Appeal," *Advertising Age* (July 17, 1989): 1 (2 pp.).

12. Jennifer Lawrence, "Gender-Specific Works for Diapers—Almost Too Well," *Advertising Age* (February 8, 1993): S–10 (2 pp.).

13. Julie Candler, "Woman Car Buyer—Don't Call Her a Niche Anymore," *Advertising Age* (January 21, 1991): S–8.

14. "Club Med in a Family Way," *American Demographics* (January 1987): 25.

15. Stuart Elliott, "Club Med Says It's for Families," *New York Times* (October 8, 1991): D22.

16. Amy Stevens, "Where the Boys, Girls, Teens, Couples, Tots, and Washing-Machine Salesmen Are," *Wall Street Journal* (May 16, 1997): B1.

17. Richard P. Coleman, "The Continuing Significance of Social Class to Marketing," *Journal of Consumer Research* 10 (December 1983): 265–80.

18. Dan Gardner, "Immigration Ignored in Election Despite Its Impact On Future," *Vancouver Sun* (May 31, 1997): A6.

19. Eve Johnson, "Getting a Taste for Canada," *Vancouver Sun* (June 19, 1995): C1.

20. Kevin Gudrige, "High Prices Wear Well for Cataloger," *Advertising Age* (August 23, 1993): 10.

21. Jonathan Berry, "Database Marketing," *Business Week* (September 5, 1994): 56 (7 pp.).

22. Gerri Hirshey, "Gambling Nation," *The New York Times Magazine* (July 17, 1994): 36 (14 pp.).

23. Bruce Orwall, "Like Playing Slots? Casinos Know All About You," *New York Times* (December 20, 1995): B1 (2 pp.).

24. Jane Hodges and Alice Z. Cuneo, "Levi's Registration Program Will Seek to Build Database," *Advertising Age* (February 24, 1997): 86.

25. Robert C. Blattberg and John Deighton, "Interactive Marketing: Exploiting the Age of Addressability," *Sloan Management Review* 331, 1 (Fall 1991): 5–14.

26. Quoted in "Bringing Meaning to Brands," *American Demographics* (June 1997): 34.

27. Susan Fournier, "A Consumer-Brand Relationship Framework for Strategic Brand Management," Doctoral Dissertation, Department of Marketing, University of Florida, 1994.

28. See David Mick, "Consumer Research and Semiotics: Exploring the Morphology of Signs, Symbols, and Significance," *Journal of Consumer Research* 13 (September 1986): 196–213.

29. Teresa J. Domzal and Jerome B. Kernan, "Reading Advertising: The What and How of Product Meaning," *Journal of Consumer Marketing* 9 (Summer 1992): 48–64.

30. Arthur Asa Berger, *Signs in Contemporary Culture: An Introduction to Semiotics* (New York: Longman, 1984); Mick, "Consumer Research and Semiotics"; Charles Sanders Peirce, in *Collected Papers*, eds. Charles Hartshorne, Paul Weiss and Arthur W. Burks (Cambridge, MA: Harvard University Press, 1931–1958).

31. For a recent discussion of this trend, see Russell W. Belk, "Hyperreality and Globalization: Culture in the Age of Ronald McDonald," parts 1 and 2, *Journal of International Consumer Marketing* 8, 3&4.

32. Nina Munk, "The Levi Straddle," *Forbes* (January 17, 1994): 44 (2 pp.).

33. Mary Kuntz and Joseph Weber, "The New Hucksterism," *Business Week* (July 1, 1996): 75 (7 pp.).

34. "Goodbye Johnny, Hello Tic Tac," *Advertising Age* (May 25, 1992): 22; Cleveland Horton, "Hyundai Pulls Planned Ad in L.A. Beating Aftermath," *Advertising Age* (April 22, 1991): 2; Randall Rothenberg, "Does Integration Lead to Segregation?: The Ethical Problems of Integrated Marketing," in *Integrated Marketing Communications*, eds. Jeri Moore and Esther Thorson (Hillsdale, NJ: Lawrence Erlbaum, 1992).

35. Fara Warner, "Why It's Getting Harder to Tell the Shows from the Ads," *Wall Street Journal* (June 15, 1995): B1 (2 pp.).

36. Quoted in David Barboza, "Advertising: A Campaign that Keeps 'Going and Going and Going' is now Going in Some New Directions," *New York Times* (December 26, 1996): D7.

37. Randall Lane, "The Ultimate Sponsorship," *Forbes* (March 14, 1994): 106.

38. Kuntz and Weber, "The New Hucksterism."

39. Warner, "Why It's Getting Harder"; T.L. Stanley, "You Want It Where?" *PROMO Magazine* (May 1997): S4 (4 pp.).

40. Joseph Pereira, "Toys 'R' Us Says It Decided to Pull Sega's Night Trap From Store Shelves," *Wall Street Journal* (December 17, 1993): B5F.

41. American Marketing Association, *Code of Ethics*, rev. ed. (Chicago: American Marketing Association, 1985).

42. Anne Lavack, "Using Brand Image to Compete for the Youth Market: The Case of Export 'A' and Player's," in Administrative Sciences Association of Canada (ASAC) Conference Proceedings, 14(3) 1993, 142–51.

43. "Dear Chrysler: Outsiders Advice on Handling the Odometer Charge," *Wall Street Journal* (June 26, 1987): 19.

44. William Leiss, Stephen Kline and Sut Jhally, *Social Communication in Advertising: Persons, Products, & Images of Well-Being* (Toronto: Methuen, 1986); Jerry Mander, *Four Arguments for the Elimination of Television* (New York: William Morrow, 1977).

45. Matthew L. Wald, "Looking for Savings as Gas Prices Rise," *New York Times* (May 27, 1989): 48.

46. Packard, *The Hidden Persuaders* (1957): 11; quoted in Leiss, Kline and Jhally, *Social Communication.*

47. Raymond Williams, "Advertising: The Magic System," in *Problems in Materialism and Culture* (London: New Left Books, 1962).

48. Leiss, Kline and Jhally, *Social Communication.*

49. George Stigler, "The Economics of Information," *Journal of Political Economy* (1961): 69.

50. Quoted in Leiss, Kline and Jhally, *Social Communication.*

51. For consumer research and discussions related to public policy issues, see Paul N. Bloom and Stephen A. Greyser, "The Maturing of Consumerism," *Har-*

vard *Business Review* (November/December 1981): 130–39; George S. Day, "Assessing the Effect of Information Disclosure Requirements," *Journal of Marketing* (April 1976): 42–52; Dennis E. Garrett, "The Effectiveness of Marketing Policy Boycotts: Environmental Opposition to Marketing," *Journal of Marketing* 51 (January 1987): 44–53; Michael Houston and Michael Rothschild, "Policy-Related Experiments on Information Provision: A Normative Model and Explication," *Journal of Marketing Research* 17 (November 1980): 432–49; Jacob Jacoby, Wayne D. Hoyer and David A. Sheluga, *Misperception of Televised Communications* (New York: American Association of Advertising Agencies, 1980); Gene R. Laczniak and Patrick E. Murphy, *Marketing Ethics: Guidelines for Managers* (Lexington, MA: Lexington Books, 1985): 117–23; Lynn Phillips and Bobby Calder, "Evaluating Consumer Protection Laws: Promising Methods," *Journal of Consumer Affairs* 14 (Summer 1980): 9–36; Donald P. Robin and Eric Reidenbach, "Social Responsibility, Ethics, and Marketing Strategy: Closing the Gap Between Concept and Application," *Journal of Marketing* 51 (January 1987): 44–58; Howard Schutz and Marianne Casey, "Consumer Perceptions of Advertising as Misleading," *Journal of Consumer Affairs* 15 (Winter 1981): 340–57; Darlene Brannigan Smith and Paul N. Bloom, "Is Consumerism Dead or Alive? Some New Evidence," in *Advances in Consumer Research* 11, ed. Thomas C. Kinnear (Provo, UT: Association for Consumer Research, 1984): 369–73.

52. "Psychologist Warns of Internet Addiction," *Montgomery Advertiser* (August 18, 1997): 2D.

53. Thomas C. O'Guinn and Ronald J. Faber, "Compulsive Buying: A Phenomenological Explanation," *Journal of Consumer Research* 16 (September 1989): 154.

54. Quoted in Anastasia Toufexis, "365 Shopping Days Till Christmas," *Time* (December 26, 1988): 82; see also Ronald J. Faber and Thomas C. O'Guinn, "Compulsive Consumption and Credit Abuse," *Journal of Consumer Policy* 11 (1988): 109–21; Mary S. Butler, "Compulsive Buying: It's No Joke," *Consumer's Digest* (September 1986): 55.

55. Georgia Witkin, "The Shopping Fix," *Health* (May 1988): 73; see also Arch G. Woodside and Randolph J. Trappey III, "Compulsive Consumption of a Consumer Service: An Exploratory Study of Chronic Horse Race Track Gambling Behavior" (Working Paper #90–MKTG–04, A.B. Freeman School of Business, Tulane University, 1990); Rajan Nataraajan and Brent G. Goff, "Manifestations of Compulsiveness in the Consumer-Marketplace Domain," *Psychology &*

Marketing 9 (January 1992): 31–44; Joann Ellison Rodgers, "Addiction: A Whole New View," *Psychology Today* (September/October 1994): 32 (11 pp.).

56. James Barron, "Are We All Really Losers with Gambling, a Spreading Social Addiction?" *New York Times* (May 31, 1989): A18.

57. Jane Coutts, "Ontario Health-Care Cuts Hit Home," *Globe and Mail* (May 3, 1997): A6.

58. Paul Bernstein, "Cheating: The New National Pastime?" *Business* (October/December 1985): 24–33.

59. "Shoplifting: Bess Myerson's Arrest Highlights a Multibillion-Dollar Problem that Many Stores Won't Talk About," *Life* (August 1988): 32.

60. Roy Carter, "Whispering Sweet Nothings to the Shop Thief," *Retail & Distribution Management* (January/February 1986): 36.

61. Catherine A. Cole, "Deterrence and Consumer Fraud," *Journal of Retailing* 65 (Spring 1989): 107–20; Stephen J. Grove, Scott J. Vitell and David Strutton, "Non-Normative Consumer Behavior and the Techniques of Neutralization," in *Marketing Theory and Practice*, eds. Terry Childers et al. (1989 AMA Winter Educators Conference; Chicago: American Marketing Association, 1989): 131–35.

62. Anthony D. Cox, Dena Cox, Ronald D. Anderson and George P. Moschis, "Social Influences on Adolescent Shoplifting—Theory, Evidence, and Implications for the Retail Industry," *Journal of Retailing* 69, 2 (Summer 1993): 234–46.

63. Julie L. Ozanne, Ronald Paul Hill and Newell D. Wright, "Culture as Contested Terrain: The Juvenile Delinquents' Use of Consumption as Cultural Resistance" (unpublished manuscript, Virginia Polytechnic Institute and State University, 1994).

64. Morris B. Holbrook, "The Consumer Researcher Visits Radio City: Dancing in the Dark," in *Advances in Consumer Research* 12, eds. Elizabeth C. Hirschman and Morris B. Holbrook (Provo, UT: Association for Consumer Research, 1985): 28–31.

65. Alladi Venkatesh, "Postmodernism, Poststructuralism and Marketing" (paper presented at the American Marketing Association Winter Theory Conference, San Antonio, February 1992); see also A. Fuat Firat, "Postmodern Culture, Marketing and the Consumer," in *Marketing Theory and Application*, eds. T. Childers et al. (Chicago: American Marketing Association, 1991): 237–42; A. Fuat Firat and Alladi Venkatesh, "The Making of Postmodern Consumption," in *Consumption and Marketing: Macro Dimensions*, eds. Russell W. Belk and Nikhilesh Dholakia (Boston: PWS-Kent, 1993).

II

Consumers as Individuals

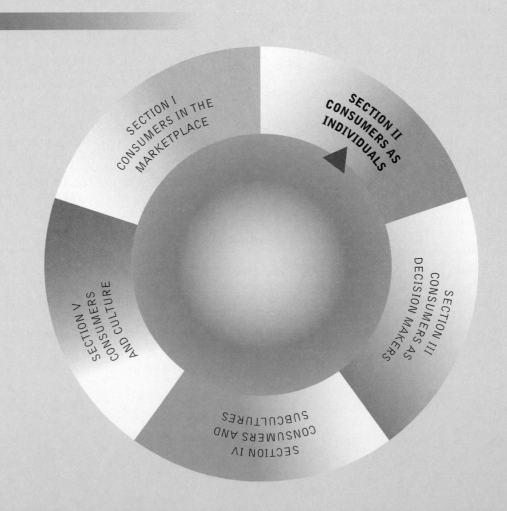

SECTION I
CONSUMERS IN THE
MARKETPLACE

SECTION II
CONSUMERS AS
INDIVIDUALS

SECTION III
CONSUMERS AS
DECISION MAKERS

SECTION IV
CONSUMERS AND
SUBCULTURES

SECTION V
CONSUMERS
AND CULTURE

In this section we focus on the internal dynamics of consumer behaviour. We are constantly confronted with advertising messages, products, other people persuading us to buy, and reflections of ourselves. Each chapter in this section will consider a different aspect of the consumer—perceptions, memories and attitudes—that is invisible to others.

Chapter 2 describes the process of perception, in which information from the outside world about products and other people is absorbed by the individual and interpreted. Chapter 3 focuses on the ways this information is mentally stored and how it adds to our existing knowledge about the world as it is learned. Chapter 4 discusses our reasons or motivations for absorbing this information and how particular needs influence the way we think about products.

Chapters 5 and 6 explore how our views about ourselves and our lifestyles affect what we do, want and buy. Chapter 5 looks at the self and gender roles in our society; we are interested in the images we portray to others and the images we aspire to. Chapter 6 takes a look at the importance of lifestyle to segmentation issues, as well as trends we can expect in the future.

Chapters 7 and 8 discuss how attitudes— our evaluations of all these products, ad messages and so on—are formed and (sometimes) changed by marketers. When all of these "internal" parts are put together, the unique role of each individual consumer as a self-contained agent in the marketplace will be clear.

Gary has his first big date with Janeen tonight. Since Janeen is a very sophisticated woman, two years older than Gary, he is sure he needs a special cologne for this occasion.

Gary drags his buddy Sanjay to the store, and the two friends check out the selections at the fragrance counter. There are so many scents to choose from. Which will send the right message? The colognes and toilet waters run the gamut, from spin-offs of women's perfumes with fancy French names, like Cacharel Pour Homme, to down-to-earth "macho" brands like Brut. After smelling a few samples, Gary realizes this won't be as easy as he thought. Some of the choices have a thick, sweet scent, while others are more crisp and even citrusy. Just as he's about to give up, Sanjay calls his attention to a cologne called Drakkar Noir, which comes in a mysterious-looking, solid black bottle. Aha! This is the image he wants to cultivate for Janeen—exotic and a bit mysterious. Gary grabs a bottle as he is sure this is the best cologne to give Janeen the right impression.

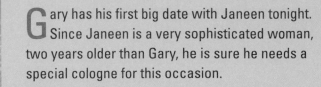

UNITED COLORS OF BENETTON.

2

Perception

INTRODUCTION

We live in a world overflowing with sensations. Wherever we turn, we are bombarded by a symphony of colours, sounds and odours. Some of the "notes" in this symphony, such as the loud barking of a dog, the shades of the evening sky or the heady smell of a rose-bush, occur naturally. Others come from people: the person sitting next to you in class might sport tinted blonde hair, bright pink pants and a vanilla-chocolate scent.

Marketers certainly contribute to this commotion. Consumers are never far from advertisements, product packages, radio and television commercials, and billboards that clamour for their attention. Each of us copes with this bombardment by paying attention to some stimuli and tuning out others. And the messages to which we do choose to pay attention often wind up differing from what the sponsors intended, as we each put our "spin" on things by taking away meanings consistent with our own unique experiences, biases and desires. This chapter focuses on the process of perception, in which sensations are absorbed by the consumer and used to interpret the surrounding world.

Sensation is the immediate response of our sensory receptors (eyes, ears, nose, mouth and fingers) to such basic stimuli as light, colour and sound. **Perception** is the process by which these sensations are selected, organized and interpreted. The study

sensation the immediate response of sensory receptors (eyes, ears, nose, mouth, fingers) to such basic stimuli as light, colour and sound

perception the process by which stimuli are selected, organized and interpreted

47

of perception focuses on what we add to or take away from these raw sensations as we choose which to notice, and then go about assigning meaning to them.

The subjective nature of perception is demonstrated by a controversial advertisement developed for Benetton by a French agency and shown at the beginning of the chapter. Because a black man and a white man are handcuffed together, the ad was the target of many complaints about racism after it appeared in magazines and on billboards around the United States, even though the company has a reputation for promoting racial tolerance. People interpreted it to depict a black man who had been arrested by a white man;[1] people's prior assumptions distorted the ad's meaning.

The perceptual process is illustrated by Gary's purchase of a new cologne. He had learned to equate cologne with romantic appeal, so he searched for cues that would increase (he believed) his attractiveness to Janeen. Gary made his selection by considering such factors as the image associated with each alternative and the design of the bottles, as well as the actual scents he detected. Gary thus accessed a small portion of the raw data available and processed it to be consistent with his needs. These expectations are largely affected by a consumer's cultural background. For example, like many Maritime men, Gary had a negative reaction to overly feminine brand names, even though his counterparts around the world might not have this reaction.

Like computers, people undergo stages of information processing in which stimuli are input and stored. Unlike computers, consumers do not passively process whatever information happens to be present. Only a very small number of the stimuli in our environment are ever noticed. Of these, an even smaller amount are attended to, and even these might not be processed objectively. The meaning of the stimulus is interpreted by the individual, who is influenced by his or her unique biases, needs and experiences. As shown in Figure 2–1, three stages—exposure, attention and interpretation—make up the process of perception. Before considering each of these stages, let's step back and consider the sensory systems that provide sensations to us in the first place.

FIGURE 2–1 • An Overview of the Perceptual Process

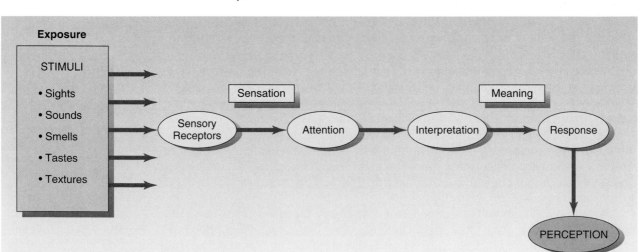

SENSORY SYSTEMS

External stimuli, or *sensory inputs,* can be received on a number of channels. We may see a billboard, hear a jingle, feel the softness of a cashmere sweater, taste a new flavour of ice cream or smell a leather jacket.

The inputs picked up by our five senses constitute the raw data that generates many types of responses. For example, sensory data emanating from the external environment (hearing a song on the radio) can generate internal sensory experiences when the song on the radio triggers a young man's memory of his first dance and brings to mind the smell of his date's perfume or the feel of her hair on his cheek.

These responses are an important part of **hedonic consumption**, or the multisensory, fantasy and emotional aspects of consumers' interactions with products.[2] The data that we receive from our sensory systems determine how we respond to products.

The unique sensory quality of a product can play an important role in helping it to stand out from the competition, especially if the brand creates a unique association with the sensation. The Owens-Corning Fiberglass Corporation trademarked the colour pink for its insulation material and adopted the Pink Panther cartoon character and pink flamingos to represent the company.[3] Harley-Davidson trademarked the distinctive "hog" sound of its revving motor.[4]

> **hedonic consumption** the multisensory, fantasy and emotional aspects of consumers' interactions with products

Vision

Marketers rely heavily on visual elements in advertising, store design and packaging. As the old saying goes, "A picture is worth a thousand words." The visual elements of a marketing message often speak volumes about a product's attributes. Meanings are communicated on the visual channel through a product's size, styling, brightness and distinctiveness from competitors' products.

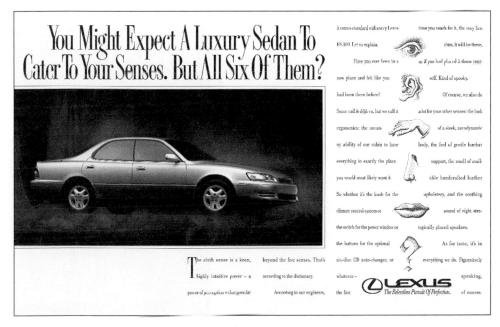

This ad for a luxury car emphasizes the contribution made by all of our senses to the evaluation of a driving experience. In addition to the five channels of sight, sound, touch, smell and taste, the ad mentions the "sixth sense" of intuition in its treatment of the "power of perception."
© 1993 by Lexus, a division of Toyota Motor Sales, USA, Inc. Used by permission.

As the old saying goes, "A picture is worth a thousand words." The visual elements of a marketing message often speak volumes about a product's attributes. In this case, the message about roominess conveyed by this Singaporean ad for Mitsubishi is clear. *Courtesy of Euro RSCG Ball Partnership, Singapore.*

Colours are rich in symbolic value and cultural meanings. For example, the display of red, white and blue evokes feelings of patriotism for both Americans and French people. Red means good luck to the Chinese and is often the main colour in their celebrations. Such powerful cultural meanings make colour a central aspect of many marketing strategies. Colour choices are made carefully with regard to packaging, advertising and even store décor. Indeed, evidence suggests that some colours (particularly red) create feelings of arousal in viewers, while others (such as blue) are more relaxing. The power of colours to evoke good and bad feelings is an important consideration in the design of advertising. Some reactions to colour come from learned associations—in Western countries, black is the colour of mourning, while in

Now that the passion for clear appears to be fading, marketers are seeing red—at least in the beer category. Beers with names like Killian's Irish Red, Boar's Head Red and Leinenkugel Red are now invading the market. Industry leader Anheuser-Busch introduced its Red Wolf brand in late 1994.
(Cyndee Miller, "What's Cool and Delicious and Red All Over?" Marketing News [November 7, 1994]: 2.) Photo courtesy of Anheuser-Busch Cos., Inc.

MULTICULTURAL DIMENSIONS

Cultural differences in colour preferences create the need for marketing strategies tailored to people in different countries. Mexican women, for example, are passionate in their love for vibrant lipsticks and fingernail polishes. Especially since the signing of the North American Free Trade Agreement (NAFTA), cosmetics companies have discovered in Mexico a market of 26 million women who are willing to pay a premium for boldly coloured nail polishes with names like "Orange Flip."

While many Canadian women believe that excessive make-up is unprofessional and not very flattering, traditional femininity tends to be more valued by Latins. In addition, Mexican women are taught to be attentive to their appearance from early childhood. Baby girls often sport pierced ears, and homemakers typically get dressed up in high heels tinted in tropical colours to go to the supermarket. For these women, the natural look is out. As one legal secretary in Mexico City explained, "When you don't wear makeup, men look at you like you are sick or something."[5]

some Eastern countries white plays this role. In addition, the colour black is associated with power and may even have an impact on people who wear it. Teams in the National Hockey League who wear black uniforms are among the most aggressive; they consistently rank near the top of the league in penalties during the season.[6]

The choice of colour is frequently a key issue in package design. These choices used to be made casually. For example, the familiar Campbell's soup can was produced in red and white because a company executive liked the football uniforms at Cornell University! Now, however, colour is a serious business, and companies often employ consultants to assist in these decisions.

Some colour combinations come to be so strongly associated with a corporation that they become known as the company's *trade dress,* and the company may even be granted exclusive use of these colours. For example, Eastman Kodak has successfully protected its trade dress of yellow, black and red in court. As a rule, however, trade dress protection is granted only when consumers might be confused about what they are buying because of similar coloration of a competitor's packages.[7]

The Federal Court of Canada recently ruled that Novopharm Ltd., a generic drug maker, could copy the colours of Eli Lilly's lucrative antidepressant Prozac. The generic drug company argued that colour was a safety factor in the drug business;[8] that is, consumers identified their medication by its colour. Successful businesses need to protect their brand equity from imitators. What strategies would you suggest to Eli Lilly and others to protect their identity from imitators?

Smell

Odours can stir emotions or create a calming feeling. They can evoke memories or relieve stress. Some of our responses to scents result from early associations that call up good or bad feelings, and that explains why businesses are exploring connections between smell, memory and mood. Fragrance is processed by the limbic system, the

ONLY NATURE COULD INSPIRE SO PERFECT A FRAGRANCE

Vanilla is the scent that appeals to the young. Coty found Vanilla to be their number-one seller.
Courtesy of Coty Canada Inc.

most primitive part of the brain and the place where immediate emotions are experienced. Smell is a direct line to feelings of happiness or hunger, and even to memories of happy times. This explains why "plain" vanilla has of late become so widely used in scented products, from perfumes and colognes to cake frosting, coffees and ice creams (Coty sold $25 million (US) worth of its Vanilla Fields cologne spray in a four-month period). An industry executive explains that vanilla "... evokes memories of home and hearth, warmth, and cuddling."[9] Another marketer noted that "... a baby-powder scent ... is frequently used in fragrances because the smell connotes comfort, warmth, and gratification."[10]

The sense of smell is not just a physiological response to a stimulus. The labels we give to odours not only help us identify them, but also influence how we perceive them. Our cognitive processes for smell help to explain why the elderly are not as good at identifying odours as the young and why women can generally name more odours than men. In an experiment, 103 blindfolded women were asked to identify 80 different substances, but they could only name 36 odours accurately. In a follow-up study, the three most identifiable products were 1) Johnson's Baby Powder; 2) chocolate; and 3) coconut. These researchers concluded that women were better at identifying smells because they learn about them directly and deliberately.[11] Maybe as the genders share more household and child-rearing duties, men and women will become more equal in their ability to identify everyday odours.

At least to some extent consumers' reactions to odours depend on their cultural background. The Gillette Co. is a master at fragrances. They realize that there is a vast difference, culture to culture, in how people want to smell. The Germans like to layer it on while American men don't like to smell "sissy," despite spending more time grooming than the French or Italians.[12] Many multinational companies adjust the scent of their products from country to country. Even Palmolive dish detergent has a different scent in Europe than in Canada. Vidal Sassoon products sold in Asia include a pine aroma that smells like floor cleaner to Americans.[13]

This ad for Everlast sports apparel pokes fun at the
proliferation of scented ads.
Courtesy of Everlast Sports, NY.

Scented advertising (now a $90-million business) is taking new turns, as marketers are experimenting with scents such as cigarettes, pizza, beer and vodka. A study by the market research department of *The New York Times* found that, when choosing between two similar food or beverage products, 81 percent of consumers would choose one they could both smell and see over one they could only see.[14] Samuel Adams beer was one of the first non-perfume products to be advertised with a scent strip that smelled of hops. Rolls-Royce also has distributed ads scented with the smell of leather. However, a note of caution: this technique adds at least 10 percent to the cost of producing an ad, so marketers will need to watch their dollars and scents.[15]

Sound

Music and sound are also important to marketers. Consumers buy millions of dollars' worth of sound recordings each year; advertising jingles maintain brand awareness; and background music creates desired moods.[16] Many aspects of sound may affect people's feelings and behaviours. Two areas of research that have widespread applications in consumer contexts are the effects of background music on mood and the influence of speaking rate on attitude change and message comprehension.

BACKGROUND TUNES: THE SOUND OF MUZAK

The Muzak Corporation estimates that its recordings are heard by 80 million people every day. This so-called "functional music" is played in stores, shopping malls and offices to either relax or stimulate consumers. Research shows that workers tend to slow down during midmorning and midafternoon, so Muzak uses a system it calls "stimulus progression," in which the tempo of its music increases during those slack times. Muzak has been linked to reductions in absenteeism among factory workers, and even the milk output of cows and egg output of chickens are claimed to increase under its influence.[17]

The research on music in the shopping environment is what we would call non-conscious. We can hear the music if we pay attention to it, but when asked if there was music in the shopping environment without being directed to its existence, most people would not be able accurately to recall the presence of music after leaving the store.[18] More research on the effect of music on our consumption environment is described in Chapter 3 under classical conditioning.

TIME COMPRESSION

Time compression is a technique used by broadcasters to manipulate perceptions of sound. It is a way to pack more information into a limited time by speeding up an announcer's voice in commercials. The speaking rate is typically accelerated to about 120 to 130 percent of normal. This effect is not detectable by most people; in fact, some tests indicate that consumers prefer a rate of transmission that is slightly faster than the normal speaking rate.[19]

The evidence for the effectiveness of time compression is mixed. It has been shown to increase persuasion in some situations and to reduce it in others. One explanation for a positive effect is that the listener uses a person's speaking rate to infer whether the speaker is confident; that is, people seem to think that fast talkers must know what they are talking about.[20] Another, more plausible explanation is that the listener is given less time to elaborate in his or her mind on the assertions made in the commercial. The acceleration disrupts normal responses to the ad and changes the cues used to form judgments about its content. This change can either hinder or facilitate attitude change, depending on other conditions.[21]

Touch

Although relatively little research has been done on the effects of tactile stimulation on consumer behaviour, common observation tells us that this sensory channel is important.[22] Moods are relaxed or stimulated on the basis of sensations of the skin, whether from a luxurious massage or the bite of a winter wind. Touch has even been shown to be a factor in sales interactions. In one study, for example, diners who were touched by waiters gave bigger tips, and food demonstrators in a supermarket who lightly touched customers had better luck in getting shoppers to try a new snack product and to redeem coupons for the brand.[23]

People associate the textures of fabrics and other products with underlying product qualities. The perceived richness or quality of the material in clothing, bedding or upholstery is linked to its "feel," that is, whether it is rough or smooth, flexible or inflexible. A smooth fabric like silk is equated with luxury, while denim is considered practical and durable. Some of these tactile/quality associations are summarized in Table 2–1. Fabrics that are composed of scarce materials or that require a high degree of processing to achieve their smoothness or fineness tend to be more expensive and thus are seen as being higher-class. Similarly, lighter, more delicate textures are assumed to be feminine. Roughness is often positively valued for men, while smoothness is sought by women. (When was the last time you saw a commercial in which a man was fretting about "dishpan hands"?)

TABLE 2–1   Tactile Oppositions in Fabrics

PERCEPTION	MALE	FEMALE	
High class	Wool	Silk	Fine
Low class	Denim	Cotton	↕
	Heavy ⟷	Light	Coarse

This ad for Lubriderm lotion relies on the vivid imagery of a rough tactile sensation to communicate a primary product benefit.
Courtesy of Warner Lambert, Inc.

MARKETING PITFALL

The Clearly Canadian beverage company recently introduced Orbitz—a "texturally enhanced" drink with numerous "flavoured gel spheres" floating in the bottle.[24] The company spent more than a year developing the technology that would keep the edible jelly balls floating in the drink. The company learned from the mistake of a competitor, Mistic Brands: when Mistic launched a similar product called "Jumpin Gems," the balls settled on the bottom, and consumers thought the drink had simply gone bad.

Clearly Canadian appears to face long odds of success. One industry consultant commented, "It's gross. It's like, when you drink a glass of milk, do you want to find lumps?" He adds, "... basically, people are taught not to drink things floating in their glass." But the company is banking on the product's weirdness to appeal to rebellious teens. It points to the success of Goldschalger, a spicy liquor with real bits of gold floating in it, and to (some) consumers' affection for tequila brands featuring a worm in the bottom of the bottle (which is taken as a sign of authenticity). Some drinks sold in Southeast Asia feature bursting malt balls or chunks of fruit, but only time will tell if Western consumers will prefer to chew rather than sip their drinks.

Taste

Our taste receptors obviously contribute to our experience of many products. Specialized companies called "flavour houses" keep busy trying to develop new tastes to please the changing palates of consumers. Their work has been especially important as consumers continue to demand good-tasting foods that are also low in calories and fat. When the Quaker Oats Company decided to capitalize on this trend by buying a small rice-cake manufacturer, consumers complained that the cakes tasted like styrofoam, and sales were disappointing. A flavour house was hired to develop a rice cake that tasted like buttered popcorn. This new taste was perfected along with several others, and industry-wide sales of rice cakes now exceed $100 million a year.[25]

Food companies go to great lengths to ensure that their products taste as they should. Consider, for example, the procedure used by Nabisco as it monitors the quality of its cookies. The company uses a group of "sensory panelists" as cookie tasters. These consumers are recruited because they have superior sensory abilities, and they are then given six months of training. In a *blind taste test* (where the specific types and brands being tested are kept secret), the panelists rate the products of Nabisco and its competitors on a number of dimensions. These include "rate of melt," "fracturability and density," "molar packing" (the amount of cookie that sticks to the teeth), and the "notes" of the cookie, such as sweetness, saltiness or bitterness. A typical evaluation session takes the group eight hours to rate just one sample of cookies.[26]

Are blind taste tests worth their salt? While taste tests often provide valuable information, their results can be misleading when it is forgotten that objective taste is only one component of product evaluation. The most famous example of this mistake concerns New Coke, Coca-Cola's answer to the Pepsi Challenge.[27] The new formulation was preferred to Pepsi in blind taste tests by an average of 55 percent to 45 percent in 17 markets, yet the maker of New Coke ran into problems when it replaced the older version. People do not buy a cola for taste alone; they are buying intangibles like brand image as well.

Just as fabrics are prized for their textures, some types of liquor are rated according to their "feel." This ad for a premium Scotch whisky emphasizes the product's "smoothness" by equating its taste with the experience of gliding over ice.
Courtesy of William Grant & Sons, Inc.

However, it is important to note that the taste of Coca-Cola actually does vary from culture to culture, sometimes even within a country. The French prefer sweeter colas, and the syrup is adjusted for those markets.

EXPOSURE

Exposure is the degree to which people notice a stimulus that is within range of their sensory receptors. Consumers concentrate on some stimuli, are unaware of others and even go out of their way to ignore some messages. An experiment by a Minneapolis bank illustrates consumers' tendencies to miss or ignore information in which they are not interested. After a state law was passed that required banks to explain details about money transfer in electronic banking, the Northwestern National Bank distributed a pamphlet to 120 000 of its customers at considerable cost to provide the required information, which was hardly exciting bedtime reading. In 100 of the mailings, a section in the middle of the pamphlet offered readers $10 merely for finding that paragraph. Not a single person claimed the reward.[28]

Before we consider what people may choose not to perceive, let's consider what they are capable of perceiving.

exposure an initial stage of perception where some sensations come within range of consumers' sensory receptors

Sensory Thresholds

If you have ever blown a dog whistle and watched pets respond to a sound you cannot hear, you know that there are some stimuli that people simply are not capable of perceiving. And, of course, some people are better able to pick up sensory information than are others. The science that focuses on how the physical environment is integrated into our personal, subjective world is known as **psychophysics.**

THE ABSOLUTE THRESHOLD

When we define the lowest intensity of a stimulus that can be registered on a sensory channel, we speak of a *threshold* for that receptor. The **absolute threshold** refers to the minimum amount of stimulation that can be detected on a sensory channel. The sound emitted by a dog whistle is too high to be detected by human ears, so this stimulus is beyond our auditory absolute threshold. The absolute threshold is an important consideration in designing marketing stimuli. A billboard might have the most entertaining copy ever written, but this genius is wasted if the print is too small for passing motorists to see from the highway.

psychophysics the science that focuses on how the physical environment is integrated into the consumer's subjective experience

absolute threshold the minimum amount of stimulation that can be detected on a sensory channel

THE DIFFERENTIAL THRESHOLD

The **differential threshold** refers to the ability of a sensory system to detect changes in or differences *between* two stimuli. The minimum change in a stimulus that can be detected is also known as the **JND,** which stands for *just noticeable difference.*

The issue of when and if a change will be noticed by consumers is relevant to many marketing situations. Sometimes a marketer may want to ensure that a change is noticed, such as when merchandise is offered at a discount. In other situations, the fact that a change has been made is downplayed, as in the case of price increases or when a product is downsized.

differential threshold the ability of a sensory system to detect changes or differences among stimuli

JND (just noticeable difference) the minimum change in a stimulus that can be detected by a perceiver

A consumer's ability to detect a difference between two stimuli is relative. A whispered conversation that might be unintelligible on a noisy street can suddenly become public and embarrassing knowledge in a quiet library. It is the relative difference between the decibel level of the conversation and its surroundings, rather than the loudness of the conversation itself, that determines whether the stimulus will register.

In the nineteenth century a psychophysicist named Ernst Weber found that the amount of change that is necessary to be noticed is systematically related to the original intensity of the stimulus. The stronger the initial stimulus, the greater the change must be for it to be noticed. This relationship is known as **Weber's Law** and is expressed in the following equation:

Weber's Law the principle that the stronger the initial stimulus, the greater its change must be for it to be noticed

$$K = \frac{\triangle I}{I}$$

where

K = the constant increase or decrease necessary for the stimulus to be noticed (this varies across the senses)

$\triangle I$ = the minimal change in intensity of the stimulus required to be just noticeable to the person (j.n.d.).

I = the intensity of the stimulus before the change occurs.

For example, consider how Weber's Law might work with respect to a product that has had its price decreased for a special sale. A rule of thumb used by some retailers is that a mark-down should be at least 20 percent for this price cut to make an impact on shoppers. If so, a pair of socks that retails for $10 should be put on sale for $8 (a $2 discount). However, a sport coat selling for $100 would not benefit from a "mere" $2 discount; it would have to be marked down to $80 to achieve the same impact.

The main point of Weber's Law is that the ratios, not the absolute differences, are important in describing the least perceptible differences in sensory discrimination. The differential threshold varies not only with consumers' sensitivity and type of stimuli, but also with the absolute intensity of the stimuli being compared. The use of Weber's Law in the selling of goods is important. Manufacturers and brand managers endeavour to determine the relevant just noticeable difference for their products for two reasons: first, so that reductions in product size, increases in product price or changes in packaging are not readily discernible to the public; and second, so that product improvements are perceived by the public. Can you give an example of each from your own buying experience?

Many companies choose to update their packages periodically, making small changes that will not necessarily be noticed at the time. When a product icon is updated, the manufacturer does not want people to lose their identification with a familiar symbol. A *corporate identity campaign*—wherein a company tries to build a distinctive image for a line of products—illustrates the importance of phasing in an identity image by making incremental changes over time. Recently, when IBM sold its line of desktop printers, typewriters and related supplies to an investment firm, the new company needed a new name and logo because the sales agreement stipulated that it would lose the rights to the IBM name in 1996. The new company

FIGURE 2–2 • Evolution of the Lexmark Logo. The four stages illustrate the company's attempt to phase in the new identity by relying on the more familiar IBM image for as long as possible.

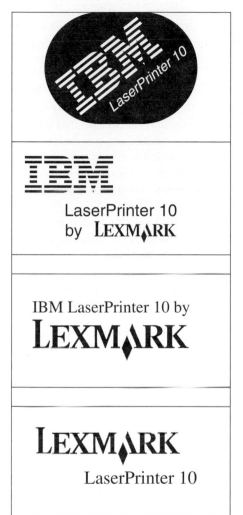

Courtesy of Lexmark International, Inc.

wanted consumers simultaneously to perceive its product line as being new but also to connect it with the more familiar IBM image. A new name, Lexmark International, was selected from an initial list of 200 candidates, and a four-stage timetable was developed to phase in the Lexmark name over the five-year period in which the new company was entitled to use the IBM logo. A corporate identity advertising campaign, initiated to assist in the transition, included an ad asking consumers to "imagine a brand-new company with more than 50 years of experience." The successive changes in the logo are shown in Figure 2–2.[29]

Subliminal Perception

Most marketers are concerned with creating advertising messages above consumers' thresholds. There is, however, another side to this story. A good number of consumers appear to believe that many advertising messages are in fact designed to be perceived unconsciously, or below the threshold of recognition. Another word for threshold is *limen,* and stimuli that fall below the limen are termed *subliminal.* **Subliminal perception** thus occurs when the stimulus is below the level of the consumer's awareness.

Subliminal perception is a topic that has captivated the public for over 30 years, despite the fact that there is virtually no proof that this process has any effect on consumer behaviour. In fact, most examples of subliminal perception that have been "discovered" are not subliminal at all; they are quite visible. Remember, if you can see it or hear it, it is *not* subliminal, because the stimulus is above the level of conscious awareness! Nonetheless, the continuing controversy about subliminal persuasion has been important in shaping the public's beliefs about advertising and the ability of marketers to manipulate consumers against their will.

The public's fear of unconscious manipulation began with a widely popularized experiment that was performed in a New Jersey drive-in movie theatre in September 1957. During a showing of the movie *Picnic,* a firm called the Subliminal Projection Company inserted messages that said "Drink Coca-Cola" and "Eat Popcorn" for 1/3000 second every 5 seconds. This rate was too fast for viewers to be aware that they had seen the images. Supposedly, sales of popcorn increased by almost 20 percent and consumption of Coke by almost 60 percent.

These claims created an uproar as journalists and social critics expressed fears that social scientists would team up with advertisers to invade privacy and control consumers against their will. As one magazine put it at the time, consumers' minds had been "broken and entered."[30] This experiment was never replicated and has repeatedly been criticized. The design of the study was flawed in that other possible effects on consumption, such as the movie itself, the weather during the showing, and so on, could not be ruled out. Indeed, the executive responsible for the test later admitted that he had made up the results to revive his failing research firm![31]

SUBLIMINAL TECHNIQUES

Embeds are tiny figures that are inserted into magazine advertising by using high-speed photography or airbrushing. These hidden figures, usually of a sexual nature, supposedly exert strong but unconscious influences on innocent readers. To date, the only real impact of this interest in hidden messages is to make consumers (and students of consumer behaviour) look a bit more closely at print ads—perhaps seeing whatever their imaginations lead them to see.

In addition to subliminal visual messages, many consumers and marketers seem to be fascinated by the possible effects of messages hidden on sound recordings. An attempt to capitalize on subliminal auditory perception techniques is found in the growing market for self-help cassettes. These tapes, which typically feature the sound of waves crashing or some other natural setting, supposedly contain subliminal messages to help the listener stop smoking, lose weight, gain confidence, etc. Despite the rapid growth of this market, there is little evidence that any subliminal stimuli transmitted on the auditory channel can bring about desired changes in behaviour.[32] In a major study conducted to obtain a definitive answer on the effect of subliminal per-

Q. CAN YOU FIND THE HIDDEN PLEASURE
IN REFRESHING SEAGRAM'S GIN?

A. If you think this
is just a bubble,
look again.

This Seagram's ad pokes fun at the belief that advertisers
frequently embed pleasurable images in the ice cubes in
pictures of drinks.
Courtesy of The House of Seagram.

suasion, groups of people were recruited to a double-blind weight loss experiment involving tapes with subaudible messages. One group had real weight loss messages in their tapes, while the other group just listened to the ocean. After many weeks of listening to the tapes, there were no differences in weight loss between the two groups.[33]

Along with the interest in hidden self-help messages on recordings, some consumers have become concerned about rumours of satanic messages recorded backwards on rock records. The popular press has devoted much attention to such stories. These backwards messages do indeed appear in some songs, including Led Zeppelin's classic "Stairway to Heaven," which contains the lyric "...there's still time to change." When played in reverse, this phrase sounds like "so here's to my sweet Satan." The novelty of such reversals might help to sell records, but the "evil" messages within have no effect:[34] humans do not have a speech perception mechanism operating at an unconscious level that is capable of decoding a reversed signal.

On the other hand, subtle acoustical messages such as "I am honest. I won't steal. Stealing is dishonest" are broadcast in more than 1000 stores in the United States to prevent shoplifting. Unlike subliminal perception, though, these messages are played at a (barely) audible level, using a technique known as threshold messaging.[35] After a nine-month test period, theft losses in one six-store chain declined almost 40 percent, saving the company $600 000. Some evidence indicates, however, that these messages are effective only on individuals whose value systems make them predisposed to suggestion. For example, someone who might be thinking about taking something on a dare but who feels guilty about it might be susceptible to these messages, but they will not sway a professional thief.[36]

DOES SUBLIMINAL PERCEPTION WORK? EVALUATING THE EVIDENCE

Some research by clinical psychologists suggests that people can be influenced by subliminal messages under very specific conditions, though it is doubtful that these techniques would be of much use in most marketing contexts. To be effective, messages must be very specifically tailored to individuals rather than to a mass audience, as required by advertising.[37] These messages should also be as close to the liminal threshold as possible. Other discouraging factors include the following:

- There are wide individual differences in threshold levels. In order for a message to avoid conscious detection by consumers who have a low threshold, it would have to be so weak that it would not reach those who have a high threshold.

- Advertisers lack control over consumers' distance and position from a screen. In a movie theatre, for example, only a small portion of the audience would be in exactly the right seats to be exposed to the subliminal message.

- The consumer must be paying absolute attention to the stimulus. People watching a television program or a movie typically shift their attention periodically and might not even be looking when the stimulus is presented.

- Even if the desired effect is induced, it operates only at a very general level. For example, a message might increase a person's thirst, but not necessarily for a specific drink. Because basic drives are affected, marketers could find that, after all the bother and expense of creating a subliminal message, demand for competitors' products increases as well! Clearly, there are better ways to get our attention. Let's see how.

ATTENTION

Although we live in an "information society," we can have too much of a good thing. Consumers are often in a state of *sensory overload*, i.e., they are exposed to far more information than they are able or willing to process. In our society, much of this bombardment comes from commercial sources, and the competition for our attention is increasing steadily. In 1971 about 2600 television commercials ran each week; now cable and network stations carry more than 6000 during the same time period.[38]

Perceptual Selection: Barriers to Reception of Marketing Messages

perceptual selectivity
process in which people attend to only a small portion of the stimuli to which they are exposed

Because the brain's capacity to process information is limited, consumers are very selective about what they pay attention to. The process of **perceptual selectivity** means that people attend to only a small portion of the stimuli to which they are exposed. Consumers practise a form of psychic economy, picking and choosing among stimuli to avoid being overwhelmed by *advertising clutter*.

PERSONAL SELECTION FACTORS

Experience, which is the result of acquiring stimulation, is one factor that determines how much exposure to a particular stimulus a person accepts. *Perceptual filters* based on consumers' past experiences influence what they decide to process.

The photograph in this ad for Pensions & Investment Age illustrates how visual stimuli can cause advertising clutter—the sensory overload to which consumers are exposed in the marketplace.
Courtesy of Pensions & Investment Age. Concept: W. Bisson; Copy: W. Bisson; Design: J. Hunt, Donna Klein.

Perceptual vigilance is a factor in selective exposure. Consumers are more likely to be aware of stimuli that relate to their current needs. These needs may be conscious or unconscious. A consumer who rarely notices car ads will become very much aware of them when he or she is in the market for a new car. A newspaper ad for a fast-food restaurant that would otherwise go unnoticed becomes significant when one glances at the paper in the middle of a five o'clock class.

The flip side of perceptual vigilance is *perceptual defence*. This means that people see what they want to see—and don't see what they don't want to see. If a stimulus is threatening to us in some way, we may not process it, or we may distort its meaning so that it is more acceptable. For example, a heavy smoker may block out images of cancer-scarred lungs because these vivid reminders hit a bit too close to home.

Another factor affecting exposure is **adaptation,** that is, the degree to which consumers continue to notice a stimulus over time. The process of adaptation occurs when consumers no longer pay attention to a stimulus because it is so familiar. Almost like drug addiction, a consumer can become "habituated" and require increasingly stronger "doses" of a stimulus for it to continue to be noticed. For example, a consumer en route to work might read a billboard message when it is first installed, but after a few days it becomes part of the passing scenery.

Generally, several factors can lead to adaptation:

- *Intensity.* Less intense stimuli (soft sounds or dim colours) habituate because they have less of a sensory impact.

- *Duration.* Stimuli that require relatively lengthy exposure in order to be processed tend to habituate because they require a long attention span.

- *Discrimination.* Simple stimuli tend to habituate because they do not require attention to detail.

- *Exposure.* Frequently encountered stimuli tend to habituate as the rate of exposure increases.

adaptation the process that occurs when a sensation becomes so familiar that it is no longer the focus of attention

- *Relevance*. Stimuli that are irrelevant or unimportant will habituate because they fail to attract attention.

STIMULUS SELECTION FACTORS

In addition to the receiver's "mind-set," characteristics of the stimulus itself play an important role in determining what gets noticed and what gets ignored.[39] These factors need to be understood by marketers, who can apply them to their messages and packages to boost their chances of cutting through the clutter and commanding attention. In general, stimuli that differ from others around them are more likely to be noticed (remember Weber's Law). This *contrast* can be created in several ways:

- *Size:* The size of the stimulus itself in contrast to the competition helps to determine if it will command attention. Readership of a magazine ad increases in proportion to the size of the ad. Drink sizes are even becoming a marketing tool, as companies scramble to eliminate anything "small" from their offerings. McDonald's offers only regular, large and supersize drinks, and 7-Eleven boasts that it makes America's biggest drink, the 64-ounce double gulp. (Note: the idea that "more is better" is largely American. The chain's international stores don't sell this version, as the company feels that in Europe and Japan small is often interpreted as luxurious and precious rather than just less of a good thing!).[40]

- *Colour:* As we've seen, colour is a powerful way to draw attention to a product or to give it a distinct identity. For example, Black & Decker recently inaugurated a new line of tools, called DeWalt, targeted to the residential construction industry. The new line was coloured yellow instead of black, which made them stand out against other "dull" tools.[41]

- *Position:* Not surprisingly, stimuli that are in places we're more likely to look stand a better chance of being noticed. That's why the competition among suppliers to have their products displayed in stores at eye level is so heated. In magazines, ads that are placed towards the front of the issue, preferably on the right-hand side, also win out in the race to get readers' attention. (Hint: the next time you read a magazine, notice which pages you're more likely to spend time looking at.)[42]

   Some advertisers don't take any chances; they buy large blocks of advertising space to be sure they get their message across. Designer Ralph Lauren filled 15 consecutive full pages in a single issue of *Vanity Fair* for this reason. For the same reason, MCA Records paid a major movie-theatre chain to play a music video by Tom Petty and the Heartbreakers prior to showing its scheduled movies, while Mercury Records launched a bus placard campaign in 18 cities to promote a new John Mellencamp album.[43]

- *Novelty:* Stimuli that appear in unexpected ways or places tend to grab our attention. These places include the backs of shopping carts, tunnels, sports stadiums and movies.[44] An executive at Campbell's Soup, commenting on the company's decision to place ads in church bulletins, noted, "We have to shake consumers up these days in order to make them take notice ... we have to hit them with our ads where they shop and play and on their way to work."[45] Some advertisers, including Clorox, McDonald's and Quaker Oats, have even taken to printing part of their ads upside down to get the reader's attention.[46]

MARKETING PITFALL

The advent of the VCR has allowed consumers armed with remote control fast-forward buttons to be much more selective about which television messages they are exposed to. By "zipping," viewers fast-forward through commercials when playing recorded tapes of their favourite programs. A VCR marketed by Mitsubishi in Japan even removes the need for zipping. It distinguishes between the different types of TV signals used to broadcast programs and commercials and automatically pauses during ads.[47]

How big an issue is zipping for marketers? The jury is still out on this question. In one survey, 69 percent of VCR owners said that they had increased their television viewing time, so overall exposure to commercials might actually increase as people continue to purchase VCRs.[48]

Zipping has enhanced the need for advertising creativity. Interesting commercials do not get zipped as frequently. Evidence indicates that viewers are willing to stop fast-forwarding to watch an enticing or novel commercial. In addition, longer commercials and those that keep a static figure on the screen (such as a brand name or a logo) appear to counteract the effects of zipping; these executions are not as affected by a speed increase, since the figure remains in place longer.[49]

INTERPRETATION

Interpretation refers to the meaning that people assign to sensory stimuli. Just as people differ in terms of the stimuli that they perceive, the eventual assignment of meanings to these stimuli varies as well. Two people can see or hear the same event, but their interpretations of it can be like night and day depending on what they had expected the stimulus to be.

Consumers assign meaning to stimuli based on the **schema**, or set of beliefs, to which the stimulus is assigned. Certain properties of a stimulus will more likely evoke a schema than others. (This process is known as **priming.**) As evidenced by Gary's cologne selection, a brand name can communicate expectations about product attributes and can colour consumers' perceptions of product performance by activating a schema. When Toro introduced a lightweight snow thrower, it was named the "Snow Pup." Sales were disappointing because the word *pup* called up a schema that grouped together things that are small and cuddly—not the desirable attributes for a snow thrower. When the product was renamed the "Snow Master," sales went up markedly.[50]

interpretation the process whereby meanings are assigned to stimuli

schema an organized collection of beliefs and feelings represented in a cognitive category

priming process in which certain properties of a stimulus are more likely to evoke a schema than others

Stimulus Organization

People do not perceive a single stimulus in isolation; they tend to view it in terms of relationships with other events, sensations or images.

When RJR Nabisco introduced a version of Teddy Grahams (a children's product) for adults, restrained packaging colours were used to reinforce the idea that the new product was for grown-ups, but sales were disappointing. The box was then changed to a bright yellow to convey the idea that this was a fun snack, and buyers' more positive association between a bright primary colour and taste led adults to start buying the cookies.[52]

Our brains tend to relate incoming sensations to others already in memory based on some fundamental organizational principles. These principles are based on work in **Gestalt psychology,** a school of thought maintaining that people derive meaning from the *totality* of a set of stimuli, rather than from any individual stimulus. The German word *gestalt* roughly means whole, pattern or configuration, and this perspective is best summarized by the saying "the whole is greater than the sum of its parts." The importance of a gestalt is underscored when consumers' interpretations of stimuli are affected by aesthetic, symbolic or sensory qualities. Set in a

Gestalt psychology a school of thought that maintains people derive meaning from the totality of a set of stimuli, rather than from any individual stimulus

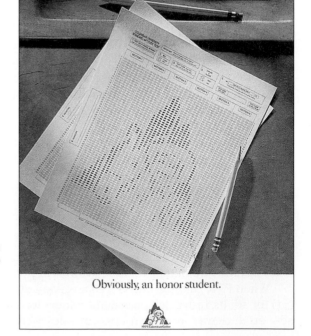

This ad for Colombian coffee illustrates Gestalt principles of perception, in which the individual parts (the coloured circles) are seen as a whole (the familiar symbol used to promote Colombian coffee). *Courtesy of the National Federation of Coffee Growers of Colombia.*

Obviously, an honor student.

FIGURE 2–3 • Principles of Stimulus Organization Derived from Gestalt Psychology

PRINCIPLE OF CLOSURE   PRINCIPLE OF SIMILARITY   PRINCIPLE OF FIGURE-GROUND

context that is painfully familiar to most students, the Colombian coffee ad shown here demonstrates the formation of a meaningful image from the individual coloured circles on a Scantron sheet when viewed in totality. A piecemeal perspective that analyzes each component of the stimulus separately will be unable to capture the total effect. The gestalt perspective provides several principles relating to the way stimuli are organized. Three of these principles, or perceptual tendencies, are illustrated in Figure 2–3.

The gestalt **principle of closure** implies that consumers tend to perceive an incomplete picture as complete. That is, we tend to fill in the blanks based on our prior experience. This principle explains why most of us have no trouble reading a neon sign even if one or two of its letters are burned out or filling in the blanks in an incomplete message. The principle of closure is also at work when we hear only part of a jingle or theme. Utilization of the principle of closure in marketing strategies encourages audience participation, which increases the chance that people will attend to the message.

principle of closure the gestalt principle that consumers tend to perceive an incomplete picture as complete

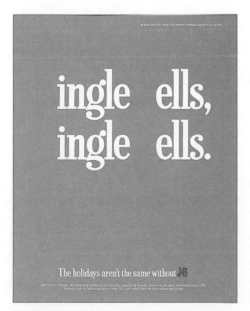

This J&B ad illustrates use of the principle of closure, in which people participate in the ad by mentally filling in the gaps.
Reprinted with permission by The Paddington Corporation ©.

This advertisement for Movado watches illustrates the figure-ground principle. The eye is immediately drawn to the oversized watch—that is, the figure that dominates the copy, or ground.
Courtesy of Movado Watch Company.

principle of similarity the gestalt principle that describes how consumers tend to group objects that share similar physical characteristics

figure-ground principle the gestalt principle whereby one part of a stimulus configuration dominates a situation while other aspects recede into the background

The **principle of similarity** tells us that consumers tend to group together objects that share similar physical characteristics; that is, they group like items into sets to form an integrated whole. Green Giant relied upon this principle when the company redesigned the packaging for its line of frozen vegetables. It created a "sea-of-green" look to unify all of its different offerings.

Another important gestalt concept is the **figure-ground principle,** in which one part of a stimulus will dominate (the *figure*) while other parts recede into the background. This concept is easy to understand if one thinks of a photograph with a clear and sharply focused object (the figure) in the centre. The figure is dominant, and the eye goes straight to it. The parts of the configuration that will be perceived as figure or ground can vary depending on the individual consumer as well as other factors. Similarly, in marketing messages that use the figure-ground principle, a stimulus can be made the focal point of the message or merely the context that surrounds the focus.

The Eye of the Beholder: Interpretation Biases

The stimuli we perceive are often ambiguous; it's up to us to determine the meaning based on our past experiences, expectations and needs. The process of "seeing what you want to see" was demonstrated in a classic experiment where students at Princeton and Dartmouth viewed a movie of a particularly rough football game between the two schools. Although everyone was exposed to the same stimulus, the degree to which students saw infractions, and the blame they assigned for those they did see, was quite different depending on which college they attended.[53]

As this experiment demonstrates, consumers tend to project their own desires or assumptions onto products and advertisements. This interpretation process can backfire for marketers, as occurred in these recent cases:

• When Ocean Spray introduced its Cranberry Juice Cocktail Refill in concentrated form, the new product came in an 8-ounce carton with a picture of the more familiar 48-ounce bottle on it. Many confused consumers thought the concentrate package was a single-serving juice carton, and many nasty surprises occurred until the company hastily added the word *refill* to the bottle.[54]

- In 1992, Planters Lifesavers Company introduced a vacuum-packed peanuts package called Planters Fresh Roast. The idea was to capitalize on consumers' growing love affair with fresh roast coffee by emphasizing the freshness of the nuts in the same way. A great idea—until irate supermarket managers began calling to ask who was going to pay to clean the peanut gook out of their stores' coffee-grinding machines.[55]

Perceptual Positioning

As we've seen, a product stimulus is often interpreted in the light of what we already know about a product category and the characteristics of existing brands. Perceptions of a brand are composed both of its functional attributes (its features, price and so on) and its symbolic attributes (its image and what we think it says about us when we use it). We'll look more closely at issues like brand image in later chapters, but for now it's important to keep in mind that our evaluation of a product typically is the result of what it means rather than what it does. This meaning, as perceived by consumers, constitutes the product's *market position*—and may have more to do with our expectations of product performance as communicated by its colour, packaging or styling than with the product itself. For example, when the background colour on Barrelhead Sugar-Free Root Beer was changed from blue to beige, consumers said it tasted more like old-fashioned root beer served in a frosty mug.[56]

A **positioning strategy** is a fundamental part of a company's marketing efforts as it uses elements of the marketing mix (product design, price, distribution and marketing communications) to influence the consumer's interpretation of its meaning. For example, while consumers' preference for the taste of one product over another are important, this functional attribute is only one component of product evaluation.[57] Coca-Cola found this out the hard way when it committed its (in)famous New Coke marketing blunder in the 1980s. New Coke was preferred to Pepsi in blind taste tests (in which the products were not identified) by an average of 55 percent to 45 percent in seventeen markets, yet New Coke ran into problems when it replaced the older version. Consumers' impassioned protests and letter-writing campaigns eventually forced the company to bring back "Coke Classic." People do not buy a cola for taste alone; they are buying intangibles like brand image as well. Coca-Cola's unique position as part of a fun-loving lifestyle is based on years of marketing efforts that involve a lot more than taste alone.

positioning strategy the place a brand occupies in the consumer's mind with regard to important attributes (such as functional features) and competitive offerings

POSITIONING DIMENSIONS

There are many dimensions that can be used to establish a brand's position in the marketplace.[58] These include:

- *Lifestyle:* Grey Poupon mustard is a "higher class" condiment.
- *Price leadership:* L'Oréal's Noisôme brand face cream is sold in upscale beauty shops, while its Plentitude brand is available for one-sixth the price in discount stores—even though both are based on the same chemical formula.
- *Attributes:* Bounty paper towels are "the quicker picker upper."

- *Product class:* The Mazda Miata is a sporty convertible.
- *Occasions:* Wrigley's gum is an alternative at times when smoking is not permitted.
- *Users:* Levi's Dockers are targeted primarily to men in their twenties, thirties and forties..
- *Quality:* At Ford, "Quality is Job 1."[59]

REPOSITIONING

repositioning the process of changing the place a brand occupies in the consumer's mind, in order to make it more competitive with other brands or to change its image

Repositioning occurs when a brand's original market position is modified. In some cases a marketer may decide that a brand is competing too closely with another of its own products, so sales are being *cannibalized* (i.e., the two brands are taking sales away from each other, rather than from competing companies). This was the reason for the decision by Cadbury Beverages to reposition Crush, an orange soda. The brand was targeted to the teen market when it was acquired from Proctor & Gamble. However, the company already marketed Sunkist to this segment, so it is taking steps to move Crush towards an all-family position.[60]

Finally, repositioning can occur when the original market evaporates or is unreceptive to the offering. *Details* magazine was initially launched as an "underground nightlife magazine," but it was relaunched as a fashion and lifestyle magazine for twentysomething males. Formerly criticized for being too raw and bold, it now strives to be more sophisticated so that advertisers wishing to reach younger males will encounter a more conducive environment in which to place their advertising.[61]

CHAPTER SUMMARY

- Perception is the process by which physical sensations such as sights, sounds and smells are selected, organized and interpreted. The eventual interpretation of a stimulus allows it to be assigned meaning. A perceptual map is a widely used marketing tool that evaluates the relative standing of competing brands along relevant dimensions.

- Marketing stimuli have important sensory qualities. We rely on colours, odours, sounds, tastes and even the "feel" of products when forming evaluations of them.

- Not all sensations make their way successfully through the perceptual process. Many stimuli compete for our attention, and the majority are not noticed or accurately comprehended.

- People have different thresholds of perception. A stimulus must be presented at a certain level of intensity before it can be detected by an individual's sensory receptors. In addition, a consumer's ability to detect whether two stimuli are different (the differential threshold) is an important issue in many marketing contexts, such as changing a package design, altering the size of a product or reducing its price.

- A lot of controversy has been sparked by so-called subliminal persuasion and related techniques, by which people are exposed to visual and audio messages below the threshold. Although evidence of subliminal persuasion's effectiveness is virtually nonexistent, many consumers continue to believe that advertisers use this technique.

- Some of the factors that determine which stimuli (above the threshold level) do get perceived are the amount of exposure to the stimulus, how much attention it generates and how it is interpreted. In an increasingly crowded stimulus environment, advertising clutter occurs when too many marketing-related messages compete for attention.

- A stimulus that is attended to is not perceived in isolation; it is classified and organized according to principles of perceptual organization. These principles are guided by a gestalt, or overall pattern. Specific grouping principles include closure, similarity and figure-ground relationships.

- The final step in the process of perception is interpretation. Symbols help us to make sense of the world by providing us with an interpretation of a stimulus that is often shared by others. The degree to which the symbolism is consistent with our previous experience affects the meaning we assign to related objects. Every marketing message contains a relationship between the product, the sign or symbol, and the interpretation of meaning. A semiotic analysis involves the correspondence between stimuli and the meaning of signs.

KEY TERMS

Absolute threshold p. 57
Adaptation p. 63
Differential threshold p. 57
Exposure p. 57
Figure-ground principle p. 68
Gestalt psychology p. 66
Hedonic consumption p. 49
Interpretation p. 65
JND p. 57
Perception p. 47
Perceptual selectivity p. 62
Positioning strategy p. 69
Priming p. 65
Principle of closure p. 67
Principle of similarity p. 68
Psychophysics p. 57
Repositioning p. 70
Schema p. 65
Sensation p. 47
Subliminal perception p. 60
Weber's Law p. 58

CONSUMER BEHAVIOUR CHALLENGE

1. Many studies have shown that our sensory detection abilities decline as we grow older. Discuss the implications of the absolute threshold for marketers attempting to appeal to the elderly.

2. Interview three to five male and three to five female friends regarding their perceptions of both men's and women's fragrances. Construct a perceptual map for each set of products. Based on your map of perfumes, do you see any areas that are not adequately served by current offerings? What (if any) gender differences did you detect regarding both the relevant dimensions used by raters and the placement of specific brands along these dimensions?

3. Assuming that some forms of subliminal persuasion may have the desired effect of influencing consumers, do you think the use of these techniques is ethical? Explain your answer.

4. Assume that you are a consultant for a marketer who wants to design a package for a new premium chocolate bar targeted to an affluent market. What recom-

mendations would you make in terms of such package elements as colour, symbolism and graphic design? Give the reasons for your suggestions.

5. Do you believe that marketers have the right to use any or all public spaces to deliver product messages? Where would you draw the line in terms of places and products that should be restricted?

6. Using magazines archived in the library, track the packaging of a specific brand over time. Find an example of gradual changes in package design that may have been below the JND.

7. Collect a set of current ads for one type of product (e.g., personal computers, perfumes, laundry detergents or athletic shoes) from magazines, and analyze the colours employed. Describe the images conveyed by different colours, and try to identify any consistency across brands in terms of the colours used in product packaging or other aspects of the ads.

8. Look through a current magazine and select one ad that captures your attention over the others. Give the reasons why.

9. Find ads that utilize the techniques of contrast and novelty. Give your opinion of the effectiveness of each ad and whether the technique is likely to be appropriate for the consumers targeted by the ad.

CBC VIDEO VIGNETTES

Concepts at Work for Scents and Sales

It has long been thought that the smell of bread baking increases the sales of baked goods in supermarkets, that the aroma of freshly baked cookies will help to sell a house, and that unpleasant smells can chase customers away from retail environments. However, North American retailers are now taking a closer look at the role of scent in marketing. Odours which evoke pleasant memories and emotions, or relieve stress, are being identified in sophisticated Canadian and American laboratories and field-tested by retailers. They are looking for the right scent to trigger purchase.

Retailers are wondering how the management of the smell in store environments might be used to augment other elements of the marketing mix. Can smell be used to evoke a certain level of perceived quality in products, to create a less intimidating sales situation, to create a buying mood, or to increase or sustain sales levels? Understanding the symbolism that a particular smell holds for consumers could elevate it to the level of importance colour has in the presentation of products. Perceptual issues that arise out of this "nosy" approach are related to the appropriate scent or combination of scents, sensory thresholds and adaptation effects. There is also some concern about the ethics of attempting to influence consumer behaviour through the sense of smell.

QUESTIONS

1. What is the present use of scent as a tool in the marketing mix?

2. Describe examples of innovative applications of scent in marketing contexts.

3. Describe in detail perceptual issues related to scent.

4. Is the use of scent to influence buying behaviour unethical?

Video Resource: "Scents in Sales," *Marketplace* #24 (April 2, 1996).

NOTES

1. Kim Foltz, "Campaign on Harmony Backfires for Benetton," *New York Times* (November 20, 1989): D8.

2. Elizabeth C. Hirschman and Morris B. Holbrook, "Hedonic Consumption: Emerging Concepts, Methods, and Propositions," *Journal of Marketing* 46 (Summer 1982): 92–101.

3. Glenn Collins, "Owens-Corning's Blurred Identity," *New York Times* (August 19, 1994): D4; Owens-Corning Fiberglass Corp., 774 F.2d 1116(Fed Cir 1985).

4. Anna D. Wilde, "Harley Hopes to add Hogs Roar to its Menagerie," *Wall Street Journal* (June 23, 1995): B1; Associated Press, "Harley Growls About Exclusive Rights on Potato-Potato-Potato Sound," *Vancouver Sun* (March 29, 1996): D1.

5. Dianne Solis, "Cost No Object for Mexico's Makeup Junkies," *Wall Street Journal* (June 7, 1994): B1.

6. Mark G. Frank and Thomas Gilovich, "The Dark Side of Self- and Social Perception: Black Uniforms and Aggression in Professional Sports," *Journal of Personality and Social Psychology* 54, 1 (1988): 74–85.

7. Ronald Alsop, "Color Grows More Important in Catching Consumers' Eyes," *Wall Street Journal* (November 29, 1984): 37; Meg Rosen and Frank Alpert, "Protecting Your Business Image: The Supreme Court Rules on Trade Dress," *Journal of Consumer Marketing* 11, 1 (1994): 50–55.

8. Marion Stinson, "Generics Win on Prozac Look-alike," *Globe and Mail* (April 27, 1997): B11.

9. Quoted in Glenn Collins, "Everything's Coming Up Vanilla," *New York Times* (June 10, 1994): D1 (2 pp.).

10. Quoted in Cynthia Morris, "The Mystery of Fragrance," *Essence* 71, 3 (May 1988): 71.

11. William S. Cain, "Educating Your Nose," *Psychology Today* (July 1981): 48–56.

12. Barbara Carton, "Thank Carl Klumpp for the Swell Smell of Right Guard," *Wall Street Journal* (May 11, 1995): A1.

13. Paulette Thomas, "Cosmetics Makers Offer World's Women an All-American Look with Local Twists," *Wall Street Journal* (May 8, 1995): B1 (2 pp.).

14. Anthony Ramirez, "Advertising: Bored to the gills with trendy new beers? How does a scratch-and-sniff magazine campaign sound?" *New York Times* (October 31, 1994): D7.

15. Tamara Cherry, "Advertising: New Scented Ads Promise Magazine Readers Aromas Mimicking Toothpaste and Leather," *New York Times* (July 9, 1996): D2.

16. Gail Tom, "Marketing with Music," *Journal of Consumer Marketing* 7 (Spring 1990): 49–53; J. Vail, "Music as a Marketing Tool," *Advertising Age* (November 4, 1985): 24. For empirical work on the effects of music on consumer behaviour, see James J. Kellaris and Robert J. Kent, "An Exploratory Investigation of Responses Elicited by Music Varying in Tempo, Tonality, and Texture," *Journal of Consumer Psychology* 2, 4 (1994): 381–401; James J. Kellaris, Anthony D. Cox and Dena Cox, "The Effect of Background Music on Ad Processing: A Contingency Explanation," *Journal of Marketing* 57, 4 (October 1993): 114–25.

17. Otto Friedrich, "Trapped in a Musical Elevator," *Time* 110 (December 10, 1984): 3.

18. Ronald E. Millman, "Using Background Music to Affect the Behaviour of Supermarket Shoppers," *Journal of Marketing* 46 (Summer 1982): 86–91.

19. James MacLachlan and Michael H. Siegel, "Reducing the Costs of Television Commercials by Use of Time Compression," *Journal of Marketing Research* 17 (February 1980): 52–57.

20. James MacLachlan, "Listener Perception of Time Compressed Spokespersons," *Journal of Advertising Research* 2 (April/May 1982): 47–51.

21. Danny L. Moore, Douglas Hausknecht and Kanchana Thamodaran, "Time Compression, Response Opportunity, and Persuasion," *Journal of Consumer Research* 13 (June 1986): 85–99.

22. See Leslie Davis Burns and Sharron J. Lennon, "The Look and the Feel: Methods for Measuring Aesthetic Perceptions of Textiles and Apparel," in M.R. DeLong and A.M. Fiore, *Aesthetics of Textiles and Clothing: Advancing Multi-Disciplinary Perspectives* (Monument, CO: International Textile and Apparel Association, 1994): 120–30.

23. Jacob Hornik, "Tactile Stimulation and Consumer Response," *Journal of Consumer Research* 19 (December 1992).

24. Robert Frank, "Yum! It's a Bottle of Soda Filled with Big Lumps of Slippery Jelly," *Wall Street Journal* (May 16, 1996): B1.

25. Eben Shapiro, "The People Who Are Putting Taste Back on the Table," *New York Times* (July 22, 1990): F5.

26. Judann Dagnoli, "Cookie Tasters Chip in for Nabisco," *Advertising Age* (August 21, 1989): 58.

27. See Tim Davis, "Taste Tests: Are the Blind Leading the Blind?" *Beverage World* (April 1987): 43.

28. "$10 Sure Thing," *Time* (August 4, 1980): 51.

29. Stuart Elliott, "Another Remarkable Story of the Brand-Name Lexicon," *New York Times* (August 13, 1992): D9. IBM is the world's ninth most popular brand.

30. *New Yorker* (September 21, 1957): 33.

31. Erv Wolk, "Can Subliminal Ads Work for You?" *Modern Floor Coverings* (June 1986): 23.

32. Philip M. Merikle, "Subliminal Auditory Messages: An Evaluation," *Psychology & Marketing* 5, 4 (1988): 355–72.

33. Eric R. Spangenberg, Carl Obermiller and Anthony G. Greenwald, "A Field Test of Subliminal Self-Help Audio-Tapes," *Journal of Public Policy and Marketing* 11, 2 (1992): 26–36.

34. Timothy E. Moore, "The Case Against Subliminal Manipulation," *Psychology & Marketing* 5 (Winter 1988): 297–316.

35. Sid C. Dudley, "Subliminal Advertising: What Is the Controversy About?" *Akron Business and Economic Review* 18 (Summer 1987): 6–18; "Subliminal Messages: Subtle Crime Stoppers," *Chain Store Age Executive* 2 (July 1987): 85; "Mind Benders," *Money* (September 1978): 24.

36. Moore, "The Case Against Subliminal Manipulation."

37. Joel Saegert, "Why Marketing Should Quit Giving Subliminal Advertising the Benefit of the Doubt," *Psychology & Marketing* 4 (Summer 1987): 107–20. See also Dennis L. Rosen and Surendra N. Singh, "An Investigation of Subliminal Embed Effect on Multiple Measures of Advertising Effectiveness," *Psychology & Marketing* 9 (March/April 1992): 157–73. For a more recent review, see Kathryn T. Theus, "Subliminal Advertising and the Psychology of Processing Unconscious Stimuli: A Review of Research," *Psychology & Marketing* (May/June 1994): 271–90.

38. Kim Foltz, *New York Times* (October 23, 1989).

39. Roger Barton, *Advertising Media* (New York: McGraw-Hill, 1964).

40. Cynthia Grossen, "Case of the Vanishing Medium: Perpetrator is Large," *Wall Street Journal* (February 26, 1996): B1, B8.

41. Suzanne Oliver, "New Personality," *Forbes* (August 15, 1994): 114.

42. Adam Finn, "Print Ad Recognition Readership Scores: An Information Processing Perspective," *Journal of Marketing Research* 25 (May 1988): 168–77.

43. Michael Lev, "Music Industry Broadens Its Campaigns," *New York Times* (January 17, 1992): D15.

44. "Traffic Now Tuned to Boston's Tunnel Radio," *New York Times* (August 1, 1982); Alison Fahey, "In the Lobby," *Advertising Age* (September 18, 1989); Kim Foltz, "Ads Popping Up All Over," *Newsweek* (August 12, 1985): 50.

45. Kim Foltz, *New York Times* (October 23, 1989): D11.

46. Stuart Elliott, "When Up Is Down, Does It Sell?" *New York Times* (February 21, 1992): D1.

47. David Kilburn, "Japanese VCR Edits Out the Ads," *Advertising Age* (August 20, 1990): 16.

48. Kate Lewin, "Getting Around Commercial Avoidance," *Marketing and Media Decisions* (December 1988): 116.

49. Craig Reiss, "Fast-Forward Ads Deliver," *Advertising Age* (October 27, 1986): 3; Steve Sternberg, "VCRs: Impact and Implications," *Marketing and Media Decisions* 22, 5 (December 1987): 100.

50. Gail Tom, Teresa Barnett, William Lew and Jodean Selmants, "Cueing the Consumer: The Role of Salient Cues in Consumer Perception," *Journal of Consumer Marketing* 4, 2 (1987): 23–27.

51. Tara Parker-Pope, "Spiked Sodas, An Illicit Hit with Kids in U.K., Head for U.S.," *Wall Street Journal* (February 12, 1996): B1.

52. Anthony Ramirez, "Lessons in the Cracker Market: Nabisco Saved New Graham Snack," *New York Times* (July 5, 1990): D1.

53. Albert H. Hastorf and Hadley Cantril, "They Saw a Game: A Case Study," *Journal of Abnormal and Social Psychology* 49 (1954): 129–34. Cf. also Roberto Friedmann and Mary R. Zimmer, "The Role of Psychological Meaning in Advertising," *Journal of Advertising* 17, 1 (1988): 31–40.

54. Thomas Hine, "Why We Buy: The Silent Persuasion of Boxes, Bottles, Cans, and Tubes," *Worth* (May 1995): 78–83.

55. Robert M. McMath, "Chock Full of (Pea)nuts," *American Demographics* (April 1997): 60.

56. Ronald Alsop, "Color Grows More Important in Catching Consumers' Eyes," *Wall Street Journal* (November 29, 1984): 37.

57. See Tim Davis, "Taste Tests: Are the Blind Leading the Blind?" *Beverage World* (April 1987) 3: 43.

58. Adapted from Michael R. Solomon and Elnora W. Stuart, *Marketing: Real People, Real Choices* (Englewood Cliffs, NJ: Prentice Hall, 1997).

59. William Echikson, "Aiming at High and Low Markets," *Fortune* (March 22, 1993): 89.

60. Patricia Winters, "Cadbury Puts Crush Back on TV," *Ad Age* (February 25, 1991): 16.

61. Scott Donaton, "Magazine of the Year," *Ad Age* (March 1, 1993): S-1 (3 pp.).

It's Saturday night, and Michelle and Debbie are getting ready for a big end-of-summer party. There is a news flash on the television that Princess Diana is critically injured after a car crash in Paris. Michelle and Debbie can hardly believe their ears. How could a car accident happen to a princess? Over the next few hours the television stays on during the party. Then the announcement is made: Princess Diana has died from her massive internal injuries. By this time the party should be rockin', but deep down inside no one is in a party mood. Their minds are far away, trying to comprehend this shocking news.

3

Learning and Memory

THE LEARNING PROCESS

Michelle, Debbie and most of the world will have memories of where they were and what they were doing the night that Princess Diana died in a fatal car crash in Paris. An estimated 2.5 billion people around the world watched the funeral service.[1] Many people over 40 will add this event to their memories of where they were when John F. Kennedy was assassinated or Marilyn Monroe died. In this chapter we'll explore how learned associations among feelings, events and products are important aspects of consumer behaviour.

   Learning refers to a relatively permanent change in behaviour that is caused by experience. This experience does not have to directly affect the learner; we can learn *vicariously* by observing events that affect others.[2] We also learn even when we are not trying. Consumers, for example, recognize many brand names and can hum many product jingles, even those for product categories they themselves do not use. This casual, unintentional acquisition of knowledge is known as *incidental learning*. Learning is an ongoing process. Our knowledge about the world is constantly being revised as we are exposed to new stimuli and receive ongoing feedback that allows us to modify behaviour in other, similar situations. The concept of learning covers a lot of ground, ranging from a consumer's simple association between a stimulus such as a product logo (Coca-Cola) and a response ("refreshing soft drink") to a complex

learning a relatively permanent change in a behaviour, caused by experience

77

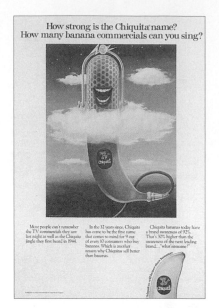

How strong is the Chiquita name?
How many banana commercials can you sing?

Many classic advertising campaigns consist of product slogans that have been repeated so many times that they are etched in consumers' minds. The ad shown here brags about the high awareness of the Chiquita banana jingle ("I'm Chiquita banana, and I'm here to say ...").
Used by permission of Chiquita Brands, Inc.

series of cognitive activities (writing an essay on learning for a Consumer Behaviour exam). Psychologists who study learning have advanced several theories to explain the learning process. These theories range from those focusing on simple stimulus-response connections (behavioural theories) to perspectives that regard consumers as complex problem solvers who learn abstract rules and concepts by observing others (cognitive theories). Understanding these theories is important to marketers as well, since basic learning principles are at the heart of many consumer purchase decisions.

BEHAVIOURAL LEARNING THEORIES

behavioural learning theories the perspectives on learning that assume that learning takes place as the result of responses to external events

Behavioural learning theories assume that learning takes place as the result of responses to external events. Psychologists who subscribe to this viewpoint do not focus on internal thought processes. Instead, they approach the mind as a "black box" and emphasize the observable aspects of behaviour.

This view is represented by two major approaches to learning: classical conditioning and instrumental conditioning. People's experiences are shaped by the feedback they receive as they go through life. Similarly, consumers respond to brand names, scents, jingles and other marketing stimuli based upon the learned connections they have formed over time. People also learn that actions they take result in rewards and punishments, and this feedback influences the way they will respond in similar situations in the future. Consumers who receive compliments on a product choice will be more likely to buy that brand again, while those who get food poisoning at a new restaurant will not be likely to patronize it in the future.

classical conditioning the learning that occurs when a stimulus eliciting a response is paired with another stimulus that initially does not elicit a response on its own but will cause a similar response over time because of its association with the first stimulus

Classical Conditioning

Classical conditioning occurs when a stimulus that elicits a response is paired with another stimulus that initially does not elicit a response on its own. Over time, this

FIGURE 3–1 • Diagram of the Classical Conditioning Process

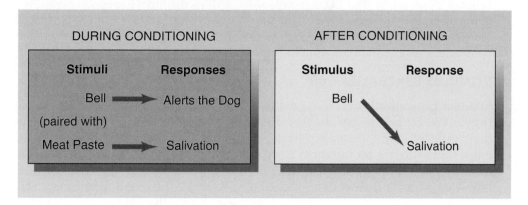

second stimulus causes a similar response because it is associated with the first stimulus. This phenomenon was first demonstrated in dogs by Ivan Pavlov, a Russian physiologist doing research on digestion in animals, and is shown in Figure 3–1.

Pavlov induced classically conditioned learning by pairing a neutral stimulus (a bell) with a stimulus known to cause a salivation response in dogs (he squirted dried meat powder into their mouths). The powder was an *unconditioned stimulus (UCS)* because it was naturally capable of causing the response. Over time, the bell became a *conditioned stimulus (CS);* it did not initially cause salivation, but the dogs learned to associate the bell with the meat powder and began to salivate at the sound of the bell only. The drooling of these canine consumers over a sound, now linked to feeding time, was a *conditioned response (CR)*.

This basic form of classical conditioning demonstrated by Pavlov primarily applies to responses controlled by the autonomic (e.g., salivation) and nervous (e.g., eyeblink) systems. That is, it focuses on visual and olfactory cues that induce hunger, thirst or sexual arousal. When these cues are consistently paired with conditioned stimuli, such as brand names, consumers may learn to feel hungry, thirsty or aroused when later exposed to the brand cues.

Classical conditioning can have similar effects for more complex reactions too. Even a credit card becomes a conditioned cue that triggers greater spending, especially since it is a stimulus that is present only in situations where consumers are spending money. People learn they can make larger purchases when using credit cards, and they also have been found to leave larger tips than they do when using cash.[3] Small wonder that American Express reminds us, "Don't leave home without it."

REPETITION

Conditioning effects are more likely to occur after the conditioned and unconditioned stimuli have been paired a number of times.[4] Repeated exposures increase the strength of stimulus-response associations and prevent the decay of these associations in memory. Many classic advertising campaigns consist of product slogans that have been repeated so many times that they are etched in consumers' minds.

Conditioning will not occur or will take longer if the CS is only occasionally presented with the UCS. One result of this lack of association may be **extinction,** which occurs when the effects of prior conditioning are reduced and finally disappear. This

extinction the process whereby a learned connection between a stimulus and response is eroded so that the response is no longer reinforced

can occur, for example, when a product is *overexposed* in the marketplace so that its original allure is lost. The Lacoste polo shirt, with its distinctive crocodile crest, is a good example of this effect. When the once-exclusive crocodile started to appear on baby clothes and many other items, it lost its cachet and was soon replaced by other contenders, such as the Lauren polo player.[5]

STIMULUS GENERALIZATION

stimulus generalization the process that occurs when the behaviour caused by a reaction to one stimulus occurs in the presence of other, similar stimuli

Stimulus generalization refers to the tendency of stimuli similar to a CS to evoke similar, conditioned responses.[6] For example, Pavlov noticed in subsequent studies that his dogs would sometimes salivate when they heard noises that only resembled a bell (keys jangling, for instance). People react to other, similar stimuli in much the same way they responded to an original stimulus. A drugstore's bottle of private-brand mouthwash deliberately packaged to resemble Listerine mouthwash may evoke a similar response among consumers who assume that this "me-too" product shares other characteristics of the original.

Indeed, consumers in one study on shampoo brands tended to rate those with similar packages as similar in quality and performance as well.[7] This "piggybacking" strategy can cut both ways: when the quality of the me-too product turns out to be lower than that of the original brand, consumers may exhibit even more positive feelings towards the original; however, if the quality of the two competitors is perceived to be about equal, consumers may conclude the price premium they are paying for the original is not worth it.[8] In addition, consumers' learned associations with a large corporation can influence what they believe about its products. The company's overall reputation has been shown to have a particularly strong impact on brand evaluations, and to a lesser extent its reputation for social responsibility can also affect these individual brand ratings.[9]

STIMULUS DISCRIMINATION

stimulus discrimination the process that occurs when behaviour caused by two stimuli is different, as when consumers learn to differentiate a brand from its competitors

Stimulus discrimination occurs when a stimulus similar to a CS is *not* followed by a UCS. In these situations, reactions are weakened and will soon disappear. Part of the learning process involves making a response to some stimuli but not to other, similar stimuli. Manufacturers of well-established brands commonly urge consumers not to buy "cheap imitations" because the results will not be what they expect.

Marketing Applications of Behavioural Learning Principles

Many marketing strategies focus on the establishment of associations between stimuli and responses. Behavioural learning principles apply to many consumer phenomena, ranging from the creation of a distinctive brand image to the perceived linkage between a product and an underlying need.

The transfer of meaning from an unconditioned stimulus to a conditioned stimulus explains why "made-up" brand names like Coca-Cola or IBM can exert such powerful effects on consumers. When nonsense syllables (meaningless sets of letters) are paired with such evaluative words as beauty or success, the meaning is transferred to the nonsense syllables. This change in the symbolic significance of initially meaningless words shows that complex meanings can be conditioned by fairly simple associations.[10]

These conditioned associations are crucial to many marketing strategies that rely on the creation and perpetuation of positive **brand equity,** in which a brand has strong positive associations in a consumer's memory and commands a lot of loyalty as a result.[11] As we will see in the following chapters, a product with brand equity holds a tremendous advantage in the marketplace.

brand equity a brand that has strong positive associations in a consumer's memory and commands a lot of loyalty as a result

REPETITION

One advertising researcher argues that more than three exposures are wasted. The first creates awareness of the product, the second demonstrates its relevance to the consumer, and the third serves as a reminder of the product's benefits.[12] However, even this bare-bones approach implies that repetition is needed to ensure that the consumer is actually exposed to (and processes) the ad at least three times. As we saw in the last chapter, this exposure is by no means guaranteed since people tend to tune out or distort many marketing communications. Marketers attempting to condition an association must ensure that the consumers they have targeted will be exposed to the stimulus a sufficient number of times to make it "stick."

On the other hand, it is possible to have too much of a good thing. Consumers can become so used to hearing or seeing a marketing stimulus that they no longer pay attention to it. This problem, known as *advertising wearout,* can be alleviated by varying the way in which the basic message is presented. For example, the tax-preparation firm H&R Block is famous for its long-standing "Another of the seventeen reasons to use H&R Block …" campaign.

CONDITIONING PRODUCT ASSOCIATIONS

Advertisements often pair a product with a positive stimulus to create a desirable association. Various aspects of a marketing message, such as music, humour or imagery, can affect conditioning. In one study, for example, subjects who viewed a slide of pens paired with either pleasant or unpleasant music were more likely later to select the pen that appeared with pleasant music.[13]

Les histoires de Mario.

Le poisson de Provigo.

One innovative way to employ repetition without causing wearout is illustrated by these related billboard images.
Courtesy of Cossette Communications Marketing for Provigo Supermarkets, 1986.

The behaviour of consumers can also be conditioned. In studies involving the effect of music on the consumption behaviour of people in supermarkets or restaurants, consumption was found to be influenced. Slow music in grocery stores led to longer visits and more money being spent.[14] Slow music in restaurants had no impact on food consumption, but patrons did tend to have one extra drink, on average.[15]

The order in which the conditioned stimulus and the unconditioned stimulus are presented can affect the likelihood that learning will occur. Generally speaking, the unconditioned stimulus should be presented prior to the conditioned stimulus. The technique of *backward conditioning,* such as showing a soft drink (the CS) and then playing a jingle (the UCS) is generally not effective.[16] Because sequential presentation is desirable for conditioning to occur, classical conditioning is not very effective in static situations, such as in magazine ads, where (in contrast to TV or radio) the marketer cannot control the order in which the CS and the UCS are perceived.

Just as product associations can be formed, they can be *extinguished.* Because of the danger of extinction, a classical conditioning strategy may not be as effective for products that are frequently encountered, since there is no guarantee they will be accompanied by the CS. A bottle of Pepsi paired with the refreshing sound of a carbonated beverage being poured over ice may seem like a good example of conditioning. Unfortunately, the product would also be seen in many other contexts where this sound was absent, reducing the effectiveness of the conditioning.

By the same reasoning, a novel tune should be chosen over a popular one to pair with a product, since the popular song might also be heard in many situations in which the product is not present.[17] Music videos in particular may serve as effective UCSs because they often have an emotional impact on viewers, and this effect may transfer to ads accompanying the video.[18]

APPLICATIONS OF STIMULUS GENERALIZATION

The process of stimulus generalization is often central to branding and packaging decisions that attempt to capitalize on consumers' positive associations with an existing brand or company name. In one 20-month period, Procter & Gamble introduced almost 90 new products. Not a single product carried a new brand name. In fact, roughly 80 percent of all new products are actually extensions of existing brands or product lines.[19] Strategies based on stimulus generalization include the following:

- *Family branding,* in which a variety of products capitalize on the reputation of a company name. Companies such as Virgin, Campbell's, Heinz and General Electric rely on their positive corporate images to sell different product lines.

- *Product line extensions,* in which related products are added to an established brand. Dole, which is associated with fruit, was able to introduce refrigerated juices and juice bars, while Sun Maid went from raisins to raisin bread. Other recent extensions include Woolite rug cleaner, Cracker Jack gourmet popping corn, and Ivory shampoo.[20]

MARKETING PITFALL

For a stimulus-response connection to be maintained, a new product must share some important characteristics with the original. Trouble can result if consumers do not make the connection between a brand and its extension. In fact, if attributes of the new products are inconsistent with the consumer's beliefs about the family brand, the overall image of the family brand runs the danger of being diluted.[21]

When Cadillac came out with the smaller Cadillac Cimarron, people who already owned Cadillacs did not regard the new model as a bona fide Cadillac. Arm & Hammer deodorant failed, possibly because consumers identified the product too strongly with something in the back of their refrigerators.[22] An extension even has the potential to weaken the parent brand, as the Carnation Company discovered. The company cancelled plans for "Lady Friskies," a contraceptive dog food, after tests indicated it would reduce sales of regular Friskies.[23]

- *Licensing,* in which well-known names are "rented" by others. This strategy is increasing in popularity as marketers try to link their products and services with well-established figures. Companies as diverse as McDonald's and Harley-Davidson have authorized the use of their names on products. Even Spam™ lovers can buy underwear, earrings, and other items bearing the logo of the canned "meat product"![24] The movie *Jurassic Park* and its sequel *The Lost World* generated over $1 billion in licensed merchandise sales, with about 5000 products crawling out of the primordial ooze and onto store shelves,[25] while the movie *Forrest Gump* inspired new products ranging from table tennis sets (inspired by his ping-pong championships) to shrimp from the Bubba Gump Seafood Company.[26] Japan Airlines recently licensed the rights to use Disney

This trade ad for King Features promotes the characters from the Blondie comic strip to potential licensers for use in their own advertising, with the expectation that positive attitudes towards these characters will be generalized to their products.
© 1986 by King Features Syndicate, Inc.

The fire that briefly raged for the *Flintstones* characters was fanned by one of the more intensive merchandising campaigns in recent memory. About 1000 products hit the market when the movie was released in May 1994. These items included a Talking Fred doll from Mattel, Flintstones children's cosmetics and Licking Dino cookies. The same marketers who were responsible for the phenomenal success of *Jurassic Park* masterminded the *Flintstones* strategy. Previous licensing winners include *Superman*, *Batman* and *Teenage Mutant Ninja Turtles*, which together sold more than $7.3 billion (US) of tie-in products. Some duds in the licensing graveyard include characters based on *Popeye*, *The Jetsons* and *The Addams Family*.
(Anthony Ramirez, "Gold in Bedrock?" New York Times [May 22, 1994]: 9–10 [2 pp.]; Glenn Heitsmith, "Licensing a Piece of the Bedrock," PROMO [June 1994]: 33 [6 pp.].)
Photo courtesy of Yvonne Hemsey/Gamma-Liason, Inc.

characters and, in addition to painting Mickey Mouse and Donald Duck on several of its planes, the carrier is requiring its flight attendants to wear mouse ears on some domestic flights![27]

- *Look-alike packaging,* in which distinctive packaging designs create strong associations with a particular brand. This linkage often is exploited by makers of generic or private-label brands who wish to communicate a quality image by putting their products in very similar packages. As one drugstore executive commented, "You want to tell the consumer that it's close to the national brand … You've got to make it look like, within the law, close to the national brand. They're at least attracted to the package."[28] This is clearly an unethical practice, which is likely to be legally pursued by the original manufacturer.

APPLICATIONS OF STIMULUS DISCRIMINATION

An emphasis on communicating a product's distinctive attributes *vis-à-vis* its competitors is an important aspect of positioning, in which consumers learn to differentiate a brand from its competitors (see Chapter 2). This is not always an easy task, especially in product categories where the brand names of many of the alternatives look and sound alike. For example, a recent survey showed that many consumers have a great deal of trouble distinguishing among products sold by the top computer manufacturers. With a blur of names like OmniPlex, OptiPlex, Premmia, Premium, ProLinea, ProLiant, etc., this confusion is not surprising.[29]

Companies with a well-established brand image try to encourage stimulus discrimination by promoting the unique attributes of their brands. Thus, the constant reminders for American Express® Travelers Cheques: "Ask for them by name …" On the other hand, a brand name that is used so widely that it is no longer distinctive becomes part of the *public domain* and can be used by competitors, as has been the case for such products as aspirin, cellophane, the yo-yo and the escalator.

Instrumental Conditioning

Instrumental conditioning, also known as *operant conditioning,* occurs as the individual learns to perform behaviours that produce positive outcomes and to avoid those that yield negative outcomes. This learning process is most closely associated with the psychologist B.F. Skinner, who demonstrated the effects of instrumental conditioning by teaching animals to dance, play ping-pong, and so on by systematically rewarding them for desired behaviours.[30]

While responses in classical conditioning are involuntary and fairly simple, those in instrumental conditioning are made deliberately to obtain a goal and may be more complex. The desired behaviour may be learned over a period of time, as intermediate actions are rewarded in a process called *shaping*. For example, the owner of a new store may award prizes to shoppers just for coming in, hoping that over time they will continue to drop in and eventually buy something.

Also, classical conditioning involves the close pairing of two stimuli. Instrumental learning occurs as a result of a reward received *following* the desired behaviour and takes place over a period in which a variety of other behaviours are attempted and abandoned because they are not reinforced. A good way to remember the difference is to keep in mind that in instrumental learning the response is performed because it is *instrumental* to gaining a reward or avoiding a punishment. Consumers over time come to associate with people who reward them and to choose products that make them feel good or satisfy some need.

HOW INSTRUMENTAL CONDITIONING OCCURS

Instrumental learning occurs in one of three ways. When the environment provides **positive reinforcement** in the form of a reward, the response is strengthened and appropriate behaviour is learned. For example, a woman who gets compliments after wearing Obsession perfume will learn that using this product has the desired effect, and she will be more likely to keep buying the product. **Negative reinforcement** also strengthens responses so that appropriate behaviour is learned. A perfume company, for example, might run an ad showing a woman sitting home alone on a Saturday night because she did not use its fragrance. The message to be conveyed is that she could have *avoided* this negative outcome if only she had used the perfume. In contrast to situations wherein we learn to do certain things in order to avoid unpleasantness, **punishment** occurs when a response is followed by unpleasant events (such as being ridiculed by friends for wearing an offensive-smelling perfume). We learn not to repeat these behaviours.

When trying to understand the differences among these mechanisms, keep in mind that reactions from a person's environment to behaviour can be either positive

instrumental conditioning the process by which the individual learns to perform behaviours that produce positive outcomes and to avoid those that yield negative outcomes

positive reinforcement the process whereby rewards provided by the environment strengthen responses to stimuli

negative reinforcement the process whereby the environment weakens responses to stimuli so that inappropriate behaviour is avoided

punishment the learning that occurs when a response is followed by unpleasant events

or negative and that these outcomes or anticipated outcomes can be applied or removed. That is, under conditions of both positive reinforcement and punishment, the person receives a reaction after doing something. In contrast, negative reinforcement occurs when a negative outcome is avoided; the removal of something negative is pleasurable and hence is rewarding.

Finally, when a positive outcome is no longer received, extinction is likely to occur, and the learned stimulus-response connection will not be maintained (as when a woman no longer receives compliments on her perfume). Thus, positive and negative reinforcement *strengthen* the future linkage between a response and an outcome because of the pleasant experience. This tie is *weakened* under conditions of both punishment and extinction because of the unpleasant experience. The relationships among these four conditions are easier to understand by referring to Figure 3–2.

An important factor in operant conditioning is the set of rules by which appropriate reinforcements are given for a behaviour. The issue of what is the most effective *reinforcement schedule* to use is important to marketers, because it relates to the amount of effort and resources they must devote to rewarding consumers in order to condition desired behaviours. Several schedules are possible:

FIGURE 3–2 • Four Types of Learning Outcomes

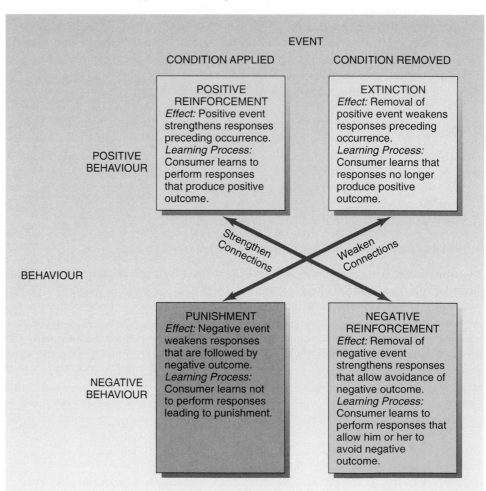

- *Fixed-interval reinforcement.* After a specified time period has passed, the first response that is made brings the reward. Under such conditions people tend to respond slowly right after being reinforced, but their responses speed up as the time for the next reinforcement looms. For example, consumers may crowd into a store for the last day of its seasonal sale and not reappear until the next one.

- *Variable-interval reinforcement.* The time that must pass before reinforcement is delivered varies around some average. Since the person does not know exactly when to expect the reinforcement, responses must be performed at a consistent rate. This logic is behind retailers' use of so-called secret shoppers—people who periodically test for service quality by posing as customers at unannounced times. Since store employees never know exactly when to expect a visit, high quality must be constantly maintained "just in case."

- *Fixed-ratio reinforcement.* Reinforcement occurs only after a fixed number of responses. This schedule motivates people to continue performing the same behaviour over and over. For example, a consumer might keep buying at the same store in order to earn a prize after collecting frequent buyer points.

- *Variable-ratio reinforcement.* The person is reinforced after a certain number of responses, but he or she does not know how many responses are required. People in such situations tend to respond at very high and steady rates, and this type of behaviour is very difficult to extinguish. This reinforcement schedule is responsible for consumers' attraction to slot machines. They learn that, if they keep throwing money into the machine, they will eventually win something (if they don't go broke first).

Applications of Instrumental Conditioning Principles

Principles of instrumental conditioning are at work when a consumer is rewarded or punished for a purchase decision. Businesspeople shape behaviour by gradually reinforcing consumers for taking appropriate actions. For example, a car dealer might encourage a reluctant buyer to just sit in a floor model, then suggest a test drive, and then try to close the deal.

REINFORCEMENT OF CONSUMPTION

Marketers have many ways to reinforce consumers, ranging from a simple thank-you after a purchase to substantial rebates and follow-up phone calls. For example, a life insurance company obtained a much higher rate of policy renewal among a group of new customers who received a thank-you letter after each payment compared to a control group that did not receive any reinforcement.[31]

FREQUENCY MARKETING

A popular technique known as **frequency marketing** reinforces regular purchasers by giving them prizes with values that increase along with the amount purchased. This operant learning strategy was pioneered by the airline industry, which introduced "frequent flyer" programs in the early 1980s to reward loyal customers. Well over 20 percent of food stores, for example, now offer some frequent-buyer promotion.

frequency marketing a marketing technique that reinforces regular purchasers by giving them prizes with values that increase along with the amount purchased

Zellers was one of the first retailers in Canada to adopt a frequency marketing program.
Courtesy of Dick Hemimgway.

COGNITIVE LEARNING THEORY

cognitive learning theory
the perspectives on learning that assume that learning takes place as the result of internal mental processes: people actively use information from the world around them to master their environment and solve problems

In contrast to behavioural theories of learning, **cognitive learning theory** stresses the importance of internal mental processes. This perspective views people as problem solvers who actively use information from the world around them to master their environment. Supporters of this viewpoint also stress the role of creativity and insight during the learning process.

MULTICULTURAL DIMENSIONS

A popular frequency marketing concept in Europe puts an interesting twist on reinforcement: customers actually pay for the privilege of belonging.[32] These programs take the form of "value clubs," where customers pay dues to receive benefits. The concept began over a decade ago and is particularly popular in Germany, where strict regulations limit the use of discounts and other price promotions. Value clubs offer two classes of rewards: 1) "soft benefits," which include premiums like T-shirts but also the use of travel services and other amenities; and 2) "hard benefits"—actual discounts on products. For example, the IKEA Family is a value club sponsored by the Swedish furniture retailer that offers a vacation-home exchange service to its members in nine European countries. The value club concept is beginning to travel across the ocean: Volkswagen and Swatch have now set up American chapters, and more companies will likely follow their lead.

Is Learning Conscious or Not?

A lot of controversy surrounds the issue of whether or when people are aware of their learning processes. While behavioural learning theorists emphasize the routine, automatic nature of conditioning, proponents of cognitive learning argue that even these simple effects are based on cognitive factors; that is, expectations are created that a stimulus will be followed by a response (the formation of expectations requires mental activity). According to this school of thought, conditioning occurs because subjects develop conscious hypotheses and then act on them.

On the one hand, there is some evidence for the existence of nonconscious procedural knowledge. People apparently do process at least some information in an automatic, passive way, which is a condition that has been termed *mindlessness*.[33] When we meet someone new or encounter a new product, for example, we have a tendency to respond to the stimulus in terms of existing categories, rather than taking the trouble to formulate different ones. Our reactions are activated by a *trigger feature*—some stimulus that cues us towards a particular pattern. For example, men in one study rated a car in an ad as superior on a variety of characteristics if a seductive woman (the trigger feature) was present, despite the fact that the men did not believe the woman's presence actually had an influence on their evaluations.[34]

Nonetheless, many modern theorists are beginning to regard some instances of conditioning as cognitive processes, especially where expectations are formed about the linkages between stimuli and responses. Indeed, studies using *masking effects*, wherein it is difficult for subjects to learn CS/UCS associations, show substantial reductions in conditioning.[35]

Observational Learning

Observational learning occurs when people watch the actions of others and note the reinforcements they receive for their behaviours; learning occurs as a result of *vicarious* rather than direct experience. This type of learning is a complex process; people store these observations in memory as they accumulate knowledge, perhaps using this information at a later point to guide their own behaviours. This process of imitating the behaviour of others is called *modelling*. For example, a woman shopping for a new kind of perfume may remember the reactions a friend received upon wearing a certain brand several months earlier, and she will base her behaviour on her friend's actions.

observational learning the process in which people learn by watching the actions of others and noting the reinforcements they receive for their behaviours

In order for observational learning in the form of modelling to occur, four conditions must be met.[36] These factors are summarized in Figure 3–3.

1. The consumer's attention must be directed to the appropriate model whom, for reasons of attractiveness, competence, status or similarity, it is desirable to emulate.

2. The consumer must remember what is said or done by the model.

3. The consumer must convert this information into actions.

4. The consumer must be motivated to perform these actions.

FIGURE 3–3 • Components of Observational Learning

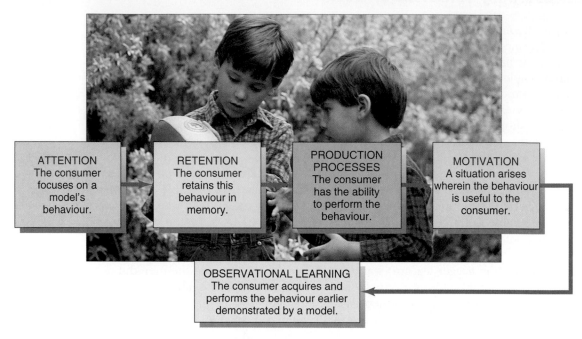

| ATTENTION
The consumer focuses on a model's behaviour. | RETENTION
The consumer retains this behaviour in memory. | PRODUCTION PROCESSES
The consumer has the ability to perform the behaviour. | MOTIVATION
A situation arises wherein the behaviour is useful to the consumer. |

OBSERVATIONAL LEARNING
The consumer acquires and performs the behaviour earlier demonstrated by a model.

Photo Courtesy of Richard Heinzen/Superstock

Applications of Cognitive Learning Principles

Consumers' ability to learn vicariously by observing how the behaviour of others is reinforced makes the lives of marketers much easier. Because people do not have to be reinforced directly for their actions, marketers do not necessarily have to reward or punish them for purchase behaviours. Instead, they can show what happens to desirable models who use or do not use their products, in the knowledge that consumers will often be motivated to imitate these actions at a later time. For example,

MARKETING PITFALL

The modelling process is a powerful form of learning, and people's tendencies to imitate others' behaviours can have negative effects. Of particular concern is the potential of television shows and movies to teach violence to children. Children may be exposed to new methods of aggression by models (such as cartoon heroes) in the shows they watch. At some later point, when the child becomes angry, these behaviours will be imitated. A classic study demonstrates the effect of modelling on children's actions. Kids who watched an adult stomp on, knock down and otherwise torture a large, inflated "Bobo doll" repeated these behaviours when later left alone in a room with the doll, in contrast to the behaviours of other children who did not witness these acts.[37] The parallel to violent programming is, unfortunately, clear.

a perfume commercial may depict a woman surrounded by a throng of admirers who are providing her with positive reinforcement for using the product. Needless to say, this learning process is more practical than providing the same personal attention to each woman who actually buys the perfume!

Consumers' evaluations of models go beyond simple stimulus-response connections. For example, a celebrity's image is often more than a simple reflexive response of good or bad;[38] it is a complex combination of many attributes. In general, the degree to which a model will be emulated depends upon his or her social attractiveness. Attractiveness can be based upon several components, including physical appearance, expertise or similarity to the evaluator.

These factors will be further addressed in Chapter 8, which discusses personal characteristics that make a communication's source more or less effective in changing consumers' attitudes. In addition, many applications of consumer problem solving are related to ways information is represented in memory and recalled at a later date. This aspect of cognitive learning is the focus of the next section.

THE ROLE OF MEMORY IN LEARNING

Memory involves a process of acquiring information and storing it over time so that it will be available when needed. Contemporary approaches to the study of memory employ an information-processing approach. They assume that the mind is in some ways like a computer: data are input, processed and output for later use in revised form. In the **encoding** stage, information is entered in a way the system will recog-

memory a process of acquiring information and storing it over time so that it will be available when needed

encoding the process in which information from short-term memory is entered into long-term memory in a recognizable form

This cosmetics ad illustrates the principle of vicarious reinforcement. The model uses the product and is shown reaping the reward—the approval of her boyfriend.
Courtesy of Maybelline, Inc.

storage the process that occurs when knowledge entered in long-term memory is integrated with what is already in memory and "warehoused" until needed

retrieval the process whereby desired information is accessed from long-term memory

nize. In the **storage** stage, this knowledge is integrated with what is already in memory and "warehoused" until needed. During **retrieval,** the person accesses the desired information.[39] The memory process is summarized in Figure 3–4.

Many of our experiences are locked inside our heads and may surface years later if prompted by the right cues. Marketers rely on consumers to retain information they have learned about products and services, trusting that it will later be applied in situations where purchase decisions must be made. During the consumer decision-making process, this *internal memory* is combined with *external memory*—which includes all of the product details on packages, in shopping lists and through other marketing stimuli—to permit brand alternatives to be identified and evaluated.[40]

Encoding of Information for Later Retrieval

The way information is *encoded,* or mentally programmed, helps to determine how it will be represented in memory. In general, incoming data that are associated with other information already in memory stand a better chance of being retained. For

This fragrance ad emphasizes that products can evoke memories of earlier experiences.
Courtesy of COMPAR.

FIGURE 3–4 • The Memory Process

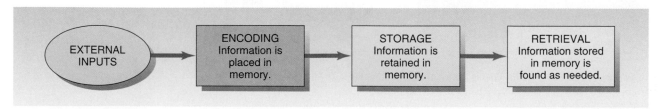

example, brand names that are linked to physical characteristics of a product category (Coffee Mate creamer or Sani-Flush toilet bowl cleaner) or that are easy to visualize (Tide detergent or Mercury Cougar cars) tend to be more easily retained in memory than more abstract brand names.[41]

However, memory for brand names may interact with one's involvement in the product class. Low-involvement products, such as household cleaners, seem to benefit from descriptive names by being easier to remember. There is no evidence that descriptive names for high-involvement products, like automobiles, are remembered any better than nondescriptive names.[42]

TYPES OF MEANING

A consumer may process a stimulus simply in terms of its *sensory meaning,* such as its colour or shape. When this occurs, the meaning may be activated when the person sees a picture of the stimulus. We may experience a sense of familiarity upon seeing an ad for a new snack food we recently tasted, for example. In many cases, though, meanings are encoded at a more abstract level. *Semantic meaning* refers to symbolic associations, such as the idea that rich people drink champagne or that fashionable men wear an earring.

PERSONAL RELEVANCE

Episodic memories are those that relate to events that are personally relevant.[43] As a result, a person's motivation to retain these memories will likely be strong. Couples often have "their song" that reminds them of their first date or wedding. The memories that might be triggered upon hearing this song would be quite different and unique for them.

Commercials sometimes attempt to activate episodic memories by focusing on experiences shared by many people. Recall of the past may have an effect on future behaviour. For example, a university fund-raising campaign can get higher donations by evoking pleasant university memories. Some especially vivid associations are called *flashbulb memories.* These are usually related to some highly significant event.

America's favorite 18 holes.

KRAFT

This Kraft cheese ad uses a play on words to link the product to consumers' pre-existing knowledge, increasing the chances that brand information will be stored in memory.
Kraft® is a registered trademark of Kraft General Foods, Inc. Used with permission.

As one example, many people can remember their first sexual encounter, their first kiss or the first time they drove a car.

Memory Systems

According to the information-processing perspective, there are three distinct memory systems: sensory memory, short-term memory (STM) and long-term memory (LTM). Each plays a role in processing brand-related information. The interrelationships of these memory systems are summarized in Figure 3–5.

sensory memory the temporary storage of information received from the senses

Sensory memory permits storage of the information we receive from our senses. This storage is very temporary; it lasts a couple of seconds at most. For example, a person might be walking past a donut shop and get a quick, enticing whiff of something baking inside. While this sensation would last for only a few seconds, it would be sufficient to allow the person to determine if he or she should investigate further. If the information is retained for further processing, it passes through an *attentional gate* and is transferred to short-term memory.

short-term memory the system that allows us to retain information for a short period of time

Short-term memory also stores information for a limited period of time, and its capacity is limited. Similar to a computer, this system can be regarded as *working memory;* it holds the information we are currently processing. Verbal input may be stored *acoustically* (in terms of how it sounds) or *semantically* (in terms of its meaning).[44]

The information is stored by combining small pieces into larger ones in a process known as *"chunking."* A chunk is a configuration that is familiar to the person and can be manipulated as a unit. For example, a brand name can be a chunk that summarizes a great deal of detailed information about the brand.

Initially, it was believed that STM was capable of processing between five and nine chunks of information at a time, and for this reason phone numbers were designed to have seven digits.[45] It now appears that three to four chunks is the opti-

FIGURE 3–5 • Relationships among Memory Systems

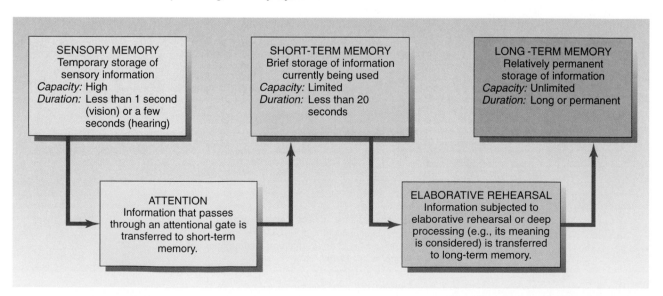

mum size for efficient retrieval (seven-digit phone numbers can be remembered because the individual digits are chunked, so we may remember a three-digit exchange as one piece of information).[46]

Long-term memory is the system that allows us to retain information for a long period of time. In order for information to enter into long-term memory from short-term memory, *elaborative rehearsal* is required. This process involves thinking about the meaning of a stimulus and relating it to other information already in memory. Marketers sometimes assist in the process by devising catchy slogans or jingles that consumers repeat on their own.

long-term memory the system that allows us to retain information for a long period of time

Storing of Information in Memory

Relationships among the types of memory are a source of some controversy. The traditional perspective, known as *multiple-store*, assumes that STM and LTM are separate systems. More recent research has moved away from the distinction between the two types of memory, instead emphasizing the interdependence of the systems. This work argues that, depending upon the nature of the processing task, different levels of processing occur that activate some aspects of memory rather than others. These approaches are called **activation models of memory**.[47] The more effort it takes to process information (so-called deep processing), the more likely it is that information will be placed in long-term memory.

activation models of memory approaches to memory stressing different levels of processing that occur and activate some aspects of memory rather than others, depending upon the nature of the processing task

ASSOCIATIVE NETWORKS

Activation models propose that an incoming piece of information is stored in an *associative network* containing many bits of related information organized according to some set of relationships. The consumer has organized systems of concepts relating to brands, stores and manufacturers.

These storage units, known as **knowledge structures,** can be thought of as complex spider webs filled with pieces of data. This information is placed into *nodes*, which are connected by *associative links* within these structures. Pieces of information that are seen as similar in some way are chunked together under some more abstract category. New, incoming information is interpreted to be consistent with the structure already in place.[48] According to the *hierarchical processing model,* a message is processed in a bottom-up fashion: processing begins at a very basic level and is subject to increasingly complex processing operations that require greater cognitive capacity. If processing at one level fails to evoke the next level, processing of the ad is terminated and capacity is allocated to other tasks.[49]

knowledge structures organized systems of concepts relating to brands, stores and other concepts

Links form between nodes as an associative network is developed. For example, a consumer might have a network for "perfumes." Each node represents a concept related to the category. This node can be an attribute, a specific brand, a celebrity identified with a perfume or even a related product. A network for perfumes might include concepts like the names Chanel, Obsession and Charlie, as well as attributes like sexy and elegant.

When asked to list perfumes, the consumer would recall only those brands contained in the appropriate category. This group constitutes that person's **evoked set**. The task of a new entrant that wants to position itself as a category member (a new luxury perfume, for example) is to provide cues that facilitate its placement in the appropriate category. A sample network for perfumes is shown in Figure 3–6.

evoked set those products already in memory plus those prominent in the retail environment that are actively considered during a consumer's choice process

FIGURE 3–6 • An Associative Network for Perfumes

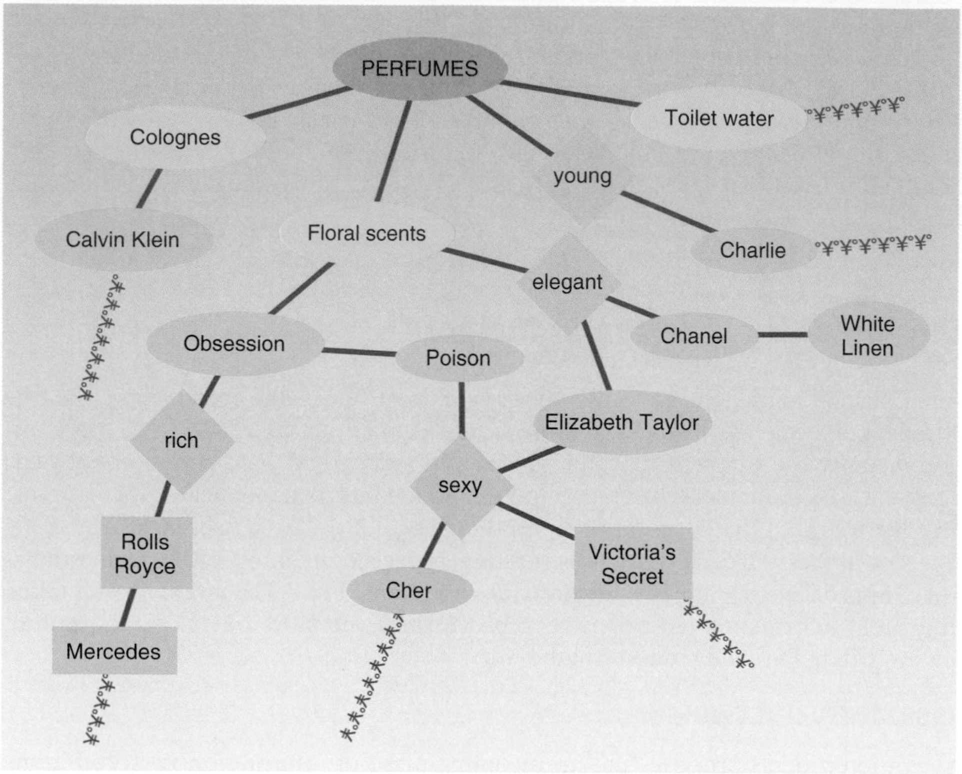

SPREADING ACTIVATION

A meaning can be activated indirectly; energy spreads across nodes of varying levels of abstraction. As one node is activated, other nodes associated with it also begin to be triggered. Meaning thus spreads across the network, bringing up concepts including competing brands and relevant attributes that are used to form attitudes towards the brand.

This process of *spreading activation* allows consumers to shift back and forth between levels of meaning. The way a piece of information is stored in memory depends upon the type of meaning assigned to it. This meaning type will, in turn, determine how and when the meaning is activated. For example, the *memory trace* for an ad could be stored in one or more of the following ways:

- Brand-specific—in terms of claims made for the brand
- Ad-specific—in terms of the medium or content of the ad itself
- Brand identification—in terms of the brand name
- Product category—in terms of how the product works, where it should be used or experiences with the product
- Evaluative reactions—in terms of whether "that looks like fun"[50]

LEVELS OF KNOWLEDGE

Knowledge is coded at different levels of abstraction and complexity. *Meaning concepts* are individual nodes (e.g., elegant). These may be combined into a larger unit, called a *proposition* (also known as a *belief*). A proposition links two nodes together to form a more complex meaning, which can serve as a single chunk of information. For example, a proposition might be that "Chanel is a perfume for elegant women."

Propositions are, in turn, integrated to produce a complex unit known as a *schema*. As was noted at the beginning of the chapter, a **schema** is a cognitive framework that is developed through experience. Information that is consistent with an existing schema is encoded more readily.[51] The ability to move up and down among levels of abstraction greatly increases processing flexibility and efficiency. For this reason, young children, who do not yet have well-developed schemas, are not able to make efficient use of purchase information compared to older children.[52]

One type of schema that is relevant to consumer behaviour is a *script*—a sequence of procedures that is expected by an individual. For example, consumers learn service scripts that guide expectations and purchasing behaviour in business settings. Consumers learn to expect a certain sequence of events and may become uncomfortable if the service departs from the script. A service script for your visit to the dentist might include such events as: 1) driving to the dentist, 2) reading old magazines in the waiting room, 3) hearing your name called and sitting in the dentist's chair, 4) having the dentist put a funny substance on your teeth, 5) having the dentist clean your teeth, and so on. This desire to follow a script helps to explain why such service innovations as automatic bank machines and self-service gas stations have met with resistance by some consumers, who have trouble adapting to a new sequence of events.[53]

schema an organized collection of beliefs and feelings represented in a cognitive category

Retrieving of Information for Purchase Decisions

Retrieval is the process whereby information is accessed from long-term memory. As evidenced by the popularity of the game Trivial Pursuit, people have a vast quantity of information stored in their heads that is not necessarily available on demand. Although most of the information entered in long-term memory does not go away, it may be difficult or impossible to retrieve unless the appropriate cues are present.

FACTORS INFLUENCING RETRIEVAL

Some differences in retrieval ability are physiological. Older adults consistently display inferior recall ability for current items, such as prescription information, though events that happened to them when they were younger may be recalled with great clarity.[54]

Other factors are situational, relating to the environment in which the message is delivered. Not surprisingly, recall is enhanced when the consumer pays more attention to the message in the first place. Some evidence indicates that information about a *pioneering brand* (the first brand to enter a market) is more easily retrieved from memory than follower brands because the product's introduction is likely to be distinctive and, for the time being, no competitors divert the consumer's attention.[55] In addition, in the case of low-involvement products, descriptive brand names are more likely to be recalled than are those that do not provide adequate cues as to what the product is.[56]

Trivial Pursuit, a popular board game developed by Canadians Scott Abbott, Chris Haney, Kohn Haney and Ed Wrener, tests consumers' memories of cultural happenings.
TRIVIAL PURSUIT® is a registered trademark of Horn Abbot Ltd., under exclusive licence to Parker Brothers and used with permission.

The viewing environment of a marketing message also can affect recall. For example, commercials shown during baseball games yield the lowest recall scores among sports programs because the activity is stop-and-go rather than continuous. Unlike football or basketball, the pacing of baseball gives many opportunities for attention to wander even during play. Similarly, General Electric found that its commercials fare better in television shows with continuous activity, such as stories or dramas, compared to variety shows or talk shows that are punctuated by a series of acts.[57]

STATE-DEPENDENT RETRIEVAL. In a process termed *state-dependent retrieval,* people are better able to access information if their internal state is the same at the time of recall as it was when the information was learned.

This phenomenon, called the *mood congruence effect,* underscores the desirability of matching a consumer's mood at the time of purchase when planning exposure to marketing communications. A consumer is more likely to recall an ad, for example, if his or her mood or level of arousal at the time of exposure is similar to that in the purchase environment. By re-creating the cues that were present when the information was first presented, recall can be enhanced. Life cereal uses a picture of "Mikey" from its commercial on the cereal box itself, which facilitates recall of brand claims and favourable brand evaluations.[58]

FAMILIARITY AND RECALL. As a general rule, prior familiarity with an item enhances its recall. Indeed, this is one of the basic goals of marketers who are trying to create and maintain awareness of their products. The more experience a consumer has with a product, the better use that person is able to make of product information.[59]

However, there is a possible fly in the ointment. As noted earlier in the chapter, some evidence indicates that extreme familiarity can result in inferior learning and/or recall. When consumers are highly familiar with a brand or an advertisement, they may attend to fewer attributes because they do not believe that any additional effort will yield a gain in knowledge.[60] For example, when consumers are exposed to the technique of *radio replay*, where the audio track from a television ad is replayed on the radio, they do very little critical, evaluative processing and instead mentally replay the video portion of the ad.[61]

SALIENCE AND RECALL. The salience of a brand refers to its prominence or level of activation in memory. As noted in Chapter 2, stimuli that stand out in contrast to their environment are more likely to command attention, which, in turn, increases the likelihood that they will be recalled. Almost any technique that increases the novelty of a stimulus also improves recall (a result known as the *von Restorff Effect*).[62] This effect explains why unusual advertising or distinctive packaging tends to facilitate brand recall.[63]

Introducing a surprise element into an ad (like the Energizer Bunny™ who unexpectedly marches through a commercial) can be particularly effective in aiding recall even if the stimulus is not relevant to the factual information being presented.[64] In addition, so-called *mystery ads,* where the brand is not identified until the end of the ad, are more effective at building associations in memory between the product category and that brand—especially in the case of relatively unknown brands.[65]

PICTORIAL VERSUS VERBAL CUES. Is a picture worth a thousand words? There is some evidence for the superiority of visual memory over verbal memory, but this advantage is unclear because it is more difficult to measure recall of pictures.[66] However, the available data indicate that information presented in picture form is more likely to be recognized later.[67] Certainly, visual aspects of an ad are more likely to grab a consumer's attention. In fact, eye-movement studies indicate that about 90 percent of viewers look at the dominant picture in an ad before they bother to view the copy.[68]

While pictorial ads may enhance recall, however, they do not necessarily improve comprehension. One study found that television news items presented with illustrations (still pictures) as a backdrop result in improved recall for details of the news story, even though understanding of the story's content does not improve.[69] The use of ethnic images in advertising was studied in Canada. The results of two experiments suggested print advertisers should be careful in using ethnic names and pictures where the product is not specifically matched to that subculture.[70]

A picture is worth a thousand words: product icons—like the Jolly Green Giant, who has appeared in ads and on packaging for more than 30 years—are a significant factor in product recognition.
Courtesy of Pillsbury.

MULTICULTURAL DIMENSIONS

Structural differences in languages can result in recall differences. One study found that Chinese consumers are more likely to recall information when brand names were presented in written rather than spoken form, while the opposite pattern was found for American consumers.[71] This suggests that the use of calligraphy or logos that reinforce the brand name will be especially effective for Chinese, while English-speaking markets have more connection with the sound qualities of brand names.

FACTORS INFLUENCING FORGETTING

Marketers obviously hope that consumers will not forget about their products. However, in a poll of more than 13 000 adults, over half were unable to remember any specific ad they had seen, heard or read in the last 30 days.[72] Forgetting is obviously a problem for marketers.

Early memory theorists assumed that memories fade due to the simple passage of time. In a process of decay, the structural changes in the brain produced by learning simply go away. Forgetting also occurs due to **interference;** as additional information is learned, it displaces earlier information.

interference a process whereby additional learned information displaces the earlier information, resulting in memory loss for the item learned previously

Stimulus-response associations will be forgotten if the consumers subsequently learn new responses to the same or similar stimuli in a process known as *retroactive interference*. Or prior learning can interfere with new learning, a process termed *proactive interference*. Since pieces of information are stored in memory as nodes that are connected to one another by links, a meaning concept that is connected by a larger number of links is more likely to be retrieved. But, as new responses are learned, a stimulus loses its effectiveness in retrieving the old response.[73]

These interference effects help to explain problems in remembering brand information. Consumers tend to organize attribute information by brand.[74] Additional attribute information regarding a brand or similar brands may limit the person's ability to recall old brand information. Recall may also be inhibited if the brand name is composed of frequently used words. These words cue competing associations and result in less retention of brand information.[75]

In one study, brand evaluations deteriorated more rapidly when ads for the brand appeared with messages for 12 other brands in the same category than when the ad was shown with ads for 12 dissimilar products.[76] By increasing the salience of a brand, the recall of other brands can be impaired.[77] On the other hand, calling a competitor by name can result in poorer recall for one's own brand.[78]

Finally, a phenomenon known as the *part-list cueing effect* allows marketers to utilize the interference process strategically. When only a portion of the items in a category are presented to consumers, the omitted items are not as easily recalled. For example, comparative advertising that mentions only a subset of competitors (preferably those that the marketer is not very worried about) may inhibit recall of the unmentioned brands with which the product does not compare favourably.[79]

You've been exposed to roughly 5,000 advertising messages in the last 24 hours. Can you remember three?

This ad for Whittle Communications emphasizes that consumers' memory for advertising is surprisingly limited and offers readers a solution to the problem of increasing an ad's memorability.
Courtesy of Whittle Communications.

Products as Memory Markers

Products and ads can themselves serve as powerful retrieval cues. Indeed, the three types of possessions most valued by consumers are furniture, visual art and photos. The most common explanation for this attachment is the ability of these things to call forth memories of the past.[80] Products are particularly important as markers when our sense of past is threatened, as when a consumer's current identity is challenged due to some change in role caused by divorce, moving, graduation and so on.[81] Products have *mnemonic* qualities that serve as a form of external memory by prompting consumers to retrieve episodic memories. For example, family photography allows consumers to create their own retrieval cues, with the 11 billion amateur photos taken annually forming a kind of external memory bank for our culture.

Researchers are just beginning to probe the effects of *autobiographical memories* on buying behaviour. These memories appear to be one way that advertisements create emotional responses. Ads that succeed in getting us to think about our own past also appear to get us to like these ads more—especially if the linkage between the nostalgia experience and the brand is strong.[82]

THE POWER OF NOSTALGIA

Nostalgia has been described as a bittersweet emotion, where the past is viewed with both sadness and longing. References to "the good old days" are increasingly common, as advertisers call up memories of distant youth—feelings they hope will translate to what they're selling today. A stimulus is at times able to evoke a weakened response much later, an effect known as *spontaneous recovery,* and this re-established connection may explain consumers' powerful nostalgic reactions to songs or pictures they have not been exposed to in many years.

Some marketers are realizing the appeal nostalgia holds for many consumers. For example, Ford tapped into nostalgic memories of its classic Mustang convertible

nostalgia a bittersweet emotion where the past is viewed with sadness and longing; many "classic" products appeal to consumers' memories of their younger days

MULTICULTURAL DIMENSIONS

Nostalgia for the "bad old days"? Parts of Eastern Europe are experiencing nostalgia for the bygone Communist era—a time of shoddy goods but no unemployment. This revival of interest in days gone by has been termed "ostalgie," an acronym for "East-Nostalgia." Berlin's Humboldt University and the City Museum even staged a fashion show of the Sixties, displaying clothes, appliances and posters from the Communist era. Ostalgie is feeding growing consumer interest in the Trabant—a car that was essentially a cardboard box powered by a lawnmower engine. The vehicle was so shoddy, a running joke was that its value could be doubled by filling it with sand. Still, renewed longing for the homely Trabant has resulted in the Son of Trabant, which is being built in the same factory used to construct the original death-trap.[83]

(first introduced in 1964) when it introduced a new model in 1993. As a senior executive at Ford observed, "Heritage [is] an integral part of the marketing effort. Even to young people who weren't born when the first Mustang came out, the Mustang does represent an American icon."[84]

Many other companies are continuing to use their old, trademark characters or are even bringing some out of retirement, including the Campbell Soup Kids, the Pillsbury Doughboy, Betty Crocker and Planters' Mr. Peanut—who recently celebrated his 75th birthday with the company.[85]

One study of network television commercials found that about 10 percent of them contained some nostalgic reference, and this appeal was especially prevalent in the food and beverage categories.[86] Recent revivals include a new advertising campaign for Shake 'N Bake by Kraft General Foods, which uses images from a commercial originally shown in the 1960s ("It's Shake 'N Bake, and I helped!"), as well as "new" footage of Colonel Sanders for KFC (even though the Colonel died in 1980).[87] In a survey of baby boomers, Bugs Bunny was the best-remembered cartoon character, Barbie was the favourite toy, and the boomers' favourite ad slogan was M&M's "Melts in your mouth, not in your hand."[88] The appeal of nostalgia is growing as the baby boomers age. As evidence of this trend, an increasing number of radio stations are converting to what the industry calls the "adult standards" format, also known as nostalgia radio.[89]

MEMORY AND AESTHETIC PREFERENCES

In addition to liking ads and products that remind us of our past, our prior experiences also help to determine what we like now. Some recent research indicates that people's tastes in such products as movies and clothing are influenced by what was popular during certain critical periods of their youth. For example, liking for specific songs appears to be related to how old a person was when those songs were popular. On average, songs that were popular when an individual was 23.5 years old are the most likely to be favoured.[90] In addition, it seems that men form preferences for women's clothing styles that were in vogue when these men were in their early twenties.[91]

MARKETING PITFALL

Some diehard fans were not pleased when the Rolling Stones sold the tune "Start Me Up" for about $4 million (US) to Microsoft, which used the classic song to promote its Windows 95 launch. The Beach Boys sold "Good Vibrations" to Cadbury Schweppes for its Sunkist soft drink; Steppenwolf's "Born to Be Wild" was used to plug the Mercury Cougar; and even Bob Dylan sold "The Times They Are A-Changin'" to Coopers & Lybrand. Other rock legends have refused to play the commercial game, including Bruce Springsteen, the Grateful Dead, Led Zeppelin, Fleetwood Mac, R.E.M. and U2. According to U2's manager, "Rock 'n roll is the last vestige of independence. It is undignified to put that creative effort and hard work to the disposal of a soft drink or beer or car." Singer Neil Young is especially adamant about selling out. In his song "This Note's For You," he croons, "Ain't singing for Pepsi, ain't singing for Coke, I don't sing for nobody, makes me look like a joke."[92]

Measuring Memory for Marketing Stimuli

Because advertisers pay so much money to place their messages in front of consumers, they are naturally concerned that people will actually remember these messages at a later point. It seems that they have good reason to be concerned. In one study, fewer than 40 percent of television viewers made positive links between commercial messages and the corresponding products; only 65 percent noticed the brand name in a commercial; and only 38 percent recognized a connection to an important point.[93]

Even more sadly, only 7 percent of television viewers can recall the product or company featured in the most recent television commercial they watched. This figure represents less than half the recall rate recorded in 1965 and may be attributed to such factors as the increase of 30- and 15-second commercials and the practice of airing television commercials in clusters rather than in connection with single-sponsor programs.[94]

RECOGNITION VERSUS RECALL

One indicator of good advertising is, of course, the impression it makes on consumers. But how can this impact be defined and measured? Two basic measures of impact are *recognition* and *recall*. In the typical recognition test, subjects are shown ads one at a time and asked if they have seen them before. In contrast, free-recall tests ask consumers to think independently of what they have seen, without being prompted for this information first; obviously, this task requires greater effort on the part of respondents.

Under some conditions these two memory measures tend to yield the same results, especially when the researchers try to keep the viewers' interest in the ads constant.[95] Generally, though, recognition scores tend to be more reliable and do not decay over time the way recall scores do.[96] Recognition scores are almost always better than recall scores because recognition is a simpler process and more retrieval cues are available to the consumer.

Both types of retrieval play important roles in purchase decisions. Recall tends to be more important in situations where consumers do not have product data at their disposal, and so they must rely upon memory to generate this information.[97] On the other hand, recognition is more likely to be an important factor in a store, where consumers are confronted with thousands of product options and information (i.e., where external memory is abundantly available) and where the task may simply be to recognize a familiar package. Unfortunately, package recognition and familiarity can have a negative consequence in that warning labels may be ignored, since their existence is taken for granted and not really noticed.[98]

THE STARCH TEST

A widely used commercial measure of advertising recall for magazines is called the Starch Test, a syndicated service founded in 1932. This service provides scores on a number of aspects of consumers' familiarity with an ad, including such categories as "noted," "associated" and "read most." It also scores the impact of the component parts of an overall ad, giving such information as "seen" for major illustrations and "read some" for a major block of copy.[99] Such factors as the size of the ad, whether it appears towards the front or the back of the magazine, if it is on the right or left page, and the size of illustrations play an important role in affecting the amount of attention given to an ad as determined by Starch scores.

PROBLEMS WITH MEMORY MEASURES

While the measurement of an ad's memorability is important, the ability of existing measures accurately to assess these dimensions has been criticized for several reasons.

RESPONSE BIASES. Results obtained from a measuring instrument are not necessarily due to what is being measured, but rather to something else about the instrument or the respondent. This form of contamination is called a **response bias.** For example, people tend to give yes responses to questions, regardless of what is asked. In addition, consumers often are eager to be "good subjects" by pleasing the experimenter. They will try to give the responses they think the experimenter is looking for. In some studies the claimed recognition of bogus ads (ads that have not been seen before) is almost as high as the recognition rate of real ads.[100]

MEMORY LAPSES. People are also prone to unintentionally forgetting information. Typical problems include *omitting* (the leaving out of facts), *averaging* (the tendency to "normalize" things and not report extreme cases) and *telescoping* (the inaccurate recall of time).[101] These distortions call into question the accuracy of various product usage databases that rely upon consumers to recall their purchase and consumption of food and household items. In one study, for example, people were asked to describe what portion of various foods—small, medium or large—they ate in a normal meal. However, different definitions of medium were used (e.g., $\frac{3}{4}$ cup versus $1\frac{1}{2}$ cups). Regardless of the measurement specified, about the same number of people claimed they normally ate medium portions.[102]

MEMORY FOR FACTS VERSUS FEELINGS. Although techniques are being developed to increase the accuracy of memory scores, these improvements do not address the more fundamental issue of whether recall is necessary for advertising to have an effect. In particular, some critics argue that these measures do not adequately tap

response bias a form of contamination in survey research where some factor, such as the desire to make a good impression on the experimenter, leads respondents to modify their true answers

the impact of "feeling" ads, where the objective is to arouse strong emotions rather than to convey concrete product benefits. Many ad campaigns, including those for Hallmark cards, Chevrolet and Pepsi, use this approach.[103] An effective strategy relies on a long-term buildup of feeling rather than on a one-shot attempt to convince consumers to buy the product.

Also, it is not clear that recall translates into preference. We may recall the benefits touted in an ad but not believe them. Or the ad may be memorable because it is so obnoxious, and the product becomes one we "love to hate." The bottom line is that, while recall is important, especially for creating brand awareness, it is not necessarily sufficient to alter consumer preferences. To accomplish this, marketers need more sophisticated attitude-change strategies. These issues will be discussed in Chapters 7 and 8.

CHAPTER SUMMARY

- Learning is a change in behaviour that is caused by experience. Learning can occur through simple associations between a stimulus and a response or via a complex series of cognitive activities.

- Behavioural learning theories assume that learning occurs as a result of responses to external events. Classical conditioning occurs when a stimulus that naturally elicits a response (an unconditioned stimulus) is paired with another stimulus that does not initially elicit this response. Over time, the second stimulus (the conditioned stimulus) comes to elicit the response as well.

- This response can also extend to other, similar stimuli in a process known as *stimulus generalization*. This process is the basis for such marketing strategies as licensing and family branding, in which a consumer's positive associations with a product are transferred to other contexts.

- Operant or instrumental conditioning occurs as the person learns to perform behaviours that produce positive outcomes and avoid those that result in negative outcomes. While classical conditioning involves the pairing of two stimuli, instrumental learning occurs when reinforcement is delivered following a response to a stimulus. Reinforcement is positive if a reward is delivered following a response. It is negative if a negative outcome is avoided by not performing a response. Punishment occurs when a response is followed by unpleasant events. Extinction of the behaviour will occur if reinforcement is no longer received.

- Cognitive learning occurs as the result of mental processes. For example, observational learning takes place when the consumer performs a behaviour as a result of seeing someone else performing it and being rewarded for it.

- Memory refers to the storage of learned information. The way information is encoded when it is perceived determines how it will be stored in memory. The memory systems known as sensory memory, short-term memory and long-term memory each play a role in retaining and processing information from the outside world.

- Information is not stored in isolation; it is incorporated into knowledge structures, where it is associated with other related data. The location of product information in associative networks, and the level of abstraction at which it is coded, help to determine when and how this information will be activated at a later time. Some factors that influence the likelihood of retrieval include the level of familiarity with an item, its salience (or prominence) in memory, and whether the information was presented in pictorial or written form.

- Products also play a role as memory markers; they are used by consumers to retrieve memories about past experiences (autobiographical memories) and are often valued for their ability to do this. This function also contributes to the use of nostalgia in marketing strategies.

- Memory of product information can be measured through either recognition or recall techniques. Consumers are more likely to recognize an advertisement if it is presented to them than to recall one without being given any cues.

KEY TERMS

CONSUMER BEHAVIOUR CHALLENGE

1. Identify three patterns of reinforcement and provide an example of how each is used in a marketing context.

2. Describe the functions of short-term and long-term memory. What is the apparent relationship between the two?

3. Devise a "product jingle memory test." Compile a list of brands that are or have been associated with memorable jingles, such as Chiquita Banana or Alka-Seltzer. Read this list to friends and see how many jingles are remembered. You may be surprised at the level of recall.

4. Identify some important characteristics for a product with a well-known brand name. Based on these attributes, generate a list of possible brand extension or licensing opportunities, as well as some others that would most likely not be accepted by consumers.

5. Collect some pictures of "classic" products that have high nostalgia value. Show these pictures to consumers and allow them to free associate. Analyze the types of memories that are evoked, and think about how these associations might be employed in a product's promotional strategy.

CBC VIDEO VIGNETTES

Concepts at Work for Air Miles

Brand loyalty, a preoccupation of marketers since the 1960s, has become more and more difficult to sustain. It is a challenge getting consumers to be loyal to a certain airline in an industry where price is controlled by fierce competition and routes are becoming deregulated due to the "Open Skies" agreement. To try to keep customers loyal to one airline, most companies have adopted "Frequent Flyer" programs, similar to the program pioneered by American Airlines that successfully encouraged and reinforced repeat purchase. In fact, this program, based on the principles of operant conditioning, has perhaps become too successful for comfort! American Airline passengers, for example, have accumulated over $25 million in travel points, and "Air Mile Addicts" have developed.

Airlines have now expanded this program to include the non-frequent-flyer public who just hope to take a free vacation someday. With empty airline seats to sell, companies began selling points to other industries at two cents a point. These points are then given as rewards to customers of grocery stores, automobile dealerships, florists and restaurants, to users of credit cards and to whomever else the airline will sell its points to. The challenge for the airlines is to retain primary brand loyalty while avoiding a run on seats—and profits!

QUESTIONS

1. Why were "Frequent Flyer" programs developed?

2. Why are "Frequent Flyer" programs so successful?

3. What options do airline companies have for relieving the pressure of a vast accumulation of "Air Mile Points"?

4. What are the limits to "Frequent Flyer" programs?

Video Resource: "Airmiles," *Venture* #588 (April 28, 1996).

NOTES

1. Ken MacQueen, "Diana: A Farewell," *Vancouver Sun* (September 6, 1997): extra section.

2. Robert A. Baron, *Psychology: The Essential Science* (Boston: Allyn & Bacon, 1989).

3. Richard A. Feinberg, "Credit Cards as Spending Facilitating Stimuli: A Conditioning Interpretation," *Journal of Consumer Research* 13 (December 1986): 348–56.

4. R.A. Rescorla, "Pavlovian Conditioning: It's Not What You Think It Is," *American Psychologist* 43 (1988): 151–60; Elnora W. Stuart, Terence A. Shimp and Randall W. Engle, "Classical Conditioning of Consumer Attitudes: Four Experiments in an Advertising Context," *Journal of Consumer Research* 14 (December 1987): 334–39; Terence A. Shimp, Elnora W. Stuart and Randall W. Engle, "A Program of Classical Conditioning Experiments Testing Variations in the Conditioned Stimulus and Context," *Journal of Consumer Research* 18, 1 (June 1991): 1–12.

5. "Anemic Crocodile," *Forbes* (August 15, 1994): 116.

6. Baron, *Psychology*.

7. James Ward, Barbara Loken, Ivan Ross and Tedi Hasapopoulous, "The Influence of Physical Similarity of Affect and Attribute Perceptions from National Brands to Private Label Brands," in *American Marketing Educators' Conference*, eds. Terence A. Shimp et al. (Chicago: American Marketing Association, 1986), pp. 51–56.

8. Judith Lynne Zaichkowsky and Richard Neil Simpson, "The Effect of Experience with a Brand Imitator on the Original Brand," *Marketing Letters* 7, 1 (1996): 31–39.

9. Tom J. Brown and Peter A. Dacin, "The Company and the Product: Corporate Associations and Consumer Product Responses," *Journal of Marketing* 61 (January 1997): 68–84.

10. Chris T. Allen and Thomas J. Madden, "A Closer Look at Classical Conditioning," *Journal of Consumer Research* 12 (December 1985): 301–15; Chester A. Insko and William F. Oakes, "Awareness and the

Conditioning of Attitudes," *Journal of Personality and Social Psychology* 4 (November 1966): 487–96; Carolyn K. Staats and Arthur W. Staats, "Meaning Established by Classical Conditioning," *Journal of Experimental Psychology* 54 (July 1957): 74–80.

11. Kevin Lane Keller, "Conceptualizing, Measuring, and Managing Customer-Based Brand Equity," *Journal of Marketing* 57 (January 1993): 1–22.

12. Herbert Krugman, "Low Recall and High Recognition of Advertising," *Journal of Advertising Research* (February/March 1986): 79–86.

13. Gerald J. Gorn, "The Effects of Music in Advertising on Choice Behavior: A Classical Conditioning Approach," *Journal of Marketing* 46 (Winter 1982): 94–101.

14. Ronald Milliman, "Using Background Music to Affect the Behavior of Supermarket Shoppers," *Journal of Marketing* 46 (Summer 1982): 86–91.

15. Ronald Milliman, "The Influence of Background Music on the Behavior of Restaurant Patrons," *Journal of Consumer Research* 13 (September 1986): 286–89.

16. Calvin Bierley, Frances K. McSweeney and Renee Vannieuwkerk, "Classical Conditioning of Preferences for Stimuli," *Journal of Consumer Research* 12 (December 1985): 316–23; James J. Kellaris and Anthony D. Cox, "The Effects of Background Music in Advertising: A Reassessment," *Journal of Consumer Research* 16 (June 1989): 113–18.

17. Frances K. McSweeney and Calvin Bierley, "Recent Developments in Classical Conditioning," *Journal of Consumer Research* 11 (September 1984): 619–31.

18. Basil G. Englis, "The Reinforcement Properties of Music Videos: 'I Want My . . . I Want My . . . I Want My . . . MTV'" (paper presented at the meetings of the Association for Consumer Research, New Orleans, 1989).

19. Bernice Kanner, "Growing Pains—and Gains: Brand Names Branch Out," *New York* (March 13, 1989): 22.

20. Peter H. Farquhar, "Brand Equity," *Marketing Insights* (Summer 1989): 59.

21. Barbara Loken and Deborah Roedder John, "Diluting Brand Beliefs: When Do Brand Extensions Have a Negative Impact?" *Journal of Marketing* 57 (July 1993): 71–84.

22. Kanner, "Growing Pains."

23. Farquhar, "Brand Equity."

24. John Marchese, "Forever Harley," *New York Times* (October 17, 1993): 10; "Spamming the Globe," *Newsweek* (August 29, 1994): 8.

25. Marcy Magiera, "Promotional Marketer of the Year," *Advertising Age* (March 21, 1994): S–1 (2 pp.).

26. Stuart Elliott, "Gump Sells, to Viacom's Surprise," *New York Times* (October 7, 1994): D1 (2 pp.).

27. Valerie Reitman, "Flight Attendants in Japan Follow in Annette Funicello's Footsteps," *Wall Street Journal* (September 1, 1994): B1.

28. Quoted in "Look-Alikes Mimic Familiar Packages," *New York Times* (August 9, 1986): D1.

29. Laurie Hays, "Too Many Computer Names Confuse Too Many Buyers," *Wall Street Journal* (June 29, 1994): B1 (2 pp.).

30. For a comprehensive approach to consumer behaviour based on operant conditioning principles, see Gordon R. Foxall, "Behavior Analysis and Consumer Psychology," *Journal of Economic Psychology* 15 (March 1994): 5–91.

31. Blaise J. Bergiel and Christine Trosclair, "Instrumental Learning: Its Application to Customer Satisfaction," *Journal of Consumer Marketing* 2 (Fall 1985): 23–28.

32. Ian P. Murphy, "Customers Can Join the Club—But at a Price," *Marketing News* (April 28, 1997): 8.

33. Ellen J. Langer, *The Psychology of Control* (Beverly Hills, CA: Sage, 1983).

34. Robert B. Cialdini, *Influence: Science and Practice*, 2nd ed. (New York: William Morrow, 1984).

35. Allen and Madden, "A Closer Look at Classical Conditioning"; see also Shimp, Stuart and Engle, "A Program of Classical Conditioning Experiments Testing Variations in the Conditioned Stimulus and Context."

36. Albert Bandura, *Social Foundations of Thought and Action: A Social Cognitive View* (Englewood Cliffs, NJ: Prentice Hall, 1986); Baron, *Psychology*.

37. Bandura, *Social Foundations of Thought and Action*.

38. Terence A. Shimp, "Neo-Pavlovian Conditioning and Its Implications for Consumer Theory and Research," in *Handbook of Consumer Behavior*, eds. Thomas S. Robertson and Harold H. Kassarjian (Englewood Cliffs, NJ: Prentice Hall, 1991).

39. R.C. Atkinson and R.M. Shiffrin, "Human Memory: A Proposed System and Its Control Processes," in *The Psychology of Learning and Motivation: Advances in Research and Theory*, eds. K.W. Spence and J.T. Spence (New York: Academic Press, 1968), pp. 89–195.

40. James R. Bettman, "Memory Factors in Consumer Choice: A Review," *Journal of Marketing* (Spring 1979): 37–53. For a study that explored the relative impact of internal versus external memory on brand choice, cf. Joseph W. Alba, Howard Marmorstein and Amitava Chattopadhyay, "Transitions in Preference Over Time: The Effects of Memory on Message Persuasiveness," *Journal of Marketing Research* 29 (November 1992): 406–17. For other research on memory and advertising, see H. Shanker Krishnan and Dipankar Chakravarti, "Varieties of Brand Memory Induced by Advertising: Determinants, Measures, and Relationships," in *Brand Equity & Advertising: Advertising's Role in Building Strong Brands,* eds. David A. Aaker and Alexander L. Biel (Hillsdale, NJ: Lawrence Erlbaum Associates, 1993), pp. 213–31; Bernd H. Schmitt, Nader T. Tavassoli and Robert T. Millard, "Memory for Print Ads: Understanding Relations Among Brand Name, Copy, and Picture,"

Journal of Consumer Psychology 2, 1 (1993): 55–81; Marian Friestad and Esther Thorson, "Remembering Ads: The Effects of Encoding Strategies, Retrieval Cues, and Emotional Response," *Journal of Consumer Psychology* 2, 1 (1993): 1–23; Surendra N. Singh, Sanjay Mishra, Neeli Bendapudi and Denise Linville, "Enhancing Memory of Television Commercials Through Message Spacing," *Journal of Marketing Research* 31 (August 1994): 384–92.

41. Kim Robertson, "Recall and Recognition Effects of Brand Name Imagery," *Psychology & Marketing* 4 (Spring 1987): 3–15.

42. Judith Lynne Zaichkowsky and Padma Vipat, "Inferences From Brand Names," in *European Advances in Consumer Research*, eds. W. Fred Van Raaij and Gary J. Bamossy (Provo, UT: Association for Consumer Research, 1993), vol. 1, pp. 534–40.

43. Endel Tulving, "Remembering and Knowing the Past," *American Scientist* 77 (July/August 1989): 361.

44. Baron, *Psychology*.

45. George A. Miller, "The Magical Number Seven, Plus or Minus Two: Some Limits on Our Capacity for Processing Information," *Psychological Review* 63 (1956): 81–97.

46. James N. MacGregor, "Short-Term Memory Capacity: Limitation or Optimization?" *Psychological Review* 94 (1987): 107–8.

47. See Catherine A. Cole and Michael J. Houston, "Encoding and Media Effects on Consumer Learning Deficiencies in the Elderly," *Journal of Marketing Research* 24 (February 1987): 55–64; A.M. Collins and E.F. Loftus, "A Spreading Activation Theory of Semantic Processing," *Psychological Review* 82 (1975): 407–28; Fergus I.M. Craik and Robert S. Lockhart, "Levels of Processing: A Framework for Memory Research," *Journal of Verbal Learning and Verbal Behavior* 11 (1972): 671–84.

48. Walter A. Henry, "The Effect of Information-Processing Ability on Processing Accuracy," *Journal of Consumer Research* 7 (June 1980): 42–48.

49. Anthony G. Greenwald and Clark Leavitt, "Audience Involvement in Advertising: Four Levels," *Journal of Consumer Research* 11 (June 1984): 581–92.

50. Kevin Lane Keller, "Memory Factors in Advertising: The Effect of Advertising Retrieval Cues on Brand Evaluations," *Journal of Consumer Research* 14 (December 1987): 316–33. For a discussion of processing operations that occur during brand choice, see Gabriel Biehal and Dipankar Chakravarti, "Consumers' Use of Memory and External Information in Choice: Macro and Micro Perspectives," *Journal of Consumer Research* 12 (March 1986): 382–405.

51. Susan T. Fiske and Shelley E. Taylor, *Social Cognition* (Reading, MA: Addison-Wesley, 1984).

52. Deborah Roedder John and John C. Whitney, Jr., "The Development of Consumer Knowledge in Children: A Cognitive Structure Approach," *Journal of Consumer Research* 12 (March 1986): 406–17.

53. Michael R. Solomon, Carol Surprenant, John A. Czepiel and Evelyn G. Gutman, "A Role Theory Perspective on Dyadic Interactions: The Service Encounter," *Journal of Marketing* 49 (Winter 1985): 99–111.

54. Roger W. Morrell, Denise C. Park and Leonard W. Poon, "Quality of Instructions on Prescription Drug Labels: Effects on Memory and Comprehension in Young and Old Adults," *The Gerontologist* 29 (1989): 345–54.

55. Frank R. Kardes, Gurumurthy Kalyanaram, Murali Chandrashekaran and Ronald J. Dornoff, "Brand Retrieval, Consideration Set Composition, Consumer Choice, and the Pioneering Advantage" (unpublished manuscript, University of Cincinnati, 1992).

56. Zaichkowsky and Vipat, "Inferences from Brand Names."

57. Krugman, "Low Recall and High Recognition of Advertising."

58. Keller, "Memory Factors in Advertising."

59. Eric J. Johnson and J. Edward Russo, "Product Familiarity and Learning New Information," *Journal of Consumer Research* 11 (June 1984): 542–50.

60. Eric J. Johnson and J. Edward Russo, "Product Familiarity and Learning New Information," in *Advances in Consumer Research 8*, ed. Kent Monroe (Ann Arbor, MI: Association for Consumer Research, 1981), pp. 151–55; John G. Lynch and Thomas K. Srull, "Memory and Attentional Factors in Consumer Choice: Concepts and Research Methods," *Journal of Consumer Research* 9 (June 1982): 18–37.

61. Julie A. Edell and Kevin Lane Keller, "The Information Processing of Coordinated Media Campaigns," *Journal of Marketing Research* 26 (May 1989): 149–64.

62. Lynch and Srull, "Memory and Attentional Factors in Consumer Choice."

63. Joseph W. Alba and Amitava Chattopadhyay, "Salience Effects in Brand Recall," *Journal of Marketing Research* 23 (November 1986): 363–70; Elizabeth C. Hirschman and Michael R. Solomon, "Utilitarian, Aesthetic, and Familiarity Responses to Verbal Versus Visual Advertisements," in *Advances in Consumer Research 11*, ed. Thomas C. Kinnear (Provo, UT: Association for Consumer Research, 1984), pp. 426–31.

64. Susan E. Heckler and Terry L. Childers, "The Role of Expectancy and Relevancy in Memory for Verbal and Visual Information: What is Incongruency?" *Journal of Consumer Research* 18 (March 1992): 475–92.

65. Russell H. Fazio, Paul M. Herr and Martha C. Powell, "On the Development and Strength of Category-Brand Associations in Memory: The Case of Mystery Ads," *Journal of Consumer Psychology* 1, 1 (1992): 1–13.

66. Hirschman and Solomon, "Utilitarian, Aesthetic, and Familiarity Responses to Verbal Versus Visual Advertisements."

67. Terry Childers and Michael Houston, "Conditions for a Picture-Superiority Effect on Consumer Memory," *Journal of Consumer Research* 11 (September 1984): 643–54; Terry Childers, Susan Heckler and Michael Houston, "Memory for the Visual and Verbal Components of Print Advertisements," *Psychology & Marketing* 3 (Fall 1986): 147–50.

68. Werner Krober-Riel, "Effects of Emotional Pictorial Elements in Ads Analyzed by Means of Eye Movement Monitoring," in *Advances in Consumer Research 11*, ed. Thomas C. Kinnear (Provo, UT: Association for Consumer Research, 1984), pp. 591–96.

69. Hans-Bernd Brosius, "Influence of Presentation Features and News Context on Learning from Television News," *Journal of Broadcasting & Electronic Media* 33 (Winter 1989): 1–14.

70. Robert M. MacGregor and Stuart J. McKelvie, "Effects of Ethnic Imagery on Recall of Brand Names," *Canadian Journal of Administrative Sciences* (September 1990): 1–9.

71. Bernd H. Schmitt and Yigang Pan, "Language and Consumer Memory: The Impact of Linguistic Differences Between Chinese and English," *Journal of Consumer Research* 21, 3 (1994): 419–31.

72. Raymond R. Burke and Thomas K. Srull, "Competitive Interference and Consumer Memory for Advertising," *Journal of Consumer Research* 15 (June 1988): 55–68.

73. Ibid.

74. Johnson and Russo, "Product Familiarity and Learning New Information."

75. Joan Meyers-Levy, "The Influence of Brand Names Association Set Size and Word Frequency on Brand Memory," *Journal of Consumer Research* 16 (September 1989): 197–208.

76. Michael H. Baumgardner, Michael R. Leippe, David L. Ronis and Anthony G. Greenwald, "In Search of Reliable Persuasion Effects: II. Associative Interference and Persistence of Persuasion in a Message-Dense Environment," *Journal of Personality and Social Psychology* 45 (September 1983): 524–37.

77. Alba and Chattopadhyay, "Salience Effects in Brand Recall."

78. Margaret Henderson Blair, Allan R. Kuse, David H. Furse and David W. Stewart, "Advertising in a New and Competitive Environment: Persuading Consumers to Buy," *Business Horizons* 30 (November/December 1987): 20.

79. Lynch and Srull, "Memory and Attentional Factors in Consumer Choice."

80. Russell W. Belk, "Possessions and the Extended Self," *Journal of Consumer Research* 15 (September 1988): 139–68.

81. Russell W. Belk, "The Role of Possessions in Constructing and Maintaining a Sense of Past," in *Advances in Consumer Research 16*, eds. Marvin E.

Goldberg, Gerald Gorn and Richard W. Pollay (Provo, UT: Association for Consumer Research, 1989), pp. 669–78.

82. Hans Baumgartner, Mita Sujan and James R. Bettman, "Autobiographical Memories, Affect and Consumer Information Processing," *Journal of Consumer Psychology* 1 (January 1992): 53–82; Mita Sujan, James R. Bettman and Hans Baumgartner, "Influencing Consumer Judgments Using Autobiographical Memories: A Self-Referencing Perspective," *Journal of Marketing Research* 30 (November 1993): 422–36.

83. Quoted in Raymond Serafin, "Mustang Love: Ford Revs Up Romantic Heritage to Sell New Model of Sports Car," *Advertising Age* (October 4, 1993): 4.

84. "Ostalgie for the Days When They'd Never Had it so Good," accessed February 10, 1997, ssnewslink, *Independent*, London.

85. Stuart Elliott, "At 75, Mr. Peanut Is Getting Expanded Role at Planters," *New York Times* (September 23, 1991): D15.

86. Lynette S. Unger, Diane M. McConocha and John A. Faier, "The Use of Nostalgia in Television Advertising: A Content Analysis," *Journalism Quarterly* 63 (Fall 1991): 345–53.

87. Kevin Goldman, "New Campaigns Tip the Hat to Nostalgia," *Wall Street Journal* (August 9, 1994): B4.

88. "For Boomers, These Were a Few of Our Favorite Things," *Adweek* 10 (February 3, 1992): 16.

89. William Dunn, "Sinatra Has the Last Dance," *American Demographics* (July 1994): 39.

90. Morris B. Holbrook and Robert M. Schindler, "Some Exploratory Findings on the Development of Musical Tastes," *Journal of Consumer Research* 16 (June 1989): 119–24.

91. Cf. Morris B. Holbrook, "Nostalgia and Consumption Preferences: Some Emerging Patterns of Consumer Tastes," *Journal of Consumer Research* 20 (September 1993): 245–56; Robert M. Schindler and Morris B. Holbrook, "Critical Periods in the Development of Men's and Women's Tastes in Personal Appearance," *Psychology & Marketing* 10, 6 (November/December 1993): 549–64; Morris B. Holbrook and Robert M. Schindler, "Age, Sex, and Attitude Toward the Past as Predictors of Consumers' Aesthetic Tastes for Cultural Products," *Journal of Marketing Research* 31 (August 1994): 412–22.

92. Quoted in Kevin Goldman, "A Few Rockers Refuse to Turn Tunes Into Ads," *New York Times* (August 25, 1995): B1.

93. "Only 38% of T.V. Audience Links Brands with Ads," *Marketing News* (January 6, 1984): 10.

94. "Terminal Television," *American Demographics* (January 1987): 15.

95. Richard P. Bagozzi and Alvin J. Silk, "Recall, Recognition, and the Measurement of Memory for Print Advertisements," *Marketing Science* (1983): 95–134.

96. Adam Finn, "Print Ad Recognition Readership Scores: An Information Processing Perspective," *Journal of Marketing Research* 25 (May 1988): 168–77.

97. Bettman, "Memory Factors in Consumer Choice."

98. Mark A. deTurck and Gerald M. Goldhaber, "Effectiveness of Product Warning Labels: Effects of Consumers' Information Processing Objectives," *Journal of Consumer Affairs* 23, 1 (1989): 111–25.

99. Finn, "Print Ad Recognition Readership Scores."

100. Surendra N. Singh and Gilbert A. Churchill, Jr., "Response-Bias-Free Recognition Tests to Measure Advertising Effects," *Journal of Advertising Research* (June/July 1987): 23–36.

101. William A. Cook, "Telescoping and Memory's Other Tricks," *Journal of Advertising Research* 27 (February/March 1987): 5–8.

102. "On a Diet? Don't Trust Your Memory," *Psychology Today* (October 1989): 12.

103. Hubert A. Zielske and Walter A. Henry, "Remembering and Forgetting Television Ads," *Journal of Advertising Research* 20 (April 1980): 7–13.

It's been two years since Basil gave up smoking, drinking and junk food. He now devotes the same enthusiasm to working out that he used to bring to partying. Basil has become a dedicated triathlete. Participating in this sport, which involves running, swimming and biking, has become so important to him that he structures his entire schedule around his training regimen. He even passed on an important class he needed for his major because the only open section was at the same time he did his daily eight-kilometre run.

Basil has been so engrossed in the sport—spending most of his free time (when not in training) reading magazines dedicated to the sport, shopping for special equipment like running shoes and Lycra tights for winter training, or travelling to triathlon events all over the country—that his friends complain they hardly see him any more.

Basil remains committed! He's nothing if not dedicated to the cause ...

IT'S A TRAIL
IF I SAY IT'S A TRAIL.

adidas

EQUIPMENT
TRIDENT

EQUIPMENT
TRIDENT

4

Motivation and Values

INTRODUCTION

Some people are so involved in an activity that they can be termed *fanatic consumers*. Whether they are training for a triathlon, watching television or playing music, these people tend to become totally engrossed in an activity to the point where such involvement has been called a "positive addiction." One survey of triathletes (like Basil), for example, found that intense commitment to the sport resulted in a highly modified daily schedule, unwillingness to stop training even if injured, major dietary changes, and—most relevant to marketers—a substantial financial commitment for travel to races, specialized clothing and health-club memberships.[1]

The forces that drive people to buy and use products are generally straightforward, as when a person purchases a pair of running shoes for everyday wear. As hard-core triathletes demonstrate, however, even the consumption of an everyday product like running shoes may also be related to deep-seated experiences. In some cases these emotional responses create a deep commitment to the product. Sometimes people are not even fully aware of the forces that drive them towards some products and away from others.

To understand motivation is to understand *why* consumers do what they do. Why do people choose to bungee-jump off a bridge or go white-water rafting in the Yukon, while others spend their leisure time playing chess or gardening? We do everything for a reason, whether to quench a thirst, to kill boredom or to attain some deep spiritual experience. Marketing students are taught from day one that the goal of marketing is to satisfy consumers' needs. However, this insight is useless unless we can discover *what* those needs are and *why* they exist. A popular beer commercial asks the question, "Why ask why?" In this chapter we'll find out.

THE MOTIVATION PROCESS

motivation an internal state that activates goal-oriented behaviour

Motivation refers to the processes that cause people to behave as they do. It occurs when a need is aroused that the consumer wishes to satisfy. Once a need has been activated, a state of tension exists that drives the consumer to attempt to reduce or eliminate the need.

This need may be utilitarian (a desire to achieve some functional or practical benefit, as when a person requires a pair of durable sneakers), or it may be hedonic (an experiential need, involving emotional responses or fantasies, as when Basil buys special running shoes for a triathlon event). The desired end state is the consumer's **goal.** Marketers try to create products and services that will provide the desired benefits and permit the consumer to reduce this tension.

goal a consumer's desired end state

Whether the need is utilitarian or hedonic, a discrepancy exists between the consumer's present state and some ideal state. This gulf creates a state of tension. The magnitude of this tension determines the urgency the consumer feels to reduce the tension. This degree of arousal is called a **drive.** A basic need can be satisfied any number of ways, and the specific path a person chooses is influenced by his or her unique set of experiences and by the values instilled by the culture in which the person has been raised.

drive the desire to satisfy a biological need in order to reduce physiological arousal

These personal and cultural factors combine to create a want, which is one manifestation of a need. For example, hunger is a basic need that must be satisfied by all; the lack of food creates a tension state that can be reduced by the intake of such products as cheeseburgers, double-fudge Oreo cookies, raw fish or bean sprouts. The specific route to hunger reduction is culturally determined.

Once the goal is attained, tension is reduced and the motivation recedes (for the time being). Motivation can be described in terms of its strength, or the pull it exerts on the consumer, and its direction, or the particular way the consumer attempts to reduce motivational tension.

MOTIVATIONAL STRENGTH

The degree to which a person is willing to expend energy to reach one goal as opposed to another reflects his or her underlying motivation to attain that goal. Many theories have been advanced to explain why people behave the way they do. Most share the basic idea that people have some finite amount of energy that must be directed towards certain goals.

Biological versus Learned Needs

Early work on motivation ascribed behaviour to instinct, the innate patterns of behaviour that are universal in a species. This view is now largely discredited. For one thing, the existence of an instinct is difficult to prove or disprove. The instinct is inferred from the behaviour it is supposed to explain (this type of circular explanation is called a *tautology*).[2] It is like saying that a consumer buys products that are status symbols because he or she is motivated to attain status, which is hardly a satisfying explanation.

Drive Theory

Drive theory focuses on biological needs that produce unpleasant states of arousal (such as your stomach grumbling during a morning class). We are motivated to reduce the tension caused by this arousal. Tension reduction has been proposed as a basic mechanism governing human behaviour.

In marketing, tension refers to the unpleasant state that exists if a person's consumption needs are not fulfilled. People may be grumpy if they haven't eaten, or dejected or angry if they cannot afford that new car. This state activates goal-oriented behaviour that attempts to reduce or eliminate this unpleasant state and return to a balanced one, called **homeostasis.**

Those behaviours that are successful in reducing the drive by eliminating the underlying need are strengthened and tend to be repeated. (This aspect of the learning process was discussed in Chapter 3.) Your motivation to leave class early to grab a snack would be greater if you hadn't eaten in 24 hours than if you had eaten only 2 hours earlier. If you did sneak out and got indigestion after, say, wolfing down a package of chips, this behaviour would be less likely to be repeated the next time you wanted a snack. One's degree of motivation, then, depends upon the distance between one's present state and the goal.

Drive theory, however, runs into difficulties when it tries to explain some facets of human behaviour that run counter to its predictions. People often do things that *increase* a drive state rather than decrease it. For example, people may delay gratification. If you know you are going out for a lavish dinner, you might decide to forgo a snack earlier in the day even though you are hungry at that time.

homeostasis the state of being where the body is in physiological balance; goal-oriented behaviour attempts to reduce or eliminate an unpleasant motivational state and return to a balanced one

Expectancy Theory

Most current explanations of motivation focus on cognitive factors rather than biological ones to understand what drives behaviour. **Expectancy theory** suggests that behaviour is largely pulled by expectations of achieving desirable outcomes—*positive incentives*—rather than pushed from within. We choose one product over another because we expect this choice to have more positive consequences for us. Thus, the term *drive* is used here more loosely to refer to both physical and cognitive processes.

expectancy theory the perspective that behaviour is largely "pulled" by expectations of achieving desirable outcomes, or positive incentives, rather than "pushed" from within

MOTIVATIONAL DIRECTION

Motives have direction as well as strength. They are goal oriented in that specific objectives are desired to satisfy a need. Most goals can be reached by a number of routes, and the objective of marketers is to convince consumers that the alternative they offer provides the best chance to attain the goal. For example, a consumer who decides that he needs a pair of jeans to help him reach his goal of being accepted by others or projecting an appropriate image can choose among Levi's, Wranglers, Guess, Calvin Klein and many other alternatives, each of which promises to deliver certain benefits.

Needs versus Wants

want the particular form of consumption chosen to satisfy a need

The specific way a need is satisfied depends upon the individual's unique history and learning experiences and his or her cultural environment. The particular form of consumption used to satisfy a need is termed a **want**. For example, two classmates may feel their stomachs rumbling during a lunchtime lecture. If neither person has eaten since the night before, the strength of their respective needs (hunger) would be about the same. However, the way each person goes about satisfying this need might be quite different. The first person may be a health-conscious individual who fantasizes about gulping down a big handful of trail mix, while the second person may be equally aroused by the prospect of a greasy cheeseburger and fries.

This distinction between needs and wants is an important one, because it relates to the issue of whether marketers are actually capable of creating needs. That issue will be considered at the end of the chapter. For now, it is important to note that a marketing strategy is more effective when it aims to influence the direction a consumer will take to satisfy a need rather than to create the need itself.

Types of Needs

People are born with a need for certain elements necessary to maintain life, such as food, water, air and shelter. These are called *biogenic needs*. People have many other needs, however, that are not innate. *Psychogenic needs* are acquired in the process of becoming a member of a culture. These include the need for status, power, affiliation and so on. Psychogenic needs reflect the priorities of a culture, and their effect on behaviour will vary in different environments. For example, Hong Kong consumers may be driven to devote a good chunk of income to products that permit them to display their wealth and status, while their Japanese counterparts may work equally hard to ensure that they do not stand out from the group. These differences in cultural values will be discussed later on in the chapter.

Consumers can also be motivated to satisfy either utilitarian or hedonic needs. The satisfaction of utilitarian needs implies that consumers will emphasize the objective, tangible attributes of products, such as kilometres per litre in a car; the amount of fat, calories and protein in a cheeseburger; and the durability of a pair of blue jeans. Hedonic needs are subjective and experiential, leading consumers to rely on a product because it meets their needs for excitement, self-confidence, fantasy and so on. Of course, consumers may be motivated to purchase a product because it provides *both* types of benefits. For example, a mink coat may be bought because of the luxurious image it portrays *and* because it keeps one warm throughout the long cold winter.

Motivational Conflicts

A goal has *valence,* which means that it can be positive or negative. A positively valued goal is one towards which consumers direct their behaviour; they are motivated to *approach* the goal and will seek out products that will be instrumental in attaining it. Basil uses his athletic equipment to help him improve his triathlon performance—his goal.

However, not all behaviour is motivated by the desire to approach a goal. As we saw in Chapter 3, sometimes consumers are motivated to *avoid* a negative outcome. They will structure their purchases or consumption activities to reduce the chances of attaining this end result. For example, many consumers work hard to avoid rejection, a negative goal. They will stay away from products that they associate with social disapproval. Products such as deodorants and mouthwash frequently rely upon consumers' negative motivation by depicting the onerous social consequences of underarm odour or bad breath. Basil would most likely be especially vigilant about avoiding junk food as he prepared for an upcoming race.

Because a purchase decision may involve more than one source of motivation, consumers often find themselves in situations where different motives, positive and negative, conflict with one another. Since marketers are attempting to satisfy consumers' needs, they can also help by providing possible solutions to these dilemmas. As shown in Figure 4–1, three general types of conflicts can occur: approach-approach, approach-avoidance and avoidance-avoidance.

APPROACH-APPROACH CONFLICT

In an approach approach conflict, a person must choose between two desirable alternatives. A student might be torn between going home for the holidays and going on a skiing trip with friends. Or he or she might have to choose between two CDs.

The **theory of cognitive dissonance** is based on the premise that people have a need for order and consistency in their lives and that a state of tension is created

theory of cognitive dissonance the perspective that cognitive discomfort results from an individual holding logically inconsistent beliefs about an object or event. The consumer is motivated to reduce dissonance through changing his or her beliefs and evaluations about the object or event.

FIGURE 4–1 • Three Types of Motivational Conflict

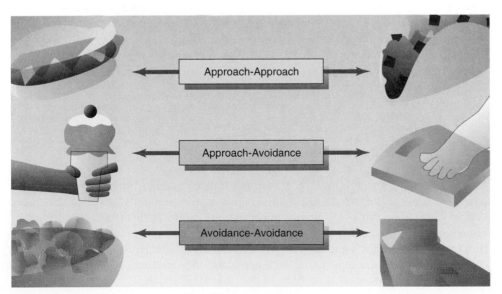

when beliefs or behaviours conflict with one another. The conflict that arises when choosing between two alternatives may be resolved through a process of cognitive dissonance reduction, in which people are motivated to reduce this inconsistency (or dissonance) and thus eliminate unpleasant tension.[3]

A state of dissonance occurs when there is a psychological inconsistency between two or more beliefs or behaviours. It often occurs when a consumer must make a choice between two products, both of which possess good and bad qualities. By choosing one product and not the other, the person gets the bad qualities of the chosen product and loses out on the good qualities of the unchosen one.

This loss creates an unpleasant, dissonant state that the person is motivated to reduce. People tend to convince themselves after the fact that choices they made were smart ones, by finding additional reasons to support the alternatives they chose or perhaps by "discovering" flaws with the options they did not choose. A marketer can resolve an approach-approach conflict by bundling several benefits together. For example, Miller Lite's claim that it is "less filling" *and* "tastes great" allows the drinker to "have his beer and drink it too."

APPROACH-AVOIDANCE CONFLICT

Many of the products and services we desire have negative consequences attached to them as well. We may feel guilty or ostentatious when buying a status-laden product like a mink coat or feel like a glutton when contemplating a bag of potato chips. When we desire a goal but wish to avoid it at the same time, an approach-avoidance conflict exists.

Some solutions to these conflicts include the proliferation of fake furs, which eliminate guilt about harming animals to make a fashion statement, and the success of diet foods, such as Weight Watchers (*www.weight-watchers.com*), which promise good food without the calories. Many marketers try to overcome guilt by convincing consumers that they are deserving of luxuries (such as when the model for L'Oréal cosmetics claims, "Because I'm worth it!").

AVOIDANCE-AVOIDANCE CONFLICT

Sometimes consumers find themselves caught "between a rock and a hard place": they face a choice between two undesirable alternatives. A person may be faced with the option of either throwing more money into an old car or buying a new one. Marketers frequently address this conflict through messages that stress the unforeseen benefits of choosing one option (emphasizing special credit plans to ease the pain of new-car payments, for example).

Classifying Consumer Needs

Much research has been done on classifying human needs. On the one hand, some psychologists have tried to define a universal inventory of needs that could be traced systematically to explain virtually all behaviour. One such effort, developed by Henry Murray, delineates a set of psychogenic needs that (sometimes in combination) result in specific behaviours. These needs, shown in Figure 4–2, include such dimensions as autonomy (being independent), defendance (defending the self against criticism) and play (engaging in pleasurable activities).[4]

FIGURE 4–2 • Levels of Needs Defined by Murray

Types of Needs Defined by Murray

Biogenic	Food
	Water
	Air
	Sleep
	Sex
	Shelter

Psychogenic	Dominance
	Superiority
	Emotional Stability
	Achievement
	Compliance
	Order
	Autonomy
	Affiliation
	Analysis
	Dependence
	Self-Depreciation
	Exhibition
	Assistance
	Change
	Endurance
	Aggression
	Defendence
	Play

Murray's need structure serves as the basis for a number of widely used personality tests, such as the Thematic Apperception Technique (TAT) and the Edward's Personal Preference Schedule (EPPS). In the TAT, test subjects are shown four to six ambiguous pictures and asked to write answers to four directing questions about the pictures. These questions are: 1) what is happening?; 2) what has led up to this situation?; 3) what is being thought?; and 4) what will happen? Four minutes of writing time is allowed for each story. Each answer is then content analyzed for references to certain needs and scored whenever that need is mentioned.

The theory behind the test is that people will freely project their own subconscious needs onto the ambiguous picture. By getting their responses to the picture,

This ambiguous picture would be suitable for the TAT.
Photo courtesy of Judy Zaichkowsky.

you are really getting at the person's true needs for achievement or affiliation or whatever other needs may dominate. Murray believed that everyone has the same basic set of needs but that individuals differ in their priority ranking of these needs.

Other motivational approaches have focused on specific needs and their ramifications for behaviour. For example, individuals with a high *need for achievement* strongly value personal accomplishment.[5] They place a premium on products and services that signify success, because these consumption items provide feedback about the realization of their goals. These consumers are good prospects for products that provide evidence of their achievements. One study of working women found that those who were high in achievement motivation were more likely to choose clothing they considered businesslike and less likely to be interested in apparel that accentuated their femininity.[6] Some other important needs that are relevant to consumer behaviour include the following:

- *Need for affiliation* (to be in the company of other people).[7] This need is relevant to products and services that are consumed among groups of people at places such as athletic venues, bars and shopping malls, and that alleviate loneliness.

- *Need for power* (to control one's environment).[8] Many products and services, ranging from "hopped-up" muscle cars to hotels, restaurants and resorts that promise to respond to the customer's every whim, allow consumers to feel that they have mastery over their surroundings.

- *Need for uniqueness* (to assert one's individual identity).[9] This need is satisfied by products that pledge to accentuate a consumer's distinctive qualities. For example, Cachet perfume claims to be "as individual as you are."

MASLOW'S HIERARCHY OF NEEDS

One influential approach to motivation was proposed by the psychologist Abraham Maslow. Maslow's approach is a general one originally developed to understand personal growth and the attainment of "peak experiences."[10] Maslow formulated a hierarchy of biogenic and psychogenic needs, in which levels of motives are specified. A hierarchical approach implies that the order of development is fixed—that is, a certain level must be attained before the next, higher one is activated. This universal approach to motivation has been adopted by marketers because it (indirectly) specifies certain types of product benefits people might be looking for, depending upon the different stages in their development and/or their environmental conditions.

These levels are summarized in Figure 4–3. At each level different priorities exist in terms of the product benefits a consumer is looking for. Ideally, an individual progresses up the hierarchy until his or her dominant motivation is a focus on "ultimate" goals, such as justice and beauty. Unfortunately, this state is difficult to achieve (at least on a regular basis); most of us have to be satisfied with occasional glimpses, or peak experiences. Examples of product appeals tailored to each level are provided in Table 4–1.

For most Canadians, the biogenic or physiological needs are regularly and easily satisfied. Thus, the higher-level needs are usually dominant. Safety and security become the next driving force of behaviour. These needs are concerned with much more than physical safety. They include order, stability, routine, familiarity and certainty—the knowledge, for example, that the individual will eat dinner not only on that day and the following day but also far into the future. Safety needs are met by unions, social welfare programs and insurance policies.

FIGURE 4–3 • Levels of Needs in the Maslow Hierarchy

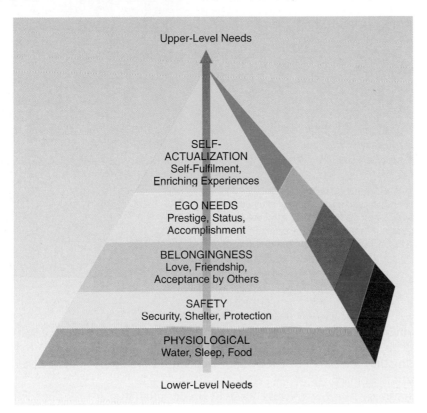

TABLE 4–1 Maslow's Hierarchy and Marketing Strategies

LEVEL OF HIERARCHY	RELEVANT PRODUCTS	EXAMPLE
Self-Actualization	Hobbies, travel, education	Marriott—"When you're comfortable you can do anything"
Ego needs	Cars, furniture, credit cards, stores, country clubs, liquors	Royal Salute Scotch—"What the rich give the wealthy"
Belongingness	Clothing, grooming products, clubs, drinks	Pepsi—"You're in the Pepsi generation."
Safety	Insurance, alarm systems, retirement investments	Allstate Insurance—"You're in good hands with Allstate."
Physiology	Medicines, staple items, generics	Quaker Oat Bran—"It's the right thing to do."

Social needs are met by seeking warm and satisfying human relationships. When the social needs are more or less satisfied, the esteem or ego needs emerge. Inwardly directed ego needs reflect an individual's need for self-acceptance, self-esteem, achievement and success. Outwardly directed ego needs include the needs for prestige, reputation, status and recognition from others. Most people spend most of their

Like many advertisements for home furnishings, this one for Waverly fabrics and wall coverings emphasizes the significance of having a secure and attractive home. The expression "There's no place like home!" is a testament to the importance of security and shelter in Maslow's hierarchy.
Reprinted by permission of Waverly. All rights reserved.

lives trying to fill their ego needs and never move on to the fifth level of self-actualization. This need refers to individuals' desire to fulfil their own potential, to become everything they are capable of becoming, so that they are totally and completely satisfied with their lives.

In summary, Maslow's Need Hierarchy predicts that higher-order needs become the driving force behind human behaviour as the consumer's lower-level needs are satisfied. The theory says, in effect, that satisfaction does not motivate behaviour; dissatisfaction does. It is important to note that lower needs are never totally satisfied but are ongoing. We do not need totally to satisfy one need before the next level of need motivates our behaviour. Sometimes certain behaviours satisfy two needs at once. For example, a Mercedes might satisfy the safety need and the ego need for prestige. You might be surprised at how often these needs are expressed. Consumers' feelings about the activity of gardening were classified according to Maslow's hierarchy and were found to express needs at all levels. This is shown in Table 4–2.

While Maslow's theory is very interesting and applicable to marketing, it has certain problems. There is no measurement tool for researchers to test the need hierarchy empirically. Also, we cannot measure precisely how well satisfied one need is before the next higher need becomes operational.

Another problem with taking Maslow's hierarchy too literally is that its assumptions may be particular to Western culture. People of other cultures may question the order of the levels as specified. Many Asian cultures operate on the premise that the welfare of the group (belongingness needs) is more highly valued than needs of the individual (esteem needs). Similarly, a religious person who has taken a vow of celibacy would not necessarily agree that his or her physiological needs must be satisfied for self-fulfilment to occur.

The point is that this hierarchy is widely applied in marketing because it reminds us that consumers may have different need priorities at different times and stages of their lives.

TABLE 4–2 Maslow's Hierarchy of Gardening

NEED	EXPRESSION OF NEED
Physiological	"I like to work in the soil"
Safety	"I feel safe in the garden"
Social	"I can share my produce with others"
Esteem	"I can create something of beauty"
Self-Actualization	"My garden gives me a sense of peace"

Source: Kansas State University, Horticulture Department, 1992, cited in "Survey Tells Why Gardening's Good," *Vancouver Sun* (April 12, 1997): B12.

CONSUMER INVOLVEMENT

As we have seen, a consumer's motivation to attain a goal influences his or her desire to expend the effort necessary to attain the products or services believed to be instrumental in satisfying that objective. However, not everyone is motivated to the same extent; that is, one person might be convinced that he or she can't live without the latest style or modern convenience, while another is only marginally interested in these items. **Involvement** can be defined as "a person's perceived relevance of the object based on their inherent needs, values, and interests."[11] The word "object" is used in the generic sense and refers to a product (or brand), an advertisement, or a purchase situation. Consumers can find involvement in all these "objects."

Since involvement is a motivational construct, it can be triggered by one or more of the different antecedents shown in Figure 4–4. The antecedents are something about the person, something about the object and something about the situation. On the right-hand side of Figure 4–4 are the results or consequences of being involved with the "object." When consumers are intent on doing what they can to satisfy a

involvement a person's perceived relevance of an object based on inherent needs, values and interests

The elegant luxury car is moving at 44 feet per second when it suddenly meets something solid.

Now it suddenly stops being an elegant luxury car. And becomes a structure for managing severe impact forces on behalf of the people within.

The fact is that the engineers of Mercedes-Benz spend most of their time thinking of all those moments when a luxury car needs to be something far more than a luxury car.

Such thinking led them to patent the concept of the impact-absorbing car body 38 years

ago, for example. And currently leads them to keep crash-testing new cars in the laboratory at the rate of one every 17 working hours, in search of further refinements.

And out in the real world, where such

engineering efforts are finally judged, it lea the thinking luxury-car buyer to think rath highly of Mercedes-Benz.

For more safety information, or the name your nearest authorized dealer, call 1-800-762-3

ENGINEERED LIKE NO OTHER CAR IN THE WORLD

This Mercedes-Benz ad responds to the perceived risk associated with physical danger by stressing that safety is a key feature of its luxury automobiles.
© Copyright of Mercedez-Benz AG; photograph provided courtesy of Mercedes-Benz AG.

FIGURE 4–4   •   Conceptualizing Involvement

Antecedents of Involvement	Possible Results of Involvement

Person Factors
— needs
— importance
— interest
— values

Object or
Stimulus Factors
— differentiation
  of alternatives
— source of
  communication
— content of
  communication

Situational Factors
— purchase/use
— occasion

Involvement
with advertisements
with products
with purchase
decisions

elicitation of counter-
arguments to ads

effectiveness of ad
to induce purchase

relative importance
of the product class

perceived differences
in product attributes

preference for a
particular brand

influence of price
on brand choice

amount of information
search

time spent deliberating
alternatives

type of decision rule
used in choice

Involvement = f (Person, Situation, Object)

Involvement = f (Person, Situation, Object)
The level of involvement may be influenced by
one or more of these three factors. Interactions
among persons, situation and object factors are
likely to occur.

Source: Judith Lynne Zaichkowsky, "Conceptualizing Involvement," *Journal of Advertising* 15, 2, (1986): 4–14

need, they will be motivated to pay attention to and process any information felt to be relevant to achieving their goals.

On the other hand, a person may not bother to pay any attention to the same information if it is not seen as relevant to satisfying some need. People who pride themselves on their knowledge of exercise equipment may read anything they can find about the subject, spend their spare time in athletics stores, and so on, while other people may skip over this information without a second thought.

Involvement can be viewed as the motivation to process information.[12] To the degree that there is a perceived linkage between a consumer's needs, goals or values and product knowledge, the consumer will be motivated to pay attention to product information. When relevant knowledge is activated in memory, a motivational state is created that drives behaviour (e.g., shopping). As involvement with a product increases, people devote more attention to ads related to the product, exert more cognitive effort to understand these ads, and focus their attention on the product-related information in them.[13]

Levels of Involvement: From Inertia to Passion

The type of information processing that will occur thus depends upon the consumer's level of involvement. It can range from *simple processing,* in which only the basic features of a message are considered, all the way to *elaboration,* in which the incoming information is linked to one's pre-existing knowledge systems.[14]

A person's degree of involvement can be conceived as a continuum, ranging from absolute lack of interest in a marketing stimulus at one end to obsession at the other. Consumption at the low end of involvement is characterized by **inertia,** where decisions are made out of habit because the consumer lacks the motivation to consider alternatives. At the high end of involvement we can expect to find the type of passionate intensity reserved for people and objects that carry great meaning to the individual. The ad for magazines published by Times Mirror Magazines shown here emphasizes this high involvement. For the most part, however, a consumer's involvement level with products falls somewhere in the middle, and the marketing strategist must determine the relative level of importance to understand how much elaboration of product information will occur.

A more sophisticated view of involvement recognizes that besides the level of involvement, there may be a type of involvement. One may be emotionally or affectively involved with an object (such as an advertisement), or one may be rationally or cognitively involved with a product, or purchase situation, and so on. The advertising industry has long held this view and advocates different types of advertising strategies depending upon the level and type of involvement. This is shown in Figure 4–5.

inertia the process whereby purchase decisions are made out of habit because the consumer lacks the motivation to consider alternatives

The Many Faces of Involvement

As previously defined, involvement can take many forms. Basil could certainly be said to be highly involved with his running shoes, since they help to define and bolster his self-concept. This involvement seems to increase at certain times, as when he must prove himself in a triathlon. Alternatively, the act of buying the shoes may be very involving for people who are passionately devoted to shopping. To complicate matters further, advertisements, such as those produced for Nike or Adidas, may themselves be involving for some reason (because they make us laugh or cry, or inspire us to work harder). It seems that involvement is a fuzzy concept, because it

This ad for lifestyle magazines targeted to men underscores the strategic value of reaching highly involved consumers.
Courtesy of Times Mirror Magazines.

FIGURE 4–5 • Foote, Cone and Belding's Involvement and Product Typology

TYPE OF INVOLVEMENT

		Cognitive	Affective
Level of Involvement	**High**	• Car • New products Media: print, information, based	• Jewellery • Motorcycles Media: TV, image based
	Low	• Ground beef • Household cleansers Media: 10 sec. IDs, POS, reminder	• Candy • Liquor Media: POS, attention grabbing

Source: Adapted from Richard Vaughn, "How Advertising Works: A Planning Model," *Journal of Advertising Research* 20 (October 1980): 31. See also Judith Lynne Zaichkowsky, "The Emotional Side of Product Involvement," in *Advances in Consomer Research*, Paul eds. Anderson and Melanie Wallendorf (Provo, UT: Association for Consumer Research), vol. 14, pp. 32–35.

overlaps with and means different things to different people. Indeed, the consensus is that there are actually several broad types of involvement—related to the product, the message or the situation:[15]

- *Product involvement* is related to a consumer's level of interest in a particular product. Many sales promotions are designed to increase this type of involvement. In a contest sponsored by Dare perfume, for example, women submitted details of their most intimate trysts by letter or by phone to radio talk shows. The winning stories were edited and published in a romance novel by Bantam Books. These books, in turn, were given away as gifts with the purchase of the perfume.[16]

- *Message-response involvement* or advertising involvement, refers to the consumer's interest in processing marketing communications.[17] Television is considered a low-involvement medium because it requires a passive viewer who exerts relatively little control over content (remote-control "zipping" notwithstanding). In contrast, print media demand high involvement. The reader is actively involved in processing the information and is able to pause and reflect on what he or she has read before moving on.[18] The role of message characteristics in changing attitudes is discussed further in Chapter 8.

- *Purchase situation involvement* refers to differences that may occur when buying the same object for different contexts. Here the person may perceive a great deal of social risk or none at all. What a person thinks when they consume the product for themselves, or when others consume the product they buy, is not always obvious or intuitive. For example, when you want to impress someone, you may try to buy a brand or product with a certain image that you think reflects good taste. When you have to buy a gift for someone in an obligatory situation, such as a wedding gift for a cousin you do not really like, you may not care what image the gift portrays; or you may actually pick something cheap that reflects your desire to distance yourself from that cousin.[19]

Measuring Involvement

The measurement of involvement is important for many marketing applications. For example, research evidence indicates that a viewer who is more involved with a television show will also respond more positively to commercials contained in that show,

TABLE 4–3 A Scale to Measure Involvement

TO ME [OBJECT TO BE JUDGED] IS

1. important	__:__:__:__:__:__	unimportant*
2. boring	__:__:__:__:__:__	interesting
3. relevant	__:__:__:__:__:__	irrelevant*
4. exciting	__:__:__:__:__:__	unexciting*
5. means nothing	__:__:__:__:__:__	means a lot to me
6. appealing	__:__:__:__:__:__	unappealing*
7. fascinating	__:__:__:__:__:__	mundane*
8. worthless	__:__:__:__:__:__	valuable
9. involving	__:__:__:__:__:__	uninvolving*
10. not needed	__:__:__:__:__:__	needed

Source: Judith Lynne Zaichkowsky, "The Personal Involvement Inventory: Reduction, Revision, and Application to Advertising," *Journal of Advertising* 23, 4 (December 1994): 59–70.

Note: Totalling the 10 items gives a score from a low of 10 to a high of 70. Items 1, 3, 5, 8 and 10 measure a more cognitive involvement, while items 2, 4, 6, 7 and 9 seem to capture a more affective type of involvement.

*Indicates item is reverse scored. For example, a score of 7 for item no. 1 (important/unimportant) would actually be scored as 1.

and that these spots will have a greater chance of influencing his or her purchase intentions.[20] Therefore, many research companies like Involvement Marketing Inc., in New York, measure the level of consumer involvement to make predictions on the success of advertising campaigns. One of the most widely used measures of the state of involvement is the scale shown in Table 4–3. It is the most widely used because it is context free and therefore applicable to products, advertisements and purchase situations.[21]

MULTICULTURAL DIMENSIONS

A study compared involvement levels of consumers from different countries for a number of products and services. Here are some differences in involvement that emerged (as measured by the scale in Table 4–3) when the researchers compared regular users of these items across countries:[22]

- The Chinese are more involved with beer than are South Americans. Otherwise, the study found little difference in this category across countries.

- Involvement with soft drinks was relatively low in Canada and Sweden, but relatively high in the former Yugoslavia and China.

- Blue jeans got the highest involvement score from Austrian consumers and the lowest from Swedes.

- Americans scored relatively high on involvement with air travel, and Swedes relatively low.

- French and Chinese subjects were most likely to be involved with going to the movies, while Mexicans were the least involved.

A pair of French researchers devised a scale to measure the antecedents of product involvement. Recognizing that consumers can be involved with a product because it is a risky purchase and/or because its use reflects upon or affects the self, they advocate the development of an *involvement profile* containing five components:[23]

1. the personal interest a consumer has in a product category; its personal meaning or importance
2. the perceived importance of the potential negative consequences associated with a poor choice of the product (risk importance)
3. probability of making a bad purchase
4. pleasure value of the product category
5. sign value of the product category.

These researchers asked a sample of women to rate a set of 14 product categories on each of the above facets of involvement. The results are shown in Table 4–4. These data indicate that no single component captures consumer involvement, since this quality can occur for different reasons. For example, the purchase of a durable product, such as a vacuum cleaner, is seen as risky because one is stuck with a bad choice for many years. However, the vacuum cleaner does not provide pleasure (hedonic value), nor is it high in sign value (i.e., its use is not related to the person's self-concept). In contrast, chocolate is high in pleasure value but is not seen as risky or closely related to the self. Dresses and bras, on the other hand, appear to be involving for a combination of reasons.

Segmenting by Involvement Levels

A measurement approach that segments involvement by levels allows consumer researchers to capture the diversity of the involvement construct, and it also provides the potential to use involvement as a basis for market segmentation. For example, a yogurt manufacturer might find that, even though its product is low in sign value for one group of consumers, it is highly related to the self-concept of another market segment, such as health-food enthusiasts or avid dieters. The company could adapt its strategy to account for the motivation of different segments to process information about the product. One study looked at the role of affective versus cognitive involvement and level of involvement (high versus low) in promoting Canadian universities. The researchers found that students cognitively high involved conducted an intense search for university information, while those students who were low and affectively involved made their university choice based mainly on emotional factors.[24] Note also that involvement with a product class may vary across cultures. While the sample of French consumers shown in Table 4–4 rated champagne high in both sign value and personal value, the ability of champagne to provide pleasure or be central to self-definition might not transfer to other countries, for example those with Islamic cultures.

Strategies to Increase Involvement

Although consumers differ in their level of involvement with respect to a product message, marketers do not have to just sit back and hope for the best. By being

TABLE 4–4 Involvement Profiles for a Set of French Consumer Products

	IMPORTANCE OF NEGATIVE CONSEQUENCES*	SUBJECTIVE PROBABILITY OF MISPURCHASE	PLEASURE VALUE	SIGN VALUE
Dresses	121	112	147	181
Bras	117	115	106	130
Washing machines	118	109	106	111
TV sets	112	100	122	95
Vacuum cleaners	110	112	70	78
Irons	103	95	72	76
Champagne	109	120	125	125
Oil	89	97	65	92
Yogurt	86	83	106	78
Chocolate	80	89	123	75
Shampoo	96	103	90	81
Toothpaste	95	95	94	105
Facial soap	82	90	114	118
Detergents	79	82	56	63

Average product score = 100.

Source: Gilles Laurent and Jean-Noël Kapferer, "Measuring Consumer Involvement Profiles," *Journal of Marketing Research* 22 (February 1985): 45, Table 3. By permission of American Marketing Association.

* Note the first two antecedents of personal importance and importance of negative consequences are combined in these data.

aware of some basic factors that increase or decrease attention, they can take steps to increase the likelihood that product information will get through. A consumer's motivation to process relevant information can be enhanced fairly easily by the marketer who uses one or more of the following techniques:[25]

- Appeal to consumers' hedonic needs. For example, ads using sensory appeals generate higher levels of attention.

- Use of novel stimuli, such as unusual cinematography, sudden silences or unexpected movements in commercials.

- Use of prominent stimuli, such as loud music and fast action, to capture attention in commercials. In print formats, larger ads increase attention. Also, viewers look longer at coloured pictures as opposed to those in black and white.

- Inclusion of celebrity endorsers to generate higher interest in commercials. This strategy will be discussed in Chapter 8.

- Building of a bond with consumers by maintaining an ongoing relationship with them. Marketers can learn from the actions of Saturn, the subsidiary of General Motors. The carmaker has cultivated a group of loyal, even fanatic, consumers. This high-involvement level was evident during the company's recent "homecoming," when 25 000 Saturn owners journeyed to the Saturn factory in Spring Hill, Tennessee, for a complimentary weekend of tours, dances and barbecues.[26] Saturn even has its own Web site to update current and potential customers

MULTICULTURAL DIMENSIONS

Quick Burger, France's second-largest fast-food chain, has discovered a route to increasing customers' involvement. The company became a partner in a marketing program called Multipoints—an interactive service that lets consumers collect points that can then be redeemed for discounts and prizes. More than 70 000 French consumers have signed up for the service. Using a device that resembles a calculator, participants enter codes they find in print ads and on billboards or hear on radio programs. They can even hold the device against their TV screens during programming that is specially encoded to dispense credits. People can win points for playing along with certain game shows and answering questions correctly. They can then redeem their points for merchandise at Quick Burger restaurants and other locations (including selected travel agencies and newsstands) by plugging their devices into computer terminals. In addition, the hamburger chain gives consumers 500 free points per week just for visiting, which gives them additional motivation to patronize Quick Burger instead of arch-rival McDonald's.[19]

(*www.saturncars.com*). The routes to cultivating brand loyalty will be discussed further in Chapter 6.

VALUES

value an enduring belief that a specific mode of conduct is personally or socially preferable to an opposite mode of conduct

A **value** is a belief that some condition is preferable to its opposite. Many people avidly pursue products and services that will make them look young, believing that this is preferable to appearing old. A person's set of values plays a very important role in his or her consumption activities, since many products and services are purchased because they will (it is believed) help us to attain a value-related goal.

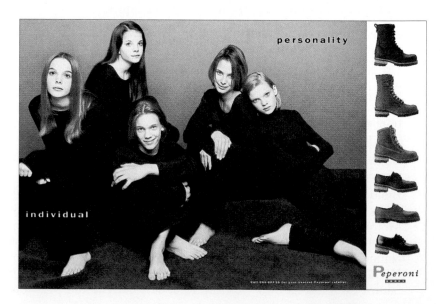

This Swedish shoe ad appeals to the value of individuality.
Courtesy of LT Skor, Sweden.

The specific values that motivate people vary across cultures, yet within each culture there is usually a set of underlying goals that most members of that culture agree are important. A study by Wirthlin Worldwide, for example, found that the most important values to Asian executives are hard work, respect for learning, and honesty. In contrast, North American respondents emphasize the values of personal freedom, self-reliance and freedom of expression.[28]

Core Values

Every culture has a set of values that it imparts to its members. For example, people in one culture might feel that being a unique individual is preferable to subordinating one's identity to the group, while another culture may emphasize the virtues of group membership. In many cases, values are universal. Who does not desire health, wisdom or world peace?

What sets cultures apart is the *relative importance,* or ranking, of these universal values. This set of rankings constitutes a culture's **value system**.[29] To illustrate a difference in value systems, consider the results of a study by Dentsu, a large Japanese advertising agency. Consumers in New York, Los Angeles and Tokyo were asked to indicate their preferences regarding the goals an ideal society should aim for. There was a high degree of consensus within the American sample: residents on each coast said their highest ideal is a "society in which people can live safely." In contrast, Tokyo residents ranked first the goal of a "society with a comprehensive welfare system." While about 45 percent of the Americans endorsed the idea of a "society which is very competitive, but in which everybody has an equal chance of success," only 25 percent of Tokyo residents echoed this sentiment.[30]

value system a culture's ranking of the relative importance of values

Every culture is characterized by its members' endorsement of a value system. These end states may not be equally endorsed by everyone, and in some cases values may even seem to contradict one another (North Americans appear to value both conformity and individuality and seek to find some accommodation between the two). Nonetheless, it is usually possible to identify a general set of *core values* that uniquely define a culture. These beliefs are taught to us by *socialization agents,* including parents, friends and teachers. The process of learning the beliefs and behaviours endorsed by one's own culture is termed **enculturation**. In contrast, the process of learning the value system and behaviours of another culture (often a priority for those who wish to understand consumers and markets in foreign countries) is called **acculturation**.

enculturation the process of learning the beliefs and behaviours endorsed by one's native culture

acculturation the process of learning the beliefs and behaviours endorsed by another culture

Core values such as equality, youthfulness, achievement, materialism and activity have been claimed to characterize most Western cultures, but even these basic beliefs are subject to change. For example, the emphasis on youth is eroding as the population ages (see Chapter 14). Table 4–5 identifies the dominant values underlying a set of American print ads representing the period from 1900 to 1980. The prevalence of product effectiveness as an underlying advertising theme is obvious.

Despite their importance, values have not been widely applied to direct examinations of consumer behaviour. One reason is that such broad-based concepts as freedom, security or inner harmony are more likely to affect general purchasing patterns than to differentiate among brands within a product category. For this reason, some researchers have found it convenient to make distinctions among such broad-based *cultural values* as security or happiness, such *consumption-specific values* as

TABLE 4–5   Cultural Values Frequently Emphasized in American Advertising: 1900–1980

OVERALL VALUE	THEMES INCLUDED	PROPORTION OF ADS USING VALUE AS CENTRAL THEME
Practical	Effectiveness, durability, convenience	44
Family	Nurturance in family, happy home, getting married	17
New	Modernism, improvement	14
Cheap	Economy, bargain, good value	13
Healthy	Fitness, vigour, athleticism	12
Sexy/vain	Good appearance, glamour, eroticism	13
Wisdom	Knowledge, experience	11
Unique	Expense, value, distinctiveness, rarity	10

Source: Adapted from Richard W. Pollay, "The Identification and Distribution of Values Manifest in Print Advertising, 1900–1980." Adapted with the permission of Lexington Books, an imprint of Macmillan, Inc., from *Personal Values and Consumer Psychology*, eds. Robert E. Pitts, Jr., and Arch G. Woodside. Copyright © 1984 by Lexington Books.

convenient shopping or prompt service, and such *product-specific values* as ease of use or durability.[31] For example, people who value group affiliation and approval have been shown to place more importance on style and brand name when evaluating the desirability of clothing products.[32]

MULTICULTURAL DIMENSIONS

Japanese culture is well known for its emphasis on cleanliness. The Shinto religion requires a ritual washing of hands and mouth before entering shrines, and people always take off their shoes at home to avoid dirtying the floors. People give money as wedding gifts and may actually iron it before putting it in the envelope. Some laundromats allow customers to rinse out the inside of a machine before using it.[33]

This value has reached new proportions since a food poisoning epidemic in the summer of 1996. Demand for products such as antiseptic bicycle grips, karaoke microphones and gauze masks is skyrocketing, and a rash of sterilized products ranging from stationery and floppy disks to telephones and dishwashers is invading the market. Pentel makes a germ-free pen decorated with a medical blue cross; the popular brand is advertised with the slogan "The pen is mightier than the bacterium." Japan's Sanwa Bank literally "launders money" for its customers in specially designed ATM machines, while Tokyo's Mitsubishi Bank opened a "Total Anti-Germ Branch" featuring ATMs with surfaces made of plastics saturated with chemicals that resist bacteria and fungus. A bank spokesperson noted that the branch is especially popular with young female customers who say they "... don't want to touch things handled by middle-aged men." But how successful are the efforts to live in a sanitized world? A Japanese sociologist comments, "Young people today think they can banish germs from their lives with a few gimmicks. But after you use your antiseptic ATM, you still walk out the door into a world of germs." Nonetheless, they keep trying ...

Since values drive much of consumer behaviour (at least in a very general sense), it could be said that virtually *all* types of consumer research ultimately are related to the identification and measurement of values. This section will describe some specific attempts by researchers to measure cultural values and apply this knowledge to marketing strategy.

The Rokeach Value Survey

The psychologist Milton Rokeach identified a set of **terminal values,** or desired end states, that apply (to various degrees) to many different cultures. The *Rokeach Value Survey,* a scale used to measure these values, also includes a set of **instrumental values,** which are composed of actions needed to achieve these terminal values.[34] These two sets of values appear in Table 4–6.

There are a great many differences in the rank importance of these values to different cultures. Since it is these values that underlie, motivate and guide our behaviour, by understanding the rank importance of values we can understand what motivates people's behaviour. For example, freedom is a very basic and important value in the United States, emanating from the history of the country. A war was

terminal values end states desired by members of a culture

instrumental values those goals that are endorsed because they are needed to achieve desired end states, or terminal values

TABLE 4–6 Two Types of Values in the Rokeach Value Survey	
INSTRUMENTAL VALUES	TERMINAL VALUES
Ambitious	A comfortable life
Broadminded	An exciting life
Capable	A sense of accomplishment
Cheerful	A world at peace
Clean	A world of beauty
Courageous	Equality
Forgiving	Family security
Helpful	Freedom
Honest	Happiness
Imaginative	Inner harmony
Independent	Mature love
Intellectual	National security
Logical	Pleasure
Loving	Salvation
Obedient	Self-respect
Polite	Social recognition
Responsible	True friendship
Self-controlled	Wisdom

Source: Richard W. Pollay, "Measuring the Cultural Values Manifest in Advertising," *Current Issues and Research in Advertising* (1983): 71–92. Reprinted by permission of University of Michigan Division of Research.

fought for "freedom" from Britain, and another was fought to "free" the slaves. The phrases "freedom" of expression, "free" to bear arms and "freedom" of speech are the basis of the American constitution and reflect US culture. In contrast, Canadians focus on equality. Equal access to health care and education, and "equality" of the provinces, underlie Canadian culture.

The List of Values (LOV) Scale

Although some evidence indicates that these global values do translate into product-specific preferences and differences in media usage, the Rokeach Value Survey has not been widely used by marketing researchers.[35] As an alternative, the *List of Values (LOV) Scale* was developed to isolate values with more direct marketing applications.

This instrument identifies nine consumer segments based on the values they endorse and relates each to differences in consumption behaviours. These segments include consumers who place a priority on such values as sense of belonging, excitement, warm relationships with others and security. For example, people who endorse the value of a sense of belonging are more likely to read *Reader's Digest* and *TV Guide,* drink and entertain frequently, prefer group activities and be older than are people who do not endorse this value as highly. In contrast, those who endorse the value of excitement prefer *Wired* and are younger than those who do not.[36]

The Means-End Chain Model

Another research approach that incorporates values is termed a *means-end chain model.* This approach assumes that very specific product attributes are linked at levels of increasing abstraction to terminal values. The individual has valued end states, and he or she chooses among alternative means to attain these goals. Products are thus valued as the means to an end. Through a technique called **laddering,** consumers' associations between specific attributes and general consequences are uncovered. Consumers are helped to climb up the "ladder" of abstraction that connects functional product attributes with desired end states.[37]

To understand how laddering works, consider the purchase of a diamond ring to symbolize an upcoming marriage. Concrete attributes like size and clarity of the stone are parlayed into abstract and emotional values of love and self-esteem. The diamond industry is very good at keeping an artificially high price on a luxury good through linking the size of the diamond to the size of your paycheque, to the size of your love, and self-worth.

The notion that products are consumed because they are instrumental to attaining more abstract values is central to one application of this technique, called the *Means-End Conceptualization of the Components of Advertising Strategy (MECCAs).* In this approach, researchers first generate a map depicting relationships between functional product or service attributes and terminal values. This information is then used to develop an advertising strategy by identifying elements such as those that follow:[38]

- *message elements*—the specific attributes or product features to be depicted
- *consumer benefit*—the positive consequences of using the product or service

laddering a technique for uncovering consumers' associations between specific attributes and general consequences

- *executional framework*—the overall style and tone of the advertisement
- *leverage point*—the way the message will activate the terminal value by linking it with specific product features
- *driving force*—the end value upon which the advertising will focus

This technique was used to develop an advertising strategy for Federal Express. The researchers developed a "hierarchical value map" for secretaries, an important group of decision makers in the category of overnight delivery services. As shown in Figure 4–6, concrete attributes of competitive services, such as having a drop box or on-time delivery, were successively related to more abstract benefits, such as "makes me look good" or "saves time." These intermediate levels were then linked, or laddered, to reveal their relationships to the terminal values of peace of mind and self-esteem.

Based on these results, an advertisement was created. Its message elements emphasized Federal Express's satellite communications network. The consumer benefit was the reliability of the service, which made work easier. The executional framework was a humorous one: A secretary is trying to track down an overnight

FIGURE 4–6 • Secretaries' Hierarchical Value Map for Overnight Delivery Services

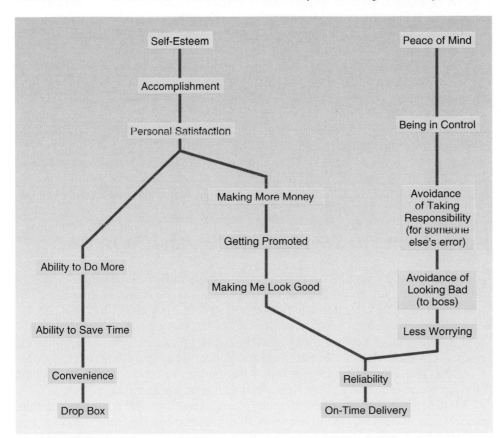

Source: Adapted from Thomas J. Reynolds and Alyce Byrd Craddock, "The Application of the MECCAs Model to the Development and Assessment of Advertising Strategy: A Case Study," *Journal of Advertising Research* (April/May 1988): 43–54.

delivery. She and her boss are interrupted and taken to view the Federal Express satellite system. As a result, the secretary sees the benefit of using the company. The leverage point is that using this service allows the secretary to be in control, which in turn provides peace of mind, the driving force (terminal value). A visit to Federal Express's Web site (**www.fedex.com**) will give the reader some insight into the sophistication of their operations.

Syndicated Surveys

A number of companies track changes in values through syndicated, large-scale surveys. The results of these studies are then sold to marketers, who pay a fee to receive regular updates on changes and trends.

This approach originated in the mid-1960s, when Playtex was concerned about sagging girdle sales.[39] The company commissioned the market research firm of Yankelovich, Skelly & White to see why. Their research determined that sales had been affected by a shift in values regarding appearance and naturalness. Playtex went on to design lighter, less restrictive garments, while Yankelovich went on to track the impact of these types of changes in a range of industries. Gradually, the firm developed the idea of one big study to track attitudes. In 1970, the Monitor was introduced. It is based on two-hour interviews with 4000 respondents.

Today, many other syndicated surveys also track changes in values. Some of these are operated by advertising agencies to allow them to stay on top of important cultural trends and help them to shape the messages they craft on behalf of their clients. In Canada, the CF Group, Goldfarb Consultants and Angus Reid regularly track consumers.

The Angus Reid Group surveys changes in values of specific groups or industry segments. For example, the Chinese consumer in Canada, the banking industry or the telecommunications industry are part of their portfolio. The cost of these surveys declines with the age of the data. They have also established a panel using the Internet to have an ongoing dialogue with the same sample over time. Details of what studies are available can be found at the Angus Reid Web site (**www.angusreid.com**).

Materialism: "He Who Dies with the Most Toys, Wins ..."

materialism the importance consumers attach to worldly possessions

One of the most relevant values to marketers is **materialism**. Materialists are people who place the acquisition and display of possessions at the centre of their lives, who view things as being central to satisfaction and well-being, and who feel that the success of themselves and others is seen in terms of the possessions they have accumulated.[40] When large segments of a society strive to consume for non-utilitarian reasons, a *consumer culture* is said to exist. A recent study that compared the extent of materialism across 12 countries found Romanians to be the most materialistic, followed by citizens of the USA, New Zealand, Germany and Turkey.[41]

Materialists are more likely to value possessions for their status and appearance-related meanings, while those who do not emphasize this value tend to prize products that connect them to other people or that provide them with pleasure by using them. As a result, products valued by high materialists are more likely to be publicly consumed and to be more expensive. A study that compared specific items valued by both types of people found that products associated with high materialists include jewellery, china or a vacation home, while those linked to low materialists included a mother's wedding gown, picture albums, a rocking chair from childhood or a garden.[42]

The Brain Waves/Market Facts survey reports that about a quarter of the population is displaying a value system characterized by a rejection of tradition and conformity. Significantly, more than half of this group is under the age of 35. They are still interested in achievement, but they are trying to balance life in the fast lane with an emphasis on developing close personal relationships and having fun. The desire to "break out of the mold" has meant big business for the "adventure travel" industry, which specializes in providing white-knuckle experiences. This helps to explain why sports like bungee-jumping, white-water rafting, skydiving, mountain biking and other physically stimulating activities now account for about one-fifth of the leisure travel market.[43]

A decade-long study by American LIVES of San Francisco, claims that about one in four Americans—a segment the firm calls Cultural Creatives—are living by a new set of values. Creatives emphasize new and unique experiences. They are altruistic and less concerned with making a lot of money—though most are middle to upper-middle income. Sixty percent are women. Their key values include:

- *Ecological sustainability*. They are eager to rebuild neighbourhoods and believe in voluntary simplicity.
- *Women's issues*. They are concerned about violence, child abuse and spouse abuse.
- *Spirituality and self-actualization*. They are into spiritual growth, and many are receptive to holistic health products and practices.
- *Social conscience and optimism*. They are willing to devote time and effort to making things better. Three-quarters are involved in volunteer activities.[44]

This shift away from traditional materialism does not mean the end of marketing! However, different approaches and products are needed to reach this new segment. Cultural Creatives tend to rely more on print and radio media rather than TV, and they try to get information from as many different sources as possible. Instead of glitzy ads, they want stories that provide details about the product itself—including where it came from. They look to *Consumer Reports* for purchasing information, they really do read labels, and they are avid consumers of the arts. This segment is looking for ecologically sound, high-mileage cars, and they are also strong purchasers of cottage beers, natural and health foods, exotic vacation travel, and older homes that they can fix up in interesting ways.

- Marketers try to satisfy consumer needs, but the reasons any product is purchased can vary widely. The identification of consumer motives is an important step in ensuring that the appropriate needs will be met by a product.

- Traditional approaches to consumer behaviour have focused on the abilities of products to satisfy rational needs (utilitarian motives), but hedonic motives (such as the needs for exploration or fun) also play a role in many purchase decisions.

CHAPTER SUMMARY

- As demonstrated by Maslow's hierarchy of needs, the same product can satisfy different needs, depending upon the consumer's state at the time (i.e., whether basic physiological needs have already been satisfied). In addition to his or her objective situation, the consumer's degree of involvement with the product must be considered.

- Consumer motivations often are driven by underlying values. In this context, products take on meaning because they are seen as being instrumental in helping the person to achieve some goal that is linked to a value, such as individuality or freedom.

KEY TERMS

Acculturation p. 131

Drive p. 114

Enculturation p. 131

Expectancy theory p. 115

Goal p. 114

Homeostasis p. 115

Inertia p. 125

Instrumental values p. 133

Involvement p. 123

Laddering p. 134

Materialism p. 136

Motivation p. 114

Terminal values p. 133

Theory of cognitive dissonance p. 117

Value p. 130

Value system p. 131

Want p. 116

CONSUMER BEHAVIOUR CHALLENGE

1. Describe three types of motivational conflict, citing an example of each from current marketing campaigns.

2. Devise separate promotional strategies for an article of clothing, each of which stresses one of the levels of Maslow's hierarchy of needs.

3. What is the difference between a want and a need? Do marketers have the power to create needs?

4. Collect several ads that seem to appeal to consumers' values. What value is being communicated in each, and how is this done? Is this an effective approach to designing a marketing communication?

5. Construct a hypothetical means-end chain model for the purchase of a bouquet of roses. How might a florist use this approach to construct a promotional strategy?

6. Describe how a man's level of involvement with his car would affect how he is influenced by different marketing stimuli. How might you design a strategy for a line of car batteries for a segment of low-involvement consumers, and how would this strategy differ from your attempts to reach a segment of men who are very involved in working on their cars?

7. Interview members of a celebrity fan club. Describe their level of involvement with the "product," and devise some marketing opportunities to reach this group.

8. "High involvement is just a fancy term for expensive." Do you agree?

CBC VIDEO VIGNETTES

Concepts at Work for Avon

Avon experienced a serious decrease in sales and profits during the 1990s. Using a metaphor for the industry, it was in need of a make-over. The person hired to develop a strategic direction was Christina Gold, a Canadian who was appointed president of the US parent company. Ms. Gold had spent 24 years working her way from inventory clerk to president of the Canadian operation. This video shows that Ms. Gold's challenge was to restore the motivation of the 400 000 sales representatives.

In the 1950s Avon sold its cosmetics through door-to-door selling in homes, and the sales representatives were compensated by straight commission. This strategy fit the lifestyles and needs of sales representatives, as well as consumers, at that time. Values and needs of consumers changed through the 1970s and 1980s. By the 1990s Avon changed its strategy, in keeping with changes they perceived in their consumers and new ways of doing business: the movement of its customer base into the paid workforce, advances in telecommunication technologies, and the trend towards scrambled merchandising in the retailing industry. This strategy resulted in a downward spiral in sales, and sales representatives who became so disenchanted that some left the company. Ms. Gold perceived a great need to integrate the sales force back into Avon's main selling system and to motivate them by setting up desirable and attainable goals. She realized that the appropriate strategy rested on understanding how customers and sales representatives were motivated and that "something old can be new again."

QUESTIONS

1. Why would customers prefer to purchase merchandise from Avon rather than other companies?

2. Provide a profile of the target segment of typical Avon customers.

3. Why do you think Avon's efforts to sell directly (through advertising) to their potential customers were unsuccessful?

4. Provide a profile of a successful Avon sales representative.

Video Resource: "Avon—Christina Gold," *Venture* #506 (September 18, 1994).

Additional Resources: Tina Parker-Hope, "Ding-Dong: Fewer Sales People Will Help Avon Come Out Ahead," *Wall Street Journal* (April 22, 1997): B1; "The battle to get women into the executive suite; what a few companies are doing," *Women in Management*, Richard Ivey School of Business, 7, 3 (March/April 1997): 5.

NOTES

1. Ronald Paul Hill and Harold Robinson, "Fanatic Consumer Behavior: Athletics as a Consumption Experience," *Psychology & Marketing* 8 (Summer 1991): 79–100.

2. Robert A. Baron, *Psychology: The Essential Science* (Needham, MA: Allyn & Bacon, 1989).

3. Leon Festinger, *A Theory of Cognitive Dissonance* (Stanford, CA: Stanford University Press, 1957).

4. See Paul T. Costa and Robert R. McCrae, "From Catalog to Classification: Murray's Needs and the Five-Factor Model," *Journal of Personality and Social Psychology* 55, 2 (1988): 258–65; Calvin S. Hall and Gardner Lindzey, *Theories of Personality,* 2nd ed. (New York: John Wiley, 1970); James U. McNeal and Stephen W. McDaniel, "An Analysis of Need-Appeals in Television Advertising," *Journal of the Academy of Marketing Science* 12 (Spring 1984): 176–90.

5. See David C. McClelland, *Studies in Motivation* (New York: Appleton-Century-Crofts, 1955).

6. Mary Kay Ericksen and M. Joseph Sirgy, "Achievement Motivation and Clothing Preferences of White-

Collar Working Women," in *The Psychology of Fashion* ed. Michael R. Solomon (Lexington, MA: Lexington Books, 1985): 357–69.

7. See Stanley Schachter, *The Psychology of Affiliation* (Stanford, CA: Stanford University Press, 1959).

8. Eugene M. Fodor and Terry Smith, "The Power Motive as an Influence on Group Decision Making," *Journal of Personality and Social Psychology* 42 (1982): 178–85.

9. C.R. Snyder and Howard L. Fromkin, *Uniqueness: The Human Pursuit of Difference* (New York: Plenum Press, 1980).

10. Abraham H. Maslow, *Motivation and Personality,* 2nd ed. (New York: Harper & Row, 1970).

11. Judith Lynne Zaichkowsky, "Measuring The Involvement Construct in Marketing," *Journal of Consumer Research* 12 (December 1985): 341–52.

12. The literature offers numerous approaches to the construct of involvement. See also Peter H. Bloch, "Involvement Beyond the Purchase Process: Conceptual Issues and Empirical Investigation," in *Advances in Consumer Research 8*, ed. Kent Monroe (Provo, UT: Association for Consumer Research, 1981): 61–65; George S. Day, *Buyer Attitudes and Brand Choice Behavior* (Chicago: Free Press, 1970); Michael J. Houston and Michael L. Rothschild, "Conceptual and Methodological Perspectives on Involvement," in *Research Frontiers in Marketing: Dialogues and Directions* ed. S.C. Jain (Chicago: American Marketing Association, 1978), pp. 184–87; John L. Lastovicka and David Gardner, "Components of Involvement," in *Attitude Research Plays for High Stakes* eds. John C. Maloney and Bernard Silverman (Chicago: American Marketing Association, 1979), pp. 53–73; Andrew Mitchell, "Involvement: A Potentially Important Mediator of Consumer Behavior," in *Advances in Consumer Research 6*, ed. William L. Wilkie (Provo, UT: Association for Consumer Research, 1979), pp. 191–96.

13. Richard L. Celsi and Jerry C. Olson, "The Role of Involvement in Attention and Comprehension Processes," *Journal of Consumer Research* 15 (September 1988): 210–24.

14. Anthony G. Greenwald and Clark Leavitt, "Audience Involvement in Advertising: Four Levels," *Journal of Consumer Research* 11 (June 1984): 581–92.

15. For a recent discussion of interrelationships between situational and enduring involvement, see Marsha L. Richins, Peter H. Bloch and Edward F. McQuarrie, "How Enduring and Situational Involvement Combine to Create Involvement Responses," *Journal of Consumer Psychology* 1, 2 (1992): 143–53.

16. Laurie Freeman, "Fragrance Sniffs Out Daring Adventures," *Advertising Age* (November 6, 1989): 47.

17. Rajeev Batra and Michael L. Ray, "Operationalizing Involvement as Depth and Quality of Cognitive Responses," in *Advances in Consumer Research 10*, eds. Alice Tybout and Richard Bagozzi (Ann Arbor, MI: Association for Consumer Research, 1983), pp. 309–13.

18. Herbert E. Krugman, "The Impact of Television Advertising: Learning Without Involvement," *Public Opinion Quarterly* 29 (Fall 1965): 349–56.

19. For more information on the involvement construct see "Special Issue on Involvement," *Psychology and Marketing* 10, 4 (July/August 1993).

20. Kevin J. Clancy, "CPMs Must Bow to Involvement Measurement," *Advertising Age* (January 20, 1992): 26.

21. The personal involvement inventory reprinted here is a very recent revision of the original Zaichkowsky involvement scale.

22. Data adapted from Judith Lynne Zaichkowsky and James H. Sood, "A Global Look at Consumers' Involvement and Use of Products," *International Marketing Review* 6, 1 (1989): 20–34.

23. For an English translation of this scale, see Jean-Noël Kapferer and Gilles Laurent, "Further Evidence on the Consumer Involvement Profile: Five Antecedents of Involvement," *Psychology and Marketing* 10, 4 (July/August 1993): 347–56; Gilles Laurent and Jean-Noël Kapferer, "Measuring Consumer Involvement Profiles," *Journal of Marketing Research* 22 (February 1985): 41–53 (this scale was recently validated on an American sample as well). Cf. William C. Rodgers and Kenneth C. Schneider, "An Empirical Evaluation of the Kapferer-Laurent Consumer Involvement Profile Scale," *Psychology & Marketing* 10, 4 (July/August 1993): 333–45.

24. Carmen W. Cullen and Scott J. Edgett, "The Role of Involvement in Promoting Management," *Journal of Promotion Management* 1, 2 (1991): 57–71.

25. Deborah J. MacInnis, Christine Moorman and Bernard J. Jaworski, "Enhancing and Measuring Consumers' Motivation, Opportunity, and Ability to Process Brand Information from Ads," *Journal of Marketing* 55 (October 1991): 332–53.

26. James Bennet, "Saturn Invites the 'Family' to a Party," *New York Times* (June 20, 1994): D1 (2 pp.).

27. Bruce Crumley, "Multipoints Add Up for Quick Burger," *Advertising Age* (November 29, 1993): 14.

28. Paul M. Sherer, "North American and Asian Executives Have Contrasting Values, Study Finds," *Wall Street Journal* (March 8, 1996): B12.

29. Milton Rokeach, *The Nature of Human Values* (New York: Free Press, 1973).

30. *A New Partnership: New Values and Attitudes of the New Middle Generation in Japan and the U.S.A.* (Tokyo: Dentsu Institute for Human Studies, 1989).

31. Donald E. Vinson, Jerome E. Scott and Lawrence R. Lamont, "The Role of Personal Values in Marketing and Consumer Behavior," *Journal of Marketing* 41 (April 1977): 44–50; John A. McCarty and L.J. Shrum,

"The Role of Personal Values and Demographics in Predicting Television Viewing Behavior: Implications for Theory and Application," *Journal of Advertising* 22, 4 (December 1993): 77–101.

32. Gregory M. Rose, Aviv Shoham, Lynn R. Kahle and Rajeev Batra, "Social Values, Conformity, and Dress," *Journal of Applied Social Psychology* 24, 17 (1994): 1501–19.

33. Quoted in "New Japanese Fads Blazing Trails in Cleanliness," *Montgomery Advertiser* (September 28, 1996): 10A. Cf. also Andrew Pollack, "Can the Pen Really be Mightier than the Germ?" *New York Times* (July 27, 1995): A4.

34. Milton Rokeach, *Understanding Human Values* (New York: Free Press, 1979). See also J. Michael Munson and Edward McQuarrie, "Shortening the Rokeach Value Survey for Use in Consumer Research," in *Advances in Consumer Research 15*, ed. Michael J. Houston (Provo, UT: Association for Consumer Research, 1988), pp. 381–86.

35. B.W. Becker and P.E. Conner, "Personal Values of the Heavy User of Mass Media," *Journal of Advertising Research* 21 (1981): 37–43; Vinson, Scott and Lamont, "The Role of Personal Values."

36. Sharon E. Beatty, Lynn R. Kahle, Pamela Homer and Shekhar Misra, "Alternative Measurement Approaches to Consumer Values: The List of Values and the Rokeach Value Survey," *Psychology & Marketing* 2 (1985): 181–200; Lynn R. Kahle and Patricia Kennedy, "Using the List of Values (LOV) to Understand Consumers," *Journal of Consumer Marketing* 2 (Fall 1988): 49–56; Lynn R. Kahle, Basil Poulos and Ajay Sukhdial, "Changes in Social Values in the United States During the Past Decade," *Journal of Advertising Research* 28 (February/March 1988): 35–41. See also Wagner A. Kamakura and Jose Afonso Mazzon, "Value Segmentation: A Model for the Measurement of Values and Value Systems,"

Journal of Consumer Research 18, 2 (September 1991): 208–18.

37. Thomas J. Reynolds and Jonathan Gutman, "Laddering Theory, Method, Analysis, and Interpretation," *Journal of Advertising Research* 28 (February/March 1988): 11–34; Beth Walker, Richard Celsi and Jerry Olson, "Exploring the Structural Characteristics of Consumers' Knowledge," in *Advances in Consumer Research 14*, eds. Melanie Wallendorf and Paul Anderson (Provo, UT: Association for Consumer Research, 1986), pp. 17–21.

38. Thomas J. Reynolds and Alyce Byrd Craddock, "The Application of the MECCAs Model to the Development and Assessment of Advertising Strategy: A Case Study," *Journal of Advertising Research* (April/May 1988): 43–54.

39. "25 Years of Attitude," *Marketing Tools* (November/December 1995): 38–39.

40. Marsha L. Richins and Floyd W. Rudmin, "Materialism and Economic Psychology," *Journal of Economic Psychology* 15 (June 1994): 217–31.

41. Güliz Ger and Russell W. Belk, "Cross-Cultural Differences in Materialism," *Journal of Economic Psychology* 17 (1996): 55–77.

42. Marsha L. Richins, "Special Possessions and the Expression of Material Values," *Journal of Consumer Research* 21 (December 1994): 522–33.

43. For an interesting ethnographic account of skydiving as voluntary high-risk consumption activity, see Richard L. Celsi, Randall L. Rose and Thomas W. Leigh, "An Exploration of High-Risk Leisure Consumption Through Skydiving," *Journal of Consumer Research* 20 (June 1993): 1–23. See also Jerry Adler, "Been There, Done That," *Newsweek* (July 19, 1993): 43 (7 pp.).

44. Paul H. Ray, "The Emerging Culture," *American Demographics* (February 1997): 29 (9 pp.).

THE ROAD NOT TAKEN

Rhoda has been trying to concentrate on the report her client is expecting by five o'clock. Rhoda has always worked hard to maintain this important account for the firm, but today she keeps getting distracted thinking about her date last night with Rob. Although things seemed to go OK, why couldn't she shake the feeling that Rob regarded her more as a friend than as a potential romantic partner?

Leafing through *Glamour* and *Cosmopolitan* during her lunch hour, Rhoda is struck by all the articles about ways to be more attractive by dieting, exercising and wearing sexy clothes. Rhoda begins to feel depressed as she looks at the models in the many advertisements for perfumes, apparel and make-up. Each woman is more glamorous and beautiful than the last. She could swear that some of them must have had breast implants and other assorted "adjustments." Women just don't look that way in real life.

In her down mood, Rhoda even entertains the thought that maybe she should look into cosmetic surgery. Even though she's never considered herself unattractive— who knows? Maybe a new nose or liposuction are what it will take for her to feel more attractive. On second thought, though, is it even worth it?...

THE ROAD NOT TAKEN.

Want to know the perfect hood ornament? A man. If ever there was a single product that captured the spirit of the American male it's the automobile. And if ever there was a magazine that did it, it's Playboy. So how come the two of us can't get together?

40 years ago we created the ideal vehicle for Detroit to talk to men, but a billion ads and a zillion readers later there's an astonishing absence of Motown messages for all those guys driven by what they see, hear, discover and believe in Playboy. Guys who go from zero to sixty on features like Automotive Report, articles like *Gotti's Fall*, and Interviews that put an Anne Rice, Betty Friedan or Barry Bonds in the passenger seat.

Yes, we're a frankly male oriented book dedicated to all the dimensions of the male mind, heart and glands, but aren't you folks in the same business? Don't you sell adrenaline? Sensuality? Fantasy? You offer the exhilaration—and acceleration—of the possible. That's what men want, that's what you give them, and that's what Playboy has always been about. A journey through all the fascinating highways, byways and hideaways in the male personality.

Almost 10 million men take that journey every month. It's a shame they're not driving your car.

40th ANNIVERSARY PLAYBOY OPEN UP YOUR MIND.

© PLAYBOY 1994

5

The Self

PERSPECTIVES ON THE SELF

Rhoda is not alone in feeling that her physical appearance and possessions affect her "value" as a person. Consumers' insecurities about their appearance are rampant: it has been estimated that 72 percent of men and 85 percent of women are unhappy with at least one aspect of their appearance.[1] Many products, from cars to cologne, are bought because people are trying to highlight or hide some aspect of the self. This chapter focuses on the self, and we'll consider how consumers' feelings about themselves shape their consumption practices, particularly as they strive to fulfil their society's expectations about how males or females should look and act.

The self can be understood from many different theoretical vantage points. As we'll see in the next chapter, from a psychoanalytic, or Freudian, perspective, the self is a system of competing forces riddled with conflict. As we saw in Chapter 3, behaviourists tend to regard the self as a collection of conditioned responses. From a cognitive orientation, the self is an information-processing system, an organizing force that serves as a nucleus around which new information is processed; more on that in Chapter 8.[2]

Does the Self Exist?

The 1980s was called the "Me Decade" because, for many, this time was marked by an absorption with the self. While it seems natural to think about each consumer as having a self, this concept is actually a relatively new way of regarding people and their relationships to society. The idea that each single human life is unique, rather than a part of a group, only developed in late medieval times (between the eleventh and fifteenth centuries). The notion that the self is an object to be pampered is even more recent. In addition, the emphasis on the unique nature of the self is much greater in Western societies.[3] Many Eastern cultures instead stress the importance of a collective self, in which the person's identity is derived in large measure from his or her social group.

Both Eastern and Western cultures see the self as divided into an inner, private self and an outer, public self. But where they differ is in terms of which part is seen as the "real you": the West tends to subscribe to an independent construal of the self, which emphasizes the inherent separateness of each individual; non-Western cultures, in contrast, tend to focus on an interdependent self, where one's identity is largely defined by the relationships one has with others.[4] For example, a Confucian perspective stresses the importance of "face"—others' perceptions of the self and maintaining one's desired status in their eyes. One dimension of face is *mien-tzu*—reputation achieved through success and ostentation. Some Asian cultures developed explicit rules about the specific garments and even colours that certain social classes and occupations were allowed to display, and these live on today in Japanese style manuals that provide very detailed instructions for dressing and for addressing particular individuals.[5] That orientation is a bit at odds with such Western conventions as "Casual Fridays," which encourage employees to express their unique selves.

Self-Concept

self-concept the attitude a person holds towards himself or herself

The **self-concept** refers to the beliefs a person holds about his or her attributes, and how he or she evaluates these qualities. While one's overall self-concept may be positive, there are certainly parts of the self that are evaluated more positively than others. For example, Rhoda felt better about her professional identity than she did about her feminine identity.

COMPONENTS OF THE SELF-CONCEPT

The self-concept is a very complex structure. It is composed of many attributes, some of which are given greater emphasis in determining overall self-attitude. Attributes of self-concept can be described along such dimensions as their content (e.g., facial attractiveness versus mental aptitude), positivity or negativity (i.e., self-esteem), intensity, stability over time, and accuracy (i.e., the degree to which one's self-assessment corresponds to reality).[6] As will be seen later in the chapter, consumers' self-assessments can be quite distorted, especially with regard to their physical appearance.

SELF-ESTEEM

Self-esteem refers to the positivity of one's attitude towards oneself. People with low self-esteem do not expect that they will perform very well, and they will try to avoid embarrassment, failure or rejection. In developing a new line of snack cakes, Sara Lee found that consumers low in self-esteem preferred portion-controlled snack items because they felt they lacked self-control.[7] In contrast, people with high self-esteem expect to be successful, will take more risks and are more willing to be the centre of attention.[8] Self-esteem often is related to acceptance by others. For example, high- school students who "hang out" in high-status "crowds" have higher self-esteem than their classmates.[9]

Marketing communications can influence a consumer's level of self-esteem. Exposure to ads can trigger a process of *social comparison,* wherein the person tries to evaluate his or her self by comparing it to other people's and those of media images. This form of comparison appears to be a basic human motive, and many marketers have tapped into this need by supplying idealized images of happy, attractive people who just happen to be using their products. A recent study illustrates this process of social comparison. It showed that female college students do tend to compare their physical appearance with that of models who appear in advertising. Furthermore, the study participants who were exposed to beautiful women in advertisements afterwards expressed lowered satisfaction with their *own* appearance, as compared to other participants who did not view ads with models.[10] Another study demonstrated that young women's perceptions of their body shapes and sizes can be altered after they are exposed to as little as 30 minutes of television programming.[11]

Self-esteem advertising attempts to change product attitudes by stimulating positive feelings about the self.[12] One strategy is to flatter the consumer, as when Virginia Slims cigarettes says, "You've come a long way, baby." Sometimes such compliments are derived by comparing the consumer to others. For instance, many consumers are socialized to consider body odours repulsive and are motivated to protect their self-image by denying the existence of these odours in themselves. This attitude explains the success of the theme for Dial soap's advertising: "Aren't you glad you use Dial? Don't you wish everyone did?"[13] Other examples of self-esteem appeals appear in Table 5–1.

TABLE 5–1 Examples of Self-Esteem Appeals in Advertising

PRODUCT	AD THEME
Virginia Slims cigarettes	"You've come a long way, baby."
Clairol hair colouring	"You're not getting older, you're getting better."
Michelob beer	"You know where you're going."
Budweiser beer	"For all you do, this Bud's for you."
Pepsi Cola	"You're feeling good about yourself and you're drinking Diet Pepsi—and it shows."
McDonald's	"You deserve a break today."

Source: Adapted from Jeffrey F. Durgee, "Self-Esteem Advertising," *Journal of Advertising* 14, 4 (1986): 21. Reprinted with permission.

REAL AND IDEAL SELVES

Self-esteem is influenced by a process where the consumer compares his or her actual standing on some attribute to an ideal. A consumer might ask, "Am I as attractive as I would like to be?" "Do I make as much money as I should?" and so on. The **ideal self** is a person's conception of how he or she would like to be, while the **actual self** is our more realistic appraisal of the qualities we do and don't have.

ideal self a person's conception of how he or she would like to be

actual self a person's realistic appraisal of his or her qualities

The ideal self is partly molded by elements of the consumer's culture, such as heroes or people depicted in advertising, that serve as models of achievement or appearance.[14] Products may be purchased because they are believed to be instrumental in helping the consumer achieve the goal of emulating these models. Some products are chosen because they are perceived to be consistent with the consumer's actual self, while others are used to help in reaching the standard set by the ideal self.

FANTASY: BRIDGING THE GAP BETWEEN THE SELVES

fantasy a self-induced shift in consciousness, often focusing on some unattainable or improbable goal; sometimes fantasy is a way of compensating for a lack of external stimulation or for dissatisfaction with the actual self

While most people experience a discrepancy between their real and ideal selves, for some consumers this gap is larger than for others. People for whom this gap is wide are especially good targets for marketing communications that employ *fantasy appeals*.[15] A **fantasy** or daydream is a self-induced shift in consciousness, which is sometimes a way of compensating for a lack of external stimulation or a means of coping with problems in the real world.[16]

Many products and services are successful because they appeal to consumers' tendencies to fantasize. These marketing strategies allow us to extend our vision of ourselves by placing us in unfamiliar, exciting situations or by permitting us to "try on" interesting or provocative roles. Nissan played on this theme in its commercials for the 240SX model. As illustrated by the storyboard shown here, a driver imagines that his girlfriend instead of his dog is with him and then makes a more unlikely substitution, fantasizing that model Christie Brinkley has taken her place.

MARKETING OPPORTUNITY

The aging of the population and the market saturation of material goods for many affluent consumers is fuelling a demand for fantasy experiences. People with ample disposable income appear to be running out of material things to buy, so their attention is instead turning inward, towards an emphasis on consuming experiences rather than status-laden goods. "Experience vacations," as they are called in the travel industry, combine physical and mental exertion and often have a large sensory component. Popular excursions include mountain climbing, going on safaris and exploring primitive countries.

A number of hotels and resorts are targeting the emerging fantasy market. The Fantasyland Hotel in the West Edmonton Mall was one of the first hotels in Canada to capture the imagination of the "local" traveller. Guests can sleep in an igloo or in the back of a pick-up truck. There are a total of 127 theme rooms, many of them with a bedside Jacuzzi. These rooms can be viewed through the mall's Web site at *www.westedmall.com.*

The West Edmonton Mall is the largest mall in the world. Besides containing over 800 shops and services, it features the world's largest indoor amusement park and the world's largest indoor lake.
Courtesy of West Edmonton Mall.

Multiple Selves

In a way, each consumer is really a number of different people. We have as many selves as we have different social roles. Depending upon the situation, we act differently, use different products and services, and even vary in terms of how much we like ourselves. A person may require a different set of products to play a number of desired roles. One may choose to consume beer with close friends but opt for a sophisticated Chardonnay when in business company. The *dramaturgical perspective* on consumer behaviour views people much like actors who play different roles. We each play many roles, and each has its own script, props and costumes.[17]

The self can be thought of as having different components or *role identities,* and only some of these are active at any given time. Some identities (husband, boss or student) are more central to the self than others, but other identities (stamp collector, dancer or advocate for the homeless) may be dominant in specific situations. For example, executives in a survey done in the United States, the United Kingdom and some Pacific Rim countries said that different aspects of their personalities come into play depending on whether they are making purchase decisions at home or at work. Not surprisingly, they report being less time conscious, more emotional and less disciplined in their home roles.[18]

SYMBOLIC INTERACTIONISM

If each person potentially has many social selves, how does each develop, and how do we decide which self to "activate" at any point in time? The sociological tradition of **symbolic interactionism** stresses that relationships with other people play a large part in forming the self.[19] This perspective maintains that people exist in a symbolic environment, and the meaning attached to any situation or object is determined by the interpretation of these symbols. As members of society we learn to agree on shared meanings. Thus we "know" that a red light means stop and the "golden arches" means fast food.

symbolic interactionism a sociological approach stressing that relationships with other people play a large part in forming the self; people live in a symbolic environment, and the meaning attached to any situation or object is determined by a person's interpretation of these symbols

If I had a Nissan 240SX ... it would be a red coupe.

Wait! A silver fastback. And I'd go for a spin up Route 7, the twisty part.

Just me and Astro ...

no, Amy.

Heck, Christie Brinkley!

Wow! Yeah, me and Christie ...

This storyboard for a Nissan 240SX ad illustrates the use of the fantasy theme, which allows consumers to try on new roles and extend their vision of the ideal self.

Reprinted by permission of Nissan Motor Corporation USA and Christie Brinkley.

in my silver—no, red 240SX ... driving into the sunset.

Like other social objects, the meanings of consumers themselves are defined by social consensus. The consumer interprets his or her own identity, and this assessment is continuously evolving as he or she encounters new situations and people. In symbolic interactionist terms, we *negotiate* these meanings over time. Essentially, the consumer poses the question, "Who am I in this situation?" The answer to this question is greatly influenced by those around us and is really an answer to the question, "Who do other people think I am?" We tend to pattern our behaviour on the perceived expectations of others in a form of *self-fulfilling prophecy*. By acting the way we *assume* others expect us to act, we often wind up confirming these perceptions.

THE LOOKING-GLASS SELF

This process of imagining the reactions of others towards us is known as "taking the role of the other," or the **looking-glass self.**[20] According to this view, a process of *reflexive evaluation* occurs when the individual attempts to define the self, and it operates as a sort of psychological sonar: we take readings of our own identity by "bouncing" signals off of others and trying to project what impression they have of us. The looking-glass image we receive will differ depending upon whose views we are considering. Like the images in distorted mirrors in a fun house, our appraisal of who we are can vary, depending upon whose perspective we are taking and how accurately we are able to predict their evaluations of us.

looking-glass self the process of imagining the reaction of others towards oneself

Self-Consciousness

There are times when people seem to be painfully aware of themselves. If you have ever walked into a class in the middle of a lecture and noticed that all eyes were on you, you can understand this feeling of self-consciousness. In contrast, consumers sometimes behave with little self-consciousness. For example, people may do things in a stadium, during a riot or at a party that they would never do if they were highly conscious of their behaviour.[21]

Some people seem, in general, to be more sensitive to the image they communicate to others; while we all know people who act as if they're oblivious to the impression they are making! A heightened concern about the nature of one's public "image" also results in more concern about the social appropriateness of products and consumption activities.

Several measures have been devised to quantify this tendency. Consumers who score high on a scale of *public self-consciousness* are also more interested in clothing and tend to be heavier users of cosmetics.[22] A similar measure is *self-monitoring*. High self-monitors are more attuned to how they present themselves in their social environments, and their product choices are influenced by their estimates of how these items will be perceived by others.[23] Self-monitoring is assessed by the extent of a consumer's agreement with such statements as "I guess I put on a show to impress or entertain others" or "I would probably make a good actor."[24]

High self-monitors are more likely than low self-monitors to evaluate products consumed in public in terms of the impressions they make on others.[25] Similarly, some recent research has looked at aspects of *vanity*, such as a fixation on physical appearance or on the achievement of personal goals. Perhaps not surprisingly, fashion models tend to score higher on this dimension.[26]

CONSUMPTION AND SELF-CONCEPT

By extending the dramaturgical perspective a bit further, one can easily see how the consumption of products and services contributes to the definition of the self. For an actor to play a role convincingly, he or she needs the correct props, stage setting and so on. Consumers learn that different roles are accompanied by *constellations* of products and activities that help to define these roles.[27] Some "props" are so important to the roles we play that they can be viewed as a part of the *extended self,* a concept to be discussed shortly.

Products That Shape the Self: You Are What You Consume

Recall that the reflected self helps to shape self-concept, which implies that people see themselves as they imagine others see them. Since what others see includes a person's clothing, jewellery, furniture, car and so on, it stands to reason that these products also help to determine the perceived self. A consumer's products place him or her into a social role, which helps to answer the question, "Who am I now?"

People use an individual's consumption behaviours to help them make judgments about who that person is. In addition to considering a person's clothes, grooming habits, and so on, we make inferences about personality based on a person's choice of leisure activities (squash versus bowling), food preferences (vegetarians versus "steak-and-potatoes" people), cars, home-decorating choices and so on. People who are shown pictures of someone's living room, for example, are able to make surprisingly accurate guesses about that consumer's personality.[28] In the same way that a consumer's use of products influences others' perceptions, the same products can help to determine his or her *own* self-concept and social identity.[29]

A consumer exhibits *attachment* to an object to the extent that it is used by that person to maintain his or her self-concept.[30] Objects can act as a sort of security blanket by reinforcing our identities, especially in unfamiliar situations. For example, students who decorate their residence rooms with personal items are less likely to drop out of university. This coping process may protect the self from being diluted in a strange environment.[31]

The use of consumption information to define the self is especially important when an identity is yet to be adequately formed, as occurs when a consumer plays a new or unfamiliar role. **Symbolic self-completion theory** predicts that people who have an incomplete self-definition tend to complete this identity by acquiring and displaying symbols associated with it.[32] Adolescent boys, for example, may use "macho" products like cars and cigarettes to bolster their developing masculinity; these products are a sort of "social crutch" to be leaned upon during a period of uncertainty.

The contribution of possessions to self-identity is perhaps most apparent when these treasured objects are lost or stolen. One of the first acts performed by institutions that want to repress individuality and encourage group identity, such as prisons or convents, is to confiscate personal possessions.[33] Victims of burglaries and natural disasters commonly report feelings of alienation, of depression, or of being "violated." One consumer's comment after being robbed is typical: "It's the next worst thing to being bereaved; it's like being raped."[34] Burglary victims exhibit a dimin-

symbolic self-completion theory the perspective that people who have an incomplete self-definition in some context will compensate by acquiring symbols associated with a desired social identity

In emphasizing the notion that looking the right way gives one confidence, this Yes Clothing ad relies on symbolic self-completion theory to appeal to consumers.
© Philippe Berthome for No Comment!

ished sense of community and fewer feelings of privacy and take less pride in their houses' appearance than do their neighbours.[35]

The dramatic impact of product loss is highlighted by studying post-disaster conditions, when consumers may literally lose almost everything but the clothes on their backs following a fire, hurricane, flood or earthquake. Some people are reluctant to undergo the process of re-creating their identity by acquiring all new possessions. Interviews with disaster victims reveal that some are reluctant to invest the self in new possessions and so become more detached about what they buy. This comment from a woman in her fifties is representative of this attitude: "I had so much love tied up in my things. I can't go through that kind of loss again. What I'm buying now won't be as important to me."[36]

Self/Product Congruence

Because many consumption activities are related to self-definition, it is not surprising to learn that consumers demonstrate consistency between their values and attitudes and the things they buy.[37] **Self-image congruence models** predict that products will be chosen when their attributes match some aspect of the self.[38] These models assume a process of cognitive matching between these attributes and the consumer's self-image.[39]

While results are somewhat mixed, the ideal self appears to be more relevant as a comparison standard for highly expressive social products, such as perfume. In contrast, the actual self is more relevant for everyday, functional products. These standards are also likely to vary by usage situation. For example, a consumer might want a functional, reliable car to commute to work every day but a flashier model with more "zing" when going out on a date in the evening.

Research tends to support the idea of congruence between product usage and self-image. One of the earliest studies to examine this process found that car owners' ratings of themselves tended to match their perceptions of their cars. Pontiac drivers, for example, saw themselves as more active and flashier than did Volkswagen drivers.[40] Congruity also has been found between consumers and their most-preferred

self-image congruence models the approaches based on the prediction that products will be chosen when their attributes match some aspect of the self

brands of beer, soap, toothpaste and cigarettes relative to their least-preferred brands, as well as between consumers' self-images and their favourite stores.[41] Some specific attributes that have been found to be useful in describing some of the matches between consumers and products include rugged/delicate, excitable/calm, rational/emotional and formal/informal.[42]

While these findings make some intuitive sense, we cannot blithely assume that consumers will always buy products whose characteristics match their own. It is not clear that consumers really see aspects of themselves in down-to-earth, functional products that don't have very complex or humanlike images. It is one thing to consider a brand personality for an expressive, image-oriented product like perfume and quite another to impute human characteristics to a toaster.

Another problem is the old "chicken-and-egg" question: do people buy products because they are seen as similar to the self, or do they *assume* that these products must be similar because they have bought them? The similarity between a person's self-image and the images of products purchased does tend to increase with ownership, so this explanation cannot be ruled out.

The Extended Self

extended self the definition of self created by the external objects with which one surrounds oneself

As noted earlier, many of the props and settings consumers use to define their social roles in a sense become a part of their selves. Those external objects that we consider a part of us comprise the **extended self.** In some cultures people literally incorporate objects into the self—that is, they lick new possessions, take the names of conquered enemies (or, in some cases, eat them) or bury the dead with their possessions.[43]

We don't usually go that far, but many people do cherish possessions as if they were a part of them. Many material objects, ranging from personal possessions and pets to national monuments or landmarks, help to form a consumer's identity. Just about everyone can name a valued possession that has a lot of the self "wrapped up" in it, whether it is a beloved photograph, a trophy, an old shirt, a car or a cat. Indeed, it is often possible to construct a pretty accurate "biography" of someone just by cataloguing the items on display in his or her bedroom or office.

In one study on the extended self, people were given a list of items that ranged from electronic equipment, facial tissues and television programs to parents, body parts and favourite clothes. They were asked to rate each in terms of its closeness to the self. Objects were more likely to be considered a part of the extended self if "psychic energy" was invested in them by expending effort to obtain them or because they were personalized and kept for a long time.[44]

Four levels of the extended self are used by consumers to define themselves. These range from very personal objects to places and things that allow people to feel as if they are rooted in their environments.[45]

1. *Individual level.* Consumers include many of their personal possessions in self-definition. These products can include jewellery, cars, clothing and so on. The saying "you are what you wear" reflects the belief that one's things are a part of what one is.

2. *Family level.* This part of the extended self includes a consumer's residence and the furnishings in it. The house can be thought of as a symbolic body for the family and is often a central aspect of identity.

3. *Community level.* It is common for consumers to describe themselves in terms of the neighbourhood or town from which they come. For farm families or residents with close ties to a community, this sense of belonging is particularly important.

4. *Group level.* Our attachments to certain social groups also can be considered a part of self. A consumer may feel that landmarks, monuments or sports teams are a part of the extended self.

GENDER ROLES

Gender identity is a very important component of a consumer's self-concept. People often conform to their culture's expectations about what those of their gender should do. Of course, these guidelines change over time, and they can differ radically across societies. It's unclear to what extent gender differences are innate versus culturally shaped, but they're certainly evident in many consumption decisions!

Consider the differences market researchers have observed when comparing the food preferences of men and women. Women eat more fruit. Men are more likely to eat meat; as one food writer put it, "Boy food doesn't grow. It is hunted or killed." Men are more likely to eat Frosted Flakes or Corn Pops, while women prefer multigrain cereals. Men are big root-beer drinkers; women account for the bulk of bottled-water sales.

And the genders differ sharply in the quantities of food they eat. When researchers at Hershey's discovered that women eat smaller amounts of candy, the company created a white chocolate confection called Hugs, one of the most successful food introductions of all time. On the other hand, men are more likely to take their food and drink in larger servings.[46]

Gender Differences in Socialization

A society's assumptions about the proper roles of men and women are communicated in terms of the ideal behaviours that are stressed for each gender (in advertising, among other places). It's likely, for instance, that many women eat smaller quantities because they have been "trained" to be more delicate and dainty.

GENDER GOALS AND EXPECTATIONS

In many societies males are controlled by **agentic goals,** which stress self-assertion and mastery. Females, on the other hand, are taught to value **communal goals,** such as affiliation and the fostering of harmonious relations.[47]

Every society creates a set of expectations regarding the behaviours appropriate for men and women, and finds ways to communicate these priorities. For example, an activity such as Christmas shopping is widely regarded as "women's work."[48] This training begins very young; even children's birthday stories reinforce gender roles. A recent analysis showed that while stereotypical depictions have decreased over time, female characters in children's books are still far more likely to take on nurturing roles such as baking and gift-giving. The adult who prepares the birthday celebration is virtually always the mother; often no adult male is present at all. On the other hand, the male figure in these stories is often cast in the role of a miraculous provider of gifts.[49]

agentic goals goals that favour the advancement of the individual

communal goals goals that favour the well-being of the group or community as a whole

This ad for Bijan illustrates how gender-role identities are culturally bound by contrasting the expectations of how women should appear in two different countries.
Courtesy of Bijan. Photographer Jim Koch.

MACHO MARKETERS

The field of marketing has historically been largely defined by men, so it still tends to be dominated by male values. Competition rather than cooperation is stressed, and the language of warfare and domination is often used. Strategists often employ distinctly masculine concepts: "market penetration" or "competitive thrusts," for example. Academic marketing articles also emphasize agentic rather than communal goals. The most pervasive theme is power and control over others. Other themes include instrumentality (manipulating people for the good of an organization) and competition.[50] This bias may diminish in coming years, as more marketing researchers begin to stress such factors as emotions and aesthetics in purchase decisions—and as increasing numbers of women major in marketing!

GENDER VERSUS SEXUAL IDENTITY

sex-typed traits characteristics that are stereotypically associated with one sex or the other

Sex-role identity is a state of mind as well as body. A person's biological gender (i.e., male or female) does not totally determine whether he or she will exhibit **sex-typed traits,** or characteristics that are stereotypically associated with one sex or the other. A consumer's subjective feelings about his or her sexuality are crucial as well.[51]

Unlike maleness and femaleness, masculinity and femininity are *not* biological characteristics. A behaviour considered masculine in one culture may not be viewed as such in another. For example, the norm that males should be "strong" and repress tender feelings ("Real men don't eat quiche") and that male friends avoid touching each other (except in "safe" situations, such as on the football field) is not universal. In some Latin and European cultures it is common for men to hug one another. Each society determines what "real" men and women should and should not do.

Androgyny

Masculinity and femininity are not opposite ends of the same dimension. **Androgyny** refers to the possession of both masculine and feminine traits.[52] Researchers make a distinction between sex-typed people, who are stereotypically masculine or feminine, and androgynous people, whose mixture of characteristics allows them to function well in a variety of social situations.

androgyny the possession of both masculine and feminine traits

Differences in gender-role orientation can influence responses to marketing stimuli, at least under some circumstances.[53] For example, research evidence indicates that females are likelier to undergo more elaborate processing of message content, so they tend to be more sensitive to specific pieces of information when forming a judgment, while males are more influenced by overall themes.[54] In addition, women with a relatively strong masculine component in their gender-role identity prefer ad portrayals that include nontraditional women.[55] Some research indicates that sex typed people are more sensitive to the sex-role depictions of characters in advertising, although women appear to be more sensitive to gender-role relationships than men.

In one study, subjects read two versions of a beer advertisement, couched in either masculine or feminine terms. The masculine version contained phrases like "X beer has the strong, aggressive flavour that really asserts itself with good food and good company ...," while the feminine version made claims like "Brewed with tender care, X beer is a full-bodied beer that goes down smooth and gentle ..." People who rated themselves as highly masculine or highly feminine preferred the version that was described in very masculine or feminine terms, respectively.[56]

Female Roles

Roles for women are changing rapidly. Social changes, such as the dramatic increase in the proportion of women working outside the home, have led to an upheaval in the way women are regarded by men, in the way they regard themselves and in the products they choose to buy. Modern women now play a greater role in decisions regarding traditionally male purchases. For example, more than six in ten new-car buyers under the age of 50 are female, and women now buy almost half of all condoms sold.[57]

MULTICULTURAL DIMENSIONS

One of the most marked changes in gender roles is occurring in Japan. Traditional Japanese wives stay home and care for children, while their husbands work late and entertain clients. The good Japanese wife is expected to walk two paces behind her husband. However, these patterns are changing as women are less willing to live vicariously through their husbands. More than half of Japanese women aged 25 to 29 are either working or looking for jobs.[58] Japanese marketers and advertisers are beginning to depict women in professional situations (though still usually in subservient roles) and are even developing female market segments for such traditionally male products as automobiles.

SEGMENTING WORKING WOMEN

In the 1949 movie *Adam's Rib,* Katharine Hepburn played a stylish and competent lawyer. This film was one of the first to show that a woman can have a successful career and still be happily married. In this century, married women have frequently worked outside the home, especially during wartime. However, the presence of women in positions of authority is a fairly recent phenomenon. The evolution of a new managerial class of women has forced marketers to change their traditional assumptions about women as they target this growing market.

Ironically, it seems that, in some cases, marketers have overcompensated for their former emphasis on women as housewives. Many attempts to target the vast female working market tend to depict all working women in glamorous, executive positions. This portrayal ignores the facts that the majority of working women do not hold such jobs and that many work because they have to, not for self-fulfilment. This diversity means that all women should not be expected to respond to marketing campaigns that stress professional achievement or the glamour of the working life. These different roles for women are further discussed in Chapter 12.

Whether or not they work outside the home, many women have come to value greater independence and respond positively to marketing campaigns that stress the freedom of women to make their own lifestyle decisions. The American Express Company has been targeting women for a long time, but the company found that its "Do-you-know-me?" campaign did not appeal to women as much as to men. A campaign aimed specifically at women instead featured confident women using their American Express cards. By depicting women in active situations, the company greatly increased its share of the women's credit card market.[59]

THE DEPICTION OF WOMEN IN ADVERTISING

As implied by the ads for Virginia Slims cigarettes—"You've come a long way, baby!"—attitudes about the female role have changed remarkably in this century. Still, women continue to be depicted by advertisers and the media in stereotypical ways. Analyses of ads in such magazines as *Time, Newsweek, Playboy* and even *Ms.* have shown that the large majority of women included were presented as sex objects or in traditional roles.[60] Similar findings have been obtained in the United Kingdom.[61] One of the biggest culprits may be rock videos, which tend to reinforce traditional women's roles. The women portrayed in these videos are usually submissive, and their primary attribute is high physical attractiveness. Recent evidence also indicates an increase in the amount of lingerie and nudity contained in rock videos.[62]

MARKETING PITFALL

Marketers are still grappling with ways to entice female customers—without offending them—to buy traditionally male-oriented products such as cars and computers. One early effort by Tandy Corp. illustrates the potential for these efforts to backfire. When the company decided to market personal computers to women in 1990, it did so by packaging them with software for doing such "feminine" tasks as making Christmas lists, taking inventory of silverware and china, and generating recipes. Women were not amused by the homemaker stereotype, and the campaign flopped.[63]

Although women continue to be depicted in traditional roles, this situation is changing as advertisers scramble to catch up with reality. For example, Avon Products is trying to shed its old-fashioned image by focusing on the concerns of contemporary women. As one recent ad proclaims, "After all, you have more on your mind than what's on your lips. And Avon thinks that's beautiful."[64] Women are now as likely as men to be central characters in television commercials. However, while males increasingly are depicted as spouses and parents, women are still more likely than men to be seen in domestic settings. Also, about 90 percent of all narrators in commercials are male. The deeper male voice apparently is perceived as more authoritative and credible.[65]

Some modern ads now feature role reversal, wherein women occupy traditional men's roles. In other cases women are portrayed in romantic situations, but they are more sexually dominant than formerly. Ironically, current advertising is freer to emphasize traditional female traits now that gender equality is becoming more of an accepted fact. This freedom is demonstrated in a German poster for a women's magazine; the caption reads, "Today's women can sometimes show weakness, because they are strong."

Male Roles

While the traditional conception of the ideal male as a tough, aggressive, muscular man who enjoys "manly" sports and activities is not dead, society's definition of the male role is evolving. Men are allowed to be more compassionate and to have close friendships with other men. In contrast to the depiction of macho men who do not show feelings, some marketers are promoting men's "sensitive side." An emphasis on male bonding has been the centrepiece of many ad campaigns, especially for beer companies.[66]

The prototype of the "new man" was expressed in the positioning statement for Paco Rabanne Pour Homme, a cologne that attempted to focus on this new lifestyle:

Although women in the latter part of this century have "borrowed" some men's colognes, this ad is very clear about Roots UniScent being for both men and women.
Courtesy of Roots Canada.

MARKETING OPPORTUNITY

As gender roles for males evolve, formerly "feminine" products, such as fragrances and hair colouring, have been successfully marketed to men in recent years. Cosmetics companies are now attempting to expand the male market even further. So far the most profitable products are treatments for baldness, but some companies are trying to go even farther.

Estée Lauder, for example, sells four different male skin-care lines. Older men are somewhat resistant to the concept of skin care, and cosmetics marketers cannot use the same appeals they might employ when communicating to female consumers. As one industry consultant noted, "If you tell a man that a product makes his razor burn feel better or it makes him look healthier, he's more likely to respond. The cosmeticky language doesn't work." As explained by an executive with the Bic Corporation, which has a new line of disposable razors for men with different skin types, "Perhaps men's changing roles make it easier for some to acknowledge they had sensitive skin."[67] Lancôme sells an Anti-Wrinkle Creme and an Anti-Aging Eye Balm for men. These and other companies are optimistic about the prospects of appealing to a generation of younger men who will be more open than their older counterparts to cosmetics and skin-care products traditionally designed for women.[68]

"Paco Rabanne Pour Homme is a prestige men's fragrance for the male who is not a clichéd stereotype, the man who understands and accepts the fluidity of male/female relationships." The ideal personality of the target consumer for the cologne was described by the company with adjectives like confident, independent, romantic, tender and playful.[69]

THE JOYS OF FATHERHOOD

Males' lifestyles are changing to allow greater freedom of expression in clothing choices, hobbies such as cooking, and so on. Men also are getting more involved in parenting, and advertising campaigns for such companies as Kodak, Omega (watches) and Pioneer (electronics) stress the theme of fatherhood.[70] Still, this change is coming slowly. A commercial for 7-Eleven stores showed two men out for a walk, each pushing a stroller. As they near a 7-Eleven, they begin to push their strollers faster until they are racing. As the campaign's creative director explained, "We showed them engaged in a competition to make it easier for men to accept the concept of taking care of children."[71]

Gay and Lesbian Consumers

The proportion of the population that is gay and lesbian is difficult to determine, and efforts to measure this group have been controversial.[72] However, the respected research company Yankelovich Partners Inc., which has tracked consumer values and attitudes since 1971 in its annual Monitor survey, now includes a question about sexual identity in its survey. This was the first commercial survey to use a sample that reflects the population as a whole instead of polling only smaller or biased groups (such as readers of gay publications) whose responses may not be representative of all consumers. About 6 percent of respondents described themselves as "gay/homosexual/lesbian."

The results, therefore, help to paint a more accurate picture of the potential size and attractiveness of this segment. For example, contrary to earlier surveys that reported homosexuals to be far more affluent than the general population, this study found few differences in household income. On the other hand, additional findings underscore the potential desirability of this segment for marketers: homosexuals are twice as likely as heterosexuals to have attended graduate school, are more concerned about physical fitness and self-improvement, experience more stress in their daily lives (making them good prospects for security systems and vacations), and are much more likely to be self-employed. This means that they are an excellent market for fax machines, cellular phones and other high-tech products.[73]

As social gains are made by gay activists, the social climate is becoming more favourable for firms targeting this market segment.[74] At least in some parts of North America, homosexuality appears to be becoming a bit more mainstream and accepted. Mattel even sold an Earring Magic Ken doll, complete with *faux*-leather vest, lavender mesh shirt and two-tone hairdo (though the company removed the product from its line following reports that it had become a favourite of gay men).[75] Nevertheless, about 40 percent of Monitor™ respondents said they would prefer not to have a homosexual as a friend. When comedian Ellen DeGeneres "came out" as a lesbian on prime-time television in 1997, many advertisers chose not to place commercials on the show. On the other hand, the episode's Nielsen rating was 144 percent higher than average, so clearly someone was watching![76] Canada has many openly gay politicians who have served their constituents over many terms. Some say their success is due to the fact that they are honest about their private lifestyle and are therefore likely to be honest and trustworthy in public life.

This German ad for New West cigarettes features a gay wedding. The headline focuses on the brand's strong taste, depicting it as the choice of fearless individuals.
Ad Age (Global Gallery), March 8, 1993, p. 40. Photo courtesy of Scholz & Friends, Hamburg.

BODY IMAGE

body image a consumer's subjective evaluation of his or her physical self

A person's physical appearance is a large part of his or her self-concept. **Body image** refers to a consumer's subjective evaluation of his or her physical self. This image is not necessarily accurate. A man may think of himself as being more muscular than he really is, or a woman may feel she appears fatter than is the case. In fact, it is not uncommon to find marketing strategies that exploit consumers' tendencies to distort their body images by preying upon insecurities about appearance, thereby creating a gap between the real and ideal physical self and, consequently, the desire to purchase products and services to narrow that gap.

Body Cathexis

body cathexis a person's feelings about aspects of his or her body

A person's feelings about his or her body can be described in terms of **body cathexis.** *Cathexis* refers to the emotional significance of some object or idea to a person, and some parts of the body are more central to self-concept than others. One study of young adults' feelings about their bodies found that these respondents were the most satisfied with their hair and eyes and had the least positive feelings about their waists. These feelings also were related to usage of grooming products. Consumers who were more satisfied with their bodies were more frequent users of such "preening" products as hair conditioner, blow-dryers, cologne, facial bronzer, tooth polish and pumice soap.[77]

Ideals of Beauty

ideal of beauty a model, or exemplar, of appearance valued by a culture

A person's satisfaction with the physical image he or she presents to others is affected by how closely that image corresponds to the image valued by his or her culture. An **ideal of beauty** is a particular model, or exemplar, of appearance. Female ideals of beauty include physical features (large lips or small lips, big breasts or small breasts) as well as such aspects as clothing styles, cosmetics, hairstyles, skin tone (pale versus tan) and body type (petite, athletic or voluptuous).

IS BEAUTY UNIVERSAL?

Recent research indicates that preferences for some physical features over others are "wired in" genetically and that these reactions tend to be the same among people around the world. Specifically, people appear to favour features associated with good health and youth, attributes linked to reproductive ability and strength. These characteristics include large eyes, high cheekbones and a narrow jaw.

Of course, the way these faces are "packaged" still varies enormously, and that's where marketers come in: advertising and other forms of mass media play a significant role in determining which forms of beauty are considered desirable at any point in time. An ideal of beauty functions as a sort of cultural yardstick. Consumers compare themselves to some standard (often advocated by fashion media) and are dissatisfied with their appearance to the extent that they don't match up to it.

These cultural ideals often are summed up in a sort of cultural shorthand. We may talk about a "vamp," a "girl next door" or an "ice queen," or we may refer to specific women who have come to embody an ideal, such as Sarah McLachlan, Mar-

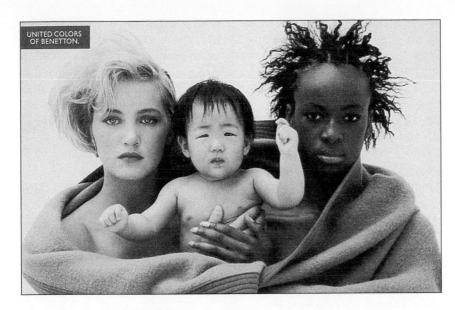

As suggested by this Benetton ad, a global perspective on ideals of beauty is resulting in more ways to be considered attractive.
Photo by Oliviero Toscani for Benetton.

ilyn Monroe or Princess Diana.[78] Similar descriptions for men include "jock," "pretty boy" and "bookworm," or a "Brad Pitt type," a "Michael Jordan type" and so on.

In retrospect, periods of history tend to be characterized by a specific "look," or ideal of beauty. For example, in sharp contrast to today's emphasis on health and vigour, in the early 1800s it was fashionable to appear delicate to the point of looking ill. The poet Keats described the ideal woman of that time as "a milk white lamb that bleats for man's protection." Other popular looks have included the voluptuous, lusty woman as epitomized by Lillian Russell; the athletic Gibson Girl of the 1890s; and the small, boyish flapper of the 1920s, exemplified by Clara Bow.[79]

In much of the nineteenth century the desirable waistline for American women was 18 inches (45 cm), a circumference that required the use of corsets pulled so tight that they routinely caused headaches, fainting spells and possibly even the uterine and spinal disorders common among women of the time. While modern women are not quite as "straightlaced," many still endure such indignities as high heels, body waxing, eye lifts and liposuction. In addition to the millions spent on cosmetics, clothing, health clubs and fashion magazines, these practices remind us that the desire to conform to current standards of beauty—rightly or wrongly—is alive and well.

The ideal body type of Western women has changed radically over time, and these changes have resulted in a realignment of *sexual dimorphic markers*—those aspects of the body that distinguish between the sexes. For example, analyses of the measurements of *Playboy* centrefolds over a 20-year period from 1958 to 1978 show that these ideals got thinner and more muscular. The average hip measurement went from 36 inches (91 cm) in 1958 to just over 34 inches (86 cm) in 1978. Average bust size shrank from almost 37 inches (94 cm) in 1958 to about 35 inches (89 cm) in 1978.[80]

The first part of the 1990s saw the emergence of the controversial "waif" look, where successful models (most notably Kate Moss) were likely to have bodies resembling those of young boys. The pendulum seems to be shifting back a bit, as the more buxom, hourglass figure popular in the 1950s (exemplified by the Marilyn

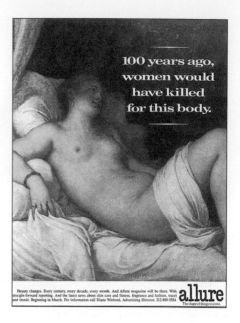

Allure magazine reminds us that ideals of beauty change over time.
Reprinted by permission of Allure magazine.
Copyright © 1990 by The Condé Nast Publications, Inc.

Monroe ideal) has reappeared.[81] One factor leading to this change has been the opposition to the use of overly thin models by feminist groups, who charge that these role models encourage starvation diets and eating disorders among women who want to emulate the look.[82] These groups have advocated boycotts against companies like Coca-Cola and Calvin Klein that have used wafer-thin models in their advertising. Some protesters have even taken to pasting stickers over these ads that read "Feed this woman" and "Give me a cheeseburger."

We can also distinguish among ideals of beauty for men in terms of facial features, musculature, facial hair and so on—who could confuse Tom Cruise with Fabio? In fact, one recent national survey that asked both men and women to comment on male aspects of appearance found that the dominant standard of beauty for men is a strongly masculine, muscled body, though women tend to prefer men with less muscle mass than men themselves strive to attain. And, at this point in time, clean-shaven men are preferred.[83]

Working on the Body

Because many consumers are motivated to match up to some ideal of appearance, they often go to great lengths to change aspects of their physical selves. From cosmetics to plastic surgery, tanning salons to diet drinks, a multitude of products and services are directed towards altering or maintaining aspects of the physical self in order to present a desirable appearance. It is difficult to overstate the importance of the physical self-concept (and the desire by consumers to improve their appearance) to many marketing activities.

HAIR AND THE SELF

Grant McCracken has provided a complete analysis of how our hair forms the basis for the presentation of self-image, and how it can be used as a tool to transform or change one's image.[84] Haircuts are a regular part of the consumption process. Many

MULTICULTURAL DIMENSIONS

Cosmetic surgeons often try to mold their patients into a standard ideal of beauty, using the features of such Caucasian classic beauties as Grace Kelly or Katharine Hepburn as guides. The aesthetic standard used by surgeons is called the *classic canon,* which spells out the ideal relationships among facial features. For example, it states that the width of the base of the nose should be the same as the distance between the eyes.

However, this standard applies to the Caucasian ideal and is being revised as people from other ethnic groups are demanding less rigidity in culture's definition of what is beautiful. Some consumers are rebelling against the need to conform to the Western ideal. For example, a rounded face is valued as a sign of beauty by many Asians, so that giving cheek implants to an Asian patient would remove much of what makes her face attractive.

Racial differences in beauty ideals also surfaced in a recent study of teenagers. White girls who were asked to describe the "ideal" girl agreed she should be 5 feet 7 inches (170 cm), weigh between 100 and 110 pounds (45–50 kg), and have blue eyes and long flowing hair—in other words, she should look a lot like a Barbie doll. Almost 90 percent of the girls in this study said they were dissatisfied with their weight.

In contrast, 70 percent of the black girls in the study responded that they were satisfied with their weight. They were much less likely to use physical characteristics to describe the ideal girl, instead emphasizing someone who has a personal sense of style and who gets along with others. It was only when prodded that they named such features as fuller hips, large thighs and a small waist, which the authors of the study say are attributes valued by black men.[85]

people, especially men, adhere to a four-week schedule for the grooming ritual. However, much of McCracken's discussion focuses around women as he found men to be much vainer about their hair and reluctant to discuss the topic. This may be because, genetically, men are more prone to lose their hair. To compensate for this male phenomena, male folklore such as "baldness is a sign of virility" has evolved. Men are also secretive about dyeing their hair. It is obvious they do it, but it is not a hot topic on the golf course.

So McCracken concentrates his analysis on women. Both hair styles and hair colour are used to project images that match the needs and social structure of the era and the individual. A blonde is not simply a blonde: she is a bombshell (Mae West), sunny (Goldie Hawn), brassy (Cybill Shepperd), dangerous (Sharon Stone), a society leader (Ivana Trump) and cool (Grace Kelly). Brunettes are said to be self-confident, because no one cares about their hair colour; it is never a topic of discussion, therefore personalities are diversified rather than stereotyped. Redheads are said to be "hot-headed" and "energetic," as typified by Lucille Ball. Red is the tint of choice for French women. There are no subtleties in the projection of the redhead's image.

The preference for long hair or short hair is reflective of the social situation. Long flowing hair is said to very sexy and maybe even dangerous. Short hair is said to be "boyish" or a signal that one is simplifying one's life. Men are said to find the "pixie" cut unthreatening and attractive. But they seem to draw the line at women

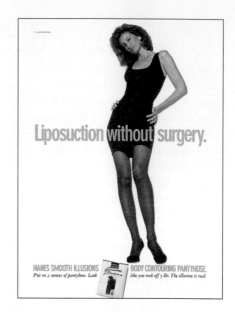

This ad for Hanes Smooth Illusions pantyhose claims to provide women who want to change their shape with an alternative to surgery.
Courtesy of Sara Lee Corporation.

shaving their heads completely bald. This style is said to portray a tough image, which is hostile and provocative.

Whenever we want to transform our image, we change our hair along with our clothes. With changes in age, lifestyle, careers and even partners comes an inevitable change in colour or style of hair.

FATTISM

As reflected in the expression "you can never be too thin or too rich," our society has an obsession with weight. Even elementary-school children perceive obesity as worse than being handicapped or disabled.[86] The pressure to be slim is continually reinforced both by advertising and by peers. North Americans in particular are preoccupied with what they weigh. We are continually bombarded by images of thin, happy people.

The desire to be thin has had a big impact on consumers' lifestyles and eating habits. A number of companies specifically target the weight conscious: Weight Watchers International, the largest weight-loss company, developed a new program called Quick Success that recognizes the new lifestyles of busy working women. This program includes eating guidelines for working lunches and cocktail parties.[87]

A similar program in Australia is called "Gut Busters." This program is for men only. The middle bulge is obvious in men who drive trucks or sit at a desk all day. The "Gut Buster" program is designed to focus particularly on male-dominated food habits. Instead of reaching for a cheeseburger and fries at a truck stop or fast-food outlet, men are conditioned to accept something less fatty and easier to digest, but more "feminine" by food image, such as fruit and salads. In Canada, "Harvey Brooker Weight Loss for Men" offers a similar program in Toronto and Montreal. Many of the clients are executives who have suffered through rich lunches and dinners and long hours at a desk.

BODY IMAGE DISTORTIONS

While many people perceive a strong link between self-esteem and appearance, some consumers unfortunately exaggerate this connection even more and make great sacrifices to attain what they consider to be a desirable body image. Women tend to be taught to a greater degree than men that the quality of their bodies reflects their self-worth, so it is not surprising that most major distortions of body image occur among females.

Men's opinions do not tend to differ in ratings of their current figure, their ideal figure and the figure they think is most attractive to women. In contrast, women rate both the figure they think is most attractive to men and their ideal figure as much thinner than their actual figure.[88] In one survey two-thirds of university women admitted resorting to unhealthy behaviour to control weight. Advertising messages that convey an image of slimness help to reinforce these activities by arousing insecurities about weight.[89]

A distorted body image has been linked to the rise of eating disorders. People with *anorexia* always see themselves as fat and virtually starve themselves in the quest for thinness. This condition often results in *bulimia,* which involves two stages. First, binge eating occurs (usually in private), where more than 5000 calories may be consumed at one time. The binge is then followed by induced vomiting, abuse of laxatives, fasting and/or overly strenuous exercise—a "purging" process that reasserts the woman's sense of control.

Most eating disorders are found in white, upper-middle-class teenaged and university-aged girls. Victims often have brothers or fathers who are hypercritical of their weight, and these disorders are also associated with a history of sexual abuse.[90]

Eating disorders have also been documented in men. They are common among male athletes, such as jockeys, boxers and male models, who must also conform to various weight requirements.[91] In general, though, most men who have distorted body images consider themselves to be too light rather than too heavy: society has taught them that they must be muscular to be masculine. Men are more likely than women to express their insecurities about their bodies by becoming addicted to exercise. In fact, striking similarities have been found between male compulsive runners and female anorexics. These include a commitment to diet and exercise as a central part of one's identity and susceptibility to body-image distortions.[92]

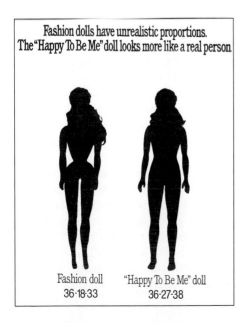

Fashion dolls have unrealistic proportions. The "Happy To Be Me" doll looks more like a real person.

Fashion doll
36-18-33

"Happy To Be Me" doll
36-27-38

To counter messages sent out to girls about what their bodies should look like, a (female) entrepreneur designed the Happy To Be Me doll.
Reprinted with permission from Marketing News, *published by the American Marketing Association.*

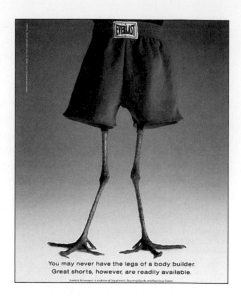

This Everlast apparel ad acknowledges the popularity of body-building in a humorous way. As marketers know well, many kinds of athletic apparel, such as shoes and warm-up suits, are purchased by "armchair athletes," who don't bother to play the sports for which these products were intended.
Winner—New York Festivals International Advertising Awards Agency: Goldsmith Jeffrey, USA. Photo courtesy of Everlast Sports, NY.

COSMETIC SURGERY

Consumers are electing in increasing numbers to have cosmetic surgery to change poor body images.[93] There is no longer much (if any) psychological stigma associated with having this type of operation; it is commonplace and accepted among many segments of consumers.[94] In fact, men now account for as much as 20 percent of plastic-surgery patients. Popular operations for men include the implantation of silicon pectoral muscles (for the chest) and calf implants to fill out "chicken legs."[95]

Many women turn to surgery either to reduce weight or to increase sexual desirability. The use of the liposuction procedure, in which fat is removed from the thighs with a vacuumlike device, has almost doubled since it was first introduced in 1982.[96]Some women feel that larger breasts will increase their allure and so undergo breast-augmentation procedures. Although some of these procedures have generated controversy due to possible negative side effects, it is unclear whether potential medical problems will deter large numbers of women from choosing surgical options to enhance their (perceived) femininity.

The importance of breast size to self-concept resulted in an interesting and successful marketing strategy undertaken by an underwear company. While conducting focus groups on bras, an analyst noted that small-chested women typically reacted with hostility when discussing the subject. They unconsciously covered their chests with their arms as they spoke, and they felt that their needs were ignored by the fashion industry. To meet this overlooked need, the company introduced a line of A-cup bras called "A-OK" and depicted wearers in a positive light. A new market segment was born.

Other companies are going in the opposite direction, pushing bras that create the illusion of a larger cleavage. In Europe and the United States, both Gossard and Playtex are aggressively marketing specially designed bras offering "cleavage enhancement" that use a combination of wires and internal pads (called "cookies" in the industry) to create the desired effect. A California company, taking a page from the craze for pump sneakers, introduced Top Secret, a bikini with built-in inflatable "falsies" as a "remedy" for flat-chested women.[97] Despite some protests by feminists, sales are booming as consumers' preferences for the ideal body type shift once again.[98]

The Body Shop positions its company and products on a positive self-image for women.
Reprinted with permission from The Body Shop.

BODY DECORATION AND MUTILATION

The body is adorned or altered in some way in every culture. Decorating the self serves a number of purposes.[99]

- *To separate group members from nonmembers.* The Chinook Indians of North America pressed the head of a newborn between two boards for a year, permanently altering its shape. In our society teens go out of their way to adopt distinctive hair and clothing styles that will separate them from adults.

- *To place the individual in the social organization.* Many cultures engage in puberty rites, wherein a boy symbolically becomes a man. Young men in Ghana paint their bodies with white stripes to resemble skeletons, symbolizing the death of their child status. In Western culture this rite may involve some form of mild self-mutilation or engagement in dangerous activities.

- *To place the person in a gender category.* The Tchikrin Indians of South America insert a string of beads in a boy's lip to enlarge it. Western women wear lipstick to enhance femininity. At the turn of the century, small lips were fashionable because they represented women's submissive role at that time.[100] Today, big red lips are provocative and indicate an aggressive sexuality. Some women, including a number of famous actresses and models, receive collagen injections or lip inserts to create large, pouting lips (known in the modelling industry as "liver lips").[101]

- *To enhance sex-role identification.* The modern use of high heels, which podiatrists agree are a prime cause of knee and hip problems, backaches and fatigue, can be compared with the traditional Asian practice of foot binding to enhance femininity. As one doctor observed, "When they [women] get home, they can't get their high-heeled shoes off fast enough. But every doctor in the world could yell from now until Doomsday, and women would still wear them."[102]

- *To provide a sense of security.* Consumers often wear lucky charms, amulets, rabbits' feet and so on to protect them from the "evil eye."

Tattoos—both temporary and permanent—are a popular form of body adornment. This body art can be used to communicate aspects of the self to onlookers and may serve some of the same functions that other kinds of body painting do in primitive cultures. Tattoos (from the Tahitian ta-tu) have deep roots in folk art. Until recently the images were crude, consisting primarily either of death symbols (such as a skull), animals (especially panthers, eagles and snakes), pin-up women or military designs. More current influences include science-fiction themes, Japanese symbolism and tribal designs.

A tattoo may be viewed as a fairly risk-free way of expressing an adventurous side of the self. Tattoos have a long history of association with people who are social outcasts. The faces and arms of criminals in sixth-century Japan were tattooed as a means to identify them, as were Massachusetts prison inmates in the nineteenth century. These emblems are often used by marginal groups, such as bikers or Japanese *yakuze* (gang members), to express group identity and solidarity.[103]

BODY PIERCING

Decorating the body with various kinds of metallic inserts also has evolved from a practice associated with some fringe groups and natives in Third World countries to become a popular fashion statement. Piercing can and is being done on all parts of the body. There are over a million Web sites related to the practice of body piercing. Publications like *Piercing Fans International Quarterly* are seeing their circulation soar, and Web sites like ***www.customdreams.com*** are attracting numerous followers. This popularity is not pleasing to hard-core piercing fans, who view the practice as a sensual consciousness-raising ritual and are concerned that people now do it simply because it's trendy. As one customer waiting for a nipple piercing remarked, "If your piercing doesn't mean anything, then it's just like buying a pair of platform shoes."[104]

CHAPTER SUMMARY

- Consumers' self-concepts are reflections of their attitudes towards themselves. Whether these attitudes are positive or negative, they will help to guide many purchase decisions; products can be used to bolster self-esteem or to "reward" the self.

- Many product choices are dictated by the consumer's perception of a similarity between his or her personality and attributes of the product. The symbolic interactionist perspective on the self implies that each of us actually has many selves, and a different set of products is required as props to play each role. Many things other than the body can also be viewed as part of the self. Valued objects, cars, homes and even attachments to sports teams or national monuments are used to define the self when these are incorporated into the extended self.

- A person's gender-role identity is a major component of self-definition. Conceptions about masculinity and femininity, largely shaped by society, guide the acquisition of "gender-typed" products and services.

- Advertising and other media play an important role in socializing consumers to be male and female. While traditional women's roles have often been perpetuated in advertising depictions, this situation is changing somewhat. The media do not always portray men accurately, either.

- A person's conception of his or her body also provides feedback to self-image. A culture communicates certain ideals of beauty, and consumers go to great lengths to attain these. Many consumer activities involve manipulating the body, whether through dieting, cosmetic surgery, tattooing or the like.

- Sometimes these activities are carried to an extreme, as people try too hard to live up to cultural ideals. One example is found in eating disorders, wherein women in particular become obsessed with thinness.

KEY TERMS

Actual self p. 146
Agentic goals p. 153
Androgyny p. 155
Body cathexis p. 160
Body image p. 160
Communal goals p. 153

Extended self p. 152
Fantasy p. 146
Ideal of beauty p. 160
Ideal self p. 146
Looking-glass self p. 149
Self-concept p. 144

Self-image congruence models p. 151
Sex-typed traits p. 154
Symbolic interactionism p. 147
Symbolic self-completion theory p. 150

CONSUMER BEHAVIOUR CHALLENGE

1. How might the creation of a self-conscious state be related to consumers who are trying on clothing in dressing rooms? Does the act of preening in front of a mirror change the dynamics by which people evaluate their product choices? Why?

2. Is it ethical for marketers to encourage infatuation with the self?

3. List three dimensions by which the self-concept can be described.

4. Compare and contrast the real versus the ideal self. List three products for which each type of self is likely to be used as a reference point when a purchase is considered.

5. Watch a set of ads on television featuring men and women. Try to imagine the characters with reversed roles (i.e., the male parts played by women and vice versa). Can you see any differences in assumptions about gender-typed behaviour?

6. To date, the bulk of advertising targeted to gay consumers has been placed in exclusively gay media. If it were your decision, would you consider using mainstream media as well to reach gays, who constitute a significant proportion of the general population? Or, remembering that members of some targeted segments have serious objections about this practice, especially when the product (e.g., liquor or cigarettes) may be viewed as harmful in some way, do you think gays should be singled out at all by marketers?

7. Do you agree that marketing strategies tend to have a male-oriented bias? If so, what are some possible consequences for specific marketing activities?

8. In the past, some marketers have been reluctant to use disabled people in advertising out of fear they would be seen as patronizing or that their ads would be depressing. Should the disabled be viewed as a distinct market segment, or

should marketers continue to assume that their wants and needs are the same as those of the rest of the mainstream market?

9. Some consumer advocates have protested the use of superthin models in advertising, claiming that these women encourage others to starve themselves in order to attain the "waif" look. Other critics respond that the media's power to shape behaviour has been overestimated and that it is insulting to people to assume that they are unable to separate fantasy from reality. What do you think?

CBC VIDEO VIGNETTES

Concepts at Work for Divorce Magazine

Some consumer purchases are motivated by a need to transform oneself, especially in a time of personal change. Clearly, services such as laser eye surgery, plastic surgery and hairstyling, alter the physical presence of consumers' social selves. However, products and services may also facilitate internal self-transformation. One example is a new entrant in the print media, Divorce Magazine (*www.divorcemag.com*). This magazine is positioned as a vehicle to help readers "start a new life" and focuses on relationships.

The prevalence of divorce has resulted in societal acceptance of this life event as worthy of personal reflection, renewal and self-transformation. Like other life events, such as marriage, the birth of a first child and graduation, a divorce marks a new beginning. Personality and purchasing behaviour often change as adjustments are made to the self-concept and the presentation of the social self. Due to the internal nature of the self, the challenge for marketers is to determine to what extent marketing strategies to help serve consumer transformations need to be tailored to micro-markets or regional markets, rather than to macro-markets or mass markets.

QUESTIONS

1. Which life events are tied closely to one's self-concept?

2. What kinds of purchasing behaviour provide self-expression of these changes?

3. Are there gender effects evident in such purchasing behaviour?

4. What are the implications of what we know about the transformation of self for the marketing strategy for *Divorce Magazine*?

Video Resource: "Divorce Magazine," *Venture* #611 (October 6, 1996).

Additional Resource: www.divorcemag.com

NOTES

1. Daniel Goleman, "When Ugliness is Only in Patient's Eye, Body Image Can Reflect Mental Disorder," *New York Times* (October 2, 1991): C13.

2. Anthony G. Greenwald and Mahzarin R. Banaji, "The Self as a Memory System: Powerful, But Ordinary," *Journal of Personality and Social Psychology* 57, 1 (1989): 41–54; Hazel Markus, "Self-Schemata and Processing Information About the Self," *Journal of Personality and Social Psychology* 35 (1977): 63–78.

3. Harry C. Triandis, "The Self and Social Behavior in Differing Cultural Contexts," *Psychological Review* 96, 3 (1989): 506–20; H. Markus and S. Kitayama, "Culture and the Self: Implications for Cognition, Emotion, and Motivation," *Psychological Review* 98 (1991): 224–53.

4. Markus and Kitayama, "Culture and the Self."

5. Nancy Wong and Aaron Ahuvia, "A Cross-Cultural Approach to Materialism and the Self," in *Cultural Dimensions of International Marketing*, ed. Dominique Bouchet (Denmark: Odense University, 1995), pp. 68–69.

6. Morris Rosenberg, *Conceiving the Self* (New York: Basic Books, 1979); M. Joseph Sirgy, "Self-Concept in Consumer Behavior: A Critical Review," *Journal of Consumer Research* 9 (December 1982): 287–300.

7. Emily Yoffe, "You Are What You Buy," *Newsweek* (June 4, 1990): 59.

8. Roy F. Baumeister, Dianne M. Tice and Debra G. Hutton, "Self-Presentational Motivations and Personality Differences in Self-Esteem," *Journal of Personality* 57 (September 1989): 547–75; Ronald J. Faber, "Are Self-Esteem Appeals Appealing?" in *Proceedings of the 1992 Conference of The American Academy of Advertising,* ed. Leonard N. Reid (1992): 230–35.

9. B. Bradford Brown and Mary Jane Lohr, "Peer-Group Affiliation and Adolescent Self-Esteem: An Integration of Ego-Identity and Symbolic-Interaction Theories," *Journal of Personality and Social Psychology* 52, 1 (1987): 47–55.

10. Marsha L. Richins, "Social Comparison and the Idealized Images of Advertising," *Journal of Consumer Research* 18 (June 1991): 71–83; Mary C. Martin and Patricia F. Kennedy, "Advertising and Social Comparison: Consequences for Female Preadolescents and Adolescents," *Psychology & Marketing* 10, 6 (November/December 1993): 513–30.

11. Philip N. Myers, Jr. and Frank A. Biocca, "The Elastic Body Image: The Effect of Television Advertising and Programming on Body Image Distortions in Young Women," *Journal of Communication* 42 (Summer 1992): 108–33.

12. Jeffrey F. Durgee, "Self-Esteem Advertising," *Journal of Advertising* 14, 4 (1986): 21.

13. Ernest Dichter, *Handbook of Consumer Motivations* (New York: McGraw-Hill, 1964).

14. Sigmund Freud, *New Introductory Lectures in Psychoanalysis* (New York: Norton, 1965).

15. Harrison G. Gough, Mario Fioravanti and Renato Lazzari, "Some Implications of Self Versus Ideal-Self Congruence on the Revised Adjective Check List," *Journal of Personality and Social Psychology* 44, 6 (1983): 1214–20.

16. Steven Jay Lynn and Judith W. Rhue, "Daydream Believers," *Psychology Today* (September 1985): 14.

17. Erving Goffman, *The Presentation of Self in Everyday Life* (Garden City, NY: Doubleday, 1959); Michael R. Solomon, "The Role of Products as Social Stimuli: A Symbolic Interactionism Perspective," *Journal of Consumer Research* 10 (December 1983): 319–29.

18. Julie Skur Hill, "Purchasing Habits Shift for Execs," *Advertising Age* (April 27, 1992): 1–16.

19. George H. Mead, *Mind, Self and Society* (Chicago: University of Chicago Press, 1934).

20. Charles H. Cooley, *Human Nature and the Social Order* (New York: Scribner's, 1902).

21. J.G. Hull and A.S. Levy, "The Organizational Functions of the Self: An Alternative to the Duval and Wicklund Model of Self-Awareness," Journal of Personality and Social Psychology 37 (1979): 756–68; Jay G. Hull et al., "Self-Consciousness and the Processing of Self-Relevant Information," Journal of Personality and Social Psychology 54, 3 (1988): 452–65.

22. Arnold W. Buss, *Self-Consciousness and Social Anxiety* (San Francisco: W.H. Freeman, 1980); Lynn Carol Miller and Cathryn Leigh Cox, "Public Self-Consciousness and Makeup Use," *Personality and Social Psychology Bulletin* 8, 4 (1982): 748–51; Michael R. Solomon and John Schopler, "Self-Consciousness and Clothing," *Personality and Social Psychology Bulletin* 8, 3 (1982): 508–14.

23. Morris B. Holbrook, Michael R. Solomon and Stephen Bell, "A Re-Examination of Self-Monitoring and Judgments of Furniture Designs," *Home Economics Research Journal* 19 (September 1990): 6–16; Mark Snyder, "Self-Monitoring Processes," in *Advances in Experimental Social Psychology,* ed. Leonard Berkowitz (New York: Academic Press, 1979): 851–928.

24. Mark Snyder and Steve Gangestad, "On the Nature of Self-Monitoring: Matters of Assessment, Matters of Validity," *Journal of Personality and Social Psychology* 51 (1986): 125–39.

25. Timothy R. Graeff, "Image Congruence Effects on Product Evaluations: The Role of Self-Monitoring and Public/Private Consumption," *Psychology & Marketing* 13, 5 (August 1996): 481–99.

26. Richard G. Netemeyer, Scot Burton and Donald R. Lichtenstein, "Trait Aspects of Vanity: Measurement and Relevance to Consumer Behavior," *Journal of Consumer Research* 21 (March 1995): 612–26.

27. Michael R. Solomon and Henry Assael, "The Forest or the Trees? A Gestalt Approach to Symbolic Consumption," in *Marketing and Semiotics: New Directions in the Study of Signs for Sale,* ed. Jean Umiker-Sebeok (Berlin: Mouton de Gruyter, 1987): 189–218.

28. Jack L. Nasar, "Symbolic Meanings of House Styles," *Environment and Behavior* 21 (May 1989): 235–57; E.K. Sadalla, B. Verschure and J. Burroughs, "Identity Symbolism," in *Housing, Environment and Behavior* 19 (1987): 599–687.

29. Solomon, "The Role of Products as Social Stimuli"; Robert E. Kleine III, Susan Schultz-Kleine and Jerome B. Kernan, "Mundane Consumption and the Self: A Social-Identity Perspective," *Journal of Consumer Psychology* 2, 3 (1993): 209–35; Newell D. Wright, C.B. Claiborne and M. Joseph Sirgy, "The Effects of Product Symbolism on Consumer Self-Concept," in *Advances in Consumer Research 19*, eds. John F. Sherry, Jr. and Brian Sternthal (Provo, UT: Association for Consumer Research, 1992), pp. 311–18; Susan Fournier, "A Person-Based Relationship Framework for Strategic Brand Management," Doctoral Dissertation, Department of Marketing, University of Florida, 1994.

30. A. Dwayne Ball and Lori H. Tasaki, "The Role and Measurement of Attachment in Consumer Behavior," *Journal of Consumer Psychology* 1, 2 (1992): 155–72.

31. William B. Hansen and Irwin Altman, "Decorating Personal Places: A Descriptive Analysis," *Environment and Behavior* 8 (December 1976): 491–504.

32. R.A. Wicklund and P.M. Gollwitzer, *Symbolic Self-Completion* (Hillsdale, NJ: Lawrence Erlbaum, 1982).

33. Erving Goffman, *Asylums* (New York: Doubleday, 1961).

34. Quoted in Floyd Rudmin, "Property Crime Victimization Impact on Self, on Attachment, and on Territorial Dominance, CPA Highlights," *Victims of Crime Supplement* 9, 2 (1987): 4–7.

35. Barbara B. Brown, "House and Block as Territory" (paper presented at the Conference of the Association for Consumer Research, San Francisco, 1982).

36. Quoted in Shay Sayre and David Horne, "I Shop, Therefore I Am: The Role of Possessions for Self Definition," in *Earth, Wind, and Fire and Water: Perspectives on Natural Disaster*, eds. Shay Sayre and David Horne (Pasadena, CA: Open Door Publishers, 1996), pp. 353–70.

37. Deborah A. Prentice, "Psychological Correspondence of Possessions, Attitudes, and Values," *Journal of Personality and Social Psychology* 53, 6 (1987): 993–1002.

38. Sak Onkvisit and John Shaw, "Self-Concept and Image Congruence: Some Research and Managerial Implications," *Journal of Consumer Marketing* 4 (Winter 1987): 13–24. For a related treatment of congruence between advertising appeals and self-concept, see George M. Zinkhan and Jae W. Hong, "Self-Concept and Advertising Effectiveness: A Conceptual Model of Congruency, Conspicuousness, and Response Mode," in *Advances in Consumer Research 18*, eds. Rebecca H. Holman and Michael R. Solomon (Provo, UT: Association for Consumer Research, 1991), pp. 348–54.

39. C.B. Claiborne and M. Joseph Sirgy, "Self-Image Congruence as a Model of Consumer Attitude Formation and Behavior: A Conceptual Review and Guide for Further Research" (paper presented at the Academy of Marketing Science Conference, New Orleans, 1990).

40. Al E. Birdwell, "A Study of Influence of Image Congruence on Consumer Choice," *Journal of Business* 41 (January 1964): 76–88; Edward L. Grubb and Gregg Hupp, "Perception of Self, Generalized Stereotypes, and Brand Selection," *Journal of Marketing Research* 5 (February 1986): 58–63.

41. Ira J. Dolich, "Congruence Relationship Between Self-Image and Product Brands," *Journal of Marketing Research* 6 (February 1969): 80–84; Danny N. Bellenger, Earle Steinberg and Wilbur W. Stanton, "The Congruence of Store Image and Self Image as It Relates to Store Loyalty," *Journal of Retailing* 52, 1 (1976): 17–32; Ronald J. Dornoff and Ronald L. Tatham, "Congruence Between Personal Image and Store Image," *Journal of the Market Research Society* 14, 1 (1972): 45–52.

42. Naresh K. Malhotra, "A Scale to Measure Self-Concepts, Person Concepts, and Product Concepts," *Journal of Marketing Research* 18 (November 1981): 456–64.

43. Ernest Beaglehole, *Property: A Study in Social Psychology* (New York: Macmillan, 1932).

44. M. Csikszentmihalyi and Eugene Rochberg-Halton, *The Meaning of Things: Domestic Symbols and the Self* (Cambridge, MA: Cambridge University Press, 1981).

45. Russell W. Belk, "Possessions and the Extended Self," *Journal of Consumer Research* 15 (September 1988): 139–68.

46. Diane Goldner, "What Men and Women Really Want ... to Eat," *New York Times* (March 2, 1994): C1 (2 pp.).

47. Joan Meyers-Levy, "The Influence of Sex Roles on Judgment," *Journal of Consumer Research* 14 (March 1988): 522–30.

48. Eileen Fischer and Stephen J. Arnold, "More Than a Labor of Love: Gender Roles and Christmas Gift Shopping," *Journal of Consumer Research* 17 (December 1990): 333–45.

49. Kimberly J. Dodson and Russell W. Belk, "Gender in Children's Birthday Stories," in *Gender, Marketing, and Consumer Behavior*, ed. Janeen Costa (Salt Lake City, UT: Association for Consumer Research, 1996), pp. 96–108.

50. Elizabeth C. Hirschman, "A Feminist Critique of Marketing Theory: Toward Agentic-Communal Balance" (working paper, School of Business, Rutgers University, New Brunswick, NJ, 1990).

51. Eileen Fischer and Stephen J. Arnold, "Sex, Gender Identity, Gender Role Attitudes, and Consumer Behavior," *Psychology & Marketing* 11, 2 (March/April 1994): 163–82.

52. Sandra L. Bem, "The Measurement of Psychological Androgyny," *Journal of Consulting and Clinical Psychology* 42 (1974): 155–62; Deborah E.S. Frable, "Sex Typing and Gender Ideology: Two Facets of the Individual's Gender Psychology That Go Together," *Journal of Personality and Social Psychology* 56, 1 (1989): 95–108.

53. See D. Bruce Carter and Gary D. Levy, "Cognitive Aspects of Early Sex-Role Development: The Influence of Gender Schemas on Preschoolers' Memories and Preferences for Sex-Typed Toys and Activities," *Child Development* 59 (1988): 782–92; Bernd H. Schmitt, France Le Clerc and Laurette Dube-Rioux, "Sex Typing and Consumer Behavior: A Test of Gender Schema Theory," *Journal of Consumer Research* 15 (June 1988): 122–27.

54. Carol Gilligan, *In a Different Voice: Psychological Theory and Women's Development* (Cambridge, MA: Harvard University Press, 1982); Joan Meyers-Levy and Durairaj Maheswaran, "Exploring Differences in Males' and Females' Processing Strategies," *Journal of Consumer Research* 18 (June 1991): 63–70.

55. Lynn J. Jaffe and Paul D. Berger, "Impact on Purchase Intent of Sex-Role Identity and Product Positioning," *Psychology & Marketing* (Fall 1988): 259–71; Lynn J. Jaffe, "The Unique Predictive Ability of Sex-Role Identity in Explaining Women's Response to Advertising," *Psychology & Marketing* 11, 5 (September/October 1994): 467–82.

56. Leila T. Worth, Jeanne Smith and Diane M. Mackie, "Gender Schematicity and Preference for Gender-Typed Products," *Psychology & Marketing* 9 (January 1992): 17–30.

57. Blayne Cutler, "Condom Mania," *American Demographics* (June 1989): 17.

58. Laurel Anderson and Marsha Wadkins, "The New Breed in Japan: Consumer Culture" (unpublished manuscript, Arizona State University, Tempe, 1990); Doris L. Walsh, "A Familiar Story," *American Demographics* (June 1987): 64.

59. B. Abrams, "American Express is Gearing New Ad Campaign to Women," *Wall Street Journal* (August 4, 1983): 23.

60. "Ads' Portrayal of Women Today is Hardly Innovative," *Marketing News* (November 6, 1989): 12; Jill Hicks Ferguson, Peggy J. Kreshel and Spencer F. Tinkham, "In the Pages of *Ms.*: Sex Role Portrayals of Women in Advertising," *Journal of Advertising* 19, 1 (1990): 40–51.

61. Sonia Livingstone and Gloria Greene, "Television Advertisements and the Portrayal of Gender," *British Journal of Social Psychology* 25 (1986): 149–54. For one of the original articles on this topic, see L.Z. McArthur and B.G. Resko, "The Portrayal of Men and Women in American Television Commercials," *Journal of Social Psychology* 97 (1975): 209–20.

62. Richard C. Vincent, "Clio's Consciousness Raised? Portrayal of Women in Rock Videos, Re-examined," *Journalism Quarterly* 66 (1989): 155.

63. Kyle Pope, "High-Tech Marketers Try to Attract Women Without Causing Offense," *Wall Street Journal* (March 17, 1994): B1 (2 pp.).

64. Stuart Elliott, "Avon Products Is Abandoning Its Old-Fashioned Image in an Appeal to Contemporary Women," *New York Times* (April 27, 1993): D21.

65. Daniel J. Brett and Joanne Cantor, "The Portrayal of Men and Women in U.S. Television Commercials: A Recent Content Analysis and Trends Over 15 Years," *Sex Roles* 18 (1988): 595–609.

66. Gordon Sumner, "Tribal Rites of the American Male," *Marketing Insights* (Summer 1989). 13.

67. Quoted in Diana Minardi, "The 90s Man: Cowboy or Wimp?" *Adweek* (June 29, 1992): 34.

68. Linda Wells, "Flirting With Men," *The New York Times Magazine* (April 9, 1989): 64.

69. Margaret G. Maples, "Beefcake Marketing: The Sexy Sell," *Marketing Communications* (April 1983): 21–25.

70. "Changing Conceptions of Fatherhood," *USA Today* (May 1988): 10.

71. Quoted in Kim Foltz, "In Ads, Men's Image Becomes Softer," *New York Times* (March 26, 1990): D12.

72. Projections of the incidence of homosexuality in the general population often are influenced by assumptions of the researchers, as well as the methodology they employ (e.g., self-report, behavioural measures, fantasy measures). For a discussion of these factors, see Edward O. Laumann et al., *The Social Organization of Homosexuality* (Chicago: University of Chicago Press, 1994).

73. Stuart Elliott, "A Sharper View of Gay Consumers," *New York Times* (June 9, 1994): D1 (2 pp.).

74. Steven Kates (1988) *Twenty Million New Customers! Understanding Gay Men's Consumer Behaviour.* New York, the Haworth Press.

75. Joseph Pereira, "These Particular Buyers of Dolls Don't Say, 'Don't Ask, Don't Tell,'" *Wall Street Journal* (August 30, 1993): B1.

76. Joe Mandese and Mark Weiner, "ABC Scores as 'Ellen' Comes Out," *Ad Age* (May 5, 1997): 6.

77. Dennis W. Rook, "Body Cathexis and Market Segmentation," in *The Psychology of Fashion,* ed. Michael R. Solomon (Lexington, MA: Lexington Books, 1985), pp. 233–41.

78. Basil G. Englis, Michael R. Solomon and Richard D. Ashmore, "Beauty *Before* the Eyes of Beholders: The Cultural Encoding of Beauty Types in Magazine Advertising and Music Television," *Journal of Advertising* 23 (June 1994): 49–64; Michael R. Solomon, Richard Ashmore and Laura Longo, "The Beauty Match-Up Hypothesis: Congruence Between Types of Beauty and Product Images in Advertising," *Journal of Advertising* 21 (December 1992): 23–34.

79. Lois W. Banner, *American Beauty* (Chicago: University of Chicago Press, 1980). For a philosophical perspective, see Barry Vacker and Wayne R. Key, "Beauty and the Beholder: The Pursuit of Beauty Through Commodities," *Psychology & Marketing* 10, 6 (November/December 1993): 471–94.

80. David M. Garner et al., "Cultural Expectations of Thinness in Women," *Psychological Reports* 47 (1980): 483–91.

81. Kathleen Boyes, "The New Grip of Girdles Is Lightened by Lycra," *USA Today* (April 25, 1991): 6D.

82. Stuart Elliott, "Ultrathin Models in Coca-Cola and Calvin Klein Campaigns Draw Fire and a Boycott Call," *New York Times* (April 26, 1994): D18; Cyndee Miller, "'Give Them a Cheeseburger,'" *Marketing News* (June 6, 1994): 1 (2 pp.).

83. Jill Neimark, "The Beefcaking of America," *Psychology Today* (November/December 1994): 32 (11 pp.).

84. Grant McCracken, *Big Hair: A Journey into the Transformation of Self* (Toronto: Penguin Books Canada, 1995).

85. Quoted in "High Heels: Ecstasy's Worth the Agony," *New York Post* (December 31, 1981).

86. "Girls at 7 Think Thin, Study Finds," *New York Times* (February 11, 1988): B9.

87. Jennifer Stoffel, "What's New in Weight Control," *New York Times* (November 26, 1989): F17.

88. Debra A. Zellner, Debra F. Harner and Robbie I. Adler, "Effects of Eating Abnormalities and Gender on Perceptions of Desirable Body Shape," *Journal of Abnormal Psychology* 98 (February 1989): 93–96.

89. Robin T. Peterson, "Bulimia and Anorexia in an Advertising Context," *Journal of Business Ethics* 6 (1987): 495–504.

90. Jane E. Brody, "Personal Health," *New York Times* (February 22, 1990): B9.

91. Judy Folkenberg, "Bulimia: Not For Women Only," *Psychology Today* (March 1984): 10.

92. Eleanor Grant, "The Exercise Fix: What Happens When Fitness Fanatics Just Can't Say No?" *Psychology Today* 22 (February 1988): 24.

93. John W. Schouten, "Selves in Transition: Symbolic Consumption in Personal Rites of Passage and Identity Reconstruction," *Journal of Consumer Research* 17 (March 1991): 412–25.

94. Annette C. Hamburger and Holly Hall, "Beauty Quest," *Psychology Today* (May 1988): 28.

95. Emily Yoffe, "Valley of the Silicon Dolls," *Newsweek* (November 26, 1990): 72.

96. Keith Greenberg, "What's Hot: Cosmetic Surgery," *Public Relations Journal* (June 1988): 23.

97. Melinda Beck, "Glad You Aren't Here," *Newsweek* (August 10, 1992): 46.

98. Joshua Levine, "Bra Wars," *Forbes* (April 25, 1994): 120; Cyndee Miller, "Bra Marketers' Cup Runneth Over With, Um, Big Success," *Marketing News* (October 24, 1994): 2 (2 pp.).

99. Ruth P. Rubinstein, "Color, Circumcision, Tattoos, and Scars," in *The Psychology of Fashion,* ed. Michael R. Solomon (Lexington, MA: Lexington Books, 1985), pp. 243–54; Peter H. Bloch and Marsha L. Richins, "You Look Mahvelous: The Pursuit of Beauty and Marketing Concept," *Psychology & Marketing* 9 (January 1992): 3–16.

100. Sondra Farganis, "Lip Service: The Evolution of Pouting, Pursing, and Painting Lips Red," *Health* (November 1988): 48–51.

101. Michael Gross, "Those Lips, Those Eyebrows; New Face of 1989 (New Look of Fashion Models)," *The New York Times Magazine* (February 13, 1989): 24.

102. "White Weight," *Psychology Today* (September/October 1994): 9.

103. See Clinton Sanders, "Customizing the Body: The Art and Culture of Tattooing" (Philadelphia: Temple University Press, 1989).

104. Quoted in Wendy Bounds, "Body-Piercing Gets Under America's Skin," *Wall Street Journal* (April 4, 1994): B1 (2 pp.).

Joshua and Hank are account executives in a high-powered Toronto advertising agency. After a particularly gruelling week they are both looking forward to a well-deserved Sunday off.

Joshua is enthusiastically telling Hank about his plans. He's going to sleep late in his new Yorkville condo. Then he's planned a luxurious, high-cholesterol champagne brunch with Anna, that creative director he's been dating. From there, it's on to the Ford Centre for a matinée of *La Traviata* and dinner at a new sushi bar he's heard a lot about.

Hank chuckles to himself. While Joshua's wasting time at some opera, he's going to pop his new Randy Travis tape in the cassette player of his Trans Am and take a morning drive out to the cottage. By four o'clock he plans to be back home, comfortably planted in front of the TV in his new Barcalounger to watch the Blue Jays play the Expos.

Hank is sometimes amazed at how different he is from Joshua, who fancies himself a real urban sophisticate. They make the same salary and have identical jobs. How can their tastes be so different away from work? Oh, well, Hank sighs to himself, that's why they make chocolate and vanilla ...

6

Personality and Lifestyles

PERSONALITY

Just what makes Hank and Joshua so different? One answer may lie in the concept of **personality,** which refers to a person's unique psychological make-up and how it consistently influences the way a person responds to his or her environment. In recent years the nature of the personality construct has been hotly debated. Many studies have found that people tend not to behave consistently across different situations and that they do not seem to exhibit stable personalities. In fact, some researchers feel that people do not exhibit a consistent personality across different situations; they argue that this is merely a convenient way to think about other people.

This argument is a bit hard to accept intuitively, possibly because we tend to see others in a limited range of situations, and so, to us, most people do act consistently. On the other hand, we each know that we are not all that consistent; we may be wild and crazy at times and the model of respectability at others. While certainly not all psychologists have abandoned the idea of personality, many now recognize that a person's underlying characteristics are but one part of the puzzle and that situational factors often play a very large role in determining behaviour.[1] Still, some aspects of personality continue to be included in marketing strategies. These dimensions are usually employed in concert with a person's choices of leisure activities, political outlook, aesthetic tastes and other individual factors to segment consumers in terms of *lifestyles,* a process we'll focus on more fully in this chapter.

personality a person's unique psychological make-up, which consistently influences the way the person responds to his or her environment

Many approaches to understanding the complex concept of personality can be traced to psychological theorists who began to develop these perspectives in the early part of the century. These perspectives were qualitative, in the sense that they were largely based on analysts' interpretations of patients' accounts of dreams, traumatic experiences and encounters with others.

Consumer Behaviour on the Couch: Freudian Theory

Sigmund Freud developed the idea that much of human behaviour stems from a fundamental conflict between a person's desire to gratify his or her physical needs and the necessity to function as a responsible member of society. This struggle is carried out in the mind among three systems. (Note that these systems do not refer to physical parts of the brain.) For the student curious about Freud, see ***www.wwhorton. com/blurbs/hpb.freud.htm.***

FREUDIAN SYSTEMS

id the system oriented towards immediate gratification

pleasure principle the belief that behaviour is guided by the desire to maximize pleasure and avoid pain

superego the system that internalizes society's rules and that works to prevent the id from seeking selfish gratification

ego the system that mediates between the id and the superego

The **id** is entirely oriented towards immediate gratification—that is, it is the "party animal" of the mind. It operates according to the **pleasure principle:** behaviour is guided by the primary desire to maximize pleasure and avoid pain. The id is selfish and illogical. It directs a person's psychic energy towards pleasurable acts without regard for any consequences.

The **superego** is the counterweight to the id. This system is essentially the person's conscience. It internalizes society's rules (especially as communicated by parents) and works to prevent the id from seeking selfish gratification.

Finally, the **ego** is the system that mediates between the id and the superego. It is, in a way, a referee in the fight between temptation and virtue. The ego tries to balance these two opposing forces according to the reality principle. It finds ways to gratify the id that will be acceptable to the outside world. These conflicts occur on an unconscious level, so the person is not necessarily aware of the underlying reasons for behaviour.

Some of Freud's ideas have also been adapted by consumer researchers. In particular, his work highlights the potential importance of unconscious motives underlying purchases. The implication is that consumers cannot necessarily tell us their true motivations for choosing a product, even if we can devise a sensitive way to ask them directly.

The Freudian perspective also hints at the possibility that the ego relies on the symbolism in products to compromise between the demands of the id and the prohibitions of the superego. The person channels his or her unacceptable desires into acceptable outlets by using products that signify these underlying desires. This is the connection between product symbolism and motivation: the product stands for, or represents, a consumer's true goal, one that is socially unacceptable or unattainable; by acquiring the product, the person is able vicariously to experience the forbidden fruit.

SOMETIMES A CIGAR IS JUST A CIGAR

Most Freudian applications in marketing are related to the sexuality of products. For example, some analysts have speculated that a sports car is a substitute for sexual gratification for many men. Indeed, some men do seem inordinately attached to

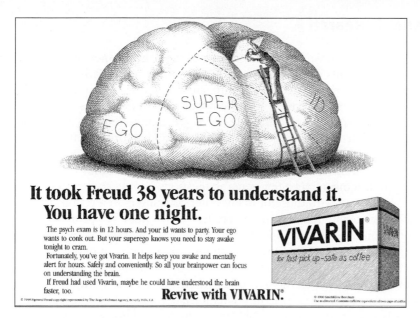

This ad for Vivarin stimulants depicts the three components of Freud's perspective on motivation and the unconscious.
Licensed by The Roger Richman Agency, Inc., Beverly Hills, CA. Courtesy of Grey Advertising, Inc.

their cars and may spend many hours lovingly washing and polishing them. The Infiniti ad shown here reinforces the belief that cars symbolically satisfy consumers' sexual needs in addition to their functional ones by describing the J30 model as "... what happens when you cross sheet metal and desire."

Others focus on male-oriented symbolism—the so-called phallic symbol—that appeals to women. Although Freud himself joked that "sometimes a cigar is just a cigar," many pop applications of Freud's ideas revolve around the use of objects that resemble sex organs (such as cigars, trees or swords for men and tunnels for women). This focus stems from Freud's analysis of dreams, which were often interpreted as communicating repressed desires through symbols.

This Infiniti ad stresses the sexual dimension of car ownership.
Courtesy of Infiniti Division, Nissan Motor Corporation U.S.A.

Motivational Research

The first attempts to apply Freudian ideas to understand the deeper meanings of products and advertisements were made in the 1950s, when a perspective known as **motivational research** was developed. This approach is largely based on psychoanalytic (Freudian) interpretations, with a heavy emphasis on unconscious motives. A basic assumption is that socially unacceptable needs are channelled into acceptable outlets. Product use or avoidance is motivated by unconscious forces that often are determined in childhood.

Motivational research relies on *depth interviews* with individual consumers. Instead of asking many consumers a few general questions about product usage and combining these responses with those of many other consumers in a representative statistical sample, this technique uses relatively few consumers but probes deeply into each person's purchase motivations. A depth interview might take several hours and is based on the assumption that the respondent cannot immediately articulate his or her latent, or underlying, motives; these can be derived only after meticulous questioning and interpretation on the part of a carefully trained interviewer.

This technique was pioneered by Ernest Dichter, a psychoanalyst who trained in Vienna in the early part of the century. Dichter conducted in-depth interview studies on over 230 different products, and many of his findings have been incorporated in actual marketing campaigns.[2] For example, Esso (now Exxon) for many years reminded consumers to "Put a tiger in your tank" after Dichter found that people responded well to this powerful animal symbolism containing vaguely suggestive overtones. A summary of major consumption motivations identified using this approach appears in Table 6–1.

Motivational research is attacked for two quite opposite reasons. Some feel it does not work, while others feel it works too well. On the one hand, social critics have reacted much the same way they have reacted to subliminal perception studies (see Chapter 2). They have attacked this school of thought for giving advertisers the power to manipulate consumers.[3] On the other hand, many consumer researchers feel the research has lacked sufficient rigour and validity, since interpretations are subjective and indirect.[4] Because conclusions are based on the analyst's own judgment and are derived from discussions with a small number of people, some researchers are dubious as to the degree to which these results can be generalized to a large market. In addition, because the original motivational researchers were heavily influenced by orthodox Freudian theory, their interpretations usually carried strong sexual overtones. This emphasis tends to overlook other plausible causes for behaviour.

Motivational research has great appeal to at least some marketers for several reasons, some of which are detailed here:

- *Cost Efficiency*: Motivational research tends to be less expensive than large-scale, quantitative surveys because interviewing and data-processing costs are relatively minimal.

- *Providing Insights:* The knowledge derived from motivational research can possibly help to develop marketing communications that appeal to deep-seated needs and thus provide a more powerful hook to relate a product to consumers. Even if they are not necessarily valid for all consumers in a target market, these insights can be valuable when used in an exploratory way. For example, the rich imagery that may be associated with a product can be used creatively when developing advertising copy.

TABLE 6–1 Major Motives for Consumption as Identified by Ernest Dichter

MOTIVE	ASSOCIATED PRODUCTS
Power–masculinity–virility	Power: Sugary products and large breakfasts (to charge oneself up), bowling, electric trains, hot rods, power tools
	Masculinity–virility: Coffee, red meat, heavy shoes, toy guns, shaving with a razor
Security	Ice cream (to feel like loved child again), full drawer of neatly ironed shirts, home baking, hospital care
Eroticism	Sweets (to lick), gloves (to be removed by women as a form of undressing), a man lighting a woman's cigarette (to create a tension-filled moment culminating in pressure, then relaxation)
Moral purity–cleanliness	White bread, cotton fabrics (to connote chastity), harsh household cleaning chemicals, bathing, oatmeal (sacrifice, virtue)
Social acceptance	Companionship: Ice cream (to share fun), coffee
	Love and affection: Toys (to express love for children), sugar and honey (to express terms of affection)
	Acceptance: Soap, beauty products
Individuality	Gourmet foods, foreign cars, cigarette holders, vodka, perfume, fountain pens
Status	Scotch, fur coats, luxury cars
Femininity	Cakes and cookies, dolls, silk, tea, household curios (to have a light, decorative and heavy tactile component)
Reward	Cigarettes, candy, alcohol, ice cream, cookies
Master over environment	Kitchen appliances, boats, sporting goods
Disalienation (a desire to feel connectedness to things)	Home decorating, skiing, morning radio broadcasts (to feel "in touch" with the world)
Magic–mystery	Soups (having healing powers), paints (change the mood of a room), carbonated drinks (magical effervescent property), vodka (romantic history), unwrapping of gifts

Source: Adapted from Jeffrey F. Durgee, "Interpreting Dichter's Interpretations: An Analysis of Consumption Symbolism in *The Handbook of Consumer Motivations*," *Marketing and Semiotics: Selected Papers from the Copenhagen Symposium,* eds. Hanne Hartvig-Larsen, David Glen Mick and Christian Alstead (Copenhagen, 1991).

- *Intuitive Sense*: Some of the findings seem intuitively plausible after the fact. For example, motivational studies concluded that coffee is associated with companionship, that people avoid prunes because they remind them of old age, and that men fondly equate the first car they owned as an adolescent with the onset of their sexual freedom.

Other interpretations are hard for some people to swallow, such as the observations that, to a woman, baking a cake symbolizes giving birth or that men are reluctant to give blood because they feel their vital fluids are being drained. On the other hand, some people do refer to a pregnant woman as "having a bun in the oven," and Pillsbury claims that "nothing says lovin' like something from the oven." Motivational research for the Red Cross (***www.redcross.ca***) did find that men (but not women) tend drastically to overestimate the amount of blood that is taken during a donation. This group counteracted the fear of loss of virility by symbolically equating the act of giving blood with fertilization: "Give the gift of life."

Despite its drawbacks, motivational research continues to be employed as a useful diagnostic tool. Its validity is enhanced, however, when used in conjunction with the other research techniques available to the consumer researcher.

NEO-FREUDIAN THEORIES

Freud's work had a huge influence on subsequent theories of personality. Although Freud opened the door to the realization that explanations for behaviour may lurk beneath the surface, many of his co-workers and students felt that an individual's personality was more influenced by how he or she handled relationships with others. These theorists are often called *neo-Freudian* (meaning following from or being influenced by Freud).

KAREN HORNEY One of the most prominent neo-Freudians was a psychoanalyst named Karen Horney. She proposed that people can be described as moving towards others (compliant), away from others (detached) or against others (aggressive).[5] Some research indicates that these three types prefer different kinds of products. For example, one study found that compliant people are more likely to gravitate towards name-brand products, detached types are more likely to be tea drinkers, while males classified as aggressive prefer brands with a strong masculine orientation (e.g., Old Spice deodorant).[6] Other well-known neo-Freudians include Alfred Adler, who proposed that many actions are motivated by people's desire to overcome feelings of inferiority relative to others, and Harry Stack Sullivan, who focused on how personality evolves to reduce anxiety in social relationships.[7]

CARL JUNG Carl Jung was also a disciple of Freud (and was being groomed by Freud to be his successor). However, Jung was unable to accept Freud's emphasis on sexual aspects of personality, and this was a contributing factor in the eventual dissolution of their relationship. Jung went on to develop his own method of psychotherapy, which became known as *analytical psychology*. This approach emphasized both the individual's development as a creative person (his or her future) and his or her individual and racial history (his or her past) in the formation of personality.

Jung believed that people are shaped by the cumulative experiences of past generations. A central part of his perspective was an emphasis on what Jung called the *collective unconscious,* which is a storehouse of memories inherited from our ancestral past. For example, Jung would argue that many people are afraid of the dark because their distant ancestors had good reason to exhibit this fear. These shared memories create **archetypes,** or universally shared ideas and behaviour patterns. Archetypes involve themes, such as birth, death or the devil, that appear frequently in myths, stories and dreams.

Jung's ideas may seem a bit far-fetched, but advertising messages often do invoke (at least intuitively) archetypes to link products with underlying meanings. For example, some of the archetypes identified by Jung and his followers include the *old wise man* and the *earth mother*.[8] These images appear frequently in marketing messages that use such characters as wizards, revered teachers or even Mother Nature to convince people of the merits of products.

archetype a universally shared idea or behaviour pattern, central to Jung's conception of personality; archetypes involve themes, such as birth, death or the devil, that appear frequently in myths, stories and dreams

Trait Theory

One approach to personality is to focus on the quantitative measurement of **traits,** or identifiable characteristics that define a person. For example, people can be distinguished by the degree to which they are socially outgoing (the trait of *extroversion*). Some specific traits that are relevant to consumer behaviour include *innovativeness* (the degree to which a person likes to try new things), *materialism* (amount of emphasis placed on acquiring and owning products), *self-consciousness* (the degree to which a person deliberately monitors and controls the image of the self that is projected to others) and *need for cognition* (the degree to which a person likes to think about things and, by extension, to expend the necessary effort to process brand information).[9]

traits the identifiable characteristics that define a person

PROBLEMS WITH TRAIT THEORY IN CONSUMER RESEARCH

Since large numbers of consumers can be categorized in terms of their standing on various traits, these approaches can, in theory, be used for segmentation purposes. If a car manufacturer could determine that drivers who fit a trait profile are more likely to prefer a car with certain features, this match could be used to great advantage. The notion that consumers buy products that are extensions of their personalities makes intuitive sense. This idea is endorsed by many marketing managers, who try to create *brand personalities* that will appeal to different types of consumers.

However, the use of standard personality-trait measurements to predict product choices has met with mixed success at best. In general, marketing researchers simply have not been able to predict consumers' behaviours on the basis of measured personality traits. A number of explanations have been offered for these equivocal results:[10]

- Many of the scales are not sufficiently valid or reliable; they do not adequately measure what they are supposed to measure, and their results may not be stable over time.

- Personality tests are often developed for specific populations (e.g., mentally ill people); these tests are then "borrowed" and applied to the general population where their relevance is questionable.

- The tests often are not administered under the appropriate conditions; they may be given in a classroom or over a kitchen table by people who are not properly trained.

- The researchers often make changes in the instruments to adapt them to their own situations, in the process deleting or adding items and renaming variables. These ad hoc changes dilute the validity of the measures and also reduce researchers' ability to compare results across consumer samples.

- Many trait scales are intended to measure gross, overall tendencies (like emotional stability or introversion); these results are then used to make predictions about purchases of specific brands.

- In many cases a number of scales are given with no advance thought about how these measures should be related to consumer behaviour. The researchers then use a shotgun approach, following up on anything that happens to look interesting.

Although the use of personality measures by marketing researchers was largely abandoned after many studies failed to yield meaningful results, some researchers have not abandoned the early promise of this line of work. More recent efforts (many in Europe) have been focused on benefiting from past mistakes. These researchers are using more specific measures of personality traits that they have reason to believe are relevant to economic behaviour. They are trying to increase the validity of these measures, primarily by using multiple measures of behaviour rather than relying on the common practice of trying to predict purchasing responses from a single item on a personality test.

In addition, researchers have toned down their expectations of what personality traits can tell them about consumers. They now recognize that traits are only part of the solution, and personality data must be incorporated with information about people's social and economic conditions in order to be useful.[11] As a result, some more recent research has had better success at relating personality traits to such consumer behaviours as alcohol consumption among young men or shoppers' willingness to try new, healthier food products.[12]

BRAND PERSONALITY

In 1886 a momentous event occurred: the Quaker Oats man first appeared on boxes of hot cereal. Quakers had a reputation in nineteenth-century America for being shrewd but fair, and peddlers sometimes dressed as Quakers for this reason. The cereal company's decision to "borrow" this imagery for its packaging signalled the recognition that purchasers might make the same associations with their product.[13] These inferences about a product's "personality" are an important part of **brand equity**, which refers to the extent that a consumer holds strong, favourable and unique associations about a brand in memory.[14] Some personality dimensions that can be used to compare and contrast the perceived characteristics of brands in various product categories include:[15]

brand equity a brand that has strong positive associations in a consumer's memory and commands a lot of loyalty as a result

- old-fashioned, wholesome, traditional
- surprising, lively, "with it"
- serious, intelligent, efficient
- glamorous, romantic, sexy
- rugged, outdoorsy, tough, athletic

Of course we all know today that packaging and other physical cues create a "personality" for a product. In addition, the marketing activities undertaken on behalf of the product also can influence inferences about its "personality," and some of these actions are shown in Table 6–2.

Indeed, consumers appear to have little trouble assigning personality qualities to all sorts of inanimate products, from personal-care products to more mundane, functional ones—even kitchen appliances. In research done by Whirlpool, its products were seen as more feminine than competing brands. They were regarded as a modern, family-oriented woman living in the suburbs—attractive but not flashy. In contrast, the company's KitchenAid brand was seen as a modern professional woman who was glamorous and wealthy and enjoyed classical music and the theatre.[16]

TABLE 6–2 Brand behaviours and Possible Personality Trait Inference

BRAND ACTION	TRAIT INFERENCE
Brand is repositioned several times or changes its slogan repeatedly	Flighty, schizophrenic
Brand uses continuing character in its advertising	Familiar, comfortable
Brand charges a high price and uses exclusive distribution	Snobbish, sophisticated
Brand frequently available on a special deal	Cheap, uncultured
Brand offers many line extensions	Versatile, adaptable
Brand sponsors show on PBS or uses recycled materials	Helpful, supportive
Brand features easy-to-use packaging or speaks at consumer's level in advertising	Warm, approachable
Brand offers seasonal clearance sale	Planful, practical
Brand offers five-year warranty or free customer hot-line	Reliable, dependable

Source: Adapted from Susan Fournier, "A Consumer–Brand Relationship Framework for Strategic Brand Management," Doctoral Dissertation, Department of Marketing, University of Florida, 1994, Table 2.2, p.24.

The creation and communication of a distinctive *brand personality* is one of the primary ways marketers can make a product stand out from the competition and inspire years of loyalty to it. This process can be understood in terms of **animism**, the practice found in many cultures whereby inanimate objects are given qualities that make them somehow alive. Animism is in some cases a part of a religion; sacred objects, animals or places are believed to have magical qualities or to contain the spirits of ancestors. In our society these objects may be "worshipped" in the sense that they are believed to impart desirable qualities to the owner, or they may in a sense become so important to a person that they can be viewed as a "friend."

animism the attribution of conscious life to inanimate objects

Three types of animism can be identified to describe the extent to which human qualities are attributed to a product:[17]

- Level 1: In the highest order of animism, the object is believed to be possessed by the soul of the being—as is sometimes the case for spokespersons in advertising. This strategy allows the consumer to feel that the spirit of the celebrity is available through the brand. In other cases a brand may be strongly associated with a loved one, alive or deceased.

- Level 2: Objects are *anthropomorphized*—given human characteristics. A cartoon character or mythical creation may be treated as if it were a person, and even assumed to have human feelings. Think about such familiar *spokescharacters* as the Jolly Green Giant, Pillsbury Dough Boy or Michelin Man.

- Level 3: The product is given selected humanlike qualities but is not treated as human. For example, products often are regarded affectionately and may even be given nicknames, such as a "Beamer" (BMW). Grey Advertising, in research for its client Sprint Business Services, found that when customers were asked to imagine long-distance carriers as animals, they envisioned AT&T as a lion, MCI as a snake and Sprint as a puma. Grey used these results to position Sprint as a company that could "help you do more business" rather than taking the more aggressive approach of its competitors.[18]

LIFESTYLES AND PSYCHOGRAPHICS

Joshua and Hank, whom we met at the beginning of the chapter, strongly resemble one another demographically. They were both raised in middle-class households, have similar educational backgrounds, are about the same age, and share the same occupation and income. However, as their leisure choices show, it would be a big mistake to assume that their consumption choices are similar as well. Joshua and Hank each choose products, services and activities that help them define a unique *lifestyle*. This section first explores how marketers approach the issue of lifestyle and then how they use information about these consumption choices to tailor products and communications to individual lifestyle segments.

Lifestyle: Who We Are, What We Do

In traditional societies one's consumption options are largely dictated by class, caste, village or family. In a modern consumer society, however, people are more free to select the set of products, services and activities that defines them and, in turn, to create a social identity that is communicated to others. One's choice of goods and services indeed makes a statement about who one is and about the types of people with whom one desires to identify—and even about those we wish to avoid.

This ad for GinsaMax relies on lifestyle symbolism to make its point. Note the sets of stereotypical products and activities associated with the before-and-after photos of a couple whose lifestyles have (supposedly) changed after using the product.
Courtesy of KAL Vitamins and Mueller and Associates.

The recreational-vehicle ad shown here demonstrates how a market segment is defined by a particular allocation of time and money to a leisure activity. The ad's claim that the RV dealer has the product that "... says you're you!" implies that dedicated RVers derive a significant portion of their self-identities from the activities associated with this lifestyle.
Courtesy of Jayco, Inc.

Lifestyle refers to a pattern of consumption reflecting a person's choices of how he or she spends time and money. Many of the factors already discussed in this book, such as a person's self-concept, ethnicity and social class, are used as "raw ingredients" to fashion a unique lifestyle. In an economic sense one's lifestyle represents the way one has elected to allocate income, in terms of relative allocations both to different products and services and to specific alternatives within these categories.[19] Other somewhat similar distinctions—such as those differentiating consumers by social class, determined by who devotes a high proportion of total expenditures to food, advanced technology or such information-intensive goods as entertainment and education—have been made to describe consumers in terms of their broad patterns of consumption.[20]

A *lifestyle marketing perspective* recognizes that people sort themselves into groups on the basis of the things they like to do, how they like to spend their leisure time and how they choose to spend their disposable income.[21] These choices in turn create opportunities for market-segmentation strategies that recognize the potency of a consumer's chosen lifestyle in determining both the types of products purchased and the specific brands more likely to appeal to a designated lifestyle segment.

lifestyle a set of shared values or tastes exhibited by a group of consumers, especially as these are reflected in consumption patterns

LIFESTYLES AS GROUP IDENTITIES

The economic approaches are useful in tracking changes in broad societal priorities, but they do not begin to embrace the symbolic nuances that separate lifestyle groups. Lifestyle is more than the allocation of discretionary income. It is a statement about who one is in society and who one is not. Group identities, whether of hobbyists, athletes or drug users, gel around forms of expressive symbolism. The self-definitions of group members are derived from the common symbol system to which the group is dedicated. Such self-definitions have been described by a number of terms, including *lifestyle, taste public, consumer group, symbolic community* and *status culture.*[22]

Patterns of consumption based on lifestyles are often composed of many ingredients that are shared by others in similar social and economic circumstances. Still, each person also provides a unique "twist" to this pattern that allows him or her to inject some individuality into a chosen lifestyle. For example, a "typical" university student (if there is such a thing) may dress much like his or her friends, hang out in the same places and like the same foods, yet still indulge a passion for marathon running, stamp collecting or community activism that makes him or her a unique person.

And lifestyles are not set in stone. Unlike deep-seated values, people's tastes and preferences evolve over time, so that consumption patterns that were viewed favourably at one point in time may be laughed at (or sneered at) a few years later. If you don't believe that, simply think back to what you, your friends and your family were wearing, doing and eating five or ten years ago. Where *did* you find those clothes?

Because people's attitudes regarding physical fitness, social activism, sex roles for men and women, the importance of home life and family, and many other things do change, it is vital for marketers to monitor continually the social landscape to try to anticipate where these changes will lead. Some of the most important lifestyle changes (known as trends) in the 1990s will be discussed later in this chapter.

Products Are the Building Blocks of Lifestyles

Consumers often choose particular products, services and activities over others because they are associated with a certain lifestyle. For this reason, lifestyle marketing strategies attempt to position a product by fitting it into an existing pattern of consumption.

Because a goal of lifestyle marketing is to allow consumers to pursue their chosen ways of enjoying their lives and expressing their social identities, a key aspect of this strategy is to focus on product usage in desirable social settings (see Chapter 10). The goal of associating a product with a social situation is a long-standing one for advertisers, whether the product is included in a round of golf, a family barbecue or a night at a glamorous disco surrounded by jet-setters.[23] Thus people, products and settings are combined to express a certain consumption style, as diagrammed in Figure 6–1.

The adoption of a lifestyle marketing perspective implies that we must look at *patterns* of behaviour to understand consumers. We can get a clearer picture of how people use products to define lifestyles by examining how they make choices in a variety of product categories. As one study noted, "... all goods carry meaning, but none by itself ... The meaning is in the relations between all the goods, just as music is in the relations marked out by the sounds and not in any one note."[24]

Indeed, many products and services do seem to "go together," usually because they tend to be selected by the same types of people. In many cases, products do not seem to "make sense" if unaccompanied by companion products (e.g., fast food and

FIGURE 6–1 • Linking Products to Lifestyles

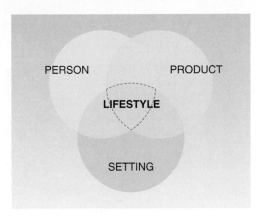

paper plates, or a suit and tie) or are incongruous in the presence of others (e.g., a Chippendale chair in a high-tech office). Therefore, an important part of lifestyle marketing is to identify the *set* of products and services that seems to be linked in consumers' minds to a specific lifestyle.

Product complementarity occurs when the symbolic meanings of different products are related to each other.[25] These sets of products, termed *consumption constellations,* are used by consumers to define, communicate and perform social roles.[26] For example, the yuppie of the 1980s was defined by such products as a Rolex watch, BMW automobile, Gucci briefcase, squash racket, fresh pesto, white wine and Brie. Somewhat similar constellations could be found for "Sloane Rangers" in the United Kingdom and "bon chic Bon genres" in France. While people today take pains to avoid being classified as yuppies, this social role had a major influence on defining cultural values and consumption priorities in the 1980s.[27] What consumption constellation might characterize you and your friends today?

product complementarity
the view that products in different functional categories have symbolic meanings that are related to one another

Psychographics

Consider a marketer who wishes to target a student population. She identifies her ideal consumer as "a 21-year-old senior marketing major living on a large university campus whose parents make between $30 000 and $60 000 per year." You may know a lot of people who fit this description. Do you think they are all the same? Would they all be likely to share common interests and buy the same products? Probably not, since their lifestyles are likely to differ considerably.

As Joshua and Hank's lifestyle choices demonstrate, consumers can share the same demographic characteristics and still be very different people. For this reason, marketers need a way to "breathe life" into demographic data to really identify, understand and target consumer segments that will share a set of preferences for their products and services. This chapter discussed some of the important differences in consumers' personalities that play a big role in determining product choices. When personality variables are combined with knowledge of lifestyle preferences, marketers have a powerful lens with which to view consumer segments.

This ad for cable television underscores the vast differences in taste and preferences among market segments and promotes the value of lifestyle segmentation.
Courtesy of National Cable Television Association (NCTA).

psychographics the use of psychological, sociological and anthropological factors to construct market segments

This tool is known as **psychographics,** which involves the "... use of psychological, sociological, and anthropological factors ... to determine how the market is segmented by the propensity of groups within the market—and their reasons—to make a particular decision about a product, person, ideology, or otherwise hold an attitude or use a medium."[28]

Psychographics can help a marketer fine-tune its offerings to meet the needs of different segments. For example, the Discovery Channel surveyed those who watch at least a half-hour of its programming a week. It found that in fact there were eight distinct groups of watchers, with different motivations and preferences—psychographic segments that were given descriptive names like Entertain-Me's, Practicals, Scholars and Escapists. Based on these results, Discovery was able to tailor its programming to different segments and increase its market share in the competitive cable industry.[29]

THE ROOTS OF PSYCHOGRAPHICS

Psychographic research was first developed in the 1960s and 1970s to address the shortcomings of two other types of consumer research: motivational research and quantitative survey research. As discussed earlier, *motivational research,* which involves intensive one-to-one interviews and projective tests, yields a lot of information about a few people. This information, however, is often idiosyncratic and not very useful or reliable. At the other extreme, *quantitative survey research,* or large-scale demographic surveys, yields only a little information about a lot of people. As some researchers observed, "... The marketing manager who wanted to know why people ate the competitor's cornflakes was told '32 percent of the respondents said taste, 21 percent said flavor, 15 percent said texture, 10 percent said price, and 22 percent said don't know or no answer.'"[30]

In many applications the term *psychographics* is used interchangeably with *lifestyle* to denote the separation of consumers into categories based on differences in choices of consumption activities and product usage. While there are many psychographic variables that can be used to segment consumers, they all share the underlying principle of going beyond surface characteristics to understand consumers' motivations for purchasing and using products.

Demographics allows us to describe *who* buys, but psychographics allows us to understand *why* they do. To illustrate how this approach works, consider a very popular campaign for Molson Export beer that based its commercials on psychographic findings. Research showed that Molson's target customers tended to be like boys who had never grown up, were uncertain about the future and were intimidated by women's new-found freedoms. Accordingly, the ads featured a group of men—"Fred and the boys"—whose get-togethers emphasized male companionship, protection against change, and the idea that the beer "keeps on tasting great."[31] Psychographics allowed the company firmly to anchor the beer in a way that was appealing to this group (even though members of this segment could not necessarily tell you *why* such commercials resonated with them).

Conducting a Psychographic Analysis

Some early attempts at lifestyle segmentation "borrowed" standard psychological scales (often used to measure pathology or personality disturbances) and tried to relate scores on these tests to product usage. As might be expected, such efforts were largely disappointing. These tests were never intended to be related to everyday consumption activities and yielded little in the way of explanation for purchase behaviours. The technique is more effective when the variables included are more closely related to actual consumer behaviours. If one wants to understand purchases of household cleaning products, it is better to ask people about their attitudes towards household cleanliness than to test for personality disorders.

Psychographic studies can take several different forms:

- a lifestyle profile that looks for items that differentiate between users and non-users of a product;
- a product-specific profile that identifies a target group and then profiles these consumers on product-relevant dimensions;
- a study that uses personality traits as descriptors, where some variable such as concern for the environment is analyzed to see which personality traits are most likely to be related to it;
- a general lifestyle segmentation, where a large sample of respondents are placed into homogenous groups based on similarities in their overall preferences; and
- a product-specific segmentation, where questions used in a general approach are tailored to a product category. For example, in a study done specifically for a stomach medicine, an item like "I worry too much" might be rephrased as "I get stomach problems if I worry too much." This allows the researcher to discriminate more finely between users of competing brands.[32]

TABLE 6–3 Lifestyle Dimensions

ACTIVITIES	INTERESTS	OPINIONS	DEMOGRAPHICS
Work	Family	Themselves	Age
Hobbies	Home	Social issues	Education
Social events	Job	Politics	Income
Vacation	Community	Business	Occupation
Entertainment	Recreation	Economics	Family size
Club membership	Fashion	Education	Dwelling
Community	Food	Products	Geography
Shopping	Media	Future	City size
Sports	Achievements	Culture	Stage in life cycle

Source: William D. Wells and Douglas J. Tigert, "Activities, Interests, and Opinions," *Journal of Advertising Research* 11 (August 1971): 27–35. ©1971 by The Advertising Research Foundation.

AIOs

AIOs (Activities, Interests and Opinions) the psychographic variables used by researchers in grouping consumers

Most contemporary psychographic research attempts to group consumers according to some combination of three categories of variables—activities, interests and opinions—known as **AIOs.** Using data from large samples, marketers create profiles of customers who resemble each other in their activities and patterns of product usage.[33] The dimensions used to assess lifestyles are listed in Table 6–3.

To group consumers into common AIO categories, researchers give respondents a long list of statements and ask them to indicate how much they agree with each one. Lifestyle is thus "boiled down" by discovering how people spend their time, what they find interesting and important, and how they view themselves and the world around them, as well as demographic information.

Typically, the first step in conducting a psychographic analysis is to determine which lifestyle segments are producing the bulk of customers for a particular product. According to a very general rule of thumb frequently used in marketing research, the **20/80 rule,** only 20 percent of a product's users account for 80 percent of the volume of product sold. Researchers attempt to determine who uses the brand and try to isolate heavy, moderate and light users. They also look for patterns of usage and attitudes towards the product. In many cases, just a few lifestyle segments account for the majority of brand users.[34] Marketers primarily target these heavy users, even though they may constitute a relatively small number of total users.

20/80 rule a rule-of-thumb in volume segmentation, which says that about 20 percent of consumers in a product category (the heavy users) account for about 80 percent of sales

After the heavy users are identified and understood, the brand's relationship to them is considered. Heavy users may have quite different reasons for using the product; they can be further subdivided in terms of the *benefits* they derive from using the product or service. For instance, marketers at the beginning of the walking-shoe craze assumed that purchasers were basically burned-out joggers. Subsequent psychographic research showed that there were actually several different groups of walkers, ranging from those who walk to get to work to those who walk for fun. This realization resulted in shoes aimed at different segments, from Footjoy Joy-Walkers to Nike Healthwalkers.

Uses of Psychographic Segmentation

Psychographic segmentation can be used in a variety of ways:

- *To define the target market.* This information allows the marketer to go beyond simple demographic or product-usage descriptions (e.g., middle-aged men or frequent users).

- *To create a new view of the market.* Sometimes the marketer creates a strategy with a "typical" customer in mind. This stereotype may not be correct because the actual customer may not match these assumptions. For example, marketers of a facial cream for women were surprised to find their key market was composed of older, widowed women rather than the younger, more sociable women to whom they were pitching their appeals.

- *To position the product.* Psychographic information can allow the marketer to emphasize features of the product that fit in with a person's lifestyle. Products targeted to people whose lifestyle profiles show a high need to be around other people might focus on the product's ability to help meet this social need.

- *To better communicate product attributes.* Psychographic information can offer very useful input to the advertising creative who must communicate something about the product. The artist or writer obtains a much richer mental image of the target consumer than that obtained through dry statistics, and this insight improves his or her ability to "talk" to that consumer.

- *To develop overall strategy.* Understanding how a product fits, or does not fit, into consumers' lifestyles allows the marketer to identify new product opportunities, chart media strategies, and create environments most consistent and harmonious with these consumption patterns.

- *To market social and political issues.* Psychographic segmentation can be an important tool in political campaigns and can also be employed to find commonalities among types of consumers who engage in destructive behaviours, such as drug use or excessive gambling.

A psychographic study of men aged 18 to 24 who drink and drive highlights the potential for this perspective to help in the eradication of harmful behaviours. This demographic segment accounts for a disproportionately high share of alcohol-related fatalities. Researchers divided this segment into four groups: "good timers," "well adjusted," "nerds" and "problem kids." They found that one group in particular—good timers—is more likely to believe that it is fun to be drunk, that the chances of a drunk driver having an accident are low, and that drinking increases one's appeal to the opposite sex. Since the study showed that this group is also the most likely to drink at rock concerts and parties, is most likely to watch MTV and tends to listen to rock-oriented radio stations, reaching good timers with a prevention campaign is made easier and more efficient.[35]

Psychographic Segmentation Typologies

Marketers are constantly on the prowl for new insights that will allow them to identify and reach groups of consumers that are united by a common lifestyle. To meet this need, many research companies and advertising agencies have developed their own *segmentation typologies* that divide people into segments. Respondents answer a battery of questions that allow the researchers to cluster them into a set of distinct lifestyle groups. The questions usually include a mixture of AIOs, plus other items relating to their perceptions of specific brands, favourite celebrities, media preferences and so on. These systems are usually sold to companies that want to learn more about their customers and potential customers.

At least at a superficial level, many of these typologies are fairly similar to one another, in that a typical typology breaks up the population into roughly five to eight segments. Each cluster is given a descriptive name, and a profile of the "typical" member is provided to the client. Unfortunately, it is often difficult to compare or evaluate different typologies, since the methods and data used to devise these systems frequently are *proprietary*—that is, the information is developed and owned by the company, and the company feels that it would not be desirable to release this information to outsiders.

VALS

VALS (Values and Lifestyles) a psychographic segmentation system used to categorize consumers into clusters, or "VALS types"

The most well-known and widely used segmentation system is **VALS (Values and Lifestyles)**, developed at what is now SRI International in California. Based on responses to a lengthy survey administered to about 1600 US households in 1980, a researcher named Arnold Mitchell initially devised a system to place consumers into one of nine lifestyle clusters, or VALS types. The VALS system has been used by well over 200 corporations and advertising agencies in their marketing efforts. It has recently been updated to a new system called VALS 2.

VALS 2 divides people into eight groups that are determined by both psychological characteristics and resources, which include such factors as income, education, energy levels and eagerness to buy. VALS 2 appears to be easier to use, but it has abandoned some of the conceptual foundation on which the original VALS was based. In the VALS 2 structure, groups are arrayed vertically by resources and horizontally by self-orientation, as shown in Figure 6–2. The new top group is termed *actualizers,* who are successful consumers with many resources. This group is concerned with social issues and is open to change. The next three groups also have sufficient resources but differ in their outlooks on life:[36]

- *Fulfilleds* are satisfied, reflective and comfortable. They tend to be practical and value functionality.
- *Achievers* are career-oriented and prefer predictability over risk or self-discovery.
- *Experiencers* are impulsive and young and enjoy offbeat or risky experiences.

The next three groups have fewer resources:

- *Believers* have strong principles and favour proven brands.
- *Strivers* are like achievers but with fewer resources. They are very concerned about the approval of others.
- *Makers* are action-oriented and tend to focus their energies on self-sufficiency. They will often be found working on their cars, canning their own vegetables or building their own houses.

Strugglers are at the bottom of the ladder. They are most concerned with meeting the needs of the moment, and thus strongly resemble the survivor and sustainer groups they replaced.

FIGURE 6–2 • Vals 2 segmentation System

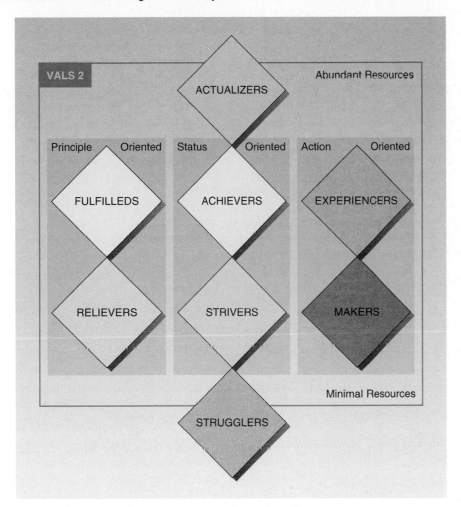

Source: SRI International, Menlo Park, CA.

VALS 2 ONLINE

You can use the VALS 2 segmentation scheme online at *future.sri.com:80/vals/survey.html*. Although the segmentation scheme is developed for citizens of the United States, the values, activities and lifestyle questions are relevant to Canadians. It will take you about ten minutes to log on, take the test and see which category best describes your approach to life. Just omit the zip code question, which is irrelevant for Canadians.

Another interesting VALS Web site is on Internet users. Check out *future.sri.com/vals/ivals/chrome.html* for profiles.

Regional Consumption Differences

If you have travelled to or lived in other parts of the country, you may have experienced the weird feeling of being slightly "out of sync" with your environment. The people may speak the same language, yet you may have difficulty understanding some things they say. Brands and store names may be confusing; some may be familiar and some not. And some familiar items may masquerade under different names. One person's hero is another's grinder is another's submarine sandwich is another's hoagie.

Citizens of Canada share the same national identity, yet the consumption patterns of different regions have been shaped by unique climates, cultural influences and resources. Such differences allow us legitimately to talk about regional personalities as well as a national personality. These regional differences often exert a big impact on consumers' lifestyles, since many of their preferences in foods, entertainment and so on are dictated by local customs and the availability of some diversions over others.

When choosing a geographical region or city for test-marketing purposes, marketers typically try to locate a place that is the most representative of the country. They want a microcosm that will allow them to predict how the mass market will react to product designs or promotional ideas. One favourite city to use as a test market is Peterborough, Ontario.

FOOD PREFERENCES

Within the regions also are some different cultural pockets and hence differences in food tastes. New Brunswick has the highest consumption of sliced white bread per capita, while Alberta leads the rest of the country in bubble-gum sales. More cornflakes are sold on the Prairies, and linguini has its highest sales in Toronto. The Québécois are the lowest consumers of frozen french fries, perhaps preferring the real thing, usually in the form of poutine.[37] Montreal is the undisputed bagel capital of Canada, while consumption of lobster is most easily enjoyed in Atlantic Canada.

Geodemography

geodemography techniques that combine consumer demographic information with geographic consumption patterns to permit precise targeting of consumers with specific characteristics

Geodemography refers to analytical techniques that combine data on consumer expenditures and other socio-economic factors with geographic information about the areas in which people live in order to identify consumers who share common consumption patterns. The assumption is that "birds of a feather flock together"—that is, people who have similar needs and tastes also tend to live near one another—so it should be possible to locate pockets of like-minded people who can then be reached more economically by direct mail and other methods.

When Western Union wanted to improve the cost-effectiveness of its network of offices, it undertook a market evaluation with the following goals:[38]

- analyze the number of Western Union agents needed in an area;
- determine where new agents would be most profitably located; and
- identify new market opportunities.

This project involved several steps. The company constructed a profile of the typical customer for money wire services and then attempted to identify areas where these customers were likely to live. It engaged a market research company to identify the geographic distribution of these customers at the area-code level and then defined areas as either unserved, partially served or saturated.

MARKETING OPPORTUNITY

With the aid of their trusty fax machines and computer modems that allow them to stay online even in remote places, growing numbers of "electronic pioneers" are forging a new lifestyle as they give up life in the big city to work in rural areas. Job growth in nonmetropolitan areas now exceeds that of metros, and counties in vacation or retirement areas or those that have a strong technology infrastructure are leading the way.

Growing numbers of middle-aged and well-educated suburbanites are trying to regain a sense of mastery over their environment by rebuilding their own homes, running their own businesses, managing their own finances, and using their own labour to buy cheaper groceries at warehouse clubs. Aided by technology, they are banking by computer, using specialized software to select mutual funds instead of relying on a broker, and using online travel agents to book vacations. The value of time spent doing tasks ourselves that could have been done by someone else is estimated to be 40 percent of the gross domestic product. Recognizing this trend, Home Depot Inc. recently opened a new store called Crossroads, which offers do-it-yourself tools and other devices needed to keep these displaced urbanites humming along in their home offices.

Their idea of precise geocoding.

Ours.

 Matchmaker/2000® for Windows™ is the only geocoding system that matches street address ranges to latitude and longitude coordinates. So you end up with a more precise and useful picture of where your customers and prospects are located. Matchmaker/2000 offers nationwide street coverage,

with more than 12 million address ranges. Other programs offer only half as many. Matchmaker/2000 is continuously updated. So your data is always current. And you'll achieve the highest match percentage available in the industry today. Matchmaker/2000 is an invaluable tool for market penetration studies. Point and cluster evaluations. Sales effectiveness analyses.

Scheduling and routing. And custom zone creation. You'll work smarter. And faster. The program is offered with a range of expandable and upgradable database options to meet your specific budget and application. Contact Geographic Data Technology, Inc., 13 Dartmouth College Highway, Lyme, NH 03768-9713. Or call 1-800-331-7881, x1101.

GEOGRAPHIC DATA TECHNOLOGY, INC.   1-800-331-7881 x1101

Reprinted from **American Demographics** magazine.

Modern geodemographic techniques allow companies to go well beyond broad regional differences. Many now segment markets down to the neighbourhood block. The provision of this type of analysis to marketers has become a profitable niche for several market research companies. *Reprinted with permission from Geographic Data Technology, Inc., Lebanon, NH.*

single-source data a compilation of information that includes different aspects of consumption and demographic data for a common consumer segment

Geographic information increasingly is being combined with other data to paint an even more complete picture of the Canadian consumer. Several marketing research ventures now employ **single-source data,** in which information about a person's actual purchasing history is combined with geodemographic data, and this method allows marketers to learn even more about the types of marketing strategies that motivate some people—but not others—to respond.

This comprehensive strategy was first implemented in the BehaviourScan project, begun in 1980 by Information Resources, Inc. The system combined UPC scanners, household panels and television to track purchases. This type of total approach allows marketers to test the impact of changes in advertising, pricing, shelf placement and promotions on consumer behaviour patterns. Similar systems are now available or under development by other organizations, such as Nielsen and SAMI/Burke.[39]

Marketers have been successful at adapting sophisticated analytical techniques originally developed for other applications, such as the military and oil and gas exploration. These techniques, which can now employ data at the neighbourhood or even household level, are being used in a variety of ways:

- A bank examined its penetration of accounts by customer area codes.

- A utility company compared demographic data with billing patterns to fine-tune energy conservation campaigns.

- A chain of ice-cream stores helped franchisees develop sales promotion programs for local markets by providing them with demographic profiles of actual users and information about the sales potential of untapped customer groups.

International Lifestyle Segmentation

Increasingly sophisticated efforts are being made to develop lifestyle typologies that transcend national borders. Many of these systems have been developed to better understand European buying habits and, in particular, to determine if it is possible to identify "Euroconsumers," who share the same lifestyle orientations despite living in, say, France and Italy. These studies have had mixed success, with most researchers reporting that people in each nation still have a lot of idiosyncracies that make it difficult to lump them together.[40] Let's take a quick look at some of these attempts.

- McCann-Erickson London, a British advertising agency, segments male and female consumers separately. Lifestyle categories in this system include such segments as "avant guardians" (those interested in change), "pontificators" (traditionalists; those who are very British), "chameleons" (those who follow the crowd) and "sleepwalkers" (contented underachievers). An ambitious project to develop a typology of consumers in the Great Britain (England, Wales and Scotland) by a company called Socioconsult is described in Figure 6–3.

- Japanese culture values conformity. One way to refer to the desire to fit in is *hitonami consciousness,* which translates as "aligning oneself with other people." Despite this overall emphasis, there is a growing segment of Japanese consumers who are fighting the tide. These people have been called "life designers" to reflect their interest in crafting their own unique lifestyle patterns. One Japanese segmentation scheme divides consumers into "tribes" and includes, among others, the "crystal tribe" (the tribe that prefers well-known brands), "my-home tribe" (the family-oriented tribe) and the "impulse-buyer tribe."[41]

FIGURE 6–3 • Social Millieus: An Example of International Lifestyle Segmentation

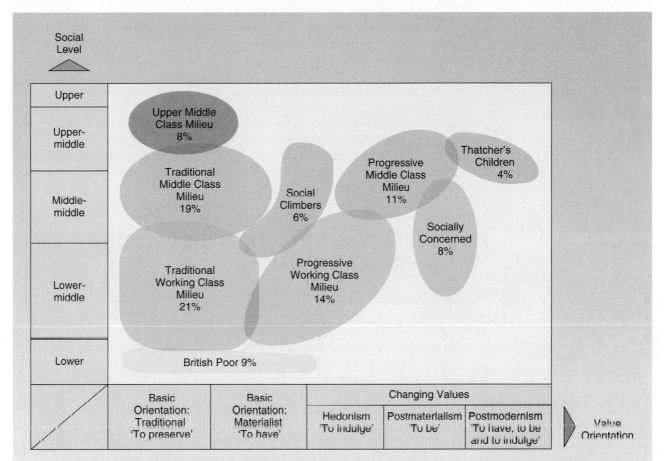

Socioconsult, based in Paris, attempts to identify segments of consumers in different countries who share common values and outlooks on life. Respondents answer a battery of questions that are designed to assess their outlook on life (including work, leisure, family, consumption and aesthetics). Based upon the responses received, consumers are grouped into what the company calls "social milieus." The nine social milieus obtained for Great Britain are shown here. These clusters are derived by using two types of information: (1) social level (i.e., income and social class) and (2) value orientation, which is related to attitudes towards change and outlook on life. Each of the nine clusters exhibits different attitudes and behaviours; this information is then provided to the company's clients, who select segments to target and who design product and promotional strategies calculated to appeal to members of that "social milieu."

Source: Socioconsult, Paris, 1994.

- As countries in eastern Europe convert to free-market economies, many marketers are exploring ways to segment these increasingly consumption-oriented societies. Some Western products such as Marlboro cigarettes and McDonald's are already firmly entrenched in Russia. The D'Arcy Masius Benton & Bowles Advertising Agency, which has offices in Moscow and St. Petersburg, conducted a psychographic study of Russian consumers and has proclaimed that the country's 150 million consumers can be divided into five segments, including "Cossacks" (status-seeking nationalists who drive BMWs, smoke Dunhill cigarettes and drink Rémy Martin cognac), *"Kuptsi"* (merchants who value practical products, tend to drive Volkswagens, smoke Chesterfields and drink Stolichnaya vodka), and "Russian souls" (passive consumers who drive Russian-made Lada cars, smoke Marlboros and drink Smirnoff).[42]

- A cross-country psychographic segmentation project conducted jointly by the Ogilvy and Mather advertising agency and an Australian research firm identified ten segments, including such categories as "basic needs" (those who are traditional and passive), "look-at-me" (seekers of exciting and prosperous lives), "visible achievement" (those with traditional values; seekers of "the good life"), "socially aware" (those involved in environmental movements) and "fairer deal" (dissatisfied with their lives). Relatively few Australians were in the "visible achievement" segment, while high numbers of consumers in the United States, Canada and Japan were. A disproportionate number of British consumers fell into the "fairer deal" group, while Germans were over-represented in the "look-at-me" segment.[43]

LIFESTYLE TRENDS: CONSUMER BEHAVIOUR IN THE MILLENNIUM

Consumer lifestyles are a moving target. Society's priorities and preferences are constantly evolving, and it is essential for marketers to track these changes and, more importantly, try to anticipate them. Of course, many lifestyle trends are rooted in economic and demographic patterns, so understanding these developments usually entails an appreciation of such factors as employment rates, educational attainment and population growth.

For example, the "go-go" economic conditions of the 1980s fed a boom in self-interest and the belief in upward mobility. In contrast, the leaner years of the 1990s have fed people's fears about their futures. As corporations continue to downsize, many consumers now face the grim prospect of downward mobility. Consumer confidence can turn into pessimism, which tends to make people more frugal, more conservative and, to some extent, more distrustful of other types of people, who are viewed as threats to the well-being of their families or important subcultures.

affinitization process where groups organize around special interests

As a result, in the 1990s we see such developments as **affinitization,** wherein groups organize around special interests, such as immigration policy, the environment or religious education. We also witness a return to an emphasis on "value" in products, as advertisers redouble their efforts to emphasize the practical benefits of products. And, as people age, they tend to become more concerned with *preservation* of assets, both financial and personal. This means a renewed interest both in products that allow consumers to conserve money to ensure an easier retirement and in those that slow the aging process.[44] In this section we'll take a final look at some of the important lifestyle issues now shaping consumer behaviour.

Trend Forecasting: Peering into the Crystal Ball of Consumer Behaviour

If a marketer could see into the future, he or she would obviously have an enormous advantage when developing products and services that will meet the needs of consumers next year, in five years or in ten years. No one is able to do that yet, but a number of marketing research firms do try very hard to predict social trends. For

FIGURE 6-4 • Highlights from 1996 Needham Lifestyle Study

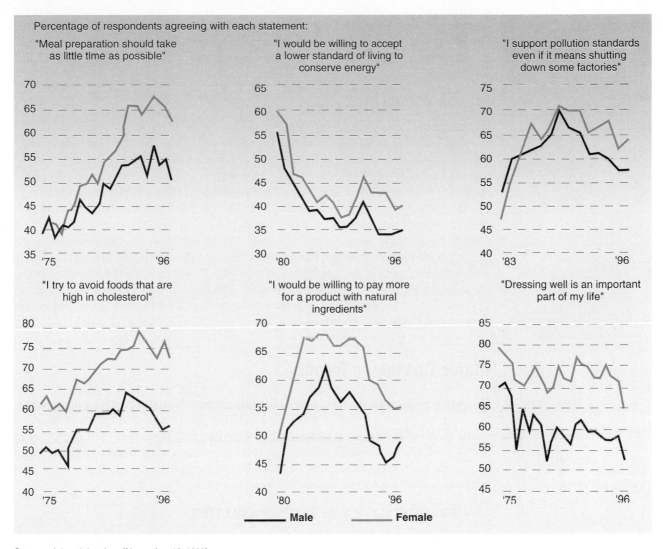

Source: *Advertising Age,* (November 18, 1996).

example, the Lifestyle Monitor, now run by the firm Yankelovich Clancy Shulman, interviews 2500 American adults annually. Advertising agency Backer Spielvogel Bates's Global Scan program divides markets in 18 countries into psychographic segments and charts changes in attitudes.

Since 1975 the DDB Needham Worldwide advertising agency has been conducting its Needham Lifestyle Study, an ongoing study of changes in consumer behaviour consisting of a sample of 4000 Americans' answers to a battery of 1000 questions. The 1996 report indicated that an earlier trend towards self-sacrifice appears to be eroding. Consumers in the late 1990s want to eat what they want, dress for comfort and embrace traditional values—as long as they don't interfere with convenience or individualism. People are paying less attention to nutrition and diet, exercise is declining as a regular activity, and fewer people believe that dressing well is important.

In addition, the study found a decrease in support for pollution standards or willingness to accept a lower standard of living to save energy. More than 85 percent of men and women say they have somewhat old-fashioned tastes and habits, yet the percentage of both sexes who say couples should live together before marriage is up, as is support for legalization of both abortion and marijuana.[45] Figure 6–4 highlights some of the long-term trends tracked by the Lifestyle Study.

TRENDS VERSUS FADS

It is important to note the difference between a lifestyle trend and a current fad. The current boom in cigar sales among 30- to 40-year-olds may be just a chance to behave in a novel manner. There is some thrill in smoking a "Cuban" cigar due to the ban on Cuban imports in the United States. Sales of this product are sure to plummet once the ban is lifted, and it is not a business that has a predictable future.[46]

Besides cigars, another old product getting a second wind is the push mower.[47] Unlike cigars, push mowers may be considered a real lifestyle trend. Many homeowners have smaller lawns to cut than they did in the Seventies. Cities have become denser, with buildings occupying more of the land. Gardens are taking over from lawns as more people are gardening as a hobby. In addition, push mowers give the consumer a sense of nostalgia and environmentalism, as well as some real exercise. They are also a lot quieter to operate. Sales are expected to grow 20 to 30 percent annually over the next few years.

Major Consumer Trends

Of course, trend forecasting is a bit like reading one's horoscope in the paper. Sometimes forecasts are so general they can't help but come true, and only a proportion of the more specific ones actually do. The problem is that we don't know until after the fact which ones will. The following sections discuss some recent predictions of trends we can expect in the rest of the 1990s (note that they sometimes contradict each other). Which will be accurate? Take your pick.

ENVIRONMENTALISM AND GREEN MARKETING

Concern for the environment, or the *green movement,* is a priority for many consumers around the world. With the introduction of its Origins line of cosmetics, the Estée Lauder Company was the first major US beauty company to bring natural, non-animal-tested products in recyclable containers into department stores.[48]

Still, although many consumers give preference to products that help the environment, there are signs that interest in the green movement is waning. Membership in environmental groups like the Sierra Club and Greenpeace is down sharply, and some marketers' abuse of the claim that their products are safe has led some consumers to discount these claims. To compound the problem, worries about crime, homelessness and other issues appear to have taken precedence over the environment for many people.[49]

A RETURN TO VALUE

Many consumers are no longer interested in the niceties provided by fancy stores, especially when the products they sell are marked up too much. These consumers are becoming what the Grey Advertising agency calls "precision shoppers"—shop-

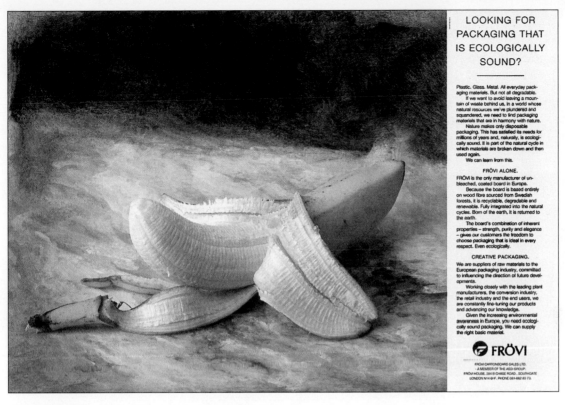

LOOKING FOR PACKAGING THAT IS ECOLOGICALLY SOUND?

Plastic. Glass. Metal. All everyday packaging materials. But not all degradable.

If we want to avoid leaving a mountain of waste behind us, in a world whose natural resources we've plundered and squandered, we need to find packaging materials that are in harmony with nature.

Nature makes only disposable packaging. This has satisfied its needs for millions of years and, naturally, is ecologically sound. It is part of the natural cycle in which materials are broken down and then used again.

We can learn from this.

FRÖVI ALONE.

FRÖVI is the only manufacturer of unbleached, coated board in Europe.

Because the board is based entirely on wood fibre sourced from Swedish forests, it is recyclable, degradable and renewable. Fully integrated into the natural cycles. Born of the earth, it is returned to the earth.

The board's combination of inherent properties – strength, purity and elegance – gives our customers the freedom to choose packaging that is ideal in every respect. Even ecologically.

CREATIVE PACKAGING.

We are suppliers of raw materials to the European packaging industry, committed to influencing the direction of future developments.

Working closely with the leading plant manufacturers, the conversion industry, the retail industry and the end users, we are constantly fine-tuning our products and advancing our knowledge.

Given the increasing environmental awareness in Europe, you need ecologically sound packaging. We can supply the right basic material.

FRÖVI

FRÖVI CARTONBOARD SALES LTD.
- A MEMBER OF THE ASSI GROUP.
FRÖVI HOUSE, 394 B CHASE ROAD , SOUTHGATE
LONDON N14 6HF. PHONE 081-882 83 73.

This Swedish ad for a manufacturer of ecologically friendly packaging materials reflects the desire of many marketers to participate in the green movement.
Courtesy of Ehrenstrahle & Co., BBDO, Stockholm, SWEDEN.

Botanical and natural extracts
No animal testing
Nothing but earth-friendly inks
Recycled packaging
And every time you buy it, money goes
to preserving the Rainforest

It's the way you
care
teach
think
dream
believe

Love's Clean & Natural™
It's the way you live.

Introducing Clean & Natural Cologne Splash, All-Over Body Spray, Shower Gel, Moisturizer, Body Powder & Deodorant.
©1994 MEM Company Inc. Northvale, N.J. 07647

This ad for a line of body powders and oils is positioned to appeal to people who are ecologically minded. It hits many of the "hot points" of the green movement: no animal testing, packaging is recycled, and a part of the profits go to help the rain forest. It is hoped that these types of value-added product attributes will sway consumers to choose one product over another.
Love's Clean & Natural, MEM Company, Inc.

"We blew a deadline, ticked everyone off, cost the company a bundle and we did the right thing."

General Motors.

What if you ran a division of General Motors and were due to debut an important flagship model...and it wasn't quite ready? Nothing drastic you understand, just a few little glitches that meant not every car coming off the line was just right. What if you'd sworn to your bosses you'd be ready? What if you had a lot of potential customers waiting to get a first look? What would you do? Here's what Chevrolet's Jim Perkins and his team did: they pulled the plug on the introduction and said, "When we know we've got it right, we'll bring out the car." That night, Jim Perkins did what people who do the right thing always do. He got a good night's sleep.

This ad for General Motors reflects the new spirit of quality and relationship-building that many marketers espouse in the 1990s.
Courtesy of General Motors Corporation.

pers who pick and choose carefully, who no longer shy away from lesser-known house brands, and who are flocking in droves to warehouse stores offering self-service and products by the case in drab surroundings.

Ironically, this emphasis on quality at a reasonable price has turned many people into more loyal shoppers. Once they find a store that provides the value they seek, they reward it with their business consistently. This type of ongoing relationship also is more efficient, since consumers no longer have to spend so much time comparing prices in different stores. Retailers are responding by offering what they call *EDLP*—everyday low prices—instead of making shoppers wait for periodic specials. This strategy adds value by making people's lives simpler.[50] Marketers of everything from automobiles to suits are scrambling to find ways to offer value and build bonds with customers who are weary of glitzy promotions and overpriced goodies.

TIME POVERTY

An increasing emphasis on the value of time as a commodity is motivating consumers to look for new ways of acquiring experiences and products in more convenient and accessible forms. Advances in technology make possible more home-centred activities, whether for entertainment (e.g., the proliferation of cable stations) or for work (e.g., the trend towards telecommuting, as more people use

This ad for John Deere reflects consumers' desire to get value for their money. The headline plays on people's frustrations about not getting their money's worth, while the rest of the ad underscores the many product attributes that make the lawnmower a good buy.
Courtesy of John Deere & Company.

MARKETING OPPORTUNITY

As one consequence of the time pressures facing many consumers, the car is becoming a popular dining room. The practice of eating on the run has become so widespread that one out of every ten meals bought in a restaurant is eaten in a car! That figure climbs even higher when convenience-store snacks are included.

Some marketers are beginning to develop new food products that make it easier to eat with at least one hand on the steering wheel. Burger King is testing a new sandwich wrapper with a pocket that is easier to pick up and put down in traffic. Southland Corp., which operates 7-Eleven convenience stores, is developing healthier alternatives that are also road-friendly, such as a grilled chicken sandwich shaped like a hot dog and a tray of bite-sized pieces of vegetables with a spill-proof receptacle for salad dressing. Still, some marketers are reluctant to push the idea of in-car dining too much further, citing the safety risks involved. Perhaps they are chastened by the recent experience of McDonald's. The company lost a multimillion-dollar lawsuit brought by a woman who was badly scalded and needed skin grafts when her too-hot coffee spilled on her in her car.[51]

their personal computers and faxes to establish offices at home).

The increase in working couples leads to greater value being placed on convenience products and services that minimize time and effort spent in purchasing. Although couples in which both partners work, as well as those in which only one person works, average two weekly trips to the market and spend about the same (US$57 per trip), working couples spend 15 percent less time in the market. To facilitate this "race" through the market, some chains now display floor plans at the entrance.[52] Home delivery of food is growing twice as fast as take-out or drive-through services. In addition, look for increased reliance on catalogues, professional shoppers and home automation.[53]

DISILLUSIONMENT OF WORKING WOMEN

As we saw in Chapter 5, changes are taking place in the gender roles of men and women as ideals about marriage, homosexuality, child-rearing and career choices evolve. As uncertainty regarding the proper roles of men and women in our culture increases, consumers will continue to be influenced by how notions of masculinity and femininity are translated into product concepts and advertising practices by marketers.

Women will discover that working outside the home is not as liberating as they thought. Look for a return to traditional husband/wife roles to occur, as women abandon careers and stay home with the children. Women are now more likely than men to say they "work very hard most of the time," and their use of pain relievers is growing dramatically. In surveys, the number of women who say they would prefer to stay home is steadily increasing. In 1976 the values most likely to be endorsed by women were security and self-respect. By 1986 the emphasis had shifted to a paramount desire for warm relationships. Many observers have noted a shift towards *neotraditionalism,* which includes a renewed commitment to the family. In the words of one observer, the 1990s have ushered in an emphasis on "romance, religion, and rattles."[54]

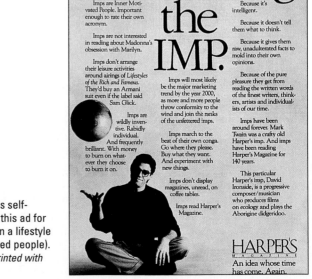

Reflecting the consumer trend towards self-fulfilment and away from materialism, this ad for *Harper's Magazine* describes people in a lifestyle segment it dubs "imps" (inner-motivated people). *Copyright © by* Harper's Magazine. *Reprinted with special permission.*

DECREASED EMPHASIS ON NUTRITION AND EXERCISE

Changing priorities regarding exercise, nutrition and self-indulgence, coupled with a premium placed on antistress services ranging from aromatherapy to personal trainers, are leading to changes as people try to cope with the numerous demands of their roles as parents and workers. The personal demands placed on us by modern society also affect the dark side of consumer behaviour, as we grapple with such problems as addiction, prostitution, compulsive shopping, theft and vandalism.

While many people still appear to be concerned about their health, the obsession of many with diet and exercise appears to be subsiding as people are adopting more of an "OK-in-moderation" outlook. An antidiet book, *Stop the Insanity!* by Susan Powter, has sold close to a million copies.[55] Such words as "real" and "rich" are being used more frequently to describe full-flavoured ice creams, peanut butter and other "comfort foods" that make people feel better in anxious times.[56] Fewer consumers are avoiding salty products or foods with additives or report a willingness to pay more for "all-natural" foods.[57] Opposition to the consumption of red meat also appears to have peaked.[58]

DEATH OF COCOONING

Ten years after Faith Popcorn baptized the phenomenon "cocooning," North Americans are officially pronouncing it dead.[59] With the growing-up of baby boomers' children, parents want to party again outside the home. Attendance at movie theatres is up for the third year in a row. The Montreal Jazz Festival has seen its audience triple to 1.5 million in the last three years. Nearly 10 million people saw dance, symphony, opera or theatre performances in 1996. Canadians are eating out more and watching 5 percent less television than they did in 1996 (20 hours a week in 1997).

The cover of this brochure focuses on acquiring the experience of "arts weekend."
Event organizer: Janet Crawford. Brochure designer: Angela Simpson.
Sculpture: Sarah Quintin-Beland.
Photography: Neil McCulloch. Reproduced with permission.

What else besides demographics accounts for this trend? Believe it or not, crime is down and people feel safer on the streets. They also want a connection with others that they cannot find in front of the television. It's party time again.

NONCONSUMPTION

People will look for products and services that will help them to shed bad habits. In recent years, abstention from certain products and practices has become a way of life for many consumers, who have adopted "non" as the code word for a lifestyle. Membership in support groups that help people to stop various forms of consumption, including alcohol, narcotics, gambling, overeating and even sex, has doubled in the last decade. Some products have succeeded at positioning themselves in terms of attributes they do *not* possess. These include 7-UP ("the UnCola"), Club Med ("the antidote to civilization") and Max Factor's "no colour mascara."[60] In addition, the concept of "lite" versions of products has permeated everything from wine to ice cream.

INDIVIDUALIZATION AND MASS CUSTOMIZATION

Modern consumers have a strong sense of individualism, partly due to the dominance of the baby boomer generation that came of age in the late 1960s. Children raised during this time grew up in a period of affluence, in which their wishes were indulged and they were encouraged to think for themselves. For better or for worse, consumers now tend to put their personal needs ahead of their loyalties to groups or organizations.[61]

Technological and marketing developments have fanned the fires of individualism. Increasing numbers of people are going to work for themselves rather than for big companies. They are communicating with one another from the isolation of their homes via the Internet, and are tailoring their own entertainment options from hundreds of offerings. Advances in database marketing are allowing marketers to target very specific groups of people with well-defined interests, who receive specialized information about products where and when they want it. Advertisers are even talking about "ad-directed channels," where cable stations are devoted to programming about specific subjects. For example, *Car & Driver* magazine recently spawned an automotive cable TV network, and its parent company is looking into creating other channels devoted to fashion or home decorating.[62]

mass customization a basic product or service is modified to meet the needs of an individual

Some forward-looking consumer-oriented companies are moving towards **mass customization,** where a basic product or service is modified to meet the needs of an individual.[63] For example, Marriott's Honoured Guest program tracks the preferences of repeat customers, so that when they check in to one of the company's hotels they are assigned a room that best conforms to their individual preferences, such as smoking or nonsmoking, on a low floor or a high floor, and so on.[64] Hallmark Cards allows buyers to create their own greeting cards by adding personal information to a basic design. Levi Strauss recently introduced made-to-order jeans called Personal Pair Line for Women. For $10 to $15 more than the cost of a mass-produced pair, customers have four measurements taken: hip, waist, inseam and rise. Women then try on a pair that corresponds to these measurements and customize for leg-cut, length and colour. In all, there are 11 544 possible size variations.[65]

As marketers continue the push to build solid relationships with customers, they will find that the ability to provide products and services that match their customers' very specific needs will be a valued commodity in the next millennium. Welcome to the new age of marketing!

A LAID-BACK LIFESTYLE

Consumers are renewing their interest in living casually, and this informality is now extending even to the workplace. Many companies are instituting a relaxed dress code, led by the "Casual Friday" movement that allows employees to leave their ties and pantyhose at home one day a week. Not surprisingly, Levi Strauss has led the charge by promoting its casual clothing lines as an alternative to suits. As one company executive observed, "Casual office dressing is becoming mainstream."[66]

LIFE IN THE FAST LANE

Consumers continue their relentless search for thrills and chills, and fantasy entertainment is growing in popularity. New attractions in Las Vegas epitomize this trend. One company blew up a real hotel on New Year's Eve 1997 in front of 200 000 tourists. This was done to make way for a 4000-room resort whose theme is an ancient forbidden city discovered on a tropical island. It will include a swim-up shark exhibit and scheduled rain showers. Other Vegas attractions include a skydiving simulator with a 160-kilometre-an-hour updraft.

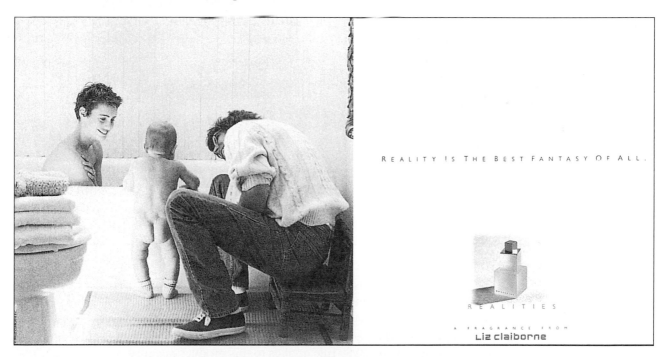

This ad for Realities by Liz Claiborne illustrates the shift in values from an emphasis in the 1980s on glitz to home-centred, down-to-earth activities in the 1990s.
Courtesy of Altschiller Reitzfeld Tracy-Locke.

CHAPTER SUMMARY

- A consumer's lifestyle refers to the ways he or she chooses to spend time and money and how his or her values and tastes are reflected by consumption choices. Lifestyle research is useful to track societal consumption preferences and also to position specific products and services to different segments.

- Marketers segment by lifestyle differences, often by grouping consumers in terms of their AIOs (activities, interests and opinions).

- Psychographic techniques attempt to classify consumers in terms of psychological, subjective variables in addition to observable characteristics (demographics). A variety of systems, such as VALS 2, have been developed to identify consumer "types" and to differentiate them in terms of their brand or product preferences, media usage, leisure-time activities, and attitudes towards such broad issues as politics and religion.

- Place of residence often is a significant determinant of lifestyle. Many marketers recognize regional differences in product preferences and develop different versions of their products for different markets. A set of techniques called geodemography analyzes consumption patterns using geographical and demographic data, and identifies clusters of consumers who exhibit similar psychographic characteristics.

KEY TERMS

Affinitization p. 200
AIOs p. 192
Animism p. 185
Archetype p. 182
Brand equity p. 184
Ego p. 178
Geodemography p. 196
Id p. 178

Lifestyle p. 187
Mass customization p. 208
Motivational research p. 180
Personality p. 177
Pleasure principle p. 178
Product complementarity p. 189

Psychographics p. 190
Single-source data p. 198
Superego p. 178
Traits p. 183
20/80 rule p. 192
VALS (Values and Lifestyles) p. 194

CONSUMER BEHAVIOUR CHALLENGE

1. Compare and contrast the concepts of lifestyle and social class.

2. In what situations is demographic information likely to be more useful than psychographic data, and vice versa?

3. Alcohol drinkers vary sharply in terms of the number of drinks they consume, from those who occasionally have one at a cocktail party to regular imbibers. Explain how the 20/80 rule applies to this product category.

4. Describe the underlying principles used to construct the VALS 2 system. What are some positive and negative aspects of this approach to lifestyle segmentation?

5. Compile a set of recent ads that attempt to link consumption of a product with a specific lifestyle. How is this goal usually accomplished?

6. The chapter mentions that psychographic analyses can be used to market politicians. Conduct research on the marketing strategies used in a recent, major election. How were voters segmented in terms of values? Can you find evidence that communications strategies were guided by this information?

7. Construct separate advertising executions for a cosmetics product targeted to the achiever, experiential and striver VALS 2 types. How would the basic appeal differ for each group?

8. Geodemographic techniques assume that people who live in the same neighbourhood have other things in common as well. Why is this assumption made, and how accurate is it?

9. Single-source data systems give marketers access to a wide range of information about a consumer, simply by knowing his or her address. Do you believe this "knowledge power" presents any ethical problems with regard to consumers' privacy? Should access to such information be regulated by the government or other bodies? Should consumers have the right to limit access to these data?

CBC VIDEO VIGNETTES

Concepts at Work for Terra Nova Shoes

Terra Nova Shoes, a family business located in Harbour Grace, Newfoundland, is a company that successfully served the construction-boot business for a generation. The second generation, however, is facing a saturated domestic market and competition from a flood of cheap imports made in countries with very low labour costs. With an investment in robotics the company is looking for expansion opportunities in international markets. They are becoming aware of how to convey quality standards for the same pair of boots through subtle changes in the presentation style used in different countries.

Recently the company explored the potential for developing a market among teens, because "the work boot look is all the rage." Terry Nova has much to learn about the lifestyle of teens, from where teens take their fashion cues to the role of advertising in establishing brand recognition and the role of retail outlets. The company is trying to cross the line to another buyer segment in a number of international markets. Competition from other manufacturers is fierce. A deep understanding of "fads" versus "fashion," as well as of cultural differences, is essential.

QUESTIONS

1. Why has Terry Nova Shoes been successful so far?

2. How has the market for work boots changed?

3. Do you think Terra Nova is in touch with the current lifestyle trends of the teen market?

4. What markets would you advise Terra Nova to pursue based on the trends and lifestyles heading into the next millennium?

Video Resource: "Terra Nova Boots," *Venture* #517 (December 4, 1994).

NOTES

1. See J. Aronoff and J.P. Wilson, *Personality in the Social Process* (Hillsdale, NJ: Erlbaum, 1985); Walter Mischel, *Personality and Assessment* (New York: Wiley, 1968).

2. Ernest Dichter, *A Strategy of Desire* (Garden City, NY: Doubleday, 1960); Ernest Dichter, *The Handbook of Consumer Motivations* (New York: McGraw-Hill, 1964); Jeffrey J. Durgee, "Interpreting Dichter's Interpretations: An Analysis of Consumption Symbolism in the Handbook of Consumer Motivations" (unpublished manuscript, Rensselaer Polytechnic Institute, Troy, NY, 1989); Pierre Martineau, *Motivation in Advertising* (New York: McGraw-Hill, 1957).

3. Vance Packard, *The Hidden Persuaders* (New York: D. McKay, 1957).

4. Harold Kassarjian, "Personality and Consumer Behavior: A Review," *Journal of Marketing Research* 8 (November 1971): 409–18.

5. Karen Horney, *Neurosis and Human Growth* (New York: Norton, 1950).

6. Joel B. Cohen, "An Interpersonal Orientation to the Study of Consumer Behavior," *Journal of Marketing Research* 6 (August 1967): 270–78; Pradeep K. Tyagi, "Validation of the CAD Instrument: A Replication," in *Advances in Consumer Research 10*, eds. Richard P. Bagozzi and Alice M. Tybout (Ann Arbor, MI: Association for Consumer Research, 1983), pp. 112–14.

7. For a comprehensive review of classic perspectives on personality theory, see Calvin S. Hall and Gardner Lindzey, *Theories of Personality,* 2nd ed. (New York: John Wiley & Sons, Inc., 1970).

8. Cf. Carl G. Jung, "The Archetypes and the Collective Unconscious," in *Collected Works,* eds. H. Read, M. Fordham and G. Adler (Princeton: Princeton University Press, 1959), vol. 9, pt. 1.

9. Linda L. Price and Nancy Ridgway, "Development of a Scale to Measure Innovativeness," in *Advances in Consumer Research 10*, eds. Richard P. Bagozzi and Alice M. Tybout (Ann Arbor, MI: Association for Consumer Research, 1983), pp. 679–84; Russell W. Belk, "Three Scales to Measure Constructs Related to Materialism: Reliability, Validity, and Relationships to Measures of Happiness," in *Advances in Consumer Research 11*, ed. Thomas C. Kinnear (Ann Arbor, MI: Association for Consumer Research, 1984), p. 291; Mark Snyder, "Self-Monitoring Processes," in *Advances in Experimental Social Psychology*, ed. Leonard Berkowitz (New York: Academic Press, 1979), pp. 851–928; Gordon R. Foxall and Ronald E. Goldsmith, "Personality and Consumer Research: Another Look," *Journal of the Market Research Society* 30, 2 (1988): 111–25; Ronald E. Goldsmith and Charles F. Hofacker, "Measuring Consumer Innovativeness," *Journal of the Academy of Marketing Science* 19, 3 (1991): 209–21; Curtis P. Haugtvedt, Richard E. Petty and John T. Cacioppo, "Need for

Cognition and Advertising: Understanding the Role of Personality Variables in Consumer Behavior," *Journal of Consumer Psychology* 1, 3 (1992): 239–60.

10. Jacob Jacoby, *Personality and Consumer Behavior: How Not to Find Relationships,* Purdue Papers in Consumer Psychology, 102 (Lafayette, IN: Purdue University, 1969); Harold H. Kassarjian and Mary Jane Sheffet, "Personality and Consumer Behavior: An Update," in *Perspectives in Consumer Behavior,* 4th ed., eds. Harold H. Kassarjian and Thomas S. Robertson (Glenview, IL: Scott, Foresman and Company, 1991), pp. 291–353; John Lastovicka and Erich Joachimsthaler, "Improving the Detection of Personality Behavior Relationships in Consumer Research," *Journal of Consumer Research* 14 (March 1988): 583–87. For an approach that ties the notion of personality more directly to marketing issues, see Jennifer L. Aaker, "Measuring Brand Personality" (unpublished manuscript, Stanford University, September 1994).

11. Cf. Girish N. Punj and David W. Stewart, "An Interaction Framework of Consumer Decision Making," *Journal of Consumer Research* 10 (September 1983): 181–96.

12. J.F. Allsopp, "The Distribution of On-Licence Beer and Cider Consumption and Its Personality Determinants Among Young Men," *European Journal of Marketing* 20, 3 (1986): 44–62; Foxall and Goldsmith, "Personality and Consumer Research: Another Look."

13. Thomas Hine, "Why We Buy: The Silent Persuasion of Boxes, Bottles, Cans, and Tubes," *Worth* (May 1995): 78–83.

14. Kevin L. Keller, "Conceptualization, Measuring, and Managing Customer-Based Brand Equity," *Journal of Marketing* 57 (January 1993): 1–22.

15. Jennifer L. Aaker, "Dimensions of Brand Personality," *Journal of Marketing Research* 34, 3 (August 1997): 347–56.

16. Tim Triplett, "Brand Personality Must be Managed or It Will Assume a Life Of Its Own," *Marketing News* (May 9, 1994): 9.

17. Susan Fournier, "A Consumer–Brand Relationship Framework for Strategic Brand Management," Doctoral Dissertation, Department of Marketing, University of Florida, 1994.

18. Rebecca Piirto Heath, "The Frontiers of Psychographics," *American Demographics* (July 1996): 38–43.

19. Benjamin D. Zablocki and Rosabeth Moss Kanter, "The Differentiation of Life-Styles," *Annual Review of Sociology* (1976): 269–97.

20. Mary Twe Douglas and Baron C. Isherwood, *The World of Goods* (New York: Basic Books, 1979).

21. Zablocki and Kanter, "The Differentiation of Life-Styles."

22. Richard A. Peterson, "Revitalizing the Culture Concept," *Annual Review of Sociology* 5 (1979): 137–66.

23. William Leiss, Stephen Kline and Sut Jhally, *Social Communication in Advertising* (Toronto: Methuen, 1986).

24. Douglas and Isherwood, *The World of Goods*, pp. 72–73.

25. Michael R. Solomon, "The Role of Products as Social Stimuli: A Symbolic Interactionism Perspective," *Journal of Consumer Research* 10 (December 1983): 319–29.

26. Michael R. Solomon and Henry Assael, "The Forest or the Trees?: A Gestalt Approach to Symbolic Consumption," in *Marketing and Semiotics: New Directions in the Study of Signs for Sale,* ed. Jean Umiker-Sebcok (Berlin: Mouton de Gruyter, 1988), pp. 189–218; Michael R. Solomon, "Mapping Product Constellations: A Social Categorization Approach to Symbolic Consumption," *Psychology & Marketing* 5, 3 (1988): 233–58. See also Stephen C. Cosmas, "Life Styles and Consumption Patterns," *Journal of Consumer Research* 8, 4 (March 1982): 453–55.

27. Russell W. Belk, "Yuppies as Arbiters of the Emerging Consumption Style," in *Advances in Consumer Research 13*, ed. Richard J. Lutz (Provo, UT: Association for Consumer Research, 1986), pp. 514–19.

28. See Lewis Alpert and Ronald Gatty, "Product Positioning by Behavioral Life Styles," *Journal of Marketing* 33 (April 1969): 65–69; Emanuel H. Demby, "Psychographics Revisited: The Birth of a Technique," *Marketing News* (January 2, 1989): 21; William D. Wells, "Backward Segmentation," in *Insights into Consumer Behavior,* ed. Johan Arndt (Boston: Allyn & Bacon, 1968), pp. 85–100.

29. Rebecca Piirto Heath, "Psychographics: Q'est-ce que c'est?" *Marketing Tools* (November/December 1995): 73 (6 pp.).

30. William D. Wells and Douglas J. Tigert, "Activities, Interests, and Opinions," *Journal of Advertising Research* 11 (August 1971): 27.

31. Ian Pearson, "Social Studies: Psychographics in Advertising," *Canadian Business* (December 1985): 67.

32. Heath, "Psychographics: Q'est-ce que c'est?"

33. Alfred S. Boote, "Psychographics: Mind Over Matter," *American Demographics* (April 1980): 26–29; William D. Wells, "Psychographics: A Critical Review," *Journal of Marketing Research* 12 (May 1975): 196–213.

34. Joseph T. Plummer, "The Concept and Application of Life Style Segmentation," *Journal of Marketing* 38 (January 1974): 33–37.

35. John L. Lastovicka et al., "A Lifestyle Typology to Model Young Male Drinking and Driving," *Journal of Consumer Research* 14 (September 1987): 257–63.

36. Martha Farnsworth Riche, "VALS 2," *American Demographics* (July 1989): 25.

37. Eve Johnson, "Getting a Taste for Canada," *Vancouver Sun* (June 19, 1995): C1.

38. Thomas W. Osborn, "Analytic Techniques for Opportunity Marketing," *Marketing Communications* (September 1987): 49–63.

39. Ibid.

40. Valerie Latham, "Do Euroconsumers Exist?" *Marketing* (June 24, 1993): 3.

41. Leiss, Kline and Jhally, *Social Communication in Advertising.*

42. Stuart Elliott, "Sampling Tastes of a Changing Russia," *New York Times* (April 1, 1992): D1.

43. "Value Segments Help Define International Market," *Marketing News* (November 21, 1988): 17.

44. Peter Francese, "The Trend Evolution," *American Demographics* (October 1993): 3.

45. Bill McDowell, "New DDB Needham Report: Consumers Want It All," *Advertising Age* (November 18, 1996): 32–33.

46. Eve Lazarus, "Cigar Café Targets Women Customers," *Marketing Magazine* (June 23, 1997): 3.

47. Bill Richards, "Push Mowers Reach the Pinnacle of Backyard Chic," *Wall Street Journal*, reprinted in *Globe and Mail* (August 9, 1997): D1.

48. Pat Sloan, "Cosmetics: Color It Green," *Advertising Age* (July 23, 1990): 1.

49. Timothy Aeppel, "Green Groups Enter a Dry Season as Movement Matures," *Wall Street Journal* (October 21, 1994): B1 (2 pp.).

50. Rahul Jacob, "Beyond Quality & Value," *Fortune* (Autumn/Winter 1993): 8 (3 pp.).

51. Kathleen Deveny, "Movable Feasts: More People Dine and Drive," *Wall Street Journal* (January 4, 1994): B1.

52. Ronald D. Michman, "New Directions for Life-Style Behavior Patterns," *Business Horizons* (July/August 1984): 60.

53. Timothy Harris, "Fast and Easy: US Supermarkets Market Convenience Foods as Lifestyles," *Marketing* (October 29, 1987): 17.

54. Sandra Pesmen, "Home Front," *Advertising Age* (September 19, 1994): 1 (2 pp.); Lenore Skenazy, "Welcome Home: Trend Experts Point to 'Neo-traditional,'" *Advertising Age* (May 16, 1988): 38; Lynn Kahle, Basil Poulos and Ajay Sukdial, "Changes in Social Values in the United States During the Past Decade," *Journal of Advertising Research* 28 (February/March 1988): 35–41; DDB Needham Worldwide Life Style Study, reported in *Advertising Age* (September 24, 1990): 25.

55. Molly O'Neill, "'Eat, Drink and Be Merry' May Be the Next Trend," *New York Times* (January 4, 1994): 1 (2 pp.); Cyndee Miller, "The 'Real Food' Movement: Consumers Stay Health-Conscious, But Now They Splurge," *Marketing News* (June 7, 1993): 1 (2 pp.).

56. Sunita Wadekar Bhargava, "Gimme a Double Shake and a Lard on White," *Business Week* (March 1, 1993): 59.

57. Kahle, Poulos and Sukhdial, "Changes in Social Values in the United States During the Past Decade"; DDB Needham Worldwide Life Style Study.

58. Burdette Breidenstein, "Changes in Consumers' Attitudes Toward Red Meat and Their Effect on Marketing Strategy," *Food Technology* (January 1988): 112–16.

59. Doug Saunders and Alana Mitchell, "The Death of Cocooning," *Globe and Mail* (September 13, 1997): C1–2.

60. Molly O'Neill, "Words to Survive Life With: None of This, None of That," *New York Times* (May 27, 1990): 1.

61. Cheryl Russell, "The Master Trend," *American Demographics* (October 1993): 28 (6 pp.).

62. Lisa Schoenfein, "Ad-Directed Channels a Reality," *Advertising Age* (April 11, 1994): S–6 (2 pp.).

63. Cf. B. Joseph Pine II, Bart Victor and Andrew C. Boynton, "Making Mass Customization Work," *Harvard Business Review* (September/October 1993): 108–19.

64. Philip Kotler, "From Mass Marketing to Mass Customization," *Planning Review* (September/October 1989): 10–47.

65. Elizabeth Church, "Levi's Sizes up its Customers," *Globe and Mail* (April 11, 1997): B9.

66. Quoted in June Weir, "Casual Look 'Defining Character of the '90s,'" *Advertising Age* (April 7, 1994): S–2 (2 pp.); Jeanne Whalen, "Casual Dining, Not Fast Food, Challenges Mom's Meatloaf," *Advertising Age* (April 7, 1994): S–6.

It's Saturday night, and Nancy, Jan and Elena are out on the town. When the bartender at Eric's Pub comes to take their drink orders, Nancy immediately orders her standard: a dry Stolichnaya martini, straight up, with a twist. Nancy takes her vodka seriously. She's tried them all, and nothing will do but Stoly.

Jan, on the other hand, is indecisive. She doesn't drink often, and she can't really tell one concoction from another. Finally she says, "Oh, I don't care. I guess your house white wine will be fine."

Elena shrugs and says, "Looks like it's going to be Pepsi for me. I'm the designated driver tonight." Dave the bartender is impressed. "Now that's a nice change for you guys. I guess all the publicity about drunk driving finally got to you." Elena replies, "Hey, things are different these days! People know they can't party without facing the consequences."

When the drinks are served, Nancy and Jan settle back and enjoy their beverages.

Elena eyes their glasses as she munches some popcorn and drinks her Pepsi. These two owe me big time, she thinks, anticipating next Saturday night ...

7

Attitudes

THE POWER OF ATTITUDES

The term *attitude* is widely used in popular culture. You might be asked, "What is your attitude towards abortion?" A parent might scold, "Young man, I don't like your attitude." Some bars even euphemistically refer to happy hour as "an attitude adjustment period."

For our purposes, an **attitude** is a lasting, general evaluation of people (including oneself), objects or issues.[1] Anything towards which one has an attitude, whether it is tangible, such as a brand of vodka, or intangible, such as drunk driving, is called an **attitude object (A_o).** An attitude is *lasting* because it tends to endure over time. It is *general* because it applies to more than a momentary event, like hearing a loud noise (though you might over time develop a negative attitude towards all loud noises). Consumers have attitudes towards very product-specific behaviours (like using Crest toothpaste rather than Colgate), as well as towards more general consumption-related behaviours (how often one should brush one's teeth). Attitudes help to determine whom a person chooses to date, what music he or she listens to, whether he or she will recycle or discard aluminum cans, and whether he or she chooses to become a consumer researcher for a living.

This chapter will consider the contents of an attitude, how attitudes are formed and how they can be measured, and will review some of the surprisingly complex relationships between attitudes and behaviour. In the next chapter we'll take a closer look at how attitudes can be changed—certainly an issue of prime importance to marketers.

attitude a lasting, general evaluation of people (including oneself), objects or issues

attitude object (A_o) anything towards which one has an attitude

217

The Functions of Attitudes

The **functional theory of attitudes** was initially developed by psychologist Daniel Katz to explain how attitudes facilitate social behaviour.[2] According to this pragmatic approach, attitudes exist *because* they serve some function for the person; that is, they are determined by a person's motives. Consumers who expect that they will need to deal with similar information at a future time will be more likely to start forming attitudes in anticipation of this event.[3]

Two people can each have the same attitude towards some object for very different reasons. As a result, it can be helpful for a marketer to know *why* an attitude is held before attempting to change it. The following are attitude functions as identified by Katz:

- *Utilitarian function.* The utilitarian function is related to the basic principles of reward and punishment. We develop some of our attitudes towards products simply on the basis of whether these products provide pleasure or pain. If a person likes the taste of a cheeseburger, that person will develop a positive attitude towards cheeseburgers. Ads that stress straightforward product benefits (e.g., you should drink Diet Coke "just for the taste of it") appeal to the utilitarian function.

- *Value-expressive function.* Attitudes that perform a value-expressive function express the consumer's central values or self-concept. A person forms a product attitude, not because of its objective benefits, but because of what the product says about him or her as a person ("What sort of man reads *Playboy*?"). Value-expressive attitudes are highly relevant to lifestyle analyses, where consumers cultivate a cluster of activities, interests and opinions to express a particular social identity (as discussed in the last chapter).

- *Ego-defensive function.* Attitudes that are formed to protect the person, either from external threats or internal feelings, perform an ego-defensive function. Products that promise to help a man project a "macho" image (such as Marlboro cigarettes) may be appealing to his insecurities about his masculinity. Another example of this function is deodorant campaigns that stress the dire, embarrassing consequences of being caught with underarm odour in public.

- *Knowledge function.* Some attitudes are formed as the result of a need for order, structure or meaning. This need is often present when a person is in an ambiguous situation or is confronted with a new product ("Bayer wants you to know about pain relievers").

An attitude can serve more than one function, but in many cases a particular one will be dominant. By identifying the dominant function a product serves for consumers (what *benefits* it provides), marketers can emphasize these benefits in their communications and packaging. Ads relevant to the function prompt more favourable thoughts about what is being marketed and can result in a heightened preference for both the ad and the product.

One study determined that for most people coffee serves more of a utilitarian function than a value-expressive function. As a consequence, subjects responded more positively to copy for a fictitious coffee that read, "The delicious, hearty flavour and aroma of Sterling Blend coffee comes from a blend of the freshest coffee beans" (i.e., utilitarian appeal) than they did to copy that read, "The coffee you drink says something about the type of person you are. It can reveal your rare, discriminating taste" (i.e., value-expressive function).[4]

The ABC Model of Attitudes and Hierarchies of Effects ✗

Most researchers agree that an attitude has three components: affect, behaviour and cognition. **Affect** refers to the way a consumer *feels* about an attitude object. **Behaviour** involves the person's intentions to do something with regard to an attitude object (but, as will be discussed at a later point, an intention does not always result in an actual behaviour). **Cognition** refers to the *beliefs* a consumer has about an attitude object. These three components of an attitude can be remembered as the *ABC model of attitudes*.

This model emphasizes the interrelationships among knowing, feeling and doing. Consumers' attitudes towards a product cannot be determined simply by identifying their beliefs about it. For example, a researcher may find that shoppers "know" a particular camcorder has an 8:1 power zoom lens, auto-focus and a flying erase head, but such findings do not indicate whether they feel these attributes are good, bad or irrelevant, or whether they would actually buy the camcorder.

affect the way a consumer feels about an attitude object

behaviour a consumer's actions with regard to an attitude object

cognition the beliefs a consumer has about an attitude object

HIERARCHIES OF EFFECTS

While all three components of an attitude are important, their relative importance will vary depending upon a consumer's level of motivation with regard to the attitude object. The differences in drink choices among the three friends at the bar illustrate how these elements can be combined in different ways to create attitudes. Attitude researchers have developed the concept of a **hierarchy of effects** to explain the relative impact of the three components. Each hierarchy specifies that a fixed sequence of steps occurs en route to an attitude. Three different hierarchies are summarized in Figure 7–1.

hierarchy of effects a fixed sequence of steps that occurs during attitude formation; this sequence varies depending upon such factors as the consumer's level of involvement with the attitude object

This *Sports Illustrated* ad, which emphasizes feelings, underscores the importance of affect in forming attitudes.
John Iacono/Sports Illustrated.

FIGURE 7-1 • Three Hierarchies of Effects

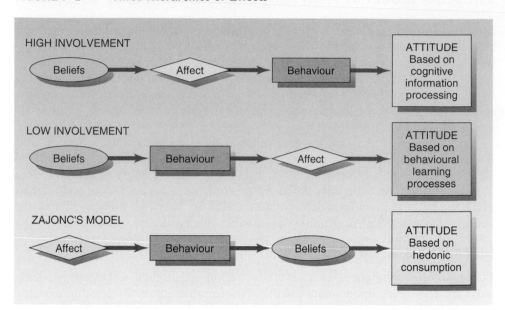

THE HIGH-INVOLVEMENT HIERARCHY

Nancy's choice of a favourite drink closely resembles the process by which most attitudes have been assumed to be constructed. A consumer approaches a product decision as a problem-solving process. First, he or she forms beliefs about a product by accumulating knowledge (beliefs) regarding relevant attributes. Next, the consumer evaluates these beliefs and forms a feeling about the product (affect). Over time, Nancy integrated information about alternative vodka brands and formed a preference for one kind. Finally, based on this evaluation, the consumer engages in a relevant behaviour, such as buying the product.

This careful choice process often results in the type of brand loyalty displayed by Nancy. The consumer "bonds" with the product over time and is not easily persuaded to experiment with other brands. The standard learning hierarchy assumes that a consumer is highly involved in making a purchase decision.[5] The person is motivated to seek out a lot of information, carefully weigh alternatives and come to a thoughtful decision.

THE LOW-INVOLVEMENT HIERARCHY

In sharp contrast to Nancy, Jan's interest in the attitude object (a particular brand of alcoholic beverage) is at best lukewarm. She has collected only a minimal amount of information before acting and has an emotional response only after consuming the beverage. Jan is typical of a consumer who forms an attitude via the *low-involvement hierarchy of effects*. In this sequence, the consumer initially does not have a strong preference for one brand over another, but he or she instead acts on the basis of limited knowledge and then forms an evaluation only after the fact.[6] The attitude is likely to come about through behavioural learning, where the consumer's choice is reinforced by good or bad experiences with the product after purchase.

The possibility that consumers simply don't care enough about many decisions to carefully assemble a set of product beliefs and then evaluate them is important, because it implies that all the concern about influencing beliefs and carefully communicating information about product attributes may largely be wasted. Consumers aren't necessarily going to pay attention anyway; they are more likely to respond to simple stimulus-response connections when making purchase decisions. For example, a consumer choosing among paper towels might remember that "Bounty is the quicker picker-upper" rather than bothering systematically to compare all the brands on the shelf.

The notion of low involvement on the part of consumers is a bitter pill for some marketers to swallow. Who wants to admit that what they market is not very important or involving? A brand manager for, say, a brand of bubble gum or cat food may find it hard to believe that consumers don't put that much thought into purchasing her product since she spends many of her waking (and perhaps sleeping) hours thinking about it.

For marketers, the ironic silver lining to this low-involvement cloud is that under these conditions consumers are not motivated to process a lot of complex brand-related information. Instead, they will be swayed by principles of behavioural learning, such as the simple responses caused by conditioned brand names, point-of-purchase displays and so on. This results in what we might call the involvement paradox: the *less* important the product is to consumers, the *more* important are many of the marketing stimuli (e.g., packages, jingles) that must be devised to sell it.

THE PREFERENCES NEED NO INFERENCES HIERARCHY BY ZAJONC

Researchers in recent years have begun to stress the significance of emotional response as a central aspect of an attitude. According to the *experiential hierarchy of effects,* consumers act on the basis of their emotional reactions (just as Elena felt strongly about drunk drivers). Although the factors of beliefs and behaviour still are recognized as playing a part, a consumer's overall evaluation of an attitude object is considered by many to be the core of an attitude.

This perspective highlights the idea that attitudes can be strongly influenced by intangible product attributes, such as package design, and by consumers' reactions towards accompanying stimuli, such as advertising and even the brand name. As discussed in Chapter 4, resulting attitudes will be affected by consumers' hedonic motivations, such as how the product makes them feel or the fun its use will provide.

One important debate about the experiential hierarchy concerns the *independence* of cognition and affect. On the one hand, the *cognitive-affective model* argues that an affective judgment is but the last step in a series of cognitive processes. Earlier steps include the sensory registration of stimuli and the retrieval of meaningful information from memory to categorize these stimuli.[7]

On the other hand, the *independence hypothesis* takes the position that affect and cognition involve two separate, partially independent systems; affective responses do not always require prior cognitions.[8] A number-one song on the *Billboard* "Top 40" may possess the same attributes as many other songs (dominant bass guitar, raspy vocals, persistent downbeat), but beliefs about these attributes cannot explain why one song becomes a classic while another sharing the same characteristics winds up in the bargain bin at the local record store. The independence hypothesis does not *eliminate* the role of cognition in experience; it simply balances this traditional, rational emphasis on calculated decision-making by paying more attention to the impact of aesthetic, subjective experience. This type of holistic processing is more likely to occur when the product is perceived as primarily expressive or delivers sensory pleasure rather than utilitarian benefits.[9]

Some advertising campaigns try to increase their entertainment value by producing spots that strongly resemble soap operas. MCI created a fictional company, called Gramercy Press, and presents different segments that show how employees are adjusting to the Information Age.
Courtesy of MCI Communications, Business Markets Div., and Messner, Vetere, Berger, McNanee, Schmetterer, NYC.

Product Attitudes Don't Tell the Whole Story

Marketers who are concerned with understanding consumers' attitudes have to contend with an even more complex issue: in decision-making situations, people form attitudes towards objects other than the product itself that can influence their ultimate selections. One additional factor to consider is *attitudes towards the act of buying* in general. As we'll see later in the chapter, sometimes people are reluctant, embarrassed or just plain too lazy to expend the effort to obtain a desired product or service.

ATTITUDE TOWARDS THE ADVERTISEMENT

In addition, consumers' reactions to a product, over and above their feelings about the product itself, are influenced by their evaluations of its advertising. Our evaluation of a product can be determined solely by our appraisal of how it's depicted in marketing communications; that is, we don't hesitate to form attitudes towards products we've never even seen in person, much less used.

attitude towards the advertisement (A_{ad}) a predisposition to respond favourably or unfavourably to a particular advertising stimulus during a particular exposure occasion

One special type of attitude object, then, is the marketing message itself. The **attitude towards the advertisement (A_{ad})** is defined as a predisposition to respond in a favourable or unfavourable manner to a particular advertising stimulus during a particular exposure occasion. Determinants of A_{ad} include the viewer's attitude towards the advertiser, evaluations of the ad execution itself, the mood evoked by the ad and the degree to which the ad affects viewers' arousal levels.[10] A viewer's feelings about the context in which an ad appears can also influence brand attitudes. For example, attitudes about an ad and the brand depicted will be influenced if the consumer sees the ad while watching a favourite TV program.[11] The effects demonstrated by A_{ad} emphasize the importance of an ad's entertainment value in the purchase process.[12]

ADS HAVE FEELINGS TOO

The feelings generated by advertising have the capacity directly to affect brand attitudes. Commercials can evoke a wide range of emotional responses, from disgust to happiness. These feelings can be influenced both by the way the ad is done (the specific advertising *execution*) and by the consumer's reactions to the advertiser's motives. For example, many advertisers who are trying to craft messages for adolescents and young adults are encountering problems because this age group, having grown up in a "marketing society," tends to be sceptical about attempts to get them to buy things.[13] These reactions can, in turn, influence memory for advertising content.[14] At least three emotional dimensions have been identified in commercials: pleasure, arousal and intimidation.[15] Specific types of feelings that can be generated by an ad include the following:[16]

MARKETING PITFALL

In a study of irritating advertising, researchers examined over 500 prime-time network commercials that had registered negative reactions by consumers. The most irritating commercials were for feminine-hygiene products, hemorrhoid medications or laxatives, and women's underwear. The researchers identified the following factors as prime offenders:[17]

- A sensitive product is shown (e.g., hemorrhoid medicine) and its use or package is emphasized.
- The situation is contrived or overdramatized.
- A person is put down in terms of appearance, knowledge or sophistication.
- An important relationship, such as a marriage, is threatened.
- There is a graphic demonstration of physical discomfort.
- Uncomfortable tension is created by an argument or by an antagonistic character.
- An unattractive or unsympathetic character is portrayed.
- A sexually suggestive scene is included.
- The commercial suffers from poor casting or execution.

This ad for EggStro'dinaire, an egg substitute, illustrates that ads are capable of communicating negative feelings.
Courtesy of Food Service Division, Sandoz Nutrition, Minneapolis, MN 55416.

- *upbeat feelings*—amused, delighted, playful
- *warm feelings*—affectionate, contemplative, hopeful
- *negative feelings*—critical, defiant, offended

FORMING ATTITUDES

We all have lots of attitudes, and we don't usually question how we got them. Certainly a person isn't born with the conviction that, say, Pepsi is better than Coke or that heavy-metal music liberates the soul. Where do these attitudes come from?

An attitude can form in several different ways, depending upon the particular hierarchy of effects in operation. It can occur because of *classical conditioning*, wherein an attitude object, such as the Pepsi name, is repeatedly paired with a catchy jingle ("You're in the Pepsi Generation ..."). Or it can be formed through *instrumental conditioning*, in which consumption of the attitude object is reinforced (e.g., Pepsi quenches one's thirst). Or the learning of an attitude can be the outcome of a very complex cognitive process. For example, a teenager may come to model the behaviour of friends and media figures who drink Pepsi because she believes that this act will allow her to fit in with the desirable images of the Pepsi Generation.

Not All Attitudes Are Created Equal

It is thus important to distinguish among types of attitudes, since not all are formed the same way.[18] For example, a highly brand-loyal consumer like Nancy, the Stolichnaya drinker, has an enduring, deeply held positive attitude towards an attitude object, and this involvement will be difficult to weaken. On the other hand, another consumer like Jan, the occasional wine drinker, may be less brand loyal; she may have a mildly positive attitude towards a product but be quite willing to abandon it when something better comes along. This section will consider the differences between strongly and weakly held attitudes and briefly review some of the major theoretical perspectives that have been developed to explain how attitudes form and relate to one another in the minds of consumers.

Levels of Commitment to an Attitude

Consumers vary in their *commitment* to an attitude. The degree of commitment is related to their level of involvement with the attitude object, as follows.[19]

- *Compliance.* At the lowest level of involvement, compliance, an attitude is formed because it helps in gaining rewards or avoiding punishments from others. This attitude is very superficial; it is likely to change when the person's behaviour is no longer monitored by others or when another option becomes available. A person may drink Pepsi because this brand is sold in the cafeteria and it is too much trouble to go elsewhere for a Coca-Cola.

- *Identification.* A process of identification occurs when attitudes are formed in order for the consumer to be similar to another person or group. Advertising that depicts the social consequences of choosing some products over others is relying on the tendency of consumers to imitate the behaviour of desirable models.

- *Internalization.* At a high level of involvement, deep-seated attitudes are internalized and become part of the person's value system. These attitudes are very difficult to change because they are so important to the individual. For example, many consumers had strong attitudes towards Coca-Cola and reacted quite negatively when the company attempted to switch to the New Coke formula. This allegiance to Coke was obviously more than a minor preference for these people; the brand had become intertwined with their social identities, taking on patriotic and nostalgic properties.

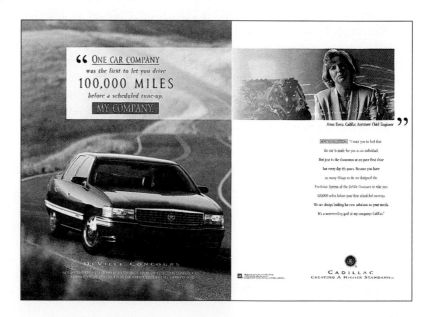

By describing Cadillac as "my company," the woman featured in this ad is exhibiting a high level of attitudinal commitment to her employer.
Courtesy of Cadillac.

The Consistency Principle

Have you ever heard someone say, "Pepsi is my favourite soft drink. It tastes terrible," or "I love my husband. He's the biggest idiot I've ever met"? Probably you have not heard these statements too often because these beliefs or evaluations are not consistent with one another. According to the **principle of cognitive consistency,** consumers value *harmony* among their thoughts, feelings and behaviours, and they are motivated to maintain uniformity among these elements. This desire means that, if necessary, consumers will *change* their thoughts, feelings or behaviours to make them consistent with their other experiences. The consistency principle is an important reminder that attitudes are not formed in a vacuum. A significant determinant of the way an attitude object will be evaluated is how it fits with other, related attitudes already held by the consumer.

principle of cognitive consistency the belief that consumers value harmony among their thoughts, feelings and behaviours and that they are motivated to maintain uniformity among these elements

COGNITIVE DISSONANCE THEORY REVISITED

In Chapter 4 we discussed the role played by cognitive dissonance when consumers are trying to choose between two desired products. Cognitive dissonance theory also has other important ramifications for attitudes, since people often are confronted with situations in which there is some conflict between their attitudes and behaviours.[20]

The theory proposes that, much like hunger or thirst, people are *motivated* to reduce this negative state by making things fit with one another. The theory focuses on situations where two *cognitive elements* are inconsistent with one another.

A cognitive element can be something a person believes about himself, a behaviour he performs or an observation about his surroundings. For example, the two cognitive elements "I know smoking cigarettes causes cancer" and "I smoke cigarettes" are *dissonant* with one another. This psychological inconsistency creates a feeling of discomfort that the smoker is motivated to reduce. The magnitude of dis-

This ad for *Woman's Day* attempts to counter the role consistency plays in shaping attitudes: consumers often distort information so that it fits with what they already know or believe. *Courtesy of* Woman's Day *(Hachette Magazines Inc.).*

sonance depends upon both the importance and the number of dissonant elements.[21] In other words, the pressure to reduce dissonance is more likely to be observed in high-involvement situations, in which the elements are more important to the individual.

Dissonance reduction can occur by either eliminating, adding or changing elements. For example, the person could stop smoking (eliminate) or remember great-aunt Sophie, who smoked until the day she died at age 90 (add). Alternatively, he might question the research that links cancer and smoking (change), perhaps by believing industry-sponsored studies that try to refute this connection.

Dissonance theory can help to explain why evaluations of a product tend to increase *after* it has been purchased, i.e., postpurchase dissonance. The cognitive element "I made a stupid decision" is dissonant with the element "I am not a stupid person," so people tend to find even more reasons to like something after it becomes theirs.

A field study performed at a horse race demonstrates postpurchase dissonance. Bettors evaluated their chosen horses more highly and were more confident of their success *after* they had placed a bet than before. Since the bettor is financially committed to the choice, he or she reduces dissonance by increasing the attractiveness of the chosen alternative relative to the unchosen ones.[22] One implication of this phenomenon is that consumers actively seek support for their purchase decisions, so marketers should supply them with additional reinforcement in order to build positive brand attitudes.

SELF-PERCEPTION THEORY

self-perception theory an alternative explanation of dissonance effects; it assumes that people use observations of their own behaviour to infer their attitudes towards some object

Do attitudes necessarily change following behaviour because people are motivated to feel good about their decisions? **Self-perception theory** provides an alternative explanation of dissonance effects.[23] It assumes that people use observations of their own behaviour to determine what their attitudes are, just as we assume that we know the attitudes of others by watching what they do. The theory states that we maintain consistency by *inferring* that we must have a positive attitude towards an object if we have bought or consumed it (assuming that we freely made this choice). Thus, Nancy might say to herself, "I guess I must like this brand of vodka, I seem to order it a lot."

Self-perception theory is relevant to the *low-involvement hierarchy,* since it involves situations in which behaviours are initially performed in the absence of a strong internal attitude. After the fact, the cognitive and affective components of attitude fall into line. Thus, buying a product out of habit may result in a positive attitude towards it *after the fact*—namely, why would I buy it if I didn't like it?

foot-in-the-door technique based on the observation that a consumer is more likely to comply with a request if he or she has first agreed to comply with a smaller request

Self-perception theory helps to explain the effectiveness of a sales strategy called the **foot-in-the-door technique,** which is based on the observation that a consumer is more likely to comply with a request if he or she has first agreed to comply with a smaller request.[24] The name for this technique comes from the practice of door-to-door selling, wherein a salesperson was taught to plant his or her foot in a door so that the prospect could not slam it shut. A good salesperson knows that he or she is more likely to get an order if the customer can be persuaded to open the door and talk. By agreeing to do so, the customer has established a willingness to listen to the salesperson. Placing an order is consistent with this self-perception. This technique is especially useful for inducing consumers to answer surveys or to donate money to charity. Such factors as the time lag between the first and second request, the similarity between the two requests and whether the same person makes both requests have been found to influence their effectiveness.[25]

SOCIAL JUDGMENT THEORY

Social judgment theory also assumes that people assimilate new information about attitude objects in light of what they already know or feel.[26] The initial attitude acts as a *frame of reference* and new information is categorized in terms of this existing standard. Just as our decision that a box is heavy depends in part on other boxes we have lifted, we develop a subjective standard when making judgments about attitude objects.

One important aspect of the theory is the notion that people differ in terms of the information they will find acceptable or unacceptable. They form **latitudes of acceptance and rejection** around an attitude standard. Ideas that fall within a latitude will be favourably received, while those falling outside this zone will not. Since Elena had a favourable attitude towards the use of designated drivers, she is likely to be receptive to communications urging her to play this role before heading out for an evening on the town. If she were opposed to this practice, these messages would probably not be considered.

Messages that fall within the latitude of acceptance tend to be seen as *more* consistent with one's position than they actually are. This process is called an *assimilation effect*. On the other hand, messages falling in the latitude of rejection tend to be seen as even *farther* from one's position than they actually are, resulting in a *contrast effect*.[27]

As a person becomes more involved with an attitude object, his or her latitude of acceptance gets smaller; in other words, the consumer accepts fewer ideas that are removed from his or her own position and tends to oppose even mildly divergent positions. This tendency is evident in ads that appeal to discriminating buyers, which claim that knowledgeable people will reject anything but the very best (e.g., "Choosy mothers choose Jif"). On the other hand, relatively uninvolved consumers will consider a wider range of alternatives. They are less likely to be brand loyal and more likely to be brand switchers.[28]

BALANCE THEORY

Balance theory considers relations among elements a person might perceive as belonging together.[29] This perspective involves relations (always from the perceiver's subjective point of view) among three elements, so the resulting attitude structures are called *triads*. Each triad contains 1) a person and his or her perceptions of 2) an attitude object and 3) some other person or object.

These perceptions can be either positive or negative. More importantly, people *alter* these perceptions in order to make relations among them consistent. The theory specifies that people desire relations among elements in a triad to be harmonious, or *balanced*. If they are not, a state of tension will result until somehow perceptions are changed and balance is restored.

Elements can be perceived as going together in one of two ways. They can have either a *unit relation*, where one element is seen as somehow belonging to or being a part of the other (something like a belief), or a *sentiment relation*, where the two elements are linked because one has expressed a preference (or dislike) for the other. A dating couple might be seen as having a positive sentiment relation. Upon getting married, they will have a positive unit relation. The process of divorce is an attempt to sever a unit relation.

To see how balance theory might work, consider the following scenario:

* Monica would like to date Jerry, who is in her Consumer Behaviour class. In balance theory terms, Monica has a positive sentiment relation with Jerry.

social judgment theory the perspective that people assimilate new information about attitude objects in light of what they already know or feel; the initial attitude acts as a frame of reference, and new information is categorized in terms of this standard

latitudes of acceptance and rejection formed around an attitude standard; ideas that fall within a latitude will be favourably received, while those falling outside this zone will not

balance theory a theory that considers relations among elements a person might perceive as belonging together, and people's tendency to change relations among elements in order to make them consistent or "balanced"

- One day Jerry shows up in class wearing an earring. Jerry has a positive unit relation with the earring. It belongs to him and is literally a part of him.

- Monica does not like men who wear earrings. She has a negative sentiment relation with men's earrings.

According to balance theory, Monica faces an unbalanced triad, and she will experience pressure to restore balance by altering some aspect of the triad, as shown in Figure 7–2. She could, for example, decide that she does not like Jerry after all. Or her liking for Jerry could prompt a change in her attitude towards earrings. She might even try to negate the unit relation between Jerry and the earring by deciding that he must be only wearing it as part of an initiation (thus reducing the free-choice element). Finally, she could choose to "leave the field" by not thinking any more about Jerry and his controversial earring.

Note that while the theory does not specify which of these routes will be taken, it does predict that one or more of Monica's perceptions will probably change in order to achieve balance. While this distortion is most likely an oversimplified representation of most attitude processes, it helps to explain a number of consumer behaviour phenomena.

MARKETING APPLICATIONS OF BALANCE THEORY Balance theory reminds us that, when perceptions are balanced, attitudes are likely to be stable. On the other hand, when inconsistencies are observed, we are more likely to observe changes in

FIGURE 7–2 • Alternative Routes to Restoring Balance in a Triad

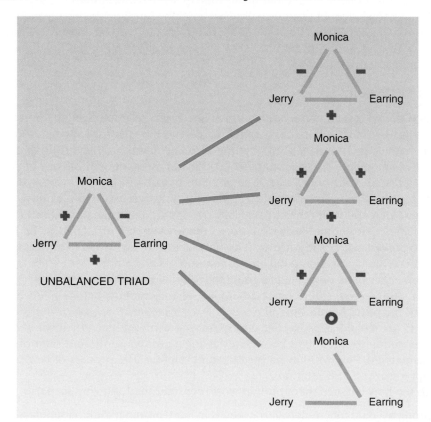

attitudes. Balance theory also helps to explain why consumers like to be associated with positively valued objects. Forming a unit relation with a popular product (buying and wearing fashionable clothing or driving a flashy car) may improve one's chances of being included as a positive sentiment relation in other people's triads.

Finally, balance theory is useful in accounting for the widespread use of celebrities to endorse products. In cases where a triad is not fully formed (e.g., one involving perceptions about a new product or one about which the consumer does not yet have a well-defined attitude), the marketer can create a positive sentiment relation between the consumer and the product by depicting a positive unit relation between the product and a well-known personality. In other cases, behaviours are discouraged when admired people argue against them, as is the goal when athletes appear in public-service advertisements against drinking and driving.

This "balancing act" is at the heart of celebrity endorsements, in which it is hoped that the star's popularity will transfer to the product. This strategy will be considered at length in the next chapter. For now, it pays to remember that this creation of a unit relation between product and star can backfire if the public's opinion of the celebrity endorser shifts from positive to negative, as happened when Madonna was associated with a controversial music video involving religion and sex: Pepsi pulled an ad featuring her. The strategy can also cause trouble if the star–product unit relation is questioned, as happened when singer Michael Jackson, who also did promotions for Pepsi, subsequently confessed that he does not drink soft drinks.

ATTITUDE MODELS

A consumer's overall evaluation of a product sometimes accounts for the bulk of his or her attitude towards it. When market researchers want to assess attitudes, it can often be sufficient for them simply to ask consumers, "How do you feel about Labatt's Blue?"

However, as we saw earlier, attitudes can be a lot more complex than that. One problem is that a product or service may be composed of many *attributes*, or qualities, some of which may be more important than others to particular people. Another problem is that a person's decision to act on his or her attitude is affected by other factors, such as whether it is felt that buying a product would be met with approval by friends or family. For these reasons *attitude models* have been developed that try to specify the different elements that might work together to influence people's evaluations of attitude objects.

Multi-Attribute Attitude Models

A simple response does not always tell us everything we need to know about either *why* the consumer feels a certain way towards a product or what marketers can do to change the consumer's attitude. For this reason **multi-attribute attitude models** have been extremely popular among marketing researchers. This type of model assumes that a consumer's attitude (evaluation) of an attitude object (A_o) will depend on the beliefs he or she has about several or many attributes of the object. The use of a multi-attribute model implies that an attitude towards a product or brand can be predicted by identifying these specific beliefs and combining them to derive a measure of the consumer's overall attitude.

multi-attribute attitude models those models that assume that a consumer's attitude (evaluation) of an attitude object depends on the beliefs he or she has about several or many attributes of the object; the use of a multi-attribute model implies that an attitude towards a product or brand can be predicted by identifying these specific beliefs and combining them to derive a measure of the consumer's overall attitude

We'll describe how these work, using the example of a consumer evaluating a complex attitude object that should be very familiar to you: a university.

Basic multi-attribute models specify three elements:[30]

1. *Attributes* are characteristics of the A_o. Most models assume that the relevant characteristics can be identified; that is, the researcher can include those attributes that consumers take into consideration when evaluating the A_o. For example, scholarly reputation is an attribute of a university.

2. *Beliefs* are cognitions about the specific A_o (usually relative to others like it). A belief measure assesses the extent to which the consumer perceives that a brand possesses a particular attribute. For example, a student might have a belief that the University of Toronto has a strong academic standing.

3. *Importance weights* reflect the relative priority of an attribute to the consumer. Although an A_o can be considered on a number of attributes, some are likely to be more important than others (i.e., they will be given greater weight). And these weights are likely to differ across consumers. In the case of universities, for example, one student might stress library resources while another might assign greater weight to athletic programs.

THE FISHBEIN MODEL

The most influential multi-attribute model is called the *Fishbein model*, named after its primary developer.[31] The model measures the following three components of attitude:

1. *salient beliefs* people have about an A_o (those beliefs about the object that are considered during evaluation);

2. *object-attribute linkages*, or the probability that a particular object has an important attribute; and

3. *evaluation* of each of the important attributes.

Note, however, that the model makes some assumptions that may not always be warranted. It assumes that we have been able adequately to specify all the relevant attributes that, for example, a student will use in evaluating his or her choice about which university to attend. The model also assumes that he or she will go through the process (formally or informally) of identifying a set of relevant attributes, weighing them and summing them. Although this particular decision is likely to be highly involving, it is still possible that his or her attitude will instead be formed by an overall affective response (a process known as *affect-referral*).

By combining these three elements, a consumer's overall attitude towards an object can be computed. (We'll see later how this basic equation has been modified to increase its accuracy.) The basic formula is

$$A_{ijk} = \Sigma B_{ijk} I_{ik}$$

where i = attribute; j = brand; k = consumer; I = the importance weight given attribute i by consumer k; B = consumer k's belief regarding the extent to which brand j possesses attribute i; and A = a particular consumer k's attitude score for brand j.

The overall attitude score (A) is obtained by multiplying a consumer's rating of each attribute for all of the brands considered by the importance rating for that attribute.

To see how this basic multi-attribute model might work, let's suppose we want to predict which university a high-school senior is likely to attend. After months of waiting, Saundra has been accepted by four universities. Since she must now decide among these, we would first like to know which attributes Saundra will consider in forming an attitude towards each school. We can then ask Saundra to assign a rating regarding how well each school performs on each attribute and also determine the relative importance of the attributes to her. An overall attitude score for each school can then be computed by summing scores on each attribute (after weighing each by its relative importance). These hypothetical ratings are shown in Table 7–1.

STRATEGIC APPLICATIONS OF THE MULTI-ATTRIBUTE MODEL

Suppose you were the director of marketing for Ryerson, another school Saundra is considering. How might you use the data from this analysis to improve your image?

CAPITALIZE ON RELATIVE ADVANTAGE. If one's brand is viewed as being superior on a particular attribute, consumers like Saundra need to be convinced that this particular attribute is an important one. For example, while Saundra rates Ryerson's social atmosphere highly, she does not believe this attribute is a valued aspect for a university. As Ryerson's marketing director, you might emphasize the importance of an active social life, varied experiences or the development of future business contacts forged through strong university friendships.

STRENGTHEN PERCEIVED PRODUCT–ATTRIBUTE LINKAGES. A marketer may discover that consumers do not equate his or her brand with a certain attribute. This problem is commonly addressed by campaigns that stress the product's qualities to consumers (e.g., "new and improved"). Saundra apparently does not think much of Ryerson's academic quality or library facilities. You might develop an information campaign to improve these perceptions (such as "little-known facts about Ryerson").

ADD A NEW ATTRIBUTE. Product marketers frequently try to create a distinctive position from their competitors by adding a product feature. Ryerson might try to

---

TABLE 7–1 The Basic Multi-Attribute Model: Saundra's University Decision

		BELIEFS (B)			
ATTRIBUTE (i)	IMPORTANCE (I)	UBC	MCGILL	YORK	RYERSON
Academic reputation	6	8	9	6	3
Cost	4	2	2	6	9
Proximity to home	3	2	2	6	9
Party atmosphere	2	1	3	7	9
Library facilities	5	7	9	7	2
Attitude score		99	119	127	109

Note: These hypothetical ratings are scored from 1 to 10, and higher numbers indicate "better" standing on an attribute. For a negative attribute (e.g., cost), higher scores indicate that the school is believed to have "less" of that attribute (i.e., to be cheaper).

This Chrysler ad is an example of comparative advertising, wherein the attributes of competitors are specifically considered in the message.
© 1989 Chrysler Corporation, used with permission.

emphasize some unique aspect, such as a hands-on internship program for business majors that takes advantage of ties to the local community.

INFLUENCE COMPETITORS' RATINGS.   Finally, you might try to decrease the positivity of competitors. This type of action is the rationale for a strategy of *comparative advertising*. One tactic might be to publish an ad that lists the employment rates for graduates of a number of universities, as well as their attributes with which Ryerson can be favourably compared, as the basis for emphasizing the value obtained for the money spent at Ryerson.

USING ATTITUDES TO PREDICT BEHAVIOUR

Although multi-attribute models have been used by consumer researchers for many years, they have been plagued by a major problem: in many cases, knowledge of a person's attitude is *not* a very good predictor of behaviour. In a classic demonstration of "do as I say, not as I do," many studies have obtained a very low correlation between a person's reported attitude towards something and his or her actual behaviour towards it. Some researchers have been so discouraged that they have questioned whether attitudes are of any use at all in understanding behaviour.[32] This questionable linkage between attitudes and behaviour can be a big headache for advertisers in that consumers can love a commercial and yet still not buy the product. For example, one of the most popular TV commercials in recent years featured basketball player Shaquille O'Neal for Pepsi. Although the company spent $67 million on this spot and other ads in 1993, sales of Pepsi fell by close to 2 percent, even as sales of archrival Coca-Cola increased by 8 percent in the same period.[33]

The Extended Fishbein Model

The original Fishbein model, which focused on measuring a consumer's attitude towards a product, has been extended in several ways to improve its predictive ability. The newer version is called the **theory of reasoned action.**[34] This model contains several important additions to the original, and while the model is still not perfect, its ability to predict relevant behaviour has been improved.[35] Some of the modifications to this model are considered here.

INTENTIONS VERSUS BEHAVIOUR

Like the motivations discussed in Chapter 4, attitudes have both direction and strength. A person may like or dislike an attitude object with varying degrees of confidence or conviction.[36] It is helpful to distinguish between firmly held attitudes and those that are more superficial, especially since an attitude held with greater conviction makes it more likely that it will be acted upon. One study on environmental issues and marketing activities found, for example, that people who express greater conviction in their feelings regarding environmentally responsible behaviours like recycling show greater consistency between attitudes and behavioural intentions.[37] However, as the old expression goes, "the road to hell is paved with good intentions."

Many factors might interfere with actual behaviour, even if the consumer has sincere intentions. He or she might save up with the intention of buying a stereo system. In the interim, though, any number of things—losing a job, getting mugged on the way to the store, or arriving at the store to find that the desired model is out of stock—could happen. It is not surprising, then, that in some instances past purchase behaviour has been found to be a better predictor of future behaviour than is a consumer's behavioural intention.[38] The theory of reasoned action aims to measure behavioural intentions, recognizing that certain uncontrollable factors inhibit prediction of actual behaviour.

SOCIAL PRESSURE

The theory acknowledges the power of other people in influencing behaviour. Many of our behaviours are not determined in a vacuum. Much as we may hate to admit it, what we think others would *like* us to do may be more crucial than our own individual preferences.

A new element, the *subjective norm* (SN), was thus added to include the effects of what we believe other people think we should do. The value of SN is arrived at by including two other factors: 1) the intensity of a *normative belief* (NB) that others think an action should be taken or not taken; and 2) the *motivation to comply* (MC) with that belief (i.e., the degree to which the consumer takes others' anticipated reactions into account when evaluating a course of action or a purchase).

ATTITUDE TOWARDS BUYING

The model now measures **attitude towards the act of buying (A_{act}),** rather than only the attitude towards the product itself. In other words, it focuses on the perceived consequences of a purchase. Knowing how someone feels about buying or using an object turns out to be more valid than merely knowing the consumer's evaluation of the object itself.[39]

To understand this distinction, consider a problem that might arise when measuring attitudes towards condoms. Although a group of college students might have a positive attitude towards condoms, does this necessarily predict that they will buy and use them? Better prediction would be obtained by asking the students how likely they are to buy condoms and use them during sex. While a person might have

theory of reasoned action an updated version of the Fishbein multi-attitude theory that considers such factors as social pressure and A_{act} (the attitude towards the act of buying a product), rather than attitudes towards just the product itself

attitude towards the act of buying (A_{act}) the perceived consequences of a purchase

a positive A_o towards condoms, A_{act} might be negative due to the embarrassment or the hassle involved.

Obstacles to Predicting Behaviour in the Theory of Reasoned Action

Despite improvements to the Fishbein model, problems arise when it is misapplied. In many cases the model is used in ways for which it was not intended or where certain assumptions about human behaviour may not be warranted.[40] Other obstacles to predicting behaviour are as follows:

- The model was developed to deal with actual behaviour (e.g., taking a diet pill), not with the outcomes of behaviour (e.g., losing weight) that are instead assessed in some studies.

- Some outcomes are beyond the consumer's control, such as when the purchase requires the cooperation of other people.

- The basic assumption that behaviour is intentional may be invalid in a variety of cases, including those involving impulsive acts, sudden changes in one's situa-

MULTICULTURAL DIMENSIONS

The theory of reasoned action has been applied primarily in Western settings. Certain assumptions inherent in the model may not necessarily apply to consumers from other cultures. Several of the following cultural roadblocks diminish the universality of the theory of reasoned action.

- The model was developed to predict the performance of any voluntary act. Across cultures, however, many consumer activities, ranging from taking exams and entering military service to receiving an inoculation or choosing a marriage partner, are not necessarily voluntary.

- The relative impact of subjective norms may vary across cultures. For example, Asian cultures tend to value conformity and face-saving, so it is possible that subjective norms involving the anticipated reactions of others to the choice will have an even greater impact on behaviour for many Asian consumers.

- The model measures behavioural intentions and thus presupposes that consumers are actively thinking ahead and planning future behaviours. The intention concept assumes that consumers have a linear time sense, i.e., that they think in terms of past, present and future. This perspective on time is not held by all cultures.

- A consumer who forms an intention is (implicitly) claiming that he or she is in control of his or her actions. Some cultures (e.g., Muslim) tend to be fatalistic and do not necessarily believe in the concept of free will. Indeed, one study comparing students from the United States, Jordan and Thailand found evidence for cultural differences in assumptions about fatalism and control over the future.[41]

tion, novelty-seeking or even simple repeat buying. One study found that such unexpected events as having guests, changes in the weather or reading articles about the healthfulness of certain foods exerted a significant effect on actual behaviours.[42]

- Measures of attitude often do not really correspond to the behaviour they are supposed to predict, either in terms of the A_o or when the act will occur. One common problem is a difference in the level of *abstraction* employed. For example, knowing a person's attitude towards sports cars may not predict whether he or she will purchase a Nissan 300ZX. It is very important to match the level of specificity between the attitude and the behavioural intention.

- A similar problem relates to the *time frame* of the attitude measure. In general, the longer the time between the attitude measurement and the behaviour it is supposed to assess, the weaker the relationship will be. For example, predictability would improve markedly by asking consumers what was the likelihood they would buy a house in the next week as opposed to within the next five years.

- Attitudes formed by direct, personal experience with an A_o are stronger and more predictive of behaviour than those formed indirectly, such as through advertising.[43] According to the *attitude accessibility* perspective, behaviour is a function of the person's immediate perceptions of the A_o in the context of the situation in which it is encountered. An attitude will guide the evaluation of the object but *only* if it is activated from memory when the object is observed. These findings underscore the importance of strategies that induce trial (by widespread product sampling to encourage the consumer to try the product at home, by taste tests, test drives, etc.) as well as those that maximize exposure to marketing communications.

Trying to Consume

Another perspective tries to address some of these problems by instead focusing on consumers' goals and what they believe is required to attain them. The *theory of trying* states that the criterion of *behaviour* in the reasoned action model should be replaced with *trying* to reach a goal.[44] This perspective recognizes that additional factors might intervene between intent and performance; both personal and environmental barriers might prevent the individual from attaining the goal. For example, a person who intends to lose weight may have to deal with numerous issues: he may not believe he is capable of slimming down, he may have a roommate who loves to cook and who leaves tempting goodies lying around the apartment, his friends may be jealous of his attempts to diet and encourage him to pig out, or he may be genetically predisposed to be heavy, so that cutting down on calories simply will not produce the desired results.

The theory of trying includes several new components that attempt to account for the complex situations where many factors either help or hurt our chances of turning intentions into actions, as shown in Figure 7–3. These factors include the amount of control the person has over the situation, his or her expectations of success or failure in achieving the goal, social norms related to attaining the goal, and his or her attitude towards the process of trying (i.e., how the action required to attain the goal makes him or her feel, regardless of the outcome). Still other new

FIGURE 7–3 • The Theory of Trying (TT)

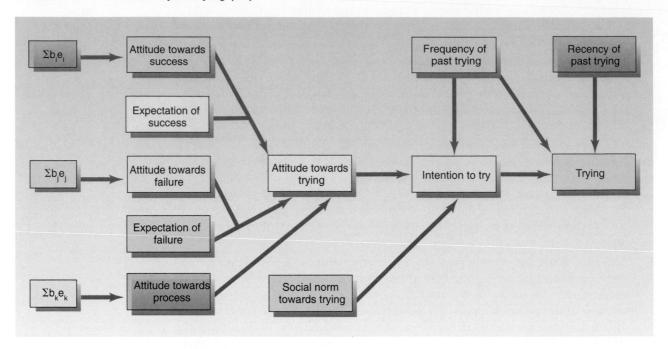

Note: Regarding the Σbe terms, the *b*'s are consequence likelihoods, the *e*'s are consequence evaluation; subscript *i* refers to consequences contingent on success, subscript *j* refers to consequences contingent on failure, and subscript *k* refers to consequences associated with the process of trying, independent of success or failure considerstions.

Source: Richard P. Bagozzi and Paul R. Warshaw, "Trying to Consume," *Journal of Consumer Research* 17, 2 (September 1990): 131.

variables are the frequency and recency of past trying of the behaviour. For example, even if a person does not have specific plans to go on a diet in the next month, the frequency with which he or she has tried to do so in the recent past (and the success—however fleeting—he or she may have experienced) would be the best predictor of future attempts to shed some pounds. To predict whether someone would try to lose weight, here are a few sample issues that might be addressed:

- *Past frequency:* Number of times in the past year the person tried to lose weight.
- *Recency:* Did he try to lose weight in the last week?
- *Beliefs:* Did he believe he would be healther if he lost weight?
- *Evaluations of consequences:* Did he believe his girlriend would be happier if he succeeded in losing weight? Did he believe his friends would make fun of him if he tried but failed to lose weight?
- *The process:* Would the diet make him uncomfortable or depressed?
- *Expectations of success and failure:* Did he believe it likely he would be able to lose weight if he tried?
- *Subjective norms towards trying:* Would the people who are important to him approve of his efforts to lose weight?

Tracking Attitudes over Time

An attitude survey is like a snapshot taken at a single point in time: it may tell us a lot about a brand's position at that moment, but it does not permit many inferences about progress the brand has made over time or any predictions about possible future changes in consumer attitudes. To accomplish these tasks it is necessary to develop an *attitude-tracking* program. This activity helps to increase the predictability of behaviour by allowing researchers to analyze attitude trends over an extended period of time. It is more like a movie than a snapshot. For example, a longitudinal survey conducted by the Food Marketing Institute of consumers' attitudes towards food content over the last decade illustrates how priorities can shift in a fairly short time (see Figure 7–4).[45]

ONGOING TRACKING STUDIES

Attitude tracking involves the administration of an attitude survey at regular intervals. Preferably, the identical methodology is used each time so that results can be reliably compared. Several syndicated services, such as the Gallup Poll or the Yankelovich Monitor, track consumer attitudes over time. Results from a tracking

FIGURE 7–4 • Changing Attitudes towards Food Content

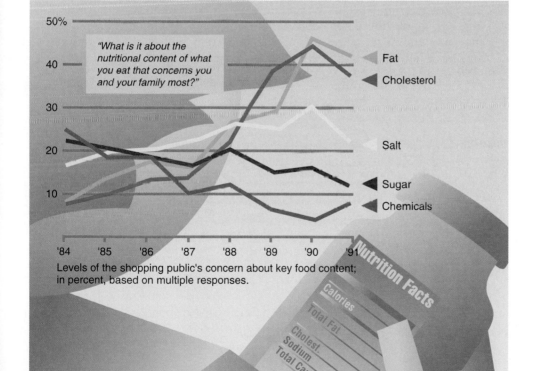

Source: Barbara Presley Noble, "After Years of Deregulation, A New Push to Inform the Public," *New York Times* (October 27, 1991): F5. Data from Food Marketing Institute. Copyright © 1991 by The New York Times Company. Reprinted by permission.

study of ecological attitudes among young people in a set of European countries are shown in Figure 7–5.

This activity can be extremely valuable for many strategic decisions. For example, one financial services firm monitored changes in consumer attitudes towards one-stop banking centres. Although a large number of consumers were warm to the idea when it was first introduced, the number of people who liked the concept did not increase over time despite the millions of dollars invested in advertising to promote the centres. This finding indicated some problems with the way the concept was being presented to consumers, and the company decided to "go back to the drawing board," eventually coming up with a new way to communicate the advantages of this service.

CHANGES TO LOOK FOR OVER TIME

Some of the dimensions that can be included in attitude tracking are the following:

• *A focus on changes in different age groups.* Attitudes tend to change as people age (a *life cycle effect*). In addition, *cohort effects* occur, where members of a particular generation (e.g., yuppies) tend to share certain outlooks. Also, *historical effects* can be observed as large groups of people are affected by profound cultural changes (such as the Great Depression or the democratization of eastern Europe).

• *Scenarios about the future.* Consumers are frequently tracked in terms of their future plans, confidence in the economy, etc. These measures can provide valuable data about future behaviour and yield insights for public policy. For example, people tend to overestimate how much they will earn after retirement, which is potentially a dangerous miscalculation.

FIGURE 7–5 • Percentage of 16–24-Year-Olds Who Agree "We Must Take Radical Action to Cut Down on How We Use Our Cars"

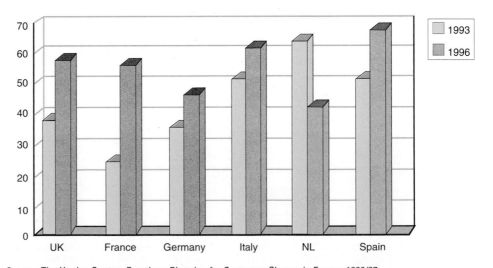
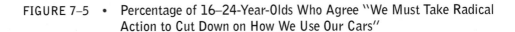

Source: The Henley Centre, *Frontiers: Planning for Consumer Change in Europe 1996/97.*

- *Identification of change agents.* Social phenomena can change people's attitudes towards basic consumption activities over time, as when consumers' willingness to buy fur products shifts. Or consumers' likelihood of desiring a divorce may be affected by such *facilitators* as changes in the legal system that make this action easier, or by *inhibitors,* such as the prevalence of AIDS and the value of two pay-cheques in today's economy.[46]

- An attitude is a predisposition to evaluate an object or product positively or negatively.
- Attitudes are made up of three components: beliefs, affect and behavioural intentions.
- Attitude researchers traditionally assumed that attitudes were learned in a fixed sequence, consisting first of the formation of beliefs (cognitions) regarding an attitude object and followed by some evaluation of that object (affect) and then some action (behaviour). Depending upon the consumer's level of involvement and the circumstances, however, attitudes can result from other hierarchies of effects as well.
- A key to attitude formation is the function the attitude plays for the consumer (e.g., is it utilitarian or ego-defensive?).
- One organizing principle of attitude formation is the importance of consistency among attitudinal components; that is, some parts of an attitude may be altered to be in line with others. Such theoretical approaches to attitudes as cognitive dissonance theory, balance theory and congruity theory stress the vital role of the need for consistency.
- The complexity of attitudes is underscored by multi-attribute attitude models, in which sets of beliefs and evaluations are identified and combined to predict an overall attitude. Factors such as subjective norms and the specificity of attitude scales have been integrated into attitude measures to improve predictability.

Affect p. 219
Attitude p. 217
Attitude object (A_o) p. 217
Attitude towards the act of buying (A_{act}) p. 235
Attitude towards the advertisement (A_{ad}) p. 224
Balance theory p. 229

Behaviour p. 219
Cognition p. 219
Foot-in-the-door technique p. 228
Functional theory of attitudes p. 218
Hierarchy of effects p. 219
Latitudes of acceptance and rejection p. 229

Multi-attribute attitude models p. 231
Principle of cognitive consistency p. 227
Self-perception theory p. 228
Social judgment theory p. 229
Theory of reasoned action p. 235

CONSUMER BEHAVIOUR CHALLENGE

1. Contrast the hierarchies of effects outlined in the chapter. How will strategic decisions related to the marketing mix be influenced by which hierarchy is operative among target consumers?

2. List three functions played by attitudes, giving an example of how each function is employed in a marketing situation.

3. Think of a behaviour exhibited by some individual that is inconsistent with his or her attitudes (e.g., attitudes towards cholesterol, drug use or buying things to attain status or to stand out). Ask the person to elaborate on why he or she does the behaviour, and try to identify the way the person has resolved dissonant elements.

4. Using a series of semantic-differential scales, devise an attitude survey for a set of competing automobiles. Identify areas of competitive advantage or disadvantage for each model you incorporate.

5. Construct a multi-attribute model for a set of local restaurants. Based on your findings, suggest how restaurant managers can improve their establishment's image via the strategies described in the chapter.

CBC VIDEO VIGNETTES

Concepts at Work for The Body Shop

According to social marketing pundits, companies can do well—that is, make profits—by doing good. The Body Shop built its company (and brand) image with a link to social causes, such as trading with developing countries, recycling, the performance of community work by their sales staff and franchisees, and taking a stand on animal testing. Its name recognition, matched only by McDonald's, was established without a penny being spent on advertising. With 1100 stores in 45 countries (100 in Canada), it has been lauded as one of the best examples of "how to do it right." However, The Body Shop is now experiencing some backlash due to having an image-building strategy that just may have worked too effectively.

Ideas about what the company stood for were passed along through word-of-mouth, leading to selective interpretations of the specific attributes of The Body Shop and its products. Consumers developed stronger beliefs about particular attributes than existed within the company. For example, some consumers thought that 90 percent of the company's products came from developing countries, when in fact up to 10 percent in any one prod-

uct category did. Over time, consumers passed along incomplete and distorted perceptions which matched their individual need for congruency, resulting in an exaggerated public image. Misperceptions developed even when consumers read the company's brochures.

Taking the high road can be treacherous without a strategy built on an understanding of how consumer attitudes are formed and changed.

QUESTIONS

1. How are attitudes towards a brand formed?

2. What was the original image of The Body Shop? How did The Body Shop build this image?

3. Explain how attitudes towards The Body Shop and its image are changing, if at all?

4. How can The Body Shop maintain its desired image or that of its brands? (Is it necessary for them to advertise?)

Video Resource: "Body Shop," *Venture* #510 (October 16, 1994).

NOTES

1. Robert A. Baron and Donn Byrne, *Social Psychology: Understanding Human Interaction*, 5th ed. (Boston: Allyn & Bacon, 1987).

2. Daniel Katz, "The Functional Approach to the Study of Attitudes," *Public Opinion Quarterly* 24 (Summer 1960): 163–204; Richard J. Lutz, "Changing Brand Attitudes through Modification of Cognitive Structure," *Journal of Consumer Research* 1 (March 1975): 49–59.

3. Russell H. Fazio, T.M. Lenn and E.A. Effrein, "Spontaneous Attitude Formation," *Social Cognition* 2 (1984): 214–34.

4. Sharon Shavitt, "The Role of Attitude Objects in Attitude Functions," *Journal of Experimental Social Psychology* 26 (1990): 124–48. See also J.S. Johar and M. Joseph Sirgy, "Value-Expressive Versus Utilitarian Advertising Appeals: When and Why to Use Which Appeal," *Journal of Advertising* 20 (September 1991): 23–34.

5. Michael Ray, "Marketing Communications and the Hierarchy-of-Effects," in *New Models for Mass Communications*, ed. P. Clarke (Beverly Hills, CA: Sage, 1973), pp. 147–76.

6. Herbert Krugman, "The Impact of Television Advertising: Learning Without Involvement," *Public Opinion Quarterly* 29 (Fall 1965): 349–56; Robert Lavidge and Gary Steiner, "A Model for Predictive Measurements of Advertising Effectiveness," *Journal of Marketing* 25 (October 1961): 59–62.

7. Punam Anand, Morris B. Holbrook and Debra Stephens, "The Formation of Affective Judgments: The Cognitive-Affective Model Versus the Independence Hypothesis," *Journal of Consumer Research* 15 (December 1988): 386–91; Richard S. Lazarus, "Thoughts on the Relations Between Emotion and Cognition," *American Psychologist* 37, 9 (1982): 1019–24.

8. Robert B. Zajonc, "Feeling and Thinking: Preferences Need No Inferences," *American Psychologist* 35, 2 (1980): 151–75.

9. Banwari Mittal, "The Role of Affective Choice Mode in the Consumer Purchase of Expressive Products," *Journal of Economic Psychology* 4, 9 (1988): 499–524.

10. Scot Burton and Donald R. Lichtenstein, "The Effect of Ad Claims and Ad Context on Attitude Toward the Advertisement," *Journal of Advertising* 17, 1 (1988): 3–11; Karen A. Machleit and R. Dale Wilson, "Emotional Feelings and Attitude Toward the Advertisement: The Roles of Brand Familiarity and Repetition," *Journal of Advertising* 17, 3 (1988): 27–35; Scott B. Mackenzie and Richard J. Lutz, "An Empirical Examination of the Structural Antecedents of Attitude Toward the Ad in an Advertising Pretesting Context," *Journal of Marketing* 53 (April 1989): 48–65; Scott B. Mackenzie, Richard J. Lutz and

George E. Belch, "The Role of Attitude Toward the Ad as a Mediator of Advertising Effectiveness: A Test of Competing Explanations," *Journal of Marketing Research* 23 (May 1986): 130–43; Darrel D. Muehling and Russell N. Laczniak, "Advertising's Immediate and Delayed Influence on Brand Attitudes: Considerations Across Message-Involvement Levels," *Journal of Advertising* 17, 4 (1988): 23–34; Mark A. Pavelchak, Meryl P. Gardner and V. Carter Broach, "Effect of Ad Pacing and Optimal Level of Arousal on Attitude Toward the Ad," in *Advances in Consumer Research 18*, eds. Rebecca H. Holman and Michael R. Solomon (Provo, UT: Association for Consumer Research, 1991), pp. 94–99. Some research evidence indicates that a separate attitude is also formed regarding the brand name itself; see George M. Zinkhan and Claude R. Martin, Jr., "New Brand Names and Inferential Beliefs: Some Insights on Naming New Products," *Journal of Business Research* 15 (1987): 157–72.

11. John P. Murry, Jr., John L. Lastovicka and Surendra N. Singh, "Feeling and Liking Responses to Television Programs: An Examination of Two Explanations for Media-Context Effects," *Journal of Consumer Research* 18 (March 1992): 441–51.

12. Barbara Stern and Judith Lynne Zaichkowsky, "The Impact of Entertaining Advertising on Consumer Responses," *Australian Marketing Researcher* 14 (August 1991): 68–80.

13. For a recent study that examined the impact of scepticism on advertising issues, see David M. Boush, Marian Friestad and Gregory M. Rose, "Adolescent Skepticism Toward TV Advertising and Knowledge of Advertiser Tactics," *Journal of Consumer Research* 21 (June 1994): 165–75.

14. Basil G. Englis, "Consumer Emotional Reactions to Television Advertising and Their Effects on Message Recall," in *Emotion in Advertising: Theoretical and Practical Explorations,* eds. S. Agres, J.A. Edell and T.M. Dubitsky (Westport, CT: Quorum Books, 1990), pp. 231–54.

15. Morris B. Holbrook and Rajeev Batra, "Assessing the Role of Emotions as Mediators of Consumer Responses to Advertising," *Journal of Consumer Research* 14 (December 1987): 404–20.

16. Marian Burke and Julie Edell, "Ad Reactions over Time: Capturing Changes in the Real World," *Journal of Consumer Research* 13 (June 1986): 114–18.

17. David A. Aaker and Donald E. Bruzzone, "Causes of Irritation in Advertising," *Journal of Marketing* 49 (Spring 1985): 47–57.

18. Herbert Kelman, "Compliance, Identification, and Internalization: Three Processes of Attitude Change," *Journal of Conflict Resolution* 2 (1958): 51–60.

19. See Sharon E. Beatty and Lynn R. Kahle, "Alternative Hierarchies of the Attitude-Behavior Relation-

ship: The Impact of Brand Commitment and Habit," *Journal of the Academy of Marketing Science* 16 (Summer 1988): 1–10.

20. Leon Festinger, *A Theory of Cognitive Dissonance* (Stanford, CA: Stanford University Press, 1957).

21. Chester A. Insko and John Schopler, *Experimental Social Psychology* (New York: Academic Press, 1972).

22. Robert E. Knox and James A. Inkster, "Postdecision Dissonance at Post Time," *Journal of Personality and Social Psychology* 8, 4 (1968): 319–23.

23. Daryl J. Bem, "Self-Perception Theory," in *Advances in Experimental Social Psychology,* ed. Leonard Berkowitz (New York: Academic Press, 1972), pp. 1–62.

24. Jonathan L. Freedman and Scott C. Fraser, "Compliance Without Pressure: The Foot-in-the-Door Technique," *Journal of Personality and Social Psychology* 4 (August 1966): 195–202. For further consideration of possible explanations for this effect, see William DeJong, "An Examination of Self-Perception Mediation of the Foot-in-the-Door Effect," *Journal of Personality and Social Psychology* 37 (December 1979): 221–31; Alice M. Tybout, Brian Sternthal and Bobby J. Calder, "Information Availability as a Determinant of Multiple-Request Effectiveness," *Journal of Marketing Research* 20 (August 1988): 280–90.

25. David H. Furse, David W. Stewart and David L. Rados, "Effects of Foot-in-the-Door, Cash Incentives and Follow-ups on Survey Response," *Journal of Marketing Research* 18 (November 1981): 473–78; Carol A. Scott, "The Effects of Trial and Incentives on Repeat Purchase Behavior," *Journal of Marketing Research* 13 (August 1976): 263–69.

26. Muzafer Sherif and Carl I. Hovland, *Social Judgment: Assimilation and Contrast Effects in Communication and Attitude Change* (New Haven, CT: Yale University Press, 1961).

27. For a recent treatment, see Joan Meyers-Levy and Brian Sternthal, "A Two-Factor Explanation of Assimilation and Contrast Effects," *Journal of Marketing Research* 30 (August 1993): 359–68.

28. Mark B. Traylor, "Product Involvement and Brand Commitment," *Journal of Advertising Research* (December 1981): 51–56.

29. Fritz Heider, *The Psychology of Interpersonal Relations* (New York: Wiley, 1958).

30. William L. Wilkie, *Consumer Behavior* (New York: Wiley, 1986).

31. Martin Fishbein, "An Investigation of the Relationships Between Beliefs About an Object and the Attitude Toward that Object," *Human Relations* 16 (1983): 233–40.

32. Allan Wicker, "Attitudes Versus Actions: The Relationship of Verbal and Overt Behavioral Responses to Attitude Objects," *Journal of Social Issues* 25 (Autumn 1969): 65.

33. Laura Bird, "Loved the Ad. May (or May Not) Buy the Product," *Wall Street Journal* (April 7, 1994): B1 (2 pp.).

34. Icek Ajzen and Martin Fishbein, "Attitude-Behavior Relations: A Theoretical Analysis and Review of Empirical Research," *Psychological Bulletin* 84 (September 1977): 888–918.

35. Morris B. Holbrook and William J. Havlena, "Assessing the Real-to-Artificial Generalizability of Multi-Attribute Attitude Models in Tests of New Product Designs," *Journal of Marketing Research* 25 (February 1988): 25–35; Terence A. Shimp and Alican Kavas, "The Theory of Reasoned Action Applied to Coupon Usage," *Journal of Consumer Research* 11 (December 1984): 795–809.

36. R.P. Abelson, "Conviction," *American Psychologist* 43 (1988): 267–75; R.E. Petty and J.A. Krosnick, *Attitude Strength: Antecedents and Consequences* (Mahwah, NJ: Erlbaum, 1995); Ida E. Berger and Linda F. Alwitt, "Attitude Conviction: A Self-Reflective Measure of Attitude Strength," *Journal of Social Behavior and Personality* 11, 3 (1996): 557–72.

37. Berger and Alwitt, "Attitude Conviction."

38. Richard P. Bagozzi, Hans Baumgartner and Youjae Yi, "Coupon Usage and the Theory of Reasoned Action," in *Advances in Consumer Research 18*, eds. Rebecca H. Holman and Michael R. Solomon (Provo, UT: Association for Consumer Research, 1991), pp. 24–27; Edward F. McQuarrie, "An Alternative to Purchase Intentions: The Role of Prior Behavior in Consumer Expenditure on Computers," *Journal of the Market Research Society* 30 (October 1988): 407–37; Arch G. Woodside and William O. Bearden, "Longitudinal Analysis of Consumer Attitude, Intention, and Behavior Toward Beer Brand Choice," in *Advances in Consumer Research 4*, ed. William D. Perrault, Jr. (Ann Arbor, MI: Association for Consumer Research, 1977), pp. 349–56.

39. Michael J. Ryan and Edward H. Bonfield, "The Fishbein Extended Model and Consumer Behavior," *Journal of Consumer Research* 2 (1975): 118–36.

40. Blair H. Sheppard, Jon Hartwick and Paul R. Warshaw, "The Theory of Reasoned Action: A Meta-Analysis of Past Research with Recommendations for Modifications and Future Research," *Journal of Consumer Research* 15 (December 1988): 325–43.

41. Joseph A. Cote and Patriya S. Tansuhaj, "Culture Bound Assumptions in Behavior Intention Models," in *Advances in Consumer Research 16*, ed. Thom Srull (Provo, UT: Association for Consumer Research, 1989), pp. 105–109.

42. Joseph A. Cote, James McCullough and Michael Reilly, "Effects of Unexpected Situations on Behavior-Intention Differences: A Garbology Analysis," *Journal of Consumer Research* 12 (September 1985): 188–94.

43. Russell H. Fazio, Martha C. Powell and Carol J. Williams, "The Role of Attitude Accessibility in the Attitude-to-Behavior Process," *Journal of Consumer Research* 16 (December 1989): 280–88; Robert E. Smith and William R. Swinyard, "Attitude-Behavior Consistency: The Impact of Product Trial Versus Advertising," *Journal of Marketing Research* 20 (August 1983): 257–67.

44. Richard P. Bagozzi and Paul R. Warshaw, "Trying to Consume," *Journal of Consumer Research* 17, 2 (September 1990): 127–40.

45. Barbara Presley Noble, "After Years of Deregulation, a New Push to Inform the Public," *New York Times* (October 27, 1991): F5.

46. Matthew Greenwald and John P. Katosh, "How to Track Changes in Attitudes," *American Demographics* (August 1987): 46.

Sharon's big promotion is the opportunity she's been waiting for. She has always wanted a fur coat, even though this symbol of luxury has lost some of its appeal as people have become more concerned about animal rights. Just this morning, a newspaper columnist observed that the "... dried, dead, hairy animal skin—or if you insist, luxurious fur coat—has become as passé and vulgarly uncivilized as flogging one's servants."[1]

"I'd rather go naked than wear fur."
—Christy Turlington

PeTA
PEOPLE FOR THE ETHICAL
TREATMENT OF ANIMALS

Sharon has also heard about the animal rights activists who have made it increasingly difficult to buy, sell and wear fur. She has read about furriers who have had their store locks glued shut and received death threats. She has also seen a news report about fur wearers being doused with red dye representing animal blood.

Nevertheless, now that Sharon can afford to reward herself in a big way, she thinks about that coat she's always wanted and is eager to find a reason to justify her passion. She browses through Sunday's newspaper ads and finds a few for furs—most of them on sale. That convinces her: she *will* buy her coat.

But she will be really careful about where she wears it ...

8

Attitude Change and Interactive Communications

CHANGING ATTITUDES THROUGH COMMUNICATION

As consumers, we are constantly bombarded by messages inducing us to change our attitudes. The passionate debate about whether consumers should wear fur illustrates some of the tactics used to change attitudes (fur sales have declined 25 percent since the 1980s).[2] For example, groups such as People for the Ethical Treatment of Animals have run hard-hitting ads to influence consumers' opinions about buying fur. In a parody of the long-running ads for Blackglama furs—which depict famous women wrapped in furs and bear the caption "What Becomes a Legend Most?"— this group ran ads with such celebrities as Cassandra Petersen (a.k.a. horror-show hostess and cult heroine Elvira) asking, "What Disgraces a Legend Most?"

On the other hand, the fur industry claims that the animals, which often kill each other in the wild anyway, are treated humanely.[3] Research conducted by the fur industry showed that most consumers felt they were entitled to wear fur but needed reassurance in the face of the social pressures confronting them. As a result of such efforts, some fur wearers are beginning to flaunt their furs to show their resentment at being told what to wear. In London, women staged a "National Wear Your Fur Day" and demonstrated in Berkeley Square with posters demanding freedom of dress.[4] Others are trying to "have their cake and eat it, too" as *faux* fur is becoming fashionable.[5]

This anti-fur ad ran in Hong Kong. It relies upon a graphic description of fur-industry practices to discourage consumers from considering the purchase of a fur coat.
Courtesy of Bates Hong Kong Ltd.

As the battle over wearing fur illustrates, persuasion attempts can range from logical arguments to graphic pictures, and from intimidation by peers to celebrity spokespeople. This chapter will review some of the factors that help to determine the effectiveness of such communication devices.

Our focus will be on some basic aspects of communication that specifically help to determine how and if attitudes will be created or modified. This objective relates to **persuasion,** which refers to an active attempt to change attitudes. Persuasion is the central goal of many marketing communications.

persuasion an active attempt to change attitudes

One way that the fur industry is trying to counteract the graphic messages of anti-fur groups is to position the debate as one involving the curtailment of the personal right to buy what one chooses. This ad, which was placed by a Scandinavian fur marketer, is typical: it wraps the fur wearer in images of a wholesome family scene and positions the decision to buy a fur as representing freedom of choice.
Courtesy of Saga Furs of Scandinavia.

Decisions, Decisions: Tactical Communications Options

Suppose that a perfume company wants to create an advertising campaign for a new fragrance. As it plans this campaign, it must develop a message that will create desire for the perfume in potential consumers. To craft persuasive messages a number of questions must be answered:

- Who will be depicted as using the scent in an ad? Should it be linked to a glamorous celebrity? a career woman? a rock star? The source of a message helps to determine consumers' acceptance of it, as well as their desire to try the product.

- How should the message be constructed? Should it emphasize the negative consequences of smelling badly? Should it directly compare the fragrance with others already on the market or maybe present a fantasy where a princess is swept off her feet by a dashing knight after she applies the scent? Product benefits can be expressed in many ways.

- What media should be used to transmit the message? Should it be depicted in a print ad? On television? Sold door-to-door? If a print ad is produced, should it be run in the pages of *Vogue*? *Good Housekeeping*? *Details*? Sometimes *where* something is said can be as important as *what* is said. Ideally, the attributes of the product should be matched to those of the medium. For example, magazines with high prestige are more effective at communicating messages about overall product image and quality, while specialized, expert magazines do a better job at conveying factual information.[6]

- What characteristics of the target market might influence the ad's acceptance? If targeted users are frustrated in their daily lives, these women might be more receptive to a fantasy appeal. If they don't tend to wear perfume, they may not pay any attention to a traditional perfume ad at all.

The Elements of Communication

Marketers and advertisers have traditionally tried to understand how marketing messages change consumers' attitudes by thinking in terms of the **communications model,** which specifies that a number of elements are necessary for communication to be achieved. This chapter focuses on two important components of this model—the source and the message—and, in the final section, compares their effectiveness in persuading consumers to change their attitudes.

In this model a *source* must choose and encode a *message* (i.e., initiate the transfer of meaning by choosing appropriate symbolic images that represent this meaning). There are many ways to say something, and the structure of the message has a big effect on how it is perceived. The message must be transmitted via a *medium*, which could be television, radio, magazines, billboards or even a T-shirt. The message is then decoded by one or more *receivers*, who interpret the symbols in light of their own experiences. Finally, *feedback* must be received by the source, who uses the reactions of receivers to modify aspects of the message. The communications process is depicted in Figure 8–1.

communications model a framework specifying that a number of elements are necessary for communication to be achieved, including a source, a message, a medium, receivers and feedback

FIGURE 8–1 • The Communications Model

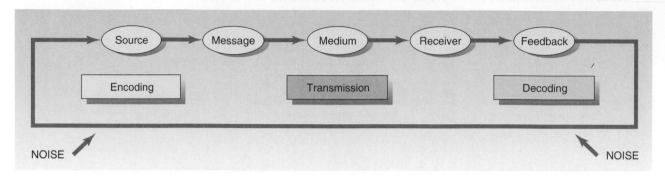

AN UPDATED VIEW: INTERACTIVE COMMUNICATIONS

While the traditional communications model is not entirely wrong, it doesn't tell the whole story—especially in today's dynamic world of interactivity.[7] The traditional model was developed in order to understand mass communications, where information is transferred from a producer (source) to many consumers (receivers) at one time—typically via print, television or radio. This perspective essentially views advertising as the process of transferring information to the buyer before a sale. A message is seen as perishable; it is repeated (perhaps frequently) for a fairly short period of time and then it "vanishes" as a new campaign eventually takes its place.

This model was strongly influenced by a group of theorists known as the *Frankfurt School,* which dominated mass-communications research for most of this century. In this view the media exert direct and powerful effects on individuals, and often are used by those in power to brainwash and exploit them. The receiver is basically a passive being—a "couch potato" who simply is the receptacle for many messages, and who is often duped or persuaded to act based on the information he or she is "fed" by the media.

Uses and Gratifications

uses and gratifications theory the perspective that the consumer uses the media to meet more than strictly informational needs

Is this an accurate picture of the way we relate to marketing communications? Proponents of **uses and gratifications theory** argue instead that consumers are an active, goal-directed audience that draws on mass media as a resource to satisfy needs. Instead of asking what media do for or to people, they ask what people do *with* their media.[8]

The uses and gratifications approach emphasizes that media compete with other sources to satisfy needs, and that these needs include diversion and entertainment as well as information. This also means that the line between marketing information and entertainment is continuing to blur—especially as companies are being forced to design more attractive retail outlets, catalogues and Web sites in order to induce consumers to stop at them. For example, Toyota's site (***www.toyota.com***) provides a lot more than the latest specs about available engine horsepower options; it also addresses interests like gardening, travel and sports.

Indeed, research with young people in Great Britain finds that they rely on advertising for many gratifications including entertainment (some report that the "adverts" are better than the programs), escapism, play (some report singing along with jingles, others make posters out of magazine ads) and self-affirmation (ads can reinforce their own values or provide role models). It's important to note that this perspective is not arguing that media play a uniformly positive role in our lives, only that recipients are making use of the information in a number of ways.[9]

Who's in Charge of the Remote?

Whether for good or bad, though, exciting technological and social developments certainly are forcing us to rethink the picture of the passive consumer, as people increasingly are playing a proactive role in communications. In other words, they are to a greater extent becoming partners—rather than potatoes—in the communications process; their input is helping to shape the messages they and others like them receive, and furthermore they may seek out these messages rather than sit home and wait to see them on TV or in the paper. This updated approach to interactive communications is illustrated in Figure 8-2.

Consider, for example, an interactive music sampling kiosk called the iStation. In 300 retail locations the installation offers online information and sound bites from more than 37 000 recordings. Consumers can also listen to cuts from a CD sitting on a store shelf by passing a laser over its bar code. They essentially are choosing which products they wish to sample, rather than being spoonfed the Top 40 of that week. Users must register with the company, giving information about their musical preferences, ethnic background and electronics usage in the home. The company then uses the data it obtains to send targeted mailings informing subscribers of upcoming concerts and releases tailored to their musical preferences.[10]

FIGURE 8–2 • The Interactive Communication Model

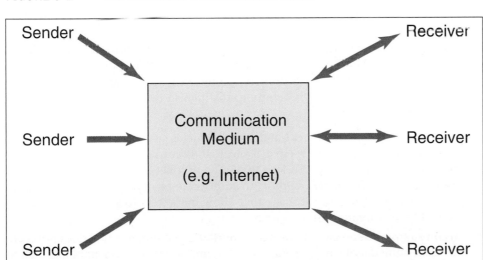

Source: Adapted from Donna L. Hoffman and Thomas P. Novak, "Marketing in Hypermedia Computer-Mediated Environments: Conceptual Foundations," *Journal of Marketing* 60, 3 (July 1996), Fig. 4.

One of the early signs of this communications revolution was the humble hand-held remote control device. As VCRs began to be commonplace in homes, suddenly consumers had more input into what they wanted to watch—and when. No longer were they at the mercy of the TV networks to decide when to see their favourite shows, and neither did they necessarily have to forsake a show because it conflicted with another's time slot.

Since that time, of course, our ability to control our media environment has mushroomed. Many people have access to video-on-demand or pay-per-view TV. Home shopping networks encourage us to call in and discuss our passion for cubic zirconium live on the air. Caller ID devices and answering machines allow us to decide if we will accept a phone call during dinner time, and to know the source of the message before picking up the phone. A bit of Web surfing allows us to identify kindred spirits around the globe, to request information about products, and even to provide suggestions to product designers and market researchers.

For example, a technology called the *radio data system* (R.D.S.) allows a radio station to transmit data on the unused portion of its frequency, known as a subcarrier. The system has been adopted in Europe by the British Broadcasting Corporation and is slowly coming to North America. R.D.S. is the concept behind Coupon Radio, a car radio system now being tested that lets listeners "capture" information and give stations and advertisers feedback about their choices. A driver who hears a new song he or she likes could request more information about the musicians, and this person could also get the names and addresses of retailers that sell an advertised product.[11]

Levels of Interactive Response

A key to understanding the dynamics of interactive marketing communications is to consider exactly what is meant by a response.[12] The early perspective on communications primarily regarded feedback in terms of behaviour: did the recipient run out and buy the laundry detergent after being exposed to an ad for it?

However, a variety of other responses are possible as well, including building awareness of the brand, informing us about product features, reminding us to buy a new package when we've run out, and—perhaps most importantly—building a long-term relationship. Therefore, a transaction is *one* type of response, but forward-thinking marketers realize that customers can interact with them in other valuable ways as well. For this reason it is helpful to distinguish between two basic types of feedback:

- *First-Order Response.*   Direct-marketing vehicles such as catalogues and television infomercials are interactive; if successful they result in an order, which is most definitely a response! So, let's think of a product offer that directly yields a transaction as a *first-order response*. In addition to providing revenue, sales data are a valuable source of feedback that allow marketers to gauge the effectiveness of their communications efforts.

- *Second-Order Response.*   However, a marketing communication does not have to result immediately in a purchase to be an important component of interactive marketing. Messages can prompt useful responses from customers, even though these recipients do not necessarily place an order immediately after being exposed to the communication. Customer feedback in response to a marketing message that is not in the form of a transaction is a *second-order response*.

A second-order response may take the form of a request for more information about a good, service or organization, or perhaps receipt of a "wish list" from the customer that specifies the types of product information he or she would like to get in the future. This response may even be in the form of referrals to other potential customers.

THE SOURCE

Common sense tells us that the same words uttered by different people can have very different effects. Research on *source effects* has been carried out for over 30 years. By attributing the same message to different sources and measuring the degree of attitude change that occurs after listeners hear it, researchers have found it is possible to determine what aspects of a communicator will induce attitude change.[13]

Under most conditions the source of a message can have a big impact on the likelihood the message will be accepted. The choice of a source to maximize attitude change can tap into several dimensions. The source can be chosen because he or she is an expert, attractive, famous or even a "typical" consumer who is both likeable and trustworthy. Two important source characteristics are *credibility* and *attractiveness*.[14]

Source Credibility

Source credibility refers to the source's perceived expertise, objectivity or trustworthiness. This characteristic relates to consumers' beliefs that a communicator is competent and willing to provide the necessary information adequately to evaluate competing products. A credible source can be particularly persuasive when the consumer has not yet learned much about a product or formed an opinion of it.[15]

source credibility a communications source's perceived expertise, objectivity or trustworthiness

BUILDING CREDIBILITY

Credibility can be enhanced if the source's qualifications are perceived as relevant to the product being endorsed. This linkage can overcome other objections people may have to the endorser or the product. When former baseball pitcher Jim Palmer endorsed Jockey International products, his athleticism was instrumental in reassuring men that it was acceptable for them to wear skimpy underwear in unusual colours.[16] Similarly, Ronald Biggs, whose claim to fame was taking part in the 1963 Great Train Robbery in the United Kingdom, successfully served as a spokesman in Brazil for a company that makes door locks—a topic about which he is presumably knowledgeable![17]

SOURCE BIASES

A consumer's beliefs about a product's attributes can be weakened if the source is perceived to be the victim of bias in presenting information.[18] *Knowledge bias* implies that a source's knowledge about a topic is not accurate. *Reporting bias* occurs where a source has the required knowledge but his or her willingness to convey it accurately is compromised, as when a star tennis-player is paid by a racket manufacturer to use its products exclusively. While his or her credentials might be appropriate, the fact that the expert is perceived as a "hired gun" compromises believability.

Source Attractiveness

source attractiveness

refers to the source's
perceived social value

Source attractiveness refers to the source's perceived social value. This quality can emanate from the person's physical appearance, personality or social status, or from his or her similarity to the receiver (we like to listen to people who are like us).

STAR POWER: CELEBRITIES AS COMMUNICATIONS SOURCES

The use of celebrity endorsers, including athletes, musicians and movie stars, is an expensive but common strategy—as golfing sensation Tiger Woods discovered when Nike signed him as its premier endorser in 1997.

While a celebrity endorsement strategy is expensive, it can pay off handsomely.[19] When used properly, famous or expert spokespeople can be of great value in improving the fortunes of a product. Celebrities increase the public awareness of a firm's advertising and enhance both company image and brand attitudes.[20] This technique is effective because consumers are better able to identify products that are associated with a well-known spokesperson.[21]

More generally, star power works because celebrities embody *cultural meanings*; they symbolize important categories such as status and social class (e.g., a "working-class heroine" like Roseanne), gender (a "manly man" like Sylvester Stallone), age (the boyish Michael J. Fox) and personality types (the eccentric Kramer on "Seinfeld"). Ideally, the advertiser decides what meanings the product should

One of the most successful athlete endorsers in recent times is basketball star Shaquille O'Neal. Unlike other athletes, who tend to wait until they have become big stars before signing lucrative endorsement contracts, Shaq had signed a multiyear contract with Reebok, valued at close to $20 million, before he even set foot on an NBA court. In his rookie year Shaq earned another $8 million in endorsements for Pepsi, Spalding and Kenner Toys. In a poll conducted among marketing professionals by the trade paper *Advertising Age*, 75 percent of those surveyed predicted that Shaq would be the most likely successor to the current endorsement champ, fellow hoopster Michael Jordan—who was raking in an estimated $32 million per year in endorsements at the time he retired (for the first time, anyway) in 1993.
Source: Patrick Goldstein, "Shaquille O'Neal: He Jams. He Raps. He Acts. He Sells," Rolling Stone *(November 25, 1993): 52 (6 pp.)*; Stuart Elliott, "The Records May Continue to Fall for Michael Jordan's Career as a Marketing All-Star," New York Times *(October 7, 1993): D20. Photo: Reprinted by permission of Pepsi Co, Inc., 1995, Purchase, NY.*

MARKETING PITFALL

For celebrity campaigns to be effective, the endorser must have a clear and popular image. In addition, the celebrity's image and that of the product he or she endorses should be similar; this effect is known as the **match-up hypothesis**.[22] Many promotional strategies employing stars fail because the endorser has not been selected very carefully; some marketers just assume that because a person is "famous" he or she will serve as a successful spokesperson. The use of Don Cherry by Irwin Toy may be just such an example.

The images of celebrities can, however, be pre-tested to increase the probability of consumer acceptance. One widely used technique is the so-called *"Q" rating* (Q stands for quality) developed by a market research company. This rating considers two factors in surveys: consumers' level of familiarity with a name, and the number of respondents who indicate that a person, program or character is a favourite. While it yields a rather rough measure, the Q rating acknowledges that mere familiarity with a celebrity's name is not sufficient to gauge popularity, since some widely known people are also widely disliked. Celebrities with low Q ratings include Michael Jackson, Gene Simmons, Wayne Newton, Madonna and Cyndi Lauper. Some with high ratings are Stevie Wonder, Billy Joel, Phil Collins, George Michael, Whitney Houston, Cher and Dolly Parton.[23] However, even a high Q rating does not guarantee success if the celebrity's specific image doesn't match up with the featured product.

Another potential problem is what to do about celebrity endorsers who "misbehave." Pepsi had to abandon its sponsorship of Michael Jackson after the singer was accused of child molestation, and the company had to drop boxer Mike Tyson following allegations of wife beating. Madonna met a similar fate following the release of her controversial *Like a Prayer* music video. Then, of course, there's always O.J. Simpson ... To avoid some of these problems, most endorsement contracts now contain a morality clause that allows the company to release the celebrity if so warranted.[24] Still, some advertisers are looking a lot more favourably at animated spokescharacters like Bugs Bunny, who tend to stay out of trouble!

match-up hypothesis the theory that the dominant characteristics of a product should match the dominant features of the communication source

convey (that is, how it should be positioned in the marketplace) and then chooses a celebrity who has come to evoke a similar meaning. The product's meaning thus moves from the manufacturer to the consumer, using the star as a vehicle.[25] The use of k.d. lang and Ru Paul as spokespersons for M.A.C. cosmetics was a special twist on this unique company. k.d. lang, a lesbian known not to wear make-up, and Ru Paul, a transvestite known to lather it on, gave M.A.C. the image congruency they wanted as an alternative cosmetics company.

Famous people can be effective because they are credible, attractive or both, depending on the reasons for their fame. Businessman/politician Paul Martin Jr. is unlikely to be a "sex symbol," but he may be quite effective at advocating use of a financial product. On the other hand, Vanna White may not be perceived as highly expert (except perhaps at turning letters on game shows), but she might be a persuasive source for a message about perfume or clothing.

The use of Ru Paul gives M.A.C. the image they desire of being a unique alternative to mainstream cosmetics.
Courtesy of M.A.C. Cosmetics.

The effectiveness of celebrities as communications sources often depends upon their perceived credibility. Consumers may not trust a celebrity's motives for endorsing a product, or they may question the star's competence critically to evaluate the product's claims. This "credibility gap" appears to be widening. In a recent one-year period, for example, the number of consumers who found celebrity advertising "less than credible" jumped to 52 percent. The greatest erosion of confidence came from younger consumers, 64 percent of whom thought that celebrities appeared in ads just for the money.[26] The lack of credibility is aggravated by incidences where celebrities endorse products that they do not really believe in or in some cases do not use.

MULTICULTURAL DIMENSIONS

Some celebrities choose to maintain their credibility by endorsing products only in other countries, so these ads will not be seen by consumers in their own land. Many celebrities who do not do many American advertisements appear frequently in Japan. Mel Gibson endorses Asahi beer, Sly Stallone appears for Kirin beer, Sean Connery plugs Ito hams, and the singer Sheena Easton—dressed in a kimono and wig—was featured in ads for Shochu liquor. Even the normally reclusive comedian and film director Woody Allen was featured in a campaign for a large Tokyo department store.[27]

This ad uses a good-looking male model to make its points. Brut's advertising campaign was based on research indicating that men are feeling more comfortable with their masculinity.
Source: Cyndee Miller, "They're Macho, and They're Back," Marketing News Nov 22, 1993: 1. Photo: Courtesy of Faberge Company.

WHAT IS BEAUTIFUL IS GOOD

Almost everywhere we turn, beautiful people are trying to persuade us to buy or do something. Our society places a very high premium on physical attractiveness, and we tend to assume that people who are good-looking are smarter, cooler and happier. Such an assumption is called a *halo effect,* which occurs when persons who are rated highly on one dimension are assumed to excel on others as well. The effect can be explained in terms of the consistency principle, discussed in Chapter 7, which states that people are more comfortable when all of their judgments about a person go together. This notion has been termed the "what-is-beautiful-is-good" stereotype.[28]

A physically attractive source tends to facilitate attitude change. His or her degree of attractiveness exerts at least a modest effect on consumers' purchase intentions or product evaluation.[29] How does this happen?

One explanation is that physical attractiveness functions as a cue that facilitates or modifies information processing by directing consumers' attention to relevant marketing stimuli. Some evidence indicates that consumers pay more attention to ads that contain attractive models, though not necessarily to the ad copy.[30] In other words, an ad with a beautiful person may stand a better chance of getting noticed but not necessarily of being read. While we may enjoy looking at a beautiful or handsome person, these positive feelings do not necessarily affect product attitudes or purchase intentions.[31]

Beauty can also function as a source of information. The effectiveness of highly attractive spokespeople in ads appears to be largely limited to those situations where the advertised product is overtly related to attractiveness or sexuality.[32] The *social adaptation perspective* assumes that information seen to be instrumental in forming an attitude will be more heavily weighted by the perceiver; we filter out irrelevant information to minimize cognitive effort. Under the right circumstances an endorser's level of attractiveness constitutes a source of information instrumental to the attitude-change process.[33] An attractive spokesperson, for this reason, is more likely to be an effective source when the product is relevant to attractiveness. For example, attractiveness affects attitudes towards ads about perfume or cologne (where attractiveness is relevant) but not towards coffee ads, where attractiveness is not relevant.[34]

CREDIBILITY VERSUS ATTRACTIVENESS

How do marketing specialists decide whether to stress credibility or attractiveness when choosing a message source? There should be a match between the needs of the recipient and the potential rewards offered by the source. When this match occurs, the recipient is more motivated to process the message. People who tend to be sensitive about social acceptance and the opinions of others, for example, are more persuaded by an attractive source, while those who are more internally oriented are swayed by a credible, expert source.[35]

The choice may also depend on the type of product. While a positive source can help to reduce risk and increase message acceptance, particular types of sources are more effective at reducing different kinds of risk. Experts are effective at changing attitudes towards utilitarian products that have high *performance risk,* such as vacuums (i.e., they may be complex and not work as expected). Celebrities are more effective when they focus on products such as jewellery and furniture, which have high *social risk*: the user of such products is aware of their effect on others' impression of him or her. Finally, "typical" consumers, who are appealing sources because of their similarity to the recipient, tend to be most effective when providing "man-in-the-street" endorsements for everyday products that are low risk, such as cookies.[36]

THE SLEEPER EFFECT

While, in general, more positive sources tend to increase attitude change, exceptions can occur. Sometimes a source can be obnoxious or disliked and still manage to be effective at getting the product's message across. A case in point is Mr. Whipple, the irritating but well-known character in toilet-paper commercials who, for many years, scolded customers, "Please don't squeeze the Charmin!"

In some instances the differences in attitude change between positive sources and less positive sources seem to get erased over time. After a while, people appear to "forget" about the negative source and wind up changing their attitudes anyway. This process is known as the **sleeper effect.**[37]

sleeper effect the process whereby differences in attitude change between positive and negative sources seem to diminish over time

The explanation for the sleeper effect is a subject of debate, as is the more basic question regarding whether and when it really exists. Initially, the *dissociative cue hypothesis* proposed that over time the message and the source become disassociated in the consumer's mind. The message remains on its own in memory, causing a delayed attitude change—the sleeper effect.[38]

A more recent explanation is the *availability-valence hypothesis,* which emphasizes the selectivity of memory owing to limited capacity.[39] If the associations linked to the negative source are less available than those linked to the message information, the residual impact of the message enhances persuasion. Consistent with this view, the sleeper effect has been obtained only when the message was encoded deeply; that is, it had stronger associations in memory than did the source.[40]

THE MESSAGE

A major study of over 1000 commercials identified factors that appear to determine whether or not a commercial message will be persuasive. The single most important

TABLE 8–1 Positive and Negative Effects of Elements in Television Commercials

POSITIVE EFFECTS	NEGATIVE EFFECTS
Showing convenience of use	Extensive information on components, ingredients or nutrition
Showing new product or improved features	Outdoor setting (message gets lost)
Casting background (i.e., people are incidental to message)	Large number of on-screen characters
Indirect comparison to other products	Graphic displays
Demonstration of the product in use	
Demonstration of tangible results (e.g., bouncy hair)	
An actor playing the role of an ordinary person	
No principal character (i.e., more time is devoted to the product)	

Source: Adapted from David W. Stewart and David H. Furse, "The Effects of Television Advertising Execution on Recall, Comprehension, and Persuasion," *Psychology & Marketing* 2 (Fall 1985): 135–60. Copyright © 1985 by John Wiley & Sons, Inc. Reprinted by permission.

feature was whether the communication contained a brand-differentiating message. In other words, did the communication stress a unique attribute or benefit of the product? Other good and bad elements are depicted in Table 8–1.[41]

Message Elements

The characteristics of the commercial message itself help to determine the impact of that message on attitudes. These variables may include how the message is said, as well as what is actually said. Some of the issues facing marketers include the following:

- Should the message be conveyed in words or pictures?
- How concrete or vivid should the arguments and imagery be?
- How often should the message be repeated?
- Should both sides of an argument be presented?
- Should a conclusion be drawn, or should this be left up to the listener?
- Is it effective to explicitly compare one's product with that of competitors?
- Should a blatant sexual appeal be used?
- Should the ad be funny?
- Should negative emotions, such as fear, ever be aroused?

Sending the Message

The saying "one picture is worth a thousand words" captures the idea that visual stimuli can economically deliver big impact, especially when the communicator wants to influence receivers' emotional responses. For this reason, advertisers often place great emphasis on vivid and creative illustrations or photography.[42]

This ad pokes fun at the typical elements one would expect to see in a persuasive communication targeted to beer drinkers.
Courtesy of Heineken USA, Inc., White Plains, NY.

On the other hand, a picture is not always as effective at communicating factual information. Ads that contain the same information, presented in either visual or verbal form, have been found to elicit different reactions. The verbal version affects ratings on the utilitarian aspects of a product, while the visual version affects aesthetic evaluations.[43] Verbal elements are more effective when reinforced by an accompanying picture, especially if the illustration is *framed* (i.e., the message in the picture is strongly related to the copy).[44]

Because it requires more effort to process, a verbal message is most appropriate for high-involvement situations, such as in print contexts where readers are motivated to pay attention to the advertising. Because verbal material decays more rapidly in memory, more frequent exposures are needed to obtain the desired effect. Visual images, in contrast, allow the receiver to *chunk* information at the time of encoding (see Chapter 3 on memory processes). Chunking results in a stronger memory trace, which aids retrieval over time.[45]

Visual elements may affect brand attitudes in one of two ways. First, the consumer may form inferences about the brand and change his or her beliefs because of an illustration's imagery. For example, people who saw an ad for a facial tissue accompanied by a photo of a sunset were more likely to believe that the brand came in attractive colours.

Second, brand attitudes may be affected more directly. A strong positive or negative reaction elicited by the visual elements will influence the consumer's attitude towards the ad (A_{ad}), which will then affect brand attitudes (A_b). This *dual-component model* of brand attitudes is illustrated in Figure 8–3.[46]

FIGURE 8–3 • Effects of Visual and Verbal Components of Advertisements on
Brand Attitudes

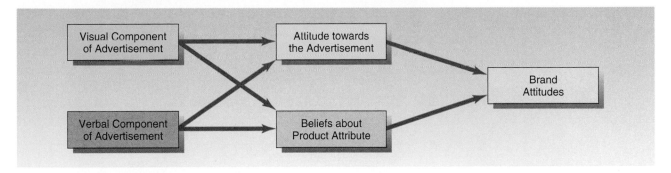

Source: Andrew A. Mitchell, "The Effect of Verbal and Visual Components of Advertisements on Brand Attitudes
and Attitude Toward the Advertisement," *Journal of Consumer Research* 13 (June 1986): 21. Reprinted by permission of The University of Chicago Press.

VIVIDNESS

Both pictures and words can differ in *vividness*. Powerful descriptions or graphics command attention and are more strongly embedded in memory. The reason may be that they tend to activate mental imagery, while abstract stimuli inhibit this process.[47] Of course, this effect can cut both ways. Negative information presented in a vivid manner may result in more negative evaluations at a later time.[48]

The concrete discussion of a product attribute in ad copy also influences the importance of that attribute because more attention is drawn to it. For example, the copy for a watch that read "According to industry sources, three out of every four watch breakdowns are due to water getting into the case" was more effective than the version that read "According to industry sources, many watch breakdowns are due to water getting into the case."[49]

REPETITION

Repetition can be a two-edged sword for marketers. As noted in Chapter 3, multiple exposures to a stimulus are usually required for learning (especially conditioning) to occur. Contrary to the saying "familiarity breeds contempt," people tend to like things that are more familiar to them, even if they were not that keen on them initially.[50] This phenomenon is known as the *mere exposure effect*. Positive effects for advertising repetition are found even in mature product categories; repeating product information has been shown to boost consumers' awareness of the brand, even though nothing new has been said.[51] On the other hand, too much repetition creates *habituation*, wherein the consumer no longer pays attention to the stimulus because of fatigue or boredom. Excessive exposure can cause *advertising wear-out*, which can result in negative reactions to an ad after seeing it too much.[52]

The fine line between familiarity and boredom has been explained by the **two-factor theory,** which proposes that two separate psychological processes are operating when a person is repeatedly exposed to an ad. The positive side of repetition is that it increases familiarity and thus reduces uncertainty about the product. The negative side is that, over time, boredom increases with each exposure. At some point the amount of boredom incurred begins to exceed the amount of uncertainty reduced, resulting in wear-out. This pattern is depicted in Figure 8–4. Its effect is

two-factor theory the perspective that two separate psychological processes are operating when a person is repeatedly exposed to an ad: repetition increases familiarity and thus reduces uncertainty about the product, but over time boredom increases with each exposure, and at some point the amount of boredom incurred begins to exceed the amount of uncertainty reduced, resulting in wear-out

FIGURE 8-4 • Two-Factor Theory and Advertising Wear-Out

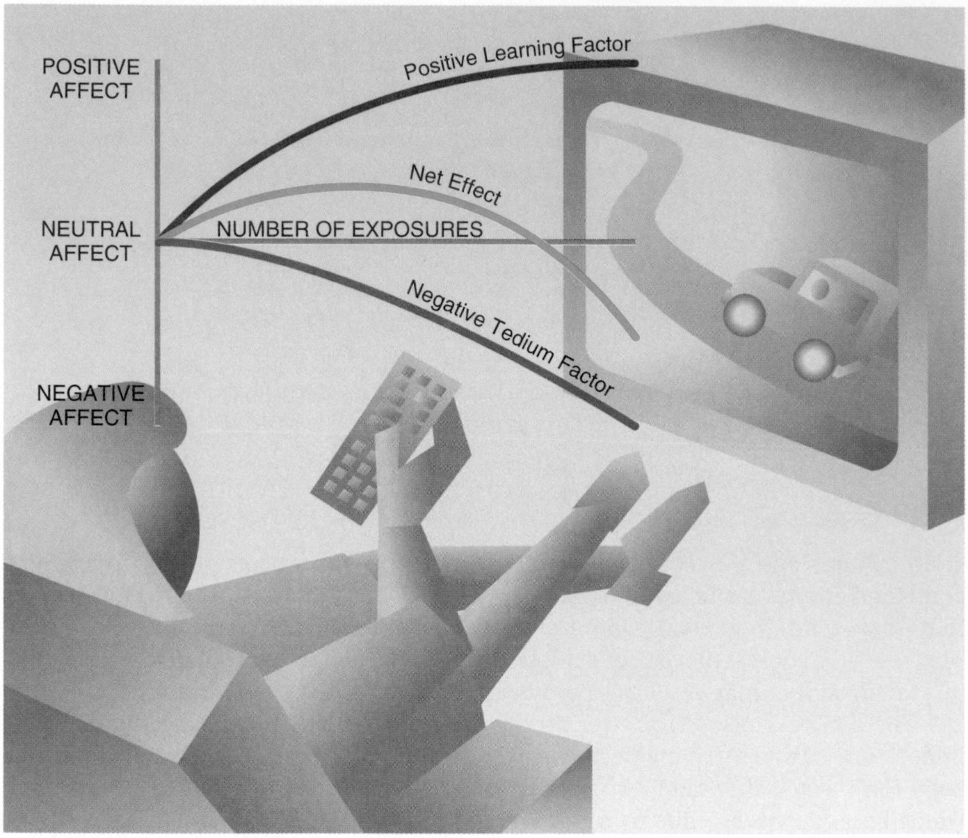

Source: Adapted from Arno J. Rathans, John L. Swasy and Lawrence Marks, "Effects of Television Commercial Repetition. Receiver Knowledge," *Journal of Marketing Research* 23 (February 1986): 50–61, Fig. 1. By permission of American Marketing Association.

especially pronounced in cases where each exposure is of a fairly long duration (such as a 60-second commercial).[53]

The theory implies that advertisers can overcome this problem by limiting the amount of exposure per repetition (for example, by using 15-second spots). They can also maintain familiarity but alleviate boredom by slightly varying the content of ads over time through campaigns that revolve around a common theme (although each spot may be different). Recipients who are exposed to varied ads about the product absorb more information about product attributes and experience more positive thoughts about the brand than do those exposed repeatedly to the same information. This additional information allows the person to resist attempts to change his or her attitude in the face of a counterattack by a competing brand.[54] H&R Block systematically presents different reasons to use its firm for tax preparation.

Constructing the Argument

Many marketing messages are similar to debates or trials, in which someone presents arguments and tries to convince the receiver to shift his or her opinion accordingly. The way the argument is presented can thus be very important.

ONE- VERSUS TWO-SIDED ARGUMENTS

Most messages merely present one or more positive attributes about the product or reasons to buy it. These are known as *supportive arguments*. An alternative is to use a *two-sided message,* in which both positive and negative information are presented. Research has indicated that two-sided ads can be quite effective, yet they are not widely used.[55]

Why would a marketer want to devote advertising space to publicizing a product's negative attributes? Under the right circumstances the use of *refutational arguments,* in which a negative issue is raised and then dismissed, can be quite effective. This approach can increase source credibility by reducing reporting bias. Also, people who are skeptical about the product may be more receptive to a balanced argument as opposed to a "whitewash."[56] In one novel application, a Château Potelle winery ad included both positive and negative reviews of a wine by two experts. The ad suggested that consumers develop their own taste rather than rely on reviews in wine magazines.[57]

This is not to say that the marketer should go overboard in presenting major problems with the product. In the typical refutational strategy, relatively minor attributes are discussed that may present a problem or fall short when a product is compared with competitors. These drawbacks are then refuted by emphasizing positive, important attributes. Avis got a lot of mileage out of claiming to be only "No. 2," while an ad for Volkswagen woefully described one of its cars as a "lemon" because there was a scratch on the glove-compartment chrome strip.[58]

A two-sided strategy appears to be most effective when the audience is well educated (and presumably more impressed by a balanced argument).[59] It is also best to use when receivers are not already loyal to the product; "preaching to the converted" about possible drawbacks may raise doubts unnecessarily.

DRAWING CONCLUSIONS

A related issue is whether the argument should draw conclusions or whether the points should merely be presented, permitting the consumer to arrive at his or her own conclusion. Should the message say only, "Our brand is superior," or should it add, "You should buy our brand"? On the one hand, consumers who make their own inferences instead of having them spoonfed will form stronger, more accessible attitudes. On the other, leaving the conclusion ambiguous increases the chance that the desired attitude will not be formed.

The response to this issue depends upon the consumers' motivation to process the ad and the complexity of the arguments. If the message is personally relevant, people will pay attention to it and spontaneously form inferences. However, if the arguments are hard to follow or consumers' motivation to follow them is lacking, it is safer for the ad to draw conclusions.[60]

COMPARATIVE ADVERTISING

Comparative advertising refers to a strategy wherein a message identifies two or more specifically named or recognizably presented brands and compares them in terms of one or more specific attributes.[61] For example, Schering-Plough claimed that "New OcuClear relieves three times longer than Visine," and Bristol-Myers stated that "New Liquid Vanish really does clean tough rust stains below the water line better than Lysol."

comparative advertising a strategy in which a message compares two or more specifically named or recognizably presented brands and makes a comparison of them in terms of one or more specific attributes

This strategy has yielded mixed results. While some comparative ads result in desired attitude change, or positive A_{ad}, they have also been found to be lower in believability and may result in more source derogation (i.e., the consumer may doubt the credibility of a biased presentation).[62] Indeed, in some cultures (such as in Asia) comparative advertising is rare because people find such a confrontational approach offensive.

Comparative ads do appear to be effective in the case of new products. Here, they are superior in anchoring a new brand closer to a dominant one and in building a clear brand image. However, if the aim is to compare the new brand with the market leader in terms of specific product attributes, merely saying it is as good as or better than the leader is not sufficient. For example, the use in a study of the claim "Spring has the same fluoride as Crest" resulted in attitude change for the fictitious product, while the more global statement "Preferred by Europeans in comparison with Crest" did not.[63]

Types of Message Appeals

The way something is said can be as significant as what is said; the same idea can be encoded in many different ways. It can tug at the heartstrings or scare you, make you laugh, make you cry or leave you wanting to learn more. In this section we'll review the major alternatives available to communicators who wish to *appeal* to a message recipient.

MARKETING PITFALL

Many consumers are sceptical about claims made or implied in advertising, and some ads are challenged after being aired, by either the government, concerned citizens or a competitor. About half of those challenged are either modified or taken off the air completely. In some cases the company makes an attempt to correct the misinformation. An example is a recent Volvo ad that was challenged by the Texas attorney general's office. In an ad showing a row of cars being crushed by a pick-up truck, only the Volvo was unharmed. However, investigation revealed that the Volvo used in the ad had been specially reinforced for the shoot. The company later ran ads acknowledging that the dramatization had been faked.

When a marketer makes a specific comparative claim relative to a competing product, he or she must be prepared for the possibility that the rival company will respond with a lawsuit. Many companies have got involved in complex lawsuits after using the comparative approach, and the costs of such litigation are high for both parties. As one judge who was involved in a 10-year court battle between two makers of rival analgesics noted, "Small nations have fought for their very survival with less resources."

As a result of these and other incidents, marketers are learning to exercise extra care when making product claims, and some are beginning to supply disclaimers to protect themselves against lawsuits.[64]

EMOTIONAL VERSUS RATIONAL APPEALS

A few years ago both Toyota and Nissan introduced large luxury cars that sold for over $40 000. The two companies chose very different ways to communicate their products' attributes, as seen in the ads shown below.

Toyota's advertising for its Lexus model used a rational appeal, with ads concentrating on the large number of technical advancements incorporated in the car's design. Print ads were dominated by copy describing these engineering features.

In sharp contrast, Nissan's controversial campaign for its Infiniti used an emotional appeal. The new model was introduced with a series of print and television ads that did not even discuss the car. The ads instead focused on the Zen-like experience of driving and featured long shots of serene landscapes. As one executive involved with the campaign explained, "We're not selling the skin of the car; we're selling the spirit."[65] While these ads were innovative, most American consumers had trouble grasping the Japanese conception of luxury. Later ads for the Infiniti emphasized functional features of the car to compensate for this initial confusion.

The goal of an emotional appeal is to establish a connection between the product and the consumer, a strategy known as *bonding*.[66] Emotional appeals have the potential to increase the chance that the message will be perceived; they may be more likely to be retained in memory; and they can also increase the consumer's involvement with the product. Although Nissan's gamble on emphasizing the aesthetic aspects of its product did not pay off in this case, other emotional appeals are quite effective. Indeed, Nissan's more recent campaign revolves around a mysterious, impish man in a baseball cap who appears at the end of offbeat vignettes that have little to do with the company's actual cars.

Many companies turned to this strategy after realizing that consumers do not find many differences among brands, especially those in well-established, mature categories. Ads for products ranging from cars (Lincoln Mercury) to cards (Hallmark) focus instead on emotional aspects. Mercury's capitalization on emotional

These ads demonstrate rational versus emotional message appeals. At the time of the initial ad campaign for the new Infiniti automobiles, the ads for rival Lexus (top) emphasized design and engineering, while the ads for Infiniti (bottom) did not even show the car. Courtesy of Lexus.
Courtesy of INFINITI®. *A division of Nissan Motor Corporation, USA.*

attachments to old rock songs succeeded in lowering the median age of its consumers for some models by 10 years.[67]

The precise effects of rational versus emotional appeals are hard to gauge. Though recall of ad contents tends to be better for "thinking" ads than for "feeling" ads, conventional measures of advertising effectiveness (like day-after recall) may not be adequate to assess cumulative effects of emotional ads. These open-ended measures are oriented towards cognitive responses, and feeling ads may be penalized because the reactions are not as easy to articulate.[68]

While they can make strong impressions, emotional appeals also run the risk of not getting across an adequate amount of product-related information. This potential problem is reminding some advertisers that the arousal of emotions is functional only to the extent that it sells the product. Procter & Gamble's original ads for Bounce fabric softener showed a happy young couple dancing to the song "Jump," with the message that Bounce is for clothes "you can't wait to jump into." Later spots show a woman discussing why the product makes her clothes feel and smell better. The ads are still somewhat emotional and experiential, but the main selling point of "softness without static cling" is driven home.[69]

SEX APPEALS

Under the assumption that "sex sells," many campaigns—for everything from perfumes to automobiles—feature heavy doses of erotic suggestions that range from subtle hints to blatant displays of skin. Perhaps not surprisingly, female nudity in

MULTICULTURAL DIMENSIONS

Nike is the master craftsman of "in your face" emotional messages about sports that barely acknowledge the shoes they are trying to sell. These appeals have played very well in North America, but now the company has hit some bumps in the road as it tries to export this attitude overseas. As the company searches for new markets, it is trying to conquer soccer the way it did basketball. An ad in *Soccer America* magazine announced the impending invasion: "Europe, Asia, and Latin America: Barricade your stadiums. Hide your trophies. Invest in some deodorant." This message was not very well received in some soccer quarters, and similarly a successful American TV commercial featuring Satan and his demons playing soccer against Nike endorsers was banned by some European stations on the grounds that it was too scary for children to see and offensive to boot. A British TV ad featuring a French soccer player saying how his spitting at a fan and insulting his coach won him a Nike contract resulted in a scathing editorial against Nike in the sport's international-federation newsletter.

Nike has a tough task ahead of it: to win over European soccer fans where rival Adidas is king—in a game that traditionally doesn't have the glitz and packaging of basketball. Now a bit chastized, Nike is modifying its "question authority" approach as it tries to win over the sports organizations in each country that don't appreciate its violent messages and anti-establishment themes. Only time will tell if the athletic giant will get "red-carded" by European fans and game officials.[70]

print ads generates negative feelings and tension among female consumers, while men's reactions are more positive.[71]

DOES SEX WORK? Although the use of sex does appear to draw attention to an ad, its use may actually be counterproductive to the marketer. Ironically, a provocative picture can be too effective: it attracts so much attention that it hinders processing and recall of the ad's contents. Sexual appeals appear to be ineffective when used merely as a "trick" to grab attention. They do, however, appear to work when the product is *itself* sexually related.

HUMOROUS APPEALS

The use of humour can be tricky, particularly since what is funny to one person may be offensive or incomprehensible to another. Specific cultures may have different senses of humour and also use funny material in diverse ways. For example, commercials in the United Kingdom and Canada are more likely to use puns and satire than those in the United States.[72]

DOES HUMOUR WORK? Overall, humorous advertisements do get attention. One study found that recognition scores for humorous liquor ads were better than average. However, the verdict is mixed as to whether humour affects recall or product attitudes in a significant way.[73] Humour can be effective when it provides a source of *distraction*. A funny ad inhibits the consumer from counterarguing. This, in turn, increases the likelihood of message acceptance.[74]

Humour is more likely to be effective when the brand is clearly identified and the funny material does not "swamp" the message. This danger is similar to that of beautiful models diverting attention from copy points. Subtle humour is usually better, as is humour that does not make fun of the potential consumer.

This humorous ad for Dristan cold medicine, which ran in Hong Kong, reads: "Is this the only way to get rid of a stuffed-up runny nose and the headaches a cold can bring?" Visual humour is often an effective way to get attention and cut through advertising clutter.
Courtesy of Bates Hong Kong, Ltd.

Finally, humour should be appropriate to the product's image. An undertaker or a bank might want to avoid humour, while other products adapt to it quite well. Sales of Sunsweet pitted prunes improved dramatically based on the claim, "Today the pits, tomorrow the wrinkles."[75]

FEAR APPEALS

fear appeal an attempt to change attitudes or behaviour through the use of threats or by the highlighting of negative consequences of non-compliance with the request

Fear appeals highlight the negative consequences that can occur if the consumer fails to change a behaviour or attitude. The arousal of fear is a common tactic for public-policy issues, such as convincing consumers to stop smoking or to drive safely (i.e., to reduce physical risk).

This tactic can also be applied to social-risk issues by appealing to people's anxieties about their careers or love lives. This tactic has been half-jokingly called the "slice-of-death" approach. One increasingly common fear appeal is to prey on people's insecurity about being laid off from their jobs. In a spot for Contac cold medicine, a construction worker wades through a rainstorm. He says that he needed to take Contac in order to get to work that day, adding, "No work, no pay." This ad was developed after interviews with about 800 consumers indicated widespread anxiety about losing their jobs.[76]

DOES FEAR WORK? Fear appeals are usually most effective when only a moderate amount of fear is induced. The relationship between fear and attitude change is *nonmonotonic*.[77] As shown in Figure 8–5, this means that increasing levels of fear do not result in increased change; the relationship instead resembles an inverted U-shaped curve. If the threat is too great, the audience tends to deny that it exists as a way of rationalizing the danger.

Fear appeals appear to be most effective when the consumer is already afraid of the problem discussed in the ad. The threats should not be excessive, and a solution to the problem should be presented (otherwise, consumers will tune out the ad since they can do nothing to solve the problem).[78] Fear appeals also work better when source credibility is high.[79]

Fear appeals have a greater chance of being effective if they also provide consumers with a possible solution to the problem. Here, celebrity Cher gives concrete advice about breast self-examinations.
Courtesy of Coors Brewing Company and AMC Cancer Research Center.

FIGURE 8–5 • The Relationship between Fear and Attitude Change

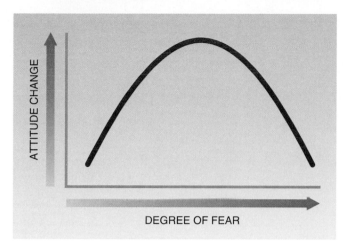

A study that manipulated subjects' degrees of anxiety about AIDS, for example, found that condom ads were evaluated most positively when a moderate amount of fear was induced. In this context, copy that promoted the use of the condom because "sex is a risky business" (moderate fear) resulted in more attitude change than either a low-fear appeal that emphasized the product's sensitivity or a high-fear appeal that discussed the certainty of death from AIDS.[80] Similarly, scare tactics have not been as effective as hoped in getting teenagers to decrease their use of alcohol or drugs. Teens simply tune out the message or deny its relevance to them.[81]

The Message as Art Form: Metaphors Be with You

Marketers may be thought of as storytellers who supply visions of reality similar to those provided by authors, poets and artists. These communications take the form of stories because the product benefits they describe are intangible and must be given tangible meaning by being expressed in a form that is concrete and visible. Advertising creatives rely (consciously or not) on various literary devices to communicate these meanings. For example, a product or service might be personified by a character such as Mr. Goodwrench, the Jolly Green Giant or the California Raisins. Many

MARKETING PITFALL

Social research tells us that teenagers are far more worried about their relationship with their peers and friends than with their physical health. Unfortunately, most people who create ads for antismoking campaigns for teens are adults focused on health issues. An analysis of 150 antismoking ads that aired between 1980 and 1994 in five English-speaking countries found that 75 percent of the ads mentioned negative effects of smoking. However, the majority of these threats (90 percent) were health-related; only 10 percent of the fear threats depicted social consequences.[82]

Reebok uses the metaphor "Pretty as a picture" to promote its line of Metaphors shoes.
Reprinted by permission of Reebok International Ltd.

ads take the form of an allegory, wherein a story is told about an abstract trait or concept that has been personified as a person, animal or vegetable.

metaphor the use of an explicit comparison ("A" is "B") between a product and some other person, place or thing

A **metaphor** involves the use of an explicit comparison, such as A is B ("Air Canada is your friend in faraway places"). The device was used literally by Reebok to equate its Metaphors line of shoes with comfort, as seen in the ad shown here. Metaphors allow the marketer to activate meaningful images and apply them to everyday events. In the stock market, "white knights" battle "hostile raiders" using "poison pills," while Tony the Tiger allows us to equate cereal with strength, and the Merrill Lynch bull sends the message that the company is "a breed apart."[83]

resonance a literary device, frequently used in advertising, that employs a play on words (a double meaning) to communicate a product benefit

Resonance is another type of literary device that is frequently used in advertising. It is a form of presentation that combines a play on words with a relevant picture. Table 8–2 gives some examples of actual ads that rely on the principle of resonance. While metaphor substitutes one meaning for another by connecting two things that are in some way similar, resonance uses an element that has a double meaning, such as a pun, in which there is a similarity in the sound of a word but a difference in meaning. For example, an ad for a diet strawberry shortcake dessert might bear the copy "berried treasure" so that qualities associated with buried treasure—being rich, hidden and associated with adventurous pirates—are conveyed for the brand. Because the text departs from expectations, it creates a state of tension or uncertainty in the viewer until he or she figures out the wordplay. Once the consumer "gets it," he or she may prefer the ad over a more straightforward message.[84]

FORMS OF STORY PRESENTATION

Just as a story can be told in words or pictures, the way the audience is addressed can also make a difference. Commercials are structured like other art forms, borrowing conventions from literature and art as they communicate their messages.[85]

One important distinction is between a *drama* and a *lecture*.[86] A lecture is like a speech where the source speaks directly to the audience members in an attempt to

TABLE 8–2 Some Examples of Advertising Resonance	
PRODUCT/HEADLINE	VISUAL
Embassy Suites: "This Year, We're Unwrapping Suites by the Dozen"	Chocolate kisses with hotel names underneath each
Toyota auto parts: "Our Lifetime Guarantee May Come as a Shock"	Man holding a shock absorber
Bounce fabric softener: "Is There Something Creeping Up Behind You?"	Woman's dress bunched up on the back of her due to static
Pepsi: "This Year, Hit the Beach Topless"	Pepsi bottle cap lying on the sand
ASICS athletic shoes: "We Believe Women Should Be Running the Country"	Woman jogging in a rural setting

Source: Adapted from Edward F. McQuarrie and David Glen Mick, "On Resonance: A Critical Pluralistic Inquiry into Advertising Rhetoric," *Journal of Consumer Research* 19 (September 1992): 182, Table 1. Reprinted with permission of The University of Chicago Press.

inform them about a product or persuade them to buy it. Because a lecture clearly implies an attempt at persuasion, the audience will regard it as such. Assuming listeners are motivated to do so, the merits of the message will be weighed, along with the credibility of the source. Cognitive responses, such as counterargumentation, will occur. The appeal will be accepted to the extent that it overcomes the consumer's objections and is congruent with his or her beliefs.

In contrast, a drama is similar to a play or movie. While an argument holds the viewer at arm's length, a drama draws the viewer into the action. The characters address the audience only indirectly; they interact with each other about a product or service in an imaginary setting. Dramas attempt to be experiential—to involve the audience emotionally. In *transformational* advertising, the consumer associates the experience of product usage with some subjective sensation. Thus, ads for the Infiniti attempted to transform the "driving experience" into a mystical, spiritual event.

THE SOURCE VERSUS THE MESSAGE: SELL THE STEAK OR THE SIZZLE?

Two major components of the communications model—the source and the message—have been reviewed. Which aspect has the most impact on persuading consumers to change their attitudes? Should marketers worry more about *what* is said or *how* it's said and *who* says it?

The answer is that it depends. Variations in a consumer's level of involvement, as discussed in Chapter 4, result in the activation of very different cognitive processes when a message is received. Research indicates that this level of involvement will determine which aspects of a communication are processed. The situation appears to resemble that of a traveller who comes to a fork in the road: one or the other path is chosen, and this path has a big impact on the factors that will make a difference in persuasion attempts.

The Elaboration Likelihood Model

elaboration likelihood model (ELM) the approach that one of two routes to persuasion (central versus peripheral) will be followed, depending upon the personal relevance of a message; the route taken determines the relative importance of message contents versus other characteristics, such as source attractiveness

The **elaboration likelihood model (ELM)** assumes that, once a consumer receives a message, he or she begins to process it.[87] Depending upon the personal relevance of this information, one of two routes to persuasion will be followed. Under conditions of high involvement, the consumer takes the *central route to persuasion*. Under conditions of low involvement, a *peripheral route* is taken instead. This model is diagrammed in Figure 8–6.

THE CENTRAL ROUTE TO PERSUASION

When the consumer finds the information in a persuasive message to be relevant or somehow interesting, he or she will carefully attend to the message content. The person is likely to think actively about the arguments presented and generate *cognitive responses* to these arguments. Upon hearing a radio message warning about drinking while pregnant, an expectant mother might say to herself, "She's right. I really should stop drinking alcohol now that I'm pregnant." Or she might offer *counterarguments*, such as "That's a bunch of baloney. My mother had a cocktail every night when she was pregnant with me, and I turned out fine." If a person generates counterarguments in response to a message, it is less likely that he or she will yield to the message, while the generation of further supporting arguments increases the probability of compliance.[88]

The central route to persuasion is likely to involve the traditional hierarchy of effects, as discussed in Chapter 7. Beliefs are carefully formed and evaluated, and strong attitudes that are then formed will be likely to guide behaviour. The implication is that message factors, such as the quality of arguments presented, will be important in determining attitude change. Prior knowledge about a topic may result

FIGURE 8–6 • The Elaboration Likelihood Model of Persuasion

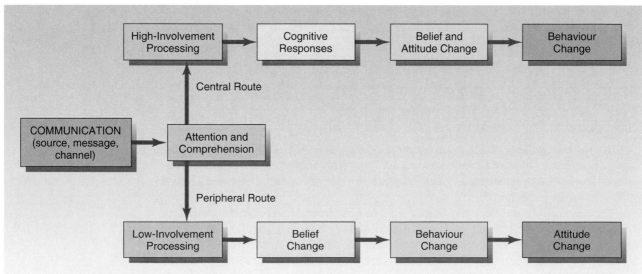

in more thoughts about the message and will also increase the number of counter arguments.[89]

THE PERIPHERAL ROUTE TO PERSUASION

In contrast, the peripheral route is taken when the person is not motivated to think about the arguments presented. Instead, the consumer is likely to use other cues in deciding on the suitability of the message. These cues might include the product's package, the attractiveness of the source or the context in which the message is presented. Sources of information extraneous to the actual message content are called *peripheral cues* because they surround the actual message.

The peripheral route to persuasion highlights the paradox of low involvement discussed in Chapter 4: when consumers do not care about a product, the stimuli associated with it *increase* in importance. The implication here is that low-involvement products may be purchased chiefly because the marketer has done a good job in designing a "sexy" package, choosing a popular spokesperson or perhaps just creating a pleasant shopping environment.

Support for the ELM Model

The ELM approach has received a lot of research support.[90] In one typical study, undergraduates were exposed to one of several mock advertisements for Break, a new brand of low-alcohol beer. Using the technique of *thought-listing* or cognitive responses, they were asked to provide their thoughts about the ads, which were later analyzed by the researchers. Two versions of the ads are shown here.[91] Three independent variables crucial to the ELM were manipulated:

1. *Message-processing involvement.* Some subjects were motivated to be highly involved with the ads. They were promised a gift of low-alcohol beer for participating in the study and were told that the brand would soon be available in

Source: J. Craig Andrews and Terence A. Shimp, "Effects of Involvement, Argument, Strength, and Source Characteristics on Central and Peripheral Processing in Advertising," Psychology & Marketing *7 (Fall 1990): 195–214.*

their area. Low-involvement subjects were not promised a gift and were told that the brand would be introduced in a distant area.

2. *Argument strength.* One version of the ad used strong, compelling arguments to drink Break ("Break contains one-half of the amount of alcohol of regular beers and, therefore, has less calories than regular beer ..."), while the other listed only weak arguments ("Break is just as good as any other regular beer").

3. *Source characteristics.* While both ads contained a photo of a couple drinking the beer, their relative social attractiveness was varied by their dress, posture and nonverbal expressions, and by the background information given about their educational achievements and occupations.

Consistent with the ELM model, high-involvement subjects had more thoughts related to the ad messages than did low-involvement subjects, who devoted more cognitive activity to the sources used in the ad. The attitudes of high-involvement subjects were more likely to be swayed by powerful arguments, while the attitudes of low-involvement subjects were more likely to be influenced by the ad version using attractive sources. The results of this study, paired with that of others, indicate that the relative effectiveness of a strong message and a favourable source depends upon consumers' level of involvement with the product being advertised.

These results underscore the basic idea that highly involved consumers look for the "steak" (strong, rational arguments), while those who are less involved are more affected by the "sizzle" (the colours and images used in packaging, or endorsements by famous people). It is important to remember, however, that the *same* communications variable can be both a central and a peripheral cue, depending upon its relation to the attitude object. The physical attractiveness of a model might serve as a peripheral cue in a car commercial, but her beauty might be a central cue for a product such as shampoo, where the product's benefits are directly tied to enhancing attractiveness.[92]

CHAPTER SUMMARY

- *Persuasion* refers to an attempt to change consumers' attitudes.
- The communications model specifies the elements needed to transmit meaning. These include a source, a message, a medium, a receiver and feedback.
- Two important characteristics that determine the effectiveness of a source are its attractiveness and credibility. While celebrities often serve this purpose, their credibility is not always as strong as marketers hope.
- Some elements of a message that help to determine its effectiveness are whether it is conveyed in words or pictures, whether an emotional or a rational appeal is employed, the frequency with which it is repeated, whether a conclusion is drawn, whether both sides of the argument are presented, and whether the message includes fear, humour or sexual references.
- Advertising messages often incorporate such elements from art or literature as drama, lecture, metaphor, allegory and resonance.
- The relative influence of the source versus the message depends upon the receiver's level of involvement with the communication. The elaboration likelihood model specifies that a less involved consumer will more likely be swayed by source effects, while a more involved consumer will more likely attend to and process components of the actual message.

KEY TERMS

CONSUMER BEHAVIOUR CHALLENGE

1. A government agency wants to encourage the use of designated drivers by people who have been drinking. What advice could you give the organization about constructing persuasive communications? Discuss some factors that might be important, including the structure of the communications, where they should appear and who should deliver them. Should fear appeals be used, and, if so, how?

2. Are infomercials ethical? Should marketers be allowed to use any format they want to present product-related information?

3. Discuss some conditions where it would be advisable to use a comparative advertising strategy.

4. Why would a marketer consider saying negative things about his or her product? When is this strategy feasible? Can you find examples of it?

5. A marketer must decide whether to incorporate rational or emotional appeals in its communications strategy. What factors would favour choosing one approach over the other?

6. Collect ads that rely on sex appeal to sell products. How often are benefits of the actual products communicated to the reader?

7. To observe the process of counterargumentation, ask a friend to talk out loud while watching a commercial. Ask him or her to respond to each point in the ad or to write down reactions to the claims made. How much scepticism regarding the claims can you detect?

8. Make a log of all the commercials shown on one network television channel over a six-hour period. Categorize each according to product category and whether they are presented as drama or argument. Describe the types of messages used (e.g., two-sided arguments) and keep track of the types of spokespeople (e.g., television actors, famous people or animated characters). What can you conclude about the dominant forms of persuasion tactics currently employed by marketers?

9. Collect examples of ads that rely on the use of metaphors or resonance. Do you feel these ads are effective? If you were working with the products, would you feel more comfortable with ads that use a more straightforward, "hard-sell" approach? Why or why not?

10. Create a list of celebrities representing cultural categories and match them with products they might promote.

CBC VIDEO VIGNETTES

Concepts at Work for 1-800-ADS

Quality Records & Special Products of Toronto is a TV mass-marketer with sales of over $25 million annually. Direct marketers pick products, make commercials and get them television air time in the United States and Canada. They specialize in "instantaneous" success in the fast-paced, tough, competitive market of novelty products with high potential for "knock-offs." For every product that is successful, another dozen are failures. There is a narrow window of opportunity for capturing the customer's perceived need of the product. Whether a product sells quickly, goes to a sudden death or is copied, Quality's interest in it is short-lived: it is usually removed between ten days and three months after initial market exposure.

Quality thought Larry Friedman had a winning product for direct selling. Larry's product, called Lassage, was a hand-held massager that cost $100 000 to develop. After receiving orders through a low-budget advertisement on a local television station, Quality took on the Lassage eagerly. In fact, they felt so certain of success that they committed to retail distribution for six weeks after the launch. As usual, a strategy built on persuasive advertisements, a focus on the unique benefits of the product and a 1-800-number for immediate order placement was used. However, after daily adjustments in the encoded advertising messages, the time slot and tie-in promotional gimmicks, Lassage's denouement in the US market was brought about. Larry was left with complete freedom to pursue other marketing approaches to convince consumers that the Lassage was a product they needed.

QUESTIONS

1. What are the mechanisms for effective advertisements in the marketplace?
2. What is Quality's formula for success?
3. Why was the Lassage unsuccessful while the Abdomenizer sold millions?
4. Can needs be created by advertisements?

Video Resource: "1-800-ADS," *Venture* #495 (July 3, 1994).

Dr. Dennis Colonello designed the Abdomenizer in 1986 while practising as a chiropractor in northern Ontario.

NOTES

1. Quoted in Cyndee Miller, "The Fur Flies as Fashion Foes Pelt It Out Over Animal Rights," *Marketing News* 2 (December 4, 1989): 2.

2. Nina Darnton, "Revolt of the Fur Bearers," *Newsweek* (January 6, 1992): 49.

3. Quoted in Miller, "The Fur Flies": 8.

4. Darnton, "Revolt of the Fur Bearers."

5. Vida Roberts, "Phony Express: Faux Fur a Reality in Fashion World," *Asbury Park Press* (September 18, 1994): D2.

6. Gert Assmus, "An Empirical Investigation into the Perception of Vehicle Source Effects," *Journal of Advertising* 7 (Winter 1978): 4–10. For a more thorough discussion of the pros and cons of different media, see Stephen Baker, *Systematic Approach to Advertising Creativity* (New York: McGraw-Hill, 1979).

7. Alladi Venkatesh, Ruby Roy Dholakia and Nikhilesh Dholakia, "New Visions of Information Technology and Postmodernism: Implications for Advertising and Marketing Communications," in *The Information Superhighway and Private Households: Case Studies of Business Impacts*, eds. Walter Brenner and Lutz Kolbe (Heidelberg: Physical-Verlag, 1966), pp. 319–37; Donna L. Hoffman and Thomas P. Novak, "Marketing in Hypermedia Computer-Mediated Environments: Conceptual Foundations," *Journal of Marketing* 60, 3 (July 1996): 50–68. For an early theoretical discussion of interactivity in communications paradigms, cf. Gratif R. Aubrey Fisher, *Perspectives on Human Communication* (New York: Macmillan, 1978).

8. First proposed by Elihu Katz, "Mass Communication Research and the Study of Popular Culture: An Editorial Note on a Possible Future for this Journal," *Studies in Public Communication* 2 (1959): 1–6. For a recent discussion on this approach, cf. Stephanie O'Donohoe, "Advertising Uses and Gratifications," *European Journal of Marketing* 28, 8/9 (1994): 52–75.

9. Quoted in O'Donohoe, "Advertising Uses and Gratifications," p. 66.

10. Alice Z. Cuneo, "With an 'i' Toward Music Lovers," *Advertising Age* (August 29, 1994): 18.

11. Michael Wilke, "A Radio Entrepreneur Reaches for the Interactive Age," *New York Times* (September 4, 1994): F7.

12. This section is adapted from a discussion in Michael R. Solomon and Elnora W. Stuart, *Marketing: Real People, Real Choices* (Upper Saddle River, NJ: Prentice Hall, 1997).

13. Carl I. Hovland and W. Weiss, "The Influence of Source Credibility on Communication Effectiveness," *Public Opinion Quarterly* 15 (1952): 635–50.

14. Herbert Kelman, "Processes of Opinion Change," *Public Opinion Quarterly* 25 (Spring 1961): 57–78;

Susan M. Petroshius and Kenneth E. Crocker, "An Empirical Analysis of Spokesperson Characteristics on Advertisement and Product Evaluations," *Journal of the Academy of Marketing Science* 17 (Summer 1989): 217–26.

15. S. Ratneshwar and Shelly Chaiken, "Comprehension's Role in Persuasion: The Case of Its Moderating Effect on the Persuasive Impact of Source Cues," *Journal of Consumer Research* 18 (June 1991): 52–62.

16. "Jim Palmer Pitches Style for Jockey," *New York Times* (August 29, 1982).

17. "Robber Makes It Biggs in Ad," *Advertising Age* (May 29, 1989): 26.

18. Alice H. Eagly, Andy Wood and Shelly Chaiken, "Causal Inferences About Communicators and Their Effect in Opinion Change," *Journal of Personality and Social Psychology* 36, 4 (1978): 424–35.

19. Judith Graham, "Sponsors Line Up for Rockin' Role," *Advertising Age* (December 11, 1989): 50.

20. Michael A. Kamins, "Celebrity and Noncelebrity Advertising in a Two-Sided Context," *Journal of Advertising Research* 29 (June/July 1989): 34; Joseph M. Kamen, A.C. Azhari and J.R. Kragh, "What a Spokesman Does for a Sponsor," *Journal of Advertising Research* 15, 2 (1975): 17–24; Lynn Langmeyer and Mary Walker, "A First Step to Identify the Meaning in Celebrity Endorsers," in *Advances in Consumer Research 18*, eds. Rebecca H. Holman and Michael R. Solomon (Provo, UT: Association for Consumer Research, 1991), pp. 364–71.

21. Jeffrey Burroughs and Richard A. Feinberg, "Using Response Latency to Assess Spokesperson Effectiveness," *Journal of Consumer Research* 14 (September 1987): 295–99.

22. Michael A. Kamins, "An Investigation into the 'Match-up' Hypothesis in Celebrity Advertising: When Beauty May be Only Skin Deep," *Journal of Advertising* 19, 1 (1990): 4–13; Lynn R. Kahle and Pamela M. Homer, "Physical Attractiveness of the Celebrity Endorser: A Social Adaptation Perspective," *Journal of Consumer Research* 11 (March 1985): 954–61.

23. Bruce Haring, "Company Totes Up Popularity Quotients," *Billboard Magazine* 101 (1989): 12.

24. Larry Armstrong, "Still Starstruck," *Business Week* (July 4, 1994): 38; Jeff Giles, "The Risks of Wishing Upon a Star," *Newsweek* (September 6, 1993): 38.

25. Grant McCracken, "Who is the Celebrity Endorser? Cultural Foundations of the Endorsement Process," *Journal of Consumer Research* 16, 3 (December 1989): 310–21.

26. Thomas R. King, "Credibility Gap: More Consumers Find Celebrity Ads Unpersuasive," *Wall Street Journal* (July 5, 1989): B5; Haring, "Company Totes Up Popularity Quotients."

27. Marie Okabe, "Fading Yen for Foreign Stars in Ads," *Singapore Straits-Times* (1986).

28. Karen K. Dion, "What is Beautiful is Good," *Journal of Personality and Social Psychology* 24 (December 1972): 285–90.

29. Michael J. Baker and Gilbert A. Churchill, Jr., "The Impact of Physically Attractive Models on Advertising Evaluations," *Journal of Marketing Research* 14 (November 1977): 538–55; Marjorie J. Caballero and William M. Pride, "Selected Effects of Salesperson Sex and Attractiveness in Direct Mail Advertisements," *Journal of Marketing* 48 (January 1984): 94–100; W. Benoy Joseph, "The Credibility of Physically Attractive Communicators: A Review," *Journal of Advertising* 11, 3 (1982): 15–24; Lynn R. Kahle and Pamela M. Homer, "Physical Attractiveness of the Celebrity Endorser: A Social Adaptation Perspective," *Journal of Consumer Research* 11, 4 (1985): 954–61; Judson Mills and Eliot Aronson, "Opinion Change as a Function of Communicator's Attractiveness and Desire to Influence," *Journal of Personality and Social Psychology* 1 (1965): 173–77.

30. Leonard N. Reid and Lawrence C. Soley, "Decorative Models and the Readership of Magazine Ads," *Journal of Advertising Research* 23, 2 (1983): 27–32.

31. Marjorie J. Caballero, James R. Lumpkin and Charles S. Madden, "Using Physical Attractiveness as an Advertising Tool: An Empirical Test of the Attraction Phenomenon," *Journal of Advertising Research* (August/September 1989): 16–22.

32. Baker and Churchill, Jr., "The Impact of Physically Attractive Models on Advertising Evaluations"; George E. Belch, Michael A. Belch and Angelina Villareal, "Effects of Advertising Communications: Review of Research," in *Research in Marketing 9* (Greenwich, CT: JAI Press, 1987), pp. 59–117; A.E. Courtney and T.W. Whipple, *Sex Stereotyping in Advertising* (Lexington, MA: Lexington Books, 1983).

33. Kahle and Homer, "Physical Attractiveness of the Celebrity Endorser."

34. Baker and Churchill, Jr., "The Impact of Physically Attractive Models on Advertising Evaluations."

35. Kenneth G. DeBono and Richard J. Harnish, "Source Expertise, Source Attractiveness, and the Processing of Persuasive Information: A Functional Approach," *Journal of Personality and Social Psychology* 55, 4 (1988): 541–46.

36. Hershey H. Friedman and Linda Friedman, "Endorser Effectiveness by Product Type," *Journal of Advertising Research* 19, 5 (1979): 63–71.

37. Anthony R. Pratkanis et al., "In Search of Reliable Persuasion Effects: III. The Sleeper Effect Is Dead, Long Live the Sleeper Effect," *Journal of Personality and Social Psychology* 54 (1988): 203–18.

38. Herbert C. Kelman and Carl I. Hovland, "Reinstatement of the Communication in Delayed Measurement of Opinion Change," *Journal of Abnormal Psychology* 4, 48 (1953): 327–35.

39. Darlene Hannah and Brian Sternthal, "Detecting and Explaining the Sleeper Effect," *Journal of Consumer Research* 11 (September 1984): 632–42.

40. David Mazursky and Yaacov Schul, "The Effects of Advertisement Encoding on the Failure to Discount Information: Implications for the Sleeper Effect," *Journal of Consumer Research* 15 (June 1988): 24–36.

41. David W. Stewart and David H. Furse, "The Effects of Television Advertising Execution on Recall, Comprehension, and Persuasion," *Psychology & Marketing* 2 (Fall 1985): 135–60.

42. R.C. Grass and W.H. Wallace, "Advertising Communication: Print vs. TV," *Journal of Advertising Research* 14 (1974): 19–23.

43. Elizabeth C. Hirschman and Michael R. Solomon, "Utilitarian, Aesthetic, and Familiarity Responses to Verbal Versus Visual Advertisements," in *Advances in Consumer Research 11*, ed. Thomas C. Kinnear (Provo, UT: Association for Consumer Research, 1984), pp. 426–31.

44. Andrew A. Mitchell and Jerry C. Olson, "Are Product Attribute Beliefs the Only Mediator of Advertising Effects on Brand Attitude?" *Journal of Marketing Research* 18, 3 (1981): 318–32.

45. Terry L. Childers and Michael J. Houston, "Conditions for a Picture-Superiority Effect on Consumer Memory," *Journal of Consumer Research* 11 (September 1984): 643–54.

46. Andrew A. Mitchell, "The Effect of Verbal and Visual Components of Advertisements on Brand Attitudes and Attitude Toward the Advertisement," *Journal of Consumer Research* 13 (June 1986): 12–24.

47. John R. Rossiter and Larry Percy, "Attitude Change Through Visual Imagery in Advertising," *Journal of Advertising Research* 9, 2 (1980): 10–16.

48. Jolita Kiselius and Brian Sternthal, "Examining the Vividness Controversy: An Availability-Valence Interpretation," *Journal of Consumer Research* 12 (March 1986): 418–31.

49. Scott B. Mackenzie, "The Role of Attention in Mediating the Effect of Advertising on Attribute Importance," *Journal of Consumer Research* 13 (September 1986): 174–95.

50. Robert B. Zajonc, "Attitudinal Effects of Mere Exposure," monograph, *Journal of Personality and Social Psychology* 8 (1968): 1–29.

51. Giles D'Souza and Ram C. Rao, "Can Repeating an Advertisement More Frequently than the Competition Affect Brand Preference in a Mature Market?" *Journal of Marketing* 59 (April 1995): 32–42.

52. George E. Belch, "The Effects of Television Commercial Repetition on Cognitive Response and Message Acceptance," *Journal of Consumer Research* 9 (June 1982): 56–65; Marian Burke and Julie Edell, "Ad Reactions Over Time: Capturing Changes in the Real World," *Journal of Consumer Research* 13 (June 1986): 114–18; Herbert Krugman, "Why Three Exposures May Be Enough," *Journal of Advertising Research* 12 (December 1972): 11–14.

53. Robert F. Bornstein, "Exposure and Affect: Overview and Meta-Analysis of Research, 1968–1987," *Psychological Bulletin* 106, 2 (1989): 265–89; Arno Rethans, John Swasy and Lawrence Marks, "Effects of Television Commercial Repetition, Receiver Knowledge, and Commercial Length: A Test of the Two-Factor Model," *Journal of Marketing Research* 23 (February 1986): 50–61.

54. Curtis P. Haugtvedt et al., "Advertising Repetition and Variation Strategies: Implications for Understanding Attitude Strength," *Journal of Consumer Research* 21 (June 1994): 176–89.

55. Linda L. Golden and Mark I. Alpert, "Comparative Analysis of the Relative Effectiveness of One- and Two-Sided Communication for Contrasting Products," *Journal of Advertising* 16 (1987); Kamins, "Celebrity and Noncelebrity Advertising in a Two-Sided Context"; Robert B. Settle and Linda L. Golden, "Attribution Theory and Advertiser Credibility," *Journal of Marketing Research* 11 (May 1974): 181–85.

56. See Alan G. Sawyer, "The Effects of Repetition of Refutational and Supportive Advertising Appeals," *Journal of Marketing Research* 10 (February 1973): 23–33; George J. Szybillo and Richard Heslin, "Resistance to Persuasion: Inoculation Theory in a Marketing Context," *Journal of Marketing Research* 10 (November 1973): 396–403; Ayn E. Crowley and Wayne D. Hoyer, "An Integrative Framework for Understanding Two-Sided Persuasion," *Journal of Consumer Research* 20, 4 (March 1994): 561–74; Cornelia Pechmann, "Predicting When Two-Sided Ads Will be More Effective Than One-Sided Ads: The Role of Correlational and Correspondent Inferences," *Journal of Marketing Research* 29 (November 1992): 441–53.

57. Lawrence M. Fisher, "Winery's Answer to Critics: Print Good and Bad Reviews," *New York Times* (January 9, 1991): D5.

58. Golden and Alpert, "Comparative Analysis of the Relative Effectiveness of One- and Two-Sided Communication for Contrasting Products."

59. G. Belch, M. Belch and Villareal, "Effects of Advertising Communications."

60. Frank R. Kardes, "Spontaneous Inference Processes in Advertising: The Effects of Conclusion Omission and Involvement on Persuasion," *Journal of Consumer Research* 15 (September 1988): 225–33.

61. Cornelia Dröge and Rene Y. Darmon, "Associative Positioning Strategies Through Comparative Advertising: Attribute vs. Overall Similarity Approaches," *Journal of Marketing Research* 24 (1987): 377–89; D. Muehling and N. Kangun, "The Multidimensionality of Comparative Advertising: Implications for the FTC," *Journal of Public Policy and Marketing* (1985): 112–28; Beth A. Walker and Helen H. Anderson, "Reconceptualizing Comparative Advertising: A Framework and Theory of Effects," in *Advances in Consumer Research 18*, eds. Rebecca H. Holman and

Michael R. Solomon (Provo, UT: Association for Consumer Research, 1991), pp. 342–47; William L. Wilkie and Paul W. Farris, "Comparison Advertising: Problems and Potential," *Journal of Marketing* 39 (October 1975): 7–15; R.G. Wyckham, "Implied Superiority Claims," *Journal of Advertising Research* (February/March 1987): 54–63.

62. Stephen A. Goodwin and Michael Etgar, "An Experimental Investigation of Comparative Advertising: Impact of Message Appeal, Information Load, and Utility of Product Class," *Journal of Marketing Research* 17 (May 1980): 187–202; Gerald J. Gorn and Charles B. Weinberg, "The Impact of Comparative Advertising on Perception and Attitude: Some Positive Findings," *Journal of Consumer Research* 11 (September 1984): 719–27; Terence A. Shimp and David C. Dyer, "The Effects of Comparative Advertising Mediated by Market Position of Sponsoring Brand," *Journal of Advertising* 3 (Summer 1978): 13–19; R. Dale Wilson, "An Empirical Evaluation of Comparative Advertising Messages: Subjects, Responses to Perceptual Dimensions," in *Advances in Consumer Research 3*, ed. B.B. Anderson (Ann Arbor, MI: Association for Consumer Research, 1976), pp. 53–57; Randall L. Rose et al., "When Persuasion Goes Undetected: The Case of Comparative Advertising," *Journal of Marketing Research* 30 (August 1993): 315–30.

63. Dröge and Darmon, "Associative Positioning Strategies Through Comparative Advertising."

64. Dottie Enrico, "Guaranteed! Greatest Advertising Story Ever Told!" *Newsday* (October 16, 1991): 43; Bruce Buchanan and Doron Goldman, "Us vs. Them: The Minefield of Comparative Ads," *Harvard Business Review* 38, 7 (May/June 1989): 50.

65. Michael Lev, "For Car Buyers, Technology or Zen," *New York Times* (May 22, 1989): D1.

66. "Connecting Consumer and Product," *New York Times* (January 18, 1990): D19.

67. Edward F. Cone, "Image and Reality," *Forbes* (December 14, 1987): 226.

68. H. Zielske, "Does Day-After Recall Penalize Feeling Ads?" *Journal of Advertising Research* 22 (1982): 19–22.

69. Cone, "Image and Reality."

70. Roger Thurow, "As In-Your-Face Ads Backfire, Nike Finds a New Global Tack," *The WSJ Interactive Edition* (May 5, 1997).

71. G. Belch, M. Belch and Villareal, "Effects of Advertising Communications"; Courtney and Whipple, *Sex Stereotyping in Advertising;* Michael S. LaTour, "Female Nudity in Print Advertising: An Analysis of Gender Differences in Arousal and Ad Response," *Psychology & Marketing* 7, 1 (1990): 65–81; B.G. Yovovich, "Sex in Advertising—The Power and the Perils," *Advertising Age* (May 2, 1983): M4–M5.

72. Marc G. Weinberger and Harlan E. Spotts, "Humor in U.S. Versus U.K. TV Commercials: A Comparison," *Journal of Advertising* 18, 2 (1989): 39–44.

73. Thomas J. Madden, "Humor in Advertising: An Experimental Analysis" (working paper no. 8327, University of Massachusetts, 1984); Thomas J. Madden and Marc G. Weinberger, "The Effects of Humor on Attention in Magazine Advertising," *Journal of Advertising* 11, 3 (1982): 8–14; Weinberger and Spotts, "Humor in U.S. Versus U.K. TV Commercials."

74. David Gardner, "The Distraction Hypothesis in Marketing," *Journal of Advertising Research* 10 (1970): 25–30.

75. "Funny Ads Provide Welcome Relief During These Gloom and Doom Days," *Marketing News* (April 17, 1981): 3.

76. Kevin Goldman, "Everybody's Afraid of the Big Bad Boss," *New York Times* (January 12, 1994): B1 (2 pp.).

77. Michael L. Ray and William L. Wilkie, "Fear: The Potential of an Appeal Neglected by Marketing," *Journal of Marketing* 34, 1 (1970): 54–62; Tony L. Henthorne, Michael S. LaTour and Rajan Nataraajan, "Fear Appeals in Print Advertising: An Analysis of Arousal and Ad Response," *Journal of Advertising* 22, 2 (June 1993): 59–70; Thomas Giese, Dana-Nicoleta Lascu and Terry M. Weisenberger, "Intended and Unintended Consequences of the Use of Fear and Guilt Appeals in Marketing Communications," *Proceedings of the Southern Marketing Association* (1993): 12.

78. Judith Waldrop, "They're Coming to Take You Away (Fear as a Form of Persuasion)," *American Demographics* (June 15, 1988): 2; John F. Tanner, Jr., James B. Hunt and David R. Eppright, "The Protection Motivation Model: A Normative Model of Fear Appeals," *Journal of Marketing* 55 (July 1991): 36–45.

79. Brian Sternthal and C. Samuel Craig, "Fear Appeals: Revisited and Revised," *Journal of Consumer Research* 1 (December 1974): 22–34.

80. Ronald Paul Hill, "An Exploration of the Relationship Between AIDS-Related Anxiety and the Evaluation of Condom Advertisements," *Journal of Advertising* 17, 4 (1988): 35–42.

81. Randall Rothenberg, "Talking Too Tough on Life's Risks?" *New York Times* (February 16, 1990): D1.

82. Anne M. Lavack, "Fear Appeals in Anti-Smoking TV Commercials 1980–1994" (paper presented at the 1994 Administrative Sciences Association of Canada [ASAC] Conference, Halifax, June 25–28, 1994).

83. Barbara B. Stern, "Medieval Allegory: Roots of Advertising Strategy for the Mass Market," *Journal of Marketing* 52 (July 1988): 84–94.

84. Edward F. McQuarrie and David Glen Mick, "On Resonance: A Critical Pluralistic Inquiry into Advertising Rhetoric," *Journal of Consumer Research* 19 (September 1992): 180–97.

85. See Linda M. Scott, "The Troupe: Celebrities as Dramatis Personae in Advertisements," in *Advances in Consumer Research 18*, eds. Rebecca H. Holman and Michael R. Solomon (Provo, UT: Association for Consumer Research, 1991), pp. 355–63; Barbara Stern, "Literary Criticism and Consumer Research: Overview and Illustrative Analysis," *Journal of Consumer Research* 16 (1989): 322–34; Judith Williamson, *Decoding Advertisements* (Boston: Marion Boyars, 1978).

86. John Deighton, Daniel Romer and Josh McQueen, "Using Drama to Persuade," *Journal of Consumer Research* 16 (December 1989): 335–43.

87. Richard E. Petty, John T. Cacioppo and David Schumann, "Central and Peripheral Routes to Advertising Effectiveness: The Moderating Role of Involvement," *Journal of Consumer Research* 10, 2 (1983): 135–46.

88. Jerry C. Olson, Daniel R. Toy and Philip A. Dover, "Do Cognitive Responses Mediate the Effects of Advertising Content on Cognitive Structure?" *Journal of Consumer Research* 9, 3 (1982): 245–62.

89. Julie A. Edell and Andrew A. Mitchell, "An Information Processing Approach to Cognitive Responses," in *Research Frontiers in Marketing: Dialogues and Directions,* ed. S.C. Jain (Chicago: American Marketing Association, 1978).

90. See Mary Jo Bitner and Carl Obermiller, "The Elaboration Likelihood Model: Limitations and Extensions in Marketing," in *Advances in Consumer Research 12*, eds. Elizabeth C. Hirschman and Morris B. Holbrook (Provo, UT: Association for Consumer Research, 1985), pp. 420–25; Meryl P. Gardner, "Does Attitude Toward the Ad Affect Brand Attitude Under a Brand Evaluation Set?" *Journal of Marketing Research* 22 (1985): 192–98; C.W. Park and S.M. Young, "Consumer Response to Television Commercials: The Impact of Involvement and Background Music on Brand Attitude Formation," *Journal of Marketing Research* 23 (1986): 11–24; Petty, Cacioppo and Schumann, "Central and Peripheral Routes to Advertising Effectiveness." For a discussion of how different kinds of involvement interact with the ELM, see Robin A. Higie, Lawrence F. Feick and Linda L. Price, "The Importance of Peripheral Cues in Attitude Formation for Enduring and Task-Involved Individuals," in *Advances in Consumer Research 18*, eds. Rebecca H. Holman and Michael R. Solomon (Provo, UT: Association for Consumer Research, 1991), pp. 187–93.

91. J. Craig Andrews and Terence A. Shimp, "Effects of Involvement, Argument Strength, and Source Characteristics on Central and Peripheral Processing in Advertising," *Psychology & Marketing* 7 (Fall 1990): 195–214.

92. Richard E. Petty et al., "Affect and Persuasion: A Contemporary Perspective," *American Behavioral Scientist* 31, 3 (1988): 355–71.

Consumers as Decision Makers

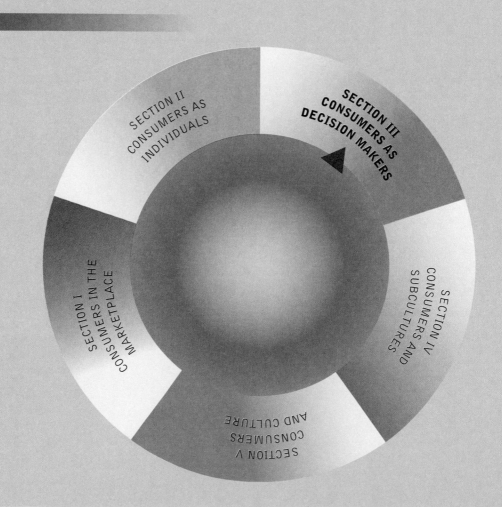

SECTION II
CONSUMERS AS
INDIVIDUALS

SECTION III
CONSUMERS AS
DECISION MAKERS

SECTION I
CONSUMERS IN THE
MARKETPLACE

SECTION IV
CONSUMERS AND
SUBCULTURES

SECTION V
CONSUMERS
AND CULTURE

This section explores how we make consumption decisions and discusses the many influences exerted by others in this process. Chapter 9 focuses on the basic sequence of steps we undergo when making a decision. Chapter 10 considers how the particular situation we find ourselves in affects these decisions, and how we go about evaluating what we've bought afterwards. Chapter 11 provides an overview of group processes and discusses the reasons we are motivated to conform to the expectations of our fellow group members. It also considers how some individuals in particular (called "opinion leaders") are likely to influence the consumption behaviour of others in a group. Chapter 12 goes on to discuss the many instances in which our purchase decisions are made in conjunction with family members.

Bill has had it. He can't go on watching his tiny, antiquated black-and-white TV set. It was bad enough listening to scratchy videos on MuchMusic and squinting at "The Simpsons" and "Beavis & Butthead," but when he couldn't tell the Canucks from the Leafs during an NHL game he went next door to watch the second period on Mark's big set and realized what he'd been missing. Budget or not, it was time to act.

Bill figures he'll get a decent selection and price at one of those new warehouse stores. At Zany Zach's Appliance Emporium he heads straight for the Video Zone, barely noticing the rows of toasters, microwave ovens and stereos on his way. In minutes he's accosted by a smiling sales-man in a cheap suit. Even though he could use some help, Bill says he's just browsing. He figures these guys don't know what they're talking about and are just out to make a sale.

Bill examines the features on the 27-inch colour sets. His friend Carol really liked her Prime Wave, and his sister Diane warned him to avoid the Kamashita. He finds a Prime Wave model with a sleep timer, on-screen programming menu, cable-compatible tuner, and remote control but chooses the less expensive Precision 2000X, with one feature that really catches his fancy: stereo broadcast reception.

Later that day, Bill is happy as he sits in his easy chair, watching the Spin Doctors on MuchMusic. If he's going to be a couch potato, he's going to be one in style ...

9

Individual Decision Making

CONSUMERS AS PROBLEM SOLVERS

A consumer purchase is a response to a problem, which in Bill's case is the perceived need for a new TV. His situation is similar to that encountered by consumers virtually every day of their lives; he realizes that he wants to make a purchase, and he goes through a series of steps in order to make it. These steps can be described as 1) problem recognition, 2) information search, 3) evaluation of alternatives, and 4) product choice. Of course, after the decision is made, the quality of that decision affects the final step in the process, when learning occurs based on how well the choice worked out. This learning process in turn influences the likelihood that the same choice will be made the next time the need for a similar decision occurs. An overview of this decision-making process appears in Figure 9–1.

This chapter begins by considering various approaches consumers use when faced with a purchase decision. It then focuses on three of the steps in the decision process: how consumers recognize the problem or need for a product; their search for information about product choices; and the ways in which they evaluate alternatives to arrive at a decision. Chapter 10 considers the actual purchase situation, as well as the person's satisfaction with the decision.

Since some purchase decisions are more important than others, the amount of effort we put into each differs. Sometimes the decision-making process is done almost automatically; we seem to make snap judgments based on very little information. At other times, coming to a purchase decision begins to resemble a full-time

FIGURE 9–1 • Stages in Consumer Decision Making

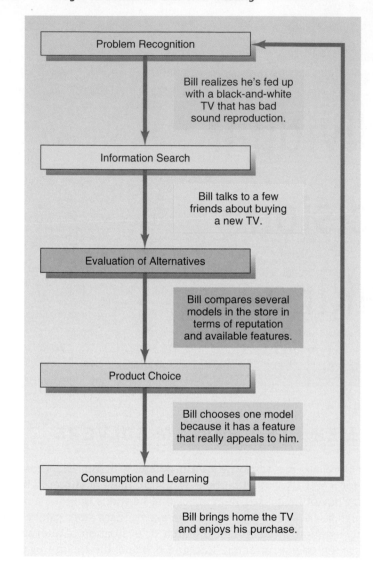

job. A person may literally spend days or weeks thinking about an important purchase such as a new home, even to the point of obsession.

Perspectives on Decision Making

rational perspective a view of the consumer as a careful, analytical decision maker who tries to maximize utility in purchase decisions

Traditionally, consumer researchers have approached decision makers from a **rational perspective.** In this view, people calmly and carefully integrate as much information as possible with what they already know about a product, painstakingly weigh the pluses and minuses of each alternative, and arrive at a satisfactory decision. This process implies that steps in decision making should be carefully studied by marketing managers to understand how information is obtained, how beliefs are formed and what product-choice criteria are specified by consumers. Products can then be developed that emphasize appropriate attributes, and promotional strategies can be tailored to deliver the types of information most likely to be desired in the most effective formats.[1]

While the steps in decision making are followed by consumers for some purchases, such a process is not an accurate portrayal of many purchase decisions.[2] Consumers simply do not go through this elaborate sequence for every decision. If they did, their entire lives would be spent making such decisions, leaving them very little time to enjoy the things they eventually decide to buy.

Researchers are now beginning to realize that decision makers actually possess a repertoire of strategies. A consumer evaluates the effort required to make a particular choice, and then he or she chooses a strategy best suited to the level of effort required. This sequence of events is known as *constructive processing*. Rather than using a big club to kill an ant, consumers tailor their degree of cognitive "effort" to the task at hand.[3]

Some decisions are made under conditions of low involvement, as discussed in Chapter 4. In many of these situations, the consumer's decision is a learned response to environmental cues (see Chapter 3), as when a person decides to buy on impulse something that is promoted as a "surprise special" in a store. A concentration on these types of decisions can be described as the **behavioural influence perspective.** Under these circumstances managers must concentrate on assessing the characteristics of the environment, such as physical surroundings and product placement, that influence members of a target market.[4]

In other cases consumers are highly involved in a decision, but it may not lend itself to the rational approach. For example, the traditional approach is hard-pressed to explain a person's choice of art, music or even a spouse. In these cases no single quality may be the determining factor. Instead, the **experiential perspective** stresses the *gestalt*, or totality, of the product or service. Marketers focus on measuring consumers' affective responses to products or services and develop offerings that elicit appropriate subjective reactions.

Types of Consumer Decisions

One helpful way to characterize the decision making process is to consider the amount of effort that goes into the decision each time it must be made. Consumer researchers have found it convenient to think in terms of a continuum, which is anchored on one end by **habitual decision making** and at the other extreme by **extended problem solving.** Many decisions fall somewhere in the middle and are characterized by **limited problem solving.** This continuum is presented in Figure 9–2.

EXTENDED PROBLEM SOLVING

Decisions involving extended problem solving correspond most closely to the traditional decision-making perspective. As indicated in Table 9–1, the extended problem-solving process is usually initiated by a motive that is fairly central to the self-concept (see Chapter 5), and the eventual decision is perceived to carry a fair degree of risk. The consumer tries to collect as much information as possible, both from memory (internal search) and from outside sources (external search). Based on the importance of the decision, each product alternative is carefully evaluated. The evaluation is often done by considering the attributes of one brand at a time and seeing how each brand's attributes shape up to some set of desired characteristics.

behavioural influence perspective the view that consumer decisions are learned responses to environmental cues

experiential perspective an approach stressing the gestalt, or totality, of the product or service experience, focusing on consumers' affective responses in the marketplace

habitual decision making the consumption choices that are made out of habit, without additional information search or deliberation among products

extended problem solving an elaborate decision-making process, often initiated by a motive that is fairly central to the self-concept and accompanied by perceived risk; the consumer tries to collect as much information as possible, and carefully weighs product alternatives

limited problem solving a problem-solving process in which consumers are not motivated to search for information or to evaluate each alternative rigorously; they instead use simple decision rules to arrive at a purchase decision

FIGURE 9–2 • A Continuum of Buying Decision Behaviour

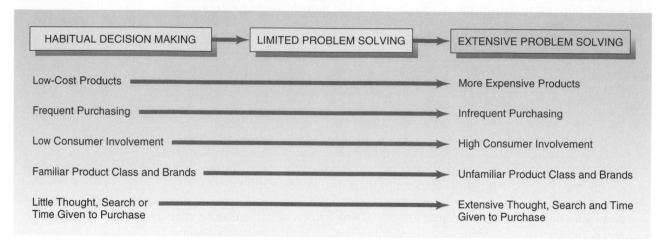

LIMITED PROBLEM SOLVING

Limited problem solving is usually more straightforward and simple. Buyers are not as motivated to search for information or to rigorously evaluate each alternative. People instead use simple *decision rules* to choose among alternatives. These cognitive shortcuts enable them to fall back on general guidelines instead of having to start from scratch every time a decision is to be made.

TABLE 9–1   Characteristics of Limited versus Extended Problem Solving

	LIMITED PROBLEM SOLVING	EXTENDED PROBLEM SOLVING
Motivation	Low risk and involvement	High risk and involvement
Information Search	Little search	Extensive search
	Information processed passively	Information processed actively
	In-store decision likely	Multiple sources consulted prior to store visits
Alternative Evaluation	Weakly held beliefs	Strongly held beliefs
	Only most prominent criteria used	Many criteria used
	Alternatives perceived as basically similar	Significant differences perceived among alternatives
	Noncompensatory strategy used	Compensatory strategy used
Purchase	Limited shopping time; may prefer self-service	Many outlets shopped if needed
	Choice often influenced by store displays	Communication with store personnel often desirable

HABITUAL DECISION MAKING

Both extended and limited problem-solving modes involve some degree of information search and deliberation, varying in the degree to which these activities are undertaken. At the other end of the choice continuum, however, are decisions that are made with little or no conscious effort. Many purchase decisions are so routinized that we may not realize we've made them until we look in our shopping carts. Choices characterized by *automaticity* are performed with minimal effort and without conscious control.[5] While this kind of thoughtless activity may seem dangerous or, at best, stupid, it is actually an efficient way to operate. The development of habitual, repetitive behaviour allows consumers to minimize the time and energy spent on mundane purchase decisions.

PROBLEM RECOGNITION

Problem recognition occurs whenever the consumer sees a significant difference between his or her current state of affairs and some desired or ideal state. The consumer perceives there is a problem to be solved, which may be small or large, simple or complex. A person who unexpectedly runs out of gas on the highway has a problem, as does the person who becomes dissatisfied with the image of his or her car, even though there is nothing mechanically wrong with it. For example, although the quality of Bill's TV had not changed, his standard of comparison had altered, and he was confronted with a need he did not have prior to watching his friend's TV.

problem recognition the process that occurs whenever the consumer sees a significant difference between his or her current state of affairs and some desired or ideal state; this recognition initiates the decision-making process

Figure 9–3 shows that a problem can arise in one of two ways. As in the case of the person running out of gas, the quality of the consumer's actual state can move downward (*need recognition*). On the other hand, as in the case of the person who craves a newer, flashier car, the consumer's ideal state can move upward (*opportunity recognition*). Either way, a gulf occurs between the actual state and the ideal state.[6] In Bill's case, a problem was perceived as a result of opportunity recognition; his ideal state in terms of television reception was altered.

Need recognition can occur in several ways. The quality of the person's actual state can be diminished by simply running out of a product, by buying a product that turns out not to satisfy needs adequately, or by creating new needs (e.g., deciding to buy a house). Opportunity recognition often occurs when a consumer is exposed to different or better-quality products. This shift often occurs because the person's circumstances have somehow changed, as when an individual goes to college or gets a new job. As the person's frame of reference shifts, a variety of purchases are made to adapt to the new environment.

Marketers' Role in Problem Creation

While problem recognition can and does occur naturally, this process is often spurred by marketing efforts. In some cases marketers attempt to create *primary demand,* wherein consumers are encouraged to use a product or service regardless of the brand they choose. Such needs are often encouraged in the early stages of a product's life cycle, as, for example, when microwave ovens were first introduced. *Secondary demand,* in which consumers are prompted to prefer a specific brand over others, can occur only if primary demand already exists. At this point marketers must

FIGURE 9–3 • Problem Recognition: Shifts in Actual or Ideal States

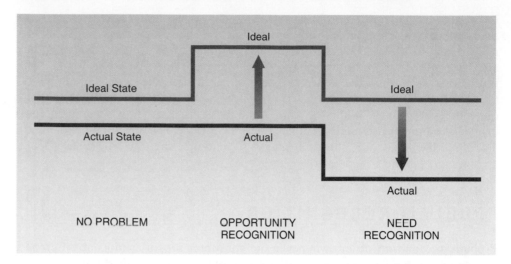

convince consumers that a problem can best be solved by choosing their brand over others in a category. For example, as the ad shown here demonstrates, Arm & Hammer has been particularly successful in identifying a succession of new problems that its product can solve. Many marketing communications are designed to make consumers aware that they have a problem and then (conveniently) provide a solution.

INFORMATION SEARCH

information search the process whereby a consumer searches for appropriate information to make a reasonable decision

Once a problem has been recognized, consumers need adequate information to resolve it. **Information search** is the process in which the consumer surveys his or her environment for appropriate data to make a reasonable decision. This section will review some of the factors involved in this search.

This ad for Arm & Hammer demonstrates the strategy of identifying new problems that an existing product can solve.
By permission of Church & Dwight Co., Inc.

MARKETING PITFALL

A common structure for advertisements has been to present a person who has a physical or social problem and then show how the product will "miraculously" resolve it. Some marketers have gone so far as to *invent* a problem and then offer a remedy for it. In the 1940s, for example, the Talon zipper was touted as a cure for "gaposis"—the horrifying condition that develops when puckers appear around the buttons on a woman's skirt. Listerine, which was originally sold to fight dandruff, carried warnings about "bottle bacillus," which caused "infectious dandruff." Geritol gave us a remedy for "tired blood" and Wisk detergent drew our attention to the shame of "ring around the collar."[7]

Even when real problems are depicted in ads, the offered solutions are sometimes overly simplistic, implying that the problem will disappear if the product is used. One analysis of over 1000 television ads found that about eight in ten suggest that the problem will be resolved within seconds or minutes after using the product. In addition, 75 percent of the ads make definite claims that the product will solve the problem, and over 75 percent imply that this solution is a one-step process—that is, all the consumer needs to do is buy the product and the problem will go away.[8] Consumers, however, are becoming more cynical and less susceptible to such claims. As many marketers are discovering, consumers of the 1990s are more receptive to realistic ads that provide solid information about the product. In addition, both the government and consumer groups are now taking a more active interest in product claims, and marketers are being more cautious about the content of their ads.

Types of Search

A consumer may explicitly search the marketplace for specific information after a need has been recognized (a process called *prepurchase search*). On the other hand, many consumers, especially veteran shoppers, enjoy hunting for information and keeping track of developments just for the fun of it (i.e., *browsing*) or because they like to maintain current information for future use. They engage in *ongoing search*.[9] Some differences between these two search modes are described in Table 9–2.

INTERNAL VERSUS EXTERNAL SEARCH

Information sources can be roughly broken down into two kinds: internal and external. As a result of prior experience and simply living in a consumer culture, each of us already has in memory some degree of knowledge about many products. When confronted with a purchase decision, we may engage in *internal search* by scanning our own memory banks to assemble information about different product alternatives (see Chapter 3). Usually, though, even the most market savvy of us need to supplement this knowledge with *external search,* where information is obtained from advertisements, friends or people watching.

TABLE 9–2 A Framework for Consumer Information Search

PREPURCHASE SEARCH	ONGOING SEARCH
Determinants	
Involvement in the purchase	Involvement with the product
Market environment	Market environment
Situational factors	Situational factors
Motives	
Making of better purchase decisions	Building of a bank of information for future use
	Experiencing of fun and pleasure
Outcome	
Increased product and market knowledge	Increased product and market knowledge leading to
Better purchase decisions	• future buying efficiencies
Increased satisfaction with the purchase outcome	• personal influence
	Increased impulse buying
	Increased satisfaction from search and other outcomes

Source: Peter H. Bloch, Daniel L. Sherrell, and Nancy M. Ridgway, "Consumer Search: An Extended Framework," *Journal of Consumer Research* 13 (June 1986): 120. Reprinted with permission by The University of Chicago Press.

This ad for The Yellow Pages highlights the use of its product by consumers during the information-search stage of making a purchase decision.
Courtesy of Yellow Pages Publishers Association.

DELIBERATE VERSUS "ACCIDENTAL" SEARCH

Our existing knowledge of a product may be the result of *directed learning,* wherein on a previous occasion we had already searched for relevant information or experienced some of the alternatives. A parent who bought a birthday cake for one child last month, for example, probably has a good idea of the best kind to buy for another child this month.

Alternatively, we may have acquired information in a more passive manner. Even though a product may not be of interest, exposure to advertising, packaging and sales promotion activities may result in *incidental learning.* Mere exposure over time to conditioned stimuli and observations of others results in the learning of much material that may not be needed for some time after the fact, if ever. For marketers, this result is a benefit of steady, "low-dose" advertising, since product associations are established and maintained until the time they are needed.[10]

In some cases we may be so expert about a product category (or at least believe we are) that no additional search is undertaken. Frequently, however, our own existing state of knowledge is not satisfactory to make an adequate decision, and we must go outside ourselves for more information. The sources we consult for advice vary. They may be impersonal and marketer-dominated sources, such as retailers and catalogues; they may be friends and family members; or they may be unbiased third parties, such as *Consumer Reports.*[11] Ironically, the problem for many is too much information rather than too little. The World Wide Web is a victim of its own success: the volume of available information is staggering, and noise and congestion makes it hard to attract visitors and keep them coming back.

Now, the ability to narrowcast is promising to turn the Web into a personalized broadcast system, where the user can obtain only the information he or she requests and not have to sift through all the rest. Programs called "tuners" organize information into "channels," and "push delivery" gets it out to "viewers" who have filled out a profile specifying what they want. Providers are gambling that viewers will be willing to pay for this customized service. Retailers like Lands' End already are experimenting with direct marketing on the Web, notifying subscribers of promotions and sending them order forms (see ***www.landsend.com***). By the year 2000 Webcasting is projected to generate a third of the $14 billion in net advertising, subscriptions and retail revenues. Major players developing push technology include America Online, Marimba (which can send programs and applets along with content), Microsoft, Netscape Constellation and Pointcast.[12]

The Adfinity software package illustrates one way push technology can simplify decision making. When a surfer first visits a Web site, he or she is asked for some basic facts in exchange for access to the site's content. Adfinity will connect with files on that user from participating company databases and send ads fine-tuned to his or her interests. For example, someone who has purchased golf vacation packages in the past might be offered a discount at a golf course as an incentive to fly a participating airline. Of course, a strategy that requires several corporations to pool their knowledge about customers can backfire, if consumers get scared away by the spectre of Big Brother, and if issues of privacy are not respected.[13] Push technology can be a two-edged sword that can cut the wrong way if it falls into the wrong hands.

The Economics of Information

The traditional decision-making perspective brings the *economics-of-information approach* to the search process; the perspective assumes that consumers will gather as much data as is needed to make an informed decision. Consumers form expectations of the value of additional information and continue to search to the extent that the rewards of doing so (the *utility*) exceed the costs. This utilitarian assumption also implies that the most valuable units of information will be collected first; additional pieces will be absorbed only to the extent that they are seen as adding to what is already known.[14] In other words, people will put themselves out to collect as much information as possible as long as the process of gathering it is not too onerous or time-consuming.[15]

DO CONSUMERS ALWAYS SEARCH RATIONALLY?

The assumption of rational search is not always supported. The amount of external search undertaken for most products is surprisingly small, even when additional information would most likely benefit the consumer. For example, lower-income shoppers, who have more to lose by making a bad purchase, actually search less prior to buying than do more affluent people.[16] Like our friend Bill, some consumers typically visit only one or two stores and rarely seek out unbiased information sources prior to making a purchase decision, especially when little time is available to do so.[17] This pattern is especially prevalent for decisions regarding durables, even when these products represent significant investments. One study of Australian car buyers found that more than a third had made only two or fewer trips to inspect cars prior to buying one.[18]

This tendency to avoid external search is less prevalent when consumers consider the purchase of symbolic items, such as clothing. In those cases, not surprisingly, people tend to do a fair amount of external search, although most of it involves seeking the opinions of peers.[19] While the stakes may be lower financially, these self-expressive decisions may be seen as having dire social consequences if the wrong choice is made. The level of perceived risk, a concept to be discussed shortly, is high.

In addition, consumers are often observed to engage in *brand switching*, even if their current brands satisfy their needs. For example, researchers who were studying the beer market for British brewer Bass Export discovered a consumer trend towards having a repertoire of two to six favourite brands rather than sticking to only one. This preference for brand switching led them to decide to begin exporting their Tennent's 1885 lager to the United States, positioning the brew as an alternative to young drinkers' usual favourite brands.[20] Sometimes it seems that people just like to try new things—that is, they are interested in *variety seeking*. The tendency of consumers to shift brand choices over time means that marketers can never rest assured that, once they have won a customer, he or she is necessarily theirs forever.[21]

BIASES IN THE DECISION-MAKING PROCESS

Consider the following scenario: You've been given a free ticket to an exciting hockey game. At the last minute a sudden snowstorm makes getting to the arena somewhat dangerous. Would you go?

Now, assume the same game and snowstorm, except this time you paid handsomely for the ticket. Would you go?

Analysis of people's responses to this situation and to others illustrates principles of mental accounting, where decisions are influenced by the way a problem is posed (called *framing*), and by whether it is put in terms of gains or losses.[22] For example, people are more likely to risk their personal safety in the storm if they paid for the hockey ticket. Only the most diehard fan would fail to recognize that this is an irrational choice, since the risk to the person is the same regardless of whether he or she got a great deal on the ticket. This decision-making bias is called the *sunk-cost fallacy*—having paid for something makes us reluctant to waste it.

Another bias is known as *loss aversion*. People place much more emphasis on loss than they do on gain. For example, for most people losing money is more unpleasant than gaining money is pleasant. Prospect theory, a descriptive model of choice, finds that utility is a function of gains and losses, and risk differs when the consumer faces options involving gains versus those involving losses.[23]

To illustrate this bias, consider the following choices. For each, would you take the safe bet or choose to gamble?

- Option #1: You're given $30 and then offered a chance to flip a coin: heads you win $9, tails you lose $9.

- Option #2: You're given a choice of getting $30 outright or accepting a coin flip that will win you either $39 or $21.

In one study 70 percent of those given option #1 chose to gamble, compared to just 43 percent of those offered option #2. Yet the odds are the same for both options! The difference is that people prefer "playing with the house money"; they are more willing to take risks when they perceive they're using someone else's resources. So, contrary to a rational decision-making perspective, we value money differently depending on where it comes from. This explains, for example, why someone might choose to blow a big bonus on some frivolous purchase, while they would never consider taking that same amount out of their savings account for this purpose.

Finally, research in mental accounting demonstrates that extraneous characteristics of the choice situation can influence our selections, even though they shouldn't if we were totally rational decision makers. As one example, participants in a survey were provided with one of two versions of this scenario:

"You are lying on the beach on a hot day. All you have to drink is ice water. For the last hour you have been thinking about how much you would enjoy a nice cold bottle of your favourite brand of beer. A companion gets up to go and make a phone call, and he offers to bring back a beer from the only nearby place where beer is sold [either a fancy resort hotel or a small, run-down grocery store, depending on the version you're given]. He says that the beer might be expensive and so asks how much you are willing to pay for it … What price do you tell him?"

In this survey the median price given by participants who were in the fancy-resort version was $5.00, while those given the grocery-store version were only willing to pay $2.25! In both versions the consumption act is the same, the beer is the same, and no "atmosphere" is consumed since the beer is being brought back to the beach.[24] So much for rational decision making!

How Much Search Occurs?

As a general rule, search activity is greater when the purchase is important, when there is a need to learn more about the purchase, and when the relevant information is easily obtained and utilized.[25] Consumers differ in the amount of search they tend to undertake, regardless of the product category in question. All things being equal, younger, better-educated people who enjoy the shopping/fact-finding process tend to conduct more information search. Women are more inclined to search than men, as are those who place greater value on style and the image they present.[26]

AMOUNT OF INFORMATION AVAILABLE

Contrary to expected behaviour, more information is not always better for the consumer. We know that consumers have limited capacity in their short-term memory and adjust to their environment by making it more manageable. Therefore, when in choice environments with more information than we can easily process, we truncate the environment to deal efficiently with a subset of it. For example, when shopping for wine or beer, one does not consider all information available, such as bottler, ingredients, price, brand, image or reputation. Shoppers only consider partial information because there are just too many combinations of all the attributes to take into short-term memory and process effectively for a decision.

THE CONSUMER'S PRIOR EXPERTISE

Should prior product knowledge make it more or less likely that a consumer will engage in a search? Product experts and novices use very different procedures during decision making. Novices who know little about a product should be the most motivated to find out more about it; however, experts, who are more familiar with the product category, should be able to better understand the meaning of any new product information they might acquire.

So, who searches more? The answer is neither: search tends to be greatest among those consumers who are *moderately* knowledgeable about the product. There is an inverted-U-shaped relationship between knowledge and external search effort, as shown in Figure 9–4. People with very limited expertise may not feel they are capable of searching extensively. In fact, they may not even know where to start. Bill, who did not spend a lot of time researching his purchase, is representative of this situation. He visited one store and only looked at brands with which he was already familiar. In addition, he focused on only a small number of product features.[27]

The *type* of search undertaken by people with varying levels of expertise differs as well. Because experts have a better sense of what information is relevant to the decision, they tend to engage in *selective search,* which means their efforts are more focused and efficient. In contrast, novices are more likely to rely upon the opinions of others and upon "nonfunctional" attributes, such as brand name and price, to distinguish among alternatives. They may also process information in a "top-down" rather than a "bottom-up" manner, focusing less on details than on the big picture. For instance, they may be more impressed by the sheer amount of technical information presented in an ad than by the actual significance of the claims made.[28]

FIGURE9–4 • The Relationship between Amount of Information Search and Product Knowledge

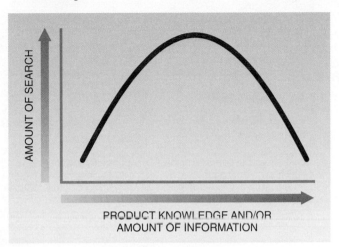

PERCEIVED RISK

As a rule, purchase decisions that involve extensive search also entail some kind of **perceived risk,** or the belief that the product has potentially negative consequences. Perceived risk may be present if the product is expensive or is complex and hard to understand. Alternatively, perceived risk can be a factor when a product choice is visible to others and we run the risk of embarrassment if the wrong choice is made.

Figure 9–5 lists five basic kinds of risk—including both objective factors (such as physical danger) and subjective factors (like social embarrassment)—as well as the products subject to each type. As this figure notes, consumers with greater "risk capital" are less affected by perceived risks associated with the products. For example, a highly self-confident person would be less worried about the social risk inherent in a

perceived risk the belief that use of a product has potentially negative consequences, either physical or social

Minolta features a No-Risk Guarantee as a way to reduce the perceived risk in buying an office copier. Newsweek, *December 6, 1993. Courtesy of Minolta Corporation.*

FIGURE 9–5 • Five Types of Perceived Risk

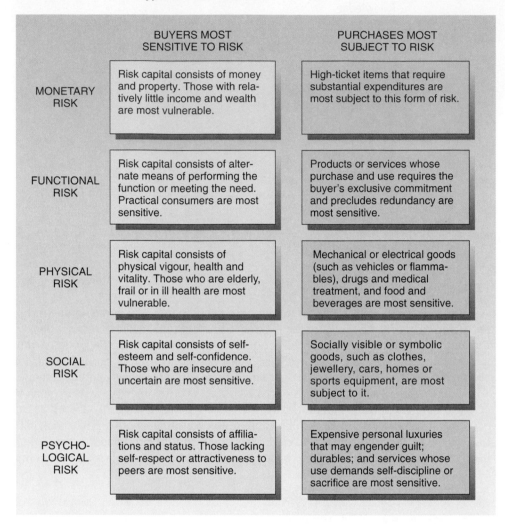

	BUYERS MOST SENSITIVE TO RISK	PURCHASES MOST SUBJECT TO RISK
MONETARY RISK	Risk capital consists of money and property. Those with relatively little income and wealth are most vulnerable.	High-ticket items that require substantial expenditures are most subject to this form of risk.
FUNCTIONAL RISK	Risk capital consists of alternate means of performing the function or meeting the need. Practical consumers are most sensitive.	Products or services whose purchase and use requires the buyer's exclusive commitment and precludes redundancy are most sensitive.
PHYSICAL RISK	Risk capital consists of physical vigour, health and vitality. Those who are elderly, frail or in ill health are most vulnerable.	Mechanical or electrical goods (such as vehicles or flammables), drugs and medical treatment, and food and beverages are most sensitive.
SOCIAL RISK	Risk capital consists of self-esteem and self-confidence. Those who are insecure and uncertain are most sensitive.	Socially visible or symbolic goods, such as clothes, jewellery, cars, homes or sports equipment, are most subject to it.
PSYCHO-LOGICAL RISK	Risk capital consists of affiliations and status. Those lacking self-respect or attractiveness to peers are most sensitive.	Expensive personal luxuries that may engender guilt; durables; and services whose use demands self-discipline or sacrifice are most sensitive.

product, while a more vulnerable, insecure consumer might be reluctant to take a chance on a product that might not be accepted by peers.

EVALUATION OF ALTERNATIVES

Much of the effort that goes into a purchase decision occurs at the stage at which a choice must be made from the available alternatives. After all, modern consumer society abounds with choices. In some cases there may be literally hundreds of different brands (as in beer) or different variations of the same brand (as in shades of lipstick), each screaming for our attention.

Just for fun, ask a friend to name all the brands of perfume she can think of. The odds are she will reel off three to five names rather quickly and then stop to think awhile before coming up with a few more. It is likely that perfumes in the first set of brands are those with which she is highly familiar, and she probably wears one or more of these. The list may also contain one or two brands that she does not like and would perhaps like to forget. Note also that there are many, many more brands on the market than she named.

If your friend were to go to the store to buy perfume, it is likely that she would consider buying some or most of the brands she listed initially. She might also consider a few more possibilities if these were forcefully brought to her attention while at the store—for example, if she were "ambushed" by an employee who sprays scent samples on shoppers, which is a common occurrence in some department stores.

Identifying Alternatives

How do we decide what criteria are important, and how do we narrow down product alternatives to an acceptable number and eventually choose one over the others? The answer varies depending upon the decision-making process used. A consumer engaged in extended problem solving may carefully evaluate several brands, while someone making a habitual decision may not consider any alternatives to his or her normal brand. And some evidence indicates that more extended processing occurs in situations where negative emotions are aroused due to conflicts among the choices available.[29]

The alternatives actively considered during a consumer's choice process are his or her **evoked set.** The evoked set is composed of those products already in memory (the retrieval set) plus those prominent in the retail environment. For example, recall that Bill did not know much about the technical aspects of television sets and that he had only a few major brands in memory. Of these, two were acceptable possibilities and one was not. The alternatives that the consumer is aware of but would not consider buying are his or her *inept set,* while those not entering the game at all comprise the *inert set.* These categories are depicted in Figure 9–6.

evoked set those products already in memory plus those prominent in the retail environment that are actively considered during a consumer's choice process

FIGURE 9–6 • Identifying Alternatives: Getting in the Game

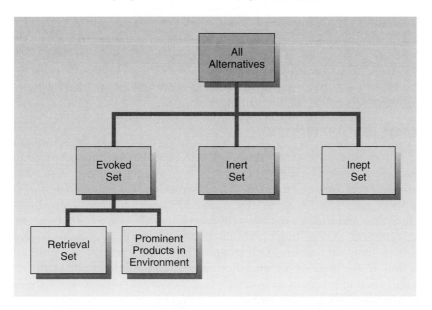

Consumers often consider a surprisingly small number of alternatives in their evoked set. One study combined results from several large-scale investigations of consumers' evoked sets and found that, although there are some marked variations by product category and across countries, the number of products included in these sets is limited. For example, the average size of the evoked set for a US beer consumer was less than three, while Canadian consumers typically considered seven brands.

For obvious reasons, a marketer who finds that her or his brand is not in the evoked set of many consumers in the target market has cause to worry. A product is not likely to be placed in the evoked set after it has previously been considered and rejected. Indeed, a new brand is more likely to be added to the evoked set than is an existing brand that was previously considered but passed over, even after additional positive information is provided for that brand.[30] For marketers, this unwillingness to give a rejected product a second chance underscores the importance of ensuring that it performs well from the time it is introduced.

Product Categorization

Remember that when consumers process product information, they do not do so in a vacuum. Instead, a product stimulus is evaluated in terms of what people already know about the product or those things it is similar to. A person evaluating a particular 35-mm camera will most likely compare it to other 35-mm cameras rather than to a Polaroid camera, and the consumer would certainly not compare it to a slide projector or VCR. Since the category in which a product is placed determines the other products it will be compared to, *categorization* is a crucial determinant of how a product is evaluated.

The products in a consumer's evoked set are likely to be those that share some similar features. It is important to understand how this knowledge is represented in a consumer's **cognitive structure,** which refers to a set of factual knowledge (i.e., beliefs) about products and the way these beliefs are organized in people's minds.[31] These knowledge structures were discussed in Chapter 4. One reason this knowledge is important is that marketers want to ensure that their products are correctly grouped. For example, General Foods brought out a new line of Jell-O flavours such as Cranberry Orange that it called Jell-O Gelatin Flavours for Salads. Unfortunately, the company discovered that people would use it only for salad since the name encouraged them to put the product in their "salad" structure rather than in their "dessert" structure. The line had to be dropped.[32]

cognitive structure the set of factual knowledge, or beliefs about a product, and the way these beliefs are organized

LEVELS OF CATEGORIZATION

Not only do people group things into categories, but these groupings occur at different levels of specificity. Typically, a product is represented in a cognitive structure at one of three levels. To understand this idea, consider how someone might respond to the following questions about an ice cream cone: what other products share similar characteristics? and which would be considered as alternatives to eating a cone?

The questions may be more complex than they first appear. At one level a cone is similar to an apple because both could be eaten as a dessert. At another level a cone is similar to a piece of pie since both are eaten for dessert and both are fattening. At still another level a cone is similar to an ice-cream sundae; both are eaten for dessert, are made of ice cream and are fattening.

FIGURE 9–7 • Levels of Abstraction in Dessert Categories

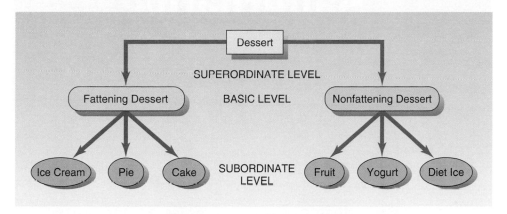

It is easy to see that the items a person associates with, say, the category "fattening dessert" influence the choices he or she will make for what to eat after dinner. The middle level, known as a *basic level category,* is typically the most useful in classifying products, since items grouped together at this level tend to have a lot in common with each other but still permit a range of alternatives to be considered. The broader *superordinate category* is more abstract, while the more specific *subordinate category* often includes individual brands.[33] These three levels are depicted in Figure 9–7. Of course not all items fit equally well into a category. Apple pie is a better example of the subordinate category "pie" than is rhubarb pie, even though both are legitimate kinds of pies. Apple pie is thus more prototypical and would tend to be considered first, especially by category novices. In contrast, pie experts will tend to have knowledge about category examples that are both typical and atypical.[34]

STRATEGIC IMPLICATIONS OF PRODUCT CATEGORIZATION

Product categorization has many strategic implications. The way a product is grouped with others has very important ramifications for determining both its competitors for adoption and what criteria will be used to make this choice.

Product Positioning. The success of a *positioning strategy* often hinges on the marketer's ability to convince the consumer that his or her product should be considered within a given category. For example, the orange-juice industry tried to reposition orange juice as a drink that could be enjoyed all day long ("It's not just for breakfast anymore"). On the other hand, soft-drink companies are now attempting to do the opposite by portraying their beverages as suitable for breakfast consumption. They are trying to make their way into consumers' "breakfast drink" category, along with orange juice, grapefruit juice and coffee.

Identifying Competitors. At the abstract, superordinate level, many different product forms compete for membership. Both bowling and ballet may be considered subcategories of "entertainment" by some people, but many would not necessarily consider the substitution of one of these activities for the other. Products and services that, on the surface, are quite different actually compete with each other at a broad level, often for consumers' discretionary dollars. While bowling or ballet may not be a likely trade-off for many people, it is feasible, for example, that a symphony might try to lure away season ticket-holders to the ballet by positioning itself as an equivalent member of the category "cultural event."[35]

This ad for Sunkist lemon juice attempts to establish a new category for the product by repositioning it as a salt substitute.
Courtesy of Sunkist Growers, Inc.

Consumers are often faced with choices between noncomparable categories, in which a number of attributes exist that cannot be directly related to one another (the old problem of comparing apples and oranges). The comparison process is easier when consumers can derive an overlapping category that encompasses both items (such as entertainment, value or usefulness) and then rate each alternative in terms of that superordinate category.[36]

Exemplar products: rhubarb versus apples, for example. If a product is a really good example of a category, it is more familiar to consumers and, as a result, is more easily recognized and recalled.[37] Judgments about category attributes tend to be disproportionately influenced by the characteristics of category exemplars.[38] In a sense, brands that are strongly associated with a category get to "call the shots" by defining the criteria that should be used to evaluate all category members.

Being a bit less than prototypical is not necessarily a bad thing. Products that are moderately unusual within their product category may stimulate more information processing and positive evaluations, since they are neither so familiar that they will be taken for granted nor so discrepant that they will be dismissed.[39] Further, a brand that is strongly discrepant may occupy a unique niche position, while those that are moderately discrepant remain in a differentiated position within the general category.[40]

Locating Products. Product categorization can also affect consumers' expectations regarding the places they can locate a desired product. If products do not clearly fit into categories (e.g., is a rug furniture?), consumers' ability to find them or make sense of them may be affected. For instance, a frozen dog-food that had to be thawed and cooked failed in the market, partly because people could not adapt to the idea of buying dog-food in the "frozen foods for people" section.

Product Choice: Selecting among Alternatives

Once the relevant options from a category have been assembled, a choice must be made among them.[41] Recall that the decision rules that guide choice can range from very simple and quick strategies to complicated processes requiring a lot of attention and cognitive processing. The choice can be influenced by integrating information from such sources as prior experience with the product, information present at the time of purchase, and beliefs about the brands that have been created by advertising.[42]

EVALUATIVE CRITERIA

When Bill was looking at different television sets, he focused on one or two product features and completely ignored several others. He narrowed down his choices by considering only two specific brand names, and from the Prime Wave and Precision models he chose the one that featured stereo capability.

Evaluative criteria are the dimensions used to judge the merits of competing options. In comparing alternative products, Bill could have chosen from among any number of criteria, ranging from very functional attributes (does this TV come with remote control?) to experiential ones (does this TV's sound reproduction make me imagine I'm in a concert hall?).

Another important point is that criteria on which products differ carry more weight in the decision process. If all brands being considered rate equally well on one attribute (e.g., if all TVs come with remote controls), consumers will have to find other attributes to use in making a choice. Those attributes that are actually used to differentiate among choices are *determinant attributes*.

Marketers can play a role in educating consumers about which criteria should be used as determinant attributes. For example, consumer research by Church & Dwight indicated that many consumers view the use of natural ingredients as a determinant attribute. The result was promotion of a toothpaste made from baking soda, which the company already manufactured for its Arm & Hammer brand.[43]

evaluative criteria the dimensions used by consumers to compare competing product alternatives

Claiming the product is "full of strength," this ad for Pucko, a Swedish chocolate drink, emphasizes an evaluation criterion based on nutritional value, whereas Canadian consumers might evaluate a similar product based on taste or calorie content.
Photographer Kurt Wass. Courtesy of Forsman and BodenFors.

The decision about which attributes to use is the result of *procedural learning,* in which a person undergoes a series of cognitive steps before making a choice. These steps include identifying important attributes, remembering whether competing brands differ on those attributes, and so on. In order for a marketer effectively to recommend a new decision criterion, his or her communication should convey three pieces of information:[44]

1. It should point out that there are significant differences among brands on the attribute.

2. It should supply the consumer with a decision-making rule, such as, "*If* [deciding among competing brands], *then* [use the attribute as a criterion]."

3. It should convey a rule that can be easily integrated with how the person has made this decision in the past. Otherwise the recommendation is likely to be ignored because it requires too much mental work.

Heuristics: Mental Shortcuts

To simplify decisions, consumers often employ decision rules that allow them to use some dimensions as substitutes for others. For example, Bill relied on certain assumptions as substitutes for a prolonged information search. In particular, he assumed the selection at Zany Zach's would be more than sufficient, so he did not bother to shop at any of Zach's competitors. This assumption served as a shortcut to more extensive information processing.[45] Especially where limited problem solving occurs prior to making a choice, consumers often fall back upon **heuristics,** or mental rules of thumb, that lead to a speedy decision. These rules range from the very general ("Higher-priced products are higher-quality products" or "I buy the same brand I bought last time") to the very specific ("I buy Domino, the brand of sugar my mother always bought").[46]

Sometimes these shortcuts may not be in consumers' best interests. For example, a consumer who personally knows one or two people who have had problems with a particular make of car might assume he or she would have similar trouble with it and thus overlook the model's overall excellent repair record.[47] The influence of such assumptions may be enhanced if the product has an unusual name, which makes it *and* the experiences with it more distinctive.[48]

RELYING ON A PRODUCT SIGNAL

One frequently used shortcut is the tendency to infer hidden dimensions of products from observable attributes. The aspect of the product that is visible acts as a *signal* of some underlying quality. Such inferences explain why someone trying to sell a used car takes great pains to be sure the car's exterior is clean and shiny: potential buyers often judge the vehicle's mechanical condition by its appearance, even though this means they may drive away in a shiny, clean clunker.[49]

When product information is incomplete, judgments are often derived from beliefs about *covariation,* or associations among events.[50] For example, a consumer may form an association between product quality and the length of time a manufacturer has been in business. Other signals or attributes believed to coexist with good or bad products include well-known brand names, country of origin, price and the retail outlets that carry the product.

heuristics the mental rules of thumb that lead to a speedy decision

Unfortunately, consumers tend to be poor estimators of covariation. Their beliefs persist despite evidence to the contrary. Similar to the consistency principle discussed in Chapter 7, people tend to see what they are looking for. They will look for product information that confirms their guesses. In one experiment consumers sampled four sets of products to determine if price and quality were related. Those who believed in this relationship prior to the study elected to sample higher-priced products, thus creating a sort of self-fulfilling prophecy.[51]

MARKET BELIEFS: IS IT BETTER IF I HAVE TO PAY MORE FOR IT?

Consumers often form specific beliefs about relationships in the marketplace. These beliefs then become the shortcuts—whether or not they are accurate—that guide their decisions.[52] Our friend Bill's decisions were influenced by his **market beliefs.** Recall, for instance, that he chose to shop at a large "electronics supermarket" because he assumed the selection would be better (though the prices would be lower). A large number of market beliefs have been identified. Some of these are listed in Table 9–3. How many do you share?

market beliefs the specific beliefs or decision rules pertaining to marketplace phenomena

Do higher prices mean higher quality? The assumption of a *price–quality relationship* is one of the most pervasive market beliefs.[53] Novice consumers may, in fact, consider price as the only relevant product attribute. Experts also consider this information, although in the case of experts price tends to be used for its informational value, especially for products (like virgin wool) that are known to have wide quality variations in the marketplace. When this quality level is more standard or strictly regulated (e.g., Harris Tweed sport coats), experts do not weigh price in their decisions. For the most part this belief is justified; you do tend to get what you pay for. However, let the buyer beware: the price–quality relationship is not always justified.[54]

COUNTRY OF ORIGIN AS A HEURISTIC

Modern consumers choose among products made in many countries. Canadians may buy Brazilian shoes, Japanese cars, clothing imported from Taiwan or microwave ovens built in South Korea. Consumers' reactions to these imports are mixed. In some cases people have come to assume that a product made overseas is of better quality (e.g., cameras or cars), while in other cases the knowledge that a product has been imported tends to lower perceptions of product quality (e.g., apparel).[55] In general, people tend to rate their own country's products more favourably than they do foreign products, and products from industrialized countries are better rated than those from developing countries.

A product's *country of origin* in some cases is an important piece of information in the decision-making process.[56] Of course, the extent to which this is a factor depends on the product category. In a Gallup Poll of US consumers, only 3 percent of respondents felt that this information is important when they buy shoes, and only 7 percent relied on it for toy purchases; but 51 percent said country of origin is a key factor when they buy clothing, and 54 percent agreed that a car's nationality is important.[57] Do you think Canadians would hold the same beliefs?

A product's origin, then, is often used as a signal of quality. Certain items are strongly associated with specific countries, and products from those countries often attempt to benefit from these linkages.

Recent evidence indicates that learning of a product's country of origin is not necessarily good or bad. Instead it has the effect of stimulating the consumer's inter-

TABLE 9–3 Common Market Beliefs	
Brand	All brands are basically the same.
	Generic products are just name brands sold under a different label at a lower price.
	The best brands are the ones that are purchased the most.
Store	Specialty stores are great places to familiarize yourself with the best brands; but once you figure out what you want, it's cheaper to buy it at a discount outlet.
	A store's character is reflected in its window displays.
	Salespeople in specialty stores are more knowledgeable than other sales personnel.
	Larger stores offer better prices than small stores.
	Locally owned stores give the best service.
	A store that offers a good value on one of its products probably offers good value on all of its items.
	Credit and return policies are most lenient at large department stores.
	Stores that have just opened usually charge attractive prices.
Prices/Discounts/Sales	Sales are typically run to get rid of slow-moving merchandise.
	Stores that are constantly having sales don't really save you money.
	Within a given store, higher prices generally indicate higher quality.
Advertising and Sales Promotion	"Hard-sell" advertising is associated with low-quality products.
	Items tied to "give-aways" are not a good value (even with the freebee).
	Coupons represent real savings for customers because they are not offered by the store.
	When you buy heavily advertised products, you are paying for the label, not for higher quality.
Product/Packaging	Largest-sized containers are almost always cheaper per unit than smaller sizes.
	New products are more expensive when they're first introduced; prices tend to settle down as time goes by.
	When you are not sure what you need in a product, it's a good idea to invest in the extra features, because you'll probably wish you had them later.
	In general, synthetic goods are lower in quality than goods made of natural materials.
	It's advisable to stay away from products when they are new to the market; it usually takes the manufacturer a little time to work the bugs out.

Source: Adapted from Calvin P. Duncan, "Consumer Market Beliefs: A Review of the Literature and an Agenda for Future Research," in *Advances in Consumer Research 17*, ed. Marvin E. Goldberg, Gerald Gorn and Richard W. Pollay (Provo, UT: Association for Consumer Research, 1990), pp. 729–35.

est in the product to a greater degree. The purchaser thinks more extensively about the product and evaluates it more carefully.[58]

Canada as a country of origin is extremely important for some products, especially bottled water and vitamins. An ad for Jamieson vitamins sold in Japan reads, "This product is imported from Canada, home of forests and lakes."[59] The image that Canada is portraying is clean, pure and trustworthy. Other research has looked at the profile of Canadians and Canadian products in terms of how these images compare against other international competitors.[60]

MULTICULTURAL DIMENSIONS

Japanese consumers have a strong interest in European and American products, and other countries work hard to cultivate favourable images in the discriminating Japanese market. Dentsu, the largest Japanese advertising agency, has conducted several studies for the Commission of the European Communities to determine how Japanese consumers perceive European countries, the United States and some Asian countries, and how they evaluate products from those countries.

One study, carried out in 1992, involved personal interviews with 1600 consumers ranging in age from 15 to 59. Respondents rated countries on such overall dimensions as "is rich in history/tradition," "has abundant natural scenery" and "would like to visit," as well as on product-related characteristics, such as "high-quality, high-performance products" and "well-designed, stylish products."

The results showed that the Japanese public associates Europe with history, tradition and well-designed products, while American advanced technology and agriculture are highly rated (products from South Korea and Taiwan tended to be rated lower than those from the United States or Europe).

Overall, respondents told the researchers that foreign products (i.e., non-Japanese) are well regarded in terms of style but are assumed to be lower in technological sophistication than are most Japanese products. There was also widespread sentiment that many non-Japanese products are not well suited to Japanese needs. These consumers felt that many foreign goods are too expensive and are in need of more thorough after-sales service.

A perceptual map summarizing Japanese consumers' images of European countries and the United States is shown in Figure 9–8 on page 314. The five countries in Group 1 have the most "image wealth"; they are strong both in overall appeal and in ratings of product quality. Germany is the sole country in Group 2, indicating that its products are better regarded than is the country as a whole. The countries in Group 3 have positive images but have yet to transfer these good feelings to their products. Finally, the countries in Group 4 appear to have their work cut out f61 them if they hope to win over the hearts and wallets of Japanese consumers.[61]

Choosing Familiar Brand Names: Loyalty or Habit?

Branding is a marketing strategy that often functions as a heuristic. People form preferences for favourite brands and then may literally never change their mind in the course of their lifetime. A study by the Boston Consulting Group of the market leaders in 30 product categories found that 27 of the brands that were number one in 1930 are still number one today. These brands include such perennial favourites as Ivory soap, Campbell's soup and Coca-Cola.[62]

A brand that exhibits that kind of staying power is treasured by marketers, and for good reason. Brands that dominate their markets are as much as 50 percent more profitable than their nearest competitors.[63] A survey of 3000 consumers on brand power in Japan, Europe and the United States combined awareness and esteem scores to produce the following list of the most positively regarded brand names around the world:[64]

FIGURE 9–8 • Perceptual Positioning by Country of Origin among Japanese Consumers

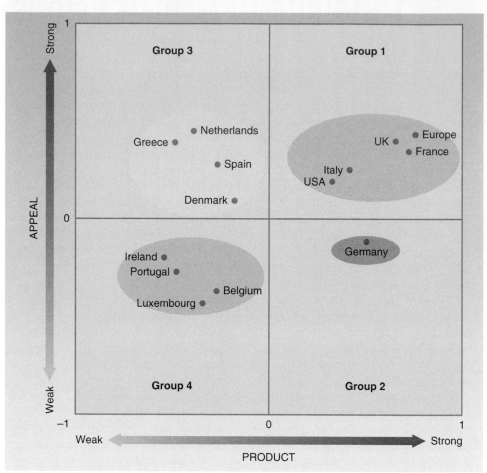

Source: *Images of Europe: A Survey of Japanese Attitudes Toward European Products* (report prepared by Dentsu Inc. for the Commission of the European Communities, Brussels, 1994): 5.

MULTICULTURAL DIMENSIONS

The French tend to be a bit finicky about their food, and products from other countries are evaluated critically. However, despite the particularly unappealing reputation of British cuisine in France, the department store Marks & Spencer is slowly making inroads by selling "produce of England" and ethnic dishes such as chicken tikka masala that are not widely found in France. The French are buying $80 000 a week of English-style sandwiches like egg and watercress on whole-wheat bread. Positioned primarily as convenience foods for young office workers, these choices are less full of calories and less expensive than the traditional French loaf split down the middle and lathered with butter and ham or camembert cheese. This modest British invasion began 20 years ago when the store began to sell tea and biscuits, in addition to jams labelled "preserves" until British managers discovered how close this word was to "préservatif," the French term for a contraceptive![65]

1. Coca-Cola
2. IBM
3. Sony
4. Porsche
5. McDonald's
6. Disney
7. Honda
8. Toyota
9. Seiko
10. BMW

Consumers' attachments to certain brands, such as Coca-Cola, Gerber and Levi's, are so powerful that this loyalty is often considered a positive product attribute in and of itself. Brand equity can actually be quantified in terms of *goodwill,* defined as the difference between the market value and the book value of a brand.

INERTIA: THE FICKLE CONSUMER

Many people tend to buy the same brand just about every time they go to the store. This consistent pattern is often due to **inertia,** where a brand is bought out of habit merely because less effort is required. If another product comes along that is for some reason easier to buy (e.g., it is cheaper or the original product is out of stock), the consumer will not hesitate to do so. A competitor who is trying to change a buying pattern based on inertia often can do so rather easily, because little resistance to brand switching will be encountered if some reason to do so is apparent.

inertia the process whereby purchase decisions are made out of habit because the consumer lacks the motivation to consider alternatives

Since there is little to no underlying commitment to the product, such promotional tools as point-of-purchase displays, extensive couponing or noticeable price reductions may be sufficient to "unfreeze" a consumer's habitual pattern.

BRAND LOYALTY: A "FRIEND," TRIED AND TRUE

This kind of fickleness will not occur if true **brand loyalty** exists. In contrast to inertia, brand loyalty is a form of repeat-purchasing behaviour reflecting a conscious decision to continue buying the same brand. This concept thus refers to a pattern of purchases over time where actual decision making occurs.[66] For brand loyalty to exist, a pattern of repeat purchasing must be accompanied by an underlying positive attitude towards the brand. Brand loyalty may be initiated by customer preference based on objective reasons, but after the brand has been around for a long time and is heavily advertised, it can also create an emotional attachment, either by being incorporated into the consumer's self-image or because it is associated with prior experiences.[67] Purchase decisions based on brand loyalty also become habitual over time, but the underlying commitment to the brand is much stronger.

brand loyalty a pattern of repeat product purchases, accompanied by an underlying positive attitude towards the brand

Compared to an inertia situation where the consumer passively accepts a brand, a brand-loyal consumer is actively (sometimes passionately) involved with his or her favourite. Because of the emotional bonds that can be created between brand-loyal consumers and products, "true-blue" users react more vehemently when these products are altered, redesigned or eliminated.[68] Witness, for example, the national call-in campaigns, boycotts and other protests when Coca-Cola replaced its tried-and-true formula with New Coke.

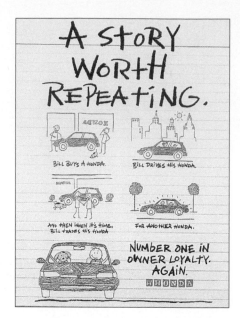

This Honda ad emphasizes the high brand loyalty of Honda owners and so portrays the act of choosing a new car as one of simple, habitual decision making. © 1992 by American Honda Motor Co., Inc. Courtesy of Rubin Poster and Associates.

In recent years marketers have struggled with the problem of *brand parity*, which refers to consumers' beliefs that there are no significant differences among brands. For example, more than one-half of consumers worldwide consider all brands of beer and cigarettes to be about the same, and more than 70 percent believe that all paper towels, soaps and snack chips are alike.[69] Some analysts even proclaimed that brand names are dead, killed off by private-label or generic products that offer the same value for less money.

However, the reports of this death appear to be premature; major brands are making a comeback. This renaissance is attributed to information overload: with too many alternatives (many of them unfamiliar names) to choose from, people are looking for a few clear signals of quality. Following a period in the late 1980s and early 1990s when people had strong doubts about the ability of large companies to produce quality products, more recent surveys indicate consumers are slowly beginning to trust major manufacturers again.[70] Brand names will be very much alive in the new millennium.

Decision Rules

Consumers consider sets of product attributes by using different rules, depending upon the complexity of the decision and the importance to them of the decision. As we have seen, in some cases these rules are quite simple: people simply rely on a "shortcut" to make a choice. In other cases, though, more effort and thought is put into carefully weighing alternatives before coming to a decision.

One way to differentiate among decision rules is to divide them into those that are *compensatory* versus those that are *noncompensatory*. Compensatory rules imply that one good attribute can "compensate" for other poorer attributes. This is

Simplify.

Sporty. Responsive. And, you won't be embarrassed to be seen with one. What decision could be easier?  HONDA
The Accord Coupe.

This ad shows the complexity of even relatively simple decision making and offers a solution.
Courtesy of Honda and Rubin, Postaer & Associates.

not the case with noncompensatory rules, where some poor attributes may eliminate
the choice despite its strength on other attributes. As an aid in the discussion, the
attributes of the TV sets that Bill considered are summarized in Table 9–4. Now let's
see if some of these rules result in different brand choices.

TABLE 9–4   Hypothetical Alternatives for a TV Set

ATTRIBUTE	PERSONAL IMPORTANCE* RATING	RANKING	PRIME WAVE	PRECISION	KAMASHITA
			BRAND RATINGS		
Size of screen	5	6	Excellent 5	Excellent 5	Excellent 5
Stereo broadcast capability	4	5	Poor 1	Excellent 5	Good 4
Brand reputation	2	4	Excellent 5	Excellent 5	Poor 1
On-screen programming	2	3	Excellent 5	Poor 1	Poor 1
Cable-ready capability	4	2	Good 4	Good 4	Good 4
Sleep timer	1	1	Excellent 5	Poor 1	Good 4

*Note that higher numbers denote more importance.

NONCOMPENSATORY DECISION RULES

noncompensatory decision rules a set of simple rules whereby a brand with a low standing on one attribute cannot make up for this position by being better on another attribute

Simple decision rules are **noncompensatory,** and a product with a low standing on one attribute cannot make up for this position by being better on another attribute. In other words, people simply eliminate all options that do not meet some basic standards. A consumer, like Bill, who uses the decision rule "Only buy well-known brand names" would not consider a new brand, even if it were equal or superior to existing ones. When people are less familiar with a product category or not very motivated to process complex information, they tend to use simple, noncompensatory rules.[71]

THE LEXICOGRAPHIC RULE. When the *lexicographic rule* is used, the brand that is the best on the most important attribute is selected. If two or more brands are seen as being equally good on that attribute, the consumer then compares them using the second most important attribute. This selection process goes on until the tie is broken. In Bill's case, since both the Prime Wave and Precision models were tied on his most important attribute (a 27-inch screen), the Precision model was chosen because of its rating on his second-most-important attribute—its stereo capability.

THE ELIMINATION-BY-ASPECTS RULE. Again, brands are evaluated on the most important attribute under the *elimination-by-aspects rule*. In this case, though, specific cut-offs are imposed. For example, if Bill had been more interested in having a sleep timer on his TV (i.e., if it had a higher importance ranking), he might have stipulated that his choice "must have a sleep timer." Since the Prime Wave model had one and the Precision did not, the Prime Wave would have been chosen.

THE CONJUNCTIVE RULE. While the two former rules involve processing by attribute, the *conjunctive rule* entails processing by brand. As with the elimination-by-aspects procedure, cut-offs are established for each attribute. A brand is chosen if it meets all the cut-offs, while failure to meet any one cut-off means rejection. If none of the brands meets all of the cut-offs, the choice may be delayed, the decision rule may be changed or the cut-offs themselves may be modified. Note that this rule rates negative data more heavily.

THE DISJUNCTIVE RULE. Here the consumer develops acceptable standards for each attribute. Usually the standards are higher than one's minimum cut-offs for attributes. If a choice alternative exceeds the standard for *any* attribute, it is accepted. While this strategy may be difficult to envisage, think about a consumer shopping for a new T-shirt or sweater to spruce up his wardrobe. Perhaps the consumer does not know exactly what he will buy before going shopping, but once in the choice environment he will select something that is exceptional in some unique way. The article may be a great new colour, style or type of fabric that exceeds his standards. When the shopper finds two great sweaters, then he must go to a different decision rule to choose between them.

If Bill had stipulated that all attributes had to be rated as "good" or better, he would not have been able to choose any of the options. He might then have modified his decision rule, conceding that it was not possible to attain these high standards in the price range he was considering. In this case Bill could perhaps decide that it was not so important to have on-screen programming, so the Precision model could again be considered.

COMPENSATORY DECISION RULES

Unlike noncompensatory decision rules, **compensatory rules** give a product a chance to make up for its shortcomings. Consumers who employ these rules tend to be more involved in the purchase and thus are willing to exert the effort to consider the entire picture in a more exacting way. The willingness to let good and bad product qualities balance out can result in quite different choices. For example, if Bill were not as concerned about having stereo reception, he might have chosen the Prime Wave model using a compensatory rule. But because this brand did not feature this highly ranked attribute, it doesn't stand a chance when he uses a noncompensatory rule.

Two basic types of compensatory rules have been identified. When using the *simple additive rule,* the consumer merely chooses the alternative having the largest number of positive attributes. This choice is most likely to occur when his or her ability or motivation to process information is limited. One drawback to this approach for the consumer is that some of these attributes may not be very meaningful or important. An ad containing a long list of product benefits may be persuasive, despite the fact that many of the benefits included are actually standard within the product class and aren't determinant attributes at all.

The more complex version is known as the *weighted additive rule.*[72] When using this rule, the consumer also takes into account the relative importance of positively rated attributes, essentially multiplying brand ratings by importance weights. If this process sounds familiar, it should. The calculation process strongly resembles the multi-attribute attitude model described in Chapter 7.

In the course of the many purchases people make in their lifetime, many different decision rules are used by the same people for different purchases. The recurring decision is when to stop acquiring additional information and commit to the leading alternative. We know that this decision is governed by the costs and benefits of the search process, as weighed by the consumer.[73] There is some attempt to model this question of how much data a consumer should acquire before choice.[74]

compensatory decision rules a set of rules that allow information about attributes of competing products to be averaged in some way; poor standing on one attribute can potentially be offset by good standing on another

---

- Consumers are faced with the need to make decisions about products all the time. Some of these decisions are very important and entail great effort, while others are made on a virtually automatic basis.

- Perspectives on decision making range from a focus on habits that people develop over time to a focus on novel situations involving a great deal of risk, wherein consumers must carefully collect and analyze information prior to making choices.

- A typical decision process involves several steps. The first is problem recognition, where the consumer first realizes that some action must be taken. This realization may be prompted in a variety of ways, ranging from the malfunction of a current purchase to a desire for new things, based on exposure to different circumstances or advertising that provides a glimpse into what is needed to "live the good life."

- Once a problem has been recognized and is seen as sufficiently important to warrant some action, information search begins. This search may range from a simple scanning of memory, to determine what has been done to resolve the

CHAPTER SUMMARY

problem in the past, to undertaking extensive fieldwork, where the consumer consults a variety of sources to amass as much information as possible. In many cases people engage in surprisingly little search. Instead, they rely upon various mental shortcuts, such as brand names or price, or they may simply imitate others.

- In the evaluation-of-alternatives stage the product alternatives that are considered comprise the individual's evoked set. Members of the evoked set usually share some characteristics; that is, they are categorized similarly. The way products are mentally grouped influences which alternatives will be considered, and some brands are more strongly associated with these categories than are others (i.e., they are more prototypical).

- Very often, heuristics, or mental rules of thumb, are used to simplify decision making. In particular, people develop many market beliefs over time. One of the most common beliefs is that price is positively related to quality. Other heuristics rely on well-known brand names or a product's country of origin as signals of product quality. When a brand is consistently purchased over time, this pattern may be due to true brand loyalty or simply to inertia (it's the easiest thing to do).

- When the consumer must eventually make a product choice from among alternatives, a number of decision rules may be used. Noncompensatory rules eliminate alternatives that are deficient on any of the criteria the consumer has chosen to use. Compensatory rules, which are more likely to be applied in high-involvement situations, allow the decision maker to consider each alternative's good and bad points more carefully to arrive at the overall best choice.

KEY TERMS

Behavioural influence perspective p. 287

Brand loyalty p. 309

Cognitive structure p. 300

Compensatory decision rules p. 312

Evaluative criteria p. 303

Evoked set p. 299

Experiential perspective p. 287

Extended problem solving p. 287

Habitual decision making p. 287

Heuristics p. 304

Inertia p. 309

Information search p. 290

Limited problem solving p. 287

Market beliefs p. 305

Noncompensatory decision rules p. 312

Perceived risk p. 297

Problem recognition p. 289

Rational perspective p. 286

1. If people are not always rational decision makers, is it worth the effort to study how their decisions are made? What techniques might be employed to understand experiential consumption and to translate this knowledge into marketing strategy?

2. List three product attributes that can be used as quality signals and provide an example of each.

3. Why is it difficult to place a product in a consumer's evoked set after it has already been rejected? What strategies might a marketer use in an attempt to accomplish this goal?

4. Define the three levels of product categorization described in the chapter. Diagram these levels for a health club.

5. Discuss two different noncompensatory decision rules, and highlight the difference(s) between them. How might the use of one rule rather than another result in a different product choice?

6. Choose a friend or parent who grocery shops on a regular basis, and keep a log of his or her purchases of common consumer products over the semester. Can you detect any evidence of brand loyalty in any categories, based upon consistency of purchases? If so, talk to the person about these purchases. Try to determine if his or her choices are based upon true brand loyalty or on inertia. What techniques might you use to differentiate between the two?

7. Form a group of three. Pick a product and develop a marketing plan based upon each of the three approaches to consumer decision making: rational, experiential and behavioural influence. What are the major differences in emphasis among the three perspectives? Which is the most likely type of problem-solving activity for the product you have selected? What characteristics of the product make this so?

8. Locate a person who is about to make a major purchase. Ask that person to make a chronological list of all the information sources consulted prior to making a decision. How would you characterize the types of sources used (i.e., internal versus external, media versus personal, etc.)? Which sources appeared to have the most impact on the person's decision?

9. Perform a survey of country-of-origin stereotypes. Compile a list of five countries and ask people what products they associate with each. What are their evaluations of the products and likely attributes of these different products? The power of a country stereotype can also be demonstrated in another way. Prepare a brief description of a product, including a list of features, and ask people to rate it in terms of quality, likelihood of purchase and so on. Make several versions of the description, varying only the country from which it comes. Do ratings change as a function of the country of origin?

10. Ask a friend to "talk through" the process he or she used to choose one brand over others during a recent purchase. Based on this description, can you identify the decision rule that was most likely employed?

CONSUMER BEHAVIOUR CHALLENGE

CBC VIDEO VIGNETTES

Concepts at Work for the Service Industry

Two-thirds of the Canadian economy is based on services. Consumers purchase services as an economic good in and of themselves (e.g., banking services), as an augmentation to product purchases (e.g., installation) and as part of the in-store experience (e.g., attentive and knowledgeable salespeople). Rapid growth and increasing consumer expectations make service, in all forms, a challenge to deliver. However, some companies see an opportunity to create customer satisfaction by paying more than lip-service to this important area of business.

Companies that provide satisfactory service seek to understand how consumers make marketplace decisions, focusing on the importance of service as an end in itself or as an attribute of a purchase. They also see the role of front-line employees and management information systems as key to service success. Solving service problems

can result in a lifetime customer and a steady stream of profits. Companies that focus on customer equity will be industry leaders in the next century.

QUESTIONS

1. List some specific complaints that consumers have about service.

2. Why do consumers complain so much about "bad service"?

3. How do companies like Federal Express, Cadet Cleaners and Delta Hotels manage service?

4. From the perspective of how consumers make decisions, why does the goal of creating "lifetime customers" make sense?

Video Resource: "Service Ha!" *Venture* #533 (March 26, 1995).

NOTES

1. John C. Mowen, "Beyond Consumer Decision Making," *Journal of Consumer Marketing* 5, 1 (1988): 15–25.

2. Richard W. Olshavsky and Donald H. Granbois, "Consumer Decision Making: Fact or Fiction," *Journal of Consumer Research* 6 (September 1989): 93–100.

3. James R. Bettman, "The Decision Maker Who Came In from the Cold," Presidential Address, in *Advances in Consumer Research 20*, eds. Leigh McAlister and Michael Rothschild (Provo, UT: Association for Consumer Research, in press); John W. Payne, James R. Bettman and Eric J. Johnson, "Behavioral Decision Research: A Constructive Processing Perspective," *Annual Review of Psychology* 4 (1992): 87–131. For an overview of recent developments in individual-choice models, see Robert J. Meyer and Barbara E. Kahn, "Probabilistic Models of Consumer Choice Behavior," in *Handbook of Consumer Behavior,* eds. Thomas S. Robertson and Harold H. Kassarjian (Englewood Cliffs, NJ: Prentice Hall, 1991): 85–123.

4. Mowen, "Beyond Consumer Decision Making."

5. Joseph W. Alba and J. Wesley Hutchinson, "Dimensions of Consumer Expertise," *Journal of Consumer Research* 13 (March 1988): 411–54.

6. Gordon C. Bruner III and Richard J. Pomazal, "Problem Recognition: The Crucial First Stage of the Consumer Decision Process," *Journal of Consumer Marketing* 5, 1 (1988): 53–63.

7. Ross K. Baker, "Textually Transmitted Diseases," *American Demographics* (December 1987): 64.

8. Julia Marlowe, Gary Selnow and Lois Blosser, "A Content Analysis of Problem-Resolution Appeals in Television Commercials," *Journal of Consumer Affairs* 23, 1 (1989): 175–94.

9. Peter H. Bloch, Daniel L. Sherrell and Nancy M. Ridgway, "Consumer Search: An Extended Framework," *Journal of Consumer Research* 13 (June 1986): 119–26.

10. Girish Punj, "Presearch Decision Making in Consumer Durable Purchases," *Journal of Consumer Marketing* 4 (Winter 1987): 71–82.

11. H. Beales et al., "Consumer Search and Public Policy," *Journal of Consumer Research* 8 (June 1981): 11–22.

12. Amy Cortese, "A Way Out of the Web Maze," *Business Week* (February 24, 1997): 93 (8 pp.).

13. Thomas E. Weber, "Advertising: New Software Lets Marketers Target Their Ads on Internet," *The Wall Street Journal Interactive Edition* (April 21, 1997).

14. Itamar Simonson, Joel Huber and John Payne, "The Relationship Between Prior Brand Knowledge and Information Acquisition Order," *Journal of Consumer Research* 14 (March 1988): 566–78.

15. John R. Hauser, Glen L. Urban and Bruce D. Weinberg, "How Consumers Allocate Their Time When Searching for Information," *Journal of Marketing Research* 30 (November 1993): 452–66; George J. Stigler, "The Economics of Information," *Journal of Political Economy* 69 (June 1961): 213–25.

16. Cathy J. Cobb and Wayne D. Hoyer, "Direct Observation of Search Behavior," *Psychology & Marketing* 2 (Fall 1985): 161–79.

17. Sharon E. Beatty and Scott M. Smith, "External Search Effort: An Investigation Across Several Product Categories," *Journal of Consumer Research* 14 (June 1987): 83–95; William L. Moore and Donald R. Lehmann, "Individual Differences in Search Behavior for a Nondurable," *Journal of Consumer Research* 7 (December 1980): 296–307.

18. Geoffrey C. Kiel and Roger A. Layton, "Dimensions of Consumer Information Seeking Behavior," *Journal of Marketing Research* 28 (May 1981): 233–39. See also Narasimhan Srinivasan and Brian T. Ratchford, "An Empirical Test of a Model of External Search for Automobiles," *Journal of Consumer Research* 18 (September 1991): 233–42.

19. David F. Midgley, "Patterns of Interpersonal Information Seeking for the Purchase of a Symbolic Product," *Journal of Marketing Research* 20 (February 1983): 74–83.

20. Cyndee Miller, "Scotland to U.S.: 'This Tennent's for You,'" *Marketing News* (August 29, 1994): 26.

21. Barbara E. Kahn, "Understanding Variety-Seeking Behavior From a Marketing Perspective" (unpublished manuscript, University of Pennsylvania, University Park, 1991); Leigh McAlister and Edgar A. Pessemier, "Variety-Seeking Behavior: An Interdisciplinary Review," *Journal of Consumer Research* 9 (December 1982): 311–22; Fred M. Feinberg, Barbara E. Kahn and Leigh McAlister, "Market Share Response When Consumers Seek Variety," *Journal of Marketing Research* 29 (May 1992): 228–37; Barbara E. Kahn and Alice M. Isen, "The Influence of Positive Affect on Variety Seeking Among Safe, Enjoyable Products," *Journal of Consumer Research* 20, 2 (September 1993): 257–70.

22. Gary Belsky, "Why Smart People Make Major Money Mistakes," *Money* (July 1995): 76 (10 pp.); Richard Thaler and Eric J. Johnson, "Gambling with the House Money or Trying to Break Even: The Effects of Prior Outcomes on Risky Choice," *Management Science* 36 (June 1990): 643–60; Richard Thaler, "Mental Accounting and Consumer Choice," *Marketing Science* 4 (Summer 1985): 199–214.

23. Daniel Kahneman and Amos Tversky, "Prospect Theory: An Analysis of Decision Under Risk," *Econometrica* 47 (March 1979): 263–91; Timothy B. Heath, Subimal Chatterjee and Karen Russo France, "Mental Accounting and Changes in Price: The Frame Dependence of Reference Dependence," *Journal of Consumer Research* 22, 1 (June 1995): 90–97.

24. Quoted in Thaler, "Mental Accounting and Consumer Choice," p. 206.

25. Girish N. Punj and Richard Staelin, "A Model of Consumer Search Behavior for New Automobiles," *Journal of Consumer Research* 9 (March 1983): 366–80.

26. Cobb and Hoyer, "Direct Observation of Search Behavior"; Moore and Lehmann, "Individual Differences in Search Behavior for a Nondurable"; Punj and Staelin, "A Model of Consumer Search Behavior for New Automobiles."

27. James R. Bettman and C. Whan Park, "Effects of Prior Knowledge and Experience and Phase of the Choice Process on Consumer Decision Processes: A Protocol Analysis," *Journal of Consumer Research* 7 (December 1980): 234–48.

28. Alba and Hutchinson, "Dimensions of Consumer Expertise"; Bettman and Park, "Effects of Prior Knowledge"; Merrie Brucks, "The Effects of Product Class Knowledge on Information Search Behavior," *Journal of Consumer Research* 12 (June 1985): 1–16; Joel E. Urbany, Peter R. Dickson and William L. Wilkie, "Buyer Uncertainty and Information Search," *Journal of Consumer Research* 16 (September 1989): 208–15.

29. Mary Frances Luce, James R. Bettman and John W. Payne, "Choice Processing in Emotionally Difficult Decisions," *Journal of Experimental Psychology*, in press.

30. Robert J. Sutton, "Using Empirical Data to Investigate the Likelihood of Brands Being Admitted or Readmitted into an Established Evoked Set," *Journal of the Academy of Marketing Science* 15 (Fall 1987): 82.

31. Alba and Hutchinson, "Dimensions of Consumer Expertise"; Joel B. Cohen and Kunal Basu, "Alternative Models of Categorization: Toward a Contingent Processing Framework," *Journal of Consumer Research* 13 (March 1987): 455–72.

32. Robert M. McMath, "The Perils of Typecasting," *American Demographics* (February 1997): 60.

33. Eleanor Rosch, "Principles of Categorization," in *Recognition and Categorization,* eds. E. Rosch and B.B. Lloyd (Hillsdale, NJ: Lawrence Erlbaum, 1978).

34. Michael R. Solomon, "Mapping Product Constellations: A Social Categorization Approach to Symbolic Consumption," *Psychology & Marketing* 5, 3 (1988): 233–58.

35. Elizabeth C. Hirschman and Michael R. Solomon, "Competition and Cooperation Among Culture Production Systems," in *Marketing Theory: Philosophy of Science Perspectives*, eds. Ronald F. Bush and Shelby D. Hunt (Chicago: American Marketing Association, 1982), pp. 269–72.

36. Michael D. Johnson, "The Differential Processing of Product Category and Noncomparable Choice Alternatives," *Journal of Consumer Research* 16 (December 1989): 300–309.

37. Mita Sujan, "Consumer Knowledge: Effects on Evaluation Strategies Mediating Consumer Judgments," *Journal of Consumer Research* 12 (June 1985): 31–46.

38. Rosch, "Principles of Categorization."

39. Joan Meyers-Levy and Alice M. Tybout, "Schema Congruity As a Basis for Product Evaluation," *Journal of Consumer Research* 16 (June 1989): 39–55.

40. Mita Sujan and James R. Bettman, "The Effects of Brand Positioning Strategies on Consumers' Brand and Category Perceptions: Some Insights from Schema Research," *Journal of Marketing Research* 26 (November 1989): 454–67.

41. Cf. William P. Putsis, Jr., and Narasimhan Srinivasan, "Buying or Just Browsing? The Duration of Purchase Deliberation," *Journal of Marketing Research* 31 (August 1994): 393–402.

42. Robert E. Smith, "Integrating Information from Advertising and Trial: Processes and Effects on Consumer Response to Product Information," *Journal of Marketing Research* 30 (May 1993): 204–19.

43. Jack Trout, "Marketing in Tough Times," *Boardroom Reports* 2 (October 1992): 8.

44. Amna Kirmani and Peter Wright, "Procedural Learning, Consumer Decision Making and Marketing Communication," *Marketing Letters* (1992).

45. Robert A. Baron, *Psychology: The Essential Science* (Boston: Allyn & Bacon, 1989); Valerie S. Folkes, "The Availability Heuristic and Perceived Risk," *Journal of Consumer Research* 15 (June 1989): 13–23; Daniel Kahneman and Amos Tversky, "Prospect Theory: An Analysis of Decision Under Risk," *Econometrica* 47 (1979): 263–91.

46. Wayne D. Hoyer, "An Examination of Consumer Decision Making for a Common Repeat Purchase Product," *Journal of Consumer Research* 11 (December 1984): 822–29; Calvin P. Duncan, "Consumer Market Beliefs: A Review of the Literature and an Agenda for Future Research," in *Advances in Consumer Research 17*, eds. Marvin E. Goldberg, Gerald Gorn and Richard W. Pollay (Provo, UT: Association for Consumer Research, 1990), pp. 729–35; Frank Alpert, "Consumer Market Beliefs and Their Managerial Implications: An Empirical Examination," *Journal of Consumer Marketing* 10, 2 (1993): 56–70.

47. Michael R. Solomon, Sarah Drenan and Chester A. Insko, "Popular Induction: When is Consensus Information Informative?" *Journal of Personality* 49, 2 (1981): 212–24.

48. Folkes, "The Availability Heuristic and Perceived Risk."

49. Beales et al., "Consumer Search and Public Policy."

50. Gary T. Ford and Ruth Ann Smith, "Inferential Beliefs in Consumer Evaluations: An Assessment of Alternative Processing Strategies," *Journal of Consumer Research* 14 (December 1987): 363–71; Deborah Roedder John, Carol A. Scott and James R. Bettman, "Sampling Data for Covariation Assessment: The Effects of Prior Beliefs on Search Patterns," *Journal of Consumer Research* 13 (June 1986): 38–47; Gary L. Sullivan and Kenneth J. Berger, "An Investigation of the Determinants of Cue Utilization," *Psychology & Marketing* 4 (Spring 1987): 63–74.

51. John, Scott and Bettman, "Sampling Data for Covariation Assessment."

52. Duncan, "Consumer Market Beliefs."

53. Chr. Hjorth-Andersen, "Price as a Risk Indicator," *Journal of Consumer Policy* 10 (1987): 267–81.

54. David M. Gardner, "Is There a Generalized Price-Quality Relationship?" *Journal of Marketing Research* 8 (May 1971): 241–43; Kent B. Monroe, "Buyers' Subjective Perceptions of Price," *Journal of Marketing Research* 10 (1973): 70–80.

55. Durairaj Maheswaran, "Country of Origin As a Stereotype: Effects of Consumer Expertise and Attribute Strength on Product Evaluations," *Journal of Consumer Research* 21 (September 1994): 354–65; Ingrid M. Martin and Sevgin Eroglu, "Measuring a Multi-Dimensional Construct: Country Image," *Journal of Business Research* 28 (1993): 191–210; Richard Ettenson, Janet Wagner and Gary Gaeth, "Evaluating the Effect of Country of Origin and the Made in the U.S.A. Campaign: A Conjoint Approach," *Journal of Retailing* 64 (Spring 1988): 85–100; C. Min Han and Vern Terpstra, "Country-of-Origin Effects for Uni-National & Bi-National Products," *Journal of International Business* 19 (Summer 1988): 235–55; Michelle A. Morganosky and Michelle M. Lazarde, "Foreign-Made Apparel: Influences on Consumers' Perceptions of Brand and Store Quality," *International Journal of Advertising* 6 (Fall 1987): 339–48.

56. See Richard Jackson Harris et al., "Effects of Foreign Product Names and Country-of-Origin Attributions on Advertisement Evaluations," *Psychology & Marketing* 11, 2 (March/April 1994): 129–45; Terence A. Shimp, Saeed Samiee and Thomas J. Madden, "Countries and Their Products: A Cognitive Structure Perspective," *Journal of the Academy of Marketing Science* 21, 4 (Fall 1993): 323–30.

57. "American Pie," *Business Week* (June 27, 1994): 6.

58. Sung-Tai Hong and Robert S. Wyer, Jr., "Effects of Country-of-Origin and Product-Attribute Informa-

tion on Product Evaluation: An Information Processing Perspective," *Journal of Consumer Research* 16 (September 1989): 175–87; Marjorie Wall, John Liefeld and Louise A. Heslop, "Impact of Country-of-Origin Cues on Consumer Judgments in Multi-Cue Situations: A Covariance Analysis," *Journal of the Academy of Marketing Science* 19, 2 (1991): 105–13.

59. Barrie McKenna, "Canada's Image Used to Sell Vitamins," *Globe and Mail* (May 6, 1997): B19.

60. Nicholas Papadopoulous, Louise A. Heslop and Gary Bamossy, "An International Comparative Analysis of Consumer Attitudes Toward Canada and Canadian Products," *Canadian Journal of Administrative Sciences* 11, 3: 224–39. See also *Product Country Images: Impact and Role in International Marketing*, eds. Nicholas Papadopoulous and Louise A. Heslop (New York: International Business Press, 1993).

61. *Images of Europe: A Survey of Japanese Attitudes Toward European Products* (report prepared by Dentsu Inc. for the Commission of the European Communities, Brussels, 1994).

62. Richard W. Stevenson, "The Brands with Billion-Dollar Names," *New York Times* (October 28, 1988): A1.

63. Ronald Alsop, "Enduring Brands Hold Their Allure by Sticking Close to Their Roots," *Wall Street Journal* (1989, centennial ed.): B4.

64. Laura Clark, "Porsche Top Auto Brand Name; Honda, Toyota, BMW Follow in U.S., Japan, Europe Survey," *Automotive News* (December 12, 1988): 62.

65. Craig R. Whitney, "Seducing France with Watercress Sandwiches," *New York Times* (May 19, 1995): A4.

66. Jacob Jacoby and Robert Chestnut, *Brand Loyalty: Measurement and Management* (New York: Wiley, 1978).

67. Anne B. Fisher, "Coke's Brand Loyalty Lesson," *Fortune* (August 5, 1985): 44.

68. Jacoby and Chestnut, *Brand Loyalty*.

69. Ronald Alsop, "Brand Loyalty is Rarely Blind Loyalty," *Wall Street Journal* (October 19, 1989): B1.

70. Betsy Morris, "The Brand's the Thing," *Fortune* (March 4, 1996): 72 (8 pp.).

71. C. Whan Park, "The Effect of Individual and Situation-Related Factors on Consumer Selection of Judgmental Models," *Journal of Marketing Research* 13 (May 1976): 144–51.

72. Joseph W. Alba and Howard Marmorstein, "The Effects of Frequency Knowledge on Consumer Decision Making," *Journal of Consumer Research* 14 (June 1987): 14–25.

73. Gad Saad and J. Edward Russo, "Stopping Criteria and Sequential Choice," *Organizational Behavior and Human Decision Processes* 67, 3 (September 1996): 258–70.

74. Gad Saad, "SMAC: An Interface for Investigating Sequential Multiattribute Choices," *Behavioral Research Methods, Instruments, and Computers* 28, 2 (1996): 259–64.

Mark is psyched. The big day has arrived. He's going to buy a car. He hasn't had time to shop around, but he's had his eye on a silver 1987 Camaro at Russ's Auto-Rama. The sticker says $2999, but Mark figures he can probably get this baby for $2000. He dreads haggling over the price but hopes to convince the salesman to take his offer, especially since he can pay the full amount today. He's been working two jobs to save up for that car, and a little more suffering will be worth it.

At the Auto-Rama, big signs proclaim that today is Russ's Auto-Rama Rip Us Off Day! This is better than Mark expected. Maybe he can get the Camaro for less than he had planned. He is surprised when a salesperson named Melanie comes over. He expected to deal with a middle-aged man in a loud sport coat—a stereotype he has about used-car salespeople—but this is more good luck: he figures he won't have to be so tough when dealing with a woman his age.

Melanie laughs at his $1800 offer and says if she takes such a low bid to her boss she'll lose her job. Her enthusiasm for the car convinces him all the more that he has to have it. When he finally writes a cheque for $2700, he's exhausted! In any case Mark figures he'll get his money back when he sells the car in a few years, and he did get the car for less than the sticker price.

Actually, he's not only pleased with the car but with himself! He's a tougher negotiator than he thought ...

10

The Purchase Situation, Postpurchase Evaluation and Product Disposal

INTRODUCTION

Many consumers dread the act of buying a car. In fact, a survey by Yankelovich Partners Inc. found that buying a car is the most anxiety-provoking and least satisfying of any retail experience.[1] But change is in the wind as the car showroom is being transformed. Car shoppers are logging on to Internet buying services, calling auto brokers who negotiate for them, buying cars at warehouse clubs and visiting giant auto malls where they can comparison shop.

In addition, although the ritual of haggling over price is a time-honoured one in the automobile industry, a growing number of dealerships (about 2 percent of the total) are responding to consumers' reluctance to enter into battle by introducing a "no-dicker" policy—a policy where the sticker price is the price people actually pay. The Saturn division of General Motors encourages this policy, as does Ford for sales of its Escort model. While the profit per car tends to be smaller, dealers who have gone this route report that they more than make up for this loss through increased sales volume. Industry research indicates that these dealers are both better liked and busier than traditional dealers. The new approach seems especially likely to benefit women and minority buyers, who are less likely (research indicates) to negotiate than white males.[2]

Car dealers are working hard to find ways to make car shopping a more pleasurable experience. Ford recently sent out a list of guidelines on how to treat shoppers, which included such directions as "customers courteously acknowledged

FIGURE 10–1 • Issues Related to Purchase and Postpurchase Activities

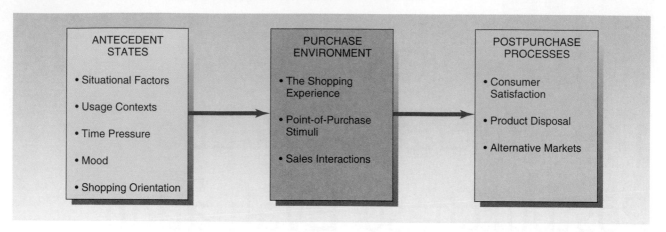

within two minutes of arrival" and "advisory relationship established by knowledge-able sales consultant who listens to customers, identifies needs, and ensures needs are met."[3] These efforts highlight the importance of the purchase situation for marketers: you can have the best car in the world, but people have to be willing to do what it takes to obtain it.

Mark's experience in buying a car illustrates some of the concepts to be discussed in this chapter. Making a purchase is often not a simple, routine matter of going to a store and quickly picking out something. As illustrated in Figure 10–1, a consumer's choices are affected by many personal factors, such as his or her mood, whether there is time pressure to make the purchase, and the particular situation or context in which the product is needed. In some situations, such as the purchase of a car or home, the salesperson or realtor plays a pivotal role in the final selection.

The store environment also exerts a big influence. Shopping is like a performance of a play, wherein the customer is involved as either an audience member or an active participant. The quality of this performance is affected by the other *cast members* (salespeople or other shoppers), as well as by the *setting* of the play (the image of a particular store and the "feeling" it imparts to the shopper) and by *props* (store decorations and promotional materials that try to influence the shopper's decisions).

In addition, a lot of important consumer activity occurs *after* a product has been purchased and brought home. After using a product, the consumer must decide whether he or she is satisfied with it. The satisfaction process is especially important to a savvy marketer who realizes that the key to success is not selling a product one time, but rather forging a relationship with the consumer so that he or she will continue to buy one's products in the future. Finally, just as Mark thought about the resale value of his car, we must also consider how consumers go about disposing of products and how secondary markets (such as used-car dealers) often play a pivotal role in product acquisition. This chapter considers many issues related to purchase and postpurchase phenomena.

SITUATIONAL EFFECTS ON CONSUMER BEHAVIOUR

A *consumption situation* is defined by factors over and above characteristics of the person and the product. Situational effects can be behavioural (e.g., entertaining friends) or perceptual (being depressed or feeling pressed for time).[4] Common sense tells us that people tailor their purchases to specific occasions or that the way they feel at a specific point in time affects what they feel like buying or doing.

Smart marketers understand these patterns and tailor their efforts to coincide with situations where people are most prone to buy. For example, book clubs tend to invest heavily in promotional campaigns in June, since many people are looking to stock up on "beach books" to read during the summer.[5] When the advertising agency Goodby, Silverstein was hired to reverse a steady decline in milk sales, it found that while milk had been depicted as a beverage that was consumed alone, in "the real world" it is consumed primarily with foods. The agency paid people not to drink any milk for a week before a focus-group meeting, and it was only then that they discovered how hard it is to go without cereal in the morning. Knowledge of this situational factor formed the basis for a successful advertising campaign that used the "got milk?" tag line. For example, one spot featuring a man taking milk from his baby's bowl was based on a focus-group participant's comment that he was so desperate he'd even steal milk from his child.[6]

In addition to the functional relationship between products and usage situation, though, another reason to take environmental circumstances seriously is that the role a person plays at any time is partly determined by his or her *situational self-image,* where he or she basically asks "Who am I right now?"[7] (see Chapter 5).

This South African ad for Volkswagen emphasizes that brand criteria can differ depending upon the situation in which the product will be used.
Courtesy of Volkswagen of South Africa.

Someone trying to impress his date by playing the role of "man about town" may spend more lavishly, ordering champagne instead of beer and buying flowers—purchases he would never consider when he is hanging around with his friends, slurping beer and playing the role of "one of the boys." As this discussion demonstrates, knowledge of what consumers are doing at the time a product is consumed can improve predictions of product and brand choice.[8] One aspect of situational role is the degree to which a consumer's ethnic identity, or *felt ethnicity,* is activated during

MARKETING PITFALL

Sometimes a marketing strategy can work *too* well. This is the case with Nabisco's Grey Poupon mustard, which the company has successfully positioned as a premium product. The problem is that consumers tend to save the brand for special occasions rather than slather it on just any old sandwich.

Grey Poupon's "special" cachet is due to its long-running ad campaign, where stuffy aristocrats pass the mustard through the windows of their limousines. The campaign is so well known that the familiar tag line, "Pardon me, would you have any Grey Poupon?" was even repeated in the movie *Wayne's World.*

To dig themselves out of this situational hole, the brand's advertising agency developed new magazine ads that feature simpler occasions, such as a picnic. In the ad shown here readers are reminded to "Poupon the potato salad" or "class up the cold cuts."[9]

Courtesy of Nabisco, Inc.

a purchase situation. When people are reminded of this connection, they are more likely to tailor their product choices along ethnic lines.[10]

By systematically identifying important usage situations, marketers can develop market segmentation strategies to position products that will meet the specific needs arising from these situations. Many product categories are amenable to this form of segmentation. For example, consumers' furniture choices are often tailored to specific settings. We prefer different styles for a city apartment, a beach house or an executive suite. Similarly, motorcycles can be distinguished in terms of what riders use them for, including commuting, riding them as dirt bikes, using them on a farm or for highway travel, and so on.[11] The South African ad for Volkswagen shown on page 323 emphasizes the versatility of the Volkswagen bus for different situations.

Table 10–1 gives one example of how situations can be used to fine-tune a segmentation strategy. By listing the major contexts where a product is used (e.g., snow skiing, sunbathing, etc., for a suntan lotion) and the different users of the product, a matrix can be constructed that identifies specific product features that should be emphasized for each situation. A lotion manufacturer might promote the fact that the bottle floats and is hard to lose during the summer, but tout its antifreeze formula during the winter season.

Physical and Social Surroundings

A consumer's physical and social environment can make a big difference in motives for product usage and also affect how the product is evaluated. Important cues include the person's physical surroundings as well as the number and type of other consumers also present in that situation. Dimensions of the physical environment, such as décor, smells and temperature, can significantly influence consumption (one study found that pumping in certain odours in a Las Vegas casino actually increased the amount of money patrons fed into slot machines!).[12] We'll take a closer look at some of these factors a bit later in the chapter when considering strategic issues related to store design.

In addition to physical cues, though, many of a consumer's purchase decisions are significantly affected by the groups or social settings. In some cases the sheer presence or absence of other patrons ("co-consumers") in a setting can function as a product attribute, such as when an exclusive resort or boutique promises to provide privacy to privileged customers. At other times the presence of others can have positive value. A sparsely attended ball game or an empty bar can be depressing sights.

The presence of large numbers of people in a consumer environment increases arousal levels, so that a consumer's subjective experience of a setting tends to be more intense. This polarization, however, can be both positive and negative. While the presence of other people creates a state of arousal, the consumer's actual experience depends upon his or her *interpretation* of this arousal. It is important to distinguish between *density* and *crowding* for this reason. The former term refers to the actual number of people occupying a space, while the psychological state of crowding exists only if a negative affective state occurs as a result of this density.[13] For example, 100 students packed into a classroom designed for 75 may be unpleasant for all concerned, but the same number of people jammed together at a party occupying a room of the same size might just make for a great party.

TABLE 10–1 A Person-Situation-Segmentation Matrix for Suntan Lotion

SITUATION	YOUNG CHILDREN		TEENAGERS		ADULT WOMEN		ADULT MEN		BENEFITS/FEATURES
	FAIR SKIN	DARK SKIN	FAIR SKIN	DARK SKIN	FAIR SKIN	DARK SKIN	FAIR SKIN	DARK SKIN	
Beach/boat sunbathing	Combined insect repellent				Summer perfume				a. Product serves as windburn protection b. Formula and container can stand heat c. Container floats and is distinctive (not easily lost)
Home-poolside sunbathing					Combined moisturizer				a. Product has large pump dispenser b. Product won't stain wood, concrete, furnishings
Sunlamp bathing					Combined moisturizer and massage oil				a. Product is designed specifically for type of lamp b. Product has an artificial tanning ingredient
Snow skiing					Winter perfume				a. Product provides special protection from special light rays and weather b. Product has antifreeze formula
Person benefit/features	Special protection a. Protection is critical b. Formula is non-poisonous		Special protection a. Product fits in jean pocket b. Product used by opinion leaders		Special protection		Special protection		
					Female perfume		Male perfume		

Source: Adapted from Peter R. Dickson, "Person-Situation: Segmentation's Missing Link," *Journal of Marketing* 46 (Fall 1982): 62. By permission of American Marketing Association.

In addition, the type of consumers who patronize a store or service can serve as an attribute. We may infer something about a store by examining its customers. For this reason some restaurants require men to wear jackets for dinner (and supply them if they don't), and bouncers of some "hot" nightspots hand-pick patrons they will admit based on whether they have the right "look" for the club. To paraphrase the comedian Groucho Marx, "I would never join a club that would have me for a member."

Temporal Factors

Time is one of consumers' most limiting resources. We talk about "making time" or "spending time," and we are frequently reminded that "time is money." Our perspectives on time can affect many stages of decision making and consumption, such as where needs are stimulated, the amount of information search we undertake and so on. Common sense tells us that more careful information search and deliberation occurs when we have the luxury of taking our time. A meticulous shopper who

MULTICULTURAL DIMENSIONS

To most Western consumers time is a neatly compartmentalized thing: we wake up in the morning, go to school or work, come home, eat dinner, go out, go to sleep ... wake up and do it all over again. This perspective is called *linear separable time* (or Christian time); events proceed in an orderly sequence and different times are well defined ("There's a time and a place for everything"). There is a clear sense of past, present and future. Many activities are performed as the means to some end that will occur later, as when people "save for a rainy day."

This conception of time is not universal. Large cultural differences exist in terms of people's time perspectives.[14] Some cultures run on *procedural time* and ignore the clock completely. People decide to do something "when the time is right." Alternatively, in *circular* or *cyclic* time, people are governed by natural cycles, such as the regular occurrence of the seasons (a perspective found in many Latin cultures). To these consumers the notion of the future does not make sense, because that time will be much like the present. Since the concept of future value does not exist, these consumers often prefer to buy an inferior product that is available now rather than wait for a better one that may be available later. Also, it is hard to convince people who function on circular time to buy insurance or save for the future when they do not endorse this concept.

Groups of university students were asked to draw a picture of time. The resulting sketches in Figure 10–2 on page 328 illustrate some of these different temporal perspectives.[15] The drawing at the top left represents procedural time; there is lack of direction from left to right and little sense of past, present and future. The two drawings in the middle and the one on the top right denote cyclical time, with regular cycles designated by markers. The bottom drawing represents linear time, with a segmented time line moving from left to right in a well-defined sequence.

FIGURE 10–2   •   Drawings of Time

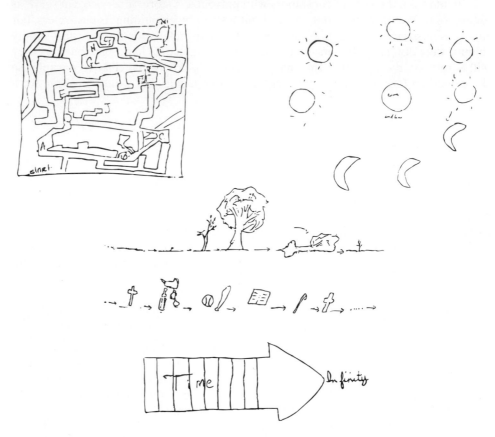

Source: Esther S. Page-Wood, Carol J. Kaufman and Paul M. Lane, "The Art of Time," *Proceedings of the Academy of Marketing Science* (1990).

would normally price an item at three different stores before buying it might be found running through the mall at 5 p.m. on Christmas Eve, furiously scooping up anything left on the shelf that might serve as a last-minute gift.

ECONOMIC TIME

Time is an economic variable; it is a resource that must be divided among activities.[16] Consumers try to maximize satisfaction by allocating time to the appropriate combination of tasks. Of course, people's allocation decisions differ; we all know people who seem to play all the time and others who are workaholics. An individual's priorities determine his or her *timestyle*.[17]

Many consumers believe they are more pressed for time than ever before. This feeling may, however, be due more to perception than to fact. People may just have more options for spending their time and feel pressured by the weight of all these choices. The average working day at the turn of the century was 10 hours (six days a week), and women did 27 hours of housework per week, compared to under 5 hours weekly now. Of course, one reason for this difference is that men are sharing these burdens more.[18]

This sense of time poverty has made consumers very responsive to marketing innovations that allow them to save time. As an executive at Campbell Soup Co.

MARKETING PITFALL

An emphasis on speed resulted in some serious public-relations problems for Domino's Pizza, which guaranteed delivery within 30 minutes. Critics claimed that this policy encouraged reckless driving and backed up this charge with some damaging statistics. In 1989 more than a dozen lawsuits, stemming from death or serious injuries caused by delivery people rushing to make the half-hour deadline, were filed against the company. The employee death rate was 50 per 100 000, a number equal to that suffered in the mining industry.[19] Domino's no longer offers the guarantee.

observed, "Time will be the currency of the 1990s."[20] This priority has created new opportunities for services as diverse as photograph processing, optometry and car repair, where speed of delivery has become an important attribute.[21]

With the increase in time poverty, researchers are also noting a rise in *polychronic activity,* wherein consumers do more than one thing at a time.[22] One area where this type of activity is especially prevalent is eating. Consumers often do not allocate a specific time to dining but instead eat on the run. In a recent poll 64 percent of respondents said they usually do something else while eating. As one food industry executive commented, "We've moved beyond grazing and into gulping."[23]

PSYCHOLOGICAL TIME

The psychological dimension of time, or how it is experienced, is an important factor in *queuing theory,* the mathematical study of waiting lines. A consumer's experience of waiting can radically influence his or her perceptions of service quality. Although we assume that something must be pretty good if we have to wait for it, the negative feelings aroused by long waits can quickly turn customers off.[24]

Marketers have adopted a variety of "tricks" to minimize psychological waiting time. These techniques range from altering customers' perceptions of a line's length to providing distractions that divert attention away from waiting.[25]

- One hotel chain, after receiving excessive complaints about the wait for elevators, installed mirrors near the elevator banks. People's natural tendency to check their appearance reduced complaints, even though the actual waiting time was unchanged.

- Airline passengers often complain of the time they must wait to claim their baggage. In one airport they walked one minute from the plane to the baggage carousel and then waited seven minutes for their luggage. By changing the layout so that the walk to the carousel took six minutes and bags arrived two minutes after that, complaints were almost entirely eliminated.

- McDonald's uses a multiple-line system, where each server deals with a separate line of people. Wendy's uses a multistage system, where the first server takes orders, the second prepares burgers, the third pours drinks, and so on. While Wendy's lines are longer, customers move continuously through stages, so signs of progress can be seen and psychological time is reduced. Similarly, Disneyland often disguises the length of its lines by bending them around corners so that customers are prevented from judging the actual size of the line and anticipated waiting time.

McDonald's' success at attracting its core market of families with kids varies dramatically by time of day. The restaurant chain earns 55 percent of its revenues during lunch-time, and only 20 percent at dinner. The company has tried luring the dinner crowd with test offerings such as pizza, pasta and skinless roast chicken, but these attempts failed. The problem: McDonald's has such a strong lunch and breakfast image that people have trouble viewing it as a dinner place, where they want a more relaxed situation. Although about 500 US outlets continue to sell McPizza, for now the company has sent its dinner plans back to the test kitchen.
Source: Marcia Berss, "Empty Tables," Forbes (December 6, 1993): 232 (2 pp.). Photo courtesy of David Young Wolfe/Photo Edit.

Some products and services are believed to be appropriate for certain times and not for others. One study of fast-food preferences found that consumers were more likely to choose Wendy's over other fast-food outlets for an evening meal when they were not rushed than when they were pressed for time.[26] Also, we may be more receptive to advertising messages at certain times (who wants to hear a beer commercial at seven o'clock in the morning?). There is some evidence that consumers' arousal levels, which affect their style and quality of information processing, are lower in the morning than in the evening.[27]

Antecedent States

A person's mood or physiological condition active at the time of purchase can have a big impact on what is bought and can also affect how products are evaluated.[28] One reason is that behaviour is directed towards certain goal states, as was discussed in Chapter 3. People spend more in the grocery store if they have not eaten for a while, because food is a priority at that time.

A consumer's mood can have a big impact on purchase decisions. For example, stress can impair information-processing and problem-solving abilities.[29] Two dimensions determine if a shopper will react positively or negatively to a store environment. These are *pleasure* and *arousal*. A person can enjoy or not enjoy a situation, and he or she can feel stimulated or not. As Figure 10–3 indicates, different combinations of pleasure and arousal levels result in a variety of emotional states. For example, an arousing situation can be either distressing or exciting depending on whether the context is positive or negative (e.g., a street riot versus a street festival, such as Mardi Gras). Maintaining an "up" feeling in a pleasant context is one factor behind the success of theme parks like Disney World, which try to provide consistent doses of carefully calculated stimulation to patrons.[30]

FIGURE 10–3 • Dimensions of Emotional States

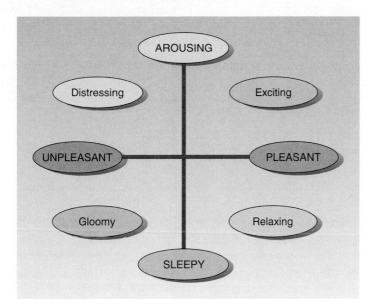

Source: James Russell and Geraldine Pratt, "A Description of the Affective Quality Attributed to Environment," *Journal of Personality and Social Psychology* 38 (August 1980): 311–22. © Copyright 1980 by the American Psychological Association. Adapted by permission.

A specific mood is some combination of these two factors. The state of happiness, for instance, is high in pleasantness and moderate in arousal, while elation would be high on both dimensions.[31] In general, a mood state (either positive or negative) biases judgments of products and services in that direction.[32] Put simply, consumers like things better when they are in a good mood (this explains the popularity of the business lunch!). Moods can be affected by store design, the weather or other factors specific to the consumer. In addition, music and television programming can affect mood, which has important consequences for commercials.[33] When consumers hear happy music or watch happy programs, they have more positive reactions to commercials and products, especially when the marketing appeals are aimed at arousing emotional reactions.[34] When in positive moods, consumers process ads with less elaboration. They pay less attention to specifics of the messages and rely more on heuristic processing (see Chapter 9).[35]

Shopping: A Job or an Adventure?

People often shop even though they do not necessarily intend to buy anything at all; others have to be dragged to a mall. Shopping is a way to acquire needed products and services, but social motives for shopping also are important. Thus, shopping is an activity that can be performed for either utilitarian (functional or tangible) or hedonic (pleasurable or intangible) reasons.[36]

REASONS FOR SHOPPING

These different motives are illustrated by scale items used by researchers to assess people's underlying reasons for shopping. One item that measures hedonic value is the statement "During the trip, I felt the excitement of the hunt." When that type of sentiment is compared to a functionally related statement, such as "I accomplished just what I wanted to on this shopping trip," the contrast between these two dimensions is clear.[37] Hedonic shopping motives can include the following:[38]

- *Social experiences.* The shopping centre or department store has replaced the traditional town square or county fair as a community gathering place. Many people (especially in suburban or rural areas) may have no place else to go to spend their leisure time.

- *Sharing of common interests.* Stores frequently offer specialized goods that allow people with shared interests to communicate.

- *Interpersonal attraction.* Shopping centres are natural places to congregate. The shopping mall has become a central hangout for teenagers. It also represents a controlled, secure environment for other groups, such as the elderly.

- *Instant status.* As every salesperson knows, some people savour the experience of being waited on, even though they may not necessarily buy anything. One men's clothing salesman offered this advice: "… remember their size, remember what you sold them last time. Make them feel important! If you can make people feel important, they are going to come back. Everybody likes to feel important!"[39]

- *The thrill of the chase.* Some people pride themselves on their knowledge of the marketplace. Unlike Mark, they may relish the process of haggling and bargaining, viewing it almost as a sport.

SHOPPING ORIENTATION

shopping orientation a consumer's general attitudes and motivations regarding the act of shopping

Which way is it? Do people hate to shop or love it? It depends. Consumers can be segmented in terms of their **shopping orientation,** or general attitudes about shopping. These orientations may vary depending on the particular product categories and store types considered. Mark hates to shop for a car, but he may love to browse in record stores. Several shopping types have been identified:[40]

- *economic consumer*—a rational, goal-oriented shopper who is primarily interested in maximizing the value of his or her money

- *personalized consumer*—a shopper who tends to form strong attachments to store personnel ("I shop where they know my name")

- *ethical consumer*—a shopper who likes to help out the underdog and will support locally owned stores against big chains

- *apathetic consumer*—one who does not like to shop and sees it as a necessary but unpleasant chore

- *recreational shopper*—a person who views shopping as a fun, social activity (a preferred way to spend leisure time)

THE PURCHASE ENVIRONMENT

The competition for customers is becoming even more intense as non-store alternatives that bring retail services to the home continue to multiply. Popular non-store alternatives include mail-order catalogues, television shopping networks and home shopping parties (like Tupperware parties).

MARKETING OPPORTUNITY

As electronic commerce mushrooms in popularity, marketers are working hard to understand better who is most likely to make purchases on the Web instead of in a store, and how they should be reached. As of now, the "typical" electronic shopper is 32 years old, male, and well educated, though many firms are optimistic that with time other segments will increase their involvement with the Web.

One source of information is the New Media Pathfinder Study conducted by Arbitron, which identified several segments of interactive shoppers.[41] Not surprisingly, younger consumers tended to be most receptive to new shopping technologies. A segment the company labelled "Fast Laners" (about 14 percent of the study population) was the most open to Web buying. This group was primarily made up of teens and people in their twenties. In contrast, another segment called "Bystanders (about 16 percent of the population) was older, and was the least confident about these possibilities and not willing to experiment.

Still, even the most diehard traditional shopper might be persuaded to try electronic shopping if the virtual environment is made sufficiently user-friendly. It's up to the next generation of marketers to figure out how to do this. Good luck!

MARKETING OPPORTUNITY

Finding that many of its female customers are no longer home during the day, Avon has expanded its distribution network to the office, where representatives make presentations during lunch and coffee breaks. Similarly, Tupperware features "rush-hour parties" at the end of the workday, and it now finds that about 20 percent of its sales are made outside of homes. An employee of Mary Kay cosmetics, another company adopting this strategy, offered another explanation for its success: "Working women buy more in the office because they are not looking at the wallpaper that needs replacing. They feel richer away from home."[42]

Retailing as Theatre

With all of these shopping alternatives available, how can a traditional store compete? Shopping malls have tried to gain the loyalty of shoppers by appealing to their social motives, as well as providing access to desired goods. The mall is often a focal point in a community. More than half of all retail purchases (excluding automobiles and gasoline) are made in a mall.[43] Malls are becoming giant entertainment centres, almost to the point where their traditional retail occupants seem like an afterthought. It is now typical to find such features as carousels, miniature golf or batting cages in a suburban mall. As one retailing executive put it, "Malls are becoming the new mini-amusement parks."[44]

The Bill Blass Swimsuit.
Now Available In Offices.

Thanks to Spiegel, the corner office is now a more convenient place to shop than the corner department store. Our Spring Catalog features the latest designs from Ralph Lauren, Gloria Sachs, Adrienne Vittadini, Mikasa, Braun and others. To receive your copy for only $3, simply call (toll-free) 1-800-345-4500 and ask for Catalog 512.

Spiegel

Recognizing that modern women have many time pressures, Spiegel brings retailing to the office.
© Copyright 1991, Spiegel, Inc.

The importance of creating a positive, vibrant and interesting image has led innovative marketers to blur the line between shopping and theatre. Both shopping malls and individual stores must create environments that stimulate people and allow them simultaneously to shop and be entertained.[45]

Retailers are seeking to combine two favourite consumer activities, shopping and eating, by developing elaborate themed environments. According to a recent Roper Starch survey, eating out is the top form of out-of-home entertainment, and innovative firms are scrambling to offer customers a chance to eat, buy and be entertained all at the same time. The Hard Rock Café, first established in London over 25 years ago, now has over 45 restaurants around the world. Planet Hollywood, which first opened in New York in 1991, is crammed full of costumes and props, and the chain now grosses over $200 million (US) a year around the world. Motown Café opened in New York, with part ownership by Diana Ross and Boyz II Men. The Harley-Davidson Café features the roar of a "Hog" engine (a sound recently copyrighted by the company). With profit margins on the merchandise sold at these restaurants as high as 60 percent, it's not surprising that as much as 50 percent of a theme chain's revenues come from T-shirts and other goods rather than T-bones and other foods![46]

Store Image

With so many stores competing for customers, how do consumers pick one over another? Like products, stores may be thought of as having "personalities." Some stores have very clearly defined images (either good or bad). Others tend to blend into the crowd; they may not have anything distinctive about them and may be overlooked for this reason. This personality, or **store image,** is composed of many different factors. Store features, coupled with such consumer characteristics as shopping orientation, help to predict which shopping outlets people will prefer.[47] Some of the important dimensions of a store's profile are location, merchandise suitability, and the knowledge and congeniality of the sales staff.[48]

store image a store's "personality," composed of such attributes as location, merchandise suitability, and the knowledge and congeniality of the sales staff

MULTICULTURAL DIMENSIONS

Retailers including Blockbuster Video, Original Levi's stores, Foot Locker, Toys 'R' Us and The Gap are exporting their version of dynamic retail environments to Europe—with some adaptations. These overseas "invasions" often begin in Britain, since bureaucratic hurdles tend to be lower and weaker unions yield reduced personnel costs. Malls are still rare in most of the European Union, so these chains must usually bid for high-rent sites on city streets. The Gap found that it needed to stock smaller sizes than in the US, and that many of its European customers prefer darker colours.[49]

These features typically work together to create an overall impression. When shoppers think about stores, they may not say, "Well, that place is fairly good in terms of convenience, the salespeople are acceptable, and services are good." They are more likely to say, "That place gives me the creeps," or "I always enjoy shopping there." Consumers evaluate stores in terms of both their specific attributes *and* a global evaluation, or *gestalt* (see Chapter 2).[50] This overall feeling may have more to do with such intangibles as interior design and the types of people one finds in the store than with such aspects as return policies or credit availability. As a result, some stores are likely to consistently be in consumers' evoked sets, while others will never be considered.[51]

ATMOSPHERICS

Because a store's image is now recognized to be a very important aspect of the retailing mix, attention is increasingly paid to **atmospherics,** or the "conscious designing of space and its various dimensions to evoke certain effects in buyers."[52] These dimensions include colours, scents and sounds. For example, stores done in red tend to make people tense, while a blue décor imparts a calmer feeling.[53]

atmospherics the use of space and physical features in store design to evoke certain effects in buyers

A store's atmosphere in turn affects purchasing behaviour. One recent study reported that the extent of pleasure reported by shoppers five minutes after entering a store was predictive of the amount of time spent in the store as well as the level of spending there.[54]

Many elements of store design can be cleverly controlled to attract customers and produce desired effects on consumers. Light colours impart a feeling of spaciousness and serenity, and signs in bright colours create excitement. In one subtle but effective application, fashion designer Norma Kamali replaced fluorescent lights with pink ones in department-store dressing rooms. The light had the effect of flattering the face and banishing wrinkles, making female customers more willing to try on (and buy) the company's bathing suits.[55] Wal-Mart found that sales were higher in areas of a prototype store lit in natural daylight compared to the more typical artificial light.[56] One study found that brighter in-store lighting influenced people to examine and handle more merchandise.[57]

In addition to visual stimuli, all sorts of cues can influence behaviours.[58] Patrons of country-and-western bars drink more when the jukebox music is slower. According to a researcher, "Hard drinkers prefer listening to slower paced, wailing, lonesome, self-pitying music ..."[59] Similarly, music can affect eating habits. A study found that diners who listened to loud, fast music ate more food. In contrast, those who listened to Mozart or Brahms ate less and more slowly. The researchers concluded that diners who choose soothing music at mealtimes can increase weight loss by at least five pounds (2.3 kg) a month![60]

MARKETING OPPORTUNITY

Shop the store, buy the soundtrack. Growing recognition of the important role played by a store or restaurant's audio environment has created a new niche, as some companies are now selling musical collections tailored to different activities. These include RCA Victor's "Classical Music for Home Improvements" and Sony Classics' "Cyber Classics," which is billed as music specifically for computer hackers to listen to while programming! In contrast, Sony's "Extreme Classics" package for bungee jumpers is claimed to be the "loudest and most dangerous music ever written." While a standard hit classical disc might sell 25 000 copies, PolyGram's Philips label has sold more than 500 000 units of its "Set Your Life to Music" series, which includes "Mozart in the Morning" and "Baroque at Bathtime." Rising Star Records shipped 10 000 copies of "Classical Erotica" in three months. Both Ralph Lauren and Victoria's Secret are packaging the music played in store outlets, and the bakery chain Au Bon Pain started selling its background music on a CD.[61] Similar spin-offs are in the works by Pottery Barn and Starbucks, which licensed the Blue Note label from Capitol Records for this purpose.[62]

In-Store Decision Making

Despite all their efforts to "presell" consumers through advertising, marketers increasingly are recognizing the significant degree to which many purchases are influenced by the store environment. It has been estimated that about two out of every three supermarket purchases are decided in the aisles. The proportion of unplanned purchases is even higher for some product categories. It is estimated that 85 percent of candy and gum, almost 70 percent of cosmetics, and 75 percent of oral-hygiene purchases are unplanned.[63]

SPONTANEOUS SHOPPING

When a shopper is prompted to buy something while in the store, one of two different processes may be at work. *Unplanned buying* may occur when a person is unfamiliar with a store's layout is under some time pressure. Or a person may be reminded to buy something by seeing it on a store shelf. About one-third of unplanned buying has been attributed to the recognition of new needs while within the store.[64]

impulse buying a process that occurs when the consumer experiences a sudden urge to purchase an item that he or she cannot resist

In contrast, **impulse buying** occurs when the person experiences a sudden urge that he or she cannot resist. The tendency to buy spontaneously is most likely to result in a purchase when the consumer believes that acting on impulse is appropriate, such as when purchasing a gift for a sick friend or picking up the tab for a meal.[65] To cater to these urges, so-called *impulse items,* such as candy and gum, are conveniently placed near the checkout. Similarly, many supermarkets have installed wider aisles to encourage browsing, and the widest tend to contain products with the highest margin. Items with low mark-up that are purchased regularly tend to be stacked high in narrower aisles, to allow shoppers to speed through.[66]

A more recent high-tech tool has been added to encourage impulse buying. A device called The Portable Shopper is a personal scanning gun that allows customers

FIGURE 10–4 • One Consumer's Image of an Impulse Buyer

DRAW-A-PICTURE

1. Think about your image of what kind of person an impulse buyer is. In the space provided below, draw a picture of your image of a typical impulse buyer who is about to make an impulse purchase. Be creative and don't worry about your artistic skills! If you feel that some features of your drawing are unclear, don't hesitate to identify them with a written label.

2. After you have completed your drawing, imagine what is going through your character's mind as he or she is about to make his or her impulse purchase. Then write down your shopper's thoughts in a speech balloon (like you might see 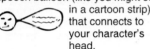 in a cartoon strip) that connects to your character's head.

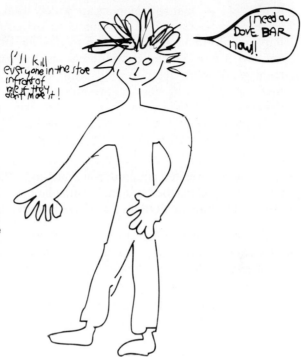

Source: Dennis Rook, "Is Impulse Buying (Yet) a Useful Marketing Concept?" (unpublished manuscript, University of Southern California, Los Angeles, 1990): Fig. 7-A.

to ring up their own purchases as they shop. The gun initially was developed for Albert Hejin, Netherlands' largest grocery chain, to move customers through the store more quickly. It's now in use in over 150 grocery chains worldwide.[67]

Shoppers can be categorized in terms of how much advance planning they do. *Planners* tend to know what products and specific brands they will buy beforehand; *partial planners* know they need certain products but do not decide on specific brands until they are in the store; and *impulse purchasers* do no advance planning whatsoever.[68] Figure 10–4 was drawn by a consumer who was participating in a study on consumers' shopping experiences and who was asked to sketch a typical impulse purchaser.

POINT-OF-PURCHASE STIMULI

Because so much decision making apparently occurs while the shopper is in the purchasing environment, retailers are beginning to pay more attention to the amount of information in their stores, as well as to the way it is presented. It has been estimated that impulse purchases increase by 10 percent when appropriate displays are used. A **point-of-purchase stimulus (POP)** can be an elaborate product display or demonstration, a coupon-dispensing machine, or someone giving out free samples of a new cookie in the grocery aisle.

In-store displays are yet another commonly used device to attract attention in the store environment. While most displays consist of simple racks that dispense the

point-of-purchase stimuli (POP) the promotional materials that are deployed in stores or other outlets to influence consumers' decisions at the time products are purchased

MARKETING PITFALL

Cents-off coupons are widely used by manufacturers and retailers to induce consumers to switch brands. While coupons are an important form of sales promotion, evidence regarding their effectiveness at luring *new* customers is mixed. Households that already use the brand offering a coupon are more likely to redeem the coupon, and most customers revert to their original brand after the promotion has expired. As a result, the company that hopes to attract brand switchers by luring them with coupon offers may instead find itself "preaching to the converted."[69]

product and/or related coupons, some highlight the value of regarding retailing as theatre by supplying the "audience" with elaborate performances and scenery. Some of the more dramatic POP displays have included the following:[70]

- *Timex.* A still-ticking watch sits in the bottom of a filled aquarium.
- *Kellogg's Corn Flakes.* A button with a picture of Cornelius the Rooster is placed within the reach of children near the Corn Flakes display. When a child presses the button, he or she hears the rooster "cock-a-doodle-do."
- *Elizabeth Arden.* The company introduced "Elizabeth," a computer and video makeover system, which allows customers to test out their images with different shades of make-up without having actually to apply the products first.
- *Tower Records.* A music sampler allows customers to hear records before buying them and to custom-design their own recordings by mixing and matching singles from assorted artists.
- *Trifari.* This company offers paper "punch-out" versions of its jewellery so that customers can try on the pieces at home.
- *Charmin.* Building on the familiar "Please don't squeeze the Charmin" theme, the company deploys the Charmin Squeeze Squad. Employees hide behind stacks of the toilet tissue and jump out and blow horns at any "squeezers" they catch in the aisles.

Advertisers are also being more aggressive about hitting consumers with their messages, wherever they may be. *Place-based media* is a growing, specialized approach featuring media that target consumers based on locations in which messages are delivered. These places can be anything from airports, doctors' offices or college campuses to health clubs. Turner Broadcasting System has begun such ventures as Checkout Channel for grocery stores and Airport Channel, and it has even tested McDTV for McDonald's restaurants.[71] Even MTV is getting into the act: its new Music Report, to be shown in record stores, is a two-hour "video capsule" featuring video spots and ads for music retailers and corporate sponsors. As an MTV executive observed, "They're already out there at the retail environment. They're ready to spend money."[72]

A company called Privy Promotions is selling ad space on restroom walls in stadiums. For $2000 the company will mount a framed ad for a year in a restroom stall, above a sink or "... wherever it looks nice and appropriate," according to Privy's president. He claims, "... it's a decided opportunity for an advertiser to reach a captive audience ..."[73]

Much of the growth in point-of-purchase activity has been in new electronic technologies.[74] Some stores feature talking posters that contain human-body sensors and that speak up when a shopper approaches. The Point-of-Purchase Radio Corporation offers in-store radio networks that are now used by about 60 grocery chains.[75] Some new shopping carts have a small screen, keyed to the specific areas of the store through which the cart is wheeled, that displays advertising.[76] In-store video displays allow advertisers to reinforce major media campaigns at the point of purchase.[77]

Some of the most interesting innovations can be found in state-of-the-art vending machines, which now dispense everything from Hormel's microwaveable chili and beef stew and Ore-Ida french fries to software. French consumers can purchase Levi's jeans from a machine called "Libre Service," which offers the pants in 10 different sizes. The customer uses a seatbelt to find his or her size, and the jeans sell for about $10 less than the same versions sold in more conventional stores. Because of their frenetic lifestyles the Japanese are particularly avid users of vending machines. These machines dispense virtually all of life's necessities, plus many luxuries people in other countries would not consider obtaining from a machine. The list includes jewellery, fresh flowers, frozen beef, pornography, business cards, underwear—and even the names of possible dates.[78]

The Salesperson

One of the most important in-store factors is the salesperson, who attempts to influence the buying behaviour of the customer.[79] This influence can be understood in terms of **exchange theory**, which stresses that every interaction involves an exchange of value; each participant gives something to the other and hopes to receive something in return.[80]

exchange theory the perspective that every interaction involves an exchange of value

RESOURCE EXCHANGE

What "value" does the customer look for in a sales interaction? There are a variety of resources a salesperson might offer. He or she might offer expertise about the product to make the shopper's choice easier. Alternatively, the customer may be reassured because the salesperson is an admired or likeable person whose tastes are similar to her own and who is therefore seen as someone to be trusted.[81] Mark's car purchase was strongly influenced by the age and sex of Melanie, the salesperson with

MARKETING PITFALL

Not exactly an ideal test drive: A woman recently sued a car dealer in Iowa, claiming that a salesman persuaded her to climb into the trunk of a Chrysler Concorde to check out its spaciousness. He then slammed the trunk shut and bounced the car several times, apparently to the delight of his co-workers. This bizarre act apparently came about because the manager offered a prize of $100 to the salesperson who could get a customer to climb in. At last report this persuasive man is now selling vacuum cleaners door to door.[82]

whom he negotiated. In fact, a long stream of research attests to the impact of a salesperson's appearance on sales effectiveness. In sales, as in much of life, attractive people appear to hold the upper hand.[83]

THE SALES INTERACTION

A buyer/seller situation is like many other dyadic encounters (those within two-person groups): it is a relationship where some agreement must be reached about the roles of each participant. In other words, a process of *identity negotiation* occurs.[84] For example, if Melanie immediately establishes herself as an all-knowing expert (and if Mark accepts this position), she is likely to have more influence over him through the course of the relationship. Some of the factors that help to determine a salesperson's role (and relative effectiveness) are his or her age, appearance, educational level and motivation to sell.[85]

In addition, more effective salespersons usually know their customers' traits and preferences better than do ineffective salespersons, since this knowledge allows them to adapt their approach to meet the needs of specific customers.[86] The ability to be adaptable is especially vital when customers and salespeople differ in terms of their *interaction styles*.[87] Consumers, for example, vary in the degree of assertiveness they bring to interactions. At one extreme, non-assertive people believe that complaining is not socially acceptable and may be intimidated in sales situations. Assertive people are more likely to stand up for themselves in firm but non-threatening ways, while aggressives may resort to rudeness and threats if they do not get their way.[88]

POSTPURCHASE SATISFACTION

consumer satisfaction/dissatisfaction (CS/D) the overall attitude a person has about a product after it has been purchased

Consumer satisfaction/dissatisfaction (CS/D) is determined by the overall feelings, or attitude, a person has about a product after it has been purchased. Consumers are engaged in a constant process of evaluating the things they buy as these products are integrated into their daily consumption activities.[89] And customer satisfaction has a real impact on the bottom line: a recent study conducted among a large sample of Swedish consumers found that product quality affects customer satisfaction, which in turn results in increased profitability among firms who provide quality products.[90] Quality is more than a marketing "buzzword."

Perceptions of Product Quality

Just what do consumers look for in products? That's easy: they want quality and value. Especially because of foreign competition, claims of product quality have become strategically crucial to maintaining a competitive advantage.[91] Consumers use a number of cues to infer quality, including brand name, price, and even their own estimates of how much money has been put into a new product's advertising campaign.[92] These cues and others, such as product warranties and follow-up letters from the company, are often used by consumers to relieve perceived risk and assure themselves that they have made smart purchase decisions.[93]

However, the weighting assigned to different cues is changing as consumers' priorities are being transformed in the 1990s. Many people are part of a trend that the

FEW THINGS IN LIFE ARE AS COMMITTED
TO YOUR SATISFACTION AS WE ARE.

This ad for Chrysler emphasizes the importance
many marketers place on earning total customer
satisfaction in the 1990s.
Newsweek 5/2/94. Photo courtesy of Chrysler Corporation.

Grey Advertising agency has called "downshifting." They are reining in spending
and trying to maximize the value of every dollar. The net result is that price has
become a bigger concern; consumers are no longer willing to pay a premium for a
brand name if they don't see a tangible difference between a well-known item and
other product alternatives.

A study done by Grey found that the definition of value has changed from "best
in class" to "best in budget range." Two factors are most likely at the heart of this
trend: 1) a sluggish economy in the early 1990s dampened people's expectations that
their financial well-being would continue to improve; and 2) there has been an
increase in the number of consumers who view many products, such as cereal, diapers or cigarettes, as commodities with very few differences among brands.[94]

While everyone wants quality, it is not clear exactly what quality means. Certainly, many manufacturers claim to provide it. The Ford Motor Company ad shown
here emphasizes "Quality is job 1." Similar claims that have been made at one time
or another by car manufacturers include the following:[95]

Lincoln-Mercury: "... the highest quality cars of any major American car company"

Chrysler: "... quality engineered to be the best"

GMC trucks: "... quality built yet economical"

Oldsmobile: "... fulfilling the quality needs of American drivers"

Audi: "... quality backed by our outstanding new warranty"

Quality Is What We Expect It to Be

In the book *Zen and the Art of Motorcycle Maintenance,* a cult hero of college students in an earlier generation literally went crazy trying to figure out the meaning of
quality.[96] Marketers appear to use the word *quality* as a catch-all for "good."
Because of its wide and imprecise usage, the attribute of "quality" threatens to
become a meaningless claim. If everyone has it, what good is it?

This ad for Ford relies on a common claim about "quality."
Courtesy of Ford Motor Company.

expectancy disconfirmation model the perspective that consumers form beliefs about product performance based upon prior experience with the product and/or communications about the product that imply a certain level of quality; their actual satisfaction depends on the degree to which performance is consistent with these expectations

To muddy the waters a bit more, satisfaction or dissatisfaction is more than a reaction to the actual performance quality of a product or service; it is influenced by prior expectations regarding the level of quality. According to the **expectancy disconfirmation model**, consumers form beliefs about product performance based upon prior experience with the product and/or upon communications about the product that imply a certain level of quality.[97] When something performs the way we thought it would, we may not think much about it. If, on the other hand, something fails to live up to expectations, a negative affect may result. And if performance happens to exceed our expectations, we are satisfied and pleased.

To understand this perspective, think about different types of restaurants. People expect to be provided with sparkling clear glassware at fancy restaurants, and they might become upset if they discover grimy glasses. On the other hand, we may not be surprised to find fingerprints on our beer mugs at a local greasy spoon; we may even shrug it off because it contributes to the "charm" of the place. An important lesson emerges for marketers from this perspective: don't overpromise.[98]

This perspective underscores the importance of *managing expectations*. Customer dissatisfaction usually is due to expectations that exceed the company's ability to deliver. Figure 10–5 illustrates the alternative strategies a firm can choose in these situations. When confronted with unrealistic expectations about what it can do, the firm can either accommodate these demands by improving the range or quality of products it offers, alter the expectations, or perhaps even choose to abandon the customer if it is not feasible to meet his or her needs.[99] Expectations are altered, for example, when waiters tell patrons in advance that the portion size they have ordered will not be very big, or when new-car buyers are warned of strange smells they will experience during the break-in period. A firm also can *underpromise*, as when Xerox inflates the time it will take for a service rep to visit.

The power of quality claims is most evident when a company's product fails in some way. Here, consumers' expectations are dashed, and dissatisfaction results. In these situations marketers immediately take steps to reassure customers. When the company confronts the problem truthfully, consumers often are willing to forgive

FIGURE 10–5 • Managing Expectations

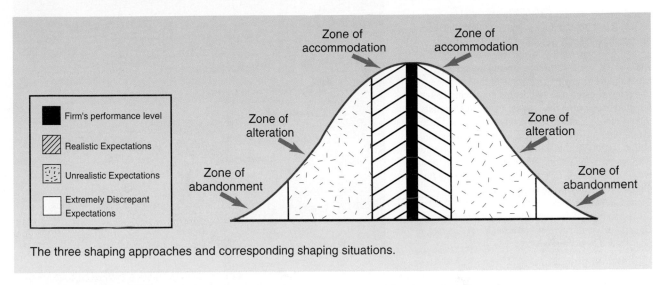

The three shaping approaches and corresponding shaping situations.

Source: Jagdish N. Sheth and Banwari Mittal, *Journal of Market Focused Management* 1 (1996): 140, fig. 2.

and forget, as was the case for Tylenol (product tampering), Chrysler (disconnecting odometers on executives' cars and reselling them as new) or Perrier (traces of benzene found in the water). When the company appears to be dragging its heels or covering up, on the other hand, consumer resentment will grow, as occurred during Union Carbide's chemical disaster in India and with Exxon following the massive Alaskan oil spill caused by its tanker *Exxon Valdez*.

Acting on Dissatisfaction

If a person is not happy with a product or service, what can be done? Essentially, a consumer has three different courses of action that can be taken (note that more than one can be taken):[100]

1. *Voice response.* The consumer can appeal directly to the retailer for redress (e.g., a refund).

2. *Private response.* The consumer can express dissatisfaction about the store or product to friends and/or can boycott the store. As will be discussed in Chapter 11, negative word of mouth (WOM) can be very damaging to a store's reputation.

3. *Third-party response.* The consumer can take legal action against the merchant, register a complaint with the Better Business Bureau or write a letter to a newspaper.

In one study, business majors wrote complaint letters to companies. Those who were sent a free sample in response indicated their image of the company significantly improved, while those who received only a letter of apology also changed their evaluations of the company. However, students who got no response reported an even more negative image than before, indicating that some form of response is better than none.[101]

In this quality-conscious era it is essential for companies to stand behind their products—even if it means destroying allegedly defective ones. That is exactly what the Nissan Motor Co. did with over 22 000 of its 1987–90 C22 vans. After announcing three safety recalls to fix problems with some of the vans, the company decided it would be easier in some cases to buy them back from their owners and simply crush them. Although some owners were not thrilled with the arrangement, others appreciated the company's attention to quality. As one van owner observed, "Anybody who would ... invest that kind of money to keep good will, they've got me forever." That is exactly the type of positive reaction Nissan is counting on.
Quoted in Neal Templin, "Nissan Recalls—and Destroys—Some Minivans," Wall Street Journal (December 9, 1993): B1 (2 pp.). Picture courtesy of Nissan North America, Inc. Reproduced by permission.

A number of factors influence which route is eventually taken. The consumer may, in general, be an assertive person or a meek one. Action is more likely to be taken for expensive products, such as household durables, cars and clothing, than for inexpensive products.[102] Also, if the consumer does not believe that the store will respond well to a complaint, the person will be more likely to simply switch brands than to fight.[103] Ironically, marketers should actually *encourage* consumers to complain to them: people are more likely to spread the word to their friends about unresolved negative experiences than they are to boast about positive occurrences.[104]

PRODUCT DISPOSAL

Because people often do form strong attachments to products, the decision to dispose of something may be a painful one. One function performed by possessions is to serve as anchors for our identities: our past lives on in our things.[105] This attachment is exemplified by the Japanese, who ritually "retire" worn-out sewing needles, chopsticks and computer chips by burning them as thanks for good service.[106]

Although some people have more trouble than others in discarding things, even a "pack rat" does not keep everything. Consumers must often dispose of things, either because they have fulfilled their designated functions or possibly because they no longer fit with consumers' views of themselves. Concern about the environment coupled with a need for convenience has made ease of product disposal a key attribute in categories from razors to diapers.

Disposal Options

When a consumer decides that a product is no longer of use, several choices are available. The person can either 1) keep the item, 2) temporarily dispose of it, or 3) permanently dispose of it. In many cases a new product is acquired even though the old one still functions. Some reasons for this replacement include a desire for

FIGURE 10–6 • Consumers' Disposal Options

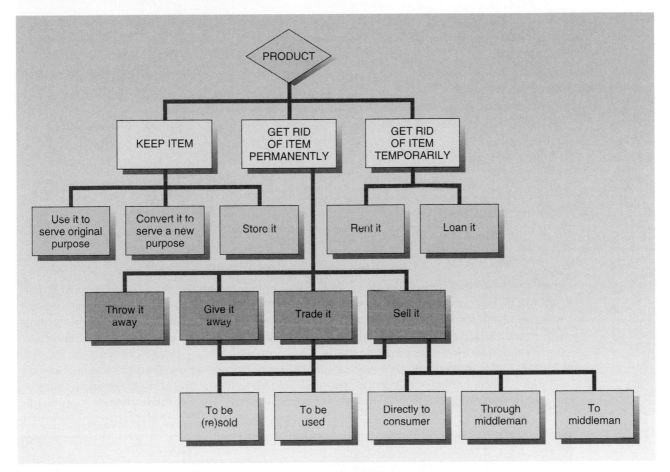

Source: Jacob Jacoby, Carol K. Berning and Thomas F. Dietvorst, "What About Disposition?" *Journal of Marketing* 41 (April 1977): 23. By permission of American Marketing Association.

new features, a change in the person's environment (e.g., a refrigerator is the wrong colour for a freshly painted kitchen), or a change in the person's role or self-image.[107] Figure 10–6 provides an overview of consumers' disposal options.

The issue of product disposal is doubly vital because of its enormous public policy implications. We live in a throw-away society, which creates problems for the environment and also results in a great deal of unfortunate waste. Training consumers to recycle has become a priority in many countries. Japan recycles about 40 percent of its garbage, and this relatively high rate of compliance is partly due to the social value the Japanese place on recycling. Citizens are encouraged by garbage trucks that periodically rumble through the streets playing classical music or children's songs.[108]

Companies continue to search for ways to use resources more efficiently, often at the prompting of activist consumer groups. McDonald's restaurants bowed to pressure by eliminating the use of styrofoam packages, and its outlets in Europe are experimenting with edible breakfast platters made of maize.[109]

A recent study examined the relevant goals consumers have in recycling. It used a means-end chain analysis of the type described in Chapter 4 to identify how spe-

This Dutch Volkswagen ad focuses on recycling. The copy says, "And when you've had enough of it, we'll clear it away nicely."
DDB Needham Worldwide, Amsterdam Lurzer's Achiv *1994. Photo courtesy of Volkswagen and DDB Needham Worldwide BV Amsterdam.*

cific instrumental goals are linked to more abstract terminal values. The most important lower-order goals identified were "avoid filling up landfills," "reduce waste," "reuse materials" and "save the environment." These were linked to the terminal values of "promote health/avoid sickness," "achieve life-sustaining ends" and "provide for future generations."

Another study reported that the perceived effort involved in recycling was the best predictor of whether people would go to the trouble; this pragmatic dimension outweighed general attitudes towards recycling and the environment in predicting

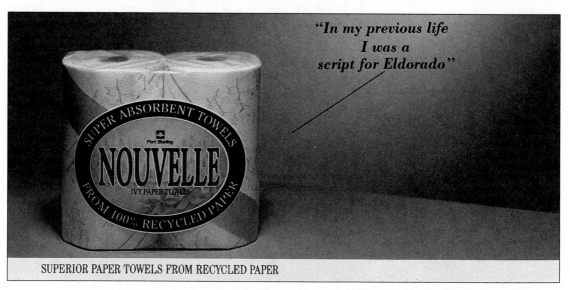

This British ad for paper towels takes a humorous route to emphasize that the paper towels are made from recycled paper.
Lurzer's Archiv, *1994, 91. Photo courtesy of BDH, Manchester, UK. Creative Team: Wayne Hanson, Graham Daldry.*

MARKETING OPPORTUNITY

Some enterprising entrepreneurs have found profitable ways to encourage recycling by creating fashion items out of recycled materials. Two young jewellery designers in New York created a fad by making necklaces out of old bottle-caps. They even pay homeless people to collect the caps. A Pittsburgh-based company called Little Earth Productions Incorporated makes all of its products from recycled materials. They sell backpacks decorated with old licence-plates, a shoulder bag made from rubber and hub-caps, and purses crafted from discarded tuna cans. In addition to selling their unusual items in American boutiques, the company has started to expand overseas. It discovered that Japanese consumers liked the concept but felt the bags were too bulky, so a line of smaller articles was designed for the Japanese market.[110]

intention to recycle.[111] By applying such techniques to study recycling and other product disposal behaviours, social marketers will find it easier to design advertising copy and other messages that tap into the underlying values that will motivate people to increase environmentally responsible behaviour.[112]

Lateral Cycling: Junk versus "Junque"

Interesting consumer processes occur during **lateral cycling,** where already purchased objects are sold to others or exchanged. Many purchases are second-hand rather than new. The reuse of other people's things is so important in our throwaway society because, as one researcher put it, "... there is no longer an 'away' to throw things to."[113]

Flea markets, garage sales, classified advertisements, bartering for services, hand-me-downs and the black market all represent important alternative marketing systems that operate in addition to the formal marketplace. For example, the number of used-merchandise retail establishments has grown at about 10 times the rate of other stores.[114] While traditional marketers have not paid much attention to used-product sellers, factors such as concern about the environment, demands for quality, and cost and fashion consciousness are conspiring to make these "secondary" markets more important.[115]

Interest in antiques, period accessories and specialty magazines catering to this niche is increasing. Other growth areas include student markets for used computers and textbooks, and ski swaps, where millions of dollars' worth of used ski equipment is exchanged.

A new generation of second-hand-store owners is developing markets for everything from used office equipment to cast-off kitchen sinks. Many are non-profit ventures started with government funding. These efforts remind us that recycling is actually the last step in the familiar mantra of the environmental movement: reduce, reuse, recycle. Only if no use is found for an item should it be shredded and made into something else.[116]

lateral cycling a process where already-purchased objects are sold to others or exchanged for other items

CHAPTER SUMMARY

- The act of purchase can be affected by many factors. These include the consumer's antecedent state (his/her mood, time pressure or disposition towards shopping). Time is an important resource that often determines how much effort and search will go into a decision. Mood can be affected by the degree of pleasure and arousal present in a store environment.

- The usage context of a product can be a basis for segmentation. Consumers look for different product attributes depending upon the uses to which they intend to put their purchases. The presence or absence of other people—and the types of people they are—can also affect a consumer's decisions.

- The shopping experience is a pivotal part of the purchase decision. In many cases retailing is like theatre; that is, the consumer's evaluation of stores and products may depend upon the type of "performance" he or she witnesses. This evaluation can be influenced by the actors (salespeople), the setting (the store environment) and props (store displays). A store image, like a brand personality, is determined by a number of factors, such as perceived convenience, sophistication, knowledgeability of salespeople and so on. With increasing competition from non-store alternatives, the creation of a positive shopping experience has never been more important.

- Since many purchase decisions are not made until the time the consumer is actually in the store, point-of-purchase (POP) stimuli are very important sales tools. These include product samples, elaborate package displays, place-based media and in-store promotional materials, such as "shelf talkers." POP stimuli are particularly useful in stimulating impulse buying, where a consumer yields to a sudden urge for a product.

- The consumer's encounter with a salesperson is a complex and important process. The outcome can be affected by such factors as the salesperson's similarity to the customer and his or her perceived credibility.

- Consumer satisfaction is determined by the person's overall feeling towards the product after purchase. Many factors influence perceptions of product quality, including price, brand name and product performance. Satisfaction is often determined by the degree to which a product's performance is consistent with the consumer's prior expectations of how well it will function.

- Product disposal is an increasingly important problem. Recycling is one option that will continue to be stressed as consumers' environmental awareness grows. Products may also be introduced by consumers into secondary markets during a process of lateral cycling, which occurs when objects are bought and sold second-hand, fenced or bartered.

KEY TERMS

Atmospherics p. 335

Consumer satisfaction/dissatisfaction (CS/D) p. 340

Exchange theory p. 339

Expectancy disconfirmation model p. 342

Impulse buying p. 336

Lateral cycling p. 347

Point-of-purchase stimuli (POP) p. 337

Shopping orientation p. 332

Store image p. 334

1. Discuss some of the motivations for shopping as described in the chapter. How might a retailer adjust his or her strategy to accommodate these motivations?

2. What are some positive and negative aspects of requiring employees who interact with customers to wear some kind of uniform, or of mandating a dress code in the office?

3. Think about exceptionally good and bad salespeople you have encountered in the past. What qualities seem to differentiate them?

4. List the five stages of a long-term service relationship. How can a practitioner of relationship marketing incorporate each stage into his or her strategy?

5. Discuss the concept of "timestyle." Based on your own experiences, how might consumers be segmented in terms of their timestyles?

6. Compare and contrast different cultures' conceptions of time. What are some implications for marketing strategy within each of these frameworks?

7. The movement away from a "disposable consumer society" towards one that emphasizes creative recycling creates many opportunities for marketers. Can you identify some?

8. Conduct naturalistic observation at a local mall. Sit in a central location and observe the activities of mall employees and patrons. Keep a log of the non-retailing activity you observe (special performances, exhibits, socializing, etc.). Does this activity enhance or detract from business conducted at the mall?

9. Select three competing clothing stores in your area and conduct a store-image study for them. Ask a group of consumers to rate each store on a set of attributes, and plot these ratings on the same graph. Based on your findings, are there any areas of competitive advantage or disadvantage you could bring to the attention of store management?

10. Using Table 10–1 as a model, construct a person/situation segmentation matrix for a brand of perfume.

11. What applications of queuing theory can you find employed among local services? Interview consumers who are waiting in lines to determine how (if at all) this experience affects their satisfaction with the service.

CBC VIDEO VIGNETTES

Concepts at Work for Getting Satisfaction in the Skies

Canadians fly millions of miles each year. Most flights depart and arrive on time, and passengers usually end up with luggage in hand. However, delays and lost luggage can be particularly harrowing experiences, leaving consumers feeling disillusioned and helpless. One of the problems is that even fairly frequent fliers do not know what to do when things go wrong. Dissatisfaction spells unhappy customers and poor word of mouth for airlines.

Customers need to learn how to act on their dissatisfaction with airline service. They need to ask what they are entitled to when flights are delayed or when their luggage does not arrive with them. The airlines in Canada have carefully worked out compensation schemes that are generous enough to create happy landings for even the most disgruntled travellers. The challenge for customers is to learn how to be proactive in looking after their rights.

QUESTIONS

1. What are the main sources of dissatisfaction with air travel?

2. How do passengers usually deal with this dissatisfaction? Why?

3. What might passengers be entitled to when flights are delayed and luggage is lost?

4. What are the principles behind achieving customer satisfaction when things go wrong with air travel?

Video Resource: "Air Travel," *Marketplace* #14 (January 23, 1996).

NOTES

1. Keith Naughton, "Revolution in the Showroom," *Business Week* (February 19, 1996): 70 (8 pp.).

2. Michelle Krebs, "Moving Out the Cars with a 'No-Dicker Sticker,'" *New York Times* (October 11, 1992): F12; "No-dicker Car Dealers Gaining Popularity," *Marketing News* (September 28, 1992): 19.

3. Paul Gray, "Nice Guys Finish First?" *Time* (July 25, 1994): 48–49.

4. Pradeep Kakkar and Richard J. Lutz, "Situational Influence on Consumer Behavior: A Review," in *Perspectives in Consumer Behavior*, 3rd ed., eds. Harold H. Kassarjian and Thomas S. Robertson (Glenview, IL: Scott, Foresman and Company, 1981), pp. 204–14.

5. Shelly Reese, "Every Product Has a Season," *American Demographics* (December 1995): 17–18.

6. Paula Mergenhagen, "How 'got milk?' Got Sales," *Marketing Tools* (September 1996): 4 (3 pp.).

7. Carolyn Turner Schenk and Rebecca H. Holman, "A Sociological Approach to Brand Choice: The Concept of Situational Self-Image," in *Advances in Consumer Research 7*, ed. Jerry C. Olson (Ann Arbor, MI: Association for Consumer Research, 1980), pp. 610–14.

8. Russell W. Belk, "An Exploratory Assessment of Situational Effects in Buyer Behavior," *Journal of Marketing Research* 11 (May 1974): 156–63; U.N. Umesh and Joseph A. Cote, "Influence of Situational Variables on Brand-Choice Models," *Journal of Business Research* 16, 2 (1988): 91–99. See also J. Wesley Hutchinson and Joseph W. Alba, "Ignoring Irrelevant Information: Situational Determinants of Consumer Learning," *Journal of Consumer Research* 18 (December 1991): 325–45.

9. Laura Bird, "Grey Poupon Tones Down Tony Image," *Wall Street Journal* (July 22, 1994): B2.

10. Peter J. Burke and Stephen L. Franzoi, "Studying Situations and Identities Using Experimental Sampling Methodology," *American Sociological Review* 53 (August 1988): 559–68; Douglas M. Stayman and Rohit Deshpande, "Situational Ethnicity and Consumer Behavior," *Journal of Consumer Research* 16 (December 1989): 361–71.

11. Peter R. Dickson, "Person-Situation: Segmentation's Missing Link," *Journal of Marketing* 46 (Fall 1982): 56–64.

12. Alan R. Hirsch, "Effects of Ambient Odors on Slot-Machine Usage in a Las Vegas Casino," *Psychology & Marketing* 12, 7 (October 1995): 585–94.

13. Daniel Stokols, "On the Distinction Between Density and Crowding: Some Implications for Future Research," *Psychological Review* 79 (1972): 275–77.

14. Robert J. Graham, "The Role of Perception of Time in Consumer Research," *Journal of Consumer Research* 7 (March 1981): 335–42.

15. Esther S. Page-Wood, Carol J. Kaufman and Paul M. Lane, "The Art of Time," in *Proceedings of the Academy of Marketing Science* (1990).

16. Carol Felker Kaufman, Paul M. Lane and Jay D. Lindquist, "Exploring More Than 24 Hours a Day: A Preliminary Investigation of Polychronic Time Use," *Journal of Consumer Research* 18 (December 1991): 392–401.

17. Laurence P. Feldman and Jacob Hornik, "The Use of Time: An Integrated Conceptual Model," *Journal of Consumer Research* 7 (March 1981): 407–19. See also Michelle M. Bergadaa, "The Role of Time in the Action of the Consumer," *Journal of Consumer Research* 17 (December 1990): 289–302.

18. Robert J. Samuelson, "Rediscovering the Rat Race," *Newsweek* (May 15, 1989): 57.

19. Eric N. Berg, "Fight on Quick Pizza Delivery Grows," *New York Times* (August 29, 1989): D6.

20. Quoted in Judann Dagnoli, "Time—The Currency of the 90s," *Advertising Age* (November 13, 1989): S2.

21. Leonard L. Berry, "Market to the Perception," *American Demographics* (February 1990): 32.

22. Kaufman, Lane and Lindquist, "Exploring More Than 24 Hours a Day."

23. Quoted in Kleiman, "Fast Food? It Just Isn't Fast Enough Anymore," *New York Times* (December 6, 1989): A1.

24. Cf. Shirley Taylor, "Waiting for Service: The Relationship Between Delays and Evaluations of Service," *Journal of Marketing* 58 (April 1994): 56–69.

25. David H. Maister, "The Psychology of Waiting Lines," in *The Service Encounter: Managing Employee/Customer Interaction in Service Businesses,* eds. John A. Czepiel, Michael R. Solomon and Carol F. Surprenant (Lexington, MA: Lexington Books, 1985), pp. 113–24.

26. Kenneth E. Miller and James L. Ginter, "An Investigation of Situational Variation in Brand Choice Behavior and Attitude," *Journal of Marketing Research* 16 (February 1979): 111–23.

27. Jacob Hornik, "Diurnal Variation in Consumer Response," *Journal of Consumer Research* 14 (March 1988): 588–91.

28. Laurette Dube and Bernd H. Schmitt, "The Processing of Emotional and Cognitive Aspects of Product Usage in Satisfaction Judgments," in *Advances in Consumer Research 18,* eds. Rebecca H. Holman and Michael R. Solomon (Provo, UT: Association for Consumer Research, 1991), pp. 52–56; Lalita A. Manrai and Meryl P. Gardner, "The Influence of Affect on Attributions for Product Failure," in *Advances in Consumer Research 18,* pp. 249–54.

29. Kevin G. Celuch and Linda S. Showers, "It's Time To Stress *Stress*: The Stress-Purchase/Consumption Relationship," in *Advances in Consumer Research 18,* pp. 284–89; Lawrence R. Lepisto, J. Kathleen Stuenkel and Linda K. Anglin, "Stress: An Ignored Situational Influence," in *Advances in Consumer Research 18,* pp. 296–302.

30. See Eben Shapiro, "Need a Little Fantasy? A Bevy of New Companies Can Help," *New York Times* (March 10, 1991): F4.

31. John D. Mayer and Yvonne N. Gaschke, "The Experience and Meta-Experience of Mood," *Journal of Personality and Social Psychology* 55 (July 1988): 102–11.

32. Meryl Paula Gardner, "Mood States and Consumer Behavior: A Critical Review," *Journal of Consumer Research* 12 (December 1985): 281–300; Scott Dawson, Peter H. Bloch and Nancy M. Ridgway, "Shopping Motives, Emotional States, and Retail Outcomes," *Journal of Retailing* 66 (Winter 1990): 408–27; Patricia A. Knowles, Stephen J. Grove and W. Jeffrey Burroughs, "An Experimental Examination of Mood States on Retrieval and Evaluation of Advertisement and Brand Information," *Journal of the Academy of Marketing Science* 21 (April 1993); Paul W. Miniard, Sunil Bhatla and Deepak Sirdeskmukh, "Mood as a Determinant of Postconsumption Product Evaluations: Mood Effects and Their Dependency on the Affective Intensity of the Consumption Experience," *Journal of Consumer Psychology* 1, 2 (1992): 173–95; Mary T. Curren and Katrin R. Harich, "Consumers' Mood States: The Mitigating Influence of Personal Relevance on Product Evaluations," *Psychology & Marketing* 11, 2 (March/April 1994): 91–107; Gerald J. Gorn, Marvin E. Rosenberg and Kunal Basu, "Mood, Awareness, and Product Evaluation," *Journal of Consumer Psychology* 2, 3 (1993): 237–56.

33. Gordon C. Bruner, "Music, Mood, and Marketing," *Journal of Marketing* 54 (October 1990): 94–104; Basil G. Englis, "Music Television and Its Influences on Consumers, Consumer Culture, and the Transmission of Consumption Messages," in *Advances in Consumer Research 18.*

34. Marvin E. Goldberg and Gerald J. Gorn, "Happy and Sad TV Programs: How They Affect Reactions to Commercials," *Journal of Consumer Research* 14 (December 1987): 387–403; Gorn, Rosenberg and Basu, "Mood, Awareness, and Product Evaluation"; Curren and Harich, "Consumers' Mood States."

35. Rajeev Batra and Douglas M. Stayman, "The Role of Mood in Advertising Effectiveness," *Journal of Consumer Research* 17 (September 1990): 203.

36. For a scale that was devised to assess these dimensions of the shopping experience, see Barry J. Babin, William R. Darden and Mitch Griffin, "Work and/or Fun: Measuring Hedonic and Utilitarian Shopping Value," *Journal of Consumer Research* 20 (March 1994): 644–56.

37. Babin, Darden and Griffin, "Work and/or Fun."

38. Edward M. Tauber, "Why Do People Shop?" *Journal of Marketing* 36 (October 1972): 47–48.

39. Quoted in Robert C. Prus, *Making Sales: Influence as Interpersonal Accomplishment* (Newbury Park, CA: Sage Library of Social Research, Sage Publications, Inc., 1989), p. 225.

40. Gregory P. Stone, "City Shoppers and Urban Identification: Observations on the Social Psychology of City Life," *American Journal of Sociology* 60 (1954): 36–45; Danny Bellenger and Pradeep K. Korgaonkar, "Profiling the Recreational Shopper," *Journal of Retailing* 56, 3 (1980): 77–92.

41. Kelly Shermach, "Study Identifies Types of Interactive Shoppers," *Marketing News* (September 25, 1995): 22.

42. Quoted in Kate Ballen, "Get Ready for Shopping at Work," *Fortune* (February 15, 1988): 95.

43. For a recent study of consumer shopping patterns in a mall that views the mall as an ecological habitat, see Peter N. Bloch, Nancy M. Ridgway and Scott A. Dawson, "The Shopping Mall as Consumer Habitat," *Journal of Retailing* 70, 1 (1994): 23–42.

44. Quoted in Jacquelyn Bivins, "Fun and Mall Games," *Stores* (August 1989): 35.

45. Sallie Hook, "All the Retail World's a Stage: Consumers Conditioned to Entertainment in Shopping Environment," *Marketing News* 21 (July 31, 1987): 16.

46. Joshua Levine, "Hamburgers and Tennis Socks," *Forbes* (November 20, 1995): 184–85; Iris Cohen Selinger, "Lights! Camera! But Can We Get a Table?" *Advertising Age* (April 17, 1995): 48.

47. Susan Spiggle and Murphy A. Sewall, "A Choice Sets Model of Retail Selection," *Journal of Marketing* 51 (April 1987): 97–111; William R. Darden and Barry J. Babin, "The Role of Emotions in Expanding the Concept of Retail Personality," *Stores* 76, 4 (April 1994): RR7–8.

48. Most measures of store image are quite similar to other attitude measures, as discussed in Chapter 5. For an excellent bibliography of store-image studies, see Mary R. Zimmer and Linda L. Golden, "Impressions of Retail Stores: A Content Analysis of Consumer Images," *Journal of Retailing* 64 (Fall 1988): 265–93.

49. "Enticing Europe's Shoppers: U.S. Way of Dressing and of Retailing Spreading Fast," *New York Times* (April 24, 1996): D1 (2 pp.).

50. Zimmer and Golden, "Impressions of Retail Stores."

51. Spiggle and Sewall, "A Choice Sets Model of Retail Selection."

52. Philip Kotler, "Atmospherics as a Marketing Tool," *Journal of Retailing* (Winter 1973/74): 10–43. For a review of some recent research, see J. Duncan Herrington, "An Integrative Path Model of the Effects of Retail Environments on Shopper Behavior," *Market-ing: Toward the Twenty-First Century*, ed. Robert L. King (Richmond, VA: Southern Marketing Association, 1991), pp. 58–62.

53. Joseph A. Bellizzi and Robert E. Hite, "Environmental Color, Consumer Feelings, and Purchase Likelihood," *Psychology & Marketing* 9, 5 (September/October 1992): 347–63.

54. Robert J. Donovan et al., "Store Atmosphere and Purchasing Behavior," *Journal of Retailing* 70, 3 (1994): 283–94.

55. Deborah Blumenthal, "Scenic Design for In-Store Try-Ons," *New York Times* (April 9, 1988).

56. John Pierson, "If Sun Shines In, Workers Work Better, Buyers Buy More," *Wall Street Journal* (November 20, 1995): B1 (2 pp.).

57. Charles S. Areni and David Kim, "The Influence of In-Store Lighting on Consumers' Examination of Merchandise in a Wine Store," *International Journal of Research in Marketing* 11, 2 (March 1994): 117–25.

58. Judy I. Alpert and Mark I. Alpert, "Music Influences on Mood and Purchase Intentions," *Psychology & Marketing* 7 (Summer 1990): 109–34.

59. Quoted in "Slow Music Makes Fast Drinkers," *Psychology Today* (March 1989): 18.

60. Brad Edmondson, "Pass the Meat Loaf," *American Demographics* (January 1989): 19.

61. Robert La Franco, "Wallpaper Sonatas," *Forbes* (March 25, 1996): 114.

62. Louise Lee, "Background Music Becomes Hoity-Toity," *Wall Street Journal* (December 22, 1995): B1 (2 pp.).

63. Marianne Meyer, "Attention Shoppers!" *Marketing and Media Decisions* 23 (May 1988): 67.

64. Easwar S. Iyer, "Unplanned Purchasing: Knowledge of Shopping Environment and Time Pressure," *Journal of Retailing* 65 (Spring 1989): 40–57; C. Whan Park, Easwar S. Iyer and Daniel C. Smith, "The Effects of Situational Factors on In-Store Grocery Shopping," *Journal of Consumer Research* 15 (March 1989): 422–33.

65. Dennis W. Rook and Robert J. Fisher, "Normative Influences on Impulsive Buying Behavior," *Journal of Consumer Research* 22 (December 1995): 305–13; Francis Piron, "Defining Impulse Purchasing," in *Advances in Consumer Research 18*, pp. 509–14; Dennis W. Rook, "The Buying Impulse," *Journal of Consumer Research* 14 (September 1987): 189–99.

66. Michael Wahl, "Eye POPping Persuasion," *Marketing Insights* (June 1989): 130.

67. "Zipping Down the Aisles," *The New York Times Magazine* (April 6, 1997).

68. Cathy J. Cobb and Wayne D. Hoyer, "Planned Versus Impulse Purchase Behavior," *Journal of Retailing* 62 (Winter 1986): 384–409; Easwar S. Iyer and Sucheta S. Ahlawat, "Deviations from a Shopping Plan: When and Why Do Consumers Not Buy as Planned," in *Advances in Consumer Research 14*, eds. Melanie

Wallendorf and Paul Anderson (Provo, UT: Association for Consumer Research, 1987), pp. 246–49.

69. See Aradhna Krishna, Imran S. Currim and Robert W. Shoemaker, "Consumer Perceptions of Promotional Activity," *Journal of Marketing* 55 (April 1991): 4–16. See also H. Bruce Lammers, "The Effect of Free Samples on Immediate Consumer Purchase," *Journal of Consumer Marketing* 8 (Spring 1991): 31–37; Kapil Bawa and Robert W. Shoemaker, "The Effects of a Direct Mail Coupon on Brand Choice Behavior," *Journal of Marketing Research* 24 (November 1987): 370–76.

70. Bernice Kanner, "Trolling in the Aisles," *New York* (January 16, 1989): 12; Michael Janofsky, "Using Crowing Roosters and Ringing Business Cards to Tap a Boom in Point-of-Purchase Displays," *New York Times* (March 21, 1994): D9.

71. John P. Cortez, "Media Pioneers Try to Corral On-the-Go Consumers," *Advertising Age* (August 17, 1992): 25.

72. Cyndee Miller, "MTV Video Capsule Features Sports for Music Retailers, Corporate Sponsors," *Marketing News* (February 3, 1992): 5.

73. Quoted in John P. Cortez, "Ads Head for Bathroom," *Advertising Age* (May 18, 1992): 24.

74. William Keenan, Jr., "Point-of-Purchase: From Clutter to Technoclutter," *Sales and Marketing Management* 141 (April 1989): 96.

75. Meyer, "Attention Shoppers!"

76. Cyndee Miller, "Videocart Spruces Up for New Tests," *Marketing News* (February 19, 1990): 19; William E. Sheeline, "User-Friendly Shopping Carts," *Fortune* (December 5, 1988): 9.

77. Paco Underhill, "In-Store Video Ads Can Reinforce Media Campaigns," *Marketing News* (May 1989): 5.

78. James Sterngold, "Why Japanese Adore Vending Machines," *New York Times* (January 5, 1992) 2: A1.

79. See Robert B. Cialdini, *Influence: Science and Practice*, 2nd. ed. (Glenview, IL: Scott, Foresman and Company, 1988).

80. Richard P. Bagozzi, "Marketing as Exchange," *Journal of Marketing* 39 (October 1975): 32–39; Peter M. Blau, *Exchange and Power in Social Life* (New York: Wiley, 1964); Marjorie Caballero and Alan J. Resnik, "The Attraction Paradigm in Dyadic Exchange," *Psychology & Marketing* 3, 1 (1986): 17–34; George C. Homans, "Social Behavior as Exchange," *American Journal of Sociology* 63 (1958): 597–606; Paul H. Schurr and Julie L. Ozanne, "Influences on Exchange Processes: Buyers' Preconceptions of a Seller's Trustworthiness and Bargaining Toughness," *Journal of Consumer Research* 11 (March 1985): 939–53; Arch G. Woodside and J.W. Davenport, "The Effect of Salesman Similarity and Expertise on Consumer Purchasing Behavior," *Journal of Marketing Research* 8 (1974): 433–36.

81. Paul Busch and David T. Wilson, "An Experimental Analysis of a Salesman's Expert and Referent Bases of Social Power in the Buyer-Seller Dyad," *Journal of Marketing Research* 13 (February 1976): 3–11; John E. Swan et al., "Measuring Dimensions of Purchaser Trust of Industrial Salespeople," *Journal of Personal Selling and Sales Management* 8 (May 1988): 1.

82. Calmetta Y. Coleman, "A Car Salesman's Bizarre Prank May End Up Backfiring in Court," *Wall Street Journal* (May 2, 1995): B1.

83. For a recent study in this area, see Peter H. Reingen and Jerome B. Kernan, "Social Perception and Interpersonal Influence: Some Consequences of the Physical Attractiveness Stereotype in a Personal Selling Setting," *Journal of Consumer Psychology* 2, 1 (1993): 25–38.

84. Mary Jo Bitner, Bernard H. Booms and Mary Stansfield Tetreault, "The Service Encounter: Diagnosing Favorable and Unfavorable Incidents," *Journal of Marketing* 54 (January 1990): 7–84; Robert C. Prus, *Making Sales* (Newbury Park, CA: Sage Publications, Inc., 1989); Arch G. Woodside and James L. Taylor, "Identity Negotiations in Buyer-Seller Interactions," in *Advances in Consumer Research 12*, eds. Elizabeth C. Hirschman and Morris B. Holbrook (Provo, UT: Association for Consumer Research, 1985), pp. 443–49.

85. Gilbert A. Churchill, Jr., et al., "The Determinants of Salesperson Performance: A Meta-Analysis," *Journal of Marketing Research* 22 (May 1985): 103–18.

86. Siew Meng Leong, Paul S. Busch and Deborah Roedder John, "Knowledge Bases and Salesperson Effectiveness: A Script-Theoretic Analysis," *Journal of Marketing Research* 26 (May 1989): 164; Harish Sujan, Mita Sujan and James R. Bettman, "Knowledge Structure Differences Between More Effective and Less Effective Salespeople," *Journal of Marketing Research* 25 (February 1988): 81–86; Robert Saxe and Barton Weitz, "The SOCCO Scale: A Measure of the Customer Orientation of Salespeople," *Journal of Marketing Research* 19 (August 1982): 343–51; David M. Szymanski, "Determinants of Selling Effectiveness: The Importance of Declarative Knowledge to the Personal Selling Concept," *Journal of Marketing* 52 (January 1988): 64–77; Barton A. Weitz, "Effectiveness in Sales Interactions: A Contingency Framework," *Journal of Marketing* 45 (Winter 1981): 85–103.

87. Jagdish M. Sheth, "Buyer-Seller Interaction: A Conceptual Framework," in *Advances in Consumer Research* (Cincinnati, OH: Association for Consumer Research, 1976), pp. 382–86; Kaylene C. Williams and Rosann L. Spiro, "Communication Style in the Salesperson-Customer Dyad," *Journal of Marketing Research* 22 (November 1985): 434–42.

88. Marsha L. Richins, "An Analysis of Consumer Interaction Styles in the Marketplace," *Journal of Consumer Research* 10 (June 1983): 73–82.

89. Rama Jayanti and Anita Jackson, "Service Satisfaction: Investigation of Three Models," in *Advances in Consumer Research 18*, pp. 603–10; David K. Tse,

Franco M. Nicosia and Peter C. Wilton, "Consumer Satisfaction as a Process," *Psychology & Marketing* 7 (Fall 1990): 177–93.

90. Eugene W. Anderson, Claes Fornell and Donald R. Lehmann, "Customer Satisfaction, Market Share, and Profitability: Findings from Sweden," *Journal of Marketing* 58, 3 (July 1994): 53–66.

91. Robert Jacobson and David A. Aaker, "The Strategic Role of Product Quality," *Journal of Marketing* 51 (October 1987): 31–44. For a recent review of issues regarding the measurement of service quality, see J. Joseph Cronin, Jr., and Steven A. Taylor, "Measuring Service Quality: A Reexamination and Extension," *Journal of Marketing* 56 (July 1992): 55–68.

92. Anna Kirmani and Peter Wright, "Money Talks: Perceived Advertising Expense and Expected Product Quality," *Journal of Consumer Research* 16 (December 1989): 344–53; Donald R. Lichtenstein and Scot Burton, "The Relationship Between Perceived and Objective Price-Quality," *Journal of Marketing Research* 26 (November 1989): 429–43; Akshay R. Rao and Kent B. Monroe, "The Effect of Price, Brand Name, and Store Name on Buyers' Perceptions of Product Quality: An Integrative Review," *Journal of Marketing Research* 26 (August 1989): 351–57.

93. Shelby Hunt, "Post-Transactional Communication and Dissonance Reduction," *Journal of Marketing* 34 (January 1970): 46–51; Daniel E. Innis and H. Rao Unnava, "The Usefulness of Product Warranties for Reputable and New Brands," in *Advances in Consumer Research 18*, pp. 317–22; Terence A. Shimp and William O. Bearden, "Warranty and Other Extrinsic Cue Effects on Consumers' Risk Perceptions," *Journal of Consumer Research* 9 (June 1982): 38–46.

94. Faye Rice, "What Intelligent Consumers Want," *Marketing Executive Report!* 3, 1 (January 1993): 1 (5 pp.).

95. Morris B. Holbrook and Kim P. Corfman, "Quality and Value in the Consumption Experience: Phaedrus Rides Again," in *Perceived Quality: How Consumers View Stores and Merchandise,* eds. Jacob Jacoby and Jerry C. Olson (Lexington, MA: Lexington Books, 1985), pp. 31–58.

96. Ibid.; Robert M. Pirsig, *Zen and the Art of Motorcycle Maintenance: An Inquiry Into Values* (New York: Bantam Books, 1974).

97. Gilbert A. Churchill, Jr., and Carol F. Surprenant, "An Investigation into the Determinants of Customer Satisfaction," *Journal of Marketing Research* 19 (November 1983): 491–504; John E. Swan and I. Frederick Trawick, "Disconfirmation of Expectations and Satisfaction with a Retail Service," *Journal of Retailing* 57 (Fall 1981): 49–67; Peter C. Wilton and David K. Tse, "Models of Consumer Satisfaction Formation: An Extension," *Journal of Marketing Research* 25 (May 1988): 204–12. For a discussion of what may occur when customers evaluate a new

service for which comparison standards do not yet exist, see Ann L. McGill and Dawn Iacobucci, "The Role of Post-Experience Comparison Standards in the Evaluation of Unfamiliar Services," in *Advances in Consumer Research 19*, eds. John F. Sherry, Jr., and Brian Sternthal (Provo, UT: Association for Consumer Research, 1992), pp. 570–78; William Boulding et al., "A Dynamic Process Model of Service Quality: From Expectations to Behavioral Intentions," *Journal of Marketing Research* 30 (February 1993): 7–27.

98. John W. Gamble, "The Expectations Paradox: The More You Offer Customer, Closer You are to Failure," *Marketing News* (March 14, 1988): 38.

99. Jagdish N. Sheth and Banwari Mittal, "A Framework for Managing Customer Expectations," *Journal of Marketing Focused Management* 1 (1996): 137–58.

100. Mary C. Gilly and Betsy D. Gelb, "Post-Purchase Consumer Processes and the Complaining Consumer," *Journal of Consumer Research* 9 (December 1982): 323–28; Diane Halstead and Cornelia Dröge, "Consumer Attitudes Toward Complaining and the Prediction of Multiple Complaint Responses," in *Advances in Consumer Research 18*, pp. 210–16; Jagdip Singh, "Consumer Complaint Intentions and Behavior: Definitional and Taxonomical Issues," *Journal of Marketing* 52 (January 1988): 93–107.

101. Gary L. Clark, Peter F. Kaminski and David R. Rink, "Consumer Complaints: Advice on How Companies Should Respond Based on an Empirical Study," *Journal of Services Marketing* 6, 1 (Winter 1992): 41–50.

102. Alan Andreasen and Arthur Best, "Consumers Complain—Does Business Respond?" *Harvard Business Review* 55 (July/August 1977): 93–101.

103. Ingrid Martin, "Expert-Novice Differences in Complaint Scripts," in *Advances in Consumer Research 18*, pp. 225–31; Marsha L. Richins, "A Multivariate Analysis of Responses to Dissatisfaction," *Journal of the Academy of Marketing Science* 15 (Fall 1987): 24–31.

104. John A. Schibrowsky and Richard S. Lapidus, "Gaining a Competitive Advantage by Analyzing Aggregate Complaints," *Journal of Consumer Marketing* 11, 1 (1994): 15–26.

105. Russell W. Belk, "The Role of Possessions in Constructing and Maintaining a Sense of Past," in *Advances in Consumer Research 17*, eds. Marvin E. Goldberg, Gerald Gorn and Richard W. Pollay (Provo, UT: Association for Consumer Research, 1989), pp. 669–76.

106. David E. Sanger, "For a Job Well Done, Japanese Enshrine the Chip," *New York Times* (December 11, 1990): A4.

107. Jacob Jacoby, Carol K. Berning and Thomas F. Dietvorst, "What About Disposition?" *Journal of Marketing* 41 (April 1977): 22–28.

108. Mike Tharp, "Tchaikovsky and Toilet Paper," *U.S. News & World Report* (December 1987): 62; B. Van Voorst, "The Recycling Bottleneck," *Time* (September 14, 1992): 52–54; Richard P. Bagozzi and Pratibha A. Dabholkar, "Consumer Recycling Goals and Their Effect on Decisions to Recycle: A Means-End Chain Analysis," *Psychology & Marketing* 11, 4 (July/August 1994): 313–40.

109. "Finally, Something at McDonald's You Can Actually Eat," *Utne Reader* (May–June 1997): 12.

110. "Cool Caps," *Newsweek* (n.d.); Timothy Aeppel, "From License Plates to Fashion Plates," *Wall Street Journal* (September 21, 1994): B1 (2 pp.).

111. Debra J. Dahab, James W. Gentry and Wanru Su, "New Ways to Reach Non-Recyclers: An Extension of the Model of Reasoned Action to Recycling Behaviors," in *Advances in Consumer Research 22*, eds. Frank R. Kardes and Mita Sujan (Provo, UT: Association for Consumer Research, 1995), pp. 251–56.

112. Bagozzi and Dabholkar, "Consumer Recycling Goals and Their Effect on Decisions to Recycle." See also L. J. Shrum, Tina M. Lowrey and John A. McCarty, "Recycling as a Marketing Problem: A Framework for Strategy Development," *Psychology & Marketing* 11, 4 (July/August 1994): 393–416; Dahab, Gentry and Su, "New Ways to Reach Non-Recyclers."

113. John F. Sherry, Jr., "A Sociocultural Analysis of a Midwestern American Flea Market," *Journal of Consumer Research* 17 (June 1990): 13–30.

114. Diane Crispell, "Collecting Memories," *American Demographics* (November 1988): 38–42.

115. Allan J. Magrath, "If Used Product Sellers Ever Get Organized, Watch Out," *Marketing News* (June 25, 1990): 9; Kevin McCrohan and James D. Smith, "Consumer Participation in the Informal Economy," *Journal of the Academy of Marketing Science* 15 (Winter 1990): 62.

116. "New Kind of Store Getting More Use Out of Used Goods," *Montgomery Advertiser* (December 12, 1996): 7A.

Carlo leads a secret life. During the week he is a straight-laced stock analyst for a major investment firm. The weekend is another story. Come Friday evening, it's off with the Harry Rosen suit and on with the black leather, as he trades in his BMW for his treasured Harley-Davidson motorcycle. A dedicated member of HOG (Harley Owners Group), Carlo belongs to the faction of Harley riders known as "RUBs" (rich urban bikers). Everyone in his group wears expensive leather vests with Harley insignias and owns a customized "Low Rider." Carlo has spent a lot on his bike and on outfitting himself to be like the rest of the group. But it's worth it. He feels a real brotherhood with his fellow RUBs. The group rides together in two-column formation to bike rallies—events that sometimes attract 300 000 cycle enthusiasts. What a sense of power he feels when they're all cruising together. It's them against the world!

Of course, an added benefit is the business networking he's been able to accomplish during his weekend jaunts with his fellow professionals—who also wait for the weekend to "ride on the wild side."[1] Sometimes sharing a secret can pay off in more ways than one ...

11

Group Influence and Opinion Leadership

REFERENCE GROUPS

Humans are social animals. We all belong to groups, try to please others, and take cues about how to behave by observing the actions of those around us. In fact our desire to "fit in" or to identify with desirable individuals or groups is the primary motivation for many of our purchases and activities. We will often go to great lengths to please the members of a group whose acceptance we covet.[2] Carlo's biker group is an important part of his identity, and this membership influences many of his buying decisions. He has spent many thousands of dollars on parts and accessories since acquiring his identity as a RUB. He and his fellow riders are united by their consumption choices to the extent that total strangers feel an immediate bond with each other when they meet.

Carlo doesn't model himself after just *any* biker. Only the people with whom he really identifies can exert that kind of influence on him. For example, his group doesn't have much to do with outlaw clubs, which are primarily composed of blue-collar riders sporting Harley tattoos (see ***www.harleycanada.com*** for more information on the Harley phenomenon). The members of his group also have only polite contact with "Ma-and-Pa" bikers, whose bikes are the epitome of comfort, featuring such niceties as radios, heated handgrips, and floorboards. Essentially, only the RUBs comprise Carlo's *reference group*.

reference group an actual or imaginary individual or group that has a significant effect upon an individual's evaluations, aspirations or behaviour

A **reference group** is "... an actual or imaginary individual or group conceived of having significant relevance upon an individual's evaluations, aspirations, or behavior."[3] Reference groups influence consumers in three ways. These influences—*informational, utilitarian* and *value-expressive*—are described in Table 11–1.

This chapter focuses on how other people, whether fellow bikers, co-workers, friends, family or just casual acquaintances, influence our purchase decisions. It considers how our preferences are shaped by our group memberships, by our desire to

TABLE 11–1 Three Forms of Reference Group Influence

Informational Influence	The individual seeks information about various brands from an association of professionals or an independent group of experts.
	The individual seeks information from those who work with the product as a profession.
	The individual seeks brand-related knowledge and experience (such as how Brand A's performance compares to Brand B's) from those friends, neighbours, relatives or work associates who have reliable information about the brands.
	The brand the individual selects is influenced by observing a seal of approval from an independent testing agency (such as Good Housekeeping).
	The individual's observation of what experts do (such as observing the type of car that police drive or the brand of television that repairmen buy) influences his or her choice of a brand.
Utilitarian Influence	So that he or she satisfies the expectations of fellow work associates, the individual's decision to purchase a particular brand is influenced by their preferences.
	The individual's decision to purchase a particular brand is influenced by the preferences of people with whom he or she has social interaction.
	The individual's decision to purchase a particular brand is influenced by the preferences of family members.
	The desire to satisfy the expectations that others have of him or her has an impact on the individual's brand choice.
Value-Expressive Influence	The individual feels that the purchase or use of a particular brand will enhance the image others have of him or her.
	The individual feels that those who purchase or use a particular brand possess the characteristics that he or she would like to have.
	The individual sometimes feels that it would be nice to be like the type of person that advertisements show using a particular brand.
	The individual feels that the people who purchase a particular brand are admired or respected by others.
	The individual feels that the purchase of a particular brand would help show others what he or she is or would like to be (such as an athlete, successful business person, good parent, etc.).

Source: Adapted from C. Whan Park and V. Parker Lessig, "Students and Housewives: Differences in Susceptibility to Reference Group Influence," *Journal of Consumer Research* 4 (September 1977): 102. Reprinted with permission by The University of Chicago Press.

Ownership of a Harley is not limited to men; women want to operate their own bike rather than piggy-back. *Courtesy of Harley Davidson Canada.*

please or be accepted by others, or by the actions of famous people whom we've never even met. Finally, it explores why some people are more influential than others in affecting consumers' product preferences, and how marketers go about finding those people and enlisting their support in the persuasion process.

Types of Reference Groups

Although two or more people are normally required to form a group, the term *reference group* often is used a bit more loosely to describe *any* external influence that provides social cues.[4] The referent may be a cultural figure and have an impact on many people (e.g., Elvis Presley) or a person or group whose influence is confined to the consumer's immediate environment (e.g., Carlo's biker club). Reference groups that affect consumption can include parents, fellow motorcycle enthusiasts, the Liberal Party, the Toronto Raptors or bands like the Barenaked Ladies.

Obviously, some groups and individuals exert a greater influence than others and for a broader range of consumption decisions. For example, our parents may play a pivotal role in forming our values towards many important issues, such as attitudes about marriage or where to go to university. This type of influence is **normative influence;** that is, the reference group helps to set and enforce fundamental standards of conduct. In contrast, a Harley-Davidson club might exert **comparative influence,** where decisions about specific brands or activities are affected.[5]

FORMAL VERSUS INFORMAL GROUPS

A reference group can take the form of a large, formal organization that has a recognized structure, complete with a charter, regular meeting times and officers. Or it can be small and informal, such as a group of friends or students living in a dormi-

normative influence the process in which a reference group helps to set and enforce fundamental standards of conduct

comparative influence the process whereby a reference group influences decisions about specific brands or activities

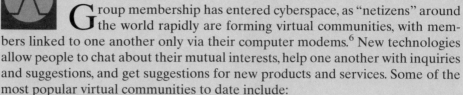

MARKETING OPPORTUNITY

Group membership has entered cyberspace, as "netizens" around the world rapidly are forming virtual communities, with members linked to one another only via their computer modems.[6] New technologies allow people to chat about their mutual interests, help one another with inquiries and suggestions, and get suggestions for new products and services. Some of the most popular virtual communities to date include:

- Tripod (*www.tripod.com*): A big hit with Web surfers in their twenties, about 270 000 people have signed up to pose questions to one another or just to sound off on issues.

- Parent Soup (*www.parentsoup.com*): More than 200 000 parents chat about the trials and tribulations of being—what else?—parents.

- Geocities (*www.geocities.com*): "Homesteaders" get free home pages and access to one of 37 themed communities, from Arts or Autos to Sports and Recreation or Travel.

- Utne Online (*www.utne.com*): Members log on to the Utne Café and discuss New Age issues and current affairs.

- Firefly Network Inc. (*www.firefly.com*): Using intelligent agent software, this Web site builds profiles of users and sorts them to recommend new music, movie and book selections based on the likes and dislikes of others with similar preferences. Users also can post their own reviews for others to read and react to.[7]

tory. Marketers tend to be more successful at influencing formal groups because they are more easily identifiable and accessible.

However, as a rule it is small, informal groups that exert a more powerful influence on individual consumers. In a recent Roper Starch Worldwide survey 34 percent of teens said that their friends' ideas had the greatest influence on how they spend their money, while only 25 percent said that advertising had the same impact.[8]

These groups tend to be more involved in individuals' day-to-day lives and to be more important to them because the groups are high in normative influence. Larger, formal groups tend to be more product- or activity-specific and thus are high in comparative influence.

MEMBERSHIP VERSUS ASPIRATIONAL REFERENCE GROUPS

While some reference groups consist of people the consumer actually knows, others are composed of people the consumer can either identify with or admire. Not surprisingly, many marketing efforts that specifically adopt a reference-group appeal concentrate on highly visible, widely admired figures (such as well-known athletes or performers).

Since people tend to compare themselves to others who are similar, they often are swayed by knowing how people like them conduct their lives. For this reason many promotional strategies include "ordinary" people whose consumption activities provide informational social influence. MasterCard shifted the focus of its advertising away from glamorous, affluent lifestyles of professionals to relatively ordinary activities like those of a young man furnishing his first apartment (and, of course, using his MasterCard to pay for it). The campaign's slogan is "For the Way We Really Live."[9]

The likelihood that people will become part of a consumer's identificational reference group is affected by several factors, including the following:

- *Propinquity.* As physical distance between people decreases and opportunities for interaction increase, relationships are more likely to form. Physical nearness is called *propinquity.* An early study on friendship patterns in a housing complex showed this factor's strong effects: residents were much more likely to be friends with the people next door than with those who lived only two doors away. And people who lived next to a staircase had more friends than those at the ends of a hall (presumably they were more likely to "bump into" people using the stairs).[10] Physical structure has a lot to do with whom we get to know and how popular we are.

MARKETING OPPORTUNITY

One of the most recent and widespread applications of reference group influences to consumer behaviour is **affinity marketing**. This strategy allows consumers to underscore their identification with some organization by attaching the group's identification to aspects of their personal lives.

In the most common form of affinity marketing, banks promote special credit cards known as *affinity cards,* that can be tied to a membership group, such as a church or university alumni organization, or to a symbolic group, such as an NFL team or a rock group.[11] Priests and nuns have been targeted to adopt the Caritas card, issued by Catholic Charities,[12] and even Elvis Presley has appeared on an affinity card.

affinity marketing a strategy that allows a consumer to emphasize his or her identification with some organization, as, for example, when organizations issue credit cards with their names on them

Dewar's has successfully used non-celebrities as endorsers in its "Profiles" campaign, which is now being adapted to other countries, as this Spanish ad illustrates.
Courtesy of Schenley Industries, Inc.

- *Mere exposure.* We come to like persons or things simply as a result of seeing them more often, which is known as the *mere exposure phenomenon.*[13] Greater frequency of contact, even if unintentional, may help to determine one's set of local referents. The same effect holds when evaluating works of art or political candidates.[14]

- *Group cohesiveness.* The degree to which members of a group are attracted to each other and value their group membership is called cohesiveness. As the value of the group to the individual increases, so too does the likelihood that the group will guide consumption decisions. Smaller groups tend to be more cohesive, because it is more difficult to relate to larger groups of people. By the same token, groups often try to restrict membership to a select few, which increases the value of membership to those who are admitted. Exclusivity of membership is a benefit often touted by credit-card companies, book clubs and so on, even though the actual membership base might be fairly large.

While the consumer may have no direct contact with reference groups, they can have powerful influences on his or her tastes and preferences, because they provide guidance as to the types of products used by admired people.[15] The MasterCard campaign noted previously takes a bit of a risk, since most credit-card advertising is "aspirational." As one executive noted, "In this industry, you market to who you want to be, rather than who you are."[16] *Aspirational reference groups* are composed of idealized figures, such as successful business people, athletes or performers. One study that included business students who aspired to the "executive" role found a strong relationship between products the students associated with their *ideal selves* (see Chapter 5) and those they assumed would be owned or used by executives.[17]

POSITIVE VERSUS NEGATIVE REFERENCE GROUPS

Reference groups may exert either a positive or a negative influence on consumption behaviours. In most cases consumers model their behaviour to be consistent with what they think the group expects of them. In some cases, though, a consumer may try to distance him- or herself from other people or groups that function as *avoidance groups.* He or she may carefully study the dress or mannerisms of a disliked group (e.g., "nerds," "druggies" or "preppies") and scrupulously avoid buying

MULTICULTURAL DIMENSIONS

"Common man" or "slice-of-life" depictions, which highlight "real" people, are more realistic and thus more credible than those featuring celebrities or superstars. While we admire perfect people, it can be frustrating to compare ourselves to them. By including people who are successful but not perfect, marketers often enhance consumers' identification with them. This strategy has been successfully employed in the classic "Dewar's Profiles," a series of ads describing the lifestyles of non-celebrity high achievers who happen to drink Dewar's Scotch. Since the strategy entails the use of real people from many different walks of life, the company has expanded its ad executions to focus on accomplished people in different countries. For example, a Thai ad highlights a successful architect who lives in Bangkok, while a Spanish campaign features a 29-year-old flight instructor.[18]

anything that might identify him or her with that group. Rebellious adolescents often resent parental influence and may deliberately do the opposite of what their parents would like as a way of making a statement about their independence. As Romeo and Juliet discovered, nothing makes a dating partner more attractive than a little parental opposition.

When Reference Groups Are Important

Reference group influences are not equally powerful for all types of products and consumption activities. For example, products that are not very complex, that are low in perceived risk and that can be tried prior to purchase are less susceptible to personal influence.[19] In addition, the specific impact of reference groups may vary. At times they may determine the use of certain products rather than others (e.g., owning or not owning a computer, or eating junk food versus health food), while at other times they may have specific effects on brand decisions within a product category (wearing Levi's jeans versus Calvin Klein jeans, or drinking Molson's rather than Labatt's).

Two dimensions that influence the degree to which reference groups are important are whether the purchase is to be consumed publicly or privately and whether it is a luxury or a necessity. As a rule, reference group effects are more robust for purchases that are: 1) luxuries (such as sailboats) rather than necessities, since products purchased with discretionary income are subject to individual tastes and preferences, and necessities do not offer this range of choices; and 2) socially conspicuous or visible to others (like living-room furniture or clothing), since consumers are not swayed as much by the opinions of others if their purchases will never be observed by anyone but themselves.[20] The relative effects of reference group influences on some specific product classes are shown in Figure 11–1.

FIGURE 11–1 • Relative Reference Group Influence on Purchase Decisions

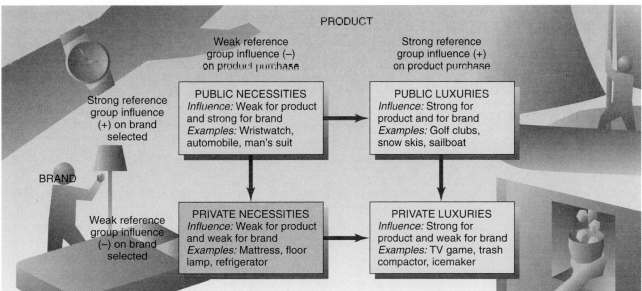

Adapted from William O. Bearden and Michael J. Etzel, "Reference Group Influence on Product and Brand Purchase Decisions," *Journal of Consumer Research* (September 1982): 185. Reprinted with permission by The University of Chicago Press.

The Power of Reference Groups

social power the capacity of
one person to alter the
actions or outcome of
another

Social power refers to "... the capacity to alter the actions of others."[21] To the degree that you are able to make someone else do something, whether they do it willingly or not, you have power over that person. The following classification of *power bases* can help us to distinguish among the reasons a person can exert power over another, the degree to which the influence is allowed voluntarily, and whether this influence will continue to have an effect in the absence of the power source.[22]

REFERENT POWER

If a person admires the qualities of an individual or a group, he or she will try to imitate those qualities by copying the referent's behaviours (e.g., choice of clothing, cars and leisure activities) as a guide to forming consumption preferences, just as Carlo's preferences are affected by his fellow bikers. Prominent people in all walks of life can affect people's consumption behaviours by virtue of product endorsements (e.g., Michael Jordan for Nike), distinctive fashion statements (Madonna's use of lingerie as outerwear) or championing of causes (Princess Diana for abolition of landmines). Referent power is important to many marketing strategies because consumers voluntarily change behaviours to please or identify with a referent.

INFORMATION POWER

A person can have information power simply because he or she knows something others would like to know. Editors of trade publications such as *Women's Wear Daily* often possess power due to their ability to compile and disseminate information that can make or break individual designers or companies. People with information power are able to influence consumer opinion by virtue of their (assumed) access to the "truth."

LEGITIMATE POWER

Sometimes people are granted power by virtue of social agreements, such as that given to policemen and professors. The legitimate power conferred by a uniform is recognized in many consumer contexts, including teaching hospitals, where medical students don white coats to enhance their aura of authority with patients, and banks, where tellers' uniforms communicate trustworthiness.[23] This form of power may be "borrowed" by marketers to influence consumers. For example, an ad featuring a model wearing a white doctor's coat can add an aura of legitimacy or authority to the presentation of the product.

EXPERT POWER

Expert power is derived from possessing a specific knowledge or skill. Consumers are often influenced by experts who are assumed to be able to evaluate products in an objective, informed way. The power of celebrity experts can be measured by their visibility on talk shows, lecture circuits and so on. Prominent economists can receive between $5000 and $20 000 for a speech, depending on their level of perceived expertise. One analysis of economist superstars noted the following requirements for success:[24]

- affiliation with an élite university, think-tank or investment house; and
- authorship of a slim, easy-to-read book that yields a vision of the future.

David Foot, author of *Boom, Bust & Echo*, has these traits and is currently racking up the consulting dollars, in addition to his university salary and book royalties. The need to provide evidence of expert power creates other marketing opportunities, ranging from the provision of certificates and diplomas to coaching for licensing exams. A number of industries in which the criteria for expertise are poorly defined are grappling with the need for *credentialling,* or defining what knowledge and experience are necessary to make a person an expert, and providing a mechanism to weed out people who do not meet these criteria.

REWARD POWER

When a person or group has the means to provide positive reinforcement (see Chapter 3), that entity will have power over a consumer to the extent that this reinforcement is valued or desired. The reward may be tangible, as occurs when an employee is given a raise. Or the reward may be intangible: social approval or acceptance is often what is exchanged in return for molding one's behaviour to a group or buying the products expected of group members. The Everlast ad shown here humorously acknowledges others' power to reward us for "correct" product choices.

COERCIVE POWER

While coercive power is often effective in the short term, it does not tend to produce permanent attitudinal or behavioural change. Surveillance of some sort is usually required to make people do something they do not wish to do. Fortunately, coercive power is rarely employed in marketing situations. However, elements of this power base are evident in fear appeals, in intimidation in personal selling, and in some campaigns that emphasize the negative consequences that might occur if people do not use a product.

This ad for Everlast pokes fun at the power of peer groups to reward people for wearing the right clothes.
Courtesy of Goldsmith/Jeffrey, Inc., N.Y.

CONFORMITY

conformity refers to a change in beliefs or actions as a reaction to real or imagined group pressure

norms the informal rules that govern what is right or wrong

Conformity refers to a change in beliefs or actions as a reaction to real or imagined group pressure. In order for a society to function, its members develop **norms,** or informal rules that govern behaviour. If such a system of agreements did not evolve, chaos would result. Imagine the confusion if a simple norm such as stopping for a red traffic-light did not exist. While norms change slowly over time, there is general agreement within a society about which ones should be obeyed, and we adjust our way of thinking to conform to these norms.

Unspoken rules govern many aspects of consumption. In addition to norms regarding appropriate use of clothing and other personal items, we conform to rules that include gift giving (we expect birthday presents from loved ones and get upset if they do not materialize), sex roles (men often are expected to pick up the check on a first date) and personal hygiene (we are expected to shower regularly to avoid offending others).

Types of Social Influence

normative social influence the conformity that occurs when a person alters his or her behaviour to meet the expectations of a person or group

Just as the bases for social power can vary, the process of social influence operates in several ways.[25] Sometimes a person is motivated to model the behaviour of others because this mimicry is believed to yield rewards, such as social approval or money. At other times the social influence process occurs simply because the person honestly does not *know* the correct way to respond and is using the behaviour of the other person or group as a cue to ensure that he or she is responding correctly.[26] **Normative social influence** occurs when a person conforms to meet the expectations of a person or group.

Cigarette smoking among youngsters is an important health issue. Although tobacco sales to minors are illegal, most smokers begin puffing before the age of 18. Much of the motivation to begin smoking at an early age is due to peer pressure; the alluring advertising images of smokers as cool, sexy or mature help to convince many young people that beginning the habit is a path to social acceptance. Because the power of advertising to influence attitudes is widely recognized, some groups have tried to fight fire with fire by creating antismoking ads that depict smoking as an ugly habit that turns people off. Are these ads effective? One recent study of non-smoking seventh-graders by a pair of consumer researchers examined the kids' perceptions of smokers after being exposed to both cigarette ads and antismoking ads. Results were promising: the researchers found that kids who saw the antismoking ads were more likely to rate smokers lower in terms of both personal appeal and common sense. These findings imply that it is possible to use advertising to debunk myths about the glamour of smoking, especially if used in tandem with other health-education efforts.
Source: Cornelia Pechmann and S. Ratneshwar, "The Effects of Antismoking and Cigarette Advertising on Young Adolescents' Perceptions of Peers Who Smoke," Journal of Consumer Research *21, 2 (September 1994): 236–51. Photo courtesy of Brogan & Partners, Detroit.*

In contrast, **informational social influence** refers to conformity that occurs because the group's behaviour is taken as evidence about reality: if other people respond in a certain way in an ambiguous situation, we may mimic their behaviour because this appears to be the correct thing to do.[27]

informational social influence the conformity that occurs because the group's behaviour is taken as evidence about reality

Conformity is not an automatic process, and many factors contribute to the likelihood that consumers will pattern their behaviour after others.[28] Among the factors that affect the likelihood of conformity are the following:

- *Cultural pressures.* Different cultures encourage conformity to a greater or lesser degree. Japanese society is characterized by the dominance of collective well-being and group loyalty over individuals' needs.

- *Fear of deviance.* The individual may have reason to believe that the group will apply *sanctions* to punish behaviour that differs from the group's. It is not unusual to observe adolescents shunning a peer who is "different," or a corporation passing over a person for promotion because he or she is not a "team player."

- *Commitment.* The more a person is dedicated to a group and values membership in it, the more motivated he or she will be to follow the dictates of the group. Rock groupies and followers of television evangelists may do anything that is asked of them, and terrorists may be willing to die for the good of their causes. According to the *principle of least interest* the person or group that is least committed to staying in a relationship has the most power, because that party won't be susceptible to threatened rejection.[29]

- *Group unanimity, size and expertise.* As groups gain in power, compliance increases. It is often harder to resist the demands of a large number of people than those of just a few, and this difficulty is compounded when the group members are perceived to know what they are talking about.

- *Gender differences.* It has often been assumed that women are more susceptible than men to interpersonal influence, since they are more sensitive to social cues and tend to be more group-oriented and cooperative by nature. However, recent indications show this reasoning as flawed: both men and women who possess feminine personality traits tend to conform more (see Chapter 5).[30]

- *Susceptibility to interpersonal influence.* This trait refers to an individual's need to identify or to enhance his or her image in the opinion of significant others. This enhancement process often is accompanied by the acquisition of products the person believes will impress his or her audience, and by the tendency to learn about products by observing how others use them.[31] Consumers who are low on this trait have been called *role-relaxed*; they tend to be older and affluent, and to have high self-confidence. Based on research identifying role-relaxed consumers, Subaru created a communications strategy to reach these people. In one commercial a man is heard saying, "I want a car ... Don't tell me about wood panelling, about winning the respect of my neighbours. They're my neighbours. They're not my heroes ..."

Social Comparison

Informational social influence implies that sometimes we look to the behaviour of others to provide a yardstick about reality. **Social comparison theory** asserts that this

social comparison theory the perspective that people compare their outcomes with others' as a way to increase the stability of their own self-evaluation, especially when physical evidence is unavailable

process occurs as a way to increase the stability of one's self-evaluation, especially when physical evidence is unavailable.[32] Social comparison even applies to choices for which there is no objectively correct answer. Such stylistic decisions as tastes in music and art are assumed to be a matter of individual choice, yet people often believe that some types are "better" or more "correct" than others.[33] If you have ever been responsible for choosing the music to play at a party, you can probably appreciate the social pressure involved in choosing the right "mix."

Although people often like to compare their judgments and actions to those of others, they tend to be selective about precisely whom they will use as benchmarks. Similarity between the consumer and others used for social comparison boosts confidence that the information is accurate and relevant (though we may find it more threatening to be outperformed by someone similar to ourselves).[34] We tend to value the views of obviously dissimilar others only when we are reasonably certain of our own.[35]

In general, people tend to choose a *co-oriented peer,* or a person of equivalent standing, when undergoing social comparison. For example, a study of adult cosmetics users found that women were more likely to seek information about product choices from similar friends in order to reduce uncertainty, and to trust the judgments of similar others.[36] The same effects have been found for evaluations of products as diverse as men's suits and coffee.[37]

Compliance and Obedience

The discussion of persuasive communications in Chapter 8 indicated that source and message characteristics have a big impact on the likelihood of influence. Influencers have been found to be more successful at gaining compliance if they are perceived to be confident or expert.[38] In addition, the way a request is phrased can influence the likelihood of compliance.

TACTICAL REQUESTS

The way a request for compliance is phrased or structured can make a difference. One well-known sales tactic (introduced in Chapter 7) is known as the *foot-in-the-door technique,* wherein the consumer is first asked a small request and then is hit up for something bigger.[39] This term is adapted from door-to-door selling. Experienced salespeople know that they are much more likely to make a sale if they first convince a customer to let them in the house to deliver a sales pitch. Once the person has agreed to this small request, it is more difficult to refuse a larger one, since the consumer has legitimized the salesperson's presence by entering into a dialogue. He or she is no longer a threatening stranger at the door.

Other variations on this strategy include the *low-ball technique,* in which a person is asked for a small favour and is informed, after agreeing to it, that it will be very costly; or the *door-in-the-face technique,* wherein a person is first asked to do something extreme (a request that is usually refused) and then is asked to do something smaller. People tend to go along with the smaller request, possibly because they feel guilty about denying the larger one.[40]

GROUP EFFECTS ON INDIVIDUAL BEHAVIOUR

With more people in a group, it becomes less likely that any one member will be singled out for attention. People in larger groups or those in situations wherein they are

MARKETING OPPORTUNITY

Home-shopping parties, as epitomized by the Tupperware Party, capitalize on group pressures to boost sales.[41] A company representative makes a sales presentation to a group of people who have gathered in the home of a friend or acquaintance. This format is effective because of informational social influence: participants model the behaviour of others who can provide them with information about how to use certain products, especially since the home party is likely to be attended by a relatively homogeneous group (e.g., neighbourhood housewives) that serves as a valuable benchmark. Normative social influence also operates because actions are publicly observed. Pressures to conform may be particularly intense and may escalate as more and more group members begin to "cave in" (this process is sometimes termed the *bandwagon* effect). In addition, deindividuation and/or the risky shift may be activated: as consumers get caught up in the group, they may find themselves willing to try new products they would not normally consider.

unlikely to be identified tend to focus less attention on themselves, so normal restraints on behaviour are reduced. You may have observed that people sometimes behave more wildly at costume parties or on Halloween night than they do normally.

There is some evidence that decisions made by groups differ from those that would be made by each individual. In many cases group members show a greater willingness to consider riskier alternatives following group discussion than they would if each member made his or her own decision with no discussion. This change is known as the *risky shift.*[42]

Several explanations have been advanced to explain this increased riskiness. One possibility is that, as more people are involved in a decision, each individual is less accountable for the outcome, so *diffusion of responsibility* occurs.[43] Another explanation is termed the *value hypothesis.* In this case, riskiness is a culturally valued characteristic, and social pressures operate on individuals to conform to attributes valued by society.[44]

Evidence for the risky shift is mixed. A more general effect appears to be that group discussion tends to increase **decision polarization.** Whichever direction the group members were leaning before discussion began—towards a risky choice or a conservative one—becomes even more extreme after discussion. Group discussions regarding product purchases tend to create a risky shift for low-risk items, but they yield even more conservative group decisions for high-risk products.[45]

Even shopping behaviour changes when people do it in groups. For example, people who shop with at least one other person tend to make more unplanned purchases, buy more and cover more areas of a store than those who go alone.[46] These effects are due to both normative and informational social influence. Group members may be convinced to buy something to gain the approval of the others, or they may simply be exposed to more products and stores by pooling information with the group. For these reasons retailers would be well advised to encourage group shopping activities.

Social loafing refers to the fact that people do not devote as much to a task when their contribution is part of a larger group effort.[47] Waitresses are painfully aware of

decision polarization the process whereby individuals' choices tend to become more extreme (polarized), in either a conservative or a risky direction, following group discussion of alternatives

social loafing: people who eat in groups tend to tip less per person than those who eat alone.[48] For this reason many restaurants automatically tack on a fixed gratuity for groups of six or more.

Resistance to Influence

Many people pride themselves on their independence, unique style, or ability to resist the best efforts of salespeople and advertisers to sell products to them.[49] Indeed, individuality should be encouraged by the marketing system: innovation creates change and demand for new products and styles.

ANTICONFORMITY VERSUS INDEPENDENCE

It is important to distinguish between *independence* and *anticonformity*, in which defiance of the group is the actual object of behaviour.[50] Some people will go out of their way *not* to buy whatever happens to be in at the moment. Indeed, they may spend a lot of time and effort to ensure that they will not be caught in style. This behaviour is a bit of a paradox, since in order to be vigilant about not doing what is expected, one must always be aware of what is expected. In contrast, truly independent people are oblivious to what is expected; like the "loner" in the Ford audio systems ad on page 371, they "march to their own drummers."

REACTANCE AND NEED FOR UNIQUENESS

reactance a "boomerang effect" that sometimes occurs when consumers are threatened with a loss of freedom of choice; they respond by doing the opposite of the behaviour advocated in a persuasive message

People have a deep-seated need to preserve freedom of choice. When they are threatened with a loss of this freedom, they try to overcome this loss. This negative emotional state is termed **reactance.**[51] For example, efforts to censor books, television shows or rock music because some people find the content objectionable may result in an *increased* desire for these products by the public.[52] Similarly, extremely

Levi Strauss promotes its jeans to women who value independence over conformity.
Photo courtesy of Levi Strauss & Company.

This ad for Ford audio systems targets nonconformists by depicting a "loner" who prefers the wide open spaces to groups of people.
Courtesy of Ford Motor Company.

overbearing promotions that tell consumers they must or should use a product may wind up losing more customers in the long run—even those who were already loyal to the advertised brand! Reactance is more likely to occur when the perceived threat to one's freedom increases and as the threatened behaviour's importance to the consumer also increases.

If you have ever shown up at a party wearing the same outfit as someone else, you know how upsetting the discovery can be. Some psychologists believe this reaction is a result of a need for uniqueness.[53] Consumers who have been led to believe they are not unique are more likely to try to compensate by increasing their creativity, or even to engage in unusual experiences. In fact the need for uniqueness could be one explanation for the purchase of relatively obscure brands; people may try to establish a unique identity by deliberately *not* buying market leaders.

This desire to carve out a unique identity was the rationale behind Saab's recent shift from stressing engineering and safety in its marketing messages to appealing to people to "find your own road." According to a Saab executive, "Research companies tell us we're moving into a period where people feel good about their choices because it fits their own self-concept rather than social conventions."[54]

WORD-OF-MOUTH COMMUNICATION

Despite the abundance of formal means of communication (such as newspapers, magazines and television), much information about the world is conveyed by individuals on an informal basis. If you think carefully about the content of your own conversations in the course of a normal day, you will probably agree that much of what you discuss with friends, family members or co-workers is product-related. Whether you compliment someone on her dress and ask her where she bought it, recommend a new restaurant to a friend or complain to your neighbour about the

word-of-mouth communication (WOM) the information transmitted by individual consumers on an informal basis

shoddy treatment you got at the bank, you are engaging in **word-of-mouth communication (WOM).** Recall, for example, that many of Carlo's biker purchases are directly initiated by comments and suggestions from his fellow RUBs.

The power of this process was recognized by Make-up Art Cosmetics Ltd. This company is an anomaly in the $6-billion cosmetics industry, because it doesn't advertise. Instead, the firm built WOM by offering discounts to professional make-up artists to encourage them to use the line.[55] By cultivating an image as the choice of beauty professionals, this company has become a huge success.

Not every firm can do without advertising (fortunately for our friends in the business!), but information obtained from those we know or talk with directly tends to be more reliable and trustworthy than that received through more formal channels, and, unlike advertising, it is often backed up by social pressure to conform with these recommendations.[56] The importance of personal, informal product communication to marketers is underscored by an advertising executive who stated, "Today, 80 percent of all buying decisions are influenced by someone's direct recommendations."[57] Sometimes these recommendations are obtained by giving out samples of the product and hoping people will talk about it.

The Dominance of WOM

Communications theorists began in the 1950s to challenge the assumption that advertising is the primary determinant of purchases. It is now generally accepted that advertising is more effective at reinforcing existing product preferences than at creating new ones.[58] Studies in both industrial and consumer-purchase settings underscore the idea that, while information from impersonal sources is important for creating brand awareness, word of mouth is relied upon in the later stages of evaluation and adoption.[59] The more positive information a consumer gets about a product from peers, the more likely he or she will adopt the product.[60] The influence

M.A.C. is one of the first cosmetics companies to have a whole store rather than just a section in a department store. This is the M.A.C. store on Robson Street in Vancouver.
Courtesy of Judy Zaichkowsky.

of others' opinions is at times even more powerful than one's own perceptions. In one study of furniture choices, consumers' estimates of how much their friends would like the furniture were better predictors of purchase than were their own evaluations of it.[61]

FACTORS ENCOURAGING WOM

Most WOM campaigns happen spontaneously, as a product begins to develop a regional following and people share their experiences about it with others. Occasionally, though, a "buzz" is intentionally created. Henry Weinhard's Private Reserve, a superpremium beer in the Pacific Northwest, was first introduced at selected bars where bartenders had been briefed on the brand's unusual brewing process. The beer was introduced to stores only after demand from bar patrons mounted.[62]

Product-related conversations can be motivated by a number of factors:[63]

- A person might be highly involved with a type of product or activity and take pleasure in talking about it. Computer hackers, avid bird-watchers and "fashion plates" seem to share the ability to steer conversations towards their particular interests.

- A person might be knowledgeable about a product and use conversations as a way to let others know it. Thus word-of-mouth communication sometimes enhances the ego of the individual who wants to impress others with his or her expertise.

- A person might initiate such a discussion out of a genuine concern for someone else. We often are motivated to ensure that people we care about buy what is good for them, do not waste their money and so on.

- One way to reduce uncertainty about the wisdom of a purchase is to talk about it. Talking gives the consumer an opportunity to generate more supporting arguments for the purchase and to garner support for this decision from others.

EFFICIENCY OF WOM

Interpersonal transmissions can be quite rapid. The producers of the movie *Batman* showed a "trailer" to 300 Batman fans months prior to the movie's release to counteract widespread anger about the casting of Michael Keaton as the star. The filmmakers attribute the film's eventual huge success to the positive word of mouth that quickly spread following the screening.[64]

WOM is especially powerful in cases where the consumer is relatively unfamiliar with the product category. Such a situation would be expected in cases where the product is new (e.g., medications to prevent hair loss) or is technologically complex (CD players). As one example, the strongest predictor of a person's intention to buy a residential solar water-heating system was found to be the number of solar-heating users the person knows.[65]

Negative WOM

Word of mouth is a two-edged sword that can cut both ways for marketers. Informal discussions among consumers can make or break a product or store. And negative word of mouth is weighted *more* heavily by consumers than are positive comments.

According to one study 90 percent of unhappy customers will not do business with a company again. Each of these people is likely to share their grievance with at least nine other people, and 13 percent of these disgruntled customers will go on to tell more than 30 people of their negative experience.[66] Especially when making a decision about trying a product innovation, the consumer is more likely to pay attention to negative information than positive information and to relate news of this experience to others.[67] Negative WOM has been shown to reduce the credibility of a firm's advertising, and to influence consumers' attitudes towards a product as well as their intention to buy it.[68]

RUMOURS: DISTORTION IN THE WORD-OF-MOUTH PROCESS

In the 1930s "professional rumour mongers" were hired to organize word-of-mouth campaigns to promote clients' products and criticize those of competitors.[69] A rumour, even if it has no basis in fact, can be a very dangerous thing. As information is transmitted among consumers, it tends to change. The resulting message usually does not at all resemble the original.

Social scientists who study rumours have examined the process by which information gets distorted. The British psychologist Frederic Bartlett used the method of *serial reproduction* to examine this phenomenon. As in the game of "Telephone," a subject is asked to reproduce a stimulus, such as a drawing or a story. Another subject is given this reproduction and asked to copy that, and so on. This technique is shown in Figure 11–2. Bartlett found that distortions almost inevitably follow a pattern. They tend to change from ambiguous forms to more conventional ones as subjects try to make them consistent with pre-existing schemas. This process, known as *assimilation,* is characterized by *levelling,* wherein details are omitted to simplify the structure, or *sharpening,* wherein prominent details are accentuated.

In general, people have been shown to prefer transmitting good news rather than bad, perhaps because they like to avoid unpleasantness or dislike arousing hostility.[70] However, this reluctance does not appear to occur when companies are the topic of conversation. Corporations such as Procter & Gamble and McDonald's have been the subjects of rumours about their products, sometimes with noticeable effects on sales.

Rumours are thought to reveal the underlying fears of a society. One rumour regarding snakes coming out of teddy bears imported from the Orient was interpreted to signify Western consumers' apprehensions about Asian influences. The Disney organization recently came under attack from conservative religious groups after a rumour spread among members that the company was sending subversive subliminal messages in its videotapes. They insisted, for example, that the character Aladdin says, "All good teenagers take off your clothes." Disney countered that the real line is, "Scat, good tiger, take off and go."[71] While rumours sometimes die out by themselves, in other instances a company may take direct action to counteract them. A French margarine was rumoured to contain contaminants, and the company addressed this in its advertising by referring to the story as "The rumour that costs you dearly."[72]

CONSUMER BOYCOTTS

Sometimes a negative experience can trigger an organized and devastating response, as when a consumer group organizes a *boycott* of a company's products. About 100 boycott campaigns (including threats to boycott if a company does not change some

FIGURE 11–2 • The Transmission of Misinformation

These drawings provide a classic example of the distortions that can occur as information is transmitted from person to person. As each participant reproduces the figure, it gradually changes from an owl to a cat.

Source: Kenneth J. Gergen and Mary Gergen, *Social Psychology* (New York: Harcourt Brace Jovanovich, 1981), p. 365, Fig. 10–3; adapted from F.C. Bartlett, *Remembering* (Cambridge: Cambridge University Press, 1932).

MULTICULTURAL DIMENSIONS

Multinational firms are especially prone to damage from rumours, since they have less control over product quality, content or word of mouth. Several marketers in Indonesia, including Nestlé, were hurt by rumours that their foods contain pork, which is prohibited to the 160 million Muslim consumers in that country. Islamic preachers, or mullahs, responded to these rumours by warning consumers not to buy products that might be tainted with pork fat. Nestlé spent more than $250 000 on an ad campaign to counteract the rumours.[73]

Pabst Blue Ribbon beer was hit by a product-tampering scare in China. Rumours about poisoned bottles spread quickly, apparently following an incident where home-brewed beer was poured into empty Pabst bottles and resold.[74]

policy) are currently in effect. These efforts can include protests against everything from the use of products from a politically undesirable country (as when Procter & Gamble used Salvadorean beans for its Folgers coffee) to the inclusion of obscene or inflammatory lyrics in songs (as when law enforcement organizations threatened to boycott Time Warner after it distributed a rap song by Ice-T entitled "Cop Killer").

OPINION LEADERSHIP

Although consumers get information from personal sources, they do not tend to ask just *anyone* for advice about purchases. If you decide to buy a new stereo, you will most likely seek advice from a friend who knows a lot about sound systems. This friend may own a sophisticated system, or she may subscribe to specialized magazines, such as *Stereo Review,* and spend free time browsing through electronics stores. On the other hand, you may have another friend who has a reputation for being stylish and who spends *his* free time reading *Gentlemen's Quarterly* and shopping at trendy boutiques. While you might not bring up your stereo problem with him, you may take him with you to shop for a new fall wardrobe.

The Nature of Opinion Leadership

opinion leaders those people who are knowledgeable about products and who are frequently able to influence others' attitudes or behaviours with regard to a product category

Everyone knows people who are knowledgeable about products and whose advice is taken seriously by others. These individuals are **opinion leaders.** An opinion leader is a person who is frequently able to influence others' attitudes or behaviours.[75]

Opinion leaders are valuable information sources for a number of reasons:

1. They are technically competent and thus are convincing, because they possess expert power.[76]

This ad for MTV focuses on the importance of young opinion leaders in shaping their friends' preferences.
Courtesy of Viacom, International.

2. They have prescreened, evaluated and synthesized product information in an unbiased way, so they possess knowledge power.[77] Unlike commercial endorsers, opinion leaders do not actually represent the interests of one company. They are more credible because they have no "axe to grind."

3. They tend to be socially active and highly interconnected in their communities.[78] They are likely to hold office in community groups and clubs and to be active outside the home. As a result, opinion leaders often have legitimate power by virtue of their social standing.

4. They tend to be similar to the consumer in terms of their values and beliefs, so they possess referent power. Note that while opinion leaders are set apart by their interest or expertise in a product category, they are more convincing to the extent that they are *homophilous* rather than *heterophilous*. *Homophily* refers to the degree that a pair of individuals is similar in terms of education, social status and beliefs.[79] Effective opinion leaders tend to be slightly higher than those they influence in terms of status and educational attainment, but not so high as to be in a different social class.

5. Opinion leaders often are among the first to buy new products, so they absorb much of the risk. This experience reduces uncertainty for others who are not as courageous. And while company-sponsored communications tend to focus exclusively on the positive aspects of a product, this hands-on experience makes opinion leaders more likely to impart both positive and negative information about product performance.

THE EXTENT OF AN OPINION LEADER'S INFLUENCE

When marketers and social scientists initially developed the concept of the opinion leader, it was assumed that certain influential people in a community would exert an overall impact on group members' attitudes. Later work, however, began to question the assumption that there is such a thing as a *generalized opinion leader*—somebody whose recommendations are sought for all types of purchases. Very few people are capable of being expert in a number of fields. Sociologists distinguish between those who are *monomorphic*, or experts in a limited field, and those who are *polymorphic*, or experts in several fields.[80] Even the opinion leaders who are polymorphic tend to concentrate on one broad domain, such as electronics or fashion.

Research on opinion leadership generally indicates that while opinion leaders do exist for multiple product categories, expertise tends to overlap across similar categories. It is rare to find a generalized opinion leader. An opinion leader for home appliances is likely to serve a similar function for home cleaners, but not for cosmetics. In contrast, a *fashion opinion leader,* whose primary influence is on clothing choices, may also be consulted for recommendations on cosmetics purchases, but not necessarily on microwave ovens.[81]

OPINION LEADERS VERSUS OTHER CONSUMER TYPES

Early conceptions of the role of the opinion leader also assumed a static process: the opinion leader absorbs information from the mass media and in turn transmits these data to opinion receivers. This view has turned out to be overly simplified; it confuses the functions of several different types of consumers.

Opinion leaders may or may not be purchasers of the products they recommend. As we will see in Chapter 17, early purchasers are known as *innovators*. Opinion leaders who are also early purchasers have been termed *innovative communicators*. One study identified a number of characteristics of college men who were innovative communicators for fashion products. These men were among the first to buy new fashions, and their fashion opinions were incorporated by other students in their own clothing decisions. Other characteristics of these men included the following:[82]

- They were socially active.
- They were appearance-conscious and narcissistic (i.e., they were quite fond of themselves and self-centred).
- They were involved in rock culture.
- They were heavy magazine readers, including *Playboy* and *Sports Illustrated*.
- They were likely to own more clothing, and a broader range of styles, than other students.
- Their intellectual interests were relatively limited.

Opinion leaders also are likely to be *opinion seekers*. They are generally more involved in a product category and actively search for information. As a result, they are more likely to talk about products with others and to solicit others' opinions as well. Contrary to the static view of opinion leadership, most product-related conversation does not take place in a "lecture" format, wherein one person does all the talking. A lot of product-related conversation is prompted by the situation and occurs in the context of a casual interaction rather than as formal instruction.[83] One study, which found that opinion seeking is especially high for food products, revealed that two-thirds of opinion seekers also view themselves as opinion leaders.[84] This updated view of interpersonal product communication is contrasted with the traditional view in Figure 11–3.

FIGURE 11–3 • Perspectives on the Communications Process

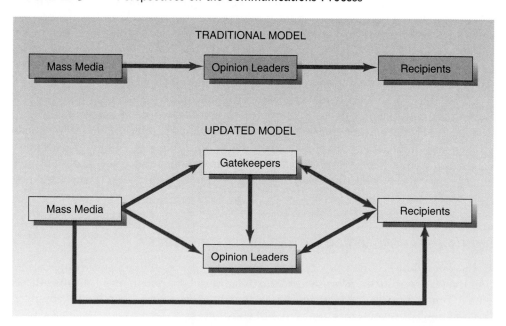

FIGURE 11–4 • Scale Items Used to Identify Market Mavens

1. I like introducing new brands and products to my friends.

2. I like helping people by providing them with information about many kinds of products.

3. People ask me for information about products, places to shop, or sales.

4. If someone asked me where to get the best buy on several types of products, I could tell him or her where to shop.

5. My friends think of me as a good source of information when it comes to new products or sales.

6. Think about a person who has information about a variety of products and likes to share this information with others. This person knows about new products, sales, stores and so on, but does not necessarily feel he or she is an expert on one particular product. How well would you say this description fits you?

Source: Adapted from Lawrence Feick and Linda Price, "The Market Maven: A Diffuser of Marketplace Information," *Journal of Marketing* 51 (January 1987): 83–87.

Consumers who are expert in a product category may not actively communicate with others, while other consumers may have a more general interest in being involved in product discussions. A consumer category called the **market maven** has been proposed to describe people who are actively involved in transmitting marketplace information of all types. Market mavens are not necessarily interested in certain products and may not necessarily be early purchasers of products. They come closer to the function of a generalized opinion leader because they tend to have a solid overall knowledge of how and where to procure products.[85] A scale that has been used to identify market mavens appears in Figure 11–4.

market maven a person who often serves as a source of information about marketplace activities

In addition to everyday consumers who are influential in affecting others' purchase decisions, a class of marketing intermediary called the **surrogate consumer** is an active player in many categories. A surrogate consumer is a person who is hired to provide input into purchase decisions. Unlike the opinion leader or market maven, the surrogate is usually compensated for this involvement.

surrogate consumer a professional who is retained to evaluate and/or make purchases on behalf of a consumer

Interior decorators, stockbrokers, professional shoppers or college consultants can all be thought of as surrogate consumers. Whether or not they actually make the purchase on behalf of the consumer, surrogates' recommendations can be enormously influential. The consumer in essence relinquishes control over several or all decision-making functions, such as information search, evaluation of alternatives or the actual purchase. For example, a client may commission an interior decorator to redo her house, while a broker may be entrusted to make crucial buy/sell decisions on behalf of investors. The involvement of surrogates in a wide range of purchase decisions tends to be overlooked by many marketers, who may be mistargeting their communications to end-consumers instead of to the surrogates who are actually sifting through product information.[86]

Identifying Opinion Leaders

Because opinion leaders are so central to consumer decision making, marketers are quite interested in identifying influential people for a product category. In fact many ads are intended to reach these influentials rather than the average consumer, especially if the ads contain a lot of technical information. The average television purchaser probably would not be excited by an ad for a Pioneer projection television that claims to have a lens with a "maximum bore of 160 mm" and a "new high-voltage stabilizing circuit." On the other hand, an electronics buff might be quite impressed by this information and, in turn, take it into consideration when recommending a projection television to a more naïve friend.

Unfortunately, since most opinion leaders are everyday consumers and are not formally included in marketing efforts, they are harder to find. A celebrity or an influential industry executive is, by definition, easy to locate. He or she has national or at least regional visibility or may be listed in published directories. In contrast, most opinion leaders tend to operate at the local level and may influence five to ten consumers rather than an entire market segment. In some cases companies have been known to identify influentials and involve them directly in their marketing efforts, hoping to create a "ripple effect" as these consumers sing the company's praises to their friends. Many department stores, for example, have "fashion panels," usually composed of adolescent girls, who provide input into fashion trends, participate in fashion shows and so on.

Because of the difficulties involved in identifying specific opinion leaders in a large market, most attempts to do so instead focus on exploratory studies in which the characteristics of representative opinion leaders can be identified and then generalized to the larger market. This knowledge helps marketers target their product-related information to appropriate settings and media. One attempt to identify financial opinion leaders found that these consumers were more likely to be involved in managing their own finances and tended to use a computer to do so. They also were more likely to follow their investments on a daily basis and to read books and watch television shows devoted to financial issues.[87]

THE SELF-DESIGNATING METHOD

The most commonly used technique to identify opinion leaders is simply to ask individual consumers whether they consider themselves to be opinion leaders. This is called the *self-designating method*.

While respondents who report a greater degree of interest in a product category are more likely to be opinion leaders, the results of surveys intended to identify self-designated opinion leaders must be viewed with some scepticism. Some people have a tendency to inflate their own importance and influence, while others who really are influential might not admit to this quality.[88] Just because we transmit advice about products does not mean other people *take* that advice. For someone to be considered a bona fide opinion leader, his or her advice must actually be heard and heeded by opinion seekers.

An alternative to self-designation is to select certain group members (*key informants*) who are then asked to identify opinion leaders. The success of this approach hinges on locating those who have accurate knowledge of the group and on minimizing their response biases (e.g., the tendency to inflate one's own influence on the choices of others).

While the self-designating method is not as reliable as a more systematic analysis (where individual claims of influence can be verified by asking others whether the person is really influential), it does have the advantage of being easy to administer to a large group of potential opinion leaders. In some cases not all members of a community are surveyed. An updated version of the original measurement scale developed for self-designation of opinion leaders is shown in Figure 11–5.[89]

FIGURE 11–5 • A Revised and Updated Version of the Opinion Leadership Scale

Please rate yourself on the following scales relating to your interactions with friends and neighbours regarding _____.

1. In general, do you talk to your friends and neighbours about _____:

very often				never
5	4	3	2	1

2. When you talk to your friends and neighbours about _____ do you:

give a great deal of information				give very little information
5	4	3	2	1

3. During the past six months, how many people have you told about a new _____?

told a number of people				told no one
5	4	3	2	1

4. Compared with your circle of friends, how likely are you to be asked about new _____?

very likely to be asked				not at all likely to be asked
5	4	3	2	1

5. In discussion of new _____, which of the following happens most?

you tell your friends about _____				your friends tell you about _____
5	4	3	2	1

6. Overall in all of your discussions with friends and neighbours are you:

often used as a source of advice				not used as a source of advice
5	4	3	2	1

Source: Adapted from Terry L. Childers, "Assessment of the Psychometric Properties of an Opinion Leadership Scale," *Journal of Marketing Research* 23 (May 1986): 184–88; Leisa Reinecke Flynn, Ronald E. Goldsmith and Jacqueline K. Eastman, "The King and Summers Opinion Leadership Scale: Revision and Refinement," *Journal of Business Research* 31 (1994): 55–64.

SOCIOMETRY

Sociometric methods, which trace communication patterns among group members, allow researchers systematically to map out interactions that take place among group members. By asking participants whom they go to for product information, those who tend to be sources of product-related information can be identified. While this method is the most precise, it is very hard and expensive to implement, since it involves very close study of interaction patterns in small groups. For this reason sociometric techniques are best applied in closed, self-contained social settings, such as hospitals, prisons and army bases, where members are largely isolated from other social networks.

sociometric methods the techniques for measuring group dynamics that involve the tracing of communication patterns in and among groups

Many professionals and services marketers depend primarily upon word of mouth to generate business. In many cases consumers recommend a service provider to a friend or co-worker, and in other cases other business people make recommendations to their customers. Only 0.2 percent of respondents in one study reported choosing physicians based on advertising; advice from family and friends was the most widely used criterion.[90]

Sociometric analyses can be used to better understand *referral behaviour* and to locate strengths and weaknesses in terms of how one's reputation is communicated through a community. *Network analysis* focuses on communication in social systems; it considers the relations among people in a *referral network* and measures the *tie strength* among them. Tie strength refers to the nature of the bond between people. It can range from strong primary (e.g., one's spouse) to weak secondary (an acquaintance that one rarely sees). A strong tie relationship may be thought of as a primary reference group, in which interactions are frequent and important to the individual.

While strong ties are important, weak ties can perform a *bridging function*. This type of connection allows a consumer access between subgroups. For example, you might have a regular group of friends who serve as a primary reference group (strong ties). If you have an interest in tennis, say, one of these friends might introduce you to a group of people in her dorm who play on the tennis team. As a result you gain access to their valuable expertise through this bridging function. This referral process demonstrates the strength of weak ties.

One study analyzed the referral networks of a services marketer (in this case a piano tuner) to demonstrate how referral patterns can be better understood. The researchers contacted all the piano tuner's customers and asked them how they found out about him (referral paths). The paths were identified, and the researchers were able to describe where business was being generated (whether through friends, business contacts, etc.) and also to pinpoint opinion leaders in the system (i.e., people who were a referral source for more than one customer).[91] This technique could conceivably be applied by many service providers to identify those customers who are responsible for generating a lot of business.

CHAPTER SUMMARY

- Consumers belong to or admire many different groups and are often influenced in their purchase decisions by a desire to be accepted by others.

- Individuals have influence in a group to the extent that they possess social power; types of power include information power, referent power, legitimate power, expert power, reward power and coercive power.

- We conform to the desires of others for one of two basic reasons. People who model their behaviour after others because they take others' behaviour as evidence of the correct way to act are conforming because of informational social influence. Those who conform to satisfy the expectations of others and/or to be accepted by the group are affected by normative social influence.

- Group members often do things they would not do as individuals because their identities become merged with the group.

- Individuals or groups whose opinions or behaviours are particularly important to consumers are *reference groups*. Both formal and informal groups influence the individual's purchase decisions, although the impact of reference-group influence is affected by such factors as the conspicuousness of the product and the relevance of the reference group for a particular purchase.

- Opinion leaders who are knowledgeable about a product and whose opinions are highly regarded tend to influence others' choices. Specific opinion leaders are somewhat hard to identify, but marketers who know their general characteristics can try to target them in their media and promotional strategies.

- Other influencers are market mavens, who have a general interest in marketplace activities, and surrogate consumers, who are compensated for their advice about purchases.

- Much of what we know about products comes about through word-of-mouth communication (WOM) rather than formal advertising. Product-related information tends to be exchanged in casual conversations.

- While word of mouth is often helpful for making consumers aware of products, it can also hurt companies when damaging product rumours or negative word of mouth occurs.
- Sociometric methods are used to trace referral patterns. This information can be used to identify opinion leaders and other influential consumers.

CONSUMER BEHAVIOUR CHALLENGE

1. Compare and contrast the five bases of power described in the text. Which are most likely to be relevant for marketing efforts?

2. Why is referent power an especially potent force for marketing appeals? What are factors that help to predict whether reference groups will or will not be a powerful influence on a person's purchase decisions?

3. Evaluate the strategic soundness of the concept of affinity marketing. For what type of linkages is this strategy most likely to be a success?

4. Discuss some factors that determine the amount of conformity likely to be observed among consumers.

5. Under what conditions are we likely to engage in social comparison with dissimilar others rather than with similar others? How might this dimension be used in the design of marketing appeals?

6. Discuss some reasons for the effectiveness of home-shopping parties as a selling tool. What factors might reduce the power of this strategy?

7. Discuss some factors that influence whether or not membership groups will have a significant influence on a person's behaviour.

8. Why is word-of-mouth communication often more persuasive than advertising?

9. Is there such a thing as a generalized opinion leader? What is likely to determine if an opinion leader will be influential with regard to a specific product category?

10. The power of unspoken social norms often becomes obvious only when these norms are violated. To witness this result firsthand, try one of the following: stand facing the back wall in an elevator; serve dessert before the main course; offer to pay cash for dinner at a friend's home; wear pajamas to class; or tell someone *not* to have a nice day.

11. Identify a set of avoidance groups for your peers. Can you identify any consumption decisions that are made with these groups in mind?

12. Identify fashion opinion leaders on your campus. Do they fit the profile discussed in the chapter?

13. Conduct a sociometric analysis within your residence or neighbourhood. For a product category such as music or cars, ask each individual to identify other individuals with whom they share information. Systematically trace all of these avenues of communication, and identify opinion leaders by locating individuals who are repeatedly named as providing helpful information.

CBC VIDEO VIGNETTES

Concepts at Work for Make-up Art Cosmetics Ltd. (M.A.C.)

M.A.C., a Canadian company started in 1985, knows firsthand the kind of impact marketplace success can have on how a company manages growth. In many ways it is a classic example of how new products diffuse among consumers. The company was born out of the insistence of one make-up artist, Frank Toscan (a cofounder), that he have the best colours for make-up for his photography work. Through experiments in his kitchen, he and his business partner, Frank Angelo, developed products that became known in the arts community after free make-up was given to other make-up artists to try. This positive word of mouth was augmented by the increasing interest of celebrities.

Within a year it was obvious that there might be mainstream demand, and so two showcases were set up in The Bay. M.A.C. lacked the sales support or advertising that were the trademarks of the marketing communications strategies employed by other cosmetics companies. Nevertheless, within two years M.A.C. had a whole aisle of selling space.

In the 1990s, while M.A.C. was busy trying to look after domestic demand, it became obvious that there was international interest. M.A.C. was being sold in countries to which the company had not been exporting; a kind of black market had developed. Retail customers were restricted to three tubes of the same colour of lipstick in an effort to prevent mass reselling abroad. In addition, M.A.C. faced increasing competition from imitators and private-label brands.

To gain access to an established international distribution network, M.A.C. went to Estée Lauder, who initially did not see M.A.C. as a successful, innovative brand. Two years later Estée Lauder realized that M.A.C.'s popularity was really taking off and that this Canadian company could provide a growth opportunity. The two companies worked out a five-year take-over plan, which retained M.A.C.'s control over creative aspects of the business while Estée Lauder provided expertise in the areas of finance and international expansion. This strategy is expected to take M.A.C. from the kitchen sink (in 1985) to a billion-dollar company by the year 2000. Only by keeping an eye on what attracts and retains M.A.C. customers can this goal be reached.

QUESTIONS

1. What was the initial appeal of M.A.C. products?

2. Why did the make-up artists act as opinion leaders?

3. How do you account for the successful consumer adoption of M.A.C. by the international market?

4. What is the future of M.A.C. cosmetics now that it is part of Estée Lauder? Do you think M.A.C. would have been a successful product if initially launched by them?

Video Resource: "M.A.C. Cosmetics," *Venture* #580 (March 3, 1996).

Additional Resource: Gayle MacDonald, "MAC makeover tightens U.S. giant's grip," *Globe and Mail* (March 14, 1997): B9.

NOTES

1. Details adapted from John W. Schouten and James H. McAlexander, "Market Impact of a Consumption Subculture: The Harley-Davidson Mystique," in *Proceedings of the 1992 European Conference of the Association for Consumer Research*, eds. Fred van Raaij and Gary Bamossy (Amsterdam, 1992).

2. Joel B. Cohen and Ellen Golden, "Informational Social Influence and Product Evaluation," *Journal of Applied Psychology* 56 (February 1972): 54–59; Robert E. Burnkrant and Alain Cousineau, "Informational and Normative Social Influence in Buyer Behavior," *Journal of Consumer Research* 2 (December 1975): 206–15; Peter H. Reingen, "Test of a List Procedure for Inducing Compliance with a Request to Donate Money," *Journal of Applied Psychology* 67 (1982): 110–18; William O. Bearden, Randall L. Rose and Jesse E. Teel, "Correlates of Conformity in the Consumption of Illicit Drugs and Alcohol," *Journal of Business Research* 30, 1 (May 1994): 25–31.

3. C. Whan Park and V. Parker Lessig, "Students and Housewives: Differences in Susceptibility to Reference Group Influence," *Journal of Consumer Research* 4 (September 1977): 102–10.

4. Kenneth J. Gergen and Mary Gergen, *Social Psychology* (New York: Harcourt Brace Jovanovich, 1981).

5. Harold H. Kelley, "Two Functions of Reference Groups," in *Basic Studies in Social Psychology,* eds. Harold Proshansky and Bernard Siedenberg (New York: Holt, Rinehart and Winston, 1965), pp. 210–14. For a recent empirical application in the area of teen apparel shopping, see Oswald A. Mascarenhas and Mary A. Higby, "Peer, Parent, and Media Influences in Teen Apparel Shopping," *Journal of the Academy of Marketing Science* 21, 1 (Winter 1993): 53–58.

6. Robert D. Hof, "Special Report: Internet Communities," *Business Week* (May 5, 1997): 63 (8 pp.).

7. Paul C. Judge, "Why Firefly Has Mad Ave. Buzzing," *Business Week* (October 7, 1996): 100 (2 pp.).

8. Carol Krol, "Survey: Friends Lead Pack in Kids' Spending Decisions," *Advertising Age* (March 10, 1997): 16.

9. Anthony Ramirez, "Mastercards Shift from Glamour," *New York Times* (April 9, 1990): D1.

10. L. Festinger, S. Schachter and K. Back, *Social Pressures in Informal Groups: A Study of Human Factors in Housing* (New York: Harper and Row, 1950).

11. Judith Waldrop, "Plastic Wars," *American Demographics* (November 1988): 6.

12. Elaine Santoro, "Catholic Charities Credit Card Unveiled," *Fund Raising Management* 20 (April 1989): 10.

13. R.B. Zajonc, H.M. Markus and W. Wilson, "Exposure Effects and Associative Learning," *Journal of Experimental Social Psychology* 10 (1974): 248–63.

14. D.J. Stang, "Methodological Factors in Mere Exposure Research," *Psychological Bulletin* 81 (1974): 1014–25; R.B. Zajonc et al., "Exposure, Satiation and Stimulus Discriminability," *Journal of Personality and Social Psychology* 21 (1972): 270–80.

15. A. Benton Cocanougher and Grady D. Bruce, "Socially Distant Reference Groups and Consumer Aspirations," *Journal of Marketing Research* 8 (August 1971): 79–81; James E. Stafford, "Effects of Group Influences on Consumer Brand Preferences," *Journal of Marketing Research* 3 (February 1966): 68–75.

16. Ramirez, "Mastercards Shift from Glamour."

17. Cocanougher and Bruce, "Socially Distant Reference Groups and Consumer Aspirations."

18. David Murrow, "Dewars Profiles Travel Well," *Advertising Age* (August 14, 1989): 28.

19. Jeffrey D. Ford and Elwood A. Ellis, "A Re-examination of Group Influence on Member Brand Preference," *Journal of Marketing Research* 17 (February 1980): 125–32; Thomas S. Robertson, *Innovative Behavior and Communication* (New York: Holt, Rinehart and Winston, 1980), ch. 8.

20. William O. Bearden and Michael J. Etzel, "Reference Group Influence on Product and Brand Purchase Decisions," *Journal of Consumer Research* 9, 2 (1982): 183–94.

21. Gergen and Gergen, *Social Psychology,* p. 312.

22. J.R.P. French, Jr., and B. Raven, "The Bases of Social Power," in *Studies in Social Power*, ed. D. Cartwright (Ann Arbor, MI: Institute for Social Research, 1959), pp. 150–67.

23. Michael R. Solomon, "Packaging the Service Provider," *Service Industries Journal* 5 (March 1985): 64–72.

24. Augustin Hedberg, "Lights! Camera! Economists! (celebrity economists)," *Money* (October 1987): 118.

25. See Robert B. Cialdini, *Influence: Science and Practice,* 2nd ed. (New York: Scott, Foresman and Company, 1988), for an excellent and entertaining treatment of this process.

26. For the seminal work on conformity and social influence, see Solomon E. Asch, "Effects of Group Pressure Upon the Modification and Distortion of Judgments," in *Group Dynamics,* eds. D. Cartwright and A. Zander (New York: Harper and Row, 1953); Richard S. Crutchfield, "Conformity and Character," *American Psychologist* 10 (1955): 191–98; Muzafer Sherif, "A Study of Some Social Factors in Perception," *Archives of Psychology* 27 (1935): 187.

27. Burnkrant and Cousineau, "Informational and Normative Social Influence in Buyer Behavior."

28. For an attempt to measure individual differences in proclivity to conformity, see William O. Bearden,

Richard G. Netemeyer and Jesse E. Teel, "Measurement of Consumer Susceptibility to Interpersonal Influence," *Journal of Consumer Research* 15 (March 1989): 473–81.

29. John W. Thibaut and Harold H. Kelley, *The Social Psychology of Groups* (New York: John Wiley, 1959); W.W. Waller and R. Hill, *The Family, a Dynamic Interpretation* (New York: Dryden, 1951).

30. Sandra L. Bem, "Sex Role Adaptability: One Consequence of Psychological Androgyny," *Journal of Personality and Social Psychology* 31 (1975): 634–43.

31. William O. Bearden, Richard G. Netemeyer and Jesse E. Teel, "Measurement of Consumer Susceptibility to Interpersonal Influence," *Journal of Consumer Research* 9, 3 (1989): 183–94; Lynn R. Kahle, "Observations: Role-Relaxed Consumers: A Trend of the Nineties," *Journal of Advertising Research* (March/April 1995): 66–71; Lynn R. Kahle and Aviv Shoham, "Observations: Role-Relaxed Consumers: Empirical Evidence," *Journal of Advertising Research* 35, 3 (May/June 1995): 59–62.

32. Leon Festinger, "A Theory of Social Comparison Processes," *Human Relations* 7 (May 1954): 117–40.

33. Chester A. Insko et al., "Conformity as a Function of the Consistency of Positive Self-Evaluation with Being Liked and Being Right," *Journal of Experimental Social Psychology* 19 (1983): 341–58.

34. Abraham Tesser, Murray Millar and Janet Moore, "Some Affective Consequences of Social Comparison and Reflection Processes: The Pain and Pleasure of Being Close," *Journal of Personality and Social Psychology* 54, 1 (1988): 49–61.

35. L. Wheeler et al., "Factors Determining the Choice of a Comparison Other," *Journal of Experimental Social Psychology* 5 (1969): 219–32.

36. George P. Moschis, "Social Comparison and Informal Group Influence," *Journal of Marketing Research* 13 (August 1976): 237–44.

37. Burnkrant and Cousineau, "Informational and Normative Social Influence in Buyer Behavior"; M. Venkatesan, "Experimental Study of Consumer Behavior Conformity and Independence," *Journal of Marketing Research* 3 (November 1966): 384–87.

38. Harvey London, *Psychology of the Persuader* (Morristown, NJ: Silver Burdett/General Learning Press, 1973); William J. McGuire, "The Nature of Attitudes and Attitude Change," in *The Handbook of Social Psychology,* eds. G. Lindzey and E. Aronson (Reading, MA: Addison-Wesley, 1968), p. 3; N. Miller et al., "Speed of Speech and Persuasion," *Journal of Personality and Social Psychology* 34 (1976): 615–24.

39. J.L. Freedman and S. Fraser, "Compliance Without Pressure: the Foot-in-the-Door Technique," *Journal of Personality and Social Psychology* 4 (1966): 195–202.

40. R.B. Cialdini et al., "Reciprocal Concessions Procedure for Inducing Compliance: The Door-in-the-Face Effect," *Journal of Personality and Social Psychology* 31 (1975): 200–215.

41. Len Strazewski, "Tupperware Locks in New Strategy," *Advertising Age* (February 8, 1988): 30.

42. Nathan Kogan and Michael A. Wallach, "Risky Shift Phenomenon in Small Decision-Making Groups: A Test of the Information Exchange Hypothesis," *Journal of Experimental Social Psychology* 3 (January 1967): 75–84; Nathan Kogan and Michael A. Wallach, *Risk Taking* (New York: Holt, Rinehart and Winston, 1964); Arch G. Woodside and M. Wayne DeLozier, "Effects of Word-of-Mouth Advertising on Consumer Risk Taking," *Journal of Advertising* (Fall 1976): 12–19.

43. Kogan and Wallach, *Risk Taking.*

44. Roger Brown, *Social Psychology* (New York: Free Press, 1965).

45. David L. Johnson and I.R. Andrews, "Risky Shift Phenomenon Tested with Consumer Product Stimuli," *Journal of Personality and Social Psychology* 20 (1971): 382–85. See also Vithala R. Rao and Joel H. Steckel, "A Polarization Model for Describing Group Preferences," *Journal of Consumer Research* 18 (June 1991): 108–18.

46. Donald H. Granbois, "Improving the Study of Customer In-Store Behavior," *Journal of Marketing* 32 (October 1968): 28–32.

47. B. Latane, K. Williams and S. Harkins, "Many Hands Make Light the Work: The Causes and Consequences of Social Loafing," *Journal of Personality and Social Psychology* 37 (1979): 822–32.

48. S. Freeman et al., "Diffusion of Responsibility and Restaurant Tipping: Cheaper by the Bunch," *Personality and Social Psychology Bulletin* 1 (1978): 584–87.

49. Gergen and Gergen, *Social Psychology.*

50. L.J. Strickland, S. Messick and D.N. Jackson, "Conformity, Anticonformity and Independence: Their Dimensionality and Generality," *Journal of Personality and Social Psychology* 16 (1970): 494–507.

51. Jack W. Brehm, *A Theory of Psychological Reactance* (New York: Academic Press, 1966).

52. R.D. Ashmore, V. Ramchandra and R. Jones, "Censorship as an Attitude Change Induction" (paper presented at meetings of Eastern Psychological Association, New York, 1971); R.A. Wicklund and J. Brehm, *Perspectives on Cognitive Dissonance* (Hillsdale, NJ: Lawrence Erlbaum, 1976).

53. C.R. Snyder and H.L. Fromkin, *Uniqueness: The Human Pursuit of Difference* (New York: Plenum Press, 1980).

54. Quoted in Raymond Serafin, "Non-conformity sparks Saab," *Advertising Age* (April 3, 1995): 27.

55. Yumiko Ono, "Earth Tones and Attitude Make a Tiny Cosmetics Company Hot," *Wall Street Journal* (February 23, 1995): B1 (2 pp.).

56. Johan Arndt, "Role of Product-Related Conversations in the Diffusion of a New Product," *Journal of Marketing Research* 4 (August 1967): 291–95.

57. Quoted in Barbara B. Stern and Stephen J. Gould, "The Consumer as Financial Opinion Leader," *Journal of Retail Banking* 10 (Summer 1988): 43–52.

58. Elihu Katz and Paul F. Lazarsfeld, *Personal Influence* (Glencoe, IL: Free Press, 1955).

59. John A. Martilla, "Word-of-Mouth Communication in the Industrial Adoption Process," *Journal of Marketing Research* 8 (March 1971): 173–78. See also Marsha L. Richins, "Negative Word-of-Mouth by Dissatisfied Consumers: A Pilot Study," *Journal of Marketing* 47 (Winter 1983): 68–78.

60. Arndt, "Role of Product-Related Conversations in the Diffusion of a New Product."

61. James H. Myers and Thomas S. Robertson, "Dimensions of Opinion Leadership," *Journal of Marketing Research* 9 (February 1972): 41–46.

62. Barnaby J. Feder, "Those with Things to Sell Love Word-of-Mouth Ads," *New York Times* (June 23, 1992): D18.

63. James F. Engel, Robert J. Kegerreis and Roger D. Blackwell, "Word of Mouth Communication by the Innovator," *Journal of Marketing* 33 (July 1969): 15–19.

64. Bill Barol, "Batmania," *Newsweek* (June 26, 1989): 70.

65. Dorothy Leonard-Barton, "Experts as Negative Opinion Leaders in the Diffusion of a Technological Innovation," *Journal of Consumer Research* 11 (March 1985): 914–26.

66. Chip Walker, "Word of Mouth," *American Demographics* (July 1995): 38–44.

67. Richard J. Lutz, "Changing Brand Attitudes Through Modification of Cognitive Structure," *Journal of Consumer Research* 1 (March 1975): 49–59. For some suggested remedies to bad publicity, see Mitch Griffin, Barry J. Babin and Jill S. Attaway, "An Empirical Investigation of the Impact of Negative Public Publicity on Consumer Attitudes and Intentions," in *Advances in Consumer Research 18*, eds. Rebecca H. Holman and Michael R. Solomon (Provo, UT: Association for Consumer Research, 1991), pp. 334–41; Alice M. Tybout, Bobby J. Calder and Brian Sternthal, "Using Information Processing Theory to Design Marketing Strategies," *Journal of Marketing Research* 18 (1981): 73–79.

68. Robert E. Smith and Christine A. Vogt, "The Effects of Integrating Advertising and Negative Word-of-Mouth Communications on Message Processing and Response," *Journal of Consumer Psychology* 4, 2 (1995): 133–51; Paula Fitzgerald Bone, "Word-of-Mouth Effects on Short-Term and Long-Term Product Judgments," *Journal of Business Research* 32 (1995): 213–23.

69. Charles W. King and John O. Summers, "Overlap of Opinion Leadership Across Consumer Product Categories," *Journal of Marketing Research* 7 (February 1970): 43–50.

70. A. Tesser and S. Rosen, "The Reluctance to Transmit Bad News," in *Advances in Experimental Social Psychology,* ed. L. Berkowitz (New York: Academic Press, 1975), p. 8.

71. Lisa Bannon, "How a Rumor Spread About Subliminal Sex in Disney's 'Aladdin,'" *Wall Street Journal* (October 24, 1995): B1 (2 pp.).

72. John Leo, "Psst! Wait Till You Hear This: A Scholar Says Rumors Reveal Our Fears and Desires," *Time* (March 16, 1987): 76.

73. Sid Astbury, "Pork Rumors Vex Indonesia," *Advertising Age* (February 16, 1989): 36.

74. Craig S. Smith, "A Beer Tampering Scare in China Shows a Peril of Global Marketing," *Wall Street Journal* (November 3, 1995): B1.

75. Everett M. Rogers, *Diffusion of Innovations,* 3rd ed. (New York: Free Press, 1983).

76. Leonard-Barton, "Experts as Negative Opinion Leaders"; Rogers, *Diffusion of Innovations.*

77. Herbert Menzel, "Interpersonal and Unplanned Communications: Indispensable or Obsolete?" in *Biomedical Innovation* (Cambridge, MA: MIT Press, 1981), pp. 155–63.

78. Meera P. Venkatraman, "Opinion Leaders, Adopters, and Communicative Adopters: A Role Analysis," *Psychology & Marketing* 6 (Spring 1989): 51–68.

79. Rogers, *Diffusion of Innovations.*

80. Robert Merton, *Social Theory and Social Structure* (Glencoe, IL: Free Press, 1957).

81. King and Summers, "Overlap of Opinion Leadership Across Consumer Product Categories." See also Ronald E. Goldsmith, Jeanne R. Heitmeyer and Jon B. Freiden, "Social Values and Fashion Leadership," *Clothing and Textiles Research Journal* 10 (Fall 1991): 37–45; J.O. Summers, "Identity of Women's Clothing Fashion Opinion Leaders," *Journal of Marketing Research* 7 (1970): 178–85.

82. Steven A. Baumgarten, "The Innovative Communicator in the Diffusion Process," *Journal of Marketing Research* 12 (February 1975): 12–18.

83. Russell W. Belk, "Occurrence of Word-of-Mouth Buyer Behavior As a Function of Situation and Advertising Stimuli," in *Combined Proceedings of the American Marketing Association,* series no. 33, ed. Fred C. Allvine (Chicago: American Marketing Association, 1971), pp. 419–22.

84. Lawrence F. Feick, Linda L. Price and Robin A. Higie, "People Who Use People: The Other Side of Opinion Leadership," in *Advances in Consumer Research 13*, ed. Richard J. Lutz (Provo, UT: Association for Consumer Research, 1986), pp. 301–5.

85. For discussion of the market-maven construct, see Lawrence F. Feick and Linda L. Price, "The Market Maven," *Managing* (July 1985): 10. Although it is possible to identify market mavens within a study population using this type of scale, to date no clear

demographic profile that characterizes this type has been identified.

86. Michael R. Solomon, "The Missing Link: Surrogate Consumers in the Marketing Chain," *Journal of Marketing* 50 (October 1986): 208–18.

87. Stern and Gould, "The Consumer as Financial Opinion Leader."

88. William R. Darden and Fred D. Reynolds, "Predicting Opinion Leadership for Men's Apparel Fashions," *Journal of Marketing Research* 1 (August 1972), pp. 324–28. A modified version of the opinion leadership scale with improved reliability and validity can be found in Terry L. Childers, "Assessment of the Psychometric Properties of an Opinion Leadership Scale," *Journal of Marketing Research* 23 (May 1986): 184–88.

89. Several studies have provided updates on the content and validity of the original King and Summers scale. The scale presented here reflects two changes from the original scale: 1) the response format has been changed to a uniform five-point format; and 2) one of the original items has been dropped due to low reliability. See Childers, "Assessment of the Psychometric Properties of an Opinion Leadership Scale"; Ronald E. Goldsmith and Rene Desborde, "A Validity Study of a Measure of Opinion Leadership," *Journal of Business Research* 22 (1991): 11–19; Leisa Reinecke Flynn, Ronald E. Goldsmith and Jacqueline K. Eastman, "The King and Summers Opinion Leadership Scale: Revision and Refinement," *Journal of Business Research* 31 (1994): 55–64.

90. "Referrals Top Ads as Influence on Patients' Doctor Selections," *Marketing News* (January 30, 1987): 22.

91. Peter H. Reingen and Jerome B. Kernan, "Analysis of Referral Networks in Marketing: Methods and Illustration," *Journal of Marketing Research* 23 (November 1986): 370–78.

Tuesday is grocery day, and P.J. is accompanying his mom. He doesn't usually go along, and he thinks Tina, his mom, would rather go alone. She spends less and gets home faster without him, she says. But he's going today anyway, partly to be sure she picks cool stuff for his eleventh birthday party. The Power Rangers tablecloth and cupcakes were OK last year, but he's a teenager now (almost) and plans to lobby heavily for the right food and decorations. Yeah, he wants stuff that's with it—maybe featuring bands like Sloan or No Doubt.

First, they get the family's regular shopping out of the way. Tina gets exasperated as P.J. and his sister argue over the best food to get for their new puppy. Finally they move on to the next aisle, where Tina throws two cans of tuna into the cart. She moves on, but from behind her she hears P.J. say, "Whoa, Ma! Just chill here! You're not going to buy that brand, are you? Don't you know they use nets to catch tuna—nets that kill hundreds of innocent dolphins every year!" This was news to Tina. Getting over her irritation at being told how to shop by a kid who can't even clean up his room, she realizes that P.J. is making sense.

As she puts the cans back on the shelf, she remarks, "Gee, P.J., I should send you to do the shopping from now on. Maybe I can take you to work, too. The guys at the office could use a little common sense when we argue about what kind of supplies to buy."

First house. First party.

Smirnoff. Two glasses. An old fridge that makes great ice.

Perfect.

12

Family
Decision
Making

INTRODUCTION

Kids are becoming a major force in persuading their parents to clean up their act when it comes to the environment. One study showed that one-third of parents have changed their shopping habits to be more environmentally conscious due to information they received from their children. "Green School" programs have been instrumental in projects ranging from home and school recycling to vermicomposting. Many companies are becoming aware of young people's influence in everyday family buying decisions, and some are trying extra hard to convince young children and teens that their products are environmentally friendly.[1]

P.J.'s influence on his mother's choice of an environmentally safe product illustrates that many consumer decisions are made jointly. The individual decision-making process described in detail in Chapter 9 is, in many cases, overly simplistic. In fact more than one person may be involved in any stage of the problem-solving sequence, from initial problem recognition and information search to evaluation of alternatives and product choice. For example, the decision to get a pet is often jointly made by family members. The kids may be instrumental in persuading their reluctant parents to get a dog or a cat, while the parents may be responsible for the information search to determine what kind to get or where to get it. Then the entire family may be involved in actually selecting the puppy or kitten that will soon become another family member.

This chapter examines issues related to *family decision making,* where more than one person is involved in the purchasing process for products or services that may be used by multiple consumers. Specifically, we'll consider how members of a family negotiate among themselves and how important changes in modern family structure are affecting this process. The chapter concludes by focusing on how children learn to be consumers.

THE FAMILY

It is not unusual to read in newspapers and magazines about the "death of the family unit." While it is true that the proportion of people living in a traditional family structure, consisting of a married couple with children, has declined (to 48 percent in 1991), many other types of families are growing rapidly. Indeed, some experts have argued that as traditional family living arrangements have waned, people are placing even greater emphasis on the roles of siblings, close friends and other relatives in providing companionship and social support.[2]

MARKETING PITFALL

Although families are "in" in the 1990s, some media critics worry that many advertisements teach undesirable lessons about what family life should be like during a time when many people are trying to juggle their desires to have successful careers *and* to be good parents. For example, a recent ad for Depo-Provera, a contraception injection, depicts a "Power Mom" in front of her word processor, engrossed in work with a phone at her ear. Sitting on her lap is her daughter, with a phone receiver glued to her ear as well. The caption reads, "Is it any wonder I sometimes forget my birth control pills?" What kind of message does this ad send?

Other popular themes include the following:[3]

- The solitary life. Many contemporary ads depict a child or a parent in solitary settings, perhaps reflecting the increasing proportion of unmarried people.

- Materialism. Some ads, it is argued, try to substitute products for family and friends. An ad for a backpack claims: "If only boyfriends came with the same guarantee we do." A record ad reads: "Prom hints from Sony 550 music: If the chaperones are like totally not cool, if your date has nothing interesting to say ..., just turn your Walkman on high and listen to the best new music."

- Narcissism. In the past, many ads promised popularity if consumers shared the product depicted. Now they are encouraged to grab it all for themselves. One example is the popular campaign for waffles where actors protest, "Leggo my Eggo!"

Industry executives argue that critics overestimate advertising's influence and that these messages merely reflect the dominant themes in society. What do you think?

This ad for *Family Circle* magazine humorously emphasizes that some traditional family values persist among young people of the 1990s.
© 1992, The Family Circle, Inc.

Many marketers have focused on the renewed interest in family life brought about by the more flexible definitions of what constitutes a family.[4] While families were indeed out of fashion in the 1960s and 1970s—being seen by some as an infringement on personal freedom—90 percent of the respondents in one recent survey confirmed that family life was one of the most important things to them.[5]

Renewed interest in the family is apparent in the success of magazines such as *Today's Parent* and *Great Expectations*. Advertisers are also climbing on the bandwagon. Companies ranging from Heinz and Polycell (in the United Kingdom) to Gitano (jeans) and Johnson (outboard motors) are revamping their campaigns.[6] In a radical departure from Club Med's old "swinging singles" days, half of the vacationers who stay at its resorts now bring their families along.[7]

Defining the Modern Family

The **extended family** was once the most common family unit. It consisted of three generations living together, and often included not only the grandparents but also aunts, uncles and cousins. As evidenced by the Cleavers of "Leave It to Beaver" and other television families of the 1950s, the **nuclear family**—a mother and a father and one or more children (perhaps with a sheepdog thrown in for good measure)— became the model family unit over time. However, many changes have occurred since the days of Beaver Cleaver. Although people may continue to conjure up an image of the typical family based on old shows, demographic data show that this ideal image of the family is no longer a realistic picture.

JUST WHAT IS A HOUSEHOLD?

In taking the national census every five years, Statistics Canada regards any occupied housing unit as a household, regardless of the relationships among people living there. A **family household,** as defined by Statistics Canada, is a household that contains at least one family (a husband and wife, married or living common law, or

extended family traditional family structure where several generations live together

nuclear family a contemporary living arrangement composed of a married couple and their children

family household a housing unit containing at least one family (a husband and wife, married or living common law, or lone-parent of any marital status with or without children who have never married living at home)

Clothing manufacturer Gitano, which traditionally positioned its jeans as a must for women who want to be seductive, spent $3 million (US) on its "Spirit of Family" campaign, which depicts an all-American family image. As a company executive explains, "Even though the Gitano ads of the past have been of a self-confident, sexy woman, they've updated with the times. Now, we see that the family is what is important." Gitano replaced its traditional focus on young, single adults (top) with a family theme (bottom). *Courtesy of THE AD GROUP, New York, N.Y., in-house agency: The Gitano Group, Inc. ("Connecting Consumer and Product," New York Times [January 18, 1990]: D19; Maryellen Gordon, "Gitano's New Ad Campaign to Emphasize Family Spirit," Women's Wear Daily [August 16, 1989]: 11; David Reed, "Heinz and Polycell Get in the Family Way," Marketing [October 27, 1988]: 9.)*

lone-parent of any marital status with or without children who have never married living at home).[8] While Statistics Canada and other survey firms compile a massive amount of data on family households, certain categories are of particular interest to marketers. In addition, changes in consumers' family structures, such as the upheaval caused by divorce, often represent opportunities for marketers as normal purchasing patterns become unfrozen and people make new choices about products and brands.[9]

MARKETING OPPORTUNITY

In recent years large numbers of women have entered, or re-entered, the workforce (among married couples, over 60 percent of mothers work outside the home).[10] Because of this trend and other changes in the family, fewer adult caretakers are available to supervise school-age children. These factors have created a generation of latchkey children—children who come home to a locked, empty home after school and who can be identified by the keys worn on chains around their necks so they won't get lost. It is estimated that almost 20 percent of Canadian kids aged 6 to 12 qualify as latchkey kids in dual-earner families.[11] Together with their parents, they represent a sizeable segment for marketers of products ranging from convenience foods to security systems.

GROWTH AND DISTRIBUTION OF FAMILY HOUSEHOLDS

The last half of the twentieth century has seen a major shift in where Canadians live. Largely through the widespread availability of automobiles, consumers have migrated, and suburban areas have grown dramatically. Recently, people have been pushing out even farther beyond cities to rural areas. However, three-quarters of Canadians were urban dwellers in 1971 and 1991. Interestingly, the growth in rural areas since 1971 has occurred east of Ontario. More than 60 percent of the population of PEI lives in rural areas. Canadian marketers play on the rural theme, and the lure of the wild and the hinterland, by offering products and services such as the Country Palette line of home furnishings and accessories (The Bombay Company), Laker beer (Lakeport Brewing Corporation), SkiDoos and Sea Doos (both manufactured by Bombardier Inc.), Sawmill Creek wine (***www.atlaswine.com/saw.html***), Canvasback ale (named by Calgary's Big Rock Brewery after the "king of the ducks"), ORCA-FM (the world's first all-whale radio station) and musk-ox burgers.[12]

Motorola recognizes the new, mobile lifestyles of many modern families. The company has positioned its paging products to meet the needs of on-the-go parents.
Courtesy of Motorola Paging Products Group.

AGE OF THE FAMILY

Most Canadians younger than 24 years have never been married or in a common-law relationship. The vast majority of 35- to 74-year-olds are in these relationships. However, as might be expected due to the baby boom effect, the 35–44 age group has the greatest number of marriages and common-law relationships.[13] An important reason for these trends is that people are waiting longer to get married: according to Statistics Canada the average age of first marriages is now 26 for women and 28 for men.[14] This trend has implications for businesses ranging from catering to cutlery. For example, since couples tend to marry later and many already have acquired basic household items, the trend is towards giving non-traditional items as wedding gifts, like home electronics and PCs.[15]

FAMILY SIZE

fertility rate a rate determined by the number of births per year per 1000 women of child- bearing age

Worldwide, surveys show that almost all women want smaller families than they did a decade ago. In 1960 the average Canadian household was close to 4 people, but today that number has slipped to 2.7 people.[16] Family size is dependent on such factors as educational level, the availability of birth control, and religion.[17] The **fertility rate** is determined by the number of births per year per 1000 Canadians. The fertility rate increased dramatically in the late 1950s and early 1960s, the period of the so-called baby boomers. It declined in the 1970s and began to climb again in the 1980s as baby boomers began to have their own children in a "baby boomlet."

Marketers keep a close eye on the population's birth rate to gauge how the pattern of births will affect demand for products in the future. Even when married couples live with kids, families are shrinking. The number of Canadian families with three or more children under age 18 living at home has fallen below 10 percent of all families.[18] Still, large families are good marketing prospects. They use a lot of cleaning products, are more likely to have pets, and typically spend more than average on games, toys and garments.[19]

The current fertility rate is about 13 babies born annually for every 1000 Canadians, a decline of 22 percent since 1971.[20] Demographers predict that the fertility rate will continue to decline, even though the number of fertile women between 15

The IWK (Isaac Walton Killam) Grace Health Centre is explicit about whom they provide service to, i.e., children, women and families.
Photo: Rosemary Polegato for Spencer Nolan MacKay.

and 44 will grow. Births will fall due to most women being on the older edge of this age group, the increased participation of Canadian women in the paid labour force, the increased acceptance and diffusion of effective contraception, and changing attitudes towards childbearing and parenting.[21]

THE HEAD OF THE FAMILY

Family households headed by a single person grew by over 20 percent between 1986 and 1994.[20] Well over one million Canadians were divorced in 1996.[23] Reflecting the prevalence of divorce situations, one Canadian entrepreneur's product provides a way for disgruntled marriage partners to rewrite history: DivorceX, a digital imaging service, removes ex-spouses from family pictures![24] *Divorce Magazine* even has an Internet site (***www.divorcemag.com***).

The number of unmarried adults is steadily rising. They now account for 22 percent of the Canadian adult population.[25] Some marketers are beginning to address the fact that this group is underrepresented in advertising. Taster's Choice coffee, for example, built a very popular campaign around a romance between two single neighbours, while Procter & Gamble introduced Folger's Singles—single-serving coffee bags for people who live alone and don't need a full pot.[26]

Single men and women are quite different markets. More than half of single men are under the age of 35, while more than half of single women are over 65. Despite single males' greater incomes, single women dominate many markets due to their spending patterns. Single women are more likely to own a home, and they spend more on housing-related items and furniture. Single men, in contrast, spend more overall in restaurants and on cars. However, these spending patterns are also significantly affected by age: middle-aged single women, for example, actually spend more than their male counterparts on cars.[27]

Folger's Coffee has addressed an important need by allowing single people to brew one cup of coffee at a time.
Courtesy of Procter & Gamble.

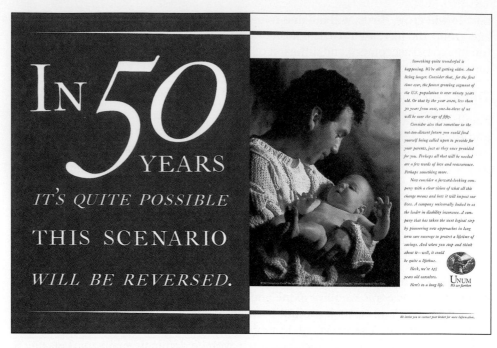

There is a famous saying, "The child is father to the man." This insurance ad reminds us that children, especially those who belong to "the sandwich generation," are often eventually put in the position of caring for their parents.
Courtesy of UNUM.

WHO'S LIVING AT HOME?

In many cases the nuclear family is being transformed to resemble the old-fashioned extended family. Many adults care for parents as well as children. In 1991 nearly 350 000 Canadians 65 years and older lived with relatives other than their spouses.[28] Middle-aged people have been termed "the sandwich generation" because they must attend to those above and below them in age.

In addition to dealing with live-in parents, many adults are surprised to find that their children are living with them longer or are moving back in, well after the "lease" has expired.[29] These returnees have been termed **boomerang kids** by demographers (you "throw them away" and they keep coming back!). If this trend continues, it will affect a variety of markets as boomerang kids spend less on housing and staples and more on discretionary purchases, such as entertainment.

boomerang kids grown children who return to their parents' home to live

ALTERNATE FAMILY STRUCTURES

As stated above, Statistics Canada regards any occupied housing unit as a household, regardless of the relationships among people living there. Thus, one person living alone, three room-mates or two lovers all constitute households. Less traditional households rapidly increased in the 1990s. For example, men head about 20 percent of lone-parent families. In 1995 there were about 430 000 step-families in Canada, nearly 65 percent of them living in Quebec and Ontario.[30] Nearly 20 percent of all children live in one-parent families.[31] The number of one-person households increased more than sevenfold between 1971 and 1991, accounting for more than one-fifth of all households in 1991.[32]

He left me. Good riddance.

He never picked up his socks. He thought I was

his mother. He didn't make me laugh anymore.

He's gone. Who cares... I kept the sofa.

This ad reflects the growing acceptance of divorce as a non-traditional family structure.
Courtesy of Montauk.

Families worldwide are becoming smaller and less traditional. Although Scandinavian countries are pacesetters in developing non-traditional forms of family living, the United States has the highest incidence of divorce and single-parent households of any country.[33] The one-person household is the fastest growing of any household size in Canada, contributing to the increase in the number of non-family household heads who are younger and older.[34]

Effects of Family Structure on Consumption

A family's needs and expenditures are affected by such factors as the number of people (children and adults) in the family, the ages of family members, and whether one, two or more adults are employed outside the home.

Two important factors that determine how a couple spends time and money are whether they have children and whether the woman works. Couples with children generally have higher expenses, such as for food and utility bills. Raising a Canadian child to age 18 can cost $150 000 or more.[35] In addition, a recently married couple makes very different expenditures than one with young children, which in turn is quite different from a couple with children in college, and so on. Families with working mothers also must often make allowances for such expenses as day care, a work wardrobe for the woman and home-cleaning services.

Social life. Sex life. Sleeping habits. Laundry powder.

Having a baby changes everything. Almost.

Sunlight actually rinses cleaner than Ivory Snow (no soapy residue is left behind), making it perfect for your entire family's wash. So even if the rest of your life has been turned upside down, when it comes to laundry, all you'll have to change are diapers.

Soft on babies. Tough on stains.

This ad for Unilever Canada's Sunlight detergent reminds new parents how much their lives will change with the arrival of a baby.
Courtesy of Unilever Canada and MacLaren Lintas, Inc.

THE FAMILY LIFE CYCLE

family life cycle (FLC) a classification scheme that segments consumers in terms of changes in income and family composition and changes in demands placed upon this income

Recognizing that family needs and expenditures change over time, the concept of the **family life cycle (FLC)** has been widely used by marketers. The FLC combines trends in income and family composition with the changes in demands placed upon this income. As we age, our preferences for products and activities tend to change. In many cases our income levels tend to rise (at least until retirement), so that we can afford more, too. In addition, many purchases that must be made at an early age do not have to be repeated very often. For example, we tend to accumulate durable goods, such as large appliances, and only replace them as necessary.

This focus on longitudinal changes in priorities is particularly valuable in predicting demand for specific product categories over time. For example, the money spent by a couple with no children on dinners out and vacations will probably be diverted for quite different purchases after the birth of a child. While a number of models have been proposed to describe family-life-cycle stages, their usefulness has been limited because, in many cases, they have failed to take into account such important social trends as the changing role of women, the acceleration of alternative lifestyles, childless and delayed-child marriages, and single-parent households. Baby showers, for example, may be considered as a rite of passage to motherhood, fatherhood or parenthood, depending on the gender ideologies and work orientation of one or both parents.[36]

Four variables are necessary to describe these trends adequately: age of the adult head of household, marital status, the presence or absence of children in the home, and the children's ages. In addition, our definition of marital status (at least for analysis purposes) must be relaxed to include any couple living together who are in a long-term relationship. Thus, while room-mates might not be considered "married," a man and woman who have established a household would be, as would two homosexual men who have a similar understanding.

When these changes are considered, this approach allows us to identify categories that include many more types of family situations.[37] These categories are listed in Table 12–1. For example, a distinction is made between the consumption needs of people in the Full Nest I category (wherein the youngest child is less than six), the Full Nest II category (wherein the youngest child is older than six), the Full Nest III category (wherein the youngest child is older than six and the parents are middle-aged) and the Delayed Full Nest (wherein the parents are middle-aged but the youngest child is younger than six).

LIFE CYCLE EFFECTS ON BUYING

As might be expected, consumers classified into these categories show marked differences in consumption patterns. Young bachelors and newlyweds have the most "modern" sex-role attitudes and are the most likely to engage in exercise; to go out to bars, concerts, movies and restaurants; to go out dancing; and to consume more alcohol. Families with young children are more likely to consume health foods, such as fruit, juice and yogurt, while those made up of single parents and older children buy more junk foods. The dollar value of homes, cars and other durables is lowest for bachelors and single parents but increases as people go through the full-nest and childless-couple stages. Perhaps reflecting the bounty of wedding gifts, newlyweds are the most likely to own such appliances as toaster ovens and electric coffee grinders. Babysitter and day-care usage is, of course, highest among single-parent and full nest households, while home-maintenance services (such as lawn mowing) are most likely to be employed by older couples and bachelors.

The increase in the number of categories creates many opportunities for enterprising marketers. For example, divorced people undergo a process of transition to a new social role. This change is often accompanied by the disposal of possessions

---

TABLE 12–1 The Family Life Cycle: An Updated View

	AGE OF HEAD OF HOUSEHOLD		
	UNDER 35	35–64	OVER 64
One adult in household	Bachelor I	Bachelor II	Bachelor III
Two adults in household	Young couple	Childless couple	Older couple
Two adults plus children in household	Full nest I Full nest II	Delayed full nest Full nest III	

Source: Adapted from Mary C. Gilly and Ben M. Enis, "Recycling the Family Life Cycle: A Proposal for Redefinition," in *Advances in Consumer Research 9*, ed. Andrew A. Mitchell (Ann Arbor, MI: Association for Consumer Research, 1982), p. 274, fig. 1.

This ad for Ethan Allen furniture borrows two categories—full house and empty nest—from the family-life-cycle concept to illustrate that its products meet people's diverse needs as they progress through life.
Courtesy of Ethan Allen, Inc.

linked to the former role and the need to acquire a set of possessions that help to express the person's new identity as he or she experiments with new lifestyles.[38]

FAMILY DECISION MAKING

The decision process within a household unit is a collective process. Certain matters are put on the table for discussion, different members may have different priorities and agendas, and there may be power struggles. In just about every living situation, whether a conventional family, students sharing a sorority house or apartment, or some other non-traditional arrangement, group members seem to take on different roles.

Household Decisions

consensual purchase decision a decision in which the group agrees on the desired purchase and differs only in terms of how it will be achieved

accommodative purchase decision the process using bargaining, coercion, compromise and the wielding of power to achieve agreement among a group whose members have different preferences or priorities

Two basic types of decisions are made by families.[39] In a **consensual purchase decision** the group agrees on the desired purchase and differs only in terms of how it will be achieved. In these circumstances the family will most likely engage in problem solving and consider alternatives until the means for satisfying the group's goal is found. A household considering adding a dog to the family but concerned about who will take care of it might decide to get a dog and draw up a chart assigning individuals to specific duties.

Unfortunately, life is not always so easy. In an **accommodative purchase decision** group members have different preferences or priorities and cannot agree on a purchase that will satisfy the minimum expectations of all involved. It is here that bargaining, coercion, compromise and the wielding of power are all likely to be used to achieve the primary goal of agreement on the purchase itself. Family decisions, such as those related to the purchase and use of a family computer, often are characterized by an accommodative rather than a consensual decision. Some Canadians use computers for work they bring home and have to jockey with other family members for time on the PC or for access to a phone line. The computer industry is gearing up to sell multiple computers to solve these problems, but for many families less expensive forms of diplomacy arc required.[40] Conflict occurs when there is not complete correspondence in family members' needs and preferences. While money is the most common source of conflict between marriage partners, television choices come in a close second![41] Some specific factors determining the degree of family-decision conflict include the following:[42]

- *Interpersonal need.* This factor depends on a person's level of investment in the group. A child in a family situation may care more about what his or her family buys for the house than will a college student who is temporarily living in a dorm.

- *Product involvement and utility.* This involves the degree to which the product in question will be used or will satisfy a need. A family member who is an avid coffee-drinker will obviously be more interested in the purchase of a new coffeemaker to replace a malfunctioning one than a similar expenditure for some other item.

MARKETING OPPORTUNITY

Many people are extremely attached to pets, to the point where companion animals might be considered part of the family. Fifty-two percent of Canadian households own a pet. Canadians spend $320 million a year on their pets.[43] This passion for pets is not confined to Canada: in France there are twice as many dogs and cats as children.[44]

The inclusion of pets as family members creates many marketing opportunities, ranging from bejewelled leashes to professional dog-walkers. Listed below are samples of some recent attempts to cater to people's pet attachments.[45]

- A 25-minute video, titled *Doggie Adventure,* was produced for dogs. Shot with a camera balanced two-thirds of a metre off the ground, it takes viewers on a romp from a dog's perspective.

- Kennelwood Village, a day-care centre for dogs in St. Louis, features a swimming pool (with a lifeguard on duty), tetherball tournaments, and whirlpool therapy for arthritic canines.

- In Britain, pet insurance is a $150-million industry. In a pet-crazed country where some restaurants feed animals but not children, more than a million pets are covered. Similarly, about 85 percent of Swedish dogs carry health and life insurance.

- Numerous specialty pet stores provide accessories and gifts to the 75 and 65 percent of Canadian pet owners who buy Christmas or birthday presents for their dogs and cats, respectively.

- *Responsibility.* Responsibility for procurement, maintenance, payment and so on influences the degree of family conflict. People are more likely to have disagreements about a decision if it entails long-term consequences and commitments. A family decision about getting a dog may involve conflict regarding who will be responsible for walking it and feeding it.

- *Power.* The degree to which one family member exerts influence over the others in making decisions is a factor. In traditional families the husband tends to have more power than the wife, who in turn has more than the oldest child, and so on. In family decisions, conflict can arise when one person continually uses the power he or she has within the group to satisfy his or her priorities. For example, if P.J. believed that his life would end if he did not have a heavy-metal birthday party, he might be more willing to resort to extreme tactics to influence his parents, perhaps by throwing a tantrum or refusing to participate in family chores.

In general, decisions will involve conflict among family members to the extent that they are somehow important or novel and/or if individuals have strong opinions about good and bad alternatives. The degree to which these factors generate conflict determines the type of decision the family will make.[46]

DECISION ROLES

A number of specific roles are played by family members when a collective decision must be made. Depending on the decision, some or all of the family members may be involved, and one person may play any number (or even all) of these roles. These roles include:[47]

- *initiator*—the family member who brings up the idea or need

- *information gatherer*—the family member who gathers information on a product or service

- *gatekeeper*—the family member who controls the flow of information available to the group

- *influencer*—the family member who tries to sway the outcome of the decision. Some family members may be more motivated to get involved, and family members also differ in terms of the amount of power they have to convince others of their choice.

- *decision maker*—the family member who holds the singular or joint power to determine whether or not to buy a product or service

- *buyer*—the family member who actually makes the purchase. The buyer may or may not actually use the product. This person may pay for the item, actually procure it, or both

- *preparer*—the family member who processes the product or directs the service into a form that can be consumed by other family members

- *user*—the family member who ultimately uses the product or service

- *maintainer*—the family member responsible for the maintenance and upkeep of a product or service

- *disposer*—the family member who discards or discontinues the use of a product or service

Gender Roles and Decision-Making Responsibilities

Traditionally, some buying decisions, termed **autocratic decisions,** were usually made by one or the other spouse. Men, for instance, often had sole responsibility for selecting a car, while most decorating choices fell to women. Other decisions, such as vacation destinations, were made jointly; these are known as **syncratic decisions.** According to a study conducted by Roper Starch Worldwide, wives tend to have the most say when buying groceries, children's toys, clothes and medicines. Syncratic decisions are common for cars, vacations, homes, appliances, furniture, home electronics, interior design and long-distance phone services. As the couple's education increases, more decisions are likely to be made together.[48]

autocratic decisions those purchase decisions that are made almost exclusively by one or the other spouse

syncratic decisions those purchase decisions that are made jointly by both spouses

IDENTIFYING THE DECISION MAKER

The nature of consumer decision making within a particular product category is an important issue for marketers, so that they know whom to target and whether or not they need to reach both spouses to influence a decision. For example, when market research in the 1980s indicated that women were playing a larger role in household purchasing decisions, lawnmower manufacturers began to emphasize the rotary mower over other power mowers. Rotary mowers, which conceal the cutting blades and engine, were often depicted being used by young women and smiling grandmothers to downplay fears of injuries.[49]

Researchers have paid special attention to which spouse plays the role of what has been called the **family financial officer (FFO),** who keeps track of the family's bills and decides how any surplus funds will be spent. Among newlyweds this role tends to be played jointly, and then, over time, one spouse or the other tends to take over these responsibilities.[50] As shown in Table 12–2 dual-earner couples in Canada differ in how they handle their respective incomes. The majority pool their income, but about 20 percent of husbands and 30 percent of wives keep their income separate.[51] Interestingly, husbands are perceived as the experts, i.e., more knowledgeable, in the area of RRSPs by both themselves and their wives, and play a fairly significant role in most stages of wives' decision making regarding their RRSPs.[52]

family financial officer (FFO) the individual in the family who is in charge of making financial decisions

TABLE 12–2 How Canadian Dual-Earner Couples Handle Their Income		
HOW INCOME IS HANDLED	HUSBANDS	WIVES
Separate—I Handle All My Income and Keep It Separate	18.9%	30.3%
Combined—I Handle Part of My Income and Give Rest to Partner or Put in Common Pool	17.2%	16.2%
Pooled—All My Income Goes into Common Pool	58.1%	52.0%
My Partner Handles All My Income	5.7%	1.5%

Source: Adapted from Judith Madill and Frances Woolley, unpublished preliminary findings of Study of Financial Management and Decision Making in Canadian Households, 1997. Used with permission.

In traditional families (and especially those with members having low educational levels) women are primarily responsible for family financial management—that is, the man makes it and the woman spends it.[53] Each spouse "specializes" in certain activities.[54] The pattern is different among families in which spouses adhere to more modern gender-role norms. These couples believe that there should be more shared participation in family-maintenance activities. In these cases husbands assume more responsibility for laundering, house-cleaning, grocery shopping, parenting and so on, while the wife shares in such traditionally "male" tasks as home maintenance and garbage removal.[55] Statistics Canada has an Internet site that outlines the average time spent on a wide range of activities by men and women (*www.statcan.ca/english/pgdb/people/families/famil36a.htm*).

Four factors appear to determine the degree to which decisions will be made jointly or by one or the other spouse:[56]

1. *Gender-role stereotypes.* Couples who believe in traditional gender-role stereotypes tend to make individual decisions for gender-typed products (i.e., those considered to be "masculine" or "feminine").

2. *Spousal resources.* The spouse who contributes more resources to the family has the greater influence.

3. *Experience.* Individual decisions are made more frequently when the couple has gained experience as a decision-making unit.

4. *Socio-economic status.* Joint decisions are made more by middle-class families than by either higher-or lower-class families.

With many women now working outside the home, men are participating more in housekeeping activities. Among married Canadian couples it was found that about one-third of the husbands did the family food shopping by themselves and at similar times during the week. However, among those same couples, nearly 80 percent of the wives versus about 25 percent of the husbands had sole responsibility for getting the family food shopping done according to expectations.[57] The spouses used similar strategies for time management, store loyalty and in-store shopping, but were different in some important tactical areas. Husbands saw budgeting as a distinct activity, while wives saw it as related to organizing and using a shopping list. Wives were also more likely to be drawn to other stores in search of bargains, and to place more importance on in-store service and product availability.[58] On the other hand, there is evidence that men enjoy cooking. Kitchenware shops across Canada report that half their customers are men.[59]

For the purpose of segmenting the household or family market, adult women can be divided into at least four groups based on their orientation towards paid work outside the home:

1. Housewives who do not plan to work outside the home.

2. Housewives who plan to work at some point. (The women in this group may be staying at home only temporarily—until small children grow old enough to enter school, for example—and are thus not to be grouped with those housewives who have voluntarily chosen a domestic lifestyle.)

3. Career-oriented working women who value professional success and the trappings of achievement.

4. "Just-a-job" women who work primarily because they need the money.[60]

Despite recent changes in decision-making responsibilities, women still are primarily responsible for the continuation of the family's **kin-network system:** they per-

kin-network system the rituals intended to maintain ties among family members both immediate and extended

MULTICULTURAL DIMENSIONS

Japanese dads spend so much time working that more than a quarter of children surveyed said their dads never take them for a walk or play games with them. Due to long work hours, a typical Japanese father has only 36 minutes a day available to spend with his kids. About 60 percent of Japanese men typically do not eat breakfast at home, and about 30 percent regularly miss dinner. Now, balancing work and family is becoming a hot topic, especially as recession weakens the guarantee of lifetime employment and men are re-examining their own priorities.[61] This change was reflected in some recent McDonald's advertising, which showed doting fathers helping kids with their bikes. This change would not be noteworthy in Canada, but it received a lot of attention in a country where fathers typically are shown as corporate warriors or even as superheroes (for example, a popular advertising character called Pepsi-Man!).

Differences have also been noted in the consumer behaviour of family segments based on the work orientation of the spouses, as shown in Table 12–3. These differences suggest that marketers need to modify or adapt product features, store environments and media messages designed for the family market.

form the rituals intended to maintain ties among family members, both immediate and extended. This function includes such activities as coordinating visits among relatives, calling and writing family members, sending greeting cards, making social engagements and elder care.[62] This organizing role means that women often make important decisions about their families' leisure activities and are more likely to decide with whom their families will socialize.

Due to corporate downsizing, dropping out of the workforce and moonlighting, both men and women are increasingly finding earning opportunities in the "party plan" format. This trend dovetails nicely with cocooning,[63] the tendency for people to spend time at home. Sales parties allow consumers to shop at home in a personalized context among friends, relatives and co-workers. Some settings serve to establish and reinforce the personal and social dimensions of women's shopping.[64] A wide

MARKETING OPPORTUNITY

Many women who work outside the home are victims of what has been termed the "juggling lifestyle"—a frenzied, guilt-ridden compromise between conflicting cultural ideals of motherhood and professionalism.[65] Some marketers are picking up on one response to this conflict. They are beginning to target what they are calling "workpausals," or women who are taking time off from careers to stay home with their children. As one advertising executive observed, "Women have stopped apologizing for staying home. Now it's a badge." Advertisers are seeking neutral territory when they design their messages, trying to avoid traditional home settings or office settings so their campaigns can be targeted both to women who work inside and outside the home. For example, a Levi's Jeans for Women commercial depicts an animated figure trading in her dress for jeans and breaking out of the "prison" that held her.[66]

TABLE 12–3 Consumer Behaviour of Family Segments Based on Work Orientation of Spouses

	DUAL CAREER	DUAL INCOME	TRADITIONAL
Grocery Shopping			
Who does it?	Whoever enjoys it	Wife usually	Wife
How often?	Once a week or once a month	Once a week or once a month	Once a week
When?	No specific day	Same day	Same day
Store loyalty	No	Yes	Yes
Household Chores			
Cooking	Both spouses	Wife usually	Wife
Cleaning & laundry	Both spouses	Wife usually	Wife
Housekeeper	Yes	No	No
Attitude towards chores	Routine during week to free weekends	Ongoing but haphazard	Ongoing but organized
Household Conveniences			
Dishwasher and microwave oven	Yes	No	No
Freezer	For bulk purchases, extra cooking	For bulk purchases	For garden harvest
Attitude towards conveniences	Appreciate time saved	To save money	To save money
Child Care			
Discipline	Both spouses	Wife, husband supportive	Wife, husband laissez-faire
Preparation for school	Both spouses	Wife	Wife
Family Finances			
Accounts	His, hers, ours	Some pooling	One account
Who keeps track of household finances?	Husband and wife	Wife	Wife
Major expenses	Conferences, each spouse contributes	Priorities determined by family needs	Priorities determined by spousal role specialization
Budget	Informal, periodic reviews	More formal	More formal
Attitude towards money	Can have what we want, "cushions"	Work to get what we want	Have what we need, some wants
Credit	Convenience, consolidation of bills	Convenience and instalment	Considered dangerous
Payment	Pay off each month	Pay interest	Pay interest
Attitude towards debt	Get rid of debt easily, even for major purchases	Debt acceptable	Debt is to be avoided
Restaurants			
How often?	Twice a week	Twice a month	Rarely
Who decides?	Either spouse	An occasion	————
With whom?	As a family; as a couple; with friends	Family usually, sometimes friends	————

TABLE 12–3 Consumer Behaviour of Family Segments continued

Where?	Fast food to fine dining	Group accommodation	Fast food
Criteria	Good food, atmosphere, discriminating	Roomy, varied menu, service	————
Cars			
How many?	Two	One or two	One
New or used car?	New	Sometimes used	Often used
Cash or credit?	Cash	Credit	Credit
Who decides?	Individual decisions	Joint decision	Husband
Criteria	Safety, mileage, size (small), investment, "experience" (e.g., sports car)	Large	Family car, large
Family Vacation			
Who decides?	Both spouses & children	Both spouses	Both spouses
Who goes?	Family, sometimes separate holiday for children	Family	Family
Arrangements	Both spouses	Wife	Wife
Criteria	Culture	Family & friends visiting	Family visits
Transportation	Fly, some driving	Drive	Drive
Places	Europe, North America	North America	Canada
Budget	Unlimited; what's needed to do it right	Limited; restricts choices	Limited
Household Durables			
Who decides?	Both spouses	Both spouses	Wife
Who buys?	Both spouses	Wife, sometimes with husband	Wife
Criteria	Time saving, style, price not a factor, very little shopping around, quality stores	Price major factor, comparison shopping, mid-quality stores	Price major factor, comparison shopping, mid-bargain stores
Lifestyle	Integration of career and family life by both spouses. Affluence allows for conveniences that make both family and individual leisure-time pursuits possible.	Both spouses focus on the family, although the wife usually tends to household and child care concerns. Both spouses work to provide needs of family.	The wife's domain is the home, the husband's domain is work. Range of individual and family activities is influenced by specialized roles and the earning power of the husband's job.

Source: Adapted from James W. Hanson and Rosemary Polegato, "Identifying Dual Career, Dual Income and Traditional Family Segments," in *Marketing*, ed. James D. Forbes (Montreal: Administrative Sciences Association of Canada, 1983), vol. 4, pp. 30–38.

array of products may be purchased within the comfort of a living room, restaurant or hotel room: raspberry salsa, Bible videos, photographic scrapbooks, art, candles, children's books, gourmet foods and personal computers.[67]

HEURISTICS IN JOINT DECISION MAKING

synoptic ideal a model of spousal decision making where the husband and wife take a common view and act as joint decision makers, assigning each other well-defined roles and making mutually beneficial decisions to maximize the couple's joint utility

The **synoptic ideal** calls for the husband and wife to take a common view and act as joint decision makers. According to this ideal they would very thoughtfully weigh alternatives, assign one another well-defined roles and calmly make mutually beneficial consumer decisions. The couple would act rationally and analytically, and would use as much information as possible to maximize joint utility. In reality, however, spousal decision making is often characterized by the use of influence or methods that are likely to reduce conflict. A couple "reaches" rather than "makes" a decision. This process has been described as "muddling through."[68]

One common technique for simplifying the decision-making process is the use of *heuristics* (see Chapter 9). Some decision-making patterns frequently observed when a couple makes decisions in buying a new house illustrate the use of heuristics:

1. The couple's areas of common preference are based upon salient, objective dimensions rather than more subtle, hard-to-define cues. For example, a couple may easily agree on the number of bedrooms they need in the new home but will have more difficulty achieving a common view of how the home should look.

2. The couple agrees on a system of task specialization, wherein each is responsible for certain duties or decision areas and does not interfere in the other's "turf." For many couples these assignments are likely to be influenced by their perceived gender roles. For example, the wife may scout out houses in advance that meet the couple's requirements, while the husband determines whether the couple can obtain a mortgage.

3. Concessions are based on the intensity of each spouse's preferences. One spouse will yield to the influence of the other in many cases simply because his or her level of preference for a certain attribute is not particularly intense, whereas in other situations he or she will be willing to exert effort to obtain a favourable decision.[69] In cases where intense preferences for different attributes exist, rather than attempt to influence each other, spouses will "trade off" a less-intense preference for a more strongly felt one. For example, a husband who is somewhat indifferent about kitchen design may defer to his wife but expect that, in turn, he will be allowed to design his own garage workshop. It is interesting to note that many men apparently want to be very involved in making some decorating decisions and setting budgets—more than women want them to be. According to one survey 70 percent of male respondents felt that husbands should be involved in decorating the den, while only 51 percent of wives wanted them to be.[70]

CHILDREN AS DECISION MAKERS: CONSUMERS-IN-TRAINING

Anyone who has had the "delightful" experience of grocery shopping with one or more children in tow knows that children often have a say in what their parents buy, especially for such products as cereal.[71] It has been estimated that children between the ages of 4 and 12 collectively spend, or influence their parents to spend, about $140 billion (US) a year.[72]

Parental yielding occurs when a parental decision maker is influenced by a child's request and "surrenders." The strategies kids use to request purchases were documented in a recent study. While most children simply asked for things, some other common tactics included saying they had seen it on television, saying that a sibling or friend has it, or bargaining by offering to do chores. Other actions were less innocuous; they included directly placing the object in the cart and continuous pleading—often a "persuasive" behaviour.[73]

Children often play important roles in family consumer decision making, and they are gaining responsibility as consumers in their own right. They continue to support the toy and candy industries, of course, but now they also buy and/or influence the purchase of many other products as well. For better or for worse, the new generation is, as the bumper sticker proclaims, "Born to Shop." Shopping now ranks among the top seven interests and activities of children.[74] Over 80 percent of young respondents in one survey said their primary wish was to have more money to buy things.[75] In this section we'll consider how kids learn to make these choices.

parental yielding the process that occurs when a parental decision maker is influenced by a child's product request

Consumer Socialization

Children do not spring from the womb with consumer skills already in memory. **Consumer socialization** has been defined as the process "... by which young people acquire skills, knowledge, and attitudes relevant to their functioning in the marketplace."[76] Where does this knowledge come from? Friends and teachers certainly par-

consumer socialization the process by which people acquire skills that enable them to function in the marketplace

Recognizing that kids influence food purchases, Oscar Mayer attempts to create a positive image for its lunch meats in this poster for use in school cafeterias.
Courtesy of Oscar Mayer Foods Corporation. The Oscar Mayer rhomboid, Lunch Is What You Make of It, and Lunchables are trademarks of Oscar Mayer Foods Corporation, Madison, Wisconsin.

MULTICULTURAL DIMENSIONS

Traditional gender roles are quite prevalent in Japan, where women have less power than in any other industrialized country. The birth control pill is banned, and a wife is legally prohibited from using a different surname than her husband. Fewer than one in ten Japanese managers are women, which is one of the lowest ratios in the world (women are twice as likely to be managers in Mexico or Zimbabwe).

However, something of a quiet revolution is happening in Japanese homes as some obedient spouses have had enough. Recently, women have started to rebel against the inevitability of getting married young and staying home with babies. The number of unmarried people older than 30 has doubled in the last 20 years.

For those women who do marry, things are changing as well. Traditionally, a wife would wait up all night for a drunken husband to come home so she could kneel down with her forehead touching the floor and proclaim, "Welcome home, honourable sir." Now she is more likely to lock him out of the house until he sobers up. Most Japanese men are given a budget by their wives for lunch, cigarettes and magazines. One woman noted, "Your home is managed very well if you make your men feel that they're in control when they are in front of others, while in reality you're in control."[77]

ticipate in this process. For instance, children talk to one another about consumer products, and this tendency increases with age.[78] Especially for young children, though, the two primary socialization sources are the family and the media.

INFLUENCE OF PARENTS

Parents' influences in consumer socialization are both direct and indirect. They deliberately try to instil their own values about consumption in their children ("You're going to learn the value of a dollar"). Parents also determine the degree to which their children will be exposed to other information sources, such as television, salespeople and peers.[79] And grown-ups serve as significant models for observational learning (see Chapter 3). Children learn about consumption by watching their parents' behaviour and imitating it. This modelling is facilitated by marketers who package adult products in child versions.

The process of consumer socialization begins with infants, who accompany their parents to stores where they are initially exposed to marketing stimuli. Within the first two years children begin to make requests for desired objects. As kids learn to walk, they also begin to make their own selections when they are in stores. By around the age of five, most kids are making purchases with the help of parents and grandparents, and by eight most are making independent purchases and have become full-fledged consumers.[80] Gentle guidance and high parental trust and expectations in giving an allowance or pocket money seem to lead to more knowledgeable eight- to ten-year-old consumers.[81] The sequence of steps involved in turning kids into consumers is summarized in Figure 12–1.

Three dimensions combine to produce different "segments" of parental styles. Parents characterized by certain styles have been found to socialize their children differently.[82] For example, "authoritarian parents," who are hostile, restrictive and emotionally uninvolved, do not have warm relationships with their children, are

FIGURE 12–1 • Five Stages of Consumer Development by Earliest Age at Onset and Median Age at Onset

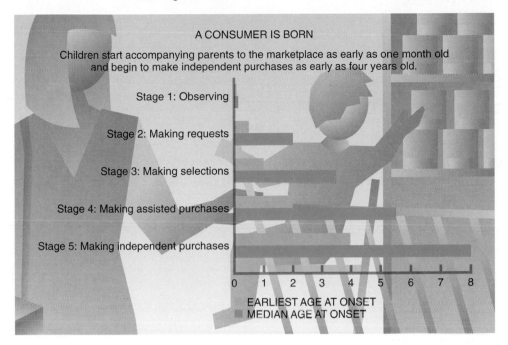

Source: Adapted from McNeal and Yeh, *American Demographics* (June 1993): 36. Reprinted by permission of American Demographics, Inc.

active in filtering the types of media to which their children are exposed, and tend to have negative views about advertising. "Neglecting parents" also do not have warm relationships, but they are more detached from their children and do not exercise much control over what their children do. In contrast, "indulgent parents" communicate more with their children about consumption-related matters and are less restrictive. They believe that children should be allowed to learn about the marketplace without much intervention.

INFLUENCE OF TELEVISION

It's no secret that children watch a lot of television. As a result, they are constantly bombarded with messages about consumption, contained both in commercials and in the shows themselves. The media teaches people about a culture's values and myths. The more a child is exposed to television—whether the show is *Friends, Traders* or *Sesame Street*—the more he or she will accept the images depicted there as real.[83] A TV show called *Tele-Tubbies* that recently debuted in the UK goes a step further: it targets viewers from three months to two years old. It's unclear if this show would succeed in Canada since babies aren't seen as a lucrative market for advertising messages (yet!).[84]

In addition to the large volume of programming targeted directly to children, kids also are exposed to idealized images of what it is like to be an adult. Since children over the age of six do about a quarter of their television viewing during prime time, they are affected by programs and commercials targeted to adults. For example, young girls exposed to adult lipstick commercials learn to associate lipstick with beauty.[85]

This L'eggs ad shows how some companies begin to cultivate future customers at an early age.
Courtesy of SARA LEE HOSIERY.

Gender-Role Socialization

Children pick up on the concept of gender identity (see Chapter 5) at an earlier age than was previously believed—perhaps as young as age one or two. By the age of three most children categorize driving a truck as masculine and cooking and cleaning as feminine.[86] Even cartoon characters who are portrayed as helpless are most likely to wear frilly or ruffled dresses.[87] Toy companies perpetuate these stereotypes by promoting gender-linked toys with commercials that reinforce gender-role expectations through their casting, emotional tone and copy.[88]

One function of children's play is to rehearse for adulthood. Children act out different roles they might assume later in life and learn about the expectations others have of them. The toy industry provides the props children use to perform these roles.[89] Depending on which side of the debate you're on, these toys either reflect or teach children about what society expects of males versus females. While preschool boys and girls do not exhibit many differences in toy preferences, after the age of five they part company: girls tend to stick with dolls, while boys gravitate towards "action figures" and high-tech diversions. Industry critics charge that this is because the toy industry is dominated by males, while toy-company executives counter that they are simply responding to the natural preferences of children.[90]

Often "traditional" gender roles are stressed in children's products; the same item may be designed and positioned differently for boys and girls. Huffy, for example, manufactures bicycles for both boys and girls. The boys' versions have names like "Sigma" and "Vortex," and they are described as having "... maxed-out features that'll pump your pulse." The girls' version of the same bike is more sedate. It is called "Sweet Style," and it comes in pink or purple. As a company executive described it in contrast to the boys' bikes, the girls' model "... is a fashion bike. It's not built for racing or jumping—just the look."[91]

Some companies have tried to level the playing field by doing research to understand differences in how boys and girls play. Lego Systems sells about 90 percent of its construction kits to boys, but the company would love to increase its sales by selling more sets to girls. When Lego introduced a special set with parts that would allow girls to make jewellery, the product bombed. Still, Lego had some success with Paradisa, a set with such colours as lavender and pink that is designed for building "socially oriented structures," such as homes, swimming pools and stables.[92] However, games like Tetris, Myst and Where in the World is Carmen Sandiego? appeal equally to girls and boys. These games are essentially non-violent and include puzzles, quizzes and intriguing narrative.[93]

Cognitive Development

The ability of children to make mature, "adult" consumer decisions obviously increases with age (not that grown-ups always make mature decisions). They can be segmented by age in terms of their stage of **cognitive development,** or ability to comprehend concepts of increasing complexity. Some recent evidence indicates that young children are able to learn consumption-related information surprisingly well, depending on the format in which the information is presented (e.g., learning is enhanced if a videotaped vignette is presented to small children repeatedly).[94]

cognitive development the ability to comprehend concepts of increasing complexity as a person ages

The foremost proponent of the idea that children pass through distinct stages of cognitive development was the Swiss psychologist Jean Piaget, who believed that each stage is characterized by a certain cognitive structure the child uses to handle information.[95] In one classic demonstration of cognitive development, Piaget poured the contents of a short, squat glass of lemonade into a taller, thinner glass. Five-year-olds, who still believed that the shape of the glass determined its contents, thought this glass held more liquid than the first glass. They are in what Piaget termed a *preoperational stage of development.* In contrast, six-year-olds tended to be unsure, but seven-year-olds knew the amount of lemonade had not changed.

Many developmental specialists no longer believe that children necessarily pass through these fixed stages at the same time. An alternative approach regards children as differing in *information processing capability,* or ability to store and retrieve information from memory (see Chapter 3). The following three segments have been identified by this approach:[96]

1. *Limited.* Below the age of 6 years, children do not employ storage-and-retrieval strategies.
2. *Cued.* Children between the ages of 6 and 12 years employ these strategies, but only when prompted.
3. *Strategic.* Children 12 years and older spontaneously employ storage-and-retrieval strategies.

This sequence of development underscores the notion that children do not think like adults and cannot be expected to use information in the same way. It also reminds us that they do not necessarily form the same conclusions as adults when presented with product information. For example, children are not as likely to realize that something they see on television is not "real," and as a result they are more vulnerable to persuasive messages.

Marketing Research and Children

Despite their buying power, relatively little real data on children's preferences or influences on spending patterns are available. Compared to adults, they are difficult subjects for market researchers. They tend to be undependable reporters of their own behaviour, they have poor recall and often do not understand abstract questions.[97] This problem is compounded in Europe, where some countries restrict marketers' ability to interview children.

Still, market research can pay off, and many companies, as well as a number of specialized firms, have been successful in researching some aspects of this segment.[98] After interviewing elementary-school kids, Campbell Soup Co. discovered that children like soup but are afraid to admit it, because they associate it with "nerds." The company decided to reintroduce the Campbell Kids in its advertising after a prolonged absence, but they are now slimmed down and more athletic to reflect an updated, "unnerdy" image.[99]

PRODUCT TESTING

A particularly helpful type of research with children is product testing. Young subjects can provide a valuable perspective on what products will succeed with other children. One candy company has a Candy Tasters Club, composed of 1200 children aged 6 to 16, that evaluates its product ideas. The group nixed the idea of a Batman lollipop, claiming that the superhero was too macho to be a sucker.[100] The Fisher-Price Company maintains a nursery known as the Playlab. Children are chosen from a waiting list of 4000 to play with new toys while staff members watch from behind a one-way mirror.[101] Heinz recently held a nationwide contest for kids to create new ketchup bottle labels and received thousands of entries, and Binney & Smith is asking children to rename its Crayola crayons after personal heroes.[102]

Other techniques include ethnographic research, where researchers hang around with children or videotape them as they shop. The most successful interviewers are those who try not to be "adultcentric" (i.e., as an adult authority figure who assumes that children's beliefs are just unreal fantasies); they act as friends to the children and are willing to use a variety of projective techniques and props to get children to express themselves in their own terms.[103]

MESSAGE COMPREHENSION

Since children differ in their abilities to process product-related information, many serious ethical issues are raised when advertisers try to appeal directly to them.[104] Children tend to accept what they see on television as real, and they do not necessarily understand the persuasive intent of commercials—that is, that they are paid advertisements. Preschool children may not have the ability to make any distinctions between programming and commercials.

Children's cognitive defences are not yet sufficiently developed to filter out commercial appeals, so, in a sense, altering their brand preferences may be likened to "shooting fish in a barrel," as one critic put it.[105] Although some ads include a disclaimer, which is a disclosure intended to clarify a potentially misleading or deceptive statement, the evidence suggests that young children do not adequately understand these.[106] The Children's Advertising Review Unit in the United States recently unveiled guidelines for child-oriented Web sites after receiving complaints that children had trouble distinguishing ads from content. These guidelines include clear identification of the sponsor and the right to cancel purchases online.[107]

Children's levels of understanding are especially hard to assess, since preschoolers are not very good at verbal responses. One way around this problem is to show children different scenarios and ask them to point to which sketch corresponds to what a commercial is trying to get children to do.

The problem with children's processing of commercials has been exacerbated by television programming that essentially showcases toys (e.g., Care Bears and Power Rangers). This format (much like that of "infomercials" for adults, described in Chapter 8) has been the target of a lot of criticism because it blurs the line between programming and commercials.[108] Parents' groups object to such shows because, as one mother put it, the "... whole show is one big commercial."[109]

Advertising to Children: An Ethical Minefield

It has been suggested that children should be better educated as to how advertising works and encouraged to question what they see on television, perhaps through public-service advertising.[110] However, there is much controversy about whether

FIGURE 12–2 • Sketches Used to Measure Children's Perception of the Intent of Commercials

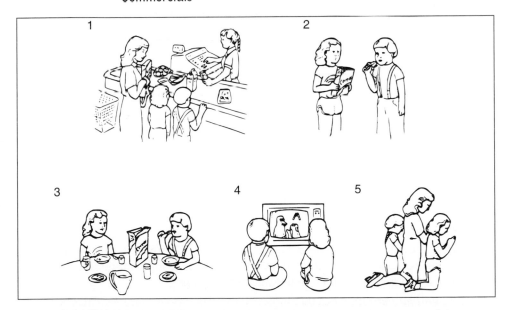

In the example shown here, a child who points to sketch 1 after seeing a cereal commercial as opposed to, say, sketches 2 or 3 would be said to understand the underlying intent of the commercial. Sketch 1 was in fact selected by only 7.5 percent of four-year-olds but 20 percent of five-year-olds.

Source: M. Carole Macklin, "Preschoolers' Understanding of the Informational Function of Television Advertising," *Journal of Consumer Research* 14 (September 1987): 234. Reprinted by permission of The University of Chicago Press.

MARKETING PITFALL

Hooper's Hooch, a lemony alcoholic beverage made by Bass PLC, is one of a dozen different brands launched in the UK that is specifically targeted to children (other popular brands include Lemonhead and Mrs. Pucker's). The drink's slogan: "One taste and you're Hooched." These drinks, known as "alcopops," are now being test-marketed in the USA in lemonade, cola and orange flavours, and contain 4 to 5.5 percent alcohol to appeal to teenagers. In Britain, alcohol laws are looser: children under 18 can't purchase booze, but they can drink it in certain restaurants and in their homes. Critics argue that this marketing strategy helps those who don't have a taste for alcohol to develop one, since children who grew up drinking Coke or Orangina will accept alcopops even more readily than wine coolers.[111] What do you think?

that education should be acquired through business partnerships with schools.[112] Of some help is "Street Cents," a children's version of "Marketplace."

In addition, the Broadcast Code for Advertising to Children of the Canadian Advertising Foundation provides industry guidelines in such areas as product claims (is it clear how the toy actually looks and works?); sales pressure techniques (do techniques used urge the child to ask parents to buy the product?); endorsements by program characters; scheduling (no more than eight minutes per hour of children's programming); safety; and social values.

Canadians are not alone in their concern about children's advertising. In the United States it was ruled recently that advertising in shows produced for children under the age of 12 cannot exceed 12 minutes an hour on weekdays and 10.5 minutes an hour on weekends. In Europe regulations are confusing, because each country still has different rules. For example, the Netherlands bars ads for sweets before 8 p.m., the ads cannot feature children under age 14, and a toothbrush must appear on the screen for at least part of the commercial; and Spain and Germany ban ads for war toys.[113] In Denmark and the United States there is also a call for rules to govern marketing operations on the Internet when children are the target.[114]

CHAPTER SUMMARY

- Many purchasing decisions are made by more than one person. Family or household decision making occurs whenever two or more people are involved in evaluating, selecting or using a product or service.

- In families, several different roles must be played during the decision-making process. These roles include initiator, information gatherer, gatekeeper (one who controls the flow of information within the group), influencer, decision maker, buyer, preparer, user, maintainer and disposer.

- *Demographics* are statistics that measure a population's characteristics. Some of the most important of these relate to family structure, e.g., the birth rate, the marriage rate and the divorce rate.

- A *household* is an occupied housing unit. The number and type of Canadian households are changing in many ways, including increasing movement by con-

Ikea recently made history by daring to create what is believed to be the first mainstream TV ad to feature a gay relationship.
Courtesy of IKEA US, Inc.

sumers to suburban and rural areas, delays in getting married and having children, and differences in the composition of family households, which increasingly are headed by a single parent. New perspectives on the family life cycle, which focus on how people's needs change as they move through different stages in their lives, are forcing marketers to consider more seriously such consumer segments as homosexuals, divorcees and childless couples when they develop targeting strategies.

- Families must be understood in terms of their decision-making dynamics. Spouses in particular have different priorities and exert varying amounts of influence in terms of effort and power. Children are also increasingly influential during a widening range of purchase decisions.

- Children undergo a process of socialization, whereby they learn how to be consumers. Some of this knowledge is instilled by parents and friends, but a lot of it comes from exposure to mass media and advertising. Since children are, in some cases, easily persuaded, the ethical aspects of marketing to them are hotly debated among consumers, academics and marketing practitioners.

KEY TERMS

CONSUMER BEHAVIOUR CHALLENGE

1. Do you think market research should be performed on children? Give the reasons for your answer.

2. What do you think of the practice of companies and survey firms collecting public data (e.g., from marriage licenses, birth records and even death announcements) to compile targeted mailing lists? State your opinion from both a consumer's and a marketer's perspective.

3. Marketers have been criticized for donating products and services to educational institutions in exchange for free promotion. Is this a fair exchange in your opinion, or should corporations be prohibited from attempting to influence youngsters in school?

4. For each of these five product categories—groceries, automobiles, vacations, furniture and appliances—describe the way in which you believe a married couple's choices would be affected if they had children.

5. In identifying and targeting newly divorced couples, do you think marketers are exploiting these couples' situations? Are there instances where you think marketers may actually be helpful to them? Support your answers with examples.

6. Arrange to interview two married couples, one younger and one older. Prepare a response form listing five product categories—groceries, furniture, appliances, vacations and automobiles—and ask each spouse to indicate, without consulting the other, whether purchases in each category are made by joint or unilateral decisions, and to indicate whether the unilateral decisions are made by the husband or the wife. Compare each couple's response for agreement between husbands and wives relative to who makes the decisions, and compare both couples' overall responses for differences relative to the number of joint versus unilateral decisions. Report your findings and conclusions.

7. Collect ads for three different product categories in which the family is targeted. Find another set of ads for different brands of the same items in which the family is not featured. Prepare a report on the effectiveness of the approaches.

8. Observe the interactions between parents and children in the cereal section of a local grocery store. Prepare a report on the number of children who expressed preferences, how they expressed their preferences and how parents responded, including the number who purchased the child's choice.

9. Watch three hours of children's programming on commercial television stations, and evaluate the marketing techniques used in the commercials in terms of the ethical issues raised in the final section of this chapter. Report your findings and conclusions.

10. Select a product category and, using the life cycle stages given in the chapter, list the variables that will affect purchase decisions for the product by consumers in each stage of the cycle.

11. Consider three important changes in modern family structure. For each, find an example of a marketer who has attempted to be conscious of this change as reflected in product communications, retailing innovations or other aspects of the marketing mix. If possible, find examples of marketers who have failed to keep up with these developments.

CBC VIDEO VIGNETTES

Concepts at Work for the V-Chip

Children are socialized as citizens and consumers by influences in their environment, ranging from their parents to schools to media exposure. As early as the 1970s, parents were active in voicing their concerns about how television advertising, for example, creates problems for them as parents and for society in general. This activism has been salved in great part by the establishment of such guidelines as the (Canadian) Code of Advertising for Children and by the banning of children's advertising in the province of Quebec. Yet these concerns persist, and they extend not only to promotion of products on television but also to the content of television programs. To tackle this issue parents have organized committees and associations in their communities and on a national level, which pay particular attention to lobbying the CRTC.

Tom Collins, an engineering professor at Simon Fraser University, just may have the answer for these anxious parents. He designed the V-Chip—V meaning violence. The V-Chip technology works in a fashion similar to the band for closed captioning. Parents would be able to set their personal tolerance levels for the amount of violence, coarse language and sex they want their children to see on television. When a program exceeds the tolerance levels, it is automatically zapped after a couple of seconds. A simple key can be used to lock and unlock the controls.

One of the challenges in getting this system to work is rating the television programs so that the parents' settings can be compared to the shows' rat-

ings. The CRTC is working with Shaw Cable and committees representing interest groups to establish the ratings. So far the Canadian constituents are working well and cooperatively with industry. However, with a concern about American television programming coming into Canada, the rating situation has become complex. Interest groups in the United States are very much divided on the issues. Some are supportive and are calling for the same spirit of cooperation and collaboration as exists in Canada. However, other groups, particularly those involved in producing or otherwise earning a living from television programming, claim that this is an unconstitutional attempt "by mothers of six-year olds" to censor the television viewing options of all Americans. There is a fear that advertisers may withdraw their support from certain programs based on the ratings.

QUESTIONS

1. Why are parents concerned about the content of television programs for children?

2. How do parents voice their concerns?

3. What role has the Canadian government and Canadian industry played in this debate?

4. Are American concerns about censorship and lack of advertising support realistic?

Video Resource: "The V Chip," *Undercurrents* #1 (October 10, 1995).

NOTES

1. Nancy Marx Better, "Green Teens," *The New York Times Magazine* (March 8, 1992): 44; Howard Schlossberg, "Kids Teach Parents How to Change Their Buying Habits," *Marketing News* (1992): 8.

2. Robert Boutilier, "Diversity in Family Structures," *American Demographics Marketing Tools* (1993): 4–6;

W. Bradford Fay, "Families in the 1990s: Universal Values, Uncommon Experiences," *Marketing Research: A Magazine of Management & Applications* 5, 1 (Winter 1993): 47. Percentage calculation based on *Market Research Handbook 1993–1994*, Statistics Canada cat. no. 63-224 (1994): 172.

3. Laura Sessions Stepp, "Where Have All the Families Gone?" *Washington Post* (March 1, 1994): C5.

4. David Cheal, "The Ritualization of Family Ties," *American Behavioral Scientist* 31 (July/August 1988): 632.

5. "Families Come First," *Psychology Today* (September 1988): 11.

6. Alison Fahey, "Lamaze Testing Seal: Program Delivers America's Newest Parents," *Advertising Age* (March 26, 1990): 4.

7. Christy Fisher, "Kidding Around Making Sense," *Advertising Age* (June 27, 1994): 34.

8. *Market Research Handbook 1993–1994*, Statistics Canada cat. no. 63-224 (1994): 631.

9. Alan R. Andreasen, "Life Status Changes and Changes in Consumer Preferences and Satisfaction," *Journal of Consumer Research* 11 (December 1984): 784–94; James H. McAlexander, John W. Schouten and Scott D. Roberts, "Consumer Behavior and Divorce," *Research in Consumer Behavior* 6 (1993): 153–84.

10. Denise Avard, "Canada's Children and Their Families," *Transition* (June 1995): 10–12.

11. Ibid.

12. Statistics from *Canada's Families: They Count* (Ottawa: The Vanier Institute of the Family, 1996). Published examples from "Big Rock brews up bucks for ducks," *Marketing* (June 23, 1997): 3; Miro Cernetig, "New radio royalty: the princes and princesses of whales," *Globe and Mail* (August 16, 1997): D1; Brian Laghi, "Coming to a grocery store near you: musk-ox burgers," *Globe and Mail* (June 15, 1996): D3.

13. *Profiling Canadian Families* (Ottawa: The Vanier Institute of the Family, 1994), p. 35.

14. Wayne W. McVey and Warren E. Kalbech, *Canadian Population* (Toronto: Nelson Canada, 1995), p. 225.

15. Cyndee Miller, "'Til Death Do They Part," *Marketing News* (March 27, 1995): 1–2.

16. John Kettle, "Smaller households are on the way," *Globe and Mail* (April 22, 1996): B7.

17. Karen Hardee-Cleaveland, "Is Eight Enough?" *American Demographics* (June 1989): 60.

18. Percentage calculation based on *Canada's Families: They Count.*

19. Diane Crispell, "Three's a Crowd," *American Demographics* (January 1989): 34.

20. *Canada's Families: They Count.*

21. McVey and Kalbech, *Canadian Population*, p. 293.

22. Percentage calculation based on *Canada's Families: They Count.*

23. *Canada's Families: They Count.*

24. Wendy Bounds, "An Easy Way to Get an Ex Out of the Picture—and No Lawyer!" *Wall Street Journal* (June 16, 1994): B1.

25. Percentage calculation based on *Canada's Families: They Count.*

26. Christy Fisher, "Census Data May Make Ads More Single-Minded," *Advertising Age* (July 20, 1992): 2.

27. Stephanie Shipp, "How Singles Spend," *American Demographics* (April 1988): 22–27; Patricia Braus, "Sex and the Single Spender," *American Demographics* (November 1993): 28–34.

28. Percentage calculation based on *Canada's Families: They Count.*

29. Thomas Exter, "Disappearing Act," *American Demographics* (January 1989): 78. See also Keren-Ami Johnson and Scott D. Roberts, "Incompletely-Launched and Returning Young Adults: Social Change, Consumption, and Family Environment," in *Enhancing Knowledge Development in Marketing*, eds. Robert P. Leone and V. Kumar (Chicago: American Marketing Association, 1992), pp. 249–54; John Burnett and Denise Smart, "Returning Young Adults: Implications for Marketers," *Psychology & Marketing* 11, 3 (May/June 1994): 253–69.

30. Percentage calculation based on *Canada's Families: They Count.*

31. Percentage calculation based on *Canada's Families: They Count.*

32. Alanna Mitchell, "Family thriving, study finds," *Globe and Mail* (November 9, 1993): A1, A7.

33. Constance Sorrentino, "The Changing Family in International Perspective," *Monthly Labor Review* (March 1990): 41.

34. McVey and Kalbech, *Canadian Population*, p. 249.

35. *Profiling Canadian Families*, p. 35.

36. Eileen Fischer and Brenda Gainer, "Baby Showers: A Rite of Passage," in *Advances in Consumer Research 20*, eds. Leigh McAlister and Michael L. Rothschild (Provo, UT: Association for Consumer Research, 1993), pp. 320–24.

37. These categories are an adapted version of an FLC model proposed by Gilly and Enis (1982). Based upon a recent empirical comparison of several competing models, Schaninger and Danko found that this framework outperformed others, especially in terms of its treatment of non-conventional households, though they recommend several improvements to this model as well. See Mary C. Gilly and Ben M. Enis, "Recycling the Family Life Cycle: A Proposal for Redefinition," in *Advances in Consumer Research 9*, ed. Andrew A. Mitchell (Ann Arbor, MI: Association for Consumer Research, 1982), pp. 271–76; Charles M. Schaninger and William P. Danko, "A Conceptual and Empirical Comparison of Alternate Household Life Cycle Markets," *Journal of Consumer Research* 19 (March 1993): 580–94; Scott D. Roberts, Patricia K. Voli and Keren-Ami Johnson, "Beyond the Family Life Cycle: An Inventory of Variables for Defining the Family as a Consumption Unit," in *Developments in Marketing Science 15*, ed. Victoria L. Crittenden

(Coral Gables, FL: Academy of Marketing Science, 1992), pp. 71–75.

38. James H. McAlexander, John W. Schouten and Scott D. Roberts, "Consumer Behavior and Divorce," in *Research in Consumer Behavior* (Greenwich, CT: JAI Press, 1992); Michael R. Solomon, "The Role of Products as Social Stimuli: A Symbolic Interactionism Perspective," *Journal of Consumer Research* 10 (December 1983): 319–29; Melissa Martin Young, "Disposition of Possession During Role Transitions," in *Advances in Consumer Research 18*, eds. Rebecca H. Holman and Michael R. Solomon (Provo, UT: Association for Consumer Research, 1991), pp. 33–39.

39. Harry L. Davis, "Decision Making Within the Household," *Journal of Consumer Research* 2 (March 1972): 241–60; Michael B. Menasco and David J. Curry, "Utility and Choice: An Empirical Study of Wife/Husband Decision Making," *Journal of Consumer Research* 16 (June 1989): 87–97. For a recent review, see Conway Lackman and John M. Lanasa, "Family Decision-Making Theory: An Overview and Assessment," *Psychology & Marketing* 10, 2 (March/April 1993): 81–94.

40. Neal Templin, "The PC Wars: Who Gets to Use the Family Computer?" *Wall Street Journal* (October 5, 1995): B1 (2 pp.).

41. Shannon Dortch, "Money and Marital Discord," *American Demographics* (October 1994): 11 (3 pp.).

42. Daniel Seymour and Greg Lessne, "Spousal Conflict Arousal: Scale Development," *Journal of Consumer Research* 11 (December 1984): 810–21.

43. "Unleash the potential (of pet product sales)," *Canadian Grocer* 111, 6 (July/August 1996): 35–37.

44. Quoted in Youssef M. Ibrahim, "French Love for Animals: Too Fervent?" *New York Times* (February 2, 1990): A5.

45. Woody Hochswender, "The Cat's Meow," *New York Times* (May 16, 1989): B7; Judann Dagnoli, "Toothcare for Terriers," *Advertising Age* (November 20, 1989): 8; "For Fido, Broccoli and Yogurt," *New York Times* (April 16, 1989); Howard G. Chua-Eoan, "Reigning Cats and Dogs," *Time* (August 16, 1993): 50 (2 pp.); William E. Schmidt, "Right, Then: Your Policy Covers Fido for Therapy," *New York Times* (May 15, 1994): 4; "Unleash the potential (of pet product sales)."

46. For research on factors affecting how much influence adolescents exert in family decision making, see Ellen Foxman, Patriya Tansuhaj and Karin M. Ekstrom, "Family Members' Perceptions of Adolescents' Influence in Family Decision Making," *Journal of Consumer Research* 15, 4 (March 1989): 482–91; Sharon E. Beatty and Salil Talpade, "Adolescent Influence in Family Decision Making: A Replication with Extension," *Journal of Consumer Research* 21, 2 (September 1994): 332–41.

47. This list of roles is adapted from Fred E. Webster and Yoram Wind, *Organizational Buying Behavior* (New York: Prentice Hall, 1972) and expanded in J. Paul

Peter, Jerry C. Olson and Jerry A. Rosenblatt, *Understanding Consumer Behavior* (Toronto: Times Mirror Professional Publishing, 1996), p. 359; John C. Mowen, *Consumer Behavior* (Englewood Cliffs, NJ: Prentice Hall, 1995), p. 658; Gail Tom, *Applications in Consumer Behavior: Readings and Exercises* (Englewood Cliffs, NJ: Prentice Hall, 1984), p. 106; and Gurprit S. Kindra, Michel Laroche and Thomas E. Muller, *The Canadian Perspective: Consumer Behavior* (Scarborough: Nelson Canada, 1994), p. 465.

48. Diane Crispell, "Dual-Earner Diversity," *American Demographics* (July 1995): 32–37.

49. Thomas Hine, *Populuxe* (New York: Alfred A. Knopf, 1986).

50. Robert Boutilier, "Targeting Families: Marketing To and Through the New Family," *American Demographics* (1993).

51. Judith Madill and Frances Woolley, unpublished preliminary findings of Study of Financial Management and Decision Making in Canadian Households, 1997.

52. Judith Madill and Frances Woolley, "The Purchase of RRSPs in Canadian Households: Husband–Wife Decision Making," abstract in *Marketing*, ed. Herbert MacKenzie (Administrative Sciences Association of Canada, 1997), vol. 18, p. 187.

53. Dennis L. Rosen and Donald H. Granbois, "Determinants of Role Structure in Family Financial Management," *Journal of Consumer Research* 10 (September 1983): 253–58.

54. Robert F. Bales, *Interaction Process Analysis: A Method for the Study of Small Groups* (Reading, MA: Addison-Wesley, 1950).

55. Alma S. Baron, "Working Parents: Shifting Traditional Roles," *Business* 37 (January/March 1987): 36; William J. Qualls, "Household Decision Behavior: The Impact of Husbands' and Wives' Sex Role Orientation," *Journal of Consumer Research* 14 (September 1987): 264–79; Charles M. Schaninger and W. Christian Buss, "The Relationship of Sex-Role Norms to Household Task Allocation," *Psychology & Marketing* 2 (Summer 1985): 93–104; John Gray, "Domesticity, Diapers and Dad," *Globe and Mail* (June 15, 1996): D1, D2.

56. Gary L. Sullivan and P.J. O'Connor, "The Family Purchase Decision Process: A Cross-Cultural Review and Framework for Research," *Southwest Journal of Business & Economics* (Fall 1988): 43; Marilyn Lavin, "Husband-Dominant, Wife-Dominant, Joint," *Journal of Consumer Marketing* 10, 3 (1993): 33–42.

57. Rosemary Polegato, "The Role of Family Members in Food Shopping: Implications for Retailers and Manufacturers," *Journal of Food Products Marketing* 2, 1 (1994): 3–15.

58. Rosemary Polegato and Judith L. Zaichkowsky, "Family Food Shopping Strategies: Strategies Used by Husbands and Wives," *The Journal of Consumer Affairs* 28, 2 (Winter 1994): 278–99.

59. Susan Kelman, "No Man's Land," *Report on Business Magazine* (August 1990): 52–57.

60. Rene Bartos, "Marketing to Women: The Quiet Revoution," *Marketing Insights* (June 1989): 61.

61. Yumiko Ono, "McDonald's Doting Dads Strike a Chord in Japan," *Wall Street Journal Interactive Edition* (May 8, 1997).

62. Micaela DiLeonardo, "The Female World of Cards and Holidays: Women, Families, and the Work of Kinship," *Signs* 12 (Spring 1942): 440–53; Dorothy Lipovenko, "Women bear brunt of elder-care," *Globe and Mail* (March 27, 1997): A1, A7.

63. Faith Popcorn, *Clicking: 16 trends to future fit your life, your work, and your business* (New York: Harper-Collins Publishers, 1996).

64. Brenda Gainer and Eileen Fischer, "To Buy or Not to Buy? That is Not the Question: Female Ritual in Home Shopping Parties," in *Advances in Consumer Research 18*, pp. 597–602.

65. Craig J. Thompson, "Caring Consumers: Gendered Consumption Meanings and the Juggling Lifestyle," *Journal of Consumer Research* 22 (March 1996): 388–407.

66. Quoted in Bernice Kanner, "Advertisers Take Aim at Women at Home," *New York Times* (January 2, 1995): 42.

67. Barbara Carton, "PCs Replace Lettuce Tubs at Sales Parties," *Wall Street Journal* (March 26, 1997): B1.

68. C. Whan Park, "Joint Decisions in Home Purchasing: A Muddling-Through Process," *Journal of Consumer Research* 9 (September 1982): 151–62. See also William J. Qualls and Françoise Jaffe, "Measuring Conflict in Household Decision Behavior: Read My Lips and Read My Mind," in *Advances in Consumer Research 19*, eds. John F. Sherry, Jr., and Brian Sternthal (Provo, UT: Association for Consumer Research, 1992), pp. 522–31.

69. Kim P. Corfman and Donald R. Lehmann, "Models of Cooperative Group Decision-Making and Relative Influence: An Experimental Investigation of Family Purchase Decisions," *Journal of Consumer Research* 14 (June 1987): 1–13.

70. Alison M. Torrillo, "Dens are Men's Territory," *American Demographics* (January 1995): 11 (2 pp.).

71. Charles Atkin, "Observation of Parent-Child Interaction in Supermarket Decision-Making," *Journal of Marketing* 42 (October 1978): 41–45.

72. Sharen Kindel, "They May Be Small, But They Spend Big," *Adweek* (February 10, 1992): 38.

73. Leslie Isler, Edward T. Popper and Scott Ward, "Children's Purchase Requests and Parental Responses: Results From a Diary Study," *Journal of Advertising Research* 27 (October/November 1987): 28–39.

74. Horst H. Stipp, "Children as Consumers," *American Demographics* (February 1988): 27.

75. Melissa Turner, "Kids Marketing Clout Man-Sized," *Atlanta Journal* (February 18, 1988): E10.

76. Scott Ward, "Consumer Socialization," in *Perspectives in Consumer Behavior,* eds. Harold H. Kassarjian and Thomas S. Robertson (Glenville, IL: Scott, Foresman and Company, 1980), p. 380.

77. Quoted in Nicholas D. Kristof, "Japan is a Woman's World Once the Front Door is Shut," *New York Times* (June 19, 1996): A1 (2 pp.).

78. Thomas Lipscomb, "Indicators of Materialism in Children's Free Speech: Age and Gender Comparisons," *Journal of Consumer Marketing* (Fall 1988): 41–46.

79. George P. Moschis, "The Role of Family Communication in Consumer Socialization of Children and Adolescents," *Journal of Consumer Research* 11 (March 1985): 898–913.

80. James U. McNeal and Chyon-Hwa Yeh, "Born to Shop," *American Demographics* (June 1993): 34–39.

81. Patricia Pliner et al., "Children's consumer behavior in a store with unattractive merchandise: The 'caveat emptorium,'" *Journal of Economic Psychology* 15 (1994): 449–65.

82. See Les Carlson, Sanford Grossbart and J. Kathleen Stuenkel, "The Role of Parental Socialization Types on Differential Family Communication Patterns Regarding Consumption," *Journal of Consumer Psychology* 1, 1 (1992): 31–52.

83. See Patricia M. Greenfield et al., "The Program-Length Commercial: A Study of the Effects of Television/Toy Tie-Ins on Imaginative Play," *Psychology & Marketing* 7 (Winter 1990): 237–56, for a study on the effects of commercial programming on creative play.

84. Jill Goldsmith, "Ga, Ga, Goo, Goo, Where's the Remote? TV Show Targets Tots," *Dow Jones Business News* (February 5, 1997), accessed via *Wall Street Journal Interactive Edition* (February 6, 1997).

85. Gerald J. Gorn and Renee Florsheim, "The Effects of Commercials for Adult Products on Children," *Journal of Consumer Research* 11 (March 1985): 962–67. For a recent study that assessed the impact of violent commercials on children, see V. Kanti Prasad and Lois J. Smith, "Television Commercials in Violent Programming: An Experimental Evaluation of Their Effects on Children," *Journal of the Academy of Marketing Science* 22, 4 (1994): 340–51.

86. Glenn Collins, "New Studies on Girl Toys and Boy Toys," *New York Times* (February 13, 1984): D1.

87. Susan B. Kaiser, "Clothing and the Social Organization of Gender Perception: A Developmental Approach," *Clothing and Textiles Research Journal* 7 (Winter 1989): 46–56.

88. D.W. Rajecki et al., "Gender Casting in Television Toy Advertisements: Distributions, Message Content Analysis, and Evaluations," *Journal of Consumer Psychology* 2, 3 (1993): 307–27.

89. Lori Schwartz and William Markham, "Sex Stereotyping in Children's Toy Advertisements," *Sex Roles* 12 (January 1985): 157–70.

90. Joseph Pereira, "Oh Boy! In Toyland, You Get More if You're Male," *Wall Street Journal* (September 23, 1994): B1 (2 pp.); Joseph Pereira, "Girls' Favorite Playthings: Dolls, Dolls, and Dolls," *Wall Street Journal* (September 23, 1994): B1 (2 pp.).

91. Brad Edmondson, "Snakes, Snails, and Puppy Dogs' Tails," *American Demographics* (October 1987): 18.

92. Laura A. Peracchio, "How Do Young Children Learn to be Consumers? A Script-Processing Approach," *Journal of Consumer Research* 18 (March 1992): 425–40; Laura A. Peracchio, "Young Children's Processing of a Televised Narrative: Is a Picture Really Worth a Thousand Words?" *Journal of Consumer Research* 20, 2 (September 1993): 281–93. See also M. Carole Macklin, "The Effects of an Advertising Retrieval Cue on Young Children's Memory and Brand Evaluations," *Psychology & Marketing* 11, 3 (May/June 1994): 291–311.

93. Jasmine Miller, "This is what little girls are made of?" *Canadian Business (Technology)* (Summer 1997): 52–56.

94. Pereira, "Girls' Favorite Playthings: Dolls, Dolls, and Dolls."

95. Jean Piaget, "The Child and Modern Physics," *Scientific American* 196, 3 (1957): 46–51. See also Kenneth D. Bahn, "How and When Do Brand Perceptions and Preferences First Form? A Cognitive Developmental Investigation," *Journal of Consumer Research* 13 (December 1986): 382–93.

96. Deborah L. Roedder, "Age Differences in Children's Responses to Television Advertising: An Information-Processing Approach," *Journal of Consumer Research* 8 (September 1981): 144–53. See also Deborah Roedder John and Ramnath Lakshmi-Ratan, "Age Differences in Children's Choice Behavior: The Impact of Available Alternatives," *Journal of Marketing Research* 29 (May 1992): 216–26; Jennifer Gregan-Paxton and Deborah Roedder John, "Are Young Children Adaptive Decision Makers? A Study of Age Differences in Information Search Behavior," *Journal of Consumer Research* 21 (March 1995): 567–80; Jennifer Gregan-Paxton and Deborah Roedder John, "The Emergence of Adaptive Decision Making in Children," *Journal of Consumer Research* 24 (June 1997): 43–56.

97. Janet Simons, "Youth Marketing: Children's Clothes Follow the Latest Fashion," *Advertising Age* (February 14, 1985): 16.

98. Stipp, "Children as Consumers." See Laura A. Peracchio, "Designing Research to Reveal the Young Child's Emerging Competence," *Psychology & Marketing* 7 (Winter 1990): 257–76, for details regarding the design of research on children.

99. "Kid Power," *Forbes* (March 30, 1987): 9–10.

100. Dena Kleiman, "Candy to Frighten Your Parents With," *New York Times* (August 23, 1989): C1.

101. Laura Shapiro, "Where Little Boys Can Play with Nail Polish," *Newsweek* (May 28, 1990): 62.

102. Matt Murray, "Marketers Want Kids' Help and Their Parents' Loyalty," *Wall Street Journal Interactive Edition* (May 6, 1997).

103. Cindy Clark, "Putting Aside Adultcentrism: Child-Centered Ethnographic Research" (unpublished manuscript, C.D. Clark Limited, 1991); Cindy Clark, "Some Practical Ins and Outs of Studying Children as Consumers" (paper presented at the AMA Research Roundtable, March 1986).

104. Gary Armstrong and Merrie Brucks, "Dealing with Children's Advertising: Public Policy Issues and Alternatives," *Journal of Public Policy and Marketing* 7 (1988): 98–113.

105. Bonnie Reece, "Children and Shopping: Some Public Policy Questions," *Journal of Public Policy and Marketing* (1986): 185–94.

106. Mary Ann Stutts and Garland G. Hunnicutt, "Can Young Children Understand Disclaimers in Television Commercials," *Journal of Advertising* 16 (Winter 1987): 41–46.

107. Ira Teinowitz, "CARU to Unveil Guidelines for Kid-Focused Web Sites," *Ad Age* (April 21, 1997): 8.

108. Steve Weinstein, "Fight Heats Up Against Kids' TV Commershows," *Marketing News* (October 9, 1989): 2.

109. Alan Bunce, "Are TV Ads Turning Kids Into Consumers?" *Christian Science Monitor* (August 11, 1988): 1.

110. Merrie Brucks, Gary M. Armstrong and Marvin E. Goldberg, "Children's Use of Cognitive Defenses Against Television Advertising: A Cognitive Response Approach," *Journal of Consumer Research* 14 (March 1988): 471–82.

111. Tara Parker-Pope, "Spiked Sodas, an Illicit Hit with Kids in U.K., Head for U.S.," *Wall Street Journal* (February 12, 1996): B1.

112. Pat Wechsler, "Hey Kid, Buy This!" *Business Week* (June 30, 1997): 62–69.

113. Edmund L. Andrews, "F.C.C. Limits Ads on TV Shows Aimed at Children," *New York Times* (April 10, 1991): D6; Laurel Wentz, "Playing by the Same Rules: Harmonization of Children's Ads Sought via Self-Regulation," *Advertising Age* (December 2, 1991): S–2.

114. See, for example, reports in *Consumer News & Reviews* (American Council on Consumer Interests, July–August 1997): "Denmark Internet Deception" (p. 2) and "On-line Marketing to Young Consumers" (p. 3).

IV

Consumers and Subcultures

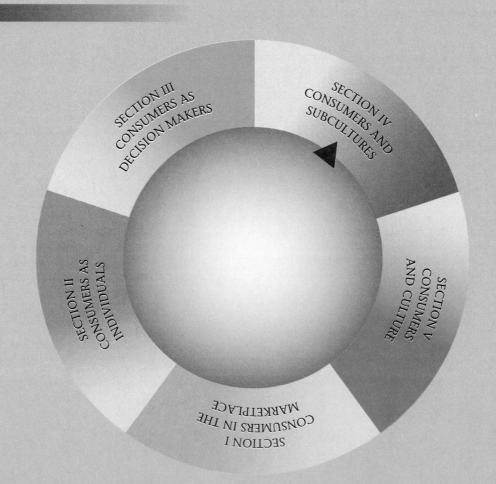

SECTION III
CONSUMERS AS
DECISION MAKERS

SECTION IV
CONSUMERS AND
SUBCULTURES

SECTION II
CONSUMERS AS
INDIVIDUALS

SECTION V
CONSUMERS
AND CULTURE

SECTION I
CONSUMERS IN THE
MARKETPLACE

The chapters in this section consider some of the social influences that help to determine who we are, with an emphasis on the various subcultures to which we belong. Chapter 13 focuses on factors that define our social classes and how membership in a social class exerts a strong pull on what we buy with the money we make. This chapter also considers more broadly how the economic conditions of a society at any point in time will affect the purchase decisions of group members. Chapters 14 and 15 discuss ways that our unique subcultural backgrounds help to stamp our social identities, and also how the bonds we share with others who were born at roughly the same time unite us.

Finally, the big day has come! Victor is going to meet Marilyn's parents. Victor was doing contracting at the publishing company where Marilyn works, and it was love at first sight. Vic attended the "School of Hard Knocks" on the streets of Toronto, and Marilyn was fresh out of Havergal College—but they knew they could work things out. Marilyn's been hinting that the Caldwells have money, but Vic isn't intimidated. He knows guys from his neighbourhood who wheeled and dealed their way into six figures; he can handle one more big shot in a silk suit, flashing a roll of bills and showing off his expensive modern furniture with mirrors and gadgets everywhere.

When they arrive in Rosedale, Victor looks for a Rolls in the driveway but sees only a Jeep Cherokee—which, he decides, must belong to a servant. Inside, Vic is surprised by how simply the house is decorated and how shabby it seems. The hall has a faded oriental rug, and all the furniture looks really old. In fact there doesn't seem to be a new stick of furniture anywhere, just a lot of antiques.

Vic is even more surprised when he meets Mr. Caldwell. He half expected Marilyn's father to wear a tuxedo and hold a glass of cognac as on "Lifestyles of the Rich and Famous." Vic even put on his best Italian silk suit and wore his large cubic zirconium "pinky ring" so this guy would know he had some money too. When Marilyn's father emerges in a rumpled cardigan and sneakers, Victor realizes he's definitely not in the old neighbourhood ...

or an agile car, the English have long known the importance of good breeding.

JAGUAR

13

Income and Social Class

INTRODUCTION

As Victor's eye-opening experience at the Caldwells' suggests, there are many ways to spend money, and a wide gulf exists between those who have it and those who don't. Perhaps an equally wide one exists between those who have had it for a long time and those who "made it the hard way—by earning it!" This chapter begins by briefly considering how general economic conditions affect the way consumers allocate their money. Then, reflecting the adage "the rich are different," it will explore how people who occupy different positions in society consume in very different ways. Whether a skilled worker like Phil or a child of privilege like Marilyn, a person's social class has a profound impact on what he or she does with money and on how consumption choices reflect the person's "place" in society.

As this chapter illustrates, these choices play another purpose as well. The specific products and services we buy are often intended to make sure *other* people know what our social standing is—or what we would like it to be. Products are frequently bought and displayed as markers of social class; they are valued as *status symbols*. Indeed, it is quite common for a product to be positioned on the basis of its (presumed) placement in the social hierarchy. The chapter concludes with an assessment of the evolving natures of such status symbols, and it considers some reasons why status-driven products are not always accurate indicators of a consumer's true social standing.

CONSUMER SPENDING AND ECONOMIC BEHAVIOUR

behavioural economics the study of the behavioural determinants of economic decisions

The field of **behavioural economics,** or economic psychology, is concerned with the "human" side of economic decisions. Beginning with the pioneering work of psychologist George Katona, this discipline studies how consumers' motives and their expectations about the future affect their current spending, and how these individual decisions add up to affect a society's economic well-being.[1]

Income Patterns

Many Canadians would probably say that they don't make enough money, but in reality the average Canadian's standard of living continues to improve. Average family income increased from $40 516 in 1970 (in 1994 dollars) to $52 858 in 1994, although there was a drop from a high of $56 145 in 1990.[2] Further, this overall increase in income was by no means shared equally among all consumer groups. In 1995 fewer than 2 percent of Canadians reported earning $100 000 or more, and 10 percent reported earning $50 000 to $100 000, while 61 percent reported earnings of less than $25 000.[3] It has been estimated that only about 40 000 Canadians earned more than $250 000 in 1994.[4] These income shifts are linked to two key factors: a shift in women's roles and increases in educational attainment.[5]

The steady increase in the numbers of working women is a primary cause of the rapid growth of middle- and upper-income families. Among about 20 percent of Canadian couples, it is the wives' paycheques that are propelling the couples up the income ladder. Nearly 30 percent of wives in dual-earner couples without children earn more than their spouses.[6]

Another factor that determines who gets a bigger piece of the pie is education. Although paying for university often entails great sacrifice, it still pays off in the long run. In 1995 just under 50 percent of Canadians had some post-secondary education; about 14 percent had a university degree. Nearly 130 000 Canadians earned baccalaureate or first professional degrees in 1995.[7]

To Spend or Not to Spend: That Is the Question

A basic assumption of economic psychology is that consumer demand for goods and services depends *both* on ability to buy and willingness to buy. While demand for necessities tends to be stable over time, other expenditures can be postponed or eliminated if people don't feel that now is a good time to spend money.[8] For example, a person may decide to "make do" with his current clunker for another year rather than buy a new car right away.

discretionary income the money available to a household over and above that required for a comfortable standard of living

Discretionary income is the money available to a household over and above that required for a comfortable standard of living. As might be expected, discretionary income increases as overall income goes up, and debt and tax burdens are relieved.

Consumers' spending decisions reverberate around the world, as the ability and interest to purchase goods and services among the citizens of one country affects the fortunes of people in other lands. As the economies of developing countries in Asia and Latin America grow, millions of new consumers from Jakarta to Mexico City are acquiring the creature comforts that people in North America and Europe have come to expect. Sometimes goods that Western consumers regard as basic necessities take on added significance as discretionary fashion items for people in other countries. For example, companies like Whirlpool typically offer refrigerators in a wide range of colours in Asian countries, since people are more likely to display these appliances in their living rooms.[9]

As the population ages and income levels rise, the typical household is changing the way it spends its money. Many consumers are experiencing doubts about their individual and collective futures and are anxious about holding on to what they have. While half of the respondents in a recent survey conducted by Roper/Starch Worldwide say they don't believe money can buy happiness, nearly 70 percent still report that if their earnings doubled, they would be happier than they are now![10]

A consumer's anxieties about money are not necessarily related to how much he or she actually has; acquiring and managing money is more a state of mind than of wallet. For many people, money is equated with security and comfort, so the prospect of losing this cushion is stressful indeed. The Roper/Starch survey found that, by far, security was the attribute most closely linked to the meaning of money. Other significant associations included comfort, being able to help one's children, freedom and pleasure.

Consumer Confidence

A consumer's beliefs about what the future holds is an indicator of **consumer confidence,** which reflects the extent to which people are optimistic or pessimistic about the future health of the economy and how they will fare down the road. These beliefs influence how much money the consumer will pump into the economy when making discretionary purchases. Thus, forecasting consumer confidence is of interest.

Many businesses take forecasts about anticipated spending very seriously, and periodic surveys attempt to "take the pulse" of the Canadian consumer. A business organization called the Conference Board of Canada conducts a survey of consumer confidence, as does the Angus Reid Group. The following are the types of questions posed to consumers in these surveys:[11]

* Would you say that you and your family are better off or worse off financially than a year ago?
* Will you be better off or worse off a year from now?
* Do you plan to buy a car in the next year?

When people are pessimistic about their prospects and about the state of the economy, they tend to cut back their spending and take on less debt. On the other hand, when they are optimistic about the future, they tend to reduce the amount they save, take on more debt and buy discretionary items. The overall **savings rate** is thus influenced by consumers' pessimism or optimism about their personal circumstances (e.g., a fear of being laid off versus a sudden increase in personal wealth due to an inheritance), as well as by national and world events (e.g., the election of a new prime minister or an international crisis), and by cultural differences in attitudes towards saving.[12]

consumer confidence the state of mind of consumers relative to their optimism or pessimism about economic conditions; people tend to make more discretionary purchases when their confidence in the economy is high

savings rate the amount of money saved for later use that is influenced by consumers' pessimism or optimism about their personal circumstances

CONSUMERS AND MARKETERS ADAPT TO CHANGING TIMES

In times of economic recession, an interesting but contradictory pattern is often observed: both discounted goods and luxury items tend to sell well. The reason is that during a recession the affluent tend to be insulated from lay-offs. Since they have cash on hand, they don't have to worry about paying high interest rates, and so they can stockpile luxury items and take on debt. In contrast, average consumers are worried about the state of the economy and their job prospects, so these people will buy frugally and engage in extensive comparison shopping. Discount chains that sell brand names for less tend to prosper in this environment.[13]

As an example of how the recent recession affected consumer spending patterns, consider the findings of recent surveys of Canadians:

- Angus Reid in his 1996 book *Shakedown* asserts that the new economy is changing Canadian consumers in many important ways: they are less loyal, more value-conscious and more involved in work (if they have a job), and they have less leisure time, value functionality over fashion, have increased the use life of durables, are increasingly interested in "self-fulfilment" experiences, and are more vocal and litigious about their dissatisfaction.[14]

- In a poll in the spring of 1996, Ernst and Young Inc. found that more than half of Canadians aged 18 to 34 said they were optimistic about their future. This consumer confidence is expected to result in the expenditure of money on such things as home furnishings and cars.[15]

- The 1994 Major Market Retail Report by Kubas Consultants states that Canadian consumers want the best value at low prices. The vast majority of adults in Canada's six major urban markets say they always check and compare prices, and look for sales and specials in ads and flyers. The intense emphasis on value surpasses variety, selection and service as a primary motivator of where to shop.[16]

In an era of diminished resources Canadians are redefining traditional relationships among price, value and quality. In the past (most notably in the "go-go" 1980s) people seemed to be willing to pay almost anything for products and services. Consumers still claim to want quality—but *quality at the right price.*

In surveys, most people now report that they regret the conspicuous consumption of the 1980s and feel the need to live with less. The attitude is more practical and reflects a "back-to-basics" orientation. People want more hard news instead of "hype" from advertising, and they appreciate ads that feature problem-solving tips or that save money or time.

SOCIAL CLASS

social class the overall rank of people in a society; people who are grouped within the same social class are approximately equal in terms of their social standing, occupations and lifestyles

All societies can be roughly divided into the "haves" and the "have-nots" (though sometimes having is a question of degree). As Victor's encounter with the Caldwells suggests, a consumer's standing in society, or **social class,** is determined by a complex set of variables, including income, family background and occupation.

The place one occupies in the social structure is an important determinant not only of *how much* money is spent; it also influences *how* it is spent. Victor is surprised that the Caldwells, who clearly have a lot of money, do not seem to flaunt it. This

Nouveau smart.

The New V6 Passat

A funny thing happened on the way to the 90's.

People came to their senses. Intelligence of all things became more socially acceptable than extravagance.

And things like common sense, honesty and good old-fashioned value were suddenly back in vogue.

In other words, people everywhere started acting, well, just like a Volkswagen.

They started believing that you don't have to show off to stand out.

That a car should cost what a car should cost. Not what a house should cost.

And by no small coincidence, they began buying the Volkswagen Passat.

A bona fide European touring sedan that asks you not to scale back your expectations, just what you pay for them.

With a heady V6, 172-horsepower engine, electronic traction control and ABS brakes, our Passat GLX is built to massage roads, not egos.

Providing all the driving exhilaration a thinking person could desire along the way.

For details, call 1-800-444-8987. Or visit your Volkswagen retailer.

Where you can discover firsthand that you don't have to be rich to have a driving experience that is.

Experience Fahrvergnügen

©1993 Volkswagen Seatbelts save lives. Don't drink and drive.

This Volkswagen ad reflects a shift in priorities in the 1990s. The headline implies that consumers are moving from "nouveau riche" to "nouveau smart."
Courtesy of Volkswagen United States, Inc.

understated way of living is a hallmark of so-called "old money"; people who have had it for a long time don't need to prove they've got it. In contrast, consumers who are relative newcomers to affluence might allocate the same amount of money very differently.

A Universal Pecking Order

In many animal species a social organization is developed whereby the most assertive or aggressive animals exert control over the others and have the first pick of food, living space and mating partners. Chickens, for example, develop a clearly defined dominance-submission hierarchy. Within this hierarchy each hen has a position in which she is submissive to all the hens above her and dominates all the ones below her (hence the origin of the term *pecking order*).[17]

People are no different. They also develop a pecking order whereby they are ranked in terms of their relative standing in society. This standing determines their access to such resources as education, housing and consumer goods. People try to improve their ranking by moving up in the social order whenever possible. This desire to improve one's lot in life—and, often, to let others know that one has done so—is at the core of many marketing strategies.

While every culture has its social hierarchies, variations exist in terms of how explicitly these distinctions are observed. Stratification of one sort or another is universal, even in societies that officially disdain such a process. In China, a supposedly

MULTICULTURAL DIMENSIONS

Avenue is an American magazine that reports on the comings and goings of New York high society. Now the magazine is launching another edition—in China. *Avenue China* made its début in October 1994 and included stories about golfing in Bali and an Italian designer, as well as profiles of top Chinese executives. The magazine cannot be found on newsstands; it is being given to the rich residents of Beijing, Shanghai, Guangzhou and Shenzhen (China's wealthiest cities). About a third of the edition's 50 000 copies will be hand-delivered to important government officials, business people and celebrities. Considering that China's per capita gross domestic product is only $370 (US) per year, it's obvious that *Avenue China* is targeting the cream of the crop of a new breed of Chinese success stories.[18]

classless society, many Chinese are irritated by the children of top party officials, who are called *gaoganzidi*. These offspring have reputations for laziness, enjoying material pleasures and getting the best jobs by virtue of their family connections. They are thus a privileged class in a classless society.[19]

SOCIAL CLASS AFFECTS ACCESS TO RESOURCES

Just as marketers try to carve society into groups for segmentation purposes, sociologists have developed ways to describe meaningful divisions of society in terms of people's relative social and economic resources. Some of these divisions involve political power, while others revolve around purely economic distinctions. Karl Marx felt that position in a society was determined by one's relationship to the *means of production*. Some people (the haves) control resources, and they use the labour of others to preserve their privileged positions. The have-nots lack control and depend on their own labour for survival, so these people have the most to gain by changing the system. Distinctions among people that entitle some to more than others are perpetuated by those who benefit by doing so.[20]

SOCIAL CLASS AFFECTS TASTES AND LIFESTYLES

The term *social class* is now used more generally to describe the overall rank of people in a society. People who are grouped within the same social class are approximately equal in terms of their social standing in the community. They work in roughly similar occupations, and they tend to have similar lifestyles by virtue of their income levels and common tastes. These people tend to socialize with one another and share many ideas and values regarding the way life should be lived.[21]

Social class is as much a state of being as it is of having. As Victor sees, class is also a question of what one *does* with one's money and how one defines one's role in society. Although people may not like the idea that some members of society are better off or "different" than others, most consumers do acknowledge the existence of different classes and the effect of class membership on consumption. As one wealthy woman observed when asked to define social class:

> I would suppose social class means where you went to school and how far. Your intelligence. Where you live ... Where you send your children to school. The hobbies you have. Skiing, for example, is higher than the snowmobile ... It can't be [just] money, because nobody ever knows that about you for sure.[22]

Social Stratification

In school it always seems that some kids are more popular. They have access to many resources, such as special privileges, fancy cars, large allowances or dates with other popular classmates. At work some people are put on the fast track and are promoted to high-prestige jobs, given higher salaries and perhaps such perks as a parking space, a large office or the keys to the executive washroom.

In virtually every context some people seem to be ranked higher than others. Patterns of social arrangements evolve whereby some members get more resources than others by virtue of their relative standing, power and/or control in the group.[23] The phenomenon of **social stratification** refers to this creation of artificial divisions in a society and can be defined as "... those processes in a social system by which scarce and valuable resources are distributed unequally to status positions that become more or less permanently ranked in terms of the share of valuable resources each receives."[24]

If you think back to groups you've belonged to, both large and small, you'll probably agree that in many instances some members seem to get more than their fair share of goodies, while other individuals are not so lucky. Some of these resources may have gone to people who earned them through hard work or diligent study. This allocation is due to *achieved status*. Other rewards may have been obtained because the person was lucky enough to be born rich or beautiful. Such good fortune reflects *ascribed status*.

Whether rewards go to the "best and the brightest" or to someone who happens to be related to the boss, allocations are rarely equal within a social group. Most groups exhibit a structure, or **status hierarchy,** in which some members are somehow better off than others. They may have more authority or power, or they are simply better liked or respected.

Canada supposedly does not have a rigid, objectively defined class system. Nevertheless, Canada has tended to maintain a stable class structure in terms of income distribution. Unlike other countries, however, what *does* change are the groups (ethnic, racial and religious) that have occupied different positions within this structure at different times.[25] The most influential and perhaps earliest attempt to describe Canadian class structure was proposed by Bernard Blishen, a sociologist, in 1958. Blishen constructed an occupational class scale incorporating assumptions about the educational, income and prestige levels attached to each occupation. The index was improved through further work with various researchers and the final version recognizes gender differences affecting occupational and social status.[26]

Among consumer researchers in North America an alternative view of social class is that proposed by Richard P. Coleman, who built on the work of earlier researchers, notably W. Lloyd Warner.[27] Their classifications imply (in ascending order) some judgment of desirability in terms of access to such resources as money, education and luxury goods. Coleman's view of American class structure, shown in Figure 13–1, can also be applied to the Canadian context, as will be discussed when measurement of social class is considered later in this chapter.

Every society has some type of hierarchical class structure, in which people's access to products and services is determined by their resources and social standing. Of course the specific "markers" of success depend on what is valued in each culture. For the Chinese, who are just beginning to experience the bounties of capitalism, one marker of success is hiring a bodyguard to protect oneself and one's newly acquired possessions![28]

social stratification the process in a social system by which scarce and valuable resources are distributed unequally to status positions that become more or less permanently ranked in terms of the share of valuable resources each receives

status hierarchy a ranking of social desirability in terms of consumers' access to such resources as money, education and luxury goods

FIGURE 13–1 • A Contemporary View of the American Class Structure

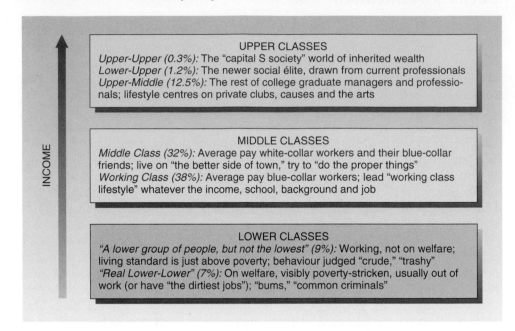

Source: Richard P. Coleman, "The Continuing Significance of Social Class to Marketing," *Journal of Consumer Research* 10 (December 1983): 265–80. Reprinted with permission of The University of Chicago Press.

Japan is a highly status-conscious society, where upscale, designer labels are quite popular and new forms of status are always being sought. To the Japanese, the traditional rock garden, formerly a vehicle for leisure and tranquillity, has become a sought-after item. Possession of a rock garden implies inherited wealth, since aristocrats traditionally were patrons of the arts. In addition, considerable assets are required to afford land in a country where real estate is extraordinarily costly. The scarcity of land also helps to explain why the Japanese are fanatic golfers: since a golf course takes up so much space, membership in a golf club is extremely valuable.[29]

On the other side of the world, there is always England. England is also an extremely class-conscious country, and, at least until recently, consumption patterns were preordained in terms of one's inherited position and family background. Members of the upper class were educated at schools like Eton and Oxford and spoke like Henry Higgins in *My Fair Lady*. Remnants of this rigid class structure can still be found. "Hooray Henrys" (wealthy young men) play polo at Windsor, and hereditary peers still dominate the House of Lords. However, the dominance of inherited wealth appears to be fading in Britain's traditionally aristocratic society. According to a recent survey, 86 of the 200 wealthiest people in England made their money the old-fashioned way: they earned it. Even the sanctity of the royal family, which epitomizes the aristocracy, has been diluted due to tabloid exposure.[30]

Social Mobility

To what degree do people tend to change their social classes? In some societies, such as India, one's social class is very difficult to change, but in Canada change is possible. **Social mobility** refers to the "... passage of individuals from one social class to another ..."[31]

This passage can be upward, downward or horizontal. *Horizontal mobility* refers to movement from one position to another that is roughly equivalent in social status, e.g., becoming a nurse instead of an elementary-school teacher. *Downward mobility* is, of course, not very desirable, but this pattern is unfortunately quite evident in recent years as farmers and other displaced workers have been forced to go on welfare rolls or have joined the ranks of the homeless. A conservative estimate is that 25 000 Torontonians and 15 000 Montrealers are homeless on any given day.[32] Despite this discouraging trend, demographics in fact decree that there must be *upward mobility* in our society.

Overall, though, the offspring of blue-collar consumers tend also to be blue-collar while the offspring of white-collar consumers tend to wind up as white-collar.[33] People in many countries do improve their positions over time, but these increases are not usually dramatic enough to catapult them from one social class to another. According to a 20-year study of 15 countries by the International Sociological Association, 90 percent of upward and downward changes were identical in every country, including Britain, the United States and East Germany.[34]

> **social mobility** the movement of individuals from one social class to another

Components of Social Class

When we think about a person's social class, there are a number of pieces of information we may consider. Two major ones are occupation and income. A third important factor is educational attainment, which is related strongly to income and occupation.

OCCUPATIONAL PRESTIGE

In a system where a consumer is defined (like it or not) to a great extent by what he or she does for a living, *occupational prestige* is one way to evaluate the "worth" of people. Hierarchies of occupational prestige tend to be quite stable over time, and they also tend to be similar in different societies. Similarities in occupational prestige have been found in countries as diverse as Brazil, Ghana, Guam, Japan and Turkey.[35]

A typical ranking includes a variety of professional and business occupations at the top (e.g., chief executive officer of a large corporation, physician and university professor), while those jobs hovering near the bottom include shoe shiner, ditch-digger and garbage collector. Because a person's occupation tends to be strongly linked to his or her use of leisure time, allocation of family resources, political orientation and so on, this variable is often considered to be the single best indicator of social class.

INCOME

The distribution of wealth is of great interest to social scientists and to marketers, since it determines what groups have the greatest buying power and market potential. Wealth is by no means distributed evenly across the classes. However, as we have seen, income *per se* is often not a very good indicator of social class, since the way money is spent is more telling. Still, people need money to allow them to obtain the goods and services they need to express their tastes, so obviously income is still very important.

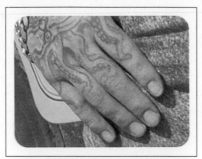

Occupational prestige is a major component of social status. This television spot, called "Valedictorian," for a school for truck drivers parodies society's emphasis on educational achievement. As the song "Pomp & Circumstance" (the traditional graduation song) plays in the background, the tattoo-covered "star" turns and spits a giant wad of tobacco.
Courtesy of Greenberg, Seronick & Partners.

THE RELATIONSHIP BETWEEN INCOME AND SOCIAL CLASS

Although consumers tend to equate money with class, the precise relationship between other aspects of social class and income is not clear and has been the subject of debate among social scientists.[36] The two are by no means synonymous, which is why many people with a lot of money try to use it to upgrade their social class.

One problem is that, even if a family increases household income by adding wage-earners, each additional job is likely to be of lower status. For example, a housewife who gets a part-time job is not likely to get one that is of equal or greater status than the primary wage-earner's. In addition, the extra money earned often is not pooled towards the common good of the family; it is instead used by the individual for his or her own personal spending. So, more money does not result in increased status or changes in consumption patterns, since it tends to be devoted to buying more of the usual rather than to upgrading to higher-status products.[37]

The following general conclusions can be made regarding the relative value of indicators of social class (i.e., place of residence, occupation, cultural interests, etc.) versus income in predicting consumer behaviour:

- Social class appears to be a better predictor of purchases that have symbolic aspects but low to moderate prices (e.g., cosmetics and liquor).
- Income is a better predictor of major expenditures that do not have status or symbolic aspects (e.g., major appliances).

Give your kids a *Royal* education.

For seventy-five wonderful years, the *Royal Agricultural Winter Fair* has been recognized as an important educational venue by both teachers and students alike. This year the *Royal* is continuing its commitment to education with the opening of the *Bank of Montreal Education Ring*. Here, in this great new 600-seat showcase, visitors will be able to see and participate in a variety of new agricultural experiences that help demonstrate the story of farm-to-table. As well, the new *Bank of Montreal Education Ring* will host breed and species shows and agricultural demonstrations. Also, performing daily during the *1997 Royal*, the Royal Notram Dogs. For additional information, call the anniversary hotline today (416) 393-7575.

The Royal 75
November 6-15

Bank of Montreal
IT *is* POSSIBLE®

This Bank of Montreal (***www.bmo.com***) ad suggests the complexity of social class, and particularly its link to education (and occupation), personal style and the "royal" benchmark.
Courtesy of Bank of Montreal and LA Ads Inc.

- Both social class and income data are needed to predict purchases of expensive, symbolic products (e.g., cars and homes).

Measurement of Social Class

Because social class is a complex concept that depends on a number of factors, it is not surprising that it is difficult to measure. Early measures included the Index of Status Characteristics developed in the 1940s and the Index of Social Position developed by Hollingshead in the 1950s.[38] These indices used various combinations of individual characteristics (e.g., income and type of housing) to arrive at a label of class standing. Blishen's Socio-economic Index for Occupations in Canada may be used when occupation is the most appropriate variable to use to collect information on socio-economic status.[39] An alternative is to adapt Coleman's example, shown in Figure 13–2, which explicitly includes four variables: education, occupational prestige, area of residence and family income.

FIGURE 13–2 • Example of a Computerized Status Index

Interviewer circles code numbers (for the computer) which in his/her judgment best fit the respondent and family. Interviewer asks for detail on occupation, then makes rating. Interviewer often asks the respondent to describe neighborhood in own words. Interviewer asks respondent to specify income—a card is presented the respondent showing the eight brackets—and records R's response. If interviewer feels this is over-statement or under, a "better judgment" estimate should be given, along with explanation.

EDUCATION:

	Respondent	Respondent's Spouse
Grammar school (8 yrs or less)	–1	–1
Some high school (9 to 11 yrs)	–2 R's Age ___	–2 Spouse's Age ___
Graduated high school (12 yrs)	–3	–3
Some post high school (business, nursing, technical, 1 yr college)	–4	–4
Two, three years of college—possibly Associate of Arts degree	–5	–5
Graduated four-year college (B.A./B.S.)	–7	–7
Master's or five-year professional degree	–8	–8
Ph.D. or six/seven-year professional degree	–9	–9

OCCUPATION PRESTIGE LEVEL OF HOUSEHOLD HEAD: Interviewer's judgement of how head of household rates in occupational status.

(Respondent's description—asks for previous occupation if retired, or if R. is widow, asks husband's: _____)

Chronically unemployed—"day" laborers, unskilled; on welfare	–0
Steadily employed but in marginal semi-skilled jobs; custodians, minimum pay factory help, service workers (gas attendants, etc.)	–1
Average-skill assembly-line workers, bus and truck drivers, police and firefighters, route deliverymen, carpenters, brickmasons	–2
Skilled craftsmen (electricians), small contractors, factory foremen, low-pay salesclerks, office workers, postal employees	–3
Owners of very small firms (2–4 employees), technicians, salespeople, office workers, civil servants with average level salaries	–4
Middle management, teachers, social workers, lesser professionals	–5
Lesser corporate officials, owners of middle-sized businesses (10–20 employees), moderate-success professionals (dentists, engineers, etc.)	–7
Top corporate executives, "big successes" in the professional world (leading doctors and lawyers), "rich" business owners	–9

AREA OF RESIDENCE: Interviewer's impressions of the immediate neighborhood in terms of its reputation in the eyes of the community.

Slum area: people on relief, common laborers	–1
Strictly working class: not slummy but some very poor housing	–2
Predominantly blue-collar with some office workers	–3
Predominantly white-collar with some well-paid blue-collar	–4
Better white-collar area: not many executives, but hardly any blue-collar either	–5
Excellent area: professionals and well-paid managers	–7
"Wealthy" or "society"-type neighborhood	–9

TOTAL SCORE _____

TOTAL FAMILY INCOME PER YEAR:

Under $5,000	–1	$20,000 to $24,999	–5
$5,000 to $9,999	–2	$25,000 to $34,999	–6
$10,000 to $14,999	–3	$35,000 to $49,999	–7
$15,000 to $19,999	–4	$50,000 and over	–8

Estimated Status _____

(Interviewer's estimate: _____ and explanation _____)

R's MARITAL STATUS: Married ___ Divorced/Separated ___ Widowed ___ Single ___ (CODE: ___)

Source: Richard P. Coleman, "The Continuing Significance of Social Class to Marketing," *Journal of Consumer Research* 10 (December 1983): 265–80. Reprinted with permission of The University of Chicago Press.

PROBLEMS WITH MEASURES OF SOCIAL CLASS

Market researchers were among the first to propose that people from different social classes can be distinguished from each other in important ways. While some of these dimensions still exist, others have changed.[40] Unfortunately, many of these measures are badly dated and are not as valid today for a variety of reasons, four of which are discussed here.[41]

CHANGES IN FAMILY STRUCTURE. Most measures of social class were designed to accommodate the traditional nuclear family, with a male wage-earner in the middle of his career and a female full-time homemaker. Such measures have trouble accounting for two-income families, young singles living alone or households headed by women—situations prevalent in today's society (see Chapter 12).

ANONYMITY. Another problem with measuring social class is attributable to the increasing anonymity of our society. Earlier studies relied on the *reputational method,* where extensive interviewing was done within a community to determine the reputations and backgrounds of individuals (see the discussion of sociometry in Chapter 11). This information, coupled with the tracing of interaction patterns among people, provided a very comprehensive view of social standing within a community.

This approach is virtually impossible to implement in most communities today. One compromise is to interview individuals to obtain demographic data and to combine these data with the subjective impressions of the interviewer regarding the person's possessions and standard of living. An example of this approach appeared in Figure 13–2. Note that the accuracy of this questionnaire relies largely on the interviewer's judgment, especially regarding the quality of the respondent's neighbourhood. These impressions are in danger of being biased by the interviewer's own circumstances, which may affect his or her standard of comparison. This potential problem highlights the need for adequate training of interviewers, as well as for some attempt to validate such data, possibly by employing multiple judges to rate the same area.

STATUS INCONSISTENCY. One problem with assigning people to a social class is that they may not be equal in their standing on all of the relevant dimensions. A person might come from a low-status ethnic group but have a high-status job, while another may live in a fancy part of town but not have finished high school. The concept of **status crystallization** was developed to assess the impact of inconsistency on the self and social behaviour.[42] It was thought that since the rewards from each part of such an "unbalanced" person's life would be variable and unpredictable, stress would result. People who exhibit such inconsistencies tend to be more receptive to social change than are those whose identities are rooted more firmly.

A related problem occurs when a person's social class standing creates expectations that are not met. Some people find themselves in the not unhappy position of making more money than is expected of those in their social class. This situation is known as an *overprivileged* condition, and is usually defined as one where an individual earns an income that is at least 25 percent to 30 percent over the median for one's class.[43] In contrast, *underprivileged* consumers, who earn at least 15 percent less than the median, must often devote their consumption priorities to sacrificing to maintain the appearance of living up to class expectations.

> **status crystallization** the extent to which different indicators of a person's status (income, ethnicity, occupation) are consistent with one another

Lottery winners are examples of consumers who become overprivileged virtually overnight. As attractive as winning is to many people, it has its problems. Consumers with a certain standard of living and level of expectations may have trouble adapting to sudden affluence, and may engage in flamboyant and irresponsible displays of wealth. Ironically, it is not unusual for lottery winners to report feelings of depression in the months after cashing in. They may have trouble adjusting to an unfamiliar world, and they frequently experience pressure from friends, relatives and business people to "share the wealth."

WOMEN AND SOCIAL CLASS. The traditional assumption is that husbands define a family's social class while wives must live it. In other words, women borrow their social status from their husbands.[44] Indeed, the evidence indicates that physically attractive women tend to "marry up" in social class to a greater extent than attractive men do. Women trade the resource of sexual appeal, which historically has been one of the few assets they were allowed to possess, for the economic resources of men.[45]

The accuracy of this assumption in today's world must be questioned. Many women now contribute equally to the family's well-being and work in positions of comparable or even greater status than their spouses. Employed women tend to average both their own and their husband's respective positions when estimating their own subjective status.[46] Nevertheless, a prospective spouse's social class is often an important "product attribute" when evaluating alternatives in the interpersonal marketplace (as Vic and Marilyn are to find out).

PROBLEMS WITH SOCIAL CLASS SEGMENTATION: A SUMMARY

Social class remains an important way to categorize consumers. Many marketing strategies do target different social classes. However, marketers have failed to use social class information as effectively as they could for the following reasons:

* They have ignored status inconsistency.
* They have ignored intergenerational mobility.
* They have ignored subjective social class (i.e., the class a consumer identifies with rather than the one to which he or she objectively belongs).
* They have ignored consumers' aspirations to change their class standing.
* They have ignored the social status of working wives.

HOW SOCIAL CLASS AFFECTS PURCHASE DECISIONS

Different products and stores are perceived by consumers to be appropriate for different social classes.[47] Working-class consumers tend to evaluate products in more utilitarian terms, such as sturdiness or comfort, rather than in terms of style or fashionability. They are less likely to experiment with new products or styles, such as modern furniture or coloured appliances.[48] In contrast, more affluent people living in the suburbs tend to be concerned about appearance and body image, so they are more avid consumers of diet foods and drinks compared to people in more downscale small towns. These differences mean that the cola market, for example, can be segmented by social class.[49]

Class Differences in World-View

A major social class difference involves the *world-view* of consumers. The world of the working class (i.e., the lower-middle class) is more intimate and constricted. For example, working-class men are likely to name local sports figures as heroes and are less likely to take long vacation trips to out-of-the-way places.[50] Immediate needs, such as a new refrigerator or TV, tend to dictate buying behaviour for these consumers, while the higher classes tend to focus on more long-term goals, such as saving for university tuition or retirement.[51] Four out of ten Canadian professionals contribute to Registered Retirement Savings Plans, and Internet usage skews very heavily to upper-income earners.[52] As income increases, gifts for people outside the household increase more rapidly.[53]

Working-class consumers depend heavily on relatives for emotional support and tend to orient themselves in terms of the community rather than the world at large. They are more likely to be conservative and family-oriented. Maintaining the appearance of one's home and property is a priority, regardless of the size of the house.

While they would like to have more in the way of material goods, working-class people do not necessarily envy those who rank above them in social standing.[54] The maintenance of a high-status lifestyle is sometimes not seen as worth the effort. As one blue-collar consumer commented: "Life is very hectic for those people. There are more breakdowns and alcoholism. It must be very hard to sustain the status, the clothes, the parties that are expected. I don't think I'd want to take their place."[55]

The blue-collar consumer quoted here may be right. While good things appear to go hand in hand with higher status and wealth, the picture is not that clear. The social scientist Emile Durkheim observed that suicide rates are much higher among the wealthy; he wrote in 1897, "... the possessors of most comfort suffer most."[56] The

This ad for Libbey Glass implies that there are social class differences in leisure activities and preferred beverages.
Courtesy of Libbey Glass Inc.

quest for riches has the potential to result in depression, deviant behaviour and ruin. In fact a recent survey of affluent consumers supports this notion: although these people are in the top income bracket, only 14 percent said they are very well off.[57]

taste culture a group of consumers who share aesthetic and intellectual preferences

The concept of **taste culture,** which differentiates people in terms of their aesthetic and intellectual preferences, is helpful in understanding the important yet subtle distinctions in consumption choices among the social classes. Taste cultures largely reflect education (and are also income-related).[58] A distinction is often made between low-culture and high-culture groups (and is discussed in more detail in Chapter 16).

While such perspectives have met with criticism due to the implicit value judgments involved, they are valuable because they recognize the existence of groupings based on shared tastes in literature, art, home decoration and so on. In one of the classic studies of social differences in taste, researchers catalogued homeowners' possessions while asking more typical questions about income and occupation. Clusters of furnishings and decorative items that seemed to appear together with some regularity were identified, and, depending upon the consumer's social status, different clusters were found (see Figure 13–3). For example, religious objects, artificial flowers and still lifes tended to be found together in relatively lower-status living rooms, while a cluster containing abstract paintings, sculptures and modern furniture was more likely to appear in a higher-status home.[59]

A semiotic approach to social class (see Chapter 2) focuses on differences in the types of *codes* (the ways meanings are expressed and interpreted by consumers) used within different social strata. Discovery of these codes is valuable to marketers, since this knowledge allows them to communicate to markets using concepts and terms most likely to be understood and appreciated by specific consumers.

restricted codes the ways of expressing and interpreting meanings that focus on the content of objects and tend to be used by the working class

elaborated codes the ways of expressing and interpreting meanings that are more complex and depend on a more sophisticated world-view, and that tend to be used by the middle and upper classes

The nature of these codes varies among social classes. **Restricted codes** are dominant among the working class, while **elaborated codes** tend to be used by the middle and upper classes. Restricted codes focus on the content of objects, not on relationships among objects. Elaborated codes, in contrast, are more complex and depend upon a more sophisticated world-view. Some differences between these two general types of codes are provided in Table 13–1. As this table indicates, these code differences extend to the way consumers approach such basic concepts as time, social relationships and objects.

Marketing appeals that are constructed with these differences in mind will result in quite different messages. For example, a life insurance ad targeted to a lower-class person might depict in simple, straightforward terms a hard-working family man who feels good immediately after purchasing a policy. A more upscale appeal might depict a more affluent older couple surrounded by photos of their children and grandchildren, and contain extensive copy emphasizing the satisfaction that comes from planning for the future and highlighting the benefits of a whole-life insurance policy.

Targeting the Poor

About 14 percent of Canadian families and 20 percent of Canadian children live below the poverty line. This segment has largely been ignored by most marketers.[60] Still, while poor people obviously have less to spend than rich ones, they have the same basic needs as everyone else. Low-income families purchase such staples as

FIGURE 13–3 • Living-Room Clusters and Social Class

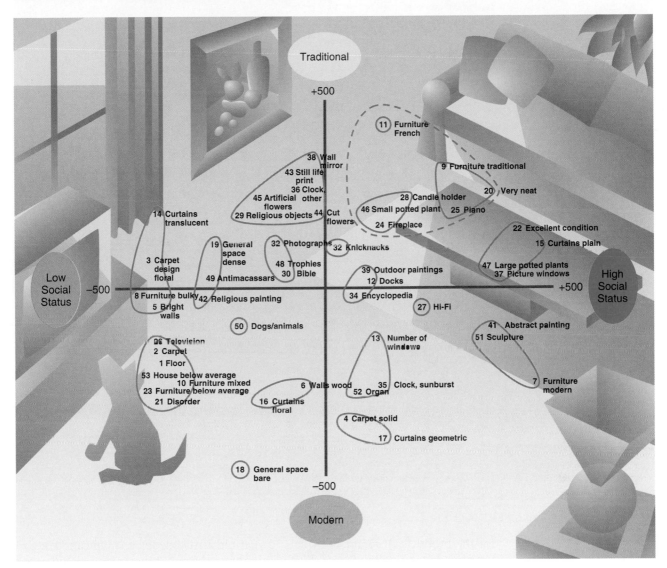

Source: Edward O. Laumann and James S. House, "Living Room Styles and Social Attributes: The Patterning of Material Artifacts in a Modern Urban Community," *Sociology and Social Research* 54 (April 1970): 321–42.

milk, orange juice and tea at the same rates as average-income families. And minimum-wage-level households spend a greater than average share on out-of-pocket costs for housing and food eaten at home.[61]

The unemployed and "working poor" do feel alienated in a consumer society, since they are unable to obtain many of the items that our culture tells us we "need" to be successful. However, idealized advertising portrayals don't appear to bother low-end consumers who have been interviewed by researchers. Apparently, one way to preserve self-esteem is by placing themselves outside the culture of consumption and emphasizing the value of a simple way of life with less emphasis on materialism. In some cases they enjoy the advertising as entertainment without actually yearning

TABLE 13–1 Effects of Restricted versus Elaborated Codes

	RESTRICTED CODES	ELABORATED CODES
General characteristics	Emphasize description and contents of objects	Emphasize analysis and inter-relationships between objects, i.e., hierarchical organization and instrumental connections
	Have implicit meanings (context-dependent)	Have explicit meanings
Language	Use few qualifiers, i.e., few adjectives or adverbs	Have language rich in personal, individual qualifiers
	Use concrete, descriptive, tangible symbolism	Use large vocabulary, complex conceptual hierarchy
Social relationships	Stress attributes of individuals over formal roles	Stress formal role structure, instrumental relationships
Time	Focus on present; have only general notion of future	Focus on instrumental relationship between present activities and future rewards
Physical space	Locate rooms, spaces in context of other rooms and places, e.g., "front room," "corner store"	Identify rooms, spaces in terms of usage; formal ordering of spaces: e.g., "dining room," "financial district"
Implications for marketers	Stress inherent product quality, contents (or trustworthiness, goodness of "real-type"), spokesperso	Stress differences, advantages vis-à-vis other products in terms of some autonomous evaluation criteria
	Stress implicit fit of product with total lifestyle	Stress product's instrumental ties to distant benefits
	Use simple adjectives, descriptors	Use complex adjectives, descriptors

Source: Adapted from Jeffrey F. Durgee, "How Consumer Sub-Cultures Code Reality: A Look at Some Code Types," in *Advances in Consumer Research 13*, ed. Richard J. Lutz (Provo, UT: Association for Consumer Research, 1986), p. 332.

for the products. A comment by one 32-year-old British woman is typical: "They're not aimed at me, definitely not. It's fine to look at them, but they're not aimed at me so in the main I just pass over them."[62]

Some marketers in the United States are developing products and services for low-income consumers. These strategies may be obvious in some cases (or even border on the insulting), as when S.C. Johnson & Son, manufacturers of Raid insect spray, regularly hosts "roach evictions" at inner-city housing developments. Still other strategies raise important ethical issues, especially when marketers of so-called "sin products" like alcohol and tobacco single out what many feel is a vulnerable audience. For example, manufacturers of malt liquors and fortified wines concentrate their efforts in poor areas where they know their products sell best.

Other marketers use much less exploitive practices in trying to tap into poor families' need to stretch their dollars and make efficient use of product information. *City Family* is a magazine targeted to poor women in New York. This target audience is concentrated in specific geographic areas, which makes readers relatively easy to reach. The magazine focuses on articles that help readers get the most out of city and

This group of magazines distributed by the Paisano Group targets young lower-class males by appealing to their interests in cars, tattoos and so on.
Courtesy of Paisano Publications.

health services. It also emphasizes the importance of home furnishings, particularly important items to consumers who cannot afford to take vacations and who often live in unsafe neighbourhoods.[63]

Residents of poor neighbourhoods must travel on average more than two miles to have the same access to supermarkets, large drugstores and banks as do residents of non-poor areas.[64] Some interesting businesses that have prospered by locating branches in more accessible areas include the following:

- Banks are trying to improve relationships with the poor by opening mobile banking centres in neighbourhoods "underserved" by financial institutions. For example, the Mobile Banking Center, a division of the Huntington National Bank in Cincinnati, works through churches to offer banking services.[65]

- Vons Companies, California's largest supermarket operator, is investing $100 million (US) in new stores that will be located in low-income urban areas.

- Fingerhut sells pots and pans, toys and many other products, but its real business is extending credit to moderate and low-income households that allows these consumers to purchase its inventory (at rates of about 24 percent a year). Even a pair of $40 sneakers can be bought on credit for 13 months at $7.49 a month.[66]

Targeting the Affluent

Many marketers try to target affluent, upscale markets. This practice often makes sense, since these consumers obviously have the resources to spend on costly products (often with higher profit margins). However, it is a mistake to assume that everyone with a high income should be placed into the same market segment. As noted earlier, social class involves more than absolute income; it is also a way of life, and affluent consumers' interests and spending priorities are significantly affected by such factors as where they got their money, how they got it and how long they have had it.[67] For example, the marginally rich tend to prefer sporting events to cultural activities, and are only half as likely as the super-rich to frequent art galleries or the opera.[68]

A recent survey of readers of *Town & Country,* a magazine that is targeted to the affluent, sheds some light on the meaning of wealth today. Very few respondents equate wealth with success; they are more likely to say that success is related to having high self-esteem, being a good parent, having a happy marriage and having a strong sense of ethics. (On the other hand, they can afford the luxury of not worrying as much about money!)

Luxury products are important to this group, but the highest-ranked symbol of achievement is being in charge of a cultural or educational institution and/or one's own business. Affluent consumers want to be seen as smart, sophisticated shoppers, and they claim they don't want to flaunt what they own. These respondents are very socially active and enjoy socializing, particularly at country clubs. They report that the top reasons to buy a product are value, durability and past experience.[69]

So, the rich *are* different. But they are different from one another as well. Income alone is not a good predictor of consumer behaviour, which reminds us that the wealthy can be further segmented in terms of attitudes, values and preferences. For example, according to industry experts, drivers in the luxury car market can be segmented as follows:

- Cadillac owners want to be chauffeured. They are not very attentive to styling details or the car's colour. Their primary interests are comfort and the impression they make on others.

Crédit Lyonnais, France's biggest commercial bank, is targeting the wealthy by opening new upscale branches and offering special services for rich customers. The bank is going after "high-net-worth individuals" who have a minimum annual income of 500 000 francs. In an unusual move, Crédit Lyonnais hopes to accomplish its objective by opening new branches in locations with heavy concentrations of wealthy people; for example, in one Paris neighbourhood four branches are clustered within a few hundred metres. At "Club Tourny," the nickname of one branch, customers do their banking in an elegant townhouse, where they sit at polished tables and discuss their financial needs over refreshments with bank staff. *Source: Nicholas Bray, "Credit Lyonnais Targets Wealthy Clients," Wall Street Journal (June 24, 1993): B7A. Photo courtesy of Bernard Annebicoue, Sygma.*

- Porsche owners prefer to drive themselves. They are more interested in performance than luxury. The colour red is a favourite.

- Jaguar owners are more austere. They are interested in elegance and prefer darker colours.

- Mercedes owners like to feel they are in control. They tend to prefer muted shades of tan, grey and silver.

OLD MONEY

When people have enough money to buy just about anything they want, social distinctions ironically no longer revolve around the amount of money they have. Instead, it appears to be important to consider *where* the money came from and *how* it is spent. The "top-out-of-sight class" or "old money" (e.g., the Bronfmans, Westons, Thomsons, Killams, McCains, etc.) live primarily on inherited money.

People who have made vast amounts of money from their own labours do not tend to be included in this select group, though their often flamboyant consumption patterns may represent an attempt to prove their wealth.[70] The mere presence of wealth thus is not sufficient to achieve social prominence. It must be accompanied by a family history of public service and philanthropy, which is often manifested in tangible markers (e.g., Ivey Business School or Zwicker's Gallery) that enable these donors to achieve a kind of immortality.[71] Old-money consumers tend to make distinctions among themselves in terms of ancestry and lineage rather than wealth.[72]

THE NOUVEAUX RICHES

Other wealthy people do not "know" how to be rich. The Horatio Alger myth, where a person goes from "rags to riches" through hard work and a bit of luck, is still a powerful force. Although many people do in fact become "self-made millionaires," they often find it challenging to adjust to wealth and higher social status. People living in Canada's 10 percent most affluent households (average income of $124 000), for example, credit hard work, education and intelligence for their financial success; however, only 20 percent of them consider themselves highly skilled at managing their money.[73] These consumers may find it helpful to visit the Web site for Canada Trust's Investor Learning Centre (***www.ctsecurities.com/ilc/index.htm***).

Consumers who have achieved extreme wealth and have relatively recently become members of upper social classes are known as the *nouveaux riches*. The *nouveau riche* phenomenon is also widespread in Russia and other eastern European countries, where the transition to capitalism has paved the way for a new class of wealthy consumers who are spending lavishly on luxury items. One study of wealthy Russians identified a group of "super spenders" who earn about $1000 a month and spend as much on discretionary items as they do on rent. They would like to spend *more* money but are frustrated by the lack of quality products and services available to them![74]

Many *nouveaux riches* are plagued by *status anxiety*. They monitor the cultural environment to ensure that they are doing the "right" thing, wearing the "right" clothes, being seen at the "right" places, using the "right" caterer, etc.[75] Flamboyant consumption can thus be viewed as a form of symbolic self-completion, where the excessive display of symbols thought to denote "class" is used to make up for an internal lack of assurance about the "correct" way to behave.[76]

Advertising directed to this group often plays on these insecurities by emphasizing the importance of "looking the part." Clever merchandising supplies these

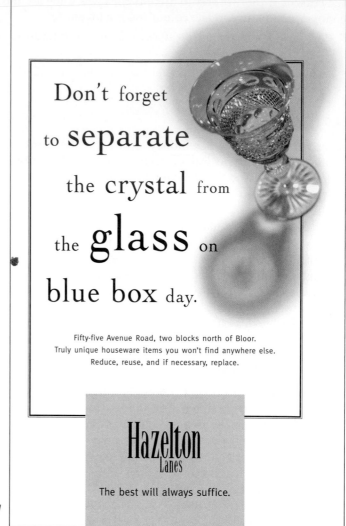

Don't forget to **separate** the crystal from the **glass** on blue box day.

Fifty-five Avenue Road, two blocks north of Bloor.
Truly unique houseware items you won't find anywhere else.
Reduce, reuse, and if necessary, replace.

Hazelton Lanes

The best will always suffice.

Hazelton Lanes is a mecca for the *nouveau riche*.
Courtesy of Hazelton Lanes and Bensiman • Byrne • DMB&B.

consumers with the props to masquerade as old-money people. For example, ads for *Colonial Homes* magazine feature consumers who "... have worked very hard to make it look like they never had to." Upscale retailing areas, such as Robson Street in Vancouver, Hazelton Lanes in Toronto and Historic Properties in Halifax, are targeted to this segment. West Edmonton Mall, the Toronto Eaton Centre and Montreal's Westmount Square are a few of Canada's largest multifaceted shopping and entertainment centres for upscale consumers. (For an interesting example of Internet marketing for malls, see ***www.torontomalls.com***.)

THE GET SET

While the possession of wealth is clearly an important dimension of affluence, this quality may be as much determined by attitudes towards consumption as it is by level of income. Some marketers have identified a consumer segment composed of well-off but not rich people who desire the best products and services, even though they may have to be more selective about those items they are able to buy. These consumers are realistic about what they can afford and prefer to sacrifice in some areas so that they can have the best in others. Various advertising and marketing research agencies have labelled this segment with such terms as the *Influentials,* the *New Grown-Ups* and the *Get Set.*

While many upper-class brands tried in the past to be downscale to attract the mass market, there are some indications that this strategy is reversing. Due to the Get Set's emphasis on quality, one scenario is that marketers will encourage the masses to "buy up" into products associated with the upper classes, even if they are forced to buy less. A print campaign for Waterford Crystal exemplifies this approach. The theme line, "Steadfast in a world of wavering standards," is calculated to appeal to consumers who desire authenticity and lasting value.[77]

STATUS SYMBOLS

People have a deep-seated tendency to evaluate themselves, their professional accomplishments, their material well-being and so on relative to others. The popular phrase "keeping up with the Joneses" (in Japan it's "keeping up with the Satos") refers to the comparison between one's standard of living and that of one's neighbours.

Satisfaction is a relative concept, however. We hold ourselves to a standard defined by others that is constantly changing. Unfortunately, a major motivation for the purchase and display of products is not to enjoy them but rather to let others know that we can afford them. In other words, these products function as **status symbols.** The desire to accumulate these "badges of achievement" is summarized by the popular bumper-sticker slogan, "He who dies with the most toys, wins." Status seeking is a significant source of the motivation (see Chapter 4) to procure appropriate products and services that will in turn (it is hoped) let others know that one has "made it."

status symbols products that are purchased and displayed to signal membership in a desirable social class

Conspicuous Consumption

The motivation to consume for the sake of consuming was first discussed by the social analyst Thorstein Veblen at the turn of the century. Veblen coined the term **conspicuous consumption** to refer to people's desire to provide prominent, visible evidence of their ability to afford luxury goods.

THE TROPHY WIFE

Veblen criticized the "decorative" role women were often forced to play as expensive clothes, pretentious homes and a life of leisure were bestowed upon them as a way to advertise the wealth of their husbands—turning them into a sort of "walking billboard." Such fashions as high heels, tight corsets, billowing trains on dresses and elaborate hairstyles all conspired to ensure that wealthy women could barely move without assistance, much less perform manual labour. Similarly, the Chinese practice of foot binding turned women into cripples, who had to be carried from place to place.

conspicuous consumption the purchase and prominent display of luxury goods to provide evidence of a consumer's ability to afford them

If you could drive one car to your high school reunion, this would be it.

AS YOU SWING INTO your alma mater in a beautiful new Jaguar XJS, you can almost see the heads turn as your classmates ask, "Isn't that...?"

A fantasy? It doesn't have to be. You can lease a new XJS for just two years, with surprisingly affordable payments. You'll enjoy two plus two seating, dual air bags,* ABS brakes, Connolly leather, and the exhilarating performance of a 219-horsepower engine.

Our commitment to quality is backed by a four-year, 50,000-mile warranty. And we'll even let you return the car within 30 days of purchase if you're not totally satisfied.**

Call 1-800-4-JAGUAR for the Jaguar dealer nearest you.

JAGUAR

This Jaguar ad uses a blatant appeal to status by playing on people's desire to show their old friends how well they've done in life.
Courtesy of Jaguar Cars.
(www.jaguar.com)

THE MODERN POTLATCH

potlatch an Indian feast where the host shows off his wealth and gives extravagant presents to guests

Veblen was inspired by anthropological studies of the Kwakiutl Indians, who lived in the Pacific Northwest. These Indians had a ceremony called a **potlatch,** a feast where the host showed off his wealth and gave extravagant presents to the guests. The more he gave away, the better he looked to the others. Sometimes the host would use an even more radical strategy to flaunt his wealth: he would publicly destroy some of his property to demonstrate how much he had.

This ritual was also used as a social weapon. Since guests were expected to reciprocate, a poorer rival could be humiliated by inviting him to a lavish potlatch. The need to give away as much as the host, even though he could not afford it, could essentially force the hapless guest into bankruptcy. If this practice sounds primitive, think for a moment about many modern weddings. Parents commonly invest huge sums of money to throw a lavish party and compete with others for the distinction of giving their daughter the "best" or most extravagant wedding, even if they have to save for 20 years to do it.

THE LEISURE CLASS

This process of conspicuous consumption was, for Veblen, most evident among what he termed the *leisure class,* people for whom productive work is taboo. In Marxist terms this reflects a desire to link oneself to ownership or control of the means of production, rather than to the production itself. Any evidence that one actually has to labour for a living is to be shunned, as suggested by the term the "idle rich."

CONSPICUOUS SUBTLETY

One of the special fabrics that distinguishes Halston as being fashion conscious yet impeccably sensible clothing is Country Silk.™

Loomed in Scotland along the river Tweed this exclusive fabric is a unique blending of high quality wool and the best of silk.

Great weight, great feel, great looks and the perfect update of a classic sport coat by none other than Halston.

THE ONE LABEL YOU DON'T HAVE TO SEE TO KNOW IT'S THERE.

HALSTON
FOR MEN
1290 AVENUE OF THE AMERICAS, NEW YORK, N.Y. 10104 (212) 581-6610

FINE FABRICS WOVEN IN SCOTLAND

In a twist on conspicuous consumption, this ad for Halston jackets appeals to people who want to avoid the blatant display of status symbols.
Courtesy of Halston For Men Tailored Clothing.

Increases heart rates.

From an award-winning diamond collection available exclusively at Birks.

BIRKS
MAKING EVERY OCCASION SPECIAL

Birks's blue box is a long-standing conspicuous symbol of elegant purchases.
Courtesy of Birks.

Like the potlatch ritual, the desire to convince others that one has a surplus of resources creates the need for evidence of this abundance. Accordingly, priority is given to consumption activities that use up as many resources as possible in non-constructive pursuits. This *conspicuous waste* in turn shows others that one has the assets to spare. Veblen noted that "... we are told of certain Polynesian chiefs, who, under the stress of good form, preferred to starve rather than carry their food to their mouths with their own hands."[78]

The Death—and Rebirth—of Status Symbols

While ostentatious products fell out of favour in the early part of the 1990s, the latter years of the decade witnessed a resurgence of interest in luxury goods. Companies such as Hermes International, LVMH Hennesey Louis Vuitton and Baccarat are enjoying sales gains of between 13 and 16 percent, as affluent customers are once again indulging their desires for the finer things in life. One market researcher has termed this trend "the pleasure revenge;" people are simply tired of buying moderately, eating low-fat foods and so on, and as a result sales are booming for self-indulgent products from fur coats to premium ice creams and caviar. The demand for upscale treats, such as premium ice cream, continues to increase: Parlour Signature (by Nestlé Canada), Cochrane's (by the MacKay sisters in Alberta) and Cows (originating in PEI).[79] As the chairman of LVMH put it, "The appetite for luxury is as strong as ever. The only difference is that in the 1980s, people would put a luxury trademark on anything. Today only the best sells."[80]

PARODY DISPLAY

parody display the deliberate avoidance of widely used status symbols, whereby the person seeks status by mocking it

As the competition to accumulate status symbols escalates, sometimes the best tactic is to switch gears and go in reverse. One way to do this is to deliberately *avoid* status symbols—that is, to seek status by mocking it. This sophisticated form of conspicuous consumption has been termed **parody display**.[81] A good example of parody display is the label image developed by The Rotting Grape Winery in

MARKETING OPPORTUNITY

Since the products and activities that connote high status are always changing, a significant amount of marketing effort goes into educating consumers as to what specific symbols they should be displaying and to ensuring that a product is accepted in the pantheon of status symbols.

The need to display the "right" symbols has been a boon to the publishing industry, where a variety of "how-to" books, magazines and videos are available to school willing students of status. The concept of "dressing for success," wherein detailed instructions are provided to allow people to dress as if they were members of the upper-middle class (or at least the authors' versions of this), is one popular example.[82] This type of guidance has now spread to other areas of consumption, including "power lunching" (e.g., order "steak tartare" to intimidate your partner, since raw meat is a power food), office furnishings and home decoration.

Kelowna, British Columbia. The label, featuring three paragraphs of text with an assertive tone, includes the line, "… it's time for a wine to be named for what it really is—rotting GRAPEs." Another example is the home-furnishing style known as High Tech, which was in vogue a few years ago. This motif incorporates the use of industrial equipment (e.g., floors are covered with plates used on the decks of destroyers), and pipes and support beams are deliberately exposed.[83] This decorating strategy is intended to show that one is so witty and "in the know" that status symbols aren't necessary. Hence the popularity of old, ripped blue jeans and utility vehicles such as Jeeps among the upper classes.

Interestingly, consumers who could afford to be conspicuous consumers in the 1980s seem to be taking the lead. A recent study by the Grocery Products Manufacturers of Canada, for example, found that 38 percent of shoppers at "club" stores (e.g., Costco) had household incomes of $50 000 and higher, while only 11 percent had incomes of less than $20 000. On a global note, in the UK younger and more upmarket consumers are creating strong demand for the new vegetarian lines under brand names, such as Birds Eye. Even second-hand stores with both upscale and downscale appeal are on an upswing in Canada and the United States.[84] Honest Ed's in Toronto (**www.canadamalls.com/honest.html**) offers social class parody in a retail setting. Thus, "true" status is shown by the adoption of deliberately unfashionable product symbolism.

- The field of behavioural economics considers how consumers decide what to do with their money. In particular, discretionary expenditures are made only when people are able and willing to spend money on items above and beyond their basic needs. Consumer confidence—the state of mind consumers have about their own personal situations, as well as their feelings about their overall economic prospects—helps to determine whether they will purchase goods and services, take on debt or save their money.

- In the 1990s, consumers overall have been relatively pessimistic about their future prospects. A lower level of resources has caused a shift towards an emphasis on quality products that are reasonably priced. Consumers are less tolerant of exaggerated or vague product claims, and they are more sceptical about marketing activities. Consumers in their twenties are particularly sceptical about the economy and about marketing messages targeted to their age group.

- A consumer's *social class* refers to his or her standing in society. It is determined by a number of factors, including education, occupation and income.

- Virtually all groups make distinctions among members in terms of relative superiority, power and access to valued resources. This social stratification creates a status hierarchy, in which some goods are preferred over others and are used to categorize their owners' social class.

- While income is an important indicator of social class, the relationship is far from perfect since social class is also determined by such factors as place of residence, cultural interests and world-view.

- Purchase decisions are sometimes influenced by the desire to "buy up" to a higher social class or to engage in the process of conspicuous consumption, wherein one's status is flaunted by the deliberate and non-constructive use of valuable resources. This spending pattern is characteristic of the *nouveaux riches,* whose relatively recent acquisition of income, rather than ancestry or breeding, is responsible for their increased social mobility.

* Products often are used as status symbols to communicate real or desired social class. Parody display occurs when consumers seek status by deliberately avoiding fashionable products.

KEY TERMS

Behavioural economics p. 430

Conspicuous consumption p. 451

Consumer confidence p. 431

Discretionary income p. 430

Elaborated codes p. 444

Parody display p. 454

Potlatch p. 452

Restricted codes p. 444

Savings rate p. 431

Social class p. 432

Social mobility p. 437

Social stratification p. 435

Status crystallization p. 441

Status hierarchy p. 435

Status symbols p. 451

Taste culture p. 444

CONSUMER BEHAVIOUR CHALLENGE

1. Sears (***www.sears.ca***) and (to a lesser degree) Kmart have made concerted efforts in recent years to upgrade their images and appeal to higher-class consumers. How successful have these efforts been? Do you believe this strategy is wise?

2. What are some of the obstacles to measuring social class in today's society? Discuss some ways to get around these obstacles.

3. What consumption differences might you expect to observe between a family characterized as underprivileged and one whose income is average for its social class?

4. When is social class likely to be a better predictor of consumer behaviour than mere knowledge of a person's income?

5. How do you assign people to social classes, or do you at all? What consumption cues (e.g., clothing, speech, cars, etc.) do you use to determine social standing?

6. Thorstein Veblen argued that women were often used as vehicles to display their husbands' wealth. Is this argument still valid today?

7. Given present environmental conditions and dwindling resources, what is the future of "conspicuous waste"? Can the desire to impress others with affluence ever be eliminated? If not, can it take on another form?

8. Some people argue that status symbols are dead. Do you agree?

9. Compile a list of occupations, and ask a sample of students in a variety of majors (both business and non-business) to rank the prestige of these jobs. Can you detect any differences in these rankings as a function of students' majors?

10. Compile a collection of ads that depict consumers of different social classes. What generalizations can you make about the reality of these ads and about the media in which they appear?

11. Identify a current set of fraudulent status symbols, and construct profiles of consumers who are wearing or using these products. Are these profiles consistent with the images portrayed in each product's promotional messages?

12. The chapter observes that some marketers are finding "greener pastures" by targeting low-income people. How ethical is it to single out consumers who cannot afford to waste their precious resources on discretionary items? Under what circumstances should this segmentation strategy be encouraged or discouraged?

CBC VIDEO VIGNETTES

Concepts at Work for Luxury Products

Despite an overall decrease in retail sales, there is a retail sector that is beginning to ride the trend towards luxury sales. Consumers are buying luxury goods to show that they can afford to buy them, to reward themselves for achieving a lifetime milestone, or just to celebrate taking a business through the worst part of an economic recession. In Canada, these goods include BMWs, Harry Rosen suits and jewellery from Chez de Versailles in Toronto. Customers are willing to pay $2600 for a suit, $12 000 for a pen or a mere $2.2 million for a wrist-watch.

Canada has no luxury index, but the movement of high-quality goods seems to be a definite trend. What's more, there is even evidence of repeat sales and brand loyalty. Sales of this sometimes inconspicuous merchandise are characterized by

the presence of a high level of service. The challenge for marketers interested in serving this segment is to understand the consumer characteristics behind these individuals' willingness to reward themselves with luxury purchases.

QUESTIONS

1. How do luxury goods differ from other goods? Provide some examples.

2. Describe the consumer who buys luxury goods.

3. Why are luxury goods recession-proof?

4. What is the relationship between social class and income?

Video Resource: "Luxury Sells," *Venture* #578 (February 18, 1996).

NOTES

1. Fred van Raaij, "Economic Psychology," *Journal of Economic Psychology* 1 (1981): 1–24.

2. *Canada's Families: They Count* (Ottawa: Vanier Institute of the Family, 1996).

3. "More Canadians in highest and lowest tax brackets," *Canadian Press Newswire* (July 15, 1997), accessed through WinSPIRS (October 8, 1997).

4. "Advisers vie for a piece of the wealthy," *Financial Post* 90, 21 (May 25/27, 1996): 44.

5. Adapted from Fabian Linden, *Consumer Affluence: The Next Wave* (New York: The Conference Board, Inc., 1994).

6. *Canada's Families: They Count.*

7. *Canada at a Glance 1996*, Statistics Canada cat. no. 12-581E.

8. Christopher D. Carroll, "How Does Future Income Affect Current Consumption?" *Quarterly Journal of Economics* 109, 1 (February 1994): 111–47.

9. Rahul Jacob, "The Big Rise," *Fortune* (May 30, 1994): 86.

10. Robert Sullivan, "Americans and Their Money," *Worth* (June 1994): 60 (12 pp.).

11. Richard T. Curtin, "Indicators of Consumer Behavior: The University of Michigan Surveys of Consumers," *Public Opinion Quarterly* (1982): 340–52.

12. George Katona, "Consumer Saving Patterns," *Journal of Consumer Research* 1 (June 1974): 1–12.

13. For an examination of how one group of consumers adapted to being unemployed, see Scott D. Roberts, "Effects of Sudden Income Loss on Consumption and Related Aspects of Life: A Study of Unemployed Steel Workers," *Research in Consumer Behavior 5* (Greenwich, CT: JAI Press, 1991), pp. 181–214.

14. Angus Reid, *Shakedown* (Toronto: Doubleday Canada, 1996).

15. "Welcome to the good times: Canada is poised for a remarkable economic rebirth," *Canadian Business* 69, 14 (November 1996): 54–57.

16. "Taking care of business: Cosmetics industry leaders speak out about recent trends and how they plan to meet the challenges of the second half of the 90s," *Cosmetics* 23, 1 (January 1995): 58–69.

17. Floyd L. Ruch and Philip G. Zimbardo, *Psychology and Life,* 8th ed. (Glenview, IL: Scott Foresman and Company, 1971).

18. Sally D. Goll, "Ignoring the Masses, Avenue Magazine Launches an Edition for China's Elite," *Wall Street Journal* (September 28, 1994): B1.

19. Louise Do Rosario, "Privilege in China's Classless Society," *World Press Review* 33 (December 1986): 58.

20. Jonathan H. Turner, *Sociology: Studying the Human System,* 2nd ed. (Santa Monica, CA: Goodyear, 1981).

21. Richard P. Coleman, "The Continuing Significance of Social Class to Marketing," *Journal of Consumer Research* 10 (December 1983): 265–80; Turner, *Sociology.*

22. Quoted by Richard P. Coleman and Lee Rainwater, *Standing in America: New Dimensions of Class* (New York: Basic Books, 1978), p. 89.

23. Coleman and Rainwater, *Standing in America.*

24. Turner, *Sociology.*

25. James Fallows, "A Talent for Disorder (Class Structure)," *U.S. News & World Report* (February 1, 1988): 83.

26. Bernard R. Blishen, William A. Carrol and Catherine Moore, "The 1981 socioeconomic index for occupations in Canada," *Canadian Review of Sociology and Anthropology* 24, 4 (1987): 465–88.

27. Coleman, "The Continuing Significance of Social Class to Marketing"; W. Lloyd Warner with Paul S. Lunt, *The Social Life of a Modern Community* (New Haven, CT: Yale University Press, 1941).

28. Nicholas D. Kristof, "Women as Bodyguards: In China, It's All the Rage," *New York Times* (July 1, 1993): A4.

29. James Sterngold, "How Do You Define Status? A New BMW in the Drive. An Old Rock in the Garden," *New York Times* (December 28, 1989): C1.

30. Robin Knight, "Just You Move Over, 'Enry 'Iggins; A New Regard for Profits and Talent Cracks Britain's Old Class System," *U.S. News & World Report* 106 (April 24, 1989): 40.

31. Turner, *Sociology,* p. 260.

32. "The visible invisible people: thousands of Canadians are homeless, yet we have few ideas about how many there are and how to help improve their lives," *Canada and the World Backgrounder* 60, 2 (November 1994): 26–27. Also see Ronald Paul Hill and Mark Stamey, "The Homeless in America: An Examination of Possessions and Consumption Behaviors," *Journal of Consumer Research* 17 (December 1990): 303–21.

33. Leonard Beeghley, *Social Stratification in America: A Critical Analysis of Theory and Research* (Santa Monica, CA: Goodyear, 1978).

34. "No art of success," *Globe and Mail* (October 25, 1995): A26.

35. Coleman and Rainwater, *Standing in America,* p. 220.

36. See Coleman, "The Continuing Significance of Social Class to Marketing"; Charles M. Schaninger, "Social Class Versus Income Revisited: An Empirical Investigation," *Journal of Marketing Research* 18 (May 1981): 192–208.

37. Coleman, "The Continuing Significance of Social Class to Marketing."

38. August B. Hollingshead and Fredrick C. Redlich, *Social Class and Mental Illness: A Community Study* (New York: John Wiley, 1958).

39. Blishen, Carrol and Moore, "The 1981 socioeconomic index for occupations in Canada."

40. Donald W. Hendon, Emelda L. Williams and Douglas E. Huffman, "Social Class System Revisited," *Journal of Business Research* 17 (November 1988): 259.

41. Coleman, "The Continuing Significance of Social Class to Marketing."

42. Gerhard E. Lenski, "Status Crystallization: A Non-Vertical Dimension of Social Status," *American Sociological Review* 19 (August 1954): 405–12.

43. Richard P. Coleman, "The Significance of Social Stratification in Selling," in *Marketing: A Maturing Discipline, Proceedings of the American Marketing Association 43rd National Conference,* ed. Martin L. Bell (Chicago: American Marketing Association, 1960), pp. 171–84.

44. E. Barth and W. Watson, "Questionable Assumptions in the Theory of Social Stratification," *Pacific Sociological Review* 7 (Spring 1964): 10–16.

45. Zick Rubin, "Do American Women Marry Up?" *American Sociological Review* 33 (1968): 750–60.

46. K.U. Ritter and L.L. Hargens, "Occupational Positions and Class Identifications of Married Working Women: A Test of the Asymmetry Hypothesis," *American Journal of Sociology* 80 (January 1975): 934–48.

47. J. Michael Munson and W. Austin Spivey, "Product and Brand-User Stereotypes Among Social Classes: Implications for Advertising Strategy," *Journal of Advertising Research* 21 (August 1981): 37–45.

48. Stuart U. Rich and Subhash C. Jain, "Social Class and Life Cycle as Predictors of Shopping Behavior,"

Journal of Marketing Research 5 (February 1968): 41–49.

49. Thomas W. Osborn, "Analytic Techniques for Opportunity Marketing," *Marketing Communications* (September 1987): 49–63.

50. Coleman, "The Continuing Significance of Social Class to Marketing."

51. Jeffrey F. Durgee, "How Consumer Sub-Cultures Code Reality: A Look at Some Code Types," in *Advances in Consumer Research 13*, ed. Richard J. Lutz (Provo, UT: Association for Consumer Research, 1986), pp. 332–37.

52. "A Marketing profile of RRSP contributors," *Marketing Magazine* (September 9, 1996): 21; "A Marketing profile of Internet users," *Marketing Magazine* (February 24, 1997): 31.

53. Thesia I. Garner and Janet Wagner, "Economic Dimensions of Household Gift Giving," *Journal of Consumer Research* 18 (December 1991): 368–79.

54. David Halle, *America's Working Man: Work, Home, and Politics Among Blue-Collar Owners* (Chicago: The University of Chicago Press, 1984); David Montgomery, "America's Working Man," *Monthly Review* (1985): 1.

55. Quoted in Coleman and Rainwater, *Standing in America*, p. 139.

56. Durkheim (1958) quoted in Roger Brown, *Social Psychology* (New York: Free Press, 1965).

57. Lenore Skenazy, "Affluent, Like Masses, Are Flush with Worries," *Advertising Age* (July 10, 1989): 55.

58. Herbert J. Gans, "Popular Culture in America: Social Problem in a Mass Society or Social Asset in a Pluralist Society?" in *Social Problems: A Modern Approach*, ed. Howard S. Becker (New York: Wiley, 1966).

59. Edward O. Laumann and James S. House, "Living Room Styles and Social Attributes: The Patterning of Material Artifacts in a Modern Urban Community," *Sociology and Social Research* 54 (April 1970): 321–42. See also Stephen S. Bell, Morris B. Holbrook and Michael R. Solomon, "Combining Esthetic and Social Value to Explain Preferences for Product Styles With the Incorporation of Personality and Ensemble Effects," *Journal of Social Behavior and Personality* (1991): 243–74.

60 *Canada's Families: They Count.*

61. Laumann and House, "Living Room Styles and Social Attributes." See also Bell, Holbrook and Solomon, "Combining Esthetic and Social Value to Explain Preferences for Product Styles."

62. Quoted in Richard Elliott, "How do the Unemployed Maintain Their Identity in a Culture of Consumption?" *European Advances in Consumer Research* 2 (1995): 1–4, p. 3.

63. Linda F. Alwitt, "Marketing and the Poor," *American Behavioral Scientist* 38 (February 1995): 564–77; Steve London, "A City Magazine for the Poor," *American*

Demographics (May 1994): 14 (2 pp.); Cyndee Miller, "The Have-Nots: Firms with the Right Products and Services Succeed Among Low-Income Consumers," *Marketing News* (August 1, 1994): 1 (2 pp.); Mark Veverka, "New Stores Planned for Inner City," *Advertising Age* (July 11, 1994): 29.

64. Linda F. Alwitt and Thomas D. Donley, "Retail Stores in Poor Urban Neighborhoods," *The Journal of Consumer Affairs* 31, 1 (1997): 108–27.

65. Chad Rubel, "Banks Go Mobile to Serve Low-Income Areas," *Marketing News* (November 20, 1995): 12.

66. Susan Chandler, "Data is Power. Just Ask Fingerhut," *Business Week* (June 3, 1996): 69.

67. "Reading the Buyer's Mind," *U.S. News & World Report* (March 16, 1987): 59.

68. Rebecca Piirto Heath, "Life on Easy Street," *American Demographics* (April 1997): 33–38.

69. *Wealth in America: A Study of Values and Attitudes Among the Wealthy Today* (Town & Country, 1994).

70. Paul Fussell, *Class: A Guide Through the American Status System* (New York: Summit Books, 1983), p. 29.

71. Elizabeth C. Hirschman, "Secular Immortality and the American Ideology of Affluence," *Journal of Consumer Research* 17 (June 1990): 31–42.

72. Coleman and Rainwater, *Standing in America*, p. 150.

73. "Lifeskills of the Rich and Famous," *Marketing Magazine* (October 23, 1995): 38.

74. M.H. Moore, "Homing in on Russian 'Super Spenders,'" *Adweek* (February 28, 1994): 14–16.

75. Jason DeParle, "Spy Anxiety; The Smart Magazine That Makes Smart People Nervous About Their Standing," *Washingtonian Monthly* (February 1989): 10.

76. For a recent examination of retailing issues related to the need for status, see Jacqueline Kilsheimer Eastman, Leisa Reinecke Flynn and Ronald E. Goldsmith, "Shopping for Status: The Retail Managerial Implications," *Association of Marketing Theory and Practice* (Spring 1994): 125–30.

77. Dennis Rodkin, "Wealthy Attitude Wins Over Healthy Wallet: Consumers Prove Affluence is a State of Mind," *Advertising Age* (July 9, 1990): S–4.

78. Thorstein Veblen, *The Theory of the Leisure Class* (1899; reprint, New York: New American Library, 1953), p. 45.

79. "Nestlé taking lick of premium ice cream," *Marketing Magazine* (July 7, 1997): 1; "Maclean's Honor Roll 1994: Robyn and Rhona MacKay," *Maclean's* (December 1994): 48–49.

80. Quoted in Cyndee Miller, "Baubles are Back," *Marketing News* (April 14, 1997): 1 (2 pp.); Elaine Underwood, "Luxury's Tide Turns," *Brandweek* (March 7, 1994): 18–22.

81. John Brooks, *Showing Off in America* (Boston: Little, Brown, 1981).

82. For examples, see John T. Molloy, *Dress For Success* (New York: Warner Books, 1975); Vicki Keltner and Mike Holsey, *The Success Image* (Houston, TX: Gulf Publishing, 1982); and William Thourlby, *You Are What You Wear* (New York: New American Library, 1978).

83. Brooks, *Showing Off in America*, pp. 31–32.

84. Virginia Matthews, "U.K. vegetarians take the bite out of their advertising," *Marketing Magazine* (July 7, 1997): 4; Marina Strauss, "Brand loyalty losing impact with shoppers," *Globe and Mail* (April 14, 1993); "Upscale Thrift Shops," in *Consumer News and Reviews*, newsletter of the American Council on Consumer Interests (March–April 1997): 3.

Ming-Ming, waking up early on Saturday, braces for a long day. As usual, her mother expects her to shop and then help prepare food for tonight's family gathering. Her brother Ho-Chiu would never be asked to do the grocery shopping or help in the kitchen. These are women's jobs.

Family gatherings make work, and Ming-Ming wishes her mother would use prepared foods, especially on a Saturday when she has errands of her own. But no! Her mother insists on preparing her food from scratch to ensure that the meals she serves are of the highest quality.

Ming-Ming watches television while getting dressed, then heads to the corner grocer to buy the *Sing Tao Daily*. There are several Chinese newspapers published in her area, and she likes to pick up new ones occasionally. Then Ming-Ming buys the groceries; the list is full of imported brand names, so she finishes quickly. With luck, she'll have a few minutes to go to the shopping centre for the new tape she's been saving to buy. She'll listen to it while she chops, peels and stirs.

Ming-Ming smiles. Vancouver is a great place, and what could be better than spending a lively, fun evening with family—parents, grandparents, brothers, aunts, uncle, her father's business partner and his son, her great-grandmother ...

14

Ethnic and Regional Subcultures

SUBCULTURES AND CONSUMER IDENTITY

Yes, Ming-Ming lives in Vancouver, not Hong Kong.

Asians have much in common with members of other ethnic groups who live in Canada. They observe the same national holidays, their expenditures are affected by the country's economic health, and they may join together in rooting for the Canadian Olympic team. Nonetheless, while Canadian citizenship provides the raw material for some consumption decisions, other decisions are profoundly affected by the enormous variations in the social fabric of Canada.

Consumers' lifestyles are affected by group memberships *within* the society at large. These groups are known as **subcultures**, whose members share beliefs and common experiences that set them apart from others. While subcultural group memberships often have a significant impact on consumer behaviour, some subcultural identifications are more powerful than others. Major subcultural groups will be discussed in detail in this chapter and the next. This chapter focuses on ethnic and regional identification, and Chapter 15 considers consumer subcultures that are defined by people of a common age. In some cases the subcultures to be considered in this chapter are already widely used by marketers as a segmentation variable (e.g., ethnicity), while the potential of others is just beginning to be recognized.

Every consumer belongs to many subcultures. These include age groups, ethnic groups and regional groups (e.g., westerners and Atlantic Canadians). Sometimes even leisure activities can evolve into a subculture, if this activity draws the con-

subculture a group whose members share beliefs and common experiences that set them apart from other members of a culture

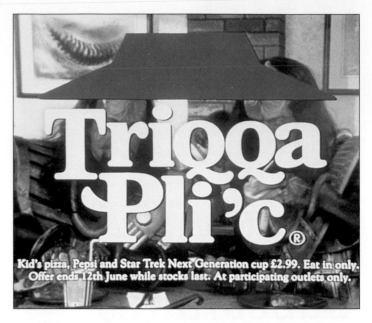

Subcultures can even gel around fictional characters. Many fans of *Star Trek* immerse themselves in a make-believe world of starships, phasers and Vulcan death grips. Some Trekkers have even specialized: there is an entire cult of fans devoted to Klingons, members of an aggressive warrior race that long battled the Federation. Devotees have their own language (*tlhIngan,* a tongue created by a linguist for one of the *Star Trek* movies), fanzines and food, and even a summer camp. Reflecting the popularity of this subculture, a commercial for Pizza Hut in the United Kingdom ran entirely in Klingonese. The warriors' words translate as "Get a kids' pizza, Pepsi and 'Star Trek: The Next Generation' cup for only £2.99." *Source: Erik Davis, "tlhIngan Hol Dajatlh'a' (Do You Speak Klingon?)," Utne Reader (March/April 1994): 122–29. Photos courtesy of Pizza Hut, Inc.*

sumer into a unique social situation with enough intensity. Consumers in these subcultures—whether they are "Dead Heads," retired people touring the country in Winnebagos or members of youth gangs—create their own worlds that are complete with their own norms, language and product insignias.

It is important to keep in mind that these are by no means the *only* important groups that marketers should know about. Canada is a mosaic of hundreds of diverse and interesting groups, from Italian and Irish Canadians to our First Nations people. Consider that in some Canadian school systems more than our two official languages are now spoken!

New products and services are springing up to address the needs of many of these groups. For example, a relatively new newspaper called the *Sing Tao Daily* targets Chinese Canadians. While this chapter addresses only the largest groups, the omission of other groups should not be taken to mean that they are not of interest or importance as well.

This chapter begins with general concepts related to ethnicity and consumer behaviour, and an overview of the ethnic diversity in the Canadian population. It continues with a look at French Canadians as an ethnic group with a long-standing presence in Canada. Chinese Canadians and the relatively recent wave of Hong Kong immigrants provide an example of acculturation processes as they relate to consumer behaviour. The analysis then proceeds to a regional level. The chapter

Different ethnic groups are represented in this ad.
Reprinted with permission of Avery-Dennison Corporation.

concludes with an examination of how the Canadian identity is manifested in consumer behaviour.

ETHNIC SUBCULTURES

Ethnic identity is often a significant component of a consumer's self-concept. An **ethnic subculture** consists of a self-perpetuating group of consumers who are held together by common cultural and/or genetic ties and which is identified both by its members and by others as a distinguishable category.[1]

In some countries, such as Japan, ethnicity is almost synonymous with the dominant culture, since most citizens claim the same homogeneous cultural ties (although Japan has sizeable minority populations, most notably people of Korean ancestry). In a heterogeneous society like Canada many different cultures are represented, and consumers may expend great effort to keep their subcultural identifications from being submerged into the mainstream of the dominant society.

Insights into the definition of ethnicity can be gained from a comprehensive study of the issues related to the measurement of English and French Canadian ethnicity that was done by a group of researchers at Concordia University. The sample consisted of 500 people who identified themselves as French Canadians and 500 who identified themselves as English Canadians in the Greater Montreal area. In addition to the self-identification measure, ethnic identity was measured by language use in various social communication settings, religious beliefs, social interaction, upbringing/background and spouse's ethnic identity. Although all six measures were

ethnic subculture a self-perpetuating group of consumers held together by common cultural ties

valid indicators of English or French Canadian ethnicity, the study suggests that the best measure is language use and the weakest measure is religion. However, language may not be the most salient dimension of a particular cultural group; for example, Jewish ethnicity may be better defined by religious beliefs. Thus, at this point in time, self-identification may be the measure that transcends various ethnicities.[2]

Interestingly, these researchers found no relationship between ethnicity and socio-economic status (as indicated by income, occupation and education). Like previous researchers they also found that there were specific types of consumer behaviour that could not be explained by socio-economic factors, suggesting that it is very important to consider cultural factors in market studies.[3]

Why It Pays to Target Ethnic Groups

Marketers can no longer ignore the stunning diversity of cultures that are reshaping mainstream society. Visible minorities (non-white, non-Caucasian and non-Aboriginal people) spend $76 billion a year on products and services in Canada.[4] The federal Multicultural Secretariat suggests that visible minorities comprise as much as 20 percent of consumer markets in urban centres.[5] Firms must devise products and communications strategies tailored to the needs of these subcultures. Some Canadian companies now have ethnic marketing programs up and running. For example, BC Tel and Bell Canada are targeting the 600 000 Chinese Canadians who live in British Columbia and Ontario with a Chinese long-distance calling card.[6] As one director of multicultural marketing observed, "Marketing today is part anthropology."[7]

ETHNICITY AND MARKETING STRATEGIES

Although some people may feel uncomfortable with the notion that people's ethnic differences should be explicitly taken into account when formulating marketing strategies, the reality is that these subcultural memberships frequently are paramount in shaping people's needs and wants. Dimensions of ethnicity that are of importance to marketers include heritage, life and consumer experiences, religion and beliefs. Membership in these groups often is predictive of such consumer variables as level and type of media exposure, food preferences, the wearing of distinctive apparel, political behaviour, leisure activities and willingness to try new products.[8]

Furthermore, research evidence indicates that members of minority groups are more likely to find an advertising spokesperson from their own group to be trustworthy, and this enhanced credibility in turn translates into more positive brand attitudes.[9] The Race Relations Advisory Council on Advertising (Canadian Advertising Foundation) provides Canadian marketers with guidelines for successful marketing to ethnic consumers. Diversity studies are being conducted by many Canadian companies to aid in understanding consumers and in recruiting marketers with ethnic insights.[10]

The way marketing messages should be structured depends on subcultural differences in how meanings are communicated. The German word for debt (*schuld*) is the same as the word for guilt, a connotation clearly extending to negative attitudes towards credit cards and bank loans.[11] Sociologists make a distinction between *high-*

context cultures and *low-context cultures*. In a high-context culture, group members tend to be tight-knit, and they are likely to infer meanings that go beyond the spoken word. Symbols and gestures, rather than words, carry much of the weight of the message. Compared to Anglos, many minority cultures are high-context and have strong oral traditions, so perceivers will be more sensitive to nuances in advertisements that go beyond the message copy.[12]

Canadian advertisers are targeting ethnic consumers in two ways: by fostering inclusiveness through putting more individuals from visible minorities into mainstream advertising, and by targeting specific ethnic groups in their mother tongue.[13] BC Hydro spends about 10 percent of its total marketing budget on ad campaigns in Chinese, Italian, Aboriginal and Jewish media, as well as mainstream vehicles. A message is "transcreated"—adapted to work in another language—or run in English in the ethnic media.[14]

There are more than 425 ethnic media outlets in Canada. Both television and radio broadcast multicultural programming. CFMT in Ontario offers programs in 15 languages, in addition to English.[15] *Maclean's* magazine and *Toronto Life* magazine both produce Chinese editions.[16] Other ethnic media include *Eyetalian,* with a readership of one million well-educated second-generation Canadians,[17] and *Telatino,* for Spanish-speaking audiences. Helpful directories include the Canadian Italian Business Directory, the Chinese Yellow Pages, the Original Jewish Pages and the Black Pages Directory.

In a study by the Canadian Advertising Foundation, 46 percent of members of visible minorities said they were more likely to buy a product if the ad included a visible minority. However, one study with students of English and French Canadian backgrounds found that ethnic brand names lowered recall. Interpretation of the findings suggested that perhaps ethnic (e.g., Spanish, black, Scottish) brand names only have salience with consumers who identify with a particular ethnicity, and that care needs to be taken not to alienate consumers of other ethnicities who may also be in the target market.[18]

Canadian marketers need to be cautious about when to segment markets by ethnicity, as the following examples indicate:

- A study of South Asian, Italian, Portuguese and Chinese consumers in Toronto by Compusearch Micromarketing Data and Systems found that these ethnic markets do more than three-quarters of their grocery shopping in supermarkets, not in local ethnic food shops. They spend more than the average Toronto household on prepackaged breakfast cereals.

- The Italian community spends $280 million a year at supermarkets—9 percent more than the average Toronto household.

- South Asians in Toronto spend $11.2 million a year on long-distance calls to their home countries.

- Italians in Toronto spend $114 million on automotive fuel—12 percent more than the average Toronto household—and 18 percent more on fresh fruits and vegetables.[19]

Products that are marketed with an ethnic appeal are not necessarily intended for consumption only by those in the ethnic subculture from which they originate. **De-ethnicitization** refers to the process whereby a product formerly associated with a specific ethnic group is detached from its roots and marketed to other subcultures. This process is illustrated by the case of bagels, a bread product formerly associated

de-ethnicitization the process whereby a product formerly associated with a specific ethnic group is detached from its roots and marketed to other subcultures

MARKETING PITFALL

The mass merchandising of ethnic products is widespread and growing. Aztec Indian designs appear on sweaters, gym shoes are sold trimmed in *kente* cloth from an African tribe, and greeting cards bear likenesses to Inuit paintings. However, many people are concerned about the borrowing—and in some cases misinterpretation—of distinctive symbolism.

Consider, for example, a recent storm of protest from the international Islamic community over what started as a simple dress design for the House of Chanel. In a fashion show, supermodel Claudia Schiffer wore a strapless evening gown designed by Karl Lagerfeld. The dress included Arabic letters that the designer believed spelled out a love poem. Instead, the message was a verse from the Koran, the Muslim holy book. To add insult to injury, the word *God* happened to appear over the model's right breast. Both the designer and the model received death threats, and the controversy subsided only after the three versions of the dress that had been made (and priced at almost $23 000) were burned.[20]

Some industry experts feel that it's all right to appropriate symbols from another culture even if the buyer does not know their original meaning. They argue that even in the host society there is often disagreement about these meanings. What do you think?

with Jewish culture and now mass-marketed. Recent variations include jalapeño bagels, blueberry bagels, and even a green bagel for St. Patrick's Day.[21] Mexican foods, such as tacos, burritos and salsa, have also become mainstream. Canada's consumption of olive oil, a staple of Mediterranean cooking for centuries, has more than doubled since the late 1980s.[22]

Ethnic Groups in Canada

Table 14–1 shows that the largest ethnic groups (by single origin) are British (21 percent), French (23 percent), German (3.4 percent), Italian (2.8 percent) and Chinese (2.2 percent). The two largest groups expand to 45 percent and 31 percent, respectively, when considered with at least one other origin.[23] Table 14–2 shows that ethnic groups are generally concentrated geographically, providing an opportunity for target marketing in a country with a widely dispersed population.[24] As mentioned previously, the French Canadian and Chinese markets will be given separate consideration in this chapter. Other ethnic markets can also be studied using the approaches and analyses used to interpret consumer behaviour in these two markets. However, one other market deserves some particular attention.

Canadians of Aboriginal origin number more than one million.[25] They dominate the ethnic composition of the Northwest Territories and represent just under 1.5 percent of the Yukon. At least 60 percent of the Aboriginal population is under 30 years old.[26] Little is known about their consumer behaviour in a scientific sense. However, work is being done to adapt the 631 characters in 19 Aboriginal languages and 5 dialects so that communication by computer is possible.[27] Building relationships

TABLE 14–1 Ethnic Origins of the Canadian Population

ETHNIC ORIGINS	NUMBER (MILLIONS)	PERCENT (%)
Total Canadian population	26 994 045	100.0
Total single origins	19 199 790	71.1
Total multiple origins	7 794 250	28.9
British alone	5 611 050	20.7
British alone or with some other origin	12 047 920	44.6
English	3 958 405	14.7
Scottish	893 125	3.3
Irish	725 660	2.7
French alone	6 129 680	22.6
French alone or with some other origin	8 389 180	31.1
Single European	4 146 065	15.2
German	911 560	3.4
Italian	750 055	2.8
Ukrainian	406 645	1.5
Dutch	358 180	1.3
Polish	272 810	1.0
Portuguese	246 890	.9
Greek	151 150	.6
Hungarian	100 725	.4
Aboriginal alone	470 615	1.7
Aboriginal alone or with some other origin	1 002 670	3.7
North American Indian	365 375	1.4
Métis	75 150	.3
Inuit	30 085	.1
Single Asian	1 607 230	5.9
Chinese	586 645	2.2
East Indian	324 840	1.2
Filipino	157 250	.6
Vietnamese	84 005	.3
Black	214 265	.8
Jewish	245 840	.9
Other single origins	1 446 355	5.4

Source: Adapted from Statistics Canada Cat. no. 93–315 (1991) and *Canada's Families: They Count* (Ottawa: The Vanier Institute for the Family, 1996).

TABLE 14–2 Dominant mother tongue by provinces and territories (single response—English or French, bilingual—English and French, and significant other languages, of at least 1 percent of the population)

PROVINCE/TERRITORY (POPULATION)	ENGLISH ONLY (%)	FRENCH ONLY (%)	ENGLISH & FRENCH (%)	OTHER (%)
Newfoundland (563 940)	98.7	0.5	—	—
Nova Scotia (890 950)	93.2	4.1	0.2	—
Prince Edward Island (128 100)	94.2	4.4	0.2	—
New Brunswick (716 495)	64.3	33.6	0.6	—
Quebec (6 810 300)	8.8	82.4	6.4	Italian (2.0)
Ontario (9 977 050)	74.0	4.5	3.0	Italian (3.3) Chinese (2.3) German (1.6) Portuguese (1.5) Polish (1.2)
Manitoba (1 079 395)	72.7	4.5	0.3	German (6.3) Ukrainian (3.4) Cree (2.0) Tagalog (1.3)
Saskatchewan (976 035)	82.7	2.2	0.2	German (4.3) Ukrainian (2.8) Cree (2.2)
Alberta (2 519 180)	80.6	2.1	0.2	German (3.2) Chinese (2.4) Ukrainian (1.7)
British Columbia (3 247 505)	78.4	1.5	0.1	Chinese (4.7) German (2.7) Punjabi (2.1)
Northwest Territories (57 435)	54.2	2.5	0.2	Inuktitut (28.7)
Yukon (27 660)	88.0	3.1	0.2	German (1.9) Aboriginal (1.5)

Source: Adapted from Statistics Canada Cat. no. 93–333 (1991).

(through activities like fishing with Native elders), providing Polaroid identification photographs, having the option of cheques with images by young Native artists, and advertising in Native people's media (such as *Windspeaker* and *Aboriginal Voices*) have attracted Indian and Métis people to the services of the Bank of Montreal, T-D Bank and CIBC.[28]

THE EFFECT OF IMMIGRATION ON CANADIAN DIVERSITY

Statistics Canada estimates that the population of Canada, numbering just under 29 million in the 1996 census, may grow to as high as 32 million by the year 2011. Much of this growth will be accounted for by members of non-white ethnic groups, and a substantial proportion will result from the immigration of people from other countries as opposed to citizens who are born in Canada.[29]

The 1991 census counted 7 million Canadians (31 percent) of single ethnic or mixed ethnic origins other than British or French—an increase of 6 percentage points since 1986.[30] A study done for the Canadian Advertising Foundation estimates that this count will increase by 5.7 million by 2001: 1.3 million Chinese-speaking, 1.3 million South Asian, and 1.1 million black. These projections represent an increase of 350 percent in the number of visible minorities in Canada over 15 years.[31]

The three groups that account for much of Canada's growth from immigration are Chinese Canadians, East Indian Canadians and Polish Canadians. These three groups, along with Italian Canadians, Portuguese Canadians and Greek Canadians, make up Canada's six largest ethnic groups outside of English and French Canadians. These consumers, 80 percent of whom live in Vancouver, Toronto and Montreal, are expected to number 2.8 million by the year 2000—an increase of one-third since the 1991 census. About 45 percent of Greater Toronto is expected to consist of visible minorities; 16 percent of Ottawa/Hull and Windsor/Sarnia; 13 percent of Hamilton and Kitchener; 11 percent of London, and over 6 percent of St. Catharine's/Niagara.[32] Ethnic diversity is expected to increase, affecting not only demand in ethnic markets but the nature of demand overall.

The potential of these markets lies not only in their size and growth patterns, but also in their household incomes. For example, 49 percent of both the Chinese and

MULTICULTURAL DIMENSIONS

Ethnic restaurants are a fast-growing segment of the food industry, whether in the United States, Canada, Europe or Japan.[33] Such restaurants are a part of the internationalization of lifestyles, in which consumers reach out for new experiences. The greatest concentration of ethnic restaurants is found in the northeastern and western parts of the United States and in urban areas of Canada. Chinese is the most frequently served ethnic cuisine and is followed closely by Mexican and Italian (these three types account for over 70 percent of all ethnic restaurants). Many other cuisines are underrepresented or not represented at all, and this fact may hint at opportunities for entrepreneurs who wish to carve out distinctive niches.

Europeans are also becoming huge fans of ethnic food. Food producers are rapidly adding international dishes to their product lines to keep pace with demand. Unilever NV's Pronto frozen foods include such choices as Indonesian "Bami Goreng" or Indian "Madras Curry." Nestlé added a "Taste of Asia" line to its Findus brand. European consumers also are beginning to show interest in more spicy foods, and they are influenced by the healthy image of Far Eastern cuisine. Tex-Mex dishes and beers are also catching fire in Europe, particularly in Britain and Scandinavia.

East Indian households, and 48 percent of the Italian households, in the three largest urban markets reported household income of $55 000 or more in 1991. The Chinese and Italian households are each expected to represent nearly 10 percent of the purchasing power in these markets by the year 2000.[34]

New arrivals are best marketed to in their native languages. They tend to cluster together geographically, which makes them easy to reach. The local community is the primary source for information and advice, so word of mouth is especially important (see Chapter 11). Advertising themes that seem to be effective among recent immigrants are based on messages of comfort, familiarity and appropriateness of language (in response to feelings of fear and insecurity on coming to a new country). Due to the forces of integration, English works well with first-generation Canadians.[35] In fact about one-half of new immigrants speak one of the official languages.[36] Ethnic consumers are also thought to be price sensitive.[37]

IS ETHNICITY A MOVING TARGET?

Although ethnic marketing is in vogue in many forms, the process of actually defining and targeting members of a distinct ethnic group is not always so easy. In the last decade there has been a continuing decline in the proportion of Canadians of British and French origin due to increasing immigration of other Europeans, Asians and other non-Europeans, stemming from various economic and political events throughout the world. In addition, ethnic intermarriage has blurred ethnic boundaries, particularly, but not solely, among first- and second-generation Canadians. Nearly 8 million Canadians reported multiple ethnic origins in the 1991 census.[38] Thus it has become increasingly difficult for marketing researchers and Statistics Canada to classify Canadians into neat ethnic categories, and comparisons across time must be done with special attention to how ethnicity is operationalized for data collection.[39]

The steady increase in the number of mixed marriages is, however, creating opportunities for some marketers who wish to meet the needs of children raised in multicultural families. Because many children are exposed to others from diverse cultural backgrounds, some marketing executives feel that their attitudes will be quite different from those of their parents. Encounters with diverse cultural traditions create the need for products and services that allow consumers to celebrate multiple heritages, including international festivals, language classes, camps with ethnic themes, and travel products and services.

Ethnic Stereotypes: The Dark Side of Multicultural Marketing

Many subcultures have powerful stereotypes associated with them. Members of a subgroup are assumed to possess certain traits, even though these assumptions are often erroneous. Also, the same trait can be cast either positively or negatively, depending upon the communicator's intentions and biases. For example, the Scottish stereotype in Canada is largely positive, so the supposed frugality of this ethnic group is viewed favourably. Scottish imagery has been used by the 3M Company to denote value (Scotch tape). However, invoking the Scottish "personality" might carry quite different connotations to consumers in Britain or Ireland. Thus, one person's "thrifty" is another's "stingy." In addition, ethnic symbolism has been used in

MARKETING OPPORTUNITY

Jost Vineyards is in many ways a quintessential example of special marketing opportunities in Canada. It is the most eastern Estate Winery operating in North America. Established in 1970 by a German immigrant family with 300 years of history in wine making, the winery is located to take advantage of the long frost-free summers of a unique microclimate on the Malagash Peninsula in Nova Scotia. The award-winning winery, which does 50 percent of its sales on its premises, also offers tours, a deli-bar, licensed patio deck, U-Barbeque, wine tasting and an artisan's cooperative.

the past by marketers as a shorthand to connote certain product attributes. The images employed were often crude and unflattering.

The Impact of Religion

An Angus Reid poll in 1996 showed that religion plays an important part in the life of nearly 60 percent of Canadians, and 60 percent think of themselves as Christians, although less than one-quarter attend church weekly.[40] In general, religion is closely associated with ethnicity, social class and geographic regions. In Canada (as in the United States), WASP (White Anglo-Saxon Protestant) values have been a dominant force.

This controversial Benetton ad was rejected by some magazines because of what some perceived to be offensive religious symbolism.
Photographer: O. Toscani for Benetton.

Religion *per se* has not been studied extensively in marketing, possibly because it is seen as a taboo subject.[41] However, the little evidence that has been accumulated indicates that religious affiliation has the potential to be a valuable predictor of consumer behaviour.[42] Religion may exert a particularly significant impact on such consumer variables as personality, attitudes towards sexuality, birth rates, household formation, income and political attitudes.

One study that examined this issue found marked differences among Catholic, Protestant and Jewish university students in preferences for weekend entertainment activities, as well as in the criteria used in making these decisions. Price was a relatively more important criterion for Protestants, while desire for companionship was highest for Jews. Catholics were more likely to designate dancing as a favoured activity than were the other two groups, but were much less likely to select sex.[43] Consumers high in religious commitment tend to look for high product quality, be worried about social risk in product purchases and be price sensitive.[44]

The WASP subculture has been a dominant force in the larger picture of Canadian (and American) culture.[45] The Protestant Establishment still dominates leadership positions in the private sector and its work ethic. In fact the WASP has been a symbol of the North American ideal for some time. For many immigrants the WASP ideal still symbolizes the light at the end of the tunnel: if one desires to assimilate, to make it, the WASP lifestyle is the goal.

As a result of this idealized view of the WASP, the formal eating rituals devised by WASPs are assumed to be the "proper" way to eat and entertain. The leisure activities associated with this subculture (e.g., golfing, yachting and squash) often are seen as socially correct.[46] Marketers have done more than their share to propagate this ideal. Idealized images of the WASP subculture are frequently employed in advertising to epitomize the good life and the amenities associated with old money (see Chapter 13).

FRENCH CANADIANS

The Nature of the French Canadian Market

French Canadians comprise a significant subculture, and account for 20 to 30 percent of the Canadian population based on ethnic origin.[47] They form the second largest ethnic market in Canada, comprising about 80 percent of the Quebec population

MARKETING OPPORTUNITY

One of the most significant Jewish-related marketing developments is the increase in demand for kosher food. Each year about 500 new kosher products appear on the market to satisfy this demand. This trend is being driven by two developments: the increased religious observance by young Jews and the belief among many Gentiles that kosher food is of higher quality. Seventh-Day Adventists and Muslims have very similar dietary requirements to some Jews and are good customers for kosher food.[48] It is estimated that fewer than a third of consumers who buy kosher products are Jewish.[49]

MARKETING OPPORTUNITY

A wide range of Canadian companies now provide ethnic market offerings:

- Knob Hill Farms, a grocery chain in Ontario, stocks products aimed at ethnic markets: canned black olives and lupini beans from Portugal; canned ackees and Pickapeppa sauce from Jamaica; and lychees and banana blossoms from Thailand.

- The Caribana Festival (Toronto's Caribbean music festival) draws more than 500 000 people each year.

- The Vancouver Symphony Orchestra and the Taiwanese Cultural Centre presented a sold-out crowd with contemporary music from Taiwan.

- Hola Sun, a Toronto-based charter tour operator, specializes in Cuban destinations for the Italian, Jewish and Polish markets. In addition to advertising in ethnic media, the company participates in the Latin Canadian Trade Show and the International Picnic sponsored by CHIN Radio.

- International Greeting Cards supplies cards for ethnic consumers sending greetings for Christmas, Hanukkah and the Chinese New Year.

- Loblaw's format for its ethnic market is Fortino's.

- The Scars catalogue portrays models of various ethnicities.

- Honest Ed's, a discount retail outlet that serves recently arrived immigrants and ethnic minority Canadians, now has a legal clinic.

- Braemar Apparel Inc. hires people who can speak Mandarin and Cantonese to sell its women's clothing in some of its Toronto and Vancouver stores.[50]

MARKETING OPPORTUNITY

The recent proliferation of ethnic dolls in toy stores reflects society's growing cultural diversity. While in the past non-Caucasian dolls appeared only in collections of dolls from around the world, all major manufacturers have now introduced ethnic dolls to the mass market.

New entrants include Kira, the Asian fashion doll, and Emmy, the black baby doll. Mattel introduced a trio of dolls named Shani (which means "marvellous" in Swahili), Asha and Nichelle, which represent the range of black facial features and skin tones (Shani also has a boyfriend named Jamal). And while Mattel has sold a black version of Barbie for over 20 years, it only recently began to promote the doll in television and print campaigns.[51]

and 34 percent of the New Brunswick population, as well as accounting for a significant number of residents in Ontario. In other words, the French Canadian market provides the advantage of geographic concentration. The market is even larger when extended to include Canadians of French with other origins.

There are more than 800 000 Anglophone consumers in Montreal, and a total of 1.5 million who speak English. A study by Le Conseil de la Langue Française notes that immigrants are generally not integrating into the French mainstream. As well, 46 percent of Montrealers whose mother tongue is French, and 60 percent whose mother tongue is English, consider themselves to be bilingual, while 48 percent of allophone Montrealers speak both official languages. According to the 1991 census, 31 percent of Anglophones and 33 percent of bilingual Francophones are middle class or affluent, compared to the Canadian average of 27 percent. More than 80 percent of both groups are employed as managers, owners, professionals or white-collar workers, compared to 69 percent in the rest of Canada.[52]

Understanding the French Canadian Identity

The work of French Canadian researchers George Henault, Bruce Mallen and Jacques Bouchard, on the nature of the French Canadian identity, has been interpreted for the English Canadian market.[53] These approaches are still informative and practical from a marketing perspective, as the French Canadian market (at least in Quebec) strives to maintain its own identity.[54]

Henault's work suggests that the cultural characteristics of English and French Canadians differ markedly. English Canadians, for example, are pragmatic, more social and conservative, and tend to save and be conformers, while French Canadians are theoretical, more individualistic and liberal, and tend to spend and be innovators.

Mallen details the sensate, conservative (unlike Henault) and non-price cognitive traits, and ties them to the consumer behaviour of French Canadians. The sensate trait speaks to the importance of all senses in French Canadian consumers, as well as their appreciation of aesthetics, fashion consciousness and social hedonism. He suggests that the conservative trait relates to low risk-taking, the emphasis on family and the strong brand loyalty of these consumers. Finally, the third trait is thought to result in accepting high price points (within reason) if a product or service meets the criteria of the first two traits.

Bouchard provides an in-depth analysis of six historical and cultural roots of French Canadians: rural, minority, North American, Catholic, Latin and French. It has been suggested that an understanding of these roots could be helpful to marketers and advertising agencies as a sort of cultural psychographic profile.

Researchers at Concordia University found that French Canadians showed more concern for their children, consumed fewer canned and frozen products, and showed less favourable attitudes towards generic products than English Canadians.[55] The Dairy Farmers of Canada switched to a different creative strategy for its butter campaign in the Quebec market because children talking on camera was well received in Quebec but not in English Canada.[56]

French Canadian Consumption Patterns

Most of what is known about the French Canadian market comes not from theoretical links to their identity (or structural theory) but from descriptive comparisons with English Canadians or segments *within* the French Canadian market. While French Canadian consumers do differ in important ways from English Canadians, the French Canadian market is not as homogeneous as many marketers seem to believe.

A study in the mid-1980s found various contrasts in consumer behaviour between French-speaking and English-speaking families. French-speaking families were found to:

- use more staples associated with original cooking, and use fewer frozen vegetables;
- consume more soft drinks and sweet instant beverages and fewer dietary beverages;
- consume more wine, beer and Geneva gin;
- own less valuable living-room and dining-room furnishings;
- purchase furniture more frequently at discount stores rather than department or furniture stores;
- have more features on appliances;
- own larger and newer primary vehicles; and
- shop at fewer and independent grocery stores.[57]

PMB'94 data show that different segments exist in the Quebec market when age is used as a segmentation variable. Francophone teenagers (12 to 17 years) differed from their Anglophone counterparts in Quebec and the rest of Canada in such shopping behaviours as being more likely to have store memberships (e.g., at Price Club) and to drink beer. In an older age group (18 to 24 years), the Francophone young adults were more likely to be involved in bicycling and dressmaking, more likely to use sunburn treatment and to have store memberships, and more likely to agree that "Dressing well is an important part of life."[58] Francophone youth (15 to 24 years) were also found to have exclusive and loyal relationships with financial institutions compared to older age cohorts.[59] More than a third of Quebec parents, and especially those in Quebec City, were influenced by their children. Mothers were most likely to be influenced in the food area, while fathers were more likely to be influenced in leisure activities and electronics.[60]

PMB'95 also showed differences in behaviour between older consumers (55 years and up) in Quebec compared to those in the rest of Canada. For example, Quebecers were more likely to use coupons and buy instant breakfast drinks, and less likely to buy generic products and use credit cards and ATM machines. They were also more liberal-minded and more open to changing women's roles in society.[61]

Le Groupe Léger & Léger Inc. found that Francophone Montrealers compared to Francophones in the rest of Quebec were greater users of banks (rather than *caisses populaires*). They were also more likely to own four credit cards, had a stronger preference for compact and subcompact Japanese cars, and spent more on long-distance phone calls.[62]

Hostess Frito-Lay developed two successful flavours for the Quebec market: Épices Mexicaines and Fromage Piquant Doritos.[63] Local heroes like Jacques Villeneuve create demand for race-car entertainment among young and old Quebecers. Jean Coutu continues to dominate the drugstore market, and Cirque du Soleil attracts local audiences as well as tourists. Further, although Quebec is behind the rest of Canada in Internet use, more than 12 000 Quebecers access IGA's Web site (*www.iga.net/gc*) for their grocery shopping. About 200 orders a week result in $20 000 worth of sales.[64]

French Canadians and the Media

In addition to using Québécois French, since the 1995 Quebec referendum some marketers have changed their advertising approaches because they think certain words and connotations have become taboo. The successful Labatt slogan, "On est six millions ... faut se pater" ("We're six million ... let's get acquainted") is no longer perceived to be appropriate in the present political climate. Words like *chez nous, ici, pays, Canada, nation* and *Québécois* are avoided in headings, as is the peace symbol (used in the Oui campaign).[65] In 1994 the maple leaf was removed from the label of Labatt Blue sold in Quebec.[66] On the other hand, Cream Ale, with its obviously Anglophone Ontario package complete with a beaver, maple leaf and the Sleeman name, is the best-selling premium beer in Quebec.[67]

Creative execution designed specifically for the Quebec market has been found to have more impact in terms of characteristics such as originality and credibility than adaptations or translations from English Canadian or American ads.[68] Appropriate advertising imagery for Quebec includes shots of the nuclear family, women and active seniors, visually powerful images (such as close-ups that fill the frame), Latin or European flair, and humour.[69] Future Shop recently moved to original creative work for its advertising in Quebec, rather than adapting material.[70]

CHINESE CANADIANS

Although their numbers are still relatively small (about 450 000), Chinese Canadians are the fastest-growing minority group in Canada.[71] Marketers are just beginning to recognize their potential as a unique market segment. This subculture is attractive to marketers because Asian Canadians typically are hard-working and many have above-average incomes. Chinese Canadians have the highest incomes of all visible minorities.[72] As one indication, readers of the nationally distributed *Ming Pao Daily* have an average family income in excess of $57 000; 60 percent are homeowners; and 65 percent have a university education.[73]

The Chinese Canadian market, however, is far from homogeneous. The attitudes and behaviour of these consumers are influenced by age, education, gender, household composition, knowledge of English, length of time in Canada, reason for immigration, working status prior to and after immigration, family size, geographic location, and marital and financial status.[74] Recent studies by Angus Reid and DSC Research have found Chinese Canadians whose mother tongue was Cantonese or Mandarin were younger and slightly less wealthy than the average Canadian. They were more likely to be married; tended towards large traditional families; were more likely to be owners of homes and consumer electronics; and played more lotteries and consumed less alcohol than Vancouverites in general.[75]

Segmenting Asian Canadians

Despite the potential, Asian Canadians are hard to market to, because they are actually composed of subgroups that are culturally diverse and speak many different languages and dialects. The term *Asian* refers to 20 ethnic groups, with Chinese being the largest.[76] Chinese Canadians still comprise less than 5 percent of the population, so mass-marketing techniques often are not viable to reach them.[77] However, opportunities exist due to the availability of Chinese Canadian media in British Columbia. Hastings Park Racecourse, for example, markets its sport to the Chinese community (many from Hong Kong) in Vancouver. The events are appealing as a family event.[78] British Columbia has 12 Chinese media outlets—two each of television and radio stations, and eight newspapers and magazines.[79]

Some attempts to translate advertising messages and concepts into Asian media have backfired. Other advertisements have overlooked the complex differences among Asian subcultures, and some have unknowingly been insensitive to cultural practices. The use of the colour red and Chinese characters, the careful use of numbers, and the delivery of high-quality service are all appreciated.[80] The Vancouver Grizzlies' club name was translated to mean "strong and powerful bear" in Cantonese and Mandarin, rather than the original "grey bear."[81]

Reaching the Chinese Canadian Consumer

Many marketers are discouraged by the lack of media available to reach Asian Canadians.[82] Practitioners generally find that advertising in English works best for broadcast ads, while print ads are more effective when executed in Asian languages.[83] However, most Asians prefer media in their own languages.[84] The most frequently spoken languages are Mandarin Chinese, Korean, Japanese and Vietnamese.[85] The *Sing Tao Daily* has been a newspaper for Chinese Canadians for about 20 years.

In the United States a crop of new magazines is trying to capture younger Asian Americans. One new offering is *A. Magazine*, which is written for and about affluent Asian Americans aged 18 to 40.[86] Even mass retailer Sears is getting into the act: the company recently became the first major department store to formally target the Asian American market by hiring an advertising agency to develop messages targeted to this segment.[87] Finally, the AsiaOne radio network provides broadcasting across the USA in seven Asian languages.[88]

Level of Acculturation

One important way to distinguish among members of a subculture is to consider the extent to which they retain a sense of identification with their country of origin as compared with their host country. **Consumer acculturation** refers to the process of movement and adaptation to one country's cultural environment by a person from another country.[89]

This factor is especially important when considering the Chinese market, since the degree to which these consumers are integrated into the Canadian way of life varies widely. Table 14–3 shows a recent attempt to segment Hong Kong immigrants

consumer acculturation
the process of movement and adaptation to one country's cultural environment by a person from another country

TABLE 14–3 Mau's 14-Item Acculturation Index

ITEM	MEASURE OF ITEM
Self-defined ethnic identity	5-point scale: 1 = Hong Kong Chinese to 5 = Canadian Chinese
Proportion of time watching English TV	Percentage of time (0–100%)
Proportion of time listening to English radio	Percentage of time (0–100%)
Proportion of time reading English newspapers	Percentage of time (0–100%)
Proportion of time reading English magazines	Percentage of time (0–100%)
Use of English at work/school	Percentage of time (0–100%)
Use of English during shopping	Percentage of time (0–100%)
Use of English among friends	Percentage of time (0–100%)
Proud of Chinese origin	5-point scale: 1 = strong disagree to 5 = strongly agree
Appreciate Chinese traditional values	5-point scale: 1 = strong disagree to 5 = strongly agree
Importance of celebrating Chinese New Year	5-point scale: 1 = strong disagree to 5 = strongly agree
Importance of children learning Chinese	5-point scale: 1 = strong disagree to 5 = strongly agree
Importance of teaching traditional values	5-point scale: 1 = strong disagree to 5 = strongly agree
Cronbach's alpha on 14 items	.79

Source: Adapted from Rosanna W.S. Mau, "The Impact of Acculturation on Decision Making: The Case of Hong Kong Immigrants in Vancouver," unpublished Master of Business Administration thesis, Simon Fraser University, 1997.

in terms of their degree of acculturation. Interestingly, the respondents identified their ethnicity on a five-point scale, ranging from Hong Kong Chinese to Canadian Chinese.[90]

DIFFERENCES IN CULTURAL INTEGRATION

Immigrants from Hong Kong represent two extremes. Annual immigration from Hong Kong has ranged from less than 1000 in 1957 to almost 15 000 in 1973 through to more than 40 000 in 1994.[91] Early immigrants worked hard for many years to establish themselves, and are now entrenched in the Canadian political and economic establishment. On the other hand, thousands of recent immigrants are trying to adapt to their new environment. These consumers may need to learn entirely new product categories. The implication for marketers is that these consumers must be taught about a product before they can be convinced to buy one brand over another.

PROGRESSIVE LEARNING

progressive learning model
the perspective that people gradually learn a new culture as they increasingly come in contact with it; consumers assimilate into a new culture, mixing practices from their old and new environments to create a hybrid culture

The acculturation of Hong Kong immigrant consumers may be understood in terms of the **progressive learning model.** This perspective assumes that people gradually learn a new culture as they increasingly come in contact with it. Thus we would expect the consumer behaviour of immigrants to be a mixture of practices taken from their original culture and those of the new culture, or *host culture.*[92]

MARKETING OPPORTUNITY

Canadian companies are serving the Chinese Canadian market successfully through various marketing strategies:

- T & T Supermarkets in Vancouver serves the Asian market by sourcing most of its stock from Asia. Brand name goods like Horlocks, Carnation, Ovaltine and Robertson Jellos are labelled in both English and Chinese.

- Twenty-five percent of the 115 Canadian branches of the Hongkong Bank of Canada are Chinese; they also have Mandarin Centres to serve people from Taiwan, China and Singapore. The Bank of Montreal has senior managers to serve the Chinese, Korean and the Indo-Canadian markets.

- Best Foods introduced trilingual labelling for its Mazola oil and distributes it to Chinese grocery stores.

- Ninety-six percent of Chinese Canadians in Toronto were found to use over-the-counter pain relievers, and they spent more than $55 million a year on dairy products.

- The Bay in Richmond, BC, which once attracted customers of European descent, had a $14-million facelift in order to appeal to the upscale tastes of its Asian base, which is about one-third of its customers.

- Manulife Financial of Toronto is targeting the Chinese market with print and television ads.[93]

Research has generally obtained results that support this pattern when such factors as shopping orientation, the importance placed on various product attributes, media preference and brand loyalty were examined.[94] When the intensity of ethnic identification was taken into account, consumers who retained a strong ethnic identification differed from their more assimilated counterparts.[95]

Leaving one's culture and family to go to a new place creates many new needs, as well as anxieties about fitting into a new environment. Recent immigrants encounter a strange culture and have often left family members behind. Word of mouth is very important in developing customer loyalty among Chinese Canadians of all ages, because the Chinese community is very interactive.[96] Canadian marketers can offer a feeling of belonging to Canadian society by including Asian models in catalogues and advertising.[97]

The nature of the transition process is affected by many factors, as shown in Figure 14–1. Individual differences, such as whether the person speaks English, influence how rocky the adjustment will be. The person's contact with **acculturation agents**—people and institutions that teach the ways of a culture—also are crucial. Some of these agents are aligned with the *culture of origin*. These include family, friends, the church, local businesses and first-language media that keep the consumer in touch with his or her country of origin. Other agents are associated with the *culture of immigration* (in this case, Canada) and help the consumer to learn how to navigate in the new environment. These include schools and English-language media.

Due partly to ESL programs in Lower Mainland Schools in British Columbia, 150 000 Hong Kong Chinese will enter their adult lives as English-speaking cultur-

acculturation agents
friends, family, local businesses and other reference groups that facilitate the learning of cultural norms

FIGURE 14–1 • A Model of Consumer Acculturation

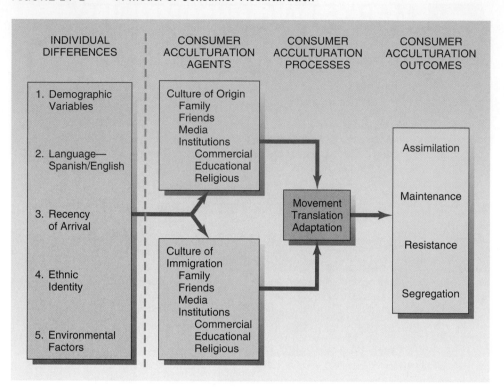

Source: Adapted from Lisa Peñaloza, "Atravesando Fronteras/Border Crossings: A Critical Ethnographic Exploration of the Consumer Acculturation of Mexican Immigrants," *Journal of Consumer Research* 21, 1 (June 1994): 32–54. Reprinted by permission of The University of Chicago Press.

ally integrated Chinese Canadians. They are expected to have some values in common with their parents (e.g., to work hard, do post-secondary studies and seek remunerative careers), but also some values picked up in Canada. The speed with which they adopt Canadian ways depends on their age, the age of their parents, where they were born, where they now live, their personal reactions to change, the attitudes of both children and parents, and their commitment to Canada.[98]

As immigrants adapt to their new surroundings, several processes come into play. *Movement* refers to the factors motivating people to uproot themselves physically from one location and go to another. Upon arrival, immigrants encounter a need for *translation*. This means attempting to master a set of rules for operating in the new environment, whether learning how to decipher a different currency or figuring out the social meanings of unfamiliar clothing styles. This cultural learning leads to a process of *adaptation,* where new consumption patterns are formed.

As consumers undergo acculturation, several things happen. Many immigrants undergo (at least to some extent) *assimilation,* where they adopt products that are identified with the mainstream culture. At the same time there is an attempt at *maintenance* of practices associated with the culture of origin. Immigrants stay in touch with their country of birth; for example, many from Hong Kong continue to eat Chinese foods and read Chinese newspapers. This continued identification with the culture of origin may cause *resistance,* as they resent the pressure to submerge their cultural identities and take on new roles. Finally, immigrants (voluntarily or not) tend to exhibit *segregation*: they are likely to live and shop in places that are physically separated from mainstream consumers.

In the book *Customers From Afar,* consultant Raymond Ng suggests five phases of adjustment for teenage and adult immigrants:

- *The honeymoon*—The immigrant marvels at the wonders of the new environment.

- *Culture shock*—The reality of the situation sets in.

- *Superficial adjustment*—The immigrant forays into the new culture and manages day-to-day life.

- *Stress and depression*—The immigrant disparages aspects of the new life: lack of high-paying job opportunities, taxes, cold and wet weather. Intergenerational conflicts arise, often over the career choices of children.

- *Integration*—The immigrant moves through society with ease comparable to the native-born.[99]

Two Chinese Canadians, Mina Shum (director) and Sandra Oh (lead actress), document the tensions between generations in the award-winning movie *Double Happiness* (1995).[100] *The Communicator,* launched in the Markam, Ontario, area in late 1996, is the first bilingual Chinese/English community newspaper. One of its objectives is to bridge cultural gaps.[101]

A 1994 study of the set of products basic and secondary to life in Canada found that about 78 percent of new immigrants and about 87 percent of long-time immigrants owned basic products (cars, houses, microwave ovens, televisions), and about 38 percent of new immigrants and about 50 percent of long-time immigrants owned secondary products (deep freezers, barbecues, dining-room sets).[102] Less acculturated immigrants from Hong Kong are more brand- and price-conscious than are more acculturated immigrants.[103]

Interestingly, some young Chinese Canadians are attached to the rapidly developing Chinese popular culture as a kind of Global Teen view akin to the Eurokids. While their parents like to hear messages of comfort and security in advertising, these young people want to hear messages of acceptance from the cultural mainstream.[104] *Jade,* an English magazine for young Chinese Canadians, focuses on fashion, cars and entertainment with an Asian flavour.[105]

REGIONAL SUBCULTURES

The four regions of Canada are usually identified as Atlantic Canada (or the East Coast), Quebec, Ontario and the west. Sometimes the Maritime provinces are defined as a region, and sometimes British Columbia is distinguished from the Prairie provinces. The northern territories are sometimes combined with the west, but with the opening of the privately funded Northwest Territories Communication Centre the stage is set for a more distinctive designation.[106] The most appropriate segmentation approach depends on the purpose for making the distinctions and whether the distinctions provide marketing leverage. NADbank Inc., which is interested in readership profiles, treats British Columbia as a separate regional market.[107]

The regions of Canada differ in weather patterns, concentration and growth of their population, age composition and ethnic mix, all of which affect regional

REGIONAL DIMENSIONS

Established in 1984, Fog Forest Gallery represents professional visual artists and craftspeople of the Atlantic region. Paintings, handmade prints, sculpture and fine crafts are featured in frequently changing exhibitions. Art workshops, a visiting artists series and a custom framing service are also offered within a friendly environment.

The name Fog Forest is taken from an article that first appeared in *Canadian Geographic* magazine. Mike Rosen, an interpreter with Parks Canada, described the area surrounding the Bay of Fundy as a fog forest. The climate, along with the additional moisture created by the fog, encourages very special plants to flourish. Even in this difficult and challenging environment, these beautiful and rare plants thrive.

Fog Forest Gallery, owned and operated by Janet Crawford, displays the special works created by fine artists and craftspeople who, like the plants in the fog forest, give the Atlantic region a distinctive and enduring quality. The Gallery represents Atlantic artists including Suezan Aikins, Alice Reed and Robert Rutherford from Nova Scotia; Alexandrya Eaton, Kathy Hooper, Peter Powning and Sarah Quintin-Beland from New Brunswick; and Debra Kuzak and Ray Mackie from Newfoundland.

lifestyles and product and service preferences. Maritimers, for example, are noted in the tea industry for preferring the Red Rose brand. Consumers in British Columbia are more likely to take cruise-ship vacations, while those in Atlantic Canada are less likely to take cruises.[108] However, it is probably fair to say that regional segments get far less attention from Canadian marketers than other bases of segmentation, and the contrasts often focus on the major urban centres in each region. Nevertheless, this section explores some of the potential for regional segmentation.

NADbank found that on average Canadians spend about three-quarters of an hour with their newspaper on weekdays; Quebecers spend the most time with their papers; and Atlantic Canadians increased their reading time by ten minutes from 1992 to 1997. They also found that Vancouverites are more likely to have investments than Torontonians and Montrealers. Department store shoppers in the Maritimes are more likely to patronize Sears, while British Columbians prefer The Bay.[109] Loblaw's format for Atlantic Canada is The Atlantic Superstore and for Western Canada is The Real Canadian Superstore.[110]

Regional identification based on ethnic overtones is tied to some consumer preferences and purchases and is perhaps most evident in the entertainment area. Celtic music in its various forms is synonymous with the Atlantic Canadian culture for many,[111] while Acadian music and cuisine are associated with the Maritimes. The long-running Festival of the Midnight Sun, the Calgary Stampede, the Natal Day Festival and the Pacific National Exhibition all bespeak the attraction to locals and tourists of regional symbols and lifestyles.

Some regions also have unique symbols that provide communication value for marketers. Inuit art styles are associated with British Columbia and the North, as is the polar bear. The Sasquatch, in British Columbia, is used to promote Kokanee beer, and Bon-Homme provides the theme for a winter carnival in Quebec City.[112]

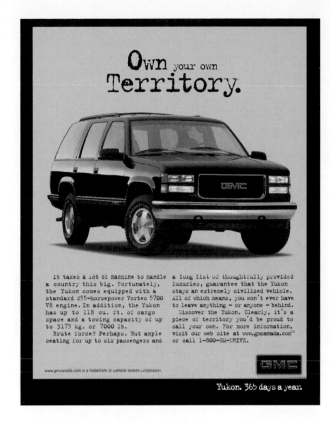

Own *your own*
Territory.

It takes a lot of machine to handle a country this big. Fortunately, the Yukon comes equipped with a standard 255-horsepower Vortec 5700 V8 engine. In addition, the Yukon has up to 118 cu. ft. of cargo space and a towing capacity of up to 3175 kg. or 7000 lb.
   Brute force? Perhaps. But ample seating for up to six passengers and a long list of thoughtfully provided luxuries, guarantee that the Yukon stays an extremely civilized vehicle. All of which means, you won't ever have to leave anything – or anyone – behind.
   Discover the Yukon. Clearly, it's a piece of territory you'd be proud to call your own. For more information, visit our web site at www.gmcanada.com™ or call 1-800-GM-DRIVE.

www.gmcanada.com is a trademark of General Motors Corporation.

GMC

Yukon. 365 days a year.

GM says: "Yukon" has a uniquely Canadian connotation and implies that this vehicle can be safely used year-round in our climate. Attention to detail in the large, luxurious interior is a particular aspect that makes this product appealing to the Canadian consumer.
Courtesty of General Motors Canada.

Regional print media, outside of newspapers, include *Up-here: Life in Canada's North, Western Living, Atlantic Progress* and *Beautiful British Columbia.* Other examples can be found at the Web site for the Canadian Magazine Publishers Association (***www.cmpa.ca***).

   Cuisine and food preferences also have regional connections. Poutine is associated with Quebec (and is now exported to Paris);[113] salmon with British Columbia and the East Coast; beef with Alberta; Oka cheese with Quebec; bakeapple with Newfoundland; and so on. Regional differences have also been found in the way common foods are consumed in the various regions, as shown in Table 14–4.

THE CANADIAN IDENTITY

Many Canadians have dedicated the latter part of the twentieth century to protecting Canadian culture—not surprising for a relatively young country among the world's industrialized nations. In 1988 an Angus Reid poll found that the most potent symbol of national unity was Medicare. Other public institutions, like Petro-Canada and CN Rail, were among the list of other public institutions that represented Canadian culture. However, with the recent wave of privatization, these symbols are being dismantled one by one.[114]

   A 1995 poll showed that 75 percent of Quebecers and 93 percent of the rest of Canadians feel proud when they see the Canadian flag or hear the national anthem.[115] Following the Quebec referendum and various political platforms, debating the concept of what Canada is as a country seems to have stirred manifestations

TABLE 14-4 Regional Comparison of Food Habits

REGION	ATTITUDES	FOOD THEMES & FAVOURITE SWEETS & SNACKS	PANTRY PRODUCTS
Atlantic Canada	More laid-back about nutrition	Fewer meatless meals; plenty of hearty suppers (steak, corn, carrots); home-baked desserts, chocolate	Instant mashed potatoes, chocolate products, corn starch, icing, molasses, peanut butter
Quebec	Take food seriously; stay at table longer (50 min.); try new recipe for main dish at least once a week (creative); more nutrition-conscious	Potato chips; cookies	Soda crackers, melba toast, raisins, dried fruit
Ontario	Believe cooking is creative & they are excellent cooks	Ready-to-eat convenience in meal components	Macaroni & cheese, ready-to-eat foods, package mixes for squares & brownies, canned pasta
Prairies	Enjoy cooking, but fewer love to cook than in any other region	Convenience (speed); eat out to save time	Individual ready-made frozen entrées; quick & easy cold cuts; packaged cake mix, dessert topping mix, canned baked beans, canned pie filling
British Columbia	Simple wholesome approach; dislike after-meals clean-up & housework	Sweet between-meals snacks	Oatmeal, cocoa, honey, nuts, herbal teas

Source: Based on a study of 1600 Canadians sponsored by the Food and Consumer Products Manufacturers of Canada, *Chatelaine* (French & English publications) and *Modern Woman*, published in "The plate of the nation," *Chatelaine* (November 1997): 38–47.

of patriotism, interspersed with some feelings of unrest. Canada Day celebrations continue to draw participation from communities across the nation, for example, and interest in the Canadian flag and its meaning seem to be increasing. In his book *Ideas of the North: A Guide to Canadian Arts and Culture*, Tom Henighan draws attention to a now-critical mass of Canadian cultural activity.[116] Interestingly, in the 1991 census nearly 800 000 respondents (more than 500 000 in Ontario) identified their ethnic origin as "Canadian."[117]

The uniquely Canadian dimension of our geography is preserved by our National Parks (e.g., Kluane, Jasper, Grasslands, Riding Mountain, Georgian Bay, Forillion, Fundy, Cape Breton Highlands). In fact marketers find opportunities in the parks located in many cities, towns and villages throughout Canada. Parks are places connected to many situational purchases—for example, wedding photos, food for picnics, and equipment for photography and wildlife enthusiasts—and are a major point of interest to tourists.

An interesting and potentially useful way to define Canadians is through their value system. Michael Adams, in his book *Sex in the Snow*, suggests that there are a dozen social-value "tribes" in Canada that are defined partly by age groupings:

The Ocean and Easterly sleeping class are meant to appeal to train passengers travelling to Atlantic Canada.
Courtesy of Via Rail Canada and Publicité Martin Inc.

Consumer purchases in all provinces and territories of Canada are influenced by the changing seasons. Home Hardware, a Canadian company, has a private label for driveway sealer, a product that prevents and solves driveway problems associated with the severity of Canadian winters. Winter brings demand for such products and services as winter clothing, snow shovels, toboggans, Skidoos, firewood, winter tires, ski wear, windshield scrapers, skates, more electricity, snow removal services and *Hockey Night in Canada*.
Courtesty of Home Hardware/Saffer Group and Canadian Gardening.

Interest in the issue of Canadian unity has increased the purchase and display of the Canadian flag on homes and businesses throughout the country. Red and white are identified as Canadian colours, not only on Canada Day, but in a wide variety of consumer purchases—from uniforms for our Olympic athletes to label designs, such as the Maple Leaf brand.
Courtesy of Rosemary Polegato.

- *The Elders* (6.6 million): Rational Traditionalists, Extroverted Traditionalists or Cosmopolitan Modernists.

- *The Boomers* (8.8 million): Disengaged Darwinists, Autonomous Rebels, Anxious Communitarians or Connected Enthusiasts.

- *The Gen-Xers* (6.8 million): Aimless Dependents, Thrill-Seeking Materialists, Autonomous Postmaterialists, Social Hedonists and New Aquarians.

Since Adams describes the motivators, values, icons and words each group lives by, there is potential to extend the descriptions to include likely purchase behaviour. For example, since the New Aquarians seek experiences, value ecologism and believe everything is interconnected,[118] they likely have an interest in ecotourism, vacation packages, travel and international cuisine.

country of origin the country in which a consumer good was produced

A study of the influence of **country of origin** on consumer behaviour suggests that Canadians appear to have trouble identifying Canadian-made products. Labelling, such as "Think Canadian" and "Canada—Buy Into It," might be one way to serve consumers more effectively. Rather than focus just on patriotic appeals, however, highlighting the already positive perceptions about factors such as reliability, performance and service would enhance the reputation of Canadian-made products by fostering positive associations through classical conditioning mechanisms.[119] The EcoLogo is one example of a labelling program that has high recognition.

Defining Canadian consumer behaviour is often done by comparison with how Americans consume. The Campbell Soup Co. Ltd. in Canada, for example, did research in the late 1980s that showed that Canadians like to eat different foods for breakfast compared to Americans. Thus, in an effort to develop microwaveable frozen breakfast entrées, they concentrated on foods like blueberry pancakes, sausages and scrambled eggs.[120] However, less than a year after the launch of the entrées, Campbell's concluded that, unlike their American counterparts, Canadians

Decks and patios (usually in backyards) are Canadian icons sometimes overlooked. These are gathering places for friends and families, and are tied to some very specialized purchase behaviour (e.g., for barbecues, games, party supplies, maintenance tools and gardening supplies), as well as consumption areas for food, beverages and clothing. The cottage or bungalow provides a similar setting for Canadian consumers on a larger scale.
Courtesy of Rosemary Polegato.

do not like to start their day with a microwaved prefabricated meal.[121] Canadians have also been found to eat out less than Americans and to have 60 food items in stock, as opposed to 20 in households in the United States.[122]

Some Canadian food habits, based on a national study, include:

Breakfast
- 94 percent eat it on weekdays, almost always at home.
- One-half have the radio on, one-third have the TV on and one-quarter read the newspaper.

Lunch
- 33 percent are "brown baggers"; 20 percent buy lunch; 10 percent microwave leftovers.

Supper/Dinner
- Most popular time is 6 p.m.
- 78 percent have a family meal, taking an average of 45 minutes.
- 67 percent eat three component meals; 83 percent have meat; favourites are ground beef and boneless chicken.
- 7 percent of weekday suppers are packaged foods, such as pasta and sauce; 10 percent use store-bought complete meals; 4 percent use take-out.

Food Preparation and Shopping Habits
- Five main dishes are rotated regularly; a new recipe is tried once a month or less frequently.
- Average amount spent on food shopping per week is $90; 20 percent use coupons on an average shopping trip.
- Young singles shop on Monday; busiest times in the supermarket are Thursdays and Saturday afternoons.[123]

CANADIAN DIMENSIONS

There are many marketing opportunities built on the Canadian identity.

- Harry Rosen ran a very successful ad campaign under a tag line referring to the Harry Rosen clothing worn by various Canadian celebrities. One ad, for example, simply said, "What Stu Jackson [of the Vancouver Grizzlies] will be wearing tonight."

- Molson had a very successful campaign with nationalist (and humorous) overtones, aimed at Generation X beer drinkers. For the independent-minded GenXers, the Molson Canadian "I am" campaign represents the identity of the brand and its take on life.

- On the electronic front, sites like The Great Canadian Restaurant Survey (*www.restaurant.ca*) allow for dining preferences in terms of location (mainly in Toronto, Vancouver, Montreal and Quebec City), cuisine, price range, features (opening hours, parking and wheelchair access) and rating (of value and service).

- *Due South,* a television series starring Canadian Paul Gross as a member of the Royal Canadian Mounted Police, is now popular as an export to countries such as the United Kingdom.

- Zeller's describes itself as "Truly Canadian," and Canadian Tire's (*www.canadiantire.ca*) company name speaks for itself.

- Canadian authors include Peter Gzowski, host of CBC Radio's "Morningside" for 15 years, Margaret Atwood, Pierre Berton, Carol Shields and Mordecai Richler.

- Successful Canadian musicians include Joni Mitchell, Bryan Adams, Alanis Morissette, Celine Dion, Leonard Cohen, Bruce Cockburn, Anne Murray, kd lang and Deborah Cox, as well as numerous bands, such as Sloan, The Odds, The Tragically Hip, Blue Rodeo, Crash Test Dummies, Barenaked Ladies and Jale. Successful Canadian musicians for children include Raffi, Fred Penner, Eric Nagler, Judy & David, Martha Johnson, and Sharon, Lois & Bram.

- Mail order services for Canadiana include catalogues for the International Native Arts Festival, Canadian Geographic, Jacaranda Tree, Images of Canada, and Decoratives & Tools for Canadian Gardeners, as well as Craft Connoisseur: A Catalogue of Fine Canadian Crafts.

- "For Better or For Worse," by cartoonist Lynn Johnston, depicts the lifestyle of Canadian families and is enjoyed by Canadians and fans in other countries.[124]

Satire, particularly of a political nature, has been called a national sport.[125] "This Hour Has 22 Minutes" and "Royal Canadian Air Farce" attract audiences of more than a million. "Double Exposure" was a popular CBC radio show. Comedy troupes, such as CODCO and Kids in the Hall, continue to develop and evolve. Toronto's Second City and Yuk Yuk's encourage Canadian comedy, and Montreal's Just for Laughs Festival is also a success. Canadian comedians and musicians are now internationally established enough to go to a city like Los Angeles and raise money for The David Suzuki Foundation.[126]

Sometimes Canadian symbols are more apparent within the context of another culture. Canadian fur coats, for example, are sold in Russia, China, South Korea, Japan and the United States.[127] In 1993 Canada's oldest independent brewery, Moosehead, became the first Canadian beer to be mass-distributed through the Scandinavian government-controlled liquor board. The Swedish campaign was successfully based on a road sign with the silhouette of a moose and traditional Canadian images of the Canadian Rockies: majestic mountains, crystal-clear lakes and deep blue skies. Like Canada, Sweden has the wilderness, the moose and the same core values.[128] (Incidentally, "moose" is the most common word in Canadian place names.)

Although the small size of the Canadian market creates challenges for publishers and other media, various target markets can be reached. Men's magazines include *Menz* and *harry*; French magazines include *L'expresse, Les affaires*, and *L'actualité*; women's magazines include *Chatelaine* (English & French), *Modern Woman, Canadian Living, Flare* and *Elm Street*; business magazines include *Maclean's, The Financial Post Magazine, Profit: The Magazine for Canadian Entrepreneurs, Canadian Business* and *Report on Business Magazine*; children's magazines include *Chickadee* and *Owl* (and its French version, *Hibou*); lifestyle and special interest magazines include *Equinox, Harrowsmith, Country Life, shift, Canadian Workshop, Canadian House & Home, Santé, Canadian Gardening* and *Canadian Wildlife*. (See the Web site for the Canadian Magazine Publishers Association—*www.cmpa.ca*—for a complete list.) CBC radio and television and Radio-Canada provide national coverage in the adult and family market, while YTV is the only national youth channel.

This ad captures the spirit of Canadian design and materials.
Courtesy of Harvest House and Robertson-Christoff Imaging Inc.

CANADIAN DIMENSIONS

The ingenuity of Canadian manufacturers helps them to serve customers in competitive markets both at home and abroad.

• Rocky Mountain Bicycle Co. is Canada's first mountain-bike company. Founder Grayson Bain thinks that being Canadian is an advantage because the products are perceived as rugged and reliable. However, producing in Delta, BC, has cost disadvantages due to the distance from material sources in Asia and the United States. A large R & D department and work with universities is helping to overcome these disadvantages. Producing 16 000 bikes a year, mostly for male buyers aged 15 to 50, brought in sales of $16 million in 1996 and provided jobs for about 100 people.[129]

• Waldale Manufacturing Ltd. in Amherst, Nova Scotia, makes about 2 million licence plates per year for more than a dozen jurisdictions, including Fiji, Mississippi, Nova Scotia, Quebec and Tahiti. Coming up with unique designs is the biggest challenge for Blake Daley, king of Canada's private licence-plate makers.[130]

CHAPTER SUMMARY

• Consumers identify with many groups that share common characteristics and identities. These large groups that exist within a society are subcultures, and membership in them often gives marketers clues about individuals' consumption decisions. A large component of a person's identity is often determined by his or her ethnic origins and regional roots. The three largest ethnic subcultures are English, French and Chinese Canadians, but consumers with many diverse backgrounds are beginning to be considered by marketers as well.

• Segmenting consumers by their ethnicity can be effective, but care must be taken not to rely on inaccurate (and sometimes offensive) ethnic stereotypes.

• While the impact of religious identification on consumer behaviour is not clear, some differences among religious subcultures do emerge. In particular, cultural characteristics of Protestants, Catholics and Jews result in varied preferences for leisure activities and orientations towards consumption. Some of these factors are closely related to social class. White Anglo-Saxon Protestants (WASPs), in particular, have played a dominant role in the formation of Canadian cultural values largely due to their cultural emphasis on achievement and their early domination of the Canadian power structure. Marketing programs based on regional subcultures and the Canadian identity are beginning to emerge.

• Both French Canadians and Chinese Canadians tend to be extremely family-oriented, and they are receptive to advertising that understands their heritage and reinforces traditional family values.

• Chinese Canadians are beginning to be actively courted by marketers. The size of this group is increasing rapidly, and in the coming years they will dominate some major markets.

- Key issues for reaching the Asian market are consumers' degree of acculturation into mainstream Canadian society and the recognition of important cultural differences among Asian subgroups.

Acculturation agents p. 481

Consumer acculturation p. 479

Country of origin p. 488

De-ethnicitization p. 467

Ethnic subculture p. 465

Progressive learning model p. 480

Subculture p. 463

CONSUMER BEHAVIOUR CHALLENGE

1. R.J. Reynolds's controversial plan to test-market a cigarette to black consumers raises numerous ethical issues about segmenting subcultures. As one observer noted, "The irony is that if R.J. Reynolds made shoes or shirts and specifically marketed to blacks, they would probably be regarded as progressive and socially positive."[131] Does a company have the right to exploit a subculture's special characteristics, especially in order to increase sales of a harmful product like cigarettes? What about the argument that successful businesses design products to meet the needs and tastes of their target markets? For example, Maybelline developed a make-up line specifically for black women, yet this did not seem to bother anyone. What do you think?

2. The chapter notes that products can function as socialization agents for ethnic groups. What examples can you find that serve this important function? What special problems do these create for marketers?

3. Describe the progressive learning model, and discuss why this phenomenon is important when marketing to subcultures.

4. How do regional and national identification affect consumer behaviour?

5. Can you locate any current examples of marketing stimuli that depend upon an ethnic stereotype to communicate a message? How effective are these appeals?

6. To understand the power of ethnic stereotypes, conduct your own poll. For a set of ethnic groups, ask people to anonymously provide, using the technique of free association, attributes (including personality traits and products) most likely to characterize each group. How much agreement do you obtain among people? Compare the associations for an ethnic group held by actual members of that group to those of non-members.

7. What are the anticipated effects of immigration patterns in the next decade on marketing activities in Canada?

8. Locate one or more consumers (perhaps family members) who have immigrated from their country of origin. Interview them about how they adapted to their host culture. In particular, what changes did they make in their consumption practices over time?

CBC VIDEO VIGNETTES

Concepts at Work for Real Estate Agents and Developers

Marketers cannot ignore the diversity of subcultures that are reshaping the mainstream culture of Canada. Subcultures offer many opportunities to marketers. Subcultures are not only distinct markets in themselves, but they also influence the marketing activities in the larger culture. To wait for a high degree of assimilation to occur is not only ethnocentric but foolhardy when new citizens are willing to spend their money to set up a new life in Canada.

The Asian subculture is one of the fastest-growing in Canada, especially in urban centres. A case in point is the Asian housing market in Vancouver. Asians are typically hard-working and many have above-average incomes. To capture their demand for housing, marketers need to understand how the principles of Feng Shui apply to house design, so that houses can be designed appropriately for new construction, renovation and resale.

Will a house with a central fireplace and a large tree out front be appealing to these house buyers? To answer this question you need to understand the philosophy of Feng Shui and its manifestations in house design.

QUESTIONS

1. Why is an understanding of ethnic subcultures of importance to Canadian marketers?

2. What are the processes of adaptation for consumers belonging to subcultures?

3. Why is the Asian subculture of particular importance in the Vancouver housing market?

4. Describe what you know about Feng Shui?

Video Resource: "Feng Shui," *Venture* #561 (October 8, 1995).

NOTES

1. See Frederik Barth, *Ethnic Groups and Boundaries: The Social Organization of Culture Difference* (London: Allen and Unwin, 1969); Michel Laroche et al., "An Examination of Ethnicity Measures: Convergent Validity and Cross-Cultural Equivalence," in *Advances in Consumer Research 18*, eds. Rebecca H. Holman and Michael R. Solomon (Provo, UT: Association for Consumer Research, 1991), pp. 150–57; Melanie Wallendorf and Michael Reilly, "Ethnic Migration, Assimilation, and Consumption," *Journal of Consumer Research* 10 (December 1983): 292–302; Milton J. Yinger, "Ethnicity," *Annual Review of Sociology* 11 (1985): 151–80.

2. Michael Hui et al., "Psychometric Properties of an Index Measure of Ethnicity in a Bicultural Environment," *Canadian Journal of Administrative Sciences* 14, 1 (March 1997):14–27. See also Anne Lavack, "Predictive Validity of Ethnic Identification Measures: An Illustration of the French–English Classification Dilemma in Canada," *Journal of the Academy of Marketing Science* 14, 2 (Summer 1986): 37–42.

3. Hui et al., "Psychometric Properties of an Index Measure of Ethnicity in a Bicultural Environment."

4. Jennifer Lynn, "Approaching diversity," *Marketing Magazine* (July 3/10, 1995): 11.

5. "TV nations: why ethnic broadcasters are booming," *Financial Post Daily* 8, 164 (November 17, 1995): 7.

6. Eve Lazarus, "Chinese calling cards dial up growing market," *Marketing Magazine* (October 21, 1996): 4.

7. Thomas McCarroll, "It's a Mass Market No More," *Time* (Fall 1993): 80–81.

8. "The ethnic market ... opportunities in the fastest growing segment," *Canadian Grocer* 109, 6 (June 1995): 5.

9. Rohit Desphandé and Douglas M. Stayman, "A Tale of Two Cities: Distinctiveness Theory and Advertising Effectiveness," *Journal of Marketing Research* 31 (February 1994): 57–64.

10. James Pollock, "Racial Minorities Become Visible," *Marketing Magazine* (March 3, 1997): 13.

11. Thomas T. Semon, "Language influences attitudes," *Marketing News* (April 14, 1997): 12.

12. Steve Rabin, "How to Sell Across Cultures," *American Demographics* (March 1994): 56–57.

13. James Pollock, "Paper tigers," *Marketing Magazine* (July 4/11, 1994): 13–14.

14. Michael McCullough, "BC Hydro Becomes Multilingual," *Marketing Magazine* (July 15, 1996): 13.

15. "Trading faces: the Chinese consumer: a marketer's challenge," *BC Business Magazine* 21, 11 (November 1993): 31.

16. "Maclean's, Toronto Life tap Chinese market," *Financial Post Daily* 8, 168 (November 24, 1995): C12.

17. "Marketers seek ways to lure ethnic consumers (Canadian Advertising Foundation study)," *Canadian Press Newswire* (September 25, 1995), accessed on WinSPIRS UNB (October 24, 1997).

18. Stuart J. McKelvie and Robert M. MacGregor, "Effects of Interactive Pictures and Ethnicity on Recall of Brand Names," *Canadian Journal of Administrative Sciences* 13, 1 (1996): 33–45.

19. "Consumer study dispels myths about ethnic market," *Canadian Press Newswire* (July 22, 1997), accessed on WinSPIRS UNB (October 24, 1997).

20. Karyn D. Collins, "Culture Clash," *Asbury Park Press* (October 16, 1994): D1 (2 pp.).

21. Eils Lotozo, "The Jalapeño Bagel and Other Artifacts," *New York Times* (June 26, 1990): C1.

22. Ann Brocklehurst, "Salad Days for Trendy Olive Oil," *Maclean's* (February 19, 1996): 58.

23. Statistics Canada cat. no. 93-315 (1996).

24. Statistics Canada cat. no. 93-333 (1996).

25. Statistics Canada cat. no. 93-315 (1996).

26. "Bankers' Indian Sunrise," *Marketing Magazine* (July 15, 1996): 13.

27. Stephen Strauss, "Native languages get with the program," *Globe and Mail* (October 16, 1997): A2.

28. "Bankers' Indian Sunrise."

29. Wayne McVey, Jr., and Warren E. Kalbech, *Canadian Population* (Toronto: Nelson Canada, 1995), pp. 47–48.

30. "Trading faces: the Chinese consumer: a marketer's challenge."

31. Pollock, "Paper tigers."

32. "The ethnic market … opportunities in the fastest growing segment."

33. Wilbur Zelinsky, "You Are Where You Eat," *American Demographics* (July 1987): 6; Cacilie Rohwedder, "Ethnic Food Whets Appetites in Europe, Enticing Producers to Add Foreign Fare," *Wall Street Journal* (November 1, 1993): B5E.

34. James Pollock, "The economics of growing communities," *Marketing Magazine* (July 3/10, 1995): 11.

35. Michael McCullough, "Ethnic Targeting Winners," *Marketing Magazine* (July 15, 1996): 13.

36. David K. Foot (with Daniel Stoffman), *Boom, Bust & Echo: How to Profit from the Coming Demographic Shift* (Toronto: Macfarlane Walter & Ross, 1996).

37. "The ethnic market … opportunities in the fastest growing segment."

38. *Canada's Families: They Count* (Ottawa: The Vanier Institute for the Family, 1996).

39. McVey, Jr., and Kalbech, *Canadian Population*, p. 348.

40. Rae Corelli, "How very different we are," *Maclean's* (November 4, 1996): 36–40.

41. Elizabeth C. Hirschman, "Religious Affiliation and Consumption Processes: An Initial Paradigm," *Research in Marketing* (Greenwich, CT: JAI Press, 1983), pp. 131–70.

42. See, for example, Nejet Delener, "The Effects of Religious Factors on Perceived Risk in Durable Goods Purchase Decisions," *Journal of Consumer Marketing* 7 (Summer 1990): 27–38.

43. Hirschman, "Religious Affiliation and Consumption Processes."

44. Malcolm C. Smith and Kristina D. Frankenberger, "The Effects of Religiosity on Selected Aspects of Consumer Behavior," *Marketing* (proceedings of the Administrative Sciences Association of Canada) 12, 6 (1991): 274–83.

45. Peter Schrag, *The Decline of the Wasp* (New York: Simon & Schuster, 1971), p. 14.

46. Elizabeth C. Hirschman, "Upper-Class WASPs as Consumers: A Humanist Inquiry," in *Research in Consumer Behavior*, eds. Jagdish N. Sheth and Elizabeth C. Hirschman (Greenwich, CT: JAI Press, 1988), pp. 115–48.

47. *Selected ethnic origins, Canada, the provinces and territories*, Statistics Canada cat. no. 93-315 (1991).

48. Isadore Barmash, "The Drive to Promote Kosher Food," *New York Times* (April 11, 1989): D25.

49. Joan Delaney, "New Kosher Products, from Tacos to Tofu," *New York Times* (December 31, 1989): F13.

50. "Strutting his stuff," *Canadian Grocer* 108, 6 (June 1994): 10–15; "Marketers warming to the Caribana festival," *Marketing Magazine* (June 30, 1997): 1; "Trading faces: the Chinese consumer: a marketer's challenge"; "Christmas in any language, but English," *Canadian Press Newswire* (December 5, 1995), accessed on WinSPIRS UNB (October 24, 1997); "Battle lines drawn as firms mobilize for grocery wars," *Financial Post Daily* (August 26, 1997): 25; "Marketers seek ways to lure ethnic consumers (Canadian Advertising Foundation study)."

51. Kim Foltz, "Mattel's Shift on Barbie Ads," *New York Times* (July 19, 1990): D17; Lora Sharpe, "Dolls in All the Colors of a Child's Dream," *Boston Globe* (February 22, 1991): 42; Barbara Brotman, "Today's Dolls Have Ethnicity That's More Than Skin Deep," *Asbury Park Press* (November 14, 1993): D6.

52. "Report on Quebec (Uncertainties have marketers treading warily)," *Marketing Magazine* 101, 11 (March 18, 1996): 9–11.

53. For an outstanding discussion of these structural approaches and various other aspects of the con-

sumer behaviour of French Canadians, see Gurprit S. Kindra, Michel Laroche and Thomas E. Muller, *Consumer Behaviour: The Canadian Perspective* (Toronto: Nelson Canada, 1994), pp. 345–51.

54. Jean-Pierre Lacroix, "As the 21st century unfolds: a look at the many influences which will impact how marketers communicate to future consumers," *Canadian Packaging* 50, 4 (April 1997): 49–50.

55. Hui et al., "Psychometric Properties of an Index Measure of Ethnicity in a Bicultural Environment."

56. Louise Gagnon, "Same Butter, Different Sell," *Marketing Magazine* (June 30, 1997): 11, 17.

57. Charles M. Schaninger, Jacques C. Bourgeois and W. Christian Buss, "French-English Canadian Subcultural Consumption Differences," *Journal of Marketing* (Spring 1985): 85–92.

58. François Vary, "Getting down to details with PMB'94," *Marketing Magazine* (February 20, 1995): 14.

59. Sylvain Gauthier, "An untapped market to bank on," *Marketing Magazine* (February 20, 1995): 15.

60. "Pushing the button: Results of a special Léger & Léger survey", *Marketing Magazine* (February 20, 1995): 17.

61. François Vary, "Sizing up 55-plus," *Marketing Magazine* (October 2, 1995): 13–14.

62. Jean-Marc Léger, "Montreal as a Distinct Society," *Marketing Magazine* (February 17, 1997): 11.

63. "Hostess gives Quebec its own Doritos flavors," *Marketing Magazine* (July 4/11, 1994): 1.

64. Brian Dunn, "IGA's online recipe," *Marketing Magazine* (May 5, 1997): 10–11.

65. "Report on Quebec (Uncertainties have marketers treading warily)," *Marketing Magazine* 101, 11 (March 18, 1996): 9–11.

66. Nicole Nolan, "Memo to Sheila Copps: forget those flags. The slickest new nationalism is in the latest wave of beer ads," *This Magazine* 30, 3 (November/December 1996): 22–25.

67. Douglas Faulkner, "The brand builder: how grand-dad's little black book made John Sleeman's microbrewery a macro player in the premium beer market," *Canadian Packaging* 50, 3 (March 1997): 15–16.

68. Louise Gagnon, "Indigenous ads have bigger bang in Quebec," *Marketing Magazine* (September 29, 1997).

69. "The right images for Quebec," *Marketing Magazine* (September 19, 1994): 12.

70. "Future Shop hires Martin for Quebec," *Marketing Magazine* (September 15, 1997): 1.

71. Statistics Canada cat. no. 93-315 (1996).

72. Michael McCullough, "The Second Chinese Wave," *BC Business Magazine* 25, 7 (July 1997): 40–41.

73. "Maclean's, Toronto Life tap Chinese market."

74. "Trading faces: the Chinese consumer: a marketer's challenge."

75. McCullough, "The Second Chinese Wave."

76. Donald Dougherty, "The Orient Express," *Marketer* (July/August 1990): 14; Cyndee Miller, "Hot Asian-American Market Not Starting Much of a Fire Yet," *Marketing News* (January 21, 1991): 12.

77. Statistics Canada cat. no. 93-315 (1996).

78. McCullough, "Ethnic Targeting Winners."

79. "Trading faces: the Chinese consumer: a marketer's challenge."

80. Ibid.

81. "Translating sport interest into gate receipts," *Financial Post Daily* 9, 151 (October 24, 1996): 26.

82. Marianne Paskowski, "Trailblazing in Asian America," *Marketing and Media Decisions* (October 1986): 75–80.

83. Ellen Schultz, "Asians in the States," *Madison Avenue* (October 1985): 78.

84. Dougherty, "The Orient Express."

85. Marty Westerman, "Fare East: Targeting the Asian-American Market," *Prepared Foods* (January 1989): 48–51.

86. "A Window on the Fast-Growing Audience of Asian-Americans," *New York Times* (March 22, 1993): D5; Elizabeth Seay, "Two English-Speaking Magazines Target Affluent Asian-Americans," *Wall Street Journal* (October 1, 1993): B5B.

87. Jeanne Whalen, "Sears Targets Asians: Retailer Names Agency to Attract Fast-Growing Segment," *Advertising Age* (October 10, 1994): 1 (2 pp.).

88. "Radio Network Targets Asian-Americans," *Marketing News* (August 29, 1994): 46.

89. Cf. Lisa Peñaloza, "Atravesando Fronteras/Border Crossings: A Critical Ethnographic Exploration of the Consumer Acculturation of Mexican Immigrants," *Journal of Consumer Research* 21, 1 (June 1994): 32–54.

90. Rosanna W.S. Mau, "The Impact of Acculturation on Decision Making: The Case of Hong Kong Immigrants in Vancouver," unpublished Master of Business Administration thesis, Simon Fraser University, 1997.

91. Statistics Canada cat. no. 93-316 (1996).

92. Melanie Wallendorf and Michael D. Reilly, "Ethnic Migration, Assimilation, and Consumption," *Journal of Consumer Research* 10 (December 1983): 292–302.

93. Eve Lazarus, "Supermarket chain caters to Asian shoppers," *Marketing Magazine* (February 24, 1997): 3; Pollock, "Racial Minorities Become Visible"; "Trading faces: the Chinese consumer: a marketer's challenge"; "Consumer study dispels myths about ethnic market"; Eve Lazarus, "The Bay 'micro-marketing' to Asians," *Marketing Magazine* (October 14, 1996): 5.

94. Ronald J. Faber, Thomas C. O'Guinn and John A. McCarty, "Ethnicity, Acculturation and the Importance of Product Attributes," *Psychology & Marketing* 4 (Summer 1987): 121–34; Humberto Valencia,

"Developing an Index to Measure Hispanicness," in *Advances in Consumer Research 12*, eds. Elizabeth C. Hirschman and Morris B. Holbrook (Provo, UT: Association for Consumer Research, 1985), pp. 118–21.

95. Rohit Deshpande, Wayne D. Hoyer and Naveen Donthu, "The Intensity of Ethnic Affiliation: A Study of the Sociology of Hispanic Consumption," *Journal of Consumer Research* 13 (September 1986): 214–20.

96. Michael McCullough, "The Second Chinese Wave."

97. Ibid.

98. Ibid.

99. Ibid.

100. Brian D. Johnson, "A bold and blissful leap of faith," *Maclean's* (July 31, 1995): 42–43.

101. Julie Wang-Morris, "Bridging the Gap," *Marketing Magazine* (March 3, 1997): 12.

102. Mau, "The Impact of Acculturation on Decision Making."

103. Wei-Na Lee and David Tse, "Becoming Canadian: Understanding How Hong Kong Immigrants Change Their Consumption," *Pacific Affairs* 67 (1994): 70–95.

104. McCullough, "The Second Chinese Wave."

105. Ibid.

106. "Empires of the North," *Profit: The Magazine for Canadian Entrepreneurs* 12, 1 (Spring 1993): 42–46.

107. Wayne Parrish, "NADbank: The Barometer of Change," *Marketing Magazine* (October 6, 1997): S3–S14.

108. "A Marketing profile of cruise ship vacationers," *Marketing Magazine* (February 20, 1995): 22.

109. Parrish, "NADbank."

110. "Battle lines drawn as firms mobilize for grocery wars," *Financial Post Daily* (August 26, 1997): 25.

111. Donalee Moulton, "East Coast Culture Ain't Fiddlin' Around," *Marketing Magazine* (August 11, 1997): 14–15.

112. "Kokanee spot revives search for Sasquatch," *Marketing Magazine* (August 18/25, 1997): 1.

113. "Putting poutine on the menu—in Paris," *Maclean's* (December 4, 1995): 13.

114. For an interesting discussion of these points, see Angus Reid, *Shakedown: How the New Economy Is Changing Our Lives* (Toronto: Doubleday Canada, 1996), pp. 36–41.

115. Anthony Wilson-Smith, "A Quiet Passion," *Maclean's* (July 1, 1996): 8–12.

116. Bronwyn Drainie, "Canadian culture viewed from the mountain top," *Globe and Mail* (August 16, 1997): D14.

117. *Selected ethnic origins, Canada, the provinces and territories, 1991*, accessed from Statistics Canada Web site at www.statcan.ca/english/Pgdb/People/Population/demo28a.htm.

118. Michael Adams, "The Demise of Demography," *Globe and Mail* (January 18, 1997): D5.

119. Nicolas Papadopoulos, Louise Heslop and Gary Bamossy, "An International Comparative Analysis of Consumer Attitudes Toward Canada and Canadian Products," *Canadian Journal of Administrative Sciences* 11, 3 (1994): 224–39.

120. Pat Davies, "The Soul of a New Instant Breakfast," *Report on Business Magazine* (September 1988): 78–92.

121. "Breakfast Blues," *Report on Business Magazine* (December 1989):109.

122. Donalee Moulton, "Canadians eating out more often," *Marketing Magazine* (May 12, 1997): 4.

123. Based on a study of 1600 Canadians sponsored by the Food and Consumer Products Manufacturers of Canada, *Chatelaine* (French & English publications), and *Modern Woman*, published in "The plate of the nation," *Chatelaine* (November 1997): 38–47.

124. Susan Kim-Kirkland, "Looking Good: Harry Rosen's monster-hit ad campaign," *Marketing Magazine* (July 21/28, 1997): 21; Nolan, "Memo to Sheila Copps"; Edward Caffyn, "Just Try to Sell to Me," *Marketing Magazine* (August 4, 1997): 13–14; "NetWatch: Food Glorious Food," *Financial Post Magazine* (September 1997): 112; "Sharing the limelight," *Maclean's* (March 18, 1996): 71.

125. Brian D. Johnson, "22 Minutes for High Schticking," *Maclean's* (February 26, 1996): 46–51; Diane Turbide, "The Air Farce Is Flying High," *Maclean's* (February 26, 1996): 52–53.

126. "Raising the Flag in L.A.," *Maclean's* (January 29, 1996): 40.

127. Robert Thompson, "Fur Fights Back," *Marketing Magazine* (September 29, 1997): 16–17.

128. Donalee Moulton, "Nova Scotia brewers find international success," *Marketing Magazine* (September 26, 1994): 8.

129. Edward Hay, "Off Road Warrior," *Canadian Business* (July 1997): 64.

130. Chris Reardon, "Hot plates," *Canadian Business* (October 1996): 140.

131. "A Cigarette Campaign Under Fire," *New York Times* (January 12, 1990): D1.

It's the end of vacation, and Morris is looking forward to going back to university. It's been a tough summer. He had trouble finding a job and was out of touch with his friends. With so much time on his hands, just hanging around, he and his mother aren't getting along. As usual, Morris is plopped on the couch eating Mexitas and watching "Friends," when his mother walks in, grabs the remote and switches the channel to CBC—yet another retrospective about student protests in the 1970s. When Morris protests, she has the nerve to say, "Keep your cool. You might actually learn something about what it was like to be in university when it really meant something."

That's when Morris loses it. He's tired of hearing about the "good old days." Besides, most of his mom's ex-hippie friends now work for the very corporations they used to protest about. Who are they to preach to him about doing something meaningful with his life? Since they've screwed up the economy so much, he'll be lucky to get a job as a bicycle messenger when he gets his degree next year.

In disgust, Morris storms into his room, puts a Skinny Puppy disc into his Discman and pulls the covers up over his head. So much for constructive use of time. What's the difference, anyway? Everyone will probably be dead from the "greenhouse effect" by the time he graduates ...

LONGEVITY MAGAZINE

A PRACTICAL GUIDE TO THE ART AND SCIENCE OF STAYING YOUNG

15

Age
Subcultures

AGE AND CONSUMER IDENTITY

The era in which a consumer is born creates for that person a cultural bond with others born during the same time period. As we grow older, our needs and preferences change, often in unison with others who are close to our own age. For this reason a consumer's age exerts a significant influence on his or her identity. All things being equal, we are more likely to have things in common with others of our own age than not.

Marketers often target products and services to one or more specific age groups. They recognize that the same offering will probably not appeal to people of different ages, so they try to craft messages with which people of a certain age will identify and place these messages in media that will reach members of this group. In addition, the buying power of different age groups shifts with the sands of time. Consumers aged 35 to 55 will increase their market dominance between now and the beginning of the next century.

In this chapter we'll explore some of the important characteristics of several age groups, and consider how marketing strategies must change when appealing to diverse age subcultures. First, though, let's take a step back and consider how best to divide people up into age subcultures.

This ad captures both the differences and the connections between generations.
Courtesy of Merck-Frosst Canada Inc.

Age Cohorts: "My Generation"

age cohort a group of consumers of the same approximate age who have undergone similar experiences

An **age cohort** consists of people of similar ages who have undergone similar experiences. An age cohort shares many common memories about cultural heroes (e.g., Mary Pickford versus Sonia Smits, or Paul Anka versus Corey Hart), important historical events (e.g., World War II versus implementation of the War Measures Act versus the Quebec referendum of 1996) and so on. Although there is no universally accepted way to divide people up into age cohorts, each of us seems to have a very good idea of what we mean when we refer to "my generation." Table 15–1 presents one of the most widely accepted schemes for defining generations in Canada.

Marketers often target products and services to one or more specific age cohorts. They recognize that the same offering will probably not appeal to people of different ages, nor will the language and images they use to reach them. In some cases separate campaigns are developed to attract consumers of different ages. The Manufacturers Life Insurance Company, for example, ran one ad with the caption, "Am I too young for life insurance?" and another with the caption, "Will I outlive my retirement savings?"[1]

The Appeal of Nostalgia

Because consumers within an age group confront crucial life changes at roughly the same time, the values and symbolism used to appeal to them can evoke powerful feelings of nostalgia (see Chapter 3). Adults over 30 are particularly susceptible to

TABLE 15–1 A Guide to Age Subcultures

SUBCULTURE	BIRTH DATE	PROPORTION OF POPULATION	COMMENTS
Most senior generation	Before 1920	4%	Most are female; major concerns about housing and health care. However, better off than preceding generation; little peer-group competition
Roaring Twenties generation	1920–1929	7%	Came of age during the Depression; many fought in WWII; are frugal
Depression generation	1930–1939	8%	Moved from hard economic conditions as children to prosperous post-war years in adulthood
War babies (WWII)	1940–1946	7%	Are worst-defined generation; usually described in terms of those that followed or preceded
Baby boomers	1947–1966	33%	Are largest generation; also known as the Hippies or Sixties generation. Generation X is a subset, born between 1960 and 1966
Baby busters	1967–1979	18%	Often described as cynical about their futures; also known as Generation X
Baby boom echo	1980–1995	23%	Primarily children of baby boomers; called the echo because births began to rise in 1980 and are gradually decreasing

Source: Adapted from David K. Foot (with Daniel Stoffman), *Boom, Bust & Echo: How to Profit from the Coming Demographic Shift* (Toronto: Macfarlane Walter & Ross, 1996), pp. 13–25; and Diane Crispell, "Where Generations Divide: A Guide," *American Demographics* (May 1993): 9–10.

MARKETING OPPORTUNITY

A reunion is an event based on a shared age cohort. People who were not necessarily fond of each other in high school or university nonetheless celebrate the common experience of having been together at the same time and place. In addition to the boon this nostalgia provides to caterers and professional reunion organizers, some marketers realize that the people who attend reunions often represent a valuable customer base. They are self-selected to be fairly successful, since the "failures" tend not to show up! Some companies are now using reunion-goers to test new products, and travel-related businesses interview attendees about their trips or provide special promotional packages for the returning consumers.[2]

this phenomenon.[3] However, young people as well as old are influenced by appeals to their past. In fact, recent research evidence indicates that some people apparently are more disposed to be nostalgic than others, regardless of age. A scale that has

TABLE 15–2 The Nostalgia Scale

SCALE ITEMS

- They don't make 'em like they used to.
- Things used to be better in the good old days.
- Products are getting shoddier and shoddier.
- Technological change will ensure a brighter future (reverse-coded).
- History involves a steady improvement in human welfare (reverse-coded).
- We are experiencing a decline in the quality of life.
- Steady growth in GNP has brought increased human happiness (reverse-coded).
- Modern business constantly builds a better tomorrow (reverse-coded).

Note: Items are presented on a nine-point scale ranging from strong disagreement (1) to strong agreement (9), and responses are summed.

Source: Morris B. Holbrook and Robert M. Schindler, "Age, Sex, and Attitude Toward the Past as Predicters of Consumers' Aesthetic Tastes for Cultural Products," *Journal of Marketing Research* 31 (August 1994): 416. Reprinted by permission of the American Marketing Assn.

been developed to measure the impact of nostalgia on individual consumers appears in Table 15–2.

Products evoke shared memories. As noted in Chapter 3, product sales can be dramatically affected by linking brands to vivid memories and experiences, especially for items that are associated with childhood or adolescence.[4] Marketers in a wide variety of industries are using several approaches to capitalize on people's fond memories of the past. Some are marketing milestones, such as the Canada Post stamp (A Bike Story) which immortalizes Canadian Tire's 75th anniversary. An entire company was revived to remarket Lola Icebergs, and there have also been successful Canadian revival campaigns for products such as Pixy Stix, Bits & Bites and Macintosh's Creamy Toffee (which is softer on baby boomers' aging dental work!). Interestingly, even push-powered lawnmowers are increasing in sales due to their appeal to baby boomers' nostalgia for upscale simplicity.[5]

While this strategy can be overdone, it is very appealing to marketers. For one thing it is virtually risk free—that is, it reminds viewers of a product's long history, anchors the item in a country's cultural history and is widely recognized by many consumers. Since awareness of the product is already high, the company does not have to work so hard to create attention and get the perceiver to think about the ad.[6]

THE TEEN MARKET: IT TOTALLY RULES

As anyone who has been there knows, the process of puberty and adolescence can be both the best of times and the worst of times. Many exciting changes happen as individuals leave the role of child and prepare to assume the role of adult. These changes create a lot of uncertainty about the self; the need to belong and to find one's unique identity as a person is paramount. At this age, choices of activities, friends and "looks" are often crucial to social acceptance. Teens actively search for cues from their peers and from advertising for the "right" way to look and behave.

This ad appeals to baby boomers' memories of childhood. Peanut butter and jam sandwiches remain a favourite among Canadian children.
Copyright 1997 Best Foods Canada Inc., used with permission.

Advertising geared to teens is typically action-oriented and depicts a group of "in" teens using the product. Teens use products to express their identities, to explore the world and their new-found freedoms in it, and also to rebel against the authority of their parents and other socializing agents.

GM says: General Motors of Canada (*www.gmcanada.com*) fosters trust, confidence and family values in its Chevrolet vehicles. Safety is a key focus. Parents will be reassured to know when their children ask for the keys, if they are Lumina keys, they will have the security of a total safety system.
Courtesy of General Motors Canada and Richard Piction Photography.

MULTICULTURAL DIMENSIONS

Japanese teens are big fans of global music and popular culture, and they're particularly fond of acquiring products associated with the American lifestyle. They love American fashions, particularly *Amekaji* (American casual). The California surfer look is also popular. In fact the University of California at Los Angeles sells about $16 million (US) worth of clothing with the UCLA logo to the Japanese each year. Surfer jackets and boards also sell well, as do skateboards and sailboards.[7] Japanese teenagers cruise down the main streets of Tokyo with surfboards on the roofs of their cars, even though they are not near the ocean. Like their Western peers, some of the favourite foods of Japanese teens are hamburgers, french fries and ice cream.[8] Some of the current hot items in Japan reflect a growing desire (as in the United States) for casual fashion and value. Hot sellers include L.L. Bean, J. Crew and Levi Strauss.[9]

And if the items are old, so much the better. Japanese teenagers especially love vintage American products. They are paying up to US$1 000 for a pair of worn-out Nike, Adidas or Converse sneakers—the more grimy and beat-up the better! Other big sellers are 40-year-old blue jeans, which can also fetch up to US$1 000 a pair, as well as a relative bargain, discarded T-shirts that go for "only" US$20. Why the fuss? Perhaps because Japanese society emphasizes order and discipline, this is one way of rebelling. As one 14-year-old explained when asked why she coveted a pair of scuffed-up sneakers, "Maybe because they are dirty. People think that's cool."[10]

Teen Values and Conflicts

Canadian teenagers spend about $6 billion annually, so naturally marketers are very interested in appealing to them. About one in ten Canadians (2.7 million) are aged 13 to 19. By 2010 there will be about 3.1 million teenagers. Some of their money comes from their parents as allowances and gifts; some is remuneration for household or neighbourhood chores. About one-third of high-schoolers also have part-time jobs.[11]

Most of teens' money is discretionary income. Creative Research International found that the average Canadian teen spends between $39 and $55 of his or her own money each week on snack food, entertainment, music and clothing. In addition, 12 percent of young teens and 27 percent of older teens have access to a credit card.[12]

Teenagers in every culture grapple with fundamental developmental issues as they make the transition from child to adult. According to research by the Saatchi & Saatchi advertising agency, there are four themes of conflict that are common to all teens:

1. *Autonomy versus belonging.* Teens need to acquire independence, so they try to break away from their families. On the other hand, they need to attach themselves to a support structure, such as peers, to avoid being alone. A thriving Internet subculture has developed among many teens to serve this purpose. The Net is a preferred method of communication for many young people, since its anonymity makes it easier to talk to people of the opposite sex, or of different ethnic groups.[13]

2. *Rebellion versus conformity*. Teens need to rebel against social standards of appearance and behaviour, yet they still need to fit in and be accepted by their peers. A Canadian company called rad cosmetics ltd. targets this dimension of teenage culture.

3. *Idealism versus pragmatism*. Teens tend to view adults as hypocrites, while they see themselves as sincere; and they work hard to reconcile their view of how the world *should* be with the realities they perceive around them.

4. *Narcissism versus intimacy*. Teens are often obsessed with their own appearances and needs. On the other hand, they also feel the desire to connect with others on a meaningful level.[14]

Teenagers throughout history have had to cope with insecurity, parental authority and peer pressure. In the 1990s, however, these issues are compounded by concerns about the environment, racism, AIDS and other pressing social problems. Today's teens often have to cope with additional family responsibilities as well, especially if they live in non-traditional families where they must help with shopping, cooking and housework. It's hard work being a teen in the 1990s. In the parlance of a recent newspaper article, "growing up goes on and on and on."[15]

Appealing to the Teen Market

Consumers in the teen subculture have a number of needs, including experimentation, belonging, independence, responsibility and approval of others. Product usage is a significant medium to express these needs. Because they are so interested in many different products and have the resources to obtain them, the teen market is avidly courted by marketers. Much of their money goes towards "feel-good" products—cosmetics, posters, music and fast food—with the occasional nose-ring thrown in as well.

Because modern teens were raised on TV and tend to be so much more "savvy" than previous generations, marketers must tread lightly when they try to reach them. In particular, the messages must be seen as authentic and not condescending. As one researcher observed: "... they have a B.S. alarm that goes off quick and fast ... They walk in and usually make up their minds very quickly about whether it's phat or not phat, and whether they want it or don't want it. They know a lot of advertising is based on lies and hype."[16] This wisdom formed the basis for Coca-Cola's introduction of OK soda, a beverage targeted to teens. After a year of field research the company found that teens responded better to a product that did not overpromise—it's just "OK."[17]

Marketers view teens as "consumers in training," since brand loyalty is often developed during this age. A teenager who is committed to a brand may continue to purchase it for many years to come. Such loyalty creates a barrier to entry for other brands that were not chosen during these pivotal years. Thus advertisers sometimes try to "lock in" consumers to certain brands so that in the future they will buy these brands more or less automatically. As one teen-magazine ad director observed, "We ... always say it's easier to start a habit than stop it."[18]

Canadian publishers and telecasters have recently developed an interest in the teen market. Many towns and cities now provide more complete coverage of high-school sports, for example. *What! A Magazine* was started in the early 1990s to target teens; national advertisers are attracted by insights to teen buyer behaviour gleaned through the marketing research conducted by the publisher. It joined other Canadian teen magazines: *In 2 Print, Jeunes pour Jeunes, La Magazine Jeunesse* and *Pop Life* (*Info Pop* is the French version), published by Pepsi-Cola. *Ego,* published by McDonald's since 1996, is targeted towards French-speaking teens in New Brunswick and Quebec.[19] YTV is a channel devoted to programming for Canadian youth. The Breakfast Zone remains one of its most popular segments.

Teens also exert a big influence on the purchase decisions of their parents (see Chapter 12).[20] In addition to providing "helpful" advice to parents, teens are increasingly *buying* products on behalf of the family, because the majority of mothers are now employed outside the home and have less time to shop for the family.

This fundamental change in family structure has altered the way marketers must view teenage consumers. Although teens are still a good market for discretionary items, in recent years their spending on such "basics" as groceries is even larger than for non-essentials. A market research firm specializing in this segment has gone so far as to label teens "skippies"—school kids with income and purchasing power.[21] One survey of 16- and 17-year-old girls found that over a three-month period a significant proportion of them had purchased such staple items as cereal, frozen meals, cheese, yogurt and salad dressing.[22] Marketers have begun to respond to these changes. The number of pages devoted to food advertising in *Seventeen* magazine increased by 31 percent in one year. Dairy Queen Canada is repositioning itself to attract teenagers to its hamburgers and other fast-food fare.[23]

BABY BUSTERS: GENERATION X

The cohort of consumers in their twenties consists of 5.4 million Canadians who will be a powerful force through the end of the 1990s and beyond.[24] This group, which has been labelled "Generation X," "slackers" or "busters," has been profoundly affected by the economic downturn in the first part of the Nineties. In Canada, Generation X also includes 2.6 million baby boomers born between 1960 and 1966. Like the "true" baby busters, this subgroup of thirtysomethings feels the pressure of the economic recession and earns about 10 percent less than their parents at the age of 30. However, unlike the younger members of Generation X, they are likely to be less well positioned (e.g., with computer skills) to participate in an economic recovery.[25]

So-called baby busters include many people, both in and out of university, whose tastes and priorities are beginning to be felt in fashion, popular culture, politics and marketing. Their sense of alienation is echoed by their choices in music (popular bands like The Tragically Hip, Crash Test Dummies, Skinny Puppy and Mitsou), media (shows with an "attitude") and fashion (the postindustrial "grunge" look of baggy or ripped jeans, tattoos and Kettle Creek Bush Pants). Two magazines that appeal to Generation X are *shift* and *Onset*.

Marketing to Busters or Marketing Bust?

Although the income of this age cohort is below expectations, they still constitute a formidable market segment—partly because so many still live at home and have more discretionary income. Because many busters have been doing the family shopping for a long time, marketers are finding that they are much more sophisticated

Hip. Cool. Rad. Awesome. Def. Fresh. Best Model In Initial Quality In Its Price Class.* Hot. Fly.

You may know Toyota Paseo has cool looks, a twin-cam 16-valve 100-horsepower engine and real responsive handling. Even a driver-side air bag** standard. What you may not know is Toyota Paseo is ranked best model in initial quality in the $12,001 to $17,000 price class. So not only is it hip, cool, rad, awesome, def and fresh, it also makes a lot of sense. Call 1-800-GO-TOYOTA for a brochure and the location of your nearest dealer.

TOYOTA Paseo
"I love what you do for me."

*J.D. Power and Associates 1993 Initial Quality Study. ** Price class claim based on $12,001 to $17,000 average median transaction price. Based on 33,691 consumer responses indicating owner-reported problems during the first 90 days of ownership. **Always use your seatbelt. Driver-side air bag is a Supplemental Restraint System (SRS). Buckle Up! Do it for those who love you.
©1994 Toyota Motor Sales, U.S.A., Inc.

Toyota hopes that the list of slang words in this ad will appeal to young people.
Courtesy of Toyota Motor Sales, USA.

Found by using yahoo.ca

Search: Body Art

What is yahoo.ca you ask?
Well, it's simple. If you use yahoo.ca for your web searches, Canadian sites will be listed first, followed by sites from around the world. In short, it just makes your life a lot less complicated.
On yeah, by the way, it's free, gratuit...no charge!
www.yahoo.ca

YAHOO! CANADA

In this ad Yahoo Canada (*www.yahoo.ca*) captures the mind and spirit of Generation X in a novel and engaging way.
Courtesy of Yahoo! Canada and Fauveshaus Advertising.

about evaluating products. Like teens, they are turned off by advertising that either contains a lot of hype or takes itself too seriously. Nike, for example, took a soft-sell approach to woo younger buyers of its athletic shoes. Its ads show little of the product, focusing instead on encouraging readers to improve themselves through exercise. Other ads make fun of advertising. An ad created for Maybelline eye-shadow depicts supermodel Christy Turlington coolly posing in a glamorous setting. She then suddenly appears on her living-room couch, where she laughs and says, "Get over it."

Advertisers have been falling all over themselves trying to craft messages that they hope will not turn off the worldly Generation X cohort. Most of these efforts to put marketing messages in contexts that busters will identify with have consisted of references to old TV shows, or vignettes featuring dishevelled actors in turned-around baseball caps expressing their alienation into the camera. This approach actually turns off a lot of busters, especially since it implies that they have nothing else to do but sit around watching old television reruns.

Perhaps one reason why marketers have not succeeded in their efforts to appeal to Xers with messages of alienation, cynicism and despair is that many people in their twenties aren't so depressed after all. Generation Xers are actually quite a diverse group; they don't all wear reversed baseball hats and work on and off as burger flippers. Despite the birth of dozens of magazines catering to "riot grrrls" and other angry Xers, the most popular magazine for twentysomething women is *Cosmopolitan* under editor-in-chief Bonnie Fuller, a Canadian.[26] What seems to make this age cohort the angriest is constantly being labelled as angry by the media![27]

The advertising agency Saatchi & Saatchi sent teams of psychologists and cultural anthropologists into the field to study the buster culture. These researchers identified four key segments:

1. *Cynical Disdainers*. These are the most pessimistic and cynical about the world.
2. *Traditional Materialists*. The most like baby boomers in their thirties and forties, these young people are upbeat, optimistic about the future and actively striving for material prosperity.
3. *Hippies Revisited*. This group tends to espouse the non-materialistic values of the Sixties. Their priorities are expressed through music, retro fashion and a strong interest in spirituality.
4. *Fifties Machos*. These consumers tend to be politically conservative. They believe in stereotyped gender roles and are the least accepting of multiculturalism.[28]

Big (Wo)Man on Campus: The University Market

Advertisers spend millions each year to influence the purchases of university students, who buy billions of dollars' worth of products annually. Food service on Canadian campuses is a $250-million-a-year industry, attracting fast-food providers like Pizza Hut, Taco Bell and Tim Hortons, as well as catering companies like Marriott, Versa and Beaver Foods.[29] After paying for books, board and tuition, the average student has hundreds of dollars per month to spend, so this interest is not surprising. As one marketing researcher observed: "... university graduates are likely to earn twice as much as their non-university peers, so their ability to buy and influence oth-

MARKETING OPPORTUNITY

Many companies are practising event marketing by participating in the ultimate event for university students: spring break. Many Canadian students now make the annual trek to points south. While beach promotions used to be dominated by suntan lotion and beer companies, many other categories are now well represented, including Chanel, Hershey, Chevrolet, Procter & Gamble and Columbia Pictures. Companies like Nintendo are developing sophisticated, interactive exhibits to grab the attention of partyers. Indeed, beer companies have been voluntarily toning down their involvement in spring break promotions. While in the past Miller Brewing Company gave out free beer samples in Daytona Beach, it now erects billboards that say, "Good beer is properly aged. You should be, too."[30]

ers is clear ... Since 90 percent of them live away from home when they attend university, they're buying all sorts of products that mom used to purchase for them. It's easier to gain them as loyal customers now when they have few brand preferences than it would be to convert them from a preferred brand later on."[31]

University students pose a special challenge for marketers, since they are hard to reach via conventional media. Students watch less television than other people, and when they do watch, they are much more likely to do so after midnight. Students also do not read newspapers as much. Some companies have found that the best way to reach students is through their campus newspapers; about 90 percent of students read their campus papers at least one day a week.[32]

Another popular way to reach students is through **event marketing,** where an organization creates a promotion, such as a volleyball tournament, that attracts students to a central location rather than trying to reach them where they live or work. About one-fourth of the promotional budgets targeted to students are allocated to the sponsorship of such events. Other strategies include the widespread distribution of sampler boxes containing a variety of personal-care products in student centres and residences, and the use of **wall media,** such as posters, to communicate with students on the run.

event marketing a promotional technique where an organization creates a promotion, such as a volleyball tournament, that attracts target consumers to a central location, rather than trying to reach them where they live or work

wall media the use of posters and other forms of announcements to promote products, services and events to hard-to-reach populations (e.g., university students)

BABY BOOMERS

The baby boomer age segment is the source of many fundamental cultural and economic phenomena. The reason: power in numbers. As Canadians returned home after World War II, they began to establish families and careers at a record pace. The children born during this era have dominated consumer culture ever since. Imagine a large python that has swallowed a pig; the pig moves down the length of the python, creating a moving bulge as it goes.[33]

Economic Power of Baby Boomers

As teenagers in the 1960s and 1970s, this age cohort created a revolution in style, politics and consumer attitudes. Now that they are older, they continue to influence popular culture in important ways. Consumers aged 35 to 44 spend the most on housing, cars and entertainment. In addition, consumers aged 45 to 54 spend the most of any age category on food, apparel and retirement programs.

Due to the size and buying power of the boomer group, marketers from the 1970s into the 1990s focused most of their attention on younger consumers, i.e., those in their twenties and thirties. The popular Sixties slogan "Don't trust anyone over 30" meant that people over 30 (and, later, those over 40) had trouble finding products appropriate to their age groups. Times have changed, and again it is the baby boomers who have changed them.

The "pig in the python" has moved into its mid-thirties to fifties, and this age group continues to exert the most impact on consumption patterns. Most of the growth in the market over the next decade will be accounted for by people who are moving into their peak earning years. As baby boomers grow older, they are moving up to more responsible and lucrative jobs. Thus consumers on average are becoming older and wealthier. By the age of 30 older baby boomers (born between 1947 and 1959) were earning 30 percent more than their fathers.[34] In a recent Royal Trust Wealth poll, about 10 percent of baby boomers were found to earn $70 000 to $1 million-plus a year.[35]

This increase in wealth, and the accompanying desire for new and better things, has prompted many marketers to develop new products or reposition old ones. Vacationing boomers are the main target for Unihost's (formerly Journey's End) Latitude 12 Degrees resorts in Barbados.[36] As they approach retirement, affluent boomers are increasing their usage of financial services, including "virtual" banking.[37]

Levi Strauss owes much of its success to baby boomers, who adopted blue jeans as a symbol of their generation. But sales of blue jeans peaked in 1981 and then fell steadily as these consumers (and their waistlines) outgrew their blue jeans. In the mid-1980s the company introduced a new line of pants that provide a looser fit, called Dockers, to win back its traditional consumers. The success of Dockers has created a new clothing category, "new casuals," as other manufacturers attempt to regear for aging boomers.[38] In the 1990s many upscale clothing companies moved into elastic waistbands, and Levi Strauss (**www.levistrauss.com**) now sells companies kits with fashion tips on casual business wear! There is also demand for fashionable eyewear, gardening supplies and light beer.[39]

As the oldest members of the baby boomer generation turned 50 in 1997, many businesses began to cash in on the mass onset of menopause, which on average begins at the age of 51. In the past this condition was largely ignored or hidden, but as assertive baby boomers are beginning to be affected, societal attitudes are changing. The new frankness about this condition has led to a boom in self-help books, estrogen supplements and exercise classes.[40]

Men are not immune to life changes either, as many fall prey to the so-called "male menopause." Their social and physical changes in mid-life can be linked to the sharp rise in the number of men undergoing hair replacement and aesthetic surgery, including nose jobs, eye lifts and liposuction (where excess fat is sucked out of body parts).[41]

In addition to the direct demand for products and services created by this age group, these consumers are also creating a new baby boom of their own to keep marketers busy in the future. However, since fertility rates have dropped, this new boom is not as big as the one that created the baby boom generation; the new upsurge in the number of births can best be described as a *baby boom echo*.

Introducing a washer so gentle, it can actually help your clothes last longer.

(Good thing it wasn't around in the seventies.)

The new Frigidaire Gallery™ Tumble Action washer. A better way to wash clothes. Instead of agitating them clean, the circular motion gently lifts and tumbles clothes through the water. Stains lift out and delicates are preserved—all with far less water and energy. (The average family can save up to 8,000 gallons of water a year.) Together with the companion wrinkle-reducing dryer, it can be installed under a counter or stacked to save floor space. Choose your clothes carefully; they'll be around for a long time. The Frigidaire Gallery Collection.
http://www.frigidaire.com

The only washer certified by the Environment Canada EcoLogo program to have less impact on the environment.

FRIGIDAIRE THE LOOK OF BETTER PERFORMANCE.

The appeal of this ad to baby boomers lies in its subtle, humorous reference to the clothing styles of their youth.
Courtesy of Frigidaire.

Many couples postponed marriage and parenthood due to the new emphasis on careers for women. These consumers are beginning to hear the ticking of the biological "time clock." They are having babies in their late twenties and early thirties, resulting in fewer (but perhaps more pampered) children per family. This new emphasis on children and the family has created opportunities for such products as cars (e.g., the success of the "mini-van" concept), services (e.g., day care) and media (e.g., magazines like *Today's Parent*).

THE GREY MARKET

The old woman sits alone in her dark apartment, while the television blares out a soap opera. Once every couple of days she slowly and painfully opens her triple-locked door with arthritic hands and ventures out to the corner store to buy essentials like tea, milk and cereal, always being sure to pick the least expensive brand. Most of the time she sits in her rocking chair, thinking sadly of her dead husband and the good times they used to have.

Is this the image you have of a typical elderly consumer? Until recently, many marketers did. As a result they largely neglected the elderly in their feverish pursuit of the baby boomer market. But as our population ages and people are living longer and healthier lives, the game is rapidly changing. A lot of businesses are beginning to replace the old stereotype of the poor recluse. The newer, more accurate image is of a mature consumer who is active, interested in what life has to offer and an enthusiastic customer with the means and willingness to buy many goods and services.[42]

Grey Power: Shattering Stereotypes

The mature market consists of approximately 5.5 million people aged 55 and older. For many purposes these consumers are classified as "senior citizens" when they reach the age of 65, when Canada Pension Plan benefits begin.[43] The number of Canadians 65 years and older more than doubled over the last 25 years and increased by 11 percent between 1991 and 1997, comprising more than 12 percent of the population. Statistics Canada predicts that they will make up 19 percent of the population in 2021, and 25 percent in 2041. Among the provinces, Saskatchewan has the highest proportion of seniors, at almost 15 percent; Alberta has 10 percent, the lowest proportion, but this number is growing due to the attraction of fewer taxes and more benefits. The Yukon and Northwest Territories have less than 5 percent of their populations in the 65-plus age group.[44]

The mature market is the second-fastest-growing market segment in Canada, lagging behind only the baby boomers. Such dramatic growth can largely be explained by improved medical diagnoses and treatment and the resulting increase in life expectancies. Many mature consumers lead more active, multidimensional lives than we assume. They devote an average of about half an hour a day to volunteer activities, and 20 percent look after children at least once a week.[45]

Still, outdated images of mature consumers persist. The editors of *Modern Maturity* magazine, which is sent to 23 million readers, reject about a third of the ads submitted to them because they portray older people in a negative light.

Economic Clout

There is abundant evidence that the economic health of elderly consumers is good and getting better. The over-50s market accounts for about 55 percent of discretionary spending power and 80 percent of personal wealth in Canada, but they are included in less than 5 percent of advertising and represent fewer than 5 percent of respondents in marketing research. Some important areas that stand to benefit from the surging grey market include exercise facilities, entertainment, cruises and tourism, cosmetic surgery, skin treatments, "how-to" books, and university courses that offer enhanced learning opportunities. Mature consumers spend more on gifts than those in younger age groups, and those 55 to 64 donate the most (an average of $1400 in 1991) to charitable organizations. Co-op housing near Toronto's lakefront and the provision of a more leisurely shopping pace and personalized service are recent examples of a consumer-based approach to the grey market.[46]

It is crucial to remember that income alone does not capture the spending power of this group. Mature consumers are finished with many of the financial obligations that siphon off the income of younger consumers. Most consumers over the age of 65 own their own home, and most of those homes are mortgage-free. In addition, child-rearing costs are over with. And, as evidenced by the popularity of the bumper sticker that proudly proclaims. "We're spending our children's inheritance," many seniors now feel better about spending money on themselves rather than skimping for the sake of children and grandchildren.

This Room Is Designed For Mature Travelers. (So Is The Discount.)

Brighter lighting

Freshly brewed coffee in your room

Bigger, easier-to-read numbers on TV remote and phone

We asked travelers 50 and over how they would re-design our hotel rooms to make their stay more comfortable. Then we took their suggestions and created the Rodeway Choice Room.

Situated on lower floors for easy access, the Rodeway Choice Room offers a host of special details

30%
Traveler's
50+ Discount

like easy-to-use lever handles on doors and faucets, and grab bars in the shower and bath. Many are no-smoking rooms, as well. Plus you'll also get to enjoy our continental breakfast—free!

No other hotel chain offers such a specially-designed room. So call 1-800-228-2000 to make your reservations now, and you'll even get our 30% discount for travelers 50 or over.* What could be more comfortable than that?

RODEWAY INN

1-800-228-2000
Or call your travel agent.

*Subject to availability;
advanced reservations required.

Several hotel chains are targeting the mature market. Choice Hotels is making adjustments to its pricing structure, room design and promotional strategy. New rooms—all on the first floor for easier access—offer brighter lighting and larger buttons on the phones and TV remote controls. The chain offers travellers over the age of 50 a 30 percent discount on rooms. This ad for Rodeway Inn shows a similar strategy.
Source: Cyndee Miller, "Seniors Lured to Hotel Rooms by Seductive Trappings," Marketing News *(December 6, 1993): 9. Photo: Courtesy of Choice Hotels International.*

Participaction uses the label "Oldtimers" hockey in the affectionate way Canadians do. The ad is testimony to the vitality of many older Canadians.
Reprinted with permission from Participaction Canada.

Key Values of Mature Consumers

Researchers have identified a set of key values that are relevant to older consumers. For marketing strategies to succeed, they should be related to one or more of these factors:[47]

- *Autonomy.* Mature consumers want to lead active lives and to be self-sufficient. The advertising strategy of Depends, undergarments for incontinent women made by Kimberly-Clark, is centred around a famous actress, June Allyson, who plays golf and goes to parties without worrying about her condition.

- *Connectedness.* Mature consumers value the bonds they have with friends and family. Quaker Oats successfully tapped into this desire with its ads featuring actor Wilford Brimely, who dispenses grandfatherly advice about eating right to the younger generation.

- *Altruism.* Mature consumers want to give something back to the world. Thrifty Car Rental found in a survey that over 40 percent of older consumers would select a rental-car company if it sponsored a program that gave discounts to senior-citizen centres that wanted to buy vans for their patrons. Based on this research the company launched its highly successful program, "Give a Friend a Lift."

- *Personal growth.* Mature consumers are very interested in trying new experiences and developing their potential. In some of its ads for health-care products, Prudential is featuring the late-in-life accomplishments of such people as Clara Barton, Benjamin Franklin and Noah Webster.

Perceived Age: You're Only as Old as You Feel

Market researchers who work with mature consumers often comment that people think of themselves as being 10 to 15 years younger than they actually are. In fact, research confirms the popular wisdom that age is more a state of mind than of body. A person's mental outlook and activity level has a lot more to do with his or her longevity and quality of life than does *chronological age,* or the actual number of years lived.

A better yardstick with which to categorize the elderly is **perceived age,** or how old a person feels. Perceived age can be measured on several dimensions, including

perceived age how old a person feels as opposed to his or her true chronological age

MARKETING OPPORTUNITY

In 1985, Peter Cook was looking for a business idea that was demographically sound, community-oriented and not capital-intensive. Thus, Seniors for Seniors was born. This company employs younger, active retirees to provide services to those who are older and frailer. They may visit their clients, live in, or do tasks such as shopping and fixing things. This Toronto-based business now has franchises in Halifax, Montreal, Hamilton and Mississauga, and it has plans to open in Ottawa, Kitchener and Vancouver. Sales have passed $3 million.[48]

MARKETING PITFALL

Some marketing efforts targeted to the elderly have backfired because they reminded people of their age or presented their age group in an unflattering way. One of the more famous blunders was committed by Heinz. A company analyst found that many elderly people were buying baby food because of the small portions and easy-chewing consistency, so it introduced a line of "Senior Foods" made especially for denture wearers. Needless to say, the product failed. Consumers did not want to admit, even to the supermarket cashier, that they required strained foods. They preferred to purchase baby foods, which they could pretend they were buying for a grandchild.

"feel-age" (how old a person feels) and "look-age" (how old a person looks).[49] The older consumers get, the younger they *feel* relative to actual age. For this reason, many marketers emphasize product benefits rather than age appropriateness in marketing campaigns, since many consumers do not relate to products targeted to their chronological age.[50]

Segmenting the Mature Market

The subculture of mature consumers represents an extremely large market: the number of Canadians 65 and older exceeds 3.5 million, and there are roughly another 2 million between the ages of 55 and 64.[51] Because this group is so large, it is helpful to think of the mature market as actually consisting of four subsegments: an "older" group (aged 55–64), an "elderly" group (65–74), an "aged" group (75–84) and finally a "very old" group (85 and up).[52]

The mature market is well suited for segmentation. Older consumers are easy to identify by age and stage in the family life cycle. Most receive benefits from the Canada Pension Plan. Many belong to organizations catering to senior citizens. Some read magazines for mature consumers, such as *Modern Maturity,* and have their interests (e.g., in benefits plans) represented by the Canadian Association of Retired Persons.

One ad agency devised a segmentation scheme for American women over the age of 65 on two dimensions: self-sufficiency and perceived opinion leadership.[53] The study yielded many important differences among the groups. The self-sufficient group was found to be more independent, cosmopolitan and outgoing. They were more likely to read books, attend concerts and sporting events, and dine out.

Several segmentation approaches begin with the premise that a major determinant of marketplace behaviour of mature consumers is the way a person deals with being old.[54] Some people become depressed, withdrawn and apathetic as they age; some are angry and resist the thought of aging; and some appear to accept the new challenges and opportunities this period of life has to offer. Table 15–3 summarizes selected findings from one current segmentation approach called Gerontographics, which divides the mature market into groups based on both level of physical well-being and social conditions, such as being a grandparent or spouse.

TABLE 15–3 Gerontographics: Selected Characteristics

SEGMENT	PERCENT OF 55+ POPULATION	PROFILE	MARKETING IMPLICATIONS
Healthy Indulgers	18%	Have experienced the fewest events related to aging, such as retirement or loss of spouse, and are most likely to behave like younger consumers. Main focus is on enjoying life.	Looking for independent living. Good customers for discretionary services, such as home cleaning and answering machines.
Healthy Hermits	36%	React to life events, such as death of a spouse, by becoming withdrawn. Resent that they are expected to behave like old people.	Emphasize conformity. They want to know their appearance is socially acceptable, and tend to be comfortable with well-known brands.
Ailing Outgoers	29%	Maintain positive self-esteem despite adverse life events. They accept limitations, but are still determined to get the most out of life.	Have health problems that may require a special diet. Special menus and promotions will bring these consumers into restaurants seen as catering to their needs.
Frail Recluses	17%	Have adjusted their lifestyles to accept old age, but have chosen to cope with negative events by becoming spiritually stronger.	Like to stay put in the same house where they raised their families. Good candidates for remodelling and for emergency-response systems.

Source: Adapted from George P. Moschis, "Life Stages of the Mature Market," *American Demographics* (September 1996): 44–50.

The Elderly and the Media

A number of specialty magazines have been introduced in recent years that focus on the active lifestyles of today's mature consumers. These include such publications as *Modern Maturity* and *50 Plus*. In addition, television is a very important medium, because the elderly often rely on TV as a window on society. They watch 60 percent more television than average households and prefer programs that provide news and current events as a way to keep up. They also watch more golf, baseball and bowling on television than the average consumer. Mature consumers tend to listen to radio news at all times of the day and are above the norm in readership of news magazines.

In general, mature consumers have been shown to respond positively to ads that provide an abundance of information. Unlike other age groups, these consumers usually are not amused or persuaded by imagery-oriented advertising. A more successful strategy involves the construction of advertising that depicts the aged as well-integrated, contributing members of society, with emphasis on them expanding their horizons rather than clinging precariously to life.

MARKETING PITFALL

Many consumer products will encounter a more sympathetic reception from the elderly if packages are designed to be sensitive to physical limitations. While aesthetically appealing, packages are often awkward and difficult to manage, especially for those who are frail or arthritic. Also, many serving sizes are not geared to smaller families, widows and other people living alone, and coupons tend to be for family-sized products rather than for single servings.

Seniors have difficulty with pull-tab cans and push-open milk cartons. Ziploc packages and clear plastic wrap are also difficult to handle. Packages need to be easier to read and should be made lighter and smaller. Finally, designers need to pay attention to contrasting colours. A slight yellowing of the lens as one ages makes it harder to see background colours on packages. Discerning between blues, greens and violets becomes especially difficult. The closer identifying-type colours are to the package's or advertisement's background colour, the less visible they are and the less attention they will command.[55]

Some basic guidelines have been suggested for effective advertising to the elderly. These include the following:[56]

- Keep language simple.
- Use clear, bright pictures.
- Use action to attract attention.
- Speak clearly, and keep the word count low.
- Use a single sales message, and emphasize brand extensions to tap consumers' familiarity.
- Avoid extraneous stimuli (i.e., excessive pictures and graphics that detract from the message).

MARKETING OPPORTUNITY

Some Canadian manufacturers are redesigning their products aimed at *all* age groups following feedback from mature consumers. For example, Tylenol's redesigned big red cap with ridges for easy turning is endorsed by the Arthritis Society of Canada. Minute Maid of Toronto has an Easy-Peel Ring on frozen-juice containers. Kraft Canada won an award for its package of Country Time iced-tea mix, which features legible type and a lid that is easy to open and doubles as a measuring container.[57]

CHAPTER SUMMARY

- People have many things in common with others merely because they are about the same age. Consumers who grew up at the same time share many cultural memories and belong to the same age cohort.

- Consumers often feel positively about products they used when they were younger, so they may be receptive to marketers' nostalgia appeals that remind them of these experiences.

- Four important age cohorts are teens, university students, baby boomers and mature consumers. Teenagers are making a transition from childhood to adulthood, and their self-concepts tend to be unstable. They are receptive to products that help them to be accepted and enable them to assert their independence. Because many teens earn money but have few financial obligations, they are a particularly important segment for many non-essential or expressive products, ranging from chewing gum to clothing fashions and music. Due to changes in family structure, many teens are also taking more responsibility for their families' day-to-day shopping and routine purchase decisions.

- University students are an important market, but they are hard to reach via conventional media. In many cases they are living alone for the first time, so they are making important decisions about setting up households. Many marketers appeal to this group by staging events or other elaborate promotions.

- Baby boomers are the most powerful age segment due to the segment's size and economic clout. The needs and desires of baby boomers affect demands for housing, child care, automobiles, clothing and financial services.

- As the population ages, the needs of mature consumers will also become increasingly influential. Many marketers traditionally ignored this age segment due to the stereotype that they are too inactive and spend too little. This stereotype is no longer accurate. Most are healthy, vigorous and interested in new products and experiences—and they have the income to purchase them. Marketing appeals to this age subculture should focus on consumers' self-concepts and perceived ages, which tend to be more youthful than their chronological ages. Marketers should also emphasize concrete benefits of products, since this group tends to be sceptical of vague, image-related promotions. Personalized service is of particular importance to this segment.

KEY TERMS

Age cohort p. 500   Perceived age p. 514   Wall media p. 509
Event marketing p. 509

CONSUMER BEHAVIOUR CHALLENGE

1. What are some possible marketing opportunities present at reunions? What effects might attending such an event have on a consumer's self-esteem, body image, affect and so on?

2. When is nostalgia an effective way to appeal to consumers? Can this technique backfire? Find ads that use a nostalgia appeal and critique their likely effectiveness.

3. Why have baby boomers had such an important impact on consumer culture in the second half of the twentieth century?

4. How has the baby boom echo changed attitudes towards child-rearing practices and created demand for different products and services?

5. Is it practical to assume that people age 55 and older constitute one large consumer market? What are some approaches to further segmenting this age subculture?

6. Find good and bad examples of advertising targeted to mature consumers. To what degree does advertising stereotype mature consumers? What elements of ads or other promotions appear to determine their effectiveness in reaching and persuading this group?

CBC VIDEO VIGNETTES

Concepts at Work with Demographics

Dr. David Foot, an economist at the University of Toronto, believes that the number of people born at a particular point in time says a lot about how each generation will affect the Canadian economy. Following trends in how each generation is aging will enable analysts in industry and government to identify opportunities and be able to anticipate problems. Foot claims that careful analysis will avoid surprises.

A focus on baby boomers—Canadians born between 1947 and 1966—illustrates his points about the high pressure put on the housing market in the 1980s and the evolving demand for stocks now that the boomers are planning for retirement. This large group of about 9 million people (about a third of the Canadian population) will create demand for many services, especially in the areas of health care, finances and leisure. They will continue to affect employment and the ability of the "baby bust" generation to get jobs and create the demand that comes from purchases made by younger consumers. The "echo" that follows will be from the boomers' 7 million children.

QUESTIONS

1. Identify the age groups that exist in the Canadian population.

2. How are these age groups likely to affect the ability of Canadians to develop spending power and to create demand for products and services?

3. What dimensions of consumer behaviour cannot be predicted through the analysis of demographic data, such as age patterns in a population?

4. What kinds of events could disrupt the age-pattern predictions that Foot makes?

Video Resource: "Footnotes on the Future," *The National* (March 7, 1996).

Additional Resources: Daniel Stoffman, "Completely Predictable People," *Report on Business Magazine* (November 1990): 78–84; David K. Foot and Daniel Stoffman, *Boom, Bust & Echo: How to Profit from the Coming Demographic Shift* (Toronto: Macfarlane Walter & Ross, 1996).

NOTES

1. Ads were run in *Maclean's,* October 28, 1996: 31–32 and October 14, 1996: 7–8, respectively.

2. Jeffrey P. Rosenfeld, "Reliving It Up," *American Demographics* (June 1987): 48.

3. Bickley Townsend, "Où sont les reiges d'antan? (Where are the snows of yesteryear?)" *American Demographics* (October 1988): 2.

4. Cf. Morris B. Holbrook, "Nostalgia and Consumption Preferences: Some Emerging Patterns of Consumer Tastes," *Journal of Consumer Research* 20 (September 1993): 245–56; Morris B. Holbrook, "Nostalgia Proneness and Consumer Tastes," in John A. Howard, *Buyer Behavior in Marketing Strategy,* 2nd ed. (Englewood Cliffs, NJ: Prentice Hall, 1994), pp. 348–64; Morris B. Holbrook and Robert M. Schindler, "Age, Sex, and Attitude Toward the Past as Predictors of Consumers' Aesthetic Tastes for Cultural Products," *Journal of Marketing Research* 31 (August 1994): 412–22.

5. Lesley Daw, "How to Market a Milestone," *Marketing Magazine* (March 10, 1997): 11–12; Joyce Lau, "It's old. It's cold. It's hot again," *Canadian Business* (August 1997): 26–30; Bill Richards, "Push mowers reach the pinnacle of backyard chic," *Globe and Mail* (August 9, 1997): D1.

6. Kevin Goldman, "New Campaigns Tip the Hat to Nostalgia," *Wall Street Journal* (August 9, 1994): B4; Raymond Serafin, "Mustang Love: Ford Revs Up Romantic Heritage to Sell New Model of Sports Cars," *Advertising Age* (October 4, 1993): 4.

7. Rose A. Horowitz, "California Beach Culture Rides Wave of Popularity in Japan," *Journal of Commerce* (August 3, 1989): 17; Elaine Lafferty, "American Casual Seizes Japan; Teenagers Go for N.F.L. Hats, Batman and the California Look," *Time* (November 13, 1989): 106.

8. Blayne Cutler, "Move Over, Miso," *American Demographics* (May 1988): 56.

9. Karen Lowry Miller, "You Just Can't Talk to These Kids," *Business Week* (April 19, 1993): 104 (2 pp.).

10. Quoted in Jennifer Cody, "Here's a New Way to Rationalize Not Cleaning Out Your Closets," *Wall Street Journal* (June 14, 1994): B1.

11. "Teens a huge force in consumer market," *Canadian Press Newswire* (November 21, 1994), accessed on WinSPIRS UNB (August 19, 1997).

12. Ibid.

13. Sara Olkon, "Black Soda with Skulls on Label Isn't Aimed at the Pepsi Generation," *Wall Street Journal* (May 24, 1995): B1.

14. Junu Bryan Kim, "For Savvy Teens: Real Life, Real Solutions," *Advertising Age* (August 23, 1993): S–1 (3 pp.).

15. Cynthia Crosseu, "Growing up Goes On and On and On," *Wall Street Journal* (March 24, 1997): B1, B3.

16. Quoted in Cyndee Miller, "Phat is Where It's At for Today's Teen Market," *Marketing News* (August 15, 1994): 6 (2 pp.).

17. Laurie M. Grossman, "Coke Hopes 'OK', New Drink, Will be the Toast of Teens," *Wall Street Journal* (April 21, 1994): B7.

18. Ellen Goodman, "The Selling of Teenage Anxiety," *Washington Post* (November 24, 1979).

19. Sue Gardiner, "During the recent hockey lockout, some editors found other ways to fill pages," *Media* 2, 1 (March 1995): 6–7; "What! A niche to grow with: national advertisers discover the power of teens," *Marketing Magazine* 99, 36 (October 3, 1994): 19; "McDonald's mag aims at teen market," *Marketing Magazine* 101, 15 (April 15, 1996): 3; "Newsstands bare of intelligent magazines for teens," *Canadian Press Newswire* (January 4, 1996), accessed on WinSPIRS UNB (August 19, 1997).

20. Ellen R. Foxman, Patriya S. Tansuhaj and Karin M. Ekstrom, "Family Members' Perceptions of Adolescents' Influence in Family Decision Making," *Journal of Consumer Research* 15 (March 1989): 482–91.

21. John Blades, "Tracking Skippies: TRU Researches Habits of Elusive Teens," *Asbury Park Press* (March 2, 1991): C1.

22. Andrew Malcolm, "Teen-Age Shoppers: Desperately Seeking Spinach," *New York Times* (November 29, 1987): 10.

23. Marina Strauss, "Dairy Queen targets teens," *Globe and Mail* (February 6, 1997): B17; James Pollock, "DQ pursues larger share of burger market," *Marketing Magazine* (March 31, 1997): 3.

24. David K. Foot (with Daniel Stoffman), *Boom, Bust & Echo: How to Profit from the Coming Demographic Shift* (Toronto: Macfarlane Walter & Ross, 1996), pp. 21–22.

25. Ibid.

26. Marci McDonald, "The new Cosmo girl," *Maclean's* (February 17, 1997): 60–63.

27. Scott Donaton, "The Media Wakes Up to Generation X," *Advertising Age* (February 1, 1993): 16 (2 pp.); Laura E. Keeton, "New Magazines Aim to Reach (and Rechristen) Generation X," *Wall Street Journal* (October 17, 1994): B1 (2 pp.); Cyndee Miller, "X Marks the Lucrative Spot, But Some Advertisers Can't Hit Target," *Marketing News* (August 2, 1993): 1 (2 pp.); Todd Pruzan, "Advertisers Wary of Generation X Titles," *Advertising Age* (October 24, 1994): S–22 (2 pp.).

28. Eben Shapiro, "New Marketing Specialists Tap College Consumers," *New York Times* (February 27, 1992): D16.

29. "The food fight: big business is battling for the hearts and palates of students," *Maclean's* 109, 48 (November 25, 1996): 56–58.

30. Stuart Elliott, "Beyond Beer and Sun Oil: The Beach-Blanket Bazaar," *New York Times* (March 18, 1992): D17; Judith Waldrop, *The Seasons of Business: The Marketer's Guide to Consumer Behavior* (New York: American Demographics, Inc., 1992).

31. Quoted in Daniel Shannon, "In a Class By Itself," *Promo: The International Magazine for Promotion Marketing* (July 1994): 51 (6 pp.).

32. Beth Bogart, "Word of Mouth Travels Fastest," *Advertising Age* (February 6, 1989): S–6; Janice Steinberg, "Media 101," *Advertising Age* (February 6, 1989): S–4.

33. David Cork, *The Pig and the Python: How to Prosper from the Aging Baby Boom* (Toronto: Stoddart, 1996).

34. Foot (with Stoffman), *Boom, Bust & Echo*, p. 21.

35. "Baby boomers with bucks," *Marketing Magazine* (October 28, 1996): 30.

36. Carolyn Leitch, "Journey's End in Barbados resort deal," *Globe and Mail* (June 10, 1997): B6.

37. "Baby boomers with bucks."

38. Andrew Pollack, "Jeans Fade but Levi Strauss Glows," *New York Times* (June 26, 1989): D1.

39. Ijeoma Ross, "Levi Strauss helps companies relax their dress codes," *Globe and Mail* (September 18, 1997): B11; Stephanie N. Mehta, "Retailer With Vision Aims to Make Fading Eyesight Chic," *Wall Street Journal* (October 23, 1996): B1; Gillian Shaw, "Raking in the Green Stuff," *The Weekend Sun* [Vancouver] (April 12, 1997): B12; Louise Gagnon, "Aging Canadians are drinking less beer," *Marketing Magazine* (July 2/28, 1997): 4.

40. Patricia Braus, "Facing Menopause," *American Demographics* (March 1993): 44 (5 pp.).

41. Quoted in Blayne Cutler, "Marketing to Menopausal Men," *American Demographics* (March 1993): 49.

42. Cf. George P. Moschis, "Gerontographics: A Scientific Approach to Analyzing and Targeting the Mature Market," *Journal of Consumer Marketing* 10, 3 (1993): 45–53; George P. Moschis, "Consumer Behavior in Later Life: Multidisciplinary Contributions and Implications for Research," *Journal of the Academy of Marketing Science* 22, 3 (1994): 195–204.

43. Foot (with Stoffman), *Boom, Bust & Echo*.

44. "Yup, Canadians are getting older," *Canadian Press Newswire* (July 29, 1997), accessed on WinSPIRS UNB (October 13, 1997); Mark Milke, "Too old to drive: a new test is developed to ease a burgeoning hazard," *Alberta Report* 24, 26 (June 9, 1997): 29; Mark Milke, "Seniors arriving by the thousands: despite cut-backs, Alberta offers a better retirement deal than BC," *Alberta Report* 24, 13 (March 10, 1997): 38–39.

45. Dorothy Lipovenko, "Male seniors better off, study finds," *Globe and Mail* (February 7, 1997): A6.

46. Klaus Rohrich, "Life after 49," *Marketing Magazine* (February 3, 1997): 18; "Seniors look to alternative housing," *Canadian Press Newswire* (February 1, 1997), accessed on WinSPIRS UNB (October 13, 1997); Lipovenko, "Male seniors better off, study finds"; "The giving feeling," *Canada and the World Backgrounder* 58, 7 (March 1993): 3; "A sense of humour, laid back attitude and dedication to customer service makes Becky Wong a winner at London Drugs," *Cosmetics* 25, 1 (January 1997): 22.

47. David B. Wolfe, "Targeting the Mature Mind," *American Demographics* (March 1994): 32–36.

48. "The ultimate gray market: with the success of Seniors for Seniors, founder Peter Cook proves that retirement is not an end, but a beginning," *Canadian Business* 70, 3 (March 1997): 16.

49. Benny Barak and Leon G. Schiffman, "Cognitive Age: A Nonchronological Age Variable," in *Advances in Consumer Research 8*, ed. Kent B. Monroe (Provo, UT: Association for Consumer Research, 1981), pp. 602–6.

50. David B. Wolfe, "An Ageless Market," *American Demographics* (July 1987): 27–55.

51. Based on *Canada's Families: They Count* (Ottawa: The Vanier Institute of the Family, 1996); and Foot (with Stoffman), *Boom, Bust & Echo*, pp. 16–17.

52. William Lazer and Eric H. Shaw, "How Older Americans Spend Their Money," *American Demographics* (September 1987): 36.

53. Ellen Day et al., "Reaching the Senior Citizen Market(s)," *Journal of Advertising Research* (December/January 1987/88): 23–30. Many studies have examined elderly consumers' shopping patterns and product choices: see J. Barry Mason and William O. Bearden, "Profiling the Shopping Behavior of Elderly Consumers," *The Gerontologist* 18, 5 (1978): 454–61; James R. Lumpkin and Barnett A. Greenberg, "Apparel-Shopping Patterns of the Elderly Consumer," *Journal of Retailing* 58 (Winter 1982): 68–89; Mary C. LaForge, "Learned Helplessness as an Explanation of Elderly Consumer Complaint Behavior," *Journal of Business Ethics* 8 (May 1989): 359–66; Betsy D. Gelb, "Exploring the Gray Market Segment," *MSU Business Topics* 26 (Spring 1978): 41–46; Elaine Sherman, "The Senior Market: Opportunities Abound," *Direct Marketing* 50 (June 1987): 82; Valarie A. Zeithaml and Mary C. Gilly, "Characteristics Affecting the Acceptance of Retailing Technologies: A Comparison of Elderly and Nonelderly Consumers," *Journal of Retailing* 83 (Spring 1987): 49–68; Mary C. Gilly and Valarie A. Zeithaml, "The Elderly Consumer and Adoption of Technologies," *Journal of Consumer Research* 12 (December 1985): 353–57.

54. Day et al., "Reaching the Senior Citizen Market(s)"; Warren A. French and Richard Fox, "Segmenting the Senior Citizen Market," *Journal of Consumer Marketing* 2 (1985): 61–74; Jeffrey G. Towle and Claude R. Martin, Jr., "The Elderly Consumer: One Segment or Many?" in *Advances in Consumer Research 3*, ed.

Beverlee B. Anderson (Provo, UT: Association for Consumer Research, 1976), p. 463.

55. "Gray Expectations: A New Force in Design," *Business Week* (April 11, 1988): 108; Mary Bender, "Packaging for the Older Consumer" (speech delivered at the Annual Winter Conference of the Gerontology Institute of New Jersey, Princeton, NJ, March 6, 1987).

56. J. Ward, "Marketers Slow to Catch Age Wave," *Advertising Age* (May 22, 1989): S–1.

57. James Pollock, "New Twists on Old Packages," *Marketing Magazine* (March 24, 1997): 8–9.

V

Consumers and Culture

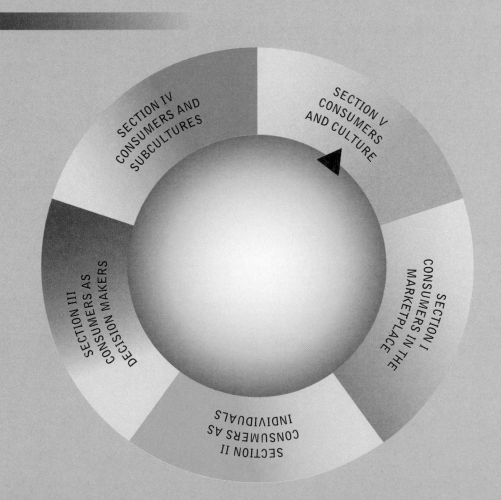

SECTION IV
CONSUMERS AND
SUBCULTURES

SECTION V
CONSUMERS
AND CULTURE

SECTION I
CONSUMERS IN THE
MARKETPLACE

SECTION II
CONSUMERS AS
INDIVIDUALS

SECTION III
CONSUMERS AS
DECISION MAKERS

The final section of this book considers consumers as members of a broad cultural system. Chapter 16 looks at some of the basic building blocks of culture and the impact these have on consumer behaviour. Chapter 17 concludes with a focus on how some of the important, emerging developments in our culture affect our lives as consumers. The theory of diffusion of innovation is used as a foundation for looking at how culture spreads and the timing of consumer change.

Whitney is at her wits' end. It's bad enough that she has a deadline looming on that new Christmas promotion for her gift shop. Now there's trouble on the home front as well: her son Stephen failed his high-school mid-terms and he's been grounded until he adjusts his study habits. To top things off, her much-anticipated vacation to Hawaii with her second husband will have to be postponed until her son gets back on track.

However, when Whitney meets up with her friend Gabrielle at the local Starbucks for their daily "retreat," her mood starts to brighten. Somehow the calm of the café rubs off onto her as she savours her grande cappuccino. Gab consoles her with her usual assurances, and then her friend prescribes the ultimate remedy to defeat the blues: go home, take a nice long aromatherapy bath, and then have a glass of Chardonnay. Yes, that's the ticket. It's amazing how the little things in life can make such a big difference. As she strolls out the door, Whitney makes a mental note to get Gab a really nice Christmas gift this year for being such a great friend …

16

Cultural Influences on Consumer Behaviour

UNDERSTANDING CULTURE

Whitney's daily coffee "fix" is mimicked in various forms around the globe, as people participate in activities that allow them to take a break and affirm their relationships with others. Of course the products that are consumed in the process can range from black Turkish coffee to Indian tea, or from lager beer to Guinness.

The Starbucks Corporation has experienced phenomenal success by turning the coffee break into a cultural event that for many has assumed almost cult-like status. The average Starbucks customer visits 18 times a month, and 10 percent of the clientele stop by twice a day.[1] Part of the appeal is that the retail outlets provide an oasis from the hectic world. Indeed, one of the advertising themes the firm is considering underscores the idea that a visit to a Starbucks is like a visit to a sacred, magical island of calm: "A little sanity, conveniently located."[2] North Americans are discovering a secret that Europeans have known for years: life is too short to spend the *whole* day behind a desk.

Culture, a concept crucial to the understanding of consumer behaviour, may be thought of as a society's personality. It includes both abstract ideas, such as values and ethics, as well as the material objects and services, such as automobiles, clothing, food, art and sports, that are produced or valued by a group of people. Culture is the accumulation of shared meanings, rituals, norms and traditions among the members of an organization or society.

culture the values, ethics, rituals, traditions, material objects and services produced or valued by the members of a society

Consumption choices simply cannot be understood without considering the cultural context in which they are made: culture is the "lens" through which people view products. Ironically, the effects of culture on consumer behaviour are so powerful and far-reaching that this importance is sometimes difficult to grasp or appreciate. Like a fish immersed in water, we do not always appreciate this power until we encounter a different environment, where suddenly many of the assumptions we had taken for granted about the clothes we wear, the food we eat, the way we address others and so on no longer seem to apply.

The importance of these cultural expectations often is only discovered when they are violated. For example, while on tour in New Zealand the British pop group The Spice Girls created a stir among New Zealand's Maoris by performing a war dance only men are supposed to do. A tribal official indignantly stated, "It is not acceptable in our culture, and especially by girlie pop stars from another culture."[3] Sensitivity to cultural issues, whether by rock stars or by brand managers, can only come by understanding these underlying dimensions; that is the goal of this chapter.

Consumer Behaviour and Culture: A Two-Way Street

A consumer's culture determines the overall priorities he or she attaches to different activities and products. It also mandates the success or failure of specific products and services. A product that provides benefits consistent with those desired by members of a culture at any point in time has a much better chance of attaining acceptance in the marketplace.

The relationship between consumer behaviour and culture is a two-way street. On the one hand, products and services that resonate with the priorities of a culture at any given time have a much better chance of being accepted by consumers. On the other hand, the study of new products and innovations in product design successfully produced by a culture at any point in time provides a window onto the dominant cultural ideals of that period. Consider, for example, some of the following products that reflect underlying cultural processes at the time they were introduced:

- the TV dinner, which hinted at changes in family structure;
- cosmetics made of natural materials and not animal-tested, which reflected consumers' apprehensions about pollution, waste, and animal rights; and
- condoms marketed in pastel carrying cases for female buyers, which signalled changes in attitudes towards sexual responsibility and frankness.

Aspects of Culture

Culture is not static. It is continuously evolving, synthesizing old ideas with new ones. A cultural system consists of three functional areas:[4]

1. *Ecology*—the way in which a system is adapted to its habitat. This area is shaped by the technology used to obtain and distribute resources (e.g., in industrialized societies versus Third World countries). The Japanese, for example, greatly value products that are designed for efficient use of space because of the cramped conditions in that island nation.[5]

2. *Social structure*—the way in which orderly social life is maintained. This area includes the domestic and political groups that are dominant within the culture (e.g., the nuclear family versus the extended family).

3. *Ideology*—the mental characteristics of a people and the way in which they relate to their environment and social groups. This area revolves around the belief that members of a society possess a common world-view; that is, they share certain ideas about principles of order and fairness. They also share an **ethos,** or a set of moral and aesthetic principles.

> **ethos** a set of moral, aesthetic and evaluative principles

Although every culture is different, four dimensions appear to account for much of this variability:[6]

1. *Power distance*—the way in which interpersonal relationships form when differences in power are perceived. Some cultures (e.g., Japan) emphasize strict, vertical relationships, while others, such as the United States, stress a greater degree of equality and informality.

2. *Uncertainty avoidance*—the degree to which people feel threatened by ambiguous situations and have beliefs and institutions that help them to avoid this uncertainty (e.g., organized religions).

3. *Masculinity/femininity*—the degree to which gender roles are clearly delineated (see Chapter 5). Traditional societies are more likely to possess very explicit rules about the acceptable behaviours of men and women, such as who is responsible for certain tasks within the family unit.

4. *Individualism*—the extent to which the welfare of the individual versus that of the group is valued (see Chapter 11). Cultures differ in their emphasis on individualism versus collectivism. In **collectivist cultures** people subordinate their personal goals to those of a stable in-group. In contrast, consumers in **individualist cultures** attach more importance to personal goals, and people are more likely to change memberships when the demands of the group (workplace, church, etc.) become too costly. Whereas a collectivist society will stress such values as self-discipline and accepting one's position in life, people in individualist cultures emphasize personal enjoyment, excitement, equality, and freedom. Some strongly individualistic cultures include those of Canada, the United States, Australia, Great Britain and the Netherlands. Venezuela, Pakistan, Taiwan, Thailand, Turkey, Greece and Portugal are some examples of strongly collectivist cultures.[7]

> **collectivist culture** a society that encourages people to subordinate their personal goals to those of a stable in-group; values such as self-discipline and group accomplishment are stressed

> **individualist culture** a society that encourages people to attach more importance to personal goals than to group goals; values such as personal enjoyment and freedom are stressed

Values are very general ideas about good and bad goals. From these flow **norms,** or rules dictating what is right or wrong, acceptable or unacceptable. Some norms, called *enacted norms,* such as the rule that a green traffic-light means "go" and a red one means "stop," are explicitly decided upon. Many norms, however, are much more subtle. These *crescive norms* are embedded in a culture and are only discovered through interaction with other members of that culture. Crescive norms include the following:[8]

> **norm** the informal rules that govern what is right or wrong

- A **custom** is a norm handed down from the past that controls basic behaviours, such as division of labour in a household or the practice of particular ceremonies.

> **custom** a norm that is derived from a traditional way of doing things

more a norm with strong moral overtones

conventions norms regarding the conduct of everyday life

- A **more** is a custom with a strong moral overtone. A more often involves a taboo, or forbidden behaviour, such as incest or cannibalism. Violation of a more often meets with strong punishment from other members of a society.

- **Conventions** are norms regarding the conduct of everyday life. These rules deal with the subtleties of consumer behaviour, including the "correct" way to furnish one's house, wear one's clothes, host a dinner party and so on.

All three types of crescive norms may operate to completely define a culturally appropriate behaviour. For example, a more may tell us what kind of food is permissible to eat. (Note that mores vary across cultures, so a meal of dog may be taboo in Canada, while Hindus would shun steaks and Muslims would avoid pork products.) A custom dictates the appropriate hour at which the meal should be served. Conventions tell us how to eat it, including such details as the utensils to be used, table etiquette and the appropriate apparel to be worn at dinner time.

We often take these conventions for granted (again, until we travel to a foreign country!), assuming that they are the "right" things to do. And it is good to remember that much of what we know about these norms is learned *vicariously* (see Chapter 3), as we observe the behaviours of actors and actresses in television commercials, sitcoms, print ads and other popular-culture media. In the long run, marketers have an awful lot to do with influencing consumers' enculturation!

MYTHS AND RITUALS

Every culture develops stories and practices that help its members to make sense of the world. When we examine these activities in other cultures, they often seem strange or even unfathomable. Yet our *own* cultural practices appear quite normal—even though a visitor may find them equally bizarre!

It Works Like Magic!

To appreciate how "primitive" belief systems that some may consider irrational or superstitious continue to influence our supposedly "modern," rational society, consider the avid interest of many consumers in magic. Marketers of health foods, anti-aging cosmetics, exercise programs and gambling casinos often imply that their offerings have "magical" properties that will ward off sickness, old age, poverty or just plain bad luck. People by the millions play their "lucky numbers" in the lottery and carry rabbits' feet and other amulets to ward off "the evil eye," and many have "lucky" clothing or other items they believe will bring them good fortune. Software developers even supply "wizards" that help to guide the uninitiated through the arcane layers of their programs!

An interest in the occult tends to be popular when members of a society feel overwhelmed or powerless. Magical remedies simplify our lives by giving us "easy" answers. Even a computer is regarded with awe by many consumers as a sort of "electronic magician," with the ability to solve our problems (or, in other cases, to make data magically disappear!).[9] This section discusses myths and rituals, two aspects of culture common to all societies from the ancients to the modern world.

Myths

Every society possesses a set of myths which define that culture. A **myth** is a story containing symbolic elements that expresses the shared emotions and ideals of a culture. The story often features some kind of conflict between two opposing forces, and its outcome serves as a moral guide for people. In this way a myth reduces anxiety by providing consumers with guidelines about their world.

An understanding of cultural myths is important to marketers, who in some cases (most likely unconsciously) pattern their strategies along mythic structures. Consider, for example, the way that a company like McDonald's takes on "mythical" qualities.[10] The "Golden Arches" are a universally recognized symbol, one that is virtually synonymous with American culture. They offer sanctuary to Americans around the world, who know exactly what to expect once they enter. Basic struggles involving good versus evil are played out in the fantasy world created by McDonald's advertising, as when Ronald McDonald confounds the Hamburglar. McDonald's even has a "seminary" (Hamburger University) where inductees go to learn appropriate behaviours.

Myths serve the following four interrelated functions in a culture:[11]

1. *Metaphysical.* They help to explain the origins of existence.

2. *Cosmological.* They emphasize that all components of the universe are part of a single picture.

3. *Sociological.* They maintain social order by authorizing a social code to be followed by members of a culture.

4. *Psychological.* They provide models for personal conduct.

Myths can be analyzed by examining their underlying structures, a technique pioneered by the anthropologist Claude Lévi-Strauss (no relation to the blue jeans company). Lévi-Strauss noted that many stories involve **binary opposition,** in which two opposing ends of some dimension are represented (good versus evil or nature versus technology). Characters and, in some cases, products are often defined by what they are not rather than what they are (e.g., "This is not your father's Oldsmobile" and "I can't believe it's not butter").

Recall from the discussion of Freudian theory in Chapter 6 that the ego functions as a kind of "referee" between the opposing needs of the id and the superego. In a similar fashion, the conflict between mythical opposing forces is sometimes resolved by a *mediating figure* who can link the opposites by sharing characteristics of each. For example, many myths contain animals that have human abilities (e.g., a talking snake) to bridge the gap between humanity and nature, just as cars (technology) are often given animal names (nature) like Cougar, Cobra or Mustang.

MYTHS ABOUND IN POPULAR CULTURE

While we generally equate myths with the ancient Greeks or Romans, modern myths are embodied in many aspects of modern popular culture, including comic books, movies, holidays and, yes, even commercials.

Comic-book superheroes demonstrate how myths can be communicated to consumers of all ages. Indeed, some of these fictional figures represent a **monomyth**—a myth that is common to many cultures.[12] The most prevalent monomyth involves a

myth a story containing symbolic elements that expresses the shared emotions and ideals of a culture

binary opposition a defining structural characteristic of many myths, where two opposing ends of some dimension are represented (e.g., good versus evil, nature versus technology)

monomyth a myth with basic characteristics that are found in many cultures

古くなった広告、お取り替え致します。

クリエイティブが元気です。

マッキャンエリクソン博報堂

This ad used in a corporate campaign for McCann-Erickson's Tokyo office plays off of the Superman myth by depicting a superhero with light beams radiating from his eyes. The headline reads: "We're ready to rejuvenate your advertising."
Courtesy of McCann-Erickson Hakuhodo Inc.

hero who emerges from the everyday world with supernatural powers and wins a decisive victory over evil forces. He then returns with the power to bestow good things on his fellow men. The recent success of the Disney movie *Hercules* reminds us that these stories are often timeless and have appealed to people through the ages.

Comic-book heroes are familiar to most consumers, and they are often viewed as more credible and effective than celebrity endorsers. Not even counting movie spin-offs or licensing deals, comic books today are a $300-million-a-year industry. The North American version of the monomyth is perhaps best epitomized by Superman, a Christlike figure who renounces worldly temptations and restores harmony to his community. This imagery is sometimes borrowed by marketers. Currently, PepsiCo is trying to enhance its position in the Japanese market by using a figure called "Pepsiman," a muscle-bound caricature of an American superhero in a skin-tight uniform, to promote the drink. Pepsiman even appears in a Sega game called *Fighting Vipers*.[13]

Many blockbuster movies and hit TV shows draw directly on mythic themes. While dramatic special effects or attractive stars certainly don't hurt, a number of these movies perhaps also owe their success to their presentation of characters and plot structures that follow mythic patterns. Three examples of these mythic blockbusters are:[14]

- *Gone with the Wind.* Myths are often set in times of upheaval, such as warfare. In this story, the North (which represents technology and democracy) is pitted against the South (which represents nature and aristocracy). The novel and movie depict a romantic era (the *ante-bellum* South) where love and honour were virtues. This era is replaced by the newer forces of materialism and industrialization (i.e., modern consumer culture). *Gone with the Wind* depicts a lost era when man and nature existed in harmony.

- *E.T.: The Extraterrestrial.* E.T. represents a familiar myth involving Messianic visitation. The gentle creature from another world visits Earth and performs miracles (e.g., reviving a dying flower). His "disciples" are neighbourhood chil-

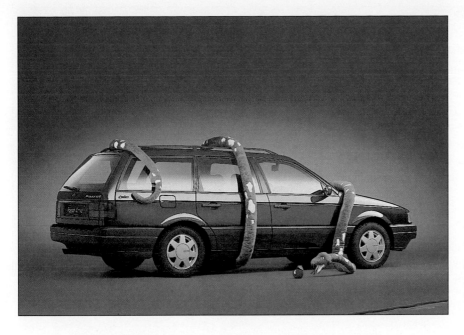

This Italian ad for Volkswagen plays upon the myth of the Garden of Eden, a classic struggle between virtue and temptation. The copy reads, "Whoever said that you would have to pay dearly for giving in to temptation?"
Courtesy of Volkswagen United States, Inc.

dren, who help him combat the forces of modern technology and an unbelieving secular society. The metaphysical function of myth is served by teaching that the humans chosen by God are pure and unselfish.

- *Star Trek.* The television series and movies documenting the adventures of the starship Enterprise are also linked to myths, such as the story of the New England Puritans exploring and conquering a new continent—"the final frontier." Encounters with the Klingons mirror skirmishes with American Native peoples. In addition, the quest for Paradise was a theme employed in at least 13 out of the original 79 episodes filmed.[15]

Rituals

A **ritual** is a set of symbolic behaviours that occur in a fixed sequence and that tend to be repeated periodically.[16] Although bizarre tribal ceremonies, perhaps involving animal or virgin sacrifice, may come to mind when people think of rituals, in reality many contemporary consumer activities are ritualistic. Just think of Whitney's daily "mental health" trip to Starbucks.

Rituals can occur at a variety of levels, as noted in Table 16–1. Some affirm broad cultural or religious values, while others occur in small groups or even in isolation. Market researchers discovered, for example, that for many people the act of late-night ice-cream eating has ritualistic overtones, often involving a favourite spoon and bowl![17] Rituals can even be invented or modified to bring about changes in consumer behaviour. In Fiji, a group of visiting doctors who were concerned about the pervasiveness of smoking (60 percent of adult men indulge) created a tobacco taboo in one village by devising a ritual involving kava, a sacred potion that is mildly hallucinogenic. After convincing the villagers that the evil spirits of cigarettes can be excised using the kava, the village became a smoke-free oasis in a tobacco-happy society.[18]

ritual a set of symbolic behaviours that occur in a fixed sequence and that tend to be repeated periodically

TABLE 16–1 Types of Ritual Experience		
PRIMARY BEHAVIOUR SOURCE	RITUAL TYPE	EXAMPLES
Cosmology	Religious	Baptism, meditation, mass
Cultural values	Rites of passage	Graduation, marriage
	Cultural	Festivals, holidays (Valentine's Day)
Group learning	Civic	Parades, elections, trials
	Group	Business negotiations, office luncheons
	Family	Mealtimes, bedtimes, birthdays, Mother's Day, Christmas
Individual aims and emotions	Personal	Grooming, household rituals

Source: Dennis W. Rook, "The Ritual Dimension of Consumer Behavior," *Journal of Consumer Research* 12 (December 1985): 251–64. Reprinted with permission of The University of Chicago Press.

ritual artifacts items (consumer goods) used in the performance of rituals

Many businesses owe their livelihood to their ability to supply **ritual artifacts**—items used in the performance of rituals—to consumers. Birthday candles, diplomas, specialized foods and beverages (wedding cakes, ceremonial wine, or even hot dogs at the ball park), trophies and plaques, band costumes and retirement watches are all used in consumer rituals. In addition, consumers often employ ritual scripts that identify the artifacts, the sequence in which they are used and who uses them. Examples include graduation programs and etiquette books.

GROOMING RITUALS

Whether brushing one's hair 100 strokes a day or talking to oneself in the mirror, virtually all consumers undergo private grooming rituals. These are sequences of behaviours that aid in the transition from the private self to the public self or back again. These rituals serve various purposes, ranging from inspiring confidence before confronting the world to cleansing the body of dirt and other profane materials.

When consumers talk about their grooming rituals, some of the dominant themes that emerge from these stories reflect the almost mystical qualities attributed to grooming products and behaviours. Many people emphasize a before-and-after phenomenon, whereby the person feels magically transformed after using certain products (similar to the Cinderella myth).[19]

Two sets of binary oppositions that are expressed in personal rituals are *private–public* and *work–leisure*. Many beauty rituals, for instance, reflect transformations from natural states to the social world (as when a woman "puts on her face") or vice versa. In these daily rituals, women reaffirm the value placed by their culture on personal beauty and the quest for eternal youth.[20] This focus is obvious in ads for Oil of Olay Beauty Cleanser, which proclaim "... And so your day begins. The Ritual of Oil of Olay." Similarly, the bath is viewed as a sacred, cleansing time, a way to wash away the sins of the profane world.[21]

GIFT-GIVING RITUALS

The promotion of appropriate gifts for every conceivable holiday and occasion provides an excellent example of the influence consumer rituals can exert on marketing phenomena. In the **gift-giving ritual** consumers procure the perfect object (artifact), meticulously remove the price tag (symbolically changing the item from a commodity to a unique good), carefully wrap it, and deliver it to the recipient.[22]

Gift giving is primarily viewed by researchers as a form of *economic exchange,* in which the giver transfers an item of value to a recipient, who in turn is obligated to reciprocate. However, gift giving can also involve *symbolic exchange,* wherein the giver is motivated by unselfish factors, such as love or admiration, and does not expect anything in return. Some research indicates that gift giving evolves as a form of social expression; it is more exchange-oriented (instrumental) in the early stages of a relationship but becomes more altruistic as the relationship develops.[23]

Every culture prescribes certain occasions and ceremonies for giving gifts, whether for personal or professional reasons. The giving of birthday presents alone is a major undertaking, and business gifts are an important component in defining professional relationships. Expenditures on business gifts exceed $1.5 billion (US) per year, and great care is often taken to ensure that the appropriate gifts are purchased.

The gift-giving ritual can be broken down into three distinct stages.[24] During *gestation,* the giver is motivated by an event to procure a gift. This event may be either *structural* (i.e., prescribed by the culture, as when people buy Christmas presents) or *emergent* (i.e., made for more personal and idiosyncratic reasons). The second stage is *presentation,* or the process of gift exchange. The recipient responds to the gift (either appropriately or not) and the donor evaluates this response. In the third stage, known as *reformulation,* the bonds between the giver and receiver are adjusted (either to be looser or tighter) to reflect the new relationship that emerges after the exchange is complete. Negativity can arise if the recipient feels that the gift is inappropriate or of inferior quality. The donor may feel the response to the gift

gift-giving ritual the events involved in the selection, presentation, acceptance and interpretation of a gift

The ritual of opening Christmas presents is one of the most familiar and beloved for many consumers.
© Julie Marcotte/TWS-Click/Chicago Ltd.

MARKETING PITFALL

*B*ride's magazine reports that a newly married couple receives an average of 171 wedding gifts, many of which they don't want or need.[25] While just about everyone has at one time or another received a ghastly gift, this "dark side" of gift giving was highlighted in a recent study by an economist, who calculated that of the $40 billion spent yearly on holiday gifts, roughly $4 billion is a "deadweight loss." This refers to the difference between the amount spent on a gift and the value the recipient assigns to it; a gift's "yield" is regarded as its perceived value compared to its true value. For example, if a tie cost $10 but you feel it's worth only $8 to you, its yield is 80 percent. The study computed the average yield of a gift to be 94.1 percent. Based on a survey of students at five universities, these yields were reported (100 percent means the gift has an intrinsic value equal to its actual value):[26]

CDs 104.4%   Books 91%   Socks, underwear 87.7%   Cosmetics 85.7%

was inadequate, insincere or a violation of the reciprocity norm, which obliges people to return the gesture of a gift with one of equal value.[27] Both participants may feel resentful for being "forced" to participate in the ritual.[28]

MULTICULTURAL DIMENSIONS

*T*he importance of gift-giving rituals is underscored by considering Japanese customs, wherein the wrapping of a gift is as important (if not more so) than the gift itself. The economic value of a gift is secondary to its symbolic meaning.[29] To the Japanese, gifts are viewed as an important aspect of one's duty to others in one's social group. Giving is a moral imperative (known as *giri*).

Highly ritualized gift giving occurs during the giving of both household/personal gifts and company/professional gifts. Each Japanese has a well-defined set of relatives and friends (usually 15 to 20) with which he or she shares reciprocal gift-giving obligations (*kosai*).[30] Japanese tourists to PEI, Banff, Whistler and Victoria are serviced by stores opened and operated by Japanese nationals. It is not uncommon for tourists to purchase five to ten of the same item to take home to Japan.

Personal gifts are given on social occasions, such as funerals, to people who are hospitalized, to mark movements from one life stage to another (e.g., weddings and birthdays) and as greetings (e.g., when one is meeting a visitor). Company gifts are given to commemorate the anniversary of a corporation's founding or the opening of a new building, and they are a routine part of doing business, as when rewards are given at trade meetings to announce new products.

Some of the items most desired by Japanese consumers as gifts include gift coupons, beer and soap.[31] In keeping with the Japanese emphasis on saving face, presents are not opened in front of the giver, so that it will not be necessary to hide one's possible disappointment with the present.

HOLIDAY RITUALS AND HEROES

On holidays consumers step back from their everyday lives and perform ritualistic behaviours unique to those times.[32] Holiday occasions are filled with ritual artifacts and scripts, and are increasingly cast by enterprising marketers as times for giving gifts. The Thanksgiving holiday is bursting with rituals; these scripts include serving (in gluttonous portions) foods like turkey and cranberry sauce that may only be consumed on that day, complaints about how much one has eaten (yet rising to the occasion to somehow find room for dessert), and (for many) a post-meal trip to the couch for the obligatory video. On Valentine's Day, standards regarding sex and love are relaxed or altered as people express feelings that may be hidden during the rest of the year.

In addition to established holidays, new occasions are invented to capitalize on the need for cards and other ritual artifacts that will then have to be acquired.[33] These cultural events often originate with the greeting-card industry, which conveniently stimulates demand for more of its products. Some recently invented holidays include Secretaries' Day and Grandparents' Day.

Most cultural holidays are based on myths, and often real or imaginary characters (e.g., Cupid on Valentine's Day) are at the centre of the stories. These holidays persist because their basic elements appeal to consumers' deep-seated needs.[34] Two of our holidays that are especially rich both in cultural symbolism and in consumption meanings are Christmas and Halloween.

The Christmas holiday is bursting with myths and rituals, from adventures at the North Pole to those that occur under the mistletoe. The meaning of Christmas has evolved quite dramatically over the last few hundred years. Few Canadians know that Boxing Day is derived from old England, where the rich "boxed" their leftovers for the poor the day after Christmas. One of the most important holiday rituals involves Santa Claus, a mythical figure eagerly awaited by children the world over. In opposition to Christ, Santa is a champion of materialism. Perhaps it is no coincidence, then, that he appears in stores and shopping malls—secular temples of consumption. Whatever his origins, the Santa Claus myth serves the purpose of socializing children by teaching them to expect rewards when they are good and that members of society get what they deserve.

Halloween is a holiday that has evolved from a pagan religious observance to a secular event. However, in contrast to Christmas, the rituals of Halloween (e.g., trick-or-treat and costume parties) primarily involve non-family members. Halloween is an unusual holiday because its rituals are the opposite of many other cultural occasions. In contrast to Christmas, it celebrates evil instead of good, and death rather than birth, and it encourages revellers to extort treats with veiled threats of "tricks" rather than rewarding only the good.

Halloween observances among adults are booming, changing the character of this holiday. Halloween is now the second most popular party night for adults (after New Year's Eve), and one in four grown-ups wears a costume.[35] The holiday is now becoming trendy in Europe as well, where the French in particular have discovered it as an occasion for festivities, dancing and the chance to show off new fashions.[36]

The shift in the Halloween ritual has been attributed to adult fears aroused by stories of children receiving tampered candy containing poison, razor blades and so on, which encourage people to plan supervised parties rather than send their children out for trick-or-treating.[37] Another factor accounting for the popularity of Halloween among adults is that, unlike other holidays, its celebration does not require a

The Coca-Cola Company claims credit for inventing the modern image of Santa, which it distributed in its advertising in 1931. Until that time (the company claims) Santa was pictured as a cartoonlike elf. More likely, the modern image of Santa Claus was shaped by the nineteenth-century cartoonist Thomas Nast, whose rendering of Santa was related to his other drawings of "fat cats" like Boss Tweed and the Robber Barons, greedy capitalists who exploited the poor and lived in useless luxury. This Thomas Nast cartoon was published in 1881. Despite this figure's resemblance to Santa Claus, it is actually a caricature of a "fat cat" Robber Baron who had accumulated a horde of worldly possessions.

Source: T. Nast, "Merry Old Santa Claus," in Russell W. Belk, Journal of American Culture *(Spring 1987): 88. NorthWind Picture Archives. Jerry Schwartz, "At Age 104, Coke Congratulates Itself,"* New York Times *(August 11, 1990): C30.*

family, which thus permits single people to participate without feeling lonely or left out.[38]

RITES OF PASSAGE

rites of passage sacred times marked by a change in social status

Examples of modern **rites of passage** are special times marked by a change in social status. Every society, both primitive and modern, sets aside times where such changes occur. Some of these changes may occur as a natural part of consumers' life cycles (e.g., puberty or death), while others are more individual in nature (getting divorced and re-entering the dating market).

Some marketers attempt to reach consumers when their products can enhance a transition from one stage of life to another.[39] For example, a chain of fur stores ran a series of ads positioning a fur coat as a way to celebrate "all of life's moments." Suggested moments included a 30th birthday, a raise and a second marriage. They even promoted a "divorce is final" fur coat. "Shed the tears and slip into a fur," reads the ad.[40]

Much like the metamorphosis of a caterpillar into a butterfly, consumers' rites of passage consist of three phases.[41] The first stage, *separation,* occurs when the individual is detached from his or her original group or status (e.g., the university student leaves home). *Liminality* is the middle stage, where the person is literally in between statuses (the new arrival on campus tries to figure out what is happening during orientation week). The last stage, *aggregation,* takes place when the person re- enters society after the rite of passage is complete (the student returns home for Christmas vacation as a university "veteran").

Rites of passage mark many consumer activities. A similar transitional state can be observed when people are prepared for certain occupational roles. For example, athletes and fashion models typically undergo a "seasoning" process. They are removed from their normal surroundings (athletes are taken to training camps,

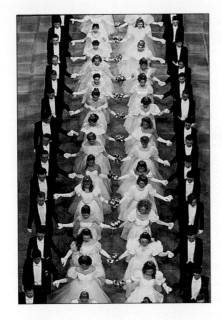

One enduring ritual undergone by many affluent young women is the debutante ball, where debs are presented in society circles. This ritual is highly scripted: debs are taught to curtsy, promenade around the dance floor and waltz with their fathers. This ritual signifies that the protected young woman has now come of age and is entering the adult world. Somewhat similar ceremonies that occur in other economic and/or ethnic subcultures include bar and bat mitzvahs, "sweet 16" parties, and proms.
Source: Jennifer Edson Escalas, "The Consumption of Insignificant Rituals: A Look at Debutante Balls," in Advances in Consumer Research 20, *eds. Leigh McAlister and Michael L. Rothschild (Provo, UT: Association for Consumer Research, 1992): 709–16. Photo courtesy of Hinterleitner/Contr and Gamma-Liason, Inc.*

while young models are often moved to Paris), indoctrinated into a new subculture and then returned to the real world in their new role.

Even the rites of passage associated with death support an entire industry. Survivors must make fairly expensive purchase decisions, often on short notice and driven by emotional and superstitious concerns. The funeral industry is beginning to be more aggressive in its marketing practices and is even targeting younger consumers who are worried about arranging for their aging parents (the prepayment of funeral and burial expenses is euphemistically known in the industry as "pre-need").[42]

Funeral ceremonies help the living to organize their relationships with the deceased, and action tends to be tightly scripted, down to the costumes (the ritual black attire, black ribbons for mourners, and the body in its best suit) and specific

MARKETING OPPORTUNITY

Hold the starch: while many rituals are strongly ingrained, sometimes pressure arises to adapt them to modern times. This is the case with the custom of throwing rice (symbolizing fertility) at a wedding. In recent years many newlyweds have substituted soap bubbles or jingling bells because of the tendency of birds to eat the rice, which can then expand inside their bodies and cause injury or death. Some enterprising businesses are springing up to work around this problem. The Hole-in-Hand Butterfly Farm in Pennsylvania ships newly hatched butterflies at $100 a dozen. They arrive in dark, cool envelopes that keep them in a resting stage until the package is opened, when they fly out in a crescendo of wagging wings. Another company sells a product called Bio Wedding Rice—reconstituted rice that dissolves in water and doesn't harm birds.[43]

behaviours (sending condolence cards or holding a wake). Mourners "pay their last respects," and seating during the ceremony is usually dictated by mourners' closeness to the individual. Even the cortège (the funeral motorcade) is accorded special status by other motorists, who recognize its separate, sacred nature by not cutting in line as it proceeds to the cemetery.[44]

SACRED AND PROFANE CONSUMPTION

As we saw when considering the structure of myths, many types of consumer activity involve the demarcation, or binary opposition, of boundaries, such as good versus bad, male versus female, or even regular versus low calorie. One of the most important of these sets of boundaries is the distinction between the sacred and the profane. **Sacred consumption** involves objects and events that are set apart from normal activities and are treated with some degree of respect or awe. They may or may not be associated with religion, but most religious items and events tend to be regarded as sacred. **Profane consumption** involves consumer objects and events that are ordinary, everyday objects, and events that do not share the "specialness" of sacred ones. (Note that profane does *not* mean vulgar or obscene in this context.)

sacred consumption the process of consuming objects and events that are set apart from normal life and treated with some degree of respect or awe

profane consumption the process of consuming objects and events that are ordinary or of the everyday world

Domains of Sacred Consumption

Sacred consumption events permeate many aspects of consumers' experiences. We find ways to set apart a variety of places, people and events. In this section we'll consider some examples of ways that "ordinary" consumption is sometimes not so ordinary after all.

SACRED PLACES

Sacred places have been set apart by a society because they have religious or mystical significance (Bethlehem, Mecca and Stonehenge) or because they commemorate some aspect of a country's heritage (the Kremlin, the Emperor's Palace in Tokyo and the Statue of Liberty). Remember that in many cases the sacredness of these places is due to the property of contamination; that is, something sacred happened on that spot, so the place itself takes on sacred qualities.

Still other places are created from the profane world and imbued with sacred qualities. Graumann's Chinese Theater in Hollywood, where movie stars leave their footprints in concrete for posterity, is one such place. Even the modern shopping mall can be regarded as a secular "cathedral of consumption," a special place where community members come to practise shopping rituals. Theme parks are a form of mass-produced fantasy that take on aspects of sacredness. In particular, Disney World and Disneyland (and their new outposts in Europe and Japan) are destinations for pilgrimages from consumers around the globe. Disney World displays many characteristics of more traditional sacred places. It is even regarded by some as having healing powers. A trip to the park is the most common last wish for terminally ill children.[45]

In many cultures the home is a particularly sacred place. It represents a crucial distinction between the harsh, external world and consumers' "inner space." Consumers all over the world go to great lengths to create special environments that allow them to create the quality of homeyness. This effect is created by personalizing the home as much as possible, using such devices as door wreaths, mantle arrangements and a "memory wall" for family photos.[46] Even public places, like Starbucks cafés, strive for a home-like atmosphere that shelters customers from the harshness of the outside world.

SACRED PEOPLE

People themselves can be sacred when they are idolized and set apart from the masses. Souvenirs, memorabilia, and even mundane items touched or used by sacred people become valuable.

Many businesses thrive on consumers' desire for products associated with famous people. There is a bustling marketplace for celebrity autographs and objects once owned by celebrities. Whether Princess Di's gowns or John Lennon's guitars, these touched objects are often sold at auction for astronomical prices. One entrepreneur dug dirt from the lawns of Johnny Carson, Shirley MacLaine, Katherine Hepburn and 43 other stars. He sold 20 000 vials of celebrity dirt in three years, at $1.95 a vial. A store called "A Star Is Worn" sells items donated by celebrities. A black bra autographed by Cher recently went for $575. As one observer commented about the store's patrons, "They want something that belonged to the stars, as if the stars have gone into sainthood and the people want their shrouds."[47]

SACRED EVENTS

For many people the world of sports is sacred and almost assumes the status of a religion. The roots of modern sports events can be found in ancient religious rites, such as fertility festivals (e.g., the original Olympics).[48] The sports pages are like the Scriptures (and we describe ardent fans as reading them "religiously"); the stadium is a house of worship; and the fans are members of the congregation. Devotees engage in group activities such as tailgate parties and the "wave," where participants rise on cue and move their arms (like at a revival meeting), creating a wavelike motion around the stadium.

MARKETING PITFALL

The public's fascination with the images of celebrities, living or dead, endures. The images of dead stars are frequently brought back to life to endorse products. James Dean hawks Jack Purcells sneakers, and Babe Ruth sells Zenith products. Licensing fees for dead celebrities now average about $100 million (US) per year.[49]

The sacredness of some celebrities has spawned a secondary industry: celebrity look-alikes and sound-alikes. The simulated voice of Louis Armstrong has appeared in ads for the Hershey Food Corporation, Canada Dry and Milk Bones.[50] Elvis Presley has imitators around the world. By one estimate, about 100 women make their living impersonating Marilyn Monroe.[51] This type of advertising is so pervasive that several lawsuits have been brought by stars (such as Woody Allen) who wished to prevent doubles from using their likenesses.[52] Nonetheless, look-alikes continue to be used, with disclaimer notices appearing in the ads.[53]

At US$15.95 per head, about 700 000 people annually make the pilgrimage to Graceland, the home of Elvis Presley. True pilgrims surround themselves with Elvis artifacts. One such fan wears an Elvis watch and earrings, has furnished her home with Elvis plates, cups, clocks, statues and rugs, and has even named her daughter Lisa (after Presley's daughter). She claimed, "There can never be too much Elvis."

Quoted in Peter Applebome, "New Stop for Elvis Fans Who Can't Get Enough," New York Times (August 7, 1989): A8. Photo courtesy of Mark E. Gibson, 1986/The Stock Market.

The athletes that fans come to see are godlike; they are reputed to have almost superhuman powers (especially superstars like Michael Jordan, who is accorded the ability to fly in his Air Nikes). Athletes are central figures in a common cultural myth, the hero tale. Often the hero must prove him- or herself under strenuous circumstances (e.g., the situation where the starter is unexpectedly injured), and victory is achieved only through sheer force of will. The signing of Mark Messier by the Vancouver Canucks was promoted by management as the road to the Stanley Cup.

Tourism is another example of a sacred, non-ordinary experience of extreme importance to marketers. When people travel on vacation, they occupy sacred time and space. The tourist is continually in search of "authentic" experiences that differ from his or her normal world.[54] The tourism experience involves binary oppositions between work and leisure, and between being at home and being away. This theme is reflected in Club Med's motto, "The antidote to civilization."

The desire of travellers to capture these sacred experiences in objects forms the bedrock of the souvenir industry, which may be said to be in the business of selling sacred memories. Whether a personalized matchbook from a wedding or Niagara Falls salt-and-pepper shakers, souvenirs represent a tangible piece of the consumer's sacred experience.[55]

In addition to personal mementos, such as ticket stubs saved from a favourite concert, the following are other sacred souvenir icons:[56]

- pictorial images (e.g., postcards);
- "piece of the rock" (e.g., sea shells and pine cones);
- symbolic shorthand in the form of literal representations of the site (e.g., a miniature Eiffel Tower); and
- markers (e.g., Hard Rock Café T-shirts).

From Sacred to Profane, and Back Again

Just to make life interesting, in recent times many consumer activities have moved from one sphere to the other. Some things that were formerly regarded as sacred have moved into the realm of the profane, while other, everyday phenomena are now regarded as sacred.[57] Both of these processes are relevant to our understanding of contemporary consumer behaviour.

DESACRALIZATION

Desacralization occurs when a sacred item or symbol is removed from its special place or is duplicated in mass quantities, becoming profane as a result. For example, souvenir reproductions of sacred monuments (such as the Eiffel Tower) or artworks (such as the *Mona Lisa*), or adaptations of important symbols (such as the Canadian flag) by clothing designers, eliminate their special aspects by turning them into unauthentic commodities, produced mechanically and possessing relatively little value.[58]

Religion itself has to some extent been desacralized. Religious symbols, such as stylized crosses or New Age crystals, have moved into the mainstream of fashion jewellery.[59] Religious holidays, particularly Christmas, are regarded by many (and criticized by some) as having been transformed into secular, materialistic occasions devoid of their original sacred significance.

Even the clergy are increasingly adopting secular marketing techniques. Televangelists rely upon the power of television, a secular medium, to convey their messages. The Catholic Church generated a major controversy after it hired a prominent public relations firm to promote its antiabortion campaign.[60]

desacralization the process that occurs when a sacred item or symbol is removed from its special place, or is duplicated in mass quantities, and becomes profane as a result

SACRALIZATION

Sacralization occurs when ordinary objects, events and people take on sacred meaning to a culture or to specific groups within a culture. For example, events like the Stanley Cup and people like Elvis Presley have become sacralized to some consumers.

Objectification occurs when sacred qualities are attributed to mundane items. One way that this process can occur is through *contamination,* where objects associated with sacred events or people become sacred in their own right. This explains the desire by many fans for items belonging to, or even touched by, famous people.

In addition to museum exhibits displaying rare objects, even mundane, inexpensive things may be set apart in *collections,* where they are transformed from profane items into sacred ones. An item is sacralized as soon as it enters a collection, and it takes on a special significance to the collector that in some cases may be hard to comprehend by the outsider.

The contents of collections range from movie memorabilia, rare books and autographs to Barbie dolls, Beatles memorabilia and junk mail.[61] Consumers are often ferociously attached to their collections. This passion is exemplified by the comment made in one study by a woman who collects teddy bears: "If my house ever burns down, I won't cry over my furniture, I'll cry over the bears."[62]

An item is sacralized as soon as it enters a collection, and it takes on special significance to the collector that in some cases may be hard for an outsider to compre-

sacralization a process that occurs when ordinary objects, events or people take on sacred meaning to a culture or to specific groups within a culture

hend. Collecting refers to the systematic acquisition of a particular object or set of objects, and this widespread activity can be distinguished from hoarding, which is merely unsystematic collecting.[63] Collecting typically involves both rational and emotional components, since collectors are frequently transfixed by their objects while also carefully organizing and exhibiting them.[64]

Some consumer researchers feel that collectors are motivated to acquire their "prizes" in order to gratify a high level of materialism in a socially acceptable manner. By systematically amassing a collection, the collector is allowed to "worship" material objects without feeling guilty or petty. Another perspective is that collecting is actually an aesthetic experience; for many collectors the pleasure emanates from being involved in creating the collection, rather than from passively admiring the items one has scavenged or bought. Whatever the motivation, hard-core collectors often devote a great deal of time and energy to maintaining and expanding their collections, so for many this activity becomes a central component of their extended self (see Chapter 5).[65]

MARKETING OPPORTUNITY

Marketers continue to find new ways to indulge consumers' passions for collecting. For example, many children and adults are avid collectors of sports trading cards. People spend about $1.5 billion (US) a year on these cards. Now, in addition to grabbing up photos and stats of baseball, football and hockey players, consumers can also collect trading cards featuring advertisements and product information for such companies as Sears, Harley-Davidson, Coca-Cola and the Hooters restaurant chain. The Sears cards feature photos of "classic" Craftsman tools, including such "valuable" items as reversible rachets and drill presses.

Some of the hottest new collectibles are phone cards. Sales of these prepaid cards are projected to reach around $3 billion by 2000. One company, called Future Call, has licensing agreements with "Star Trek," "Melrose Place" and "Mighty Morphin Power Rangers," and is issuing MCI cards with these images. The attractiveness of these cards to the phone companies is enhanced by the fact that many of them will never actually be redeemed as they are far more valuable to collectors if they are "virgins."[66]

Another "must have" for kids are Beanie Babies, a series of stuffed animals that come with distinctive names like Bubbles and Stinky and are released periodically. Ty, Inc. is doing a good job of following industry guidelines for creating collectible product lines, which include limiting the number of items available, numbering and dating each one, and offering a range to encourage people to collect the entire set.[67] Virtually no advertising is done, other than the provision of a Web site (*www.ty.com*) that gives information about the latest releases.[68] As any parent of a young girl can attest, no further encouragement is needed!

- A society's *culture* includes its values, its ethics and the material objects produced by its people. It is the accumulation of shared meanings and traditions among members of a society. A culture can be described in terms of its ecology (the way people adapt to their habitat), its social structure and its ideology (including people's moral and aesthetic principles).

- *Myths* are stories containing symbolic elements that express the shared ideals of a culture. Many myths involve some binary opposition, whereby values are defined in terms of what they are and what they are not (e.g., nature versus technology). Modern myths are transmitted through advertising, movies and other media.

- A *ritual* is a set of symbolic behaviours that occur in a fixed sequence and that tend to be repeated periodically. Rituals are related to many consumption activities that occur in popular culture. These include holiday observances, gift giving and grooming.

- A *rite of passage* is a special kind of ritual that involves the transition from one role to another. These passages typically entail the need to acquire products and services, called ritual artifacts, to facilitate the transition. Modern rites of passage include graduations, initiations, weddings, debutante balls and funerals.

- Consumer activities can be divided into sacred and profane domains. Sacred phenomena are "set apart" from everyday activities or products. People, events or objects can become sacralized. *Sacralization* occurs when sacred qualities are ascribed to products or items owned by sacred people. *Objectification* occurs when formerly sacred objects or activities become part of the everyday, as when "one-of-a-kind" works of art are reproduced in large quantities. *Descralization* occurs when objects that previously were considered sacred become commercialized and integrated into popular culture.

CHAPTER SUMMARY

KEY TERMS

Binary opposition p. 531
Collectivist cultures p. 529
Conventions p. 530
Culture p. 527
Custom p. 529
Desacralization p. 543
Ethos p. 529
Gift-giving ritual p. 535
Individualist cultures p. 529
Monomyth p. 531
More p. 530
Myth p. 531
Norms p. 529
Profane consumption p. 540
Rites of passage p. 538
Ritual p. 533
Ritual artifacts p. 534
Sacralization p. 5431
Sacred consumption p. 540

CONSUMER BEHAVIOUR CHALLENGE

1. Culture can be thought of as a society's personality. If your culture were a person, could you describe its personality traits?
2. What is the difference between an enacted norm and a crescive norm? Identify the set of crescive norms operating when a man and woman in your culture go out for dinner on a first date. What products and services are affected by these norms?

3. How do the consumer decisions involved in gift giving differ from other purchase decisions?

4. The chapter argues that not all gift giving is positive. In what ways can this ritual be unpleasant or negative?

5. Construct a ritual script for a wedding in your culture. How many artifacts can you list that are contained in this script?

6. What are some of the major motivations for the purchase of self-gifts? Discuss some marketing implications of these.

7. Describe the three stages of the rite of passage associated with graduating from university.

8. Identify the ritualized aspects of hockey that are employed in advertising.

9. "Christmas has become just another opportunity to exchange gifts and stimulate the economy." Do you agree? Why or why not?

CBC VIDEO VIGNETTES

Concepts at Work for Cross-Culture

Increasingly, Canadian companies are seeking growth and market opportunities in other countries. Canadian marketers need to understand how to do business internationally. They need to develop cultural awareness in order to be able to communicate well enough to understand consumers, make deals, advertise and set up marketing infrastructures. Even in countries that are fairly Westernized and where English is spoken as a second language, there are many challenges.

Cross-cultural issues facing marketers are related to verbal and non-verbal personal communication, and to how marketing activities are carried out in other countries. Developing cross-cultural interpersonal skills begins with a basic awareness that differences exist and a willingness to research and understand cultural variety. Language, religion, values, beliefs, norms and notions about time and space may need to be learned. Just as important is how marketing activities are managed. In Germany, for example, the hyperbole and exaggeration used to promote North American products is unacceptable and leads to perceptions that a product is actually of poor quality. In other countries there may be a need to establish a distribution network, to work carefully within legal and political frameworks, or to adjust product design. Much is learned while involved in marketing activities, but embarrassment can be avoided with some forethought and training before leaving Canada. Opportunities for developing new markets or expanding existing ones are at stake.

QUESTIONS

1. Why have Canadian companies become interested in international markets?

2. What do Canadians need to learn in order to work effectively in another country?

3. Provide examples of how to avoid blunders in cross-cultural marketing.

4. What do you think is the key to success in becoming an effective cross-cultural marketer?

Video Resource: "Cross-Culture," *Venture* #513 (November 6, 1994).

Additional Resources: "If the deal is worth it, swallow your pride," *Globe and Mail* (April 25, 1997): C2; "Learn quickly customs of new countries to avoid offending," *Globe and Mail* (April 25, 1997): C10; "When translating, get ready to alarm the porter," *Globe and Mail* (April 25, 1997): C14.

NOTES

1. Bill McDowell, "Starbucks is Ground Zero in Today's Coffee Culture," *Advertising Age* (December 9, 1996): 1 (2 pp.).

2. Seanna Browder, "Starbucks Does Not Live by Coffee Alone," *Business Week* (August 5, 1996): 76. For a discussion of the act of coffee drinking as a ritual, cf. Susan Fournier and Julie L. Yao, "Reviving Brand Loyalty: A Reconceptualization within the Framework of Consumer-Brand Relationships" (working paper no. 96-039, Harvard Business School, 1996).

3. "Spice Girls Dance into Culture Clash," *Montgomery Advertiser* (April 29, 1997): 2A.

4. Clifford Geertz, *The Interpretation of Cultures* (New York: Basic Books, 1973); Marvin Harris, *Culture, People and Nature* (New York: Crowell, 1971); John F. Sherry, Jr., "The Cultural Perspective in Consumer Research," in *Advances in Consumer Research 13*, ed. Richard J. Lutz (Provo, UT: Association for Consumer Research, 1985), pp. 573–75.

5. William Lazer, Shoji Murata and Hiroshi Kosaka, "Japanese Marketing: Towards a Better Understanding," *Journal of Marketing* 49 (Spring 1985): 69–81.

6. Geert Hofstede, *Cultures Consequences* (Beverly Hills, CA: Sage, 1980). See also Laura M. Milner, Dale Fodness and Mark W. Speece, "Hofstede's Research on Cross-Cultural Work-Related Values: Implications for Consumer Behavior," in *Proceedings of the 1992 ACR Summer Conference* (Amsterdam: Association for Consumer Research, 1992).

7. Daniel Goleman, "The Group and the Self: New Focus on a Cultural Rift," *New York Times* (December 25, 1990): 37; Harry C. Triandis, "The Self and Social Behavior in Differing Cultural Contexts," *Psychological Review* 96 (July 1989): 506; Harry C. Triandis et al., "Individualism and Collectivism: Cross-Cultural Perspectives on Self-Ingroup Relationships," *Journal of Personality and Social Psychology* 54 (February 1988): 323.

8. George J. McCall and J.L. Simmons, *Social Psychology: A Sociological Approach* (New York: Free Press, 1982).

9. Molly O'Neill, "As Life Gets More Complex, Magic Casts a Wider Spell," *New York Times* (June 13, 1994): A1 (2 pp.).

10. Conrad Phillip Kottak, "Anthropological Analysis of Mass Enculturation," in *Researching American Culture,* ed. Conrad P. Kottak (Ann Arbor, MI: University of Michigan Press, 1982), pp. 40–74.

11. Joseph Campbell, *Myths, Dreams, and Religion* (New York: E.P. Dutton, 1970).

12. Jeffrey S. Lang and Patrick Trimble, "Whatever Happened to the Man of Tomorrow? An Examination of the American Monomyth and the Comic Book Superhero," *Journal of Popular Culture* 22 (Winter 1988): 157.

13. Yumiko Ono, "PepsiCo's 'American' Superhero in Japanese Ads is Alien to U.S.," *Wall Street Journal Interactive Edition* (May 23, 1997).

14. Elizabeth C. Hirschman, "Movies as Myths: An Interpretation of Motion Picture Mythology," in *Marketing and Semiotics: New Directions in the Study of Signs for Sale,* ed. Jean Umiker-Sebeok (Berlin: Mouton de Guyter, 1987), pp. 335–74.

15. See William Blake Tyrrell, "Star Trek as Myth and Television as Mythmaker," in *The Popular Culture Reader,* eds. Jack Nachbar, Deborah Weiser, and John L. Wright (Bowling Green, OH: Bowling Green University Press, 1978), pp. 79–88.

16. See Dennis W. Rook, "The Ritual Dimension of Consumer Behavior," *Journal of Consumer Research* 12 (December 1985): 251–64; Mary A. Stansfield Tetreault and Robert E. Kleine III, "Ritual, Ritualized Behavior, and Habit: Refinements and Extensions of the Consumption Ritual Construct," in *Advances in Consumer Research 17*, eds. Marvin Goldberg, Gerald Gorn and Richard W. Pollay (Provo, UT: Association for Consumer Research, 1990), pp. 31–38.

17. Kim Foltz, "New Species for Study: Consumers in Action," *New York Times* (December 18, 1989): A1.

18. Christina Duff, "Fijian Village, Surfing Doctors Invoke Taboo Against Tobacco," *Wall Street Journal Interactive Edition* (May 19, 1997).

19. Dennis W. Rook and Sidney J. Levy, "Psychosocial Themes in Consumer Grooming Rituals," in *Advances in Consumer Research 10*, eds. Richard P. Bagozzi and Alice M. Tybout (Provo, UT: Association for Consumer Research, 1983), pp. 329–33.

20. Diane Barthel, *Putting on Appearances*.

21. Quoted in Barthel, *Putting on Appearances: Gender and Advertising* (Philadelphia: Temple University Press, 1988).

22. Russell W. Belk, Melanie Wallendorf and John F. Sherry, Jr., "The Sacred and the Profane in Consumer Behavior: Theodicy on the Odyssey," *Journal of Consumer Research* 16 (June 1989): 1–38.

23. Russell W. Belk and Gregory S. Coon, "Gift Giving as Agapic Love: An Alternative to the Exchange Paradigm Based on Dating Experiences," *Journal of Consumer Research* 20, 3 (December 1993): 393–417.

24. John F. Sherry, Jr., "Gift Giving in Anthropological Perspective," *Journal of Consumer Research* 10 (September 1983): 157–68.

25. Quoted in Cyndee Miller, "Nix the Knick-Knacks; Send Cash," *Marketing News* 1, 13 (May 26, 1997): 1.

26. Hubert B. Herring, "Dislike Those Suspenders? Don't Complain, Quantify!" *New York Times* (December 25, 1994): F3.

27. Daniel Goleman, "What's Under the Tree? Clues to a Relationship," *New York Times* (December 19, 1989): C1.

28. John F. Sherry, Jr., Mary Ann McGrath and Sidney J. Levy, "The Dark Side of the Gift," *Journal of Business Research* 28 (November 1993): 225–44.

29. Colin Camerer, "Gifts as Economics Signals and Social Symbols," *American Journal of Sociology* 94 (supplement 1988): 5180-5214.

30. Robert T. Green and Dana L. Alden, "Functional Equivalence in Cross-Cultural Consumer Behavior: Gift Giving in Japan and the United States," *Psychology & Marketing* 5 (Summer 1988): 155–68.

31. Hiroshi Tanaka and Miki Iwamura, "Gift Selection Strategy of Japanese Seasonal Gift Purchasers: An Explorative Study" (paper presented at the Association for Consumer Research, Boston, October 1994).

32. See, for example, Russell W. Belk, "Halloween: An Evolving American Consumption Ritual," in *Advances in Consumer Research 17*, eds. Richard Pollay, Jerry Gorn and Marvin Goldberg (Provo, UT: Association for Consumer Research, 1990), pp. 508–17; Melanie Wallendorf and Eric J. Arnould, "We Gather Together: The Consumption Rituals of Thanksgiving Day," *Journal of Consumer Research* 18 (June 1991): 13–31.

33. Rick Lyte, "Holidays, Ethnic Themes Provide Built-In F&B Festivals," *Hotel & Motel Management* (December 14, 1987): 56; Megan Rowe, "Holidays and Special Occasions: Restaurants are Fast Replacing Grandma's House as the Site of Choice for Special Meals," *Restaurant Management* (November 1987): 69; Judith Waldrop, "Funny Valentines," *American Demographics* (February 1989): 7.

34. Bruno Bettelheim, *The Uses of Enchantment: The Meaning and Importance of Fairy Tales* (New York: Alfred A. Knopf, 1976).

35. Andrea Adelson, "A New Spirit for Sales of Halloween Merchandise," *New York Times* (October 31, 1994): D1 (2 pp.).

36. Anne Swardson, "Trick or Treat? In Paris, It's Dress, Dance, Eat," *International Herald Tribune* (October 31, 1996): 2.

37. N.R. Kleinfeld, "The Weird, the Bad and the Scary," *New York Times* (October 15, 1989): 4.

38. Georgia Dullea, "It's the Year's No. 2 Night to Howl," *New York Times* (October 30, 1988): 20.

39. Michael R. Solomon and Punam Anand, "Ritual Costumes and Status Transition: The Female Business Suit as Totemic Emblem," in *Advances in Consumer Research 12*, eds. Elizabeth C. Hirschman and Morris Holbrook (Washington, DC: Association for Consumer Research, 1985), pp. 315–18.

40. "Divorce Can Be Furry," *American Demographics* (March 1987): 24.

41. Arnold Van Gennep, *The Rites of Passage,* trans. Maika B. Vizedom and Gabrielle L. Caffee (1908; London: Routledge and Kegan Paul, 1960); Solomon and Anand, "Ritual Costumes and Status Transition."

42. Kelly Shermach, "Pay Now, Die Later: Consumers Urged Not to Delay that Final Decision," *Marketing News* (October 24, 1994): 1 (2 pp.).

43. the Bride; Get Ready to Release a Swarm of Live Insects," *Wall Street Journal* (January 22, 1996): B1.

44. Walter W. Whitaker III, "The Contemporary American Funeral Ritual," in *Rites and Ceremonies in Popular Culture,* ed. Ray B. Browne (Bowling Green, OH: Bowling Green University Press, 1980), pp. 316–25. For a recent examination of funeral rituals, see Larry D. Compeau and Carolyn Nicholson, "Funerals: Emotional Rituals or Ritualistic Emotions" (paper presented at the Association of Consumer Research, Boston, October 1994).

45. Conrad Phillip Kottak, "Anthropological Analysis of Mass Enculturation," in *Researching American Culture*, ed. Conrad P. Kottak (Ann Arbor, MI: University of Michigan Press, 1982), pp. 40–74.

46. Grant McCracken, "Homeyness: A Cultural Account of One Constellation of Goods and Meanings," in *Interpretive Consumer Research*, ed. Elizabeth C. Hirschman (Provo, UT: Association for Consumer Research, 1989), pp. 168–84.

47. James Hirsch, "Taking Celebrity Worship to New Depths," *New York Times* (November 9, 1988): C1.

48. Susan Birrell, "Sports as Ritual: Interpretations from Durkheim to Goffman," *Social Forces* 60, 2 (1981): 354–76; Daniel Q. Voigt, "American Sporting Rituals," in *Rites and Ceremonies in Popular Culture*, ed. Ray B. Browne (Bowling Green, OH: Bowling Green University Press, 1980), pp. 125–40.

49. Mindy Weinstein, "Dead Stars Are In," *Advertising Age* (August 14, 1989): 44.

50. Judann Dagnoli, "Ads Trmpet Satchmo's Immortality," *Advertising Age* (April 30, 1990): 26.

51. Bob Greene, "Some Like It Hot," *Esquire* (October 1987): 59.

52. Fred Kirby, "Woody Allen Wins Lawsuit to Stymie National Video Lookalike," *Variety* (May 22, 1985): 84.

53. James P. Forkan, "Send in the Clones: Ads Must ID Celeb Doubles," *Advertising Age* (May 20, 1985): 2.

54. Dean MacCannell, *The Tourist: A New Theory of the Leisure Class* (New York: Shocken Books, 1976).

55. Belk, Wallendorf and Sherry, Jr., "The Sacred and the Profane in Consumer Behavior."

56. Beverly Gordon, "The Souvenir: Messenger of the Extraordinary," *Journal of Popular Culture* 20, 3 (1986): 135–46.

57. Belk, Wallendorf and Sherry, Jr., "The Sacred and the Profane in Consumer Behavior."

58. Ibid.

59. Deborah Hoffmann, "In Jewelry, Choices Sacred and Profane, Ancient and New," *New York Times* (May 7, 1989).

60. Quoted in "Public Relations Firm to Present Anti-Abortion Effort to Bishops," *New York Times* (August 14, 1990): A12.

61. For an extensive bibliography on collecting, see Russell W. Belk et al., "Collecting in a Consumer Culture," in *Highways and Buyways*, ed. Russell W. Belk (Provo, UT: Association for Consumer Research, 1991), pp. 178–215. See also Russell W. Belk, "Acquiring, Possessing, and Collecting: Fundamental Processes in Consumer Behavior," in *Marketing Theory: Philosophy of Science Perspectives*, eds. Ronald F. Bush and Shelby D. Hunt (Chicago: American Marketing Association, 1982), pp. 85–90; Werner Muensterberg, *Collecting: An Unruly Passion* (Princeton, NJ: Princeton University Press, 1994); Melanie Wallendorf and Eric J. Arnould, "'My Favorite Things': A Cross-Cultural Inquiry into Object Attachment, Possessiveness, and Social Linkage," *Journal of Consumer Research* 14 (March 1988): 531–47.

62. Quoted in Ruth Ann Smith, "Collecting as Consumption: A Grounded Theory of Collecting Behavior" (unpublished manuscript, Virginia Polytechnic Institute and State University, 1994): 14.

63. Dan L. Sherrell, Alvin C. Burns and Melodie R. Phillips, "Fixed Consumption Behavior: The Case of Enduring Acquisition in a Product Category," in *Developments in Marketing Science* XIV, ed. Robert L. King (1991), pp. 36–40.

64. Belk, "Acquiring, Possessing, and Collecting."

65. For a discussion of these perspectives, see Smith, "Collecting as Consumption."

66. Glenn J. Kalinosky, "Collecting Sales," *PROMO: The Magazine of Promotion Marketing* (May 1996): 41–47.

67. Ibid.

68. Christy Ellis, *My First Greenbook: The First, Original Complete Guide to Ty Beanie Babies* (East Setauket, NY: Greenbook, 1997).

Amy is on vacation with her Aunt Judy in France. She is awed by the fashions in the stores. They seem so cool compared with what she has seen in the malls back home, in Burlington. What particularly catches her eye are the shoes. She is determined to have a pair, even if it means using all the rest of her babysitting money and borrowing the balance from her aunt. There is nothing else she wants but these shoes.

As Amy tries on the shoes, she is envisioning the reactions of her friends in Burlington when she returns to high school. All her friends read *Seventeen* magazine and talk about the latest styles. Amy knows she will be the envy of her classmates back in Canada …

17

The Creation and Diffusion of Culture

This chapter considers how the culture in which we live creates the meanings for everyday products and how these meanings move through a society to consumers. As Figure 17–1 shows, meaning transfer is largely accomplished by such marketing

FIGURE 17–1 • The Movement of Meaning

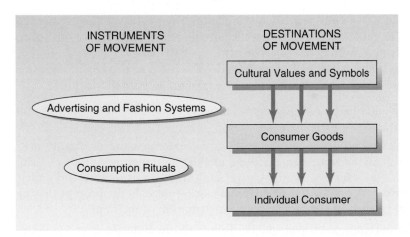

Source: Adapted from Grant McCracken, "Culture and Consumption: A Theoretical Account of the Structure and Movement of the Cultural Meaning of Consumer Goods," *Journal of Consumer Research* 13 (June 1986): 72. Reprinted with permission of The University of Chicago Press.

vehicles as the advertising and fashion industries, which associate consumer goods with symbolic qualities. These goods, in turn, impart their meanings to individual consumers as these products are used by them to create and express their identities in their daily lives.[1] Thus, this closing chapter brings us full circle, back to the issues regarding the diverse meanings of consumption that we considered in Chapter 1.

THE CREATION OF CULTURE

The Artist Formerly Known as Prince, nipple rings, platform shoes, sushi, high-tech furniture, postmodern architecture, chat rooms, double decaf cappuccino with a hint of cinnamon: we inhabit a world brimming with different styles and possibilities. The food we eat, the cars we drive, the clothes we wear, the places we live and work, the music we listen to—all are influenced by the ebb and flow of popular culture and fashion.

Consumers may at times feel overwhelmed by the sheer number of choices in the marketplace. A person trying to decide on something as routine as a necktie has many hundreds of alternatives to choose from. Despite this seeming abundance, however, the options available to consumers at any point in time actually represent only a small fraction of the total set of possibilities.

Cultural Selection

The selection of certain alternatives over others—whether automobiles, dresses, computers, recording artists, political candidates, religions or even scientific methodologies—is the culmination of a complex filtration process resembling a funnel, as depicted in Figure 17–2. Many possibilities initially compete for adoption, and these are steadily winnowed down as they make their way along the path from conception to consumption in a process of **cultural selection.**

cultural selection the process where some alternatives are selected over others by cultural gatekeepers

Our tastes and product preferences are not formed in a vacuum. Choices are driven by the images presented to us in mass media, by our observations of those around us, and by our desire to live in the fantasy worlds created by marketers. These options are constantly evolving and changing. A clothing style or type of cuisine that is "hot" one year may be "out" the next.

Amy's emulation of European style described at the beginning of the chapter illustrates some of the characteristics of fashion and popular culture:

*   Styles are often rooted in and reflect deeper societal trends (e.g., politics and social conditions).

*   Styles usually originate as an interplay between the deliberate inventions of designers and business people and the spontaneous actions of ordinary consumers. Designers, manufacturers and merchandisers who can anticipate what consumers want will succeed in the marketplace. In the process, they also help to fuel the fire by encouraging mass distribution of the item.

*   These trends can travel widely, often between countries and continents. Influential people in the media play a large role in deciding which of these trends will succeed.

FIGURE 17–2 • The Culture Production Process

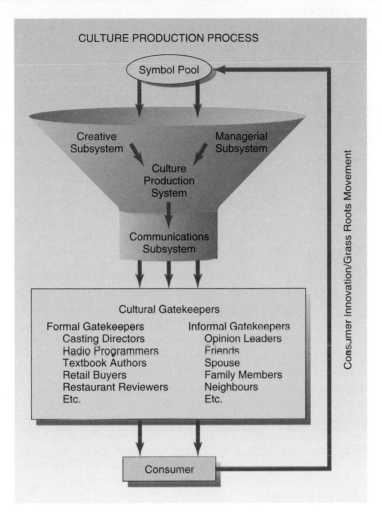

Source: Adapted from Michael R. Solomon, "Building Up and Breaking Down: The Impact of Cultural Sorting on Symbolic Consumption," in *Research in Consumer Behavior*, ed. J. Sheth and E. C. Hirschman (Greenwich, CT: JAI Press, 1988): 325–51.

- A style begins as a risky or unique statement by a relatively small group of people, and then spreads as others become increasingly aware of the style and feel confident about trying it.

- Most styles eventually wear out, as people continually search for new ways to express themselves and marketers scramble to keep up with these desires.

Culture Production Systems

No single designer, company or advertising agency is totally responsible for creating popular culture. Every product, whether a hit record, a car or a new clothing style, requires the input of many different participants. The set of individuals and organi-

culture production system (CPS) the set of individuals and organizations reponsible for creating and marketing a cultural product

zations responsible for creating and marketing a cultural product is a **culture production system (CPS).**[2]

The nature of these systems helps to determine the types of products that eventually emerge from them. Important factors include the number and diversity of competing systems and the amount of innovation versus conformity that is encouraged. For example, an analysis of the country and western music industry has shown that the hit records it produces tend to be similar to one another during time periods when it is dominated by a few large companies, whereas there is more diversity when a greater number of producers are competing within the same market.[3]

The different members of a culture production system may not necessarily be aware of or appreciate the roles played by other members, yet many diverse agents work together to create popular culture.[4] Each member does his or her best to anticipate which particular images will be most attractive to a consumer market. Of course, those who are able consistently to forecast consumers' tastes most accurately will be most successful over time.

COMPONENTS OF A CPS

A culture production system has three major subsystems: 1) a *creative subsystem* responsible for generating new symbols and/or products; 2) a *managerial subsystem* responsible for selecting, making tangible, mass producing and managing the distribution of new symbols and/or products; and 3) a *communications subsystem* responsible for giving meaning to new products and providing them with symbolic sets of attributes that are communicated to consumers.

An example of the three components of a culture production system for a record would be: 1) a singer (e.g., Coolio—a creative subsystem); 2) a company (e.g., Tommy Boy Music, which manufactures and distributes Coolio's CDs—a managerial subsystem); and 3) the advertising and publicity agencies hired to promote the CDs—a communications subsystem). Table 17–1 illustrates some of the many *cultural specialists,* operating in different subsystems, who are required to create a hit CD.

cultural gatekeepers individuals who are responsible for determining the types of messages and symbolism to which members of mass culture are exposed

CULTURAL GATEKEEPERS

Many judges or "tastemakers" influence the products that are eventually offered to consumers. These judges, or **cultural gatekeepers,** filter the overflow of information and materials intended for consumers. Gatekeepers include movie, restaurant and car reviewers, interior designers, disc jockeys, retail buyers and magazine editors. Collectively, this set of agents is known as the *through-put sector.*[5]

art product a creation viewed primarily as an object of aesthetic contemplation without any functional value

craft product a creation valued because of the beauty with which it performs some function; this type of product tends to follow a formula that permits rapid production, and it is easier to understand than an art product

High Culture and Popular Culture

Do Beethoven and Bryan Adams have anything in common? While both the famous composer and the rock singer are associated with music, many would argue that the similarity stops there. Culture production systems create many diverse kinds of products, but some basic distinctions can be offered regarding their characteristics.

One distinction can be made between arts and crafts.[6] An **art product** is viewed primarily as an object of aesthetic contemplation without any functional value. A **craft product** (e.g., a ceramic ashtray or hand-carved fishing lures), in contrast, is admired because of the beauty with which it performs some function. A piece of art

TABLE 17–1 Cultural Specialists in the Music Industry

SPECIALIST	FUNCTIONS
Songwriter(s)	Compose music and lyrics; must reconcile artistic preferences with estimates of what will succeed in the marketplace
Performer(s)	Interpret music and lyrics; may be formed spontaneously, or may be packaged by an agent to appeal to a predetermined market
Teachers and coaches	Develop and refine performers' talents
Agent	Represent performers to record companies
A&R (artist & repertoire) executive	Acquire artists for the record label
Publicists, image consultants, designers, stylists	Create an image for the group that is transmitted to the buying public
Recording technicians, producers	Create a recording to be sold
Marketing executives	Make strategic decisions regarding performers' appearances, ticket pricing, promotional strategies and so on
Video director	Interpret the song visually to create a music video that will help to promote the record
Music reviewers	Evaluate the merits of a recording for listeners
Disc Jockeys, radio program directors	Decide which records will be given airplay and/or placed in the radio stations' regular rotations
Record-store owner	Decide which of the many records produced will be stocked and/or promoted heavily in the retail environment

is original, subtle and valuable, and is associated with the élite of society. A craft tends to follow a formula that permits rapid production. According to this framework, élite culture is produced in a purely aesthetic context and is judged by reference to recognized classics. It is high culture—that is, "serious art."[7]

HIGH ART VERSUS LOW ART

The distinction between high and low culture—high art versus low art—is not as clear as it may first appear. In addition to the possible class bias that drives such a distinction (i.e., we assume that the rich have culture while the poor do not), high and low culture are blending together in interesting ways. Popular culture reflects the world around us; these phenomena touch both rich and poor. In Europe, for example, advertising is widely appreciated as an art form. Advertising executives are often public figures in Great Britain. For over ten years Europeans have paid up to $30 to watch an all-night program in a movie theatre consisting of nothing but television commercials.[8]

All cultural products that are transmitted by mass media become a part of popular culture.[9] Classical recordings are marketed in much the same way as Top 40 CDs, and museums use mass-marketing techniques to sell their wares.

Marketers often incorporate high-art imagery to promote products. They may sponsor artistic events to build public goodwill or feature works of art on shopping

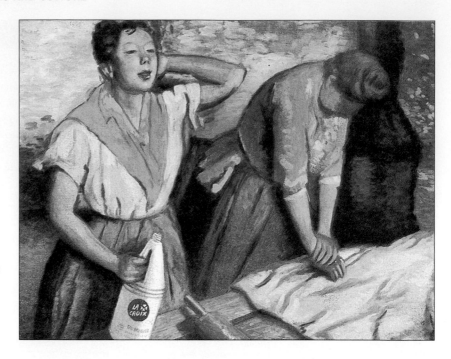

This French billboard demonstrates the adaptation of famous paintings ("high art") to sell products ("low art"). In this version of Edgar Degas's The Ironers, a brand of bleach (made by Colgate-Palmolive) replaces a bottle of wine.
Courtesy of Colgate-Palmolive.

bags.[10] When observers from Toyota watched customers in luxury-car showrooms, the company found that these consumers tended to view cars as art objects. This theme was then used in an ad for the Lexus with the caption: "Until now, the only fine arts we supported were sculpture, painting, and music."[11]

CULTURAL FORMULAE

cultural formula a sequence of media events where certain roles and props tend to occur consistently

Mass culture, in contrast, churns out products specifically for a mass market. These products aim to please the average taste of an undifferentiated audience and are predictable because they follow certain patterns. As illustrated in Table 17–2, many popular art forms, such as detective stories or science fiction, generally follow a **cultural formula,** where certain roles and props often occur consistently.[12] Romance novels are an extreme case of a cultural formula. Computer programs even allow users to "write" their own romances by systematically varying certain set elements of the story.

AESTHETIC MARKET RESEARCH

Creators of aesthetic products are increasingly adapting conventional marketing methods to fine-tune their mass-market offerings. Market research is used, for example, to test audience reactions to movie concepts. Although testing cannot account for such intangibles as acting quality or cinematography, it can determine if the basic themes of the movie strike a responsive chord in the target audience. This type of research is most appropriate for blockbuster movies, which usually follow one of the formulae described earlier.

Even the content of movies is sometimes influenced by consumer research. Typically, free invitations to prescreenings are handed out in malls and movie theatres. Attendees are asked a few questions about the movie and then some are selected to participate in focus groups. Although group members' reactions usually result in

TABLE 17–2 Cultural Formulae in Public Art Forms

ART FORM/ GENRE	CLASSIC WESTERN	SCIENCE FICTION	HARD-BOILED DETECTIVE	FAMILY SITCOM
Time	1800s	Future	Present	Anytime
Location	Edge of civilization	Space	City	Suburbs
Protagonist	Cowboy (lone individual)	Astronaut	Detective	Father (figure)
Heroine	Schoolmarm	Spacegal	Damsel in distress	Mother (figure)
Villain	Outlaws, killers	Aliens	Killer	Boss, neighbour
Secondary characters	Townfolk, Indians	Technicians in spacecraft	Cops, underworld	Kids, dogs
Plot	Restore law and order	Repel aliens	Find killer	Solve problem
Theme	Justice	Triumph of humanity	Pursuit and discovery	Chaos and confusion
Costume	Cowboy hat, boots, etc.	High-tech uniforms	Raincoat	Regular clothes
Locomotion	Horse	Spaceship	Beat-up car	Station wagon
Weaponry	Sixgun, rifle	Rayguns	Pistol, fists	Insults

Source: Arthur A. Berger, *Signs in Contemporary Culture: An Introduction to Semiotics* (New York: Longman, 1984), p. 86. Copyright ©1984. Reissued 1989 by Sheffield Publishing Company, Salem, Wisconsin. Reprinted with permission of the publisher.

only minor editing changes, more drastic effects occasionally result, such as changing the outcome of the story.

Reality Engineering

Many of the environments in which we find ourselves, whether shopping malls, sports stadiums or theme parks, are composed at least partly of images and characters drawn from products, marketing campaigns or the mass media. **Reality engineering** occurs as elements of popular culture are appropriated by marketers and

reality engineering the process whereby elements of popular culture are appropriated by marketers and become integrated into marketing strategies; examples of this phenomenon include infomercials and product placement

MARKETING PITFALL

The Web is making it easier than ever for firms to copy the designs of other companies. It's got to the point that imitations are arriving in stores at the same time as the original, high-priced version. Wildcatters such as First View have set up Web sites to show pirated versions of the latest offerings to boutiques and design houses, sometimes revealing everything from a designer's new collection. The situation is so bad that at its Spring 1997 show Chanel required photographers to sign contracts promising their shots would not be distributed on the Internet.[13]

converted to vehicles for promotional strategies.[14] These elements include sensory and spatial aspects of everyday existence in the form of products appearing in movies, odours pumped into offices and stores, billboards, theme parks, video monitors attached to shopping carts and so on.

Marketing sometimes seems to exert a self-fulfilling prophecy on popular culture. As commercial influences on popular culture increase, marketer-created symbols make their way into our daily lives to a greater degree. Historical analyses of Broadway plays, best-selling novels and the lyrics of hit songs, for example, clearly show large increases in the use of brand names over time.[15]

The melding of marketing activity with popular culture is also evident in other countries. A British coffee ad recently borrowed the words from the Beatles' song "A Day in the Life" and went so far as to include a shot of John Lennon's signature round glasses sitting on a table. The British Boy Scouts announced that they would begin accepting corporate sponsorships for merit badges. The Lost City, a new resort in South Africa, blurs the boundaries even further: it has created a "fake" Africa for affluent guests. The complex is drought-proof and disease-proof, and it features a three-storey water slide, an "ocean" with a panic button that will stop the wave motion on command, and a nightly volcanic eruption complete with non-allergenic smoke.[16]

Reality engineering is accelerating due to the current popularity of product placements by marketers. It is quite common to see real brands prominently displayed or to hear them discussed in movies and on television. In many cases these plugs are no accident. **Product placement** refers to the insertion of specific products

product placement the process of obtaining exposure for a product by arranging for it to be inserted into a movie, a television show or some other medium

These Absolut ads featuring popular artists help to blur the boundaries between marketing activities and popular culture.
Absolut Vodka logo and bottle design are trademarks owned by v&s vin & spirit ab. Imported by Carillon Importers, Ltd., Teaneck, N.J.

MARKETING PITFALL

One of the most controversial intersections between marketing and society occurs when companies provide "educational materials" to schools. In 1994 Pepsi-Cola signed an agreement with the Toronto School Board to be the official supplier of soft drinks in the school system through vending machines. The problem was that the board did not realize that many schools already had vending machines for soft drinks and agreements with other suppliers. There were profound ideological differences over the concept of "selling" the school system in exchange for corporate sponsorship. There is now a 13-point check-list for school boards that tries to ensure that any corporate involvement "enhances the quality and relevance of education" for learners. The Board also wants to make sure that corporate sponsorship does not replace public funding of education.[17]

Other manufacturers have found more creative ways to get their messages into the classroom. Campbell Soup mailed 90 000 copies of its Prego Science Challenge, a kit that allows students to determine if Prego spaghetti sauce is thicker than Ragu Old Style sauce. Commented a spokeswoman, "We thought students would be interested in connecting science to the real world." General Mills provided a kit called Gushers Wonders of the Earth that included free samples of its Fruit Gushers snack. The accompanying lesson plan encouraged kids to compare the fruit gush they experience when they bite into the snack to natural eruptions. A video by Union Carbide Corp. teaches students that chemicals "add comfort to our world." An executive at Monsanto Corp., which distributes a video promoting the use of pesticides, argues that the company has a right to counter the messages of environmental groups, which have a long history of providing educational materials to schools. Many teachers and other educators argue that these videos and kits are a godsend for resource-poor schools that otherwise would have hardly any other way to communicate with students. What do you think?[18]

and/or the use of brand names in movie and TV scripts. More than 30 companies in the United States now specialize in getting valuable exposure for products by strategically placing them in mass media. Perhaps the greatest product placement success story was Reese's Pieces; sales jumped by 65 percent after the candy appeared in the film *E.T.*[19]

Since that time, products are popping up everywhere: a Chrysler Dodge Ram is featured in the movie *Twister,* the basketball team in *Eddie* wears Knicks uniforms, and an Apple PowerBook can clearly be seen in *Mission: Impossible* (in return, Apple underwrote a television advertising campaign for the movie and also created an online Web site for the release free of charge). Sometimes these placements even result in changes to the show itself. For example, the movie *Flipper* was filmed with a Coke can in one scene. When producers signed a marketing deal with Pizza Hut (which is owned by PepsiCo), they had to spend about $40 000 to digitally change the drink label to Pepsi.[20]

Traditionally, networks demanded that brand names be "greeked" or changed before they could appear in a show, as when a Nokia cell phone is changed to Nokio on "Melrose Place."[21] Nowadays, though, real products pop up everywhere. To bypass Federal Communications Commission regulations requiring the disclosure of promotional deals, marketers typically don't pay for placements. Instead, they pay product placement firms that work with set decorators looking for free props and realism. As a result, Al on the show "Home Improvement" models a Detroit Lions jacket, while Jamie on "Mad About You" splashes on Bijan fragrances.[22]

Some critics argue that the practice of product placement has got out of hand. Shows are now created with the purpose of marketing products rather than for their entertainment value. Some children's shows have been berated for essentially being extended commercials for toys. One major film company sent a letter to large consumer products companies to solicit product placements for an upcoming movie production and even provided a fee scale: $20 000 for the product to be seen in the movie, $40 000 for an actor to mention the product by name and $60 000 for the actor actually to use the product.[23]

cultivation hypothesis a perspective emphasizing media's ability to distort consumers' perceptions of reality

Media images appear to significantly influence consumers' perceptions of reality, affecting viewers' notions about such issues as dating behaviour, racial stereotypes and occupational status.[24] Studies of the **cultivation hypothesis**, which relates to media's ability to distort consumers' perceptions of reality, have shown that heavy television viewers tend to overestimate the degree of affluence in the country, and these effects also extend to such areas as perceptions of the amount of violence in one's culture.[25] The media also tend to exaggerate or distort the frequency of behaviours like drinking or smoking. One study found that characters in movies smoke at a much higher rate than people in real life.[26]

MARKETING PITFALL

The issue of what exactly constitutes a "new" product is quite important to many businesses. It is said that "imitation is the sincerest form of flattery," and decisions regarding how much (if at all) one's product should resemble those of competitors are often a centrepiece of marketing strategy (e.g., packaging of "me-too" or look-alike products). On the other hand, the product cannot be an exact duplicate; patent law is concerned with the precise definition of what is a new product and with protecting that invention from illegal imitation.

A knockoff is a style that has deliberately been copied and modified, often with the intent to sell to a larger or different market. For example, *haute couture* clothing styles presented by top designers in Paris and elsewhere are commonly "knocked off" by other designers and sold to the mass market. It is difficult to legally protect a design (as opposed to a technological feature), but pressure is building in many industries to do just that. Manufacturers argue that a distinctive curve on a car bumper, say, is as important to the integrity of the car as is a mechanical innovation. Legislation is being considered in the United States to protect new designs with a 10-year copyright (clothing would be exempt).[27] This movement highlights the importance of the question "What exactly is an innovation?"

THE DIFFUSION OF INNOVATIONS

innovation a product or style that is perceived as new by consumers

New products and styles, termed **innovations,** constantly enter the market. These new products or services occur in both consumer and industrial settings. Innovations may take the form of a clothing style (e.g., skirts for men), a new manufacturing technique or a novel way to deliver a service. If an innovation is successful (most are not), it spreads through the population. First it is bought and/or used by only a few people, and then more and more consumers decide to adopt it, until in some cases it seems that almost everyone has bought or tried the innovation. **Diffusion of innovations** refers to the process whereby a new product, service or idea spreads through a population.

diffusion of innovation the process whereby a new product, service or idea spreads through a population

Adopting Innovations

A consumer's adoption of an innovation resembles the decision-making sequence discussed in Chapter 9. The person moves through the stages of awareness, information search, evaluation, trial and adoption, although the relative importance of each stage may differ depending upon how much is already known about a product, as well as on cultural factors that may affect people's willingness to try new things.[28]

However, even within the same culture, not all people adopt an innovation at the same rate. Some do so quite rapidly and others never do at all. Consumers can be placed into approximate categories based upon their likelihood of adopting an innovation. The categories of adopters, shown in Figure 17–3, can be related to phases of the product-life-cycle concept used widely by marketing strategists.

As can be seen in Figure 17–3, roughly one-sixth of the population (innovators and early adopters) are very quick to adopt new products, and one-sixth (laggards) are very slow. The other two-thirds are somewhere in the middle, and these majority adopters represent the mainstream public. These consumers are interested in new things, but they do not want them to be too new. In some cases people deliberately wait to adopt an innovation because they assume that its technological qualities will

FIGURE 17–3 • Types of Adopters

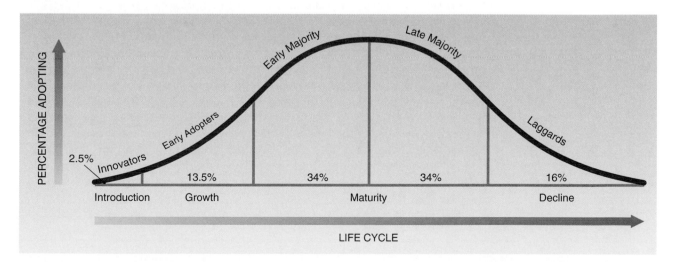

be improved or that its price will fall after it has been on the market a while.[29] Keep in mind that the proportion of consumers falling into each category is an estimate; the actual size of each depends upon such factors as the complexity of the product, its cost and so on.

Even though **innovators** represent only 2.5 percent of the population, marketers are always interested in identifying them. These are the brave souls who are always on the lookout for novel developments and will be the first to try a new offering. Just as generalized opinion leaders do not appear to exist, innovators tend to be category-specific as well. A person who is an innovator in one area may even be a laggard in another. For example, a gentleman who prides himself on being at the cutting edge of fashion may have no conception of new developments in recording technology, and stubbornly cling to his phonograph albums even while he searches for the latest *avant-garde* clothing styles in obscure boutiques.

Despite this qualification, some generalizations can be offered regarding the profile of innovators.[30] Not surprisingly, for example, they tend to have more favourable attitudes towards taking risks. They also are likely to have higher educational and income levels and to be socially active.

Early adopters share many of the same characteristics as innovators, but an important difference is their degree of concern for social acceptance, especially with regard to expressive products such as clothing and cosmetics. Generally speaking, an early adopter is receptive to new styles because he or she is involved in the product category and also places high value on being in fashion. What appears on the surface to be a fairly high-risk adoption (e.g., wearing a skirt three inches above the knee when most people are wearing them below the knee) is actually not *that* risky. The style change has already been "field tested" by innovators, who truly took the fashion risk. Early adopters are likely to be found in "fashion-forward" stores featuring the latest "hot" designers. In contrast, true innovators are more likely to be found in small boutiques featuring as-yet-unknown designers.

innovators people who are always on the lookout for novel developments and will be the first to try a new offering

early adopters people receptive to new styles because they are involved in the product category and place high value on being in fashion

MARKETING OPPORTUNITY

The race to uncover the preferences of innovators is heating up. Some companies are even hiring *coolhunters* to scout out the latest trends and report back to headquarters. For example, the US company Steven Rifkind Co. sends its "street teams"—an army of 80 kids in 28 cities—into local clubs, record stores and other hang-outs as part of an urban intelligence network on behalf of Nike, Tommy Hilfiger, Miramax Films and other corporate clients. These soldiers of cool hand out free samples of product prototypes to kids they identify as trend-setters, and then get their feedback regarding what's cool and what isn't. When client Converse was developing its model of Dennis Rodman sneakers, they were tested by coolhunters. The shoe got good marks for overall "badness," but the innovators didn't like the design of the bottom of the sole, which was half-white fading into black. The word on the street said this style would be much cooler in black and red, so Converse switched colours before introducing the shoe to the mass market.[31]

Types of Innovations

Innovations can occur on a symbolic level or a technological one. A **symbolic innovation** communicates a new social meaning (e.g., a new hairstyle or car design), while a **technological innovation** involves some functional change (e.g., central air-conditioning or car airbags).[32] Whether symbolic or functional, new products, services and ideas have characteristics that determine the degree to which they will probably diffuse. As a general rule, innovations that are more novel are least likely to diffuse, because things that are fairly similar to what is already available require fewer changes in behaviour for users. On the other hand, an innovation that radically alters a person's lifestyle requires the person to modify his or her way of doing things and thus requires more effort to adapt to the change.

symbolic innovation an innovation that communicates a new social meaning

technological innovation an innovation that involves some functional change

BEHAVIOURAL DEMANDS OF INNOVATIONS

Innovations can be categorized in terms of the degree to which they demand changes in behaviour from adopters. Three major types of innovations have been identified, though these three categories are not absolutes. They refer, in a relative sense, to the amount of disruption or change an innovation brings to people's lives.

A **continuous innovation** refers to a modification of an existing product, as when General Mills introduced a Honey Nut version of Cheerios or Levi's promoted shrink-to-fit jeans. This type of change may be used to set one brand apart from its competitors. Most product innovations are of this type; that is, they are evolutionary rather than revolutionary. Small changes are made to position the product, to add line extensions or merely to alleviate consumer boredom.

continuous innovation a product change or new product that requires relatively little adaptation by the adopter

Consumers may be lured to the new product, but adoption represents only minor changes in consumption habits, since innovation perhaps adds to the product's convenience or to the range of choices available. A typewriter company, for example, many years ago modified the shape of its product to make it more "user friendly" to secretaries. One simple change was the curving of the tops of the keys, a convention that is carried over on today's computer keyboards. The reason for the change was that secretaries had complained about the difficulty of typing with long fingernails on the flat surfaces.

A **dynamically continuous innovation** is a more pronounced change in an existing product, as represented by self-focusing 35-mm cameras or Touch-Tone telephones. These innovations have a modest impact on the way people do things, creating some behavioural changes. When introduced, the IBM Selectric typewriter, which uses a typing ball rather than individual keys, permitted secretaries to change the typeface of manuscripts instantly by replacing one Selectric ball with another.

dynamically continuous innovation a product change or new product that requires a moderate amount of adaptation by the adopter

A **discontinuous innovation** creates major changes in the way we live. Major inventions, such as the airplane, the car, the computer and the television set, have radically changed modern lifestyles. The personal computer has in many cases supplanted the typewriter, and it has created the phenomenon of "telecommuters" by allowing many consumers to work out of their homes. Of course the cycle continues, as new continuous innovations (e.g., new versions of software) are constantly being made for computers; dynamically continuous innovations, such as the keyboard "mouse," compete for adoption; and discontinuous innovations like wrist-watch personal computers loom on the horizon.

discontinuous innovation a product change or new product that requires a significant amount of adaptation by the adopter

The personal computer is an innovation that has
significantly changed the way we live.
*These photographs are reproduced courtesy of
International Business Machines Corporation.*

PREREQUISITES FOR SUCCESSFUL ADOPTION

Regardless of how much behavioural change is demanded by an innovation, several
factors are desirable for a new product to succeed:[33]

- *Compatibility.* The innovation should be compatible with consumers'
  lifestyles. As one illustration, a manufacturer of personal-care products tried
  unsuccessfully several years ago to introduce a cream hair remover for men as a
  substitute for razors and shaving cream. This formulation was similar to that
  used widely by women to remove hair from their legs. Although the product was
  simple and convenient to use, it failed because men were not interested in a
  product they perceived to be too feminine and thus threatening to their masculine self-concepts.

- *Trialability.* Since an unknown is accompanied by high perceived risk, people
  are more likely to adopt an innovation if they can experiment with it prior to
  making a commitment. To reduce risk, companies often choose the expensive
  strategy of distributing free "trial-size" samples of new products.

- *Complexity.* The product should be low in complexity. A product that is easier to understand and use will be chosen over a competitor. This strategy requires less effort from the consumer, and it also lowers perceived risk. Manufacturers of video cassette recorders, for example, have put a lot of effort into simplifying VCR usage (e.g., on-screen programming) to encourage adoption.

- *Observability.* Innovations that are easily observable are more likely to spread, since this quality makes it more likely that other potential adopters will become aware of its existence. The rapid proliferation of fanny packs (pouches worn around the waist in lieu of wallets or purses) was due to their high visibility. It was easy for others to see the convenience offered by this alternative.

- *Relative Advantage.* Most importantly, the product should offer relative advantage over other alternatives. The consumer must believe that its use will provide a benefit other products cannot offer. Two popular new products demonstrate the importance of possessing a perceived relative advantage *vis-à-vis* existing products: Energizer Green Power Batteries are promoted as being better for the environment because they contain less mercury, and the Bugchaser is a wristband containing insect repellent. Mothers with young children have liked the Bugchaser because it is non-toxic and non-staining. In contrast, the Crazy Blue Air Freshener, which was added to windshield wiper fluid and emitted a fragrance when the wipers were turned on, fizzled: people didn't see the need for the product and felt there were simpler ways to freshen their cars if they cared to.

THE FASHION SYSTEM

The **fashion system** consists of all those people and organizations involved in creating symbolic meanings and transferring these meanings to cultural goods. Although people tend to equate fashion with clothing, it is important to keep in mind that fashion processes affect *all* types of cultural phenomena, including music, art, architecture and even science (i.e., certain research topics and scientists are "hot" at any given point in time). Even business practices are subject to the fashion process; they evolve and change depending on which management techniques, such as total quality management or just-in-time inventory control, are "in vogue."

Fashion can be thought of as a *code,* or language, that helps us to decipher these meanings.[34] Unlike a language, however, fashion is *context-dependent.* The same item can be interpreted differently by different consumers and in different situations.[35] The meaning of many products is *undercoded*—that is, there is no one precise meaning, but rather plenty of room for interpretation among perceivers.

At the outset it may be helpful to distinguish among some confusing terms. **Fashion** is the process of social diffusion by which a new style is adopted by some group(s) of consumers. In contrast, *a fashion* (or style) refers to a particular combination of attributes. And, to be *in fashion* means that this combination is currently positively evaluated by some reference group. Thus, the term *Danish Modern* refers to particular characteristics of furniture design (i.e., it is a fashion in interior design); it does not necessarily imply that Danish Modern is a fashion that is currently desired by consumers (i.e., that it is in fashion).[36]

fashion system those people and organizations involved in creating symbolic meanings and transferring these meanings to cultural goods

fashion the process of social diffusion by which a new style is adopted by some group(s) of consumers

Cultural Categories

cultural categories the grouping of ideas and values that reflect the basic ways members of a society characterize the world

The meaning that does get imparted to products reflects underlying **cultural categories,** which correspond to the basic ways we characterize the world.[37] Our culture makes distinctions between different times, between leisure and work, between genders, etc. The fashion system provides us with products that signify these categories. For example, the apparel industry gives us clothing to denote certain times (e.g., evening wear, resort wear), it differentiates between leisure clothes and work clothes, and it promotes masculine and feminine styles.

These cultural categories affect many different products and styles. As a result, it is common to find that dominant aspects of a culture at any point in time tend to be reflected in the design and marketing of very different products. This concept is a bit hard to grasp, since on the surface a clothing style, say, has little in common with a piece of furniture or a car. However, an overriding concern with a value such as achievement or environmentalism can determine the types of products likely to be accepted by consumers at any point in time. These underlying or latent themes then surface in various aspects of design. A few examples of this interdependence demonstrate how a dominant fashion *motif* reverberates across industries:

- Costumes worn by political figures or movie and rock stars can affect the fortunes of the apparel and accessory industries. A movie appearance by actor Clark Gable without a T-shirt (unusual at that time) dealt a severe setback to the men's apparel industry, while Jackie Kennedy's famous pillbox hat prompted a rush for hats by women in the 1960s. Other cross-category effects include the craze for ripped sweatshirts instigated by the movie *Flashdance,* a boost for cowboy boots from the movie *Urban Cowboy,* and singer Madonna's legitimation of lingerie as an acceptable outerwear clothing style.

- The Louvre in Paris was recently remodelled to include a controversial glass pyramid at the entrance designed by the architect I.M. Pei. Shortly thereafter, several designers unveiled pyramid-shaped clothing at Paris fashion shows.[38]

- In the 1950s and 1960s much of the United States was preoccupied with science and technology. This concern with "space-age" mastery was fuelled by the Russians' launching of the Sputnik satellite, which prompted fears that the US was falling behind in the technology race. The theme of technical mastery of nature and of futuristic design became a *motif* that cropped up in many aspects of US popular culture—from car designs with prominent tail fins to high-tech kitchen styles.

Collective Selection

Fashions tend to "sweep" the country; it seems that all of a sudden "everyone" is doing the same thing or wearing the same styles. Some sociologists view fashion as a form of *collective behaviour,* or a wave of social conformity. How do so many people "get tuned in" to the same phenomenon at once, as happened with hip-hop styles?

Remember that creative subsystems within a culture production system attempt to anticipate the tastes of the buying public. Despite their unique talents, members of this subsystem are also members of mass culture. Like the fashion magazine editors discussed earlier, cultural gatekeepers are drawing from a common set of ideas and symbols and are influenced by the same cultural phenomena as the eventual consumers of their products.

The process by which certain symbolic alternatives are chosen over others has been termed **collective selection.**[39] As with the creative subsystem, members of the managerial and communications subsystems also seem to develop common frames of mind. Although products within each category must compete for acceptance in the marketplace, they can usually be characterized by their adherence to a dominant theme or *motif*—be it "The Western Look," "New Wave," "Danish Modern" or "Nouvelle Cuisine."

collective selection the process by which certain symbolic alternatives tend to be jointly chosen over others by members of a society

Behavioural Science Perspectives on Fashion

Fashion is a very complex process that operates on many levels. At one extreme, it is a macro, societal phenomenon affecting many people simultaneously. At the other, it exerts a very personal effect on individual behaviour. A consumer's purchase decisions are often motivated by his or her desire to be in fashion. Fashion products are also aesthetic objects, and their origins are rooted in art and history. Thus there are many perspectives on the origin and diffusion of fashion. Although these cannot be described in detail here, some major approaches can be briefly summarized.[40]

PSYCHOLOGICAL MODELS OF FASHION

Many psychological factors help to explain why people are motivated to be in fashion. These include conformity, variety seeking, personal creativity and sexual attraction. For example, many consumers seem to have a "need for uniqueness." These consumers want to be different, but not too different.[41] For this reason people often conform to the basic outlines of a fashion but try to improvise and make a personal statement within these guidelines.

One of the earliest theories of fashion proposed that "shifting **erogenous zones**" (sexually arousing areas of the body) accounted for fashion changes, and that different zones become the object of interest because they reflect societal trends. J.C. Flugel, a disciple of Freud, proposed in the 1920s that sexually charged areas wax and wane in order to maintain interest, and that clothing styles change to highlight or hide these parts. For example, it was common for Renaissance-era women to drape their abdomens in fabrics in order to give a swollen appearance, successful childbearing being a priority in the disease-ridden fourteenth and fifteenth centuries. Interest in the female leg in the 1920s and 1930s coincided with women's new mobility and independence, while the exposure of breasts in the 1970s signalled a renewed interest in breast-feeding. Breasts were de-emphasized in the 1980s as women concentrated on careers, but a larger bust size is now more popular as women try to combine professional activity with child rearing. Some contemporary fashion theorists suggest that the current prevalence of the exposed midriff reflects the premium our society places on fitness.[42] (Note that, until very recently, the study of fashion focused almost exclusively on its impact on women. It is to be hoped that this concentration will broaden as scholars and practitioners begin to appreciate that men are affected by many of the same fashion influences.)

erogenous zones areas of the body considered by members of a culture to be foci of sexual attractiveness

This ad for Maidenform illustrates that fashions have accentuated different parts of the female anatomy throughout history.
Copyright (c) 1990 by Maidenform, Inc.

ECONOMIC MODELS OF FASHION

Economists approach fashion in terms of the model of supply and demand. Items that are in limited supply have high value, while those readily available are less desirable. Rare items command respect and prestige.

Veblen's notion of conspicuous consumption proposed that the wealthy consume to display their prosperity, for example by wearing expensive (and at times impractical) clothing. As noted in Chapter 12, this approach is somewhat outdated, since upscale consumers often engage in *parody display,* in which they deliberately adopt formerly low-status or inexpensive products such as jeeps or jeans.

Other factors also influence the demand curve for fashion-related products. These include a *prestige-exclusivity effect,* wherein high prices still create high demand, and a *snob effect,* in which lower prices actually reduce demand ("only a lowlife would pay such a cheap price for that!").[43]

SOCIOLOGICAL MODELS OF FASHION

The collective selection model discussed previously is an example of a sociological approach to fashion. In addition, much attention has been focused on the relationship between product adoption and class structure.

trickle-down theory of fashion the perspective that fashions spread as the result of status symbols associated with the upper classes "trickling down" to other social classes as these consumers try to emulate those with greater status

The **trickle-down theory,** first proposed in 1904 by Georg Simmel, has been one of the most influential approaches to understanding fashion. It states that there are two conflicting forces that drive fashion change. First, subordinate groups try to adopt the status symbols of the groups above them as they attempt to climb up the ladder of social mobility. Dominant styles thus originate with the upper classes and *trickle down* to those below. However, this is where the second force kicks in: those people in the superordinate groups are constantly looking below them on the ladder to ensure that they are not imitated, and they respond to the attempts of lower classes to "impersonate" them by adopting even *newer* fashions. These two processes create a self-perpetuating cycle of change—the machine that drives fashion.[44]

The trickle-down theory was quite useful for understanding the process of fashion changes when applied to a society with a stable class structure that permitted the easy identification of lower- and upper-class consumers. This task is not so easy in modern times. In contemporary Western society this approach must be modified to account for new developments in mass culture:[45]

- A perspective based on class structure cannot account for the wide range of styles that are simultaneously made available in our society. Modern consumers have a much greater degree of individualized choice than they did in the past because of advances in technology and distribution. Just as an adolescent is almost instantly aware of the latest style trends by watching MuchMusic, *élite fashion* has been largely replaced by *mass fashion,* since media exposure permits many groups to become aware of a style at the same time.

- Consumers tend to be more influenced by opinion leaders who are similar to them. As a result, each social group has its own fashion innovators who determine fashion trends. It is often more accurate to speak of a *trickle-across effect,* where fashions diffuse horizontally among members of the same social group.[46]

- Finally, current fashions often originate with the lower classes and *trickle up.* Grassroots innovators typically are people who lack prestige in the dominant culture (like urban youth). Since they are less concerned with maintaining the status quo, they are more free to innovate and take risks.[47]

MARKETING PITFALL

Large companies that try to stay on top of hot fashion trends face a disturbing paradox: young consumers are drawn to happening street fashions like those produced by small entrepreneurs. For example, when Dina Mohajer was a student at the University of Southern California in 1995, she needed blue nail polish to go with her blue platform shoes, and so she mixed up her own batch. Her friends loved the idea, and she started Hard Candy with a loan from her parents. Soon Drew Barrymore, Cher and even Antonio Banderas were wearing such Hard Candy colours as Trailer Trash, Jail Bait and Fiend.[48]

However, as soon as these styles are "discovered" and mass produced, they are no longer cool. Even M.A.C. cosmetics is no longer the cool fashion statement of the times. In the old days *couture* houses and major retailers set the styles, but with the advent of the Web and numerous small 'zines produced by individuals or small companies, the big guys no longer have the final say on what is cool, and big brand names are distrusted. One way around this dilemma is to spin off a separate division and try to distance it from the parent company, as Levi Strauss did with its Silver Tab boutique label and Miller with its boutique brewery called Red Dog.

Sometimes this strategy backfires, as when a watered-down version of a product gets foisted on the market—like jeans that have an underwear-like band of cloth sewn into them to simulate the look of real underwear sticking out of slouchy pants.[49] And there is a fine line between using upstart companies' ideas as "inspiration" and blatant imitation. Another small company called Urban Decay found this out when it was forced to sue Revlon over a line of nail polishes. Its colours included Oil Slick, Rust and Pallor, and shortly thereafter Revlon introduced Tar, Blood, Rusty, Gun Metal and other selections.[50]

Cycles of Fashion Adoption

In 1996 Tickle-Me-Elmo dolls were all the rage among North American children. Faced with a limited supply of the product, some retailers reported near-riots among adults as they tried desperately to buy the dolls for their children. In Fredericton, New Brunswick, 300 parents sent a Wal-Mart employee to hospital after they rushed the store to grab one of the 48 Elmos on the shelves.[51] Although the Tickle-Me-Elmo craze lasted for a couple of months, it eventually died out and consumers moved on to other things.

Although the longevity of a particular style can range from a month to a century, fashions tend to flow in a predictable sequence. The **fashion life cycle** is quite similar to the more familiar product life cycle. An item or idea progresses through basic stages from birth to death, as shown in Figure 17–4.

The diffusion process discussed earlier in the chapter is intimately related to the popularity of fashion-related items. To illustrate how this process works, consider how the **fashion acceptance cycle** works in the popular music business. In the *introduction stage* a song is listened to by a small number of music innovators. It may be played in clubs or on "cutting-edge" university radio stations (which is exactly how "grunge rock" groups like Nirvana got their start). During the *acceptance stage* the song enjoys increased social visibility and acceptance by large segments of the pop-

fashion life cycle the "career" or stages in the life of a fashion as it progresses from introduction to obsolescence

fashion acceptance cycle the diffusion process of a style through three stages: introduction, acceptance and regression

This Jim Beam ad illustrates the cyclical nature of fashion.
Courtesy of Jim Beam Brand, Inc.

FIGURE 17–4 • Comparison of the Acceptance Cycles of Fads, Fashions and Classics

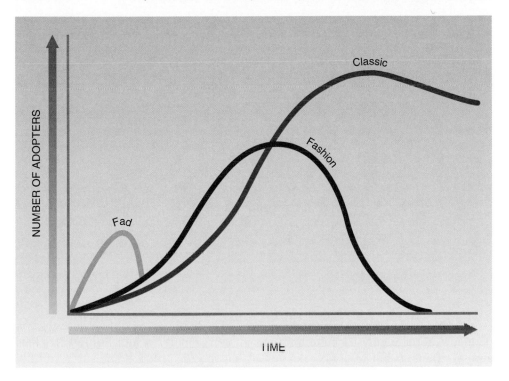

Source: Reprinted with the permission of Macmillan College Publishing Company from *The Social Psychology of Clothing* by Susan Kaiser. Copyright © 1985 by Macmillan College Publishing Company, Inc.

ulation. A record may get wide airplay on Top 40 stations, steadily rising up the charts "like a bullet." In the *regression stage* the item reaches a state of social saturation as it becomes overused, and eventually it sinks into decline and obsolescence as new songs rise to take its place. A hit record may be played once an hour on a Top 40 station for several weeks. At some point, though, people tend to get sick of it and focus their attention on newer releases. The former hit record eventually winds up in the discount rack at the local record store.

Figure 17–5 illustrates that fashions are characterized by slow acceptance at the beginning, which (if the fashion is to "make it") rapidly accelerates and then tapers off. Different classes of fashion can be identified by considering the relative length of the fashion acceptance cycle. While many fashions exhibit a moderate cycle, taking several years to work their way through the stages of acceptance and decline, others are extremely long-lived or short-lived.

A **classic** is a fashion with an extremely long acceptance cycle. It is in a sense "antifashion," since it guarantees stability and low risk to the purchaser for a long period of time. Keds sneakers, introduced in 1917, have been successful because they appeal to those who are turned off by the high-fashion, trendy appeal of L.A. Gear, Reebok and others. When consumers in focus groups were asked to project what kind of building Keds would be, a common response was a country house with a white picket fence. In other words, the shoes are seen as a stable, classic product. In contrast, Nikes were often described as steel-and-glass skyscrapers, reflecting their more modernistic image.[52]

classic a fashion with an extremely long acceptance cycle

FIGURE 17–5 • A Normal Fashion Cycle

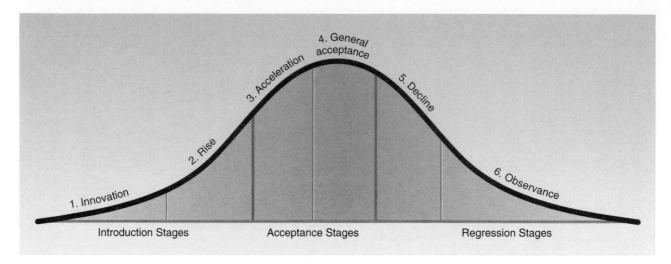

Source: Reprinted with the permission of Macmillan College Publishing Company from *The Social Psychology of Clothing* by Susan Kaiser. Copyright ©1985 by Macmillan College Publishing Company, Inc.

fad a very short-lived fashion

A **fad** is a very short-lived fashion. Fads are usually adopted by relatively few people. Adopters may all belong to a common subculture, and the fad "trickles across" members but rarely breaks out of that specific group. Some successful fad

This *House & Garden* ad illustrates the life cycle of an Emerson radio to show how ideas about a mass-produced cultural product can change over time and create a classic and valuable collector's item.
Reprinted by permission of HG Maga-zine, *Copyright © 1989 The Condé Nast Publications, Inc.*

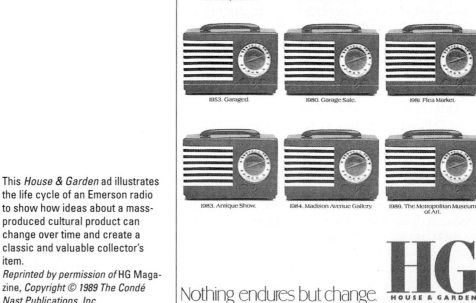

products include hula hoops, snap bracelets and "pet rocks." Streaking was a fad that hit university campuses in the mid-1970s. This term referred to students running naked through classrooms, cafeterias and dorms. Although the practice quickly spread across many campuses, it was primarily restricted to university settings. Streaking highlights several of the following important characteristics of fads:[53]

- The fad is non-utilitarian; that is, it does not perform any meaningful function.
- The fad is often adopted on impulse; people do not undergo stages of rational decision making before joining in.
- The fad diffuses rapidly, gains quick acceptance and is short-lived.

FAD OR TREND?

In 1988, Clearly Canadian began selling a clear soft drink, and over the next few years others jumped on board. Colgate-Palmolive spent $6 million developing a clear version of Palmolive dishwashing liquid, by 1992 Colgate was selling clear soap, Coors introduced a clear malt beverage called Zima, and consumers could even choose clear gasoline for their cars. Clear products were so ubiquitous that they were spoofed on "Saturday Night Live" in a fake commercial for Crystal Gravy: "you can see your meat!" It was clear that the beginning of the end was in sight and the novelty was wearing off the "clear" fad. The comments of one 25-year-old par-

MULTICULTURAL DIMENSIONS

The Japanese have a weakness for gadgets, and local companies produce toys for adults that may strike others as somewhat, well, bizarre. One recent fad is a hit series of Japanese software called "Princess Maker." Targeted to adult men, the player controls the activities, hobbies and clothing of a girl character he "raises" from childhood. The game probably would be frowned upon in the West, since this virtual daughter can be programmed to dress in lingerie or sunbathe naked. The player names her, picks her birthday and even chooses her blood type, which some Japanese believe determines character traits. His choice of activities for her affects her future success in life (and his score). For example, choosing painting lessons increases the score, while dressing her in provocative clothing reduces her moral standing and lowers the score. If a player winds up with a really low score, the daughter may face a future as a bar hostess. When this happens, she giggles while holding up a slinky dress.[54]

Another Japanese fad has now invaded American shores. It's a hand-held chicken video game—a *tamagotch*, or "cute little egg." The key-chain computer game unfolds as an egg hatches on the display screen. The owner uses three tiny buttons to feed the baby chick, play with it, clean up after it and discipline it. The game can go on for several days if the chick is cared for properly, but if the owner forgets to feed it, he or she hears a loud "peep, peep, peep," and eventually the chick grows sickly and dies. Nearly 2000 people showed up at one store in Japan when word leaked out that a new shipment had been received, and many slept outside in the cold to be first in line.[55] In late 1997 the concept invaded the USA, with about 6 million units of American versions such as Microchimp and Compu Kitty preordered in anticipation of the next craze for these "giga pets."[56]

ticipant in a research study of clear drinks sums up the problem: "When I first started drinking them, I thought they were interesting. But once it became a fad I thought, 'this isn't cool anymore.'"[57]

The first company to identify a trend and act on it has an advantage, whether the firm is Starbucks (gourmet coffee), Nabisco (Snackwell's low-fat cookies and crackers) or Taco Bell (value pricing). While nothing is certain, some guidelines help to predict if the innovation will endure as a long-term trend or is just a fad, destined to go the way of mood rings, Cabbage Patch dolls and Wally Wallwalkers:[58]

- Does it fit with basic lifestyle changes? If a new hairstyle is hard to care for, this innovation will not be consistent with women's increasing time demands. On the other hand, the movement to shorter-term vacations is more likely to last since this innovation makes trip planning easier for harried consumers.

- What are the benefits? The switch to poultry and fish from beef came about because these meats are healthier, so a real benefit is evident.

- Can it be personalized? Enduring trends tend to accommodate a desire for individuality, while styles like mohawk haircuts or the grunge look are inflexible and don't allow people to express themselves.

- Is it a trend or a side-effect? An increased interest in exercise is part of a basic trend towards health consciousness, while the specific form of exercise that is "in" at any given time will vary (e.g., low-impact aerobics vs. in-line skating).

- What other changes have occurred in the market? Sometimes the popularity of products is influenced by *carryover effects*. The miniskirt fad in the 1960s brought about a major change in the hosiery market, as sales of pantyhose and tights grew from 10 percent of this product category to more than 80 percent in two years. Now, sales of these items are declining due to the casual emphasis in dressing.

- Who has adopted the change? If the innovation is not adopted by working mothers, baby boomers or some other important market segment, it is not likely to become a trend.

TRANSFERRING PRODUCT MEANINGS TO OTHER CULTURES

Innovations know no country boundaries; in modern times they travel across oceans and deserts with blinding speed. Just as Marco Polo brought spice from China and colonial settlers introduced Europeans to the "joys" of tobacco, today multinational firms seeking to expand their markets are constantly working to conquer new markets and convince legions of foreign consumers to desire their offerings.

As if understanding the dynamics of one's own culture weren't hard enough, these issues get even more complicated when we take on the daunting—but essential—task of learning about the practices of other cultures. The consequences of ignoring cultural sensitivities can be costly. This oversight became evident, for example, during the 1994 soccer World Cup. Both McDonald's and Coca-Cola made the mistake of reprinting the Saudi Arabian flag, which includes sacred words from the Koran, on disposable packaging used in promotions. Despite their delight at having a Saudi team in contention for the Cup, Muslims around the world protested this borrowing of sacred imagery, and both companies had to scramble to rectify the situation.[59]

In this section we'll consider some of the issues confronting marketers who seek to understand the cultural dynamics of other countries. We'll also consider the consequences of global culture, as Western marketers continue to export popular culture to a globe full of increasingly affluent consumers, many of whom are eagerly waiting to replace their traditional products and practices with those of McDonald's, Levi's and MTV.

Think Globally, Act Locally

As corporations increasingly find themselves competing in many markets around the world, the debate has intensified regarding the necessity of developing separate marketing plans for each culture. A lively debate has ensued about the need to "fit in" to the local culture. Let's briefly consider each viewpoint.

ADOPTING A STANDARDIZED STRATEGY

Proponents of a standardized marketing strategy argue that many cultures, especially those of relatively industrialized countries, have become so homogenized that the same approach will work throughout the world. By developing one approach for multiple markets, a company can benefit from economies of scale, since it does not have to incur the substantial time and expense of developing a separate strategy for each culture.[60] This viewpoint represents an **etic perspective,** which focuses upon commonalities across cultures. An etic approach to a culture is objective and analytical; it reflects impressions of a culture as viewed by outsiders.

etic perspective an approach to studying cultures that stresses commonalities across cultures

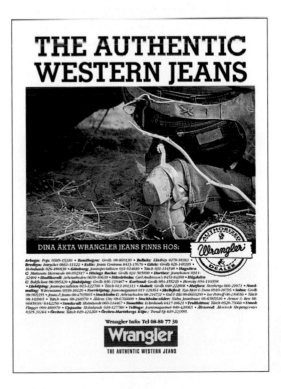

As this Swedish ad for Wrangler jeans shows, products associated with the "authentic" American West are in demand around the world.
Courtesy of Wrangler Europe.

ADOPTING A LOCALIZED STRATEGY

emic perspective an approach to studying cultures that stresses the unique aspects of each culture

In contrast, many marketers endorse an **emic perspective,** which focuses on variations within a culture. They feel that each culture is unique, with its own value system, conventions and regulations. This perspective argues that each country has a national character, a distinctive set of behaviour and personality characteristics.[61] An effective strategy must therefore be tailored to the sensibilities and needs of each specific culture. An emic approach to a culture is subjective and experiential; it attempts to explain a culture as it is experienced by insiders.

Sometimes this strategy involves modifying a product or the way it is positioned to make it acceptable to local tastes. For example, consider the challenge faced by the brewing industry in the Middle East. Alcohol-free beers are growing in popularity, and Saudi market leader Moussey has been doing business there for over 20 years. Still, selling such a product in a country where alcohol consumption is punishable by flogging can be tricky. These drinks are called malt beverages instead of beer, and they can only be marketed through special promotions. Stroh's Schlitz No-Alcohol brand is touted vaguely as "The famous American beverage."[62]

In other contexts adaptation demands more than wordplay. For example, consumers in some cultures simply do not like tastes that are popular elsewhere. Snapple failed in Japan because consumers there didn't like the drink's cloudy appearance or the stuff floating in the bottles. Similarly, Frito-Lay Inc. stopped selling Ruffles potato chips (too salty) and Cheetos (the Japanese didn't appreciate having their fingers turn orange after eating a handful).[63] Cheetos are being made in China, but the local version doesn't contain any cheese, which is not a staple of the Chinese diet. Instead, local flavours will be available in varieties like Savory American Cream and Japanese Steak.[64] Even the venerable McDonald's, which has won Big Mac fans the world over, is finding the need to make changes in order to meet local competition in the Phillipines from Jobilee Foods Corporation. This chain, which has 46 percent of the Filipino market compared to McDonald's 16 percent, caters to the local preference for sweet and spicy flavours, and offers rice with its entrées that is similar to what a Filipino mother would cook at home. In response, McDonald's was forced to offer its own version of spicy burgers, one of the few times it has actually changed the composition of its regular burger patty.[65]

Mainland China is one of the newest markets to be opened up to American business and culture. Chinese television now carries commercials for the likes of Coca-Cola, Tang and Contac cold capsules. Procter & Gamble manufactures goods like Pantene shampoo and Oil of Ulan locally (known as Oil of Olay in the United States). McDonald's recently opened a restaurant in Beijing that is the largest of its outlets in the world (and the only one with a Communist Party secretary). It has more than 700 seats and nearly 1000 employees, a few of whom are shown in the photo here. Many competed for these highly valued positions that are perceived to offer prestige and upward mobility.
Nicholas D. Kristof, "'Billions Served' (and That Was Without China)," New York Times (April 24, 1992): A4; James Sterngold, "The Awakening Chinese Consumer," New York Times (October 11, 1992): F1. Photo courtesy of © Kees/Sygma.

CULTURAL DIFFERENCES RELEVANT TO MARKETERS

So, which perspective is correct—the emic or the etic? Perhaps it will be helpful to consider some of the ways that cultures vary in terms of their product preferences and norms regarding what types of products are appropriate or desirable.

Given the sizeable variations in tastes within Canada alone, it is hardly surprising that people around the world have developed their own unique preferences. For example, Europeans favour dark chocolate over milk chocolate, which they regard as suitable only for children. Sara Lee sells its pound cake with chocolate chips in the United States, with raisins in Australia and with coconut in Hong Kong. Whisky is considered a "classy" drink in France and Italy but not in England. Crocodile bags are popular in Asia and Europe but not in the United States. Americans' favourite tie colours are red and blue, while the Japanese prefer olive, brown and bronze.[66]

Consumers in different countries are also accustomed to different forms of advertising. In general, ads that focus on such universal values as love of family travel fairly well, while those with a specific focus on lifestyles do not. In some cases advertising content is regulated by the local government. For example, pricing in Germany is controlled, and special sales can be held only for a particular reason, such as going out of business or the end of the season. Advertising also focuses more on the provision of factual information than on the aggressive hard sell. Indeed, it is illegal to mention the names of competitors.[67] A similar emphasis on facts can be found in Spain and Denmark. In contrast, the British and the Japanese regard advertising as a form of entertainment. Compared to the United States, British television commercials contain less information[68] and Japanese advertising is more likely to feature emotional appeals.[69] As in Germany, comparative advertising is rare in Japan, but for a different reason: the Japanese consider this practice impolite. They

MULTICULTURAL DIMENSIONS

The etic approach has been chosen by many companies who have adopted a standardized strategy for marketing products in Europe. Although the unification of the European Union has not happened as smoothly as many predicted, the prospect of many separate economies eventually being massed into one market of 325 million consumers has led many companies to begin to standardize their prices, brand names and advertising.[70]

Many companies are responding to this dramatic change by consolidating the different brands sold in individual countries into common *Eurobrands*. In the United Kingdom and France, for example, the Marathon candy bar sold by Mars, Inc., is becoming the Snickers bar (a somewhat risky move, considering that the British refer to women's underwear as "knickers").[71]

Wella, the hair-care company, is aggressively developing a European strategy. Eighty percent of its product line either has been or soon will be introduced or relaunched as pan-European brands. Other companies that have "gone global" include Merrill Lynch, Xerox and Chase Manhattan Bank. After testing four campaigns in seven countries, Seagram's Chivas Regal scotch chose a series of 24 ads, each featuring a Chivas crest and the theme line, "There will always be a Chivas Regal."[72]

instead value commercial messages that contain a lot of references to nature and sensory experiences.

Marketers must be aware of a culture's norms regarding such sensitive topics as taboos and sexuality. Opals signify bad luck to the British, while hunting-dog or pig emblems are offensive to Muslims. The Japanese are superstitious about the number four. Shi, the word for four, is also the word for death. For this reason Tiffany sells glassware and china in sets of five in Japan.

Cultures vary sharply in the degree to which references to sex and bodily functions are permitted. Many North American consumers pride themselves on their sophistication. However, some would blush at much European advertising, in which sexuality is more explicit. North Americans are considered prudish by Australians and many Europeans.

MULTICULTURAL DIMENSIONS

Strongly held values can make life very difficult for marketers, especially when they are selling sensitive products. This is the case with tampons. While 70 percent of North American women use them, only 100 million out of a potential market of 1.7 billion eligible women in the rest of the world do. Resistance to the product posed a major problem for Tambrands, which does not make other products and must expand its customer base to remain viable.

The company has found it difficult to sell its feminine hygiene products in cultures such as Brazil, where many young women fear they will lose their virginity if they use a tampon. A commercial developed for this market included an actress who says in a reassuring voice, "Of course, you're not going to lose your virginity," while a second woman adds, "That will happen, in a much more romantic way."

To counteract this problem prior to launching a new global advertising campaign for Tampax in 26 countries, the firm's advertising agency conducted research and divided the world into three clusters based on residents' resistance to using tampons. Resistance was so intense in Muslim countries that the agency didn't even attempt to reach women in those places!

- Cluster One (including the USA, Canada, the UK and Australia): Women felt comfortable with the idea and offered little resistance. A teaser ad was developed to encourage more frequency of use: "Should I sleep with it, or not?"

- Cluster Two (including France, Israel and South Africa): About 50 percent of women use the product, but some concerns about virginity remain. To counteract these objections the marketing strategy focused on obtaining the endorsements of gynecologists within each country.

- Cluster Three (including Brazil, China and Russia): The greatest resistance was encountered. To try to make inroads in these countries the researchers found that the first priority is simply to explain how to use the product, without making women feel squeamish—a challenge they still are trying to puzzle out.[73]

Does Global Marketing Work?

So, after briefly considering some of the many differences one encounters across cultures, do you think global marketing works? Perhaps the more appropriate question is, "*When* does it work?"

Although the argument for a homogeneous world culture is appealing in principle, in practice it has met with mixed results. One reason for the failure of global marketing is that consumers in different countries have different conventions and customs, so they simply do not use products the same way. Kellogg, for example, discovered that in Brazil big breakfasts are not traditional, and cereal is more commonly eaten as a dry snack.

In fact significant cultural differences can show up within the *same* country. Advertisers know that when they target consumers in French-speaking Quebec, their messages must be much different than they are when talking to their fellow Canadians who speak English. Ads in Montreal tend to be a lot racier than those in Toronto, reflecting differences in attitudes towards sexuality between consumers with French versus British roots.[74]

Some large corporations, such as Coca-Cola, have been successful in crafting a single, international image. Still, even Coca-Cola must make minor modifications to the way it presents itself in each culture. Although Coke commercials are largely standardized, local agencies are permitted to edit them to highlight close-ups of local faces.[75]

As the world's borders shrink due to advances in communications, many companies continue to develop global advertising campaigns. In some cases they are encountering obstacles to acceptance, especially in less-developed countries or in those areas, such as eastern Europe, that are only beginning to embrace Western-style materialism as a way of life.[76]

To maximize the chances of success for these multicultural efforts, marketers must locate consumers in different countries who nonetheless share a common world-view. This is more likely to be the case among people whose frames of reference are relatively more international or cosmopolitan and/or who receive much of their information about the world from sources that incorporate a worldwide perspective.

Who is likely to fall into this category? Two consumer segments are particularly good candidates: 1) affluent people who are "global citizens" and who are exposed to ideas from around the world through their travels, business contacts and media experiences, and who, as a result, share common tastes; and 2) young people whose tastes in music and fashion are strongly influenced by MTV and other media that broadcast many of the same images worldwide. For example, viewers of MTV Europe in Rome or Zurich can check out the same "buzz clips" as their counterparts in London or Luxembourg.[77] Benetton, the Italian clothing manufacturer, has been at the forefront in creating vivid (and often controversial) messages about AIDS, racial equality, warfare and other subjects that transcend national boundaries.[78]

The Diffusion of Western Consumer Culture

The allure of Western consumer culture has spread throughout the world, as people in other societies slowly but surely fall under the spell of far-reaching advertising campaigns, contact with tourists and the desire to form attachments with other parts of the world. This attraction sometimes results in bizarre permutations of products and services, as they are modified to be compatible with local customs. Consider these events, for example:[79]

- In Peru, Indian boys can be found carrying rocks painted to look like transistor radios.
- In highland Papua New Guinea, tribesmen put Chivas Regal wrappers on their drums and wear Pentel pens instead of nosebones.
- Bana tribesmen in the remote highlands of Kako, Ethiopia, pay to watch "Pluto the Circus Dog" on a Viewmaster.
- When a Swazi princess marries a Zulu king, she wears red touraco wing feathers around her forehead and a cape of windowbird feathers and oxtails. He is wrapped in a leopard skin. All is recorded on a Kodak movie camera while the band plays "The Sound of Music."
- In addition to traditional gifts of cloth, food and cosmetics, Nigerian Hausa brides receive cheap quartz watches—although they cannot tell time.

"I'D LIKE TO BUY THE WORLD A COKE ..."

As indicated by the above examples, many formerly isolated cultures now incorporate Western objects into their traditional practices. In the process, the meanings of these objects are transformed and adapted to local tastes (at times in seemingly bizarre ways). Sometimes the process enriches local cultures; sometimes it produces painful stresses and strains the local fabric.

back-translation to ensure accurate translation of research materials or advertising messages, a process whereby a translated message is translated back into its original language by a different interpreter, to verify its correctness

MARKETING PITFALL

The language barrier is one problem confronting marketers who wish to break into foreign markets. One technique that is used to avoid this problem is **back-translation**, where a translated ad is retranslated into the original language by a different interpreter, in order to catch errors. Some specific translation obstacles that have been encountered around the world include the following:[80]

- *Fresca* (the name of a soft drink) is Mexican slang for *lesbian*.
- When spelled phonetically, *Esso* means *stalled car* in Japan.
- Ford had several problems in Spanish markets. The company discovered that a truck model it called *Fiera* means *ugly old woman* in Spanish. Its *Caliente*, the name of a model sold in Mexico, is slang for *streetwalker*. In Brazil, *Pinto* is a slang term meaning *small male appendage*.
- When Rolls-Royce introduced its Silver Mist model in Germany, it found that the word *mist* is translated as *excrement*. Similarly, Sunbeam's curling iron, called the *Mist-Stick*, translated as *manure wand*. To add insult to injury, *Vicks* is German slang for *sexual intercourse,* so that company's name had to be changed to Wicks in this market.

The West is a *net exporter* of popular culture. Western symbols in the form of images, words and products have diffused throughout the world. This influence is eagerly sought by many consumers, who have learned to equate Western lifestyles in general and the English language in particular with modernization and sophistication. As a result, people around the world are being exposed to a blizzard of American products that their producers are attempting to make part of local lifestyles.

Levi's jeans, for example, are a status symbol among upwardly mobile Asian and European consumers, who snap them up even though they retail at over $100 in many countries. Recent attempts by American marketers to "invade" other countries include the following:

- Kellogg Co. is trying to carve out a market for breakfast cereal in India, even though currently only about 3 percent of Indian households eat such products. Most middle-class Indians eat traditional hot breakfasts that include such dishes as *chapatis* (unleavened bread) and *dosas* (fried pancakes), but the company is confident that it can entice them to make the switch to Corn Flakes, Froot Loops and other American delicacies.[81]

- The British are avid tea drinkers, but how will they react to American-style iced tea? US companies such as Snapple are hoping they can convince the British that iced tea is more than hot tea that got cold. These firms may have a way to go, based on the reaction of one British construction worker who tried a canned iced tea for the first time and said, "It was bloody awful."[82]

- Pizza Hut is invading, of all places, Italy. The country that invented pizza will be exposed to the mass-produced version, quite a different dish than the local pizza, which is often served on porcelain dishes and eaten with a knife and fork. On the other hand, one of Pizza Hut's top-performing restaurants is now located in Paris, a centre of fine cuisine, so only time will tell if Italians will embrace pizza "American-style."[83]

THE INVASION OF ASIA

Although a third of the world's countries have a per capita gross national product of less than US$500, people around the world now have access to Western media, where they can watch reruns of shows like "The X-Files" and "Baywatch." To illustrate the impact of this imagery around the world, we will compare its impact in two very different Asian countries.

Consider how the material expectations of consumers in the People's Republic of China have escalated. Twenty years ago the Chinese strove to attain what they called the "three bigs"—bikes, sewing machines and wrist-watches. This wish list was later modified to become the "new big six," adding refrigerators, washing machines and televisions. At last count the ideal was the "eight new things." The list now includes *colour* televisions, cameras and video recorders.[84] Chinese women are starting to demand Western cosmetics costing up to a quarter of their salaries and ignoring domestically produced competitors. As one Chinese executive noted, "Some women even buy a cosmetic just because it has foreign words on the package."[85]

In contrast to people in China, the Japanese have already become accustomed to a bounty of consumer goods. Still, the Japanese too are particularly enthusiastic borrowers of Western culture. Some Japanese pay the equivalent of half a million dollars for shrunken versions of US homes, and the more avid Americophiles have been known to stage cookouts around imported brick barbecues and to trade in their Toyotas for expensive imports like Chevy vans.[86]

This movie poster promotes the Tom Cruise film *Far and Away* to the Japanese, who are huge fans of American popular culture.
© *Jeffrey Aaronson/Aspen Network.*

One of the latest fads is *Bassu Boomu*. Inspired by the popularity of the American film *A River Runs Through It,* thousands of Japanese are dressing up like American fishermen and heading for the water. Some years ago a wealthy businessman imported American black bass to Japan, and they spread through the country but were considered a pest—until now. According to one importer of expensive fishing gear, "To consumers, bass fishing is equal to America." Sixteen million foreign fishing rods were imported in one year, and magazines like *Basser* and *LureFreak* have sprung up to meet the needs of Japanese hooked on American outdoor culture.[87]

The Japanese often use Western words as a shorthand for anything new and exciting, even if they do not understand their meaning. The resulting phenomenon is known as "Japlish," where new Western-sounding words are merged with Japanese. Cars are given names like Fairlady, Gloria and Bongo Wagon. Consumers buy *deodoranto* (deodorant) and *appuru pai* (apple pie). Ads urge shoppers to *stoppu rukku* (stop and look), and products are claimed to be *yuniku* (unique).[88] Coca-Cola cans say, "I feel Coke & sound special," and a company called Cream Soda sells products with the slogan, "Too old to die, too young to happy."[89] Other Japanese products with English names include Mouth Pet (breath freshener), Pocari Sweat (refreshment water), Armpit (electric razor), Brown Gross Foam (hair-colouring mousse), Virgin Pink Special (skin cream), Cow Brand (beauty soap) and Mymorning Water (canned water).[90]

EMERGING CONSUMER CULTURES IN TRANSITIONAL ECONOMIES

In the early 1980s the American TV show "Dallas" was broadcast by the Romanian Communist government to show off the decadence of Western capitalism. This strategy backfired, and instead the devious (but rich!) J.R. became a revered icon in parts of eastern Europe and the Middle East—to the extent that a tourist attraction outside Bucharest includes a big white log gate that announces (in English) the name, "South Fork Ranch."[91] Western "decadence" appears to be infectious.[92]

After the downfall of Communism, eastern Europeans emerged from a long winter of deprivation into a springtime of abundance. The picture is not all rosy, however, since attaining consumer goods is not easy for many in *transitional economies,* where the economic system still is "neither fish nor fowl," and governments ranging from China to Portugal struggle with the difficult adaptation from a controlled, centralized economy to a free-market system. These problems stem from such factors as the unequal distribution of income among citizens, as well as striking rural–urban differences in expectations and values. The key aspect of a transitional economy is the rapid change required on social, political and economic dimensions as the populace suddenly is exposed to global communications and external market pressures.[93]

Some of the consequences of the transition to capitalism include a loss of confidence and pride in the local culture, as well as alienation, frustration and an increase in stress as leisure time is sacrificed to work ever harder to buy consumer goods. The yearning for the trappings of Western material culture is perhaps most evident in parts of eastern Europe, where citizens who threw off the shackles of Communism now have direct access to coveted consumer goods from the USA and Western Europe—if they can afford them. One analyst observed, "... as former subjects of the Soviet empire dream it, the American dream has very little to do with liberty and justice for all and a great deal to do with soap operas and the Sears Catalogue.[94]

In 1990 well over 60 countries had a Gross National Product of less than $10 billion, while more than 135 international companies had revenues greater than that. The dominance of these marketing powerhouses has helped to create a *globalized consumption ethic:* as people the world over are increasingly surrounded by goods and tempting images of them, a material lifestyle becomes more important to attain. Shopping evolves from a wearying, task-oriented struggle to locate even basic necessities to become a leisure activity, and possessing luxury items becomes a mechanism to display one's status (see Chapter 13)—often at great personal sacrifice. In Romania, for example, Kent cigarettes became an underground currency, even though the cost of smoking a pack a day of foreign cigarettes would cost the average Romanian his or her entire yearly salary. As the global consumption ethic spreads, the products wished for in different cultures become homogenized. For example, Christmas is now celebrated among some urbanites in Muslim Turkey, although gift giving even on birthdays is not customary in many parts of that country.

In some cases the meanings of these desired products are adapted to local customs and needs. For example, in Turkey some urban women use ovens to dry clothes and dishwashers to wash muddy spinach. The process of **creolization** occurs when foreign influences are absorbed and integrated with local meanings—just as modern Christianity incorporated the pagan Christmas tree into its own rituals. Thus a traditional clothing style such as a *bilum* worn in Papua New Guinea may be combined with Western items like Mickey Mouse shirts or baseball caps.[95] These processes make it unlikely that global homogenization will overwhelm local cultures, but rather that there will be multiple consumer cultures, each blending global icons, such as Nike's pervasive "swoosh," with indigenous products and meanings.

creolization the process whereby foreign customs are integrated into a local culture, producing a blend of foreign and local practices

CREEPING AMERICANISM: A NEGATIVE BACKLASH

Despite the proliferation of Western culture around the world, there are signs that this invasion is slowing. Japanese consumers, for example, are beginning to show signs of waning interest in foreign products as the health of their country's economy declines. Some of the latest "hot" products in Japan include green tea and *yukata,* traditional printed cotton robes donned after the evening bath.[96] Several locally made products are catching on in parts of eastern Europe due to their lower prices, improved quality and the problem that the imported products are sometimes inferior versions. Some Muslims are rejecting Western symbols as they adhere to a green Islam philosophy that includes using natural, traditional products.[97]

Critics in other countries deplore the creeping Americanization of their cultures. Debates continue in many countries on the imposition of quotas that limit American television programming.[98] The conflict created by the exporting of American culture was brought to a head in recent trade negotiations on the General Agreement on Tariffs and Trade (GATT), which were deadlocked over the export of American movies to Europe (the United States' share of the European cinema market is about 75 percent). As one French official put it, "French films are the cinema of creation. American films are products of marketing."[99]

Reacting to the growing popularity of country music, the Canadian government decided a few years ago to prohibit Nashville-based Country Music Television, a network that had been available to viewers in this country for over a decade, from broadcasting here. Instead, it was replaced by the Country Network, based in Canada. The new service has content that is 30 percent Canadian.[100] The French have been the most outspoken opponents of creeping Americanization. They have even tried to ban the use of such "Franglais" terms as *le drugstore, le fast food* and even *le marketing,* though this effort was recently ruled unconstitutional.[101] The French debate over cultural contamination was brought to a head by the 1992 opening of Euro Disney in a Paris suburb. In addition to the usual attractions, hotels with names like Hotel New York, Newport Bay Club and Hotel Cheyenne attempt to re-create portions of the USA. In addition to encountering serious financial problems, some Europeans have been less than enthusiastic about the cultural messages being

MARKETING PITFALL

Cigarettes are among the most successful of Western exports. Asian consumers alone spend $90 billion (US) a year on cigarettes, and US tobacco manufacturers continue to push relentlessly into these markets. Cigarette advertising, often depicting glamorous Western models and settings, is found just about everywhere—on billboards, buses, storefronts and clothing—and many major sports and cultural events are sponsored by tobacco companies. Some companies even hand out cigarettes and gifts in amusement areas, often to preteens.

A few countries have taken steps to counteract this form of Westernization. Singapore bans all promotions that mention products' names. Hong Kong has prohibited cigarette ads from appearing on radio and TV. Japan and South Korea do not allow ads to appear in women's magazines. Industry executives argue that they are simply competing in markets that do little to discourage smoking (e.g., Japan issues the health warning, "Please don't smoke too much"), often against heavily subsidized local brands with names like Long Life (a cigarette made in Taiwan). The warnings and restrictions are likely to increase, however: smoking-related deaths have now overtaken communicable diseases for the "honour" of being Asia's number-one killer.[102]

sent by the Disney organization. One French critic described the theme park as "a horror made of cardboard, plastic, and appalling colours—a construction of hardened chewing gum and idiotic folklore taken straight out of comic books written for obese Americans."[103]

- The styles prevalent in a culture at any given point in time often reflect underlying political and social conditions. The set of agents responsible for creating stylistic alternatives is termed *a culture production system*. Factors such as the types of people involved in this system and the amount of competition by alternative product forms influence the choices that eventually make their way to the marketplace for consideration by end consumers.

- Culture is often described in terms of high (or élite) forms and low (or popular) forms. Products of popular culture tend to follow a cultural formula and contain predictable components. On the other hand, these distinctions are blurring in modern society as imagery from "high art" is increasingly being incorporated into marketing efforts.

- Reality engineering occurs as elements of popular culture are appropriated by marketers and converted to vehicles for promotional strategies.[104] These elements include sensory and spatial aspects of everyday existence, whether in the form of products appearing in movies, odours pumped into offices and stores, billboards, theme parks or video monitors attached to shopping carts.

- *Diffusion of innovations* refers to the process whereby a new product, service or idea spreads through a population. Innovators and early adopters are quick to adopt new products, while laggards are very slow. A consumer's decision to adopt a new product depends on his or her personal characteristics as well as on characteristics of the innovation itself. Products stand a better chance of being adopted if they demand relatively little change in behaviour from users, are easy to understand and provide a relative advantage compared to existing products.

- The fashion system includes everyone involved in the creation and transference of symbolic meanings. Meanings that express common cultural categories (e.g., gender distinctions) are conveyed by many different products. New styles tend to be adopted by many people simultaneously in a process known as *collective selection*. Perspectives on motivations for adopting new styles include psychological, economic and sociological models of fashion.

- Fashions tend to follow cycles that resemble the product life cycle. The two extremes of fashion adoption—classics and fads—can be distinguished in terms of the length of this cycle.

- Because a consumer's culture exerts such a big influence on his or her lifestyle choices, marketers must learn as much as possible about differences in cultural norms and preferences when marketing in more than one country. One important issue is the extent to which marketing strategies must be tailored to each culture rather than standardized across cultures. Followers of an etic perspective believe that the same universal messages will be appreciated by people in many cultures. Believers in an emic perspective argue that individual cultures are too unique to permit such standardization; marketers must instead adapt their approaches to be consistent with local values and practices. Attempts at global marketing have met with mixed success; in many cases this approach is more likely to work if the messages appeal to basic values and/or if the target markets consist of consumers who are more internationally rather than locally oriented.

KEY TERMS

Art product p. 554

Back-translation p. 580

Classic p. 571

Collective selection p. 567

Continuous innovation p. 563

Craft product p. 554

Creolization p. 583

Cultivation hypothesis p. 560

Cultural categories p. 566

Cultural formula p. 556

Cultural gatekeepers p. 554

Cultural selection p. 552

Culture production system (CPS) p. 554

Diffusion of innovation p. 561

Discontinuous innovation p. 563

Dynamically continuous innovation p. 563

Early adopters p. 562

Emic perspective p. 576

Erogenous zones p. 567

Etic perspective p. 575

Fad p. 572

Fashion p. 565

Fashion acceptance cycle p. 570

Fashion life cycle p. 570

Fashion system p. 565

Innovation p. 561

Innovators p. 562

Product placement p. 558

Reality engineering p. 557

Symbolic innovation p. 563

Technological innovation p. 563

Trickle-down theory p. 568

CONSUMER BEHAVIOUR CHALLENGE

1. Is it appropriate for large corporations to market small boutique brands as they hide the true origins of these products?

2. Some consumers complain that they are "at the mercy" of designers: they are forced to buy whatever styles are in fashion because nothing else is available. Do you agree that there is such a thing as a "designer conspiracy"?

3. What is the basic difference between a fad, a fashion and a classic? Provide examples of each.

4. What is the difference between an art and a craft? Where would you characterize advertising within this framework?

5. The chapter mentions some instances where market research findings influenced artistic decisions, as when a movie ending was reshot to accommodate consumers' preferences. Many people would most likely oppose this practice, claiming that books, movies, records or other artistic endeavours should not be designed merely to conform to what people want to read, see or hear. What do you think?

6. Due to increased competition and market saturation, marketers in industrialized countries increasingly are trying to develop Third World markets by encouraging people in underdeveloped countries to desire Western products. Should this practice be encouraged, even if the products being marketed may be harmful to consumers' health (e.g., cigarettes) or divert needed money away from the purchase of essentials? If you were a trade or health official in a Third World country, what guidelines, if any, might you suggest to regulate the import of luxury goods from advanced economies?

7. Comment on the growing practices described as reality engineering. Do marketers "own" our culture, and should they?

NOTES

1. Grant McCracken, "Culture and Consumption: A Theoretical Account of the Structure and Movement of the Cultural Meaning of Consumer Goods," *Journal of Consumer Research* 13 (June 1986): 71–84.

2. Richard A. Peterson, "The Production of Culture: A Prolegomenon," in *The Production of Culture*, ed. Richard A. Peterson, Sage Contemporary Social Science Issues (Beverly Hills: Sage, 197Q6), p. 722.

3. Richard A. Peterson and D.G. Berger, "Entrepreneurship in Organizations: Evidence from the Popular Music Industry," *Administrative Science Quarterly* 16 (1971): 97–107.

4. Elizabeth C. Hirschman, "Resource Exchange in the Production and Distribution of a Motion Picture," *Empirical Studies of the Arts* 8, 1 (1990): 31–51; Michael R. Solomon, "Building Up and Breaking Down: The Impact of Cultural Sorting on Symbolic Consumption," in *Research in Consumer Behavior,* eds. J. Sheth and E.C. Hirschman (Greenwich, CT: JAI Press, 1988), pp. 325–51.

5. See Paul M. Hirsch, "Processing Fads and Fashions: An Organizational Set Analysis of Cultural Industry Systems," *American Journal of Sociology* 77, 4 (1972): 639–59; Russell Lynes, *The Tastemakers* (New York: Harper and Brothers, 1954); Michael R. Solomon, "The Missing Link: Surrogate Consumers in the Marketing Chain," *Journal of Marketing* 50 (October 1986): 208–19.

6. Howard S. Becker, "Arts and Crafts," *American Journal of Sociology* 83 (January 1987): 862–89.

7. Herbert J. Gans, "Popular Culture in America: Social Problem in a Mass Society or Social Asset in a Pluralist Society?" in *Social Problems: A Modern Approach,* ed. Howard S. Becker (New York: Wiley, 1966).

8. Peter S. Green, "Moviegoers Devour Ads," *Advertising Age* (June 26, 1989): 36.

9. Michael R. Real, *Mass-Mediated Culture* (Englewood Cliffs, NJ: Prentice Hall, 1977).

10. Annetta Miller, "Shopping Bags Imitate Art: Seen the Sacks? Now Visit the Museum Exhibit," *Newsweek* (January 23, 1989): 44.

11. Kim Foltz, "New Species for Study: Consumers in Action," *New York Times* (December 18, 1989): A1.

12. Arthur A. Berger, *Signs in Contemporary Culture: An Introduction to Semiotics* (New York: Longman, 1984).

13. Robin Givhan, "Designers Caught in a Tangled Web," *Washington Post* (April 5, 1997): C1 (2 pp.).

14. Michael R. Solomon and Basil G. Englis, "Reality Engineering: Blurring the Boundaries Between Marketing and Popular Culture," *Journal of Current Issues and Research in Advertising* 16, 2 (Fall 1994): 1–17.

15. Monroe Friedman, "The Changing Language of a Consumer Society: Brand Name Usage in Popular American Novels in the Postwar Era," *Journal of Consumer Research* 11 (March 1985): 927–37; Monroe Friedman, "Commercial Influences in the Lyrics of Popular American Music of the Postwar Era," *Journal of Consumer Affairs* 20 (Winter 1986): 193.

16. Bill Keller, "For Rich Tourists (and Not Too African)," *New York Times* (December 3, 1992): A1.

17. Jennifer Lewington, "Pepsi Ignites Corporate Debate," *Globe and Mail* (March 27, 1997).

18. Suzanne Alexander Ryan, "Companies Teach All Sorts of Lessons with Educational Tools They Give Away," *Wall Street Journal* (April 19, 1994): B1 (2 pp.); Cyndee Miller, "Marketers Find a Seat in the Classroom," *Marketing News* (June 20, 1994): 2.

19. Benjamin M. Cole, "Products That Want to Be in Pictures," *Los Angeles Herald Examiner* (March 5, 1985): 36. See also Stacy M. Vollmers and Richard W. Mizerski, "A Review and Investigation into the Effectiveness of Product Placements in Films," in *Proceedings of the 1994 Conference of the American Academy of Advertising*, ed. Karen Whitehill King: 97–102; Solomon and Englis, "Reality Engineering."

20. David Leonhardt, "Cue the Soda Can," *Business Week* (June 24, 1996): 64 (2 pp.).

21. Fara Warner, "Why It's Getting Harder to Tell the Shows from the Ads," *Wall Street Journal* (June 15, 1995): B1 (2 pp.).

22. Ibid.

23. Randall Rothenberg, "Is It a Film? Is It an Ad? Harder to Tell?" *New York Times* (March 13, 1990): D23.

24. George Gerbner et al., "Aging with Television: Images on Television Drama and Conceptions of Social Reality," *Journal of Communication* 30 (1980): 37–47.

25. Stephen Fox and William Philber, "Television Viewing and the Perception of Affluence," *Sociological Quarterly* 19 (1978): 103–12; W. James Potter, "Three Strategies for Elaborating the Cultivation Hypothesis," *Journalism Quarterly* 65 (Winter 1988): 930–39; Gabriel Weimann, "Images of Life in America: The Impact of American T.V. in Israel," *International Journal of Intercultural Relations* 8 (1984): 185–97.

26. "Movie Smoking Exceeds Real Life," *Asbury Park Press* (June 20, 1994): A4.

27. Edmund L. Andrews, "When Imitation Isn't the Sincerest Form of Flattery," *New York Times* (August 9, 1990): 20.

28. Eric J. Arnould, "Toward a Broadened Theory of Preference Formation and the Diffusion of Innovations: Cases from Zinder Province, Niger Republic," *Journal of Consumer Research* 16 (September 1989): 239–67; Susan B. Kaiser, *The Social Psychology of Clothing* (New York: Macmillan, 1985); Thomas S. Robertson, *Innovative Behavior and Communication*

(New York: Holt, Rinehart and Winston, 1971).

29. Susan L. Holak, Donald R. Lehmann and Fareena Sultan, "The Role of Expectations in the Adoption of Innovative Consumer Durables: Some Preliminary Evidence," *Journal of Retailing* 63 (Fall 1987): 243–59.

30. Hubert Gatignon and Thomas S. Robertson, "A Propositional Inventory for New Diffusion Research," *Journal of Consumer Research* 11 (March 1985): 849–67.

31. Joshua Levine, "The Streets Don't Lie," *Forbes* (April 21, 1997): 145.

32. Elizabeth C. Hirschman, "Symbolism and Technology as Sources of the Generation of Innovations," in *Advances in Consumer Behavior 9,* ed. Andrew Mitchell (Provo, UT: Association for Consumer Research, 1981), pp. 537–41.

33. Everett M. Rogers, *Diffusion of Innovations,* 3rd ed. (New York: Free Press, 1983).

34. Umberto Eco, *A Theory of Semiotics* (Bloomington, IN: Indiana University Press, 1979).

35. Fred Davis, "Clothing and Fashion as Communication," in *The Psychology of Fashion,* ed. Michael R. Solomon (Lexington, MA: Lexington Books, 1985), pp. 15–28.

36. Melanie Wallendorf, "The Formation of Aesthetic Criteria Through Social Structures and Social Institutions," in *Advances in Consumer Research 7,* ed. Jerry C. Olson (Ann Arbor, MI: Association for Consumer Research, 1980), p. 36.

37. McCracken, "Culture and Consumption."

38. "The Eternal Triangle," *Art in America* (February 1989): 23.

39. Herbert Blumer, *Symbolic Interactionism: Perspective and Method* (Englewood Cliffs, NJ: Prentice Hall, 1969); Howard S. Becker, "Art as Collective Action," *American Sociological Review* 39 (December 1973); Richard A. Peterson, "Revitalizing the Culture Concept," *Annual Review of Sociology* 5 (1979): 137–66.

40. For more details, see Kaiser, *The Social Psychology of Clothing*; George B. Sproles, "Behavioral Science Theories of Fashion," in *The Psychology of Fashion,* ed. Solomon, pp. 55–70.

41. C.R. Snyder and Howard L. Fromkin, *Uniqueness: The Human Pursuit of Difference* (New York: Plenum Press, 1980).

42. Linda Dyett, "Desperately Seeking Skin," *Psychology Today* (May/June 1996): 14; Alison Lurie, *The Language of Clothes* (New York: Random House, 1981).

43. Harvey Leibenstein, *Beyond Economic Man: A New Foundation for Microeconomics* (Cambridge, MA: Harvard University Press, 1976).

44. Georg Simmel, "Fashion," *International Quarterly* 10 (1904): 130–55.

45. Grant D. McCracken, "The Trickle-Down Theory Rehabilitated," in *The Psychology of Fashion,* ed. Solomon, pp. 39–54.

46. Charles W. King, "Fashion Adoption: A Rebuttal to the Trickle-Down Theory," in *Toward Scientific Marketing,* ed. Stephen A. Greyser (Chicago: American Marketing Association, 1963), pp. 108–25.

47. Alf H. Walle, "Grassroots Innovation," *Marketing Insights* (Summer 1990): 44–51.

48. Gregory Beals and Leslie Kaufman, "The Kids Know Cool," *Newsweek* (March 31, 1997): 48–49.

49. Marc Spiegler, "Marketing Street Culture: Bringing Hip-Hop Style to the Mainstream," *American Demographics* (November 1996): 29–34.

50. Beals and Kaufman, "The Kids Know Cool."

51. Petti Fong, "Trample Me Elmo to Arrive in Vancouver Before Christmas," *Vancouver Sun* (December 18, 1996): B1.

52. Anthony Ramirez, "The Pedestrian Sneaker Makes a Comeback," *New York Times* (October 14, 1990): F17.

53. B.E. Aguirre, E.L. Quarantelli and Jorge L. Mendoza, "The Collective Behavior of Fads: The Characteristics, Effects, and Career of Streaking," *American Sociological Review* (August 1989): 569.

54. Associated Press, "Hit Japanese Software lets Players Raise 'Daughter,'" *Montgomery Advertiser* (April 7, 1996): 14A.

55. "Japanese Flock to Stores for Virtual Chicken Game," *Montgomery Advertiser* (January 27, 1997): 6A.

56. Joseph Pereira, "Retailers Bet Virtual Pets Will be the Next Toy Craze," *Wall Street Journal Interactive Edition* (May 2, 1997).

57. Quoted in Kathleen Deveny, "Anatomy of a Fad: How Clear Products Were Hot and Then Suddenly Were Not," *Wall Street Journal* (March 15, 1994): B8.

58. Martin G. Letscher, "How to Tell Fads from Trends," *American Demographics* (December 1994): 38-45.

59. "Packaging Draws Protest," *Marketing News* (July 4, 1994): 1.

60. Theodore Levitt, *The Marketing Imagination* (New York: Free Press, 1983).

61. Terry Clark, "International Marketing and National Character: A Review and Proposal for an Integrative Theory," *Journal of Marketing* 54 (October 1990): 66–79.

62. Tara Parker-Pope, "Nonalcoholic Beer Hits the Spot in Mideast," *Wall Street Journal* (December 6, 1995): B1 (2 pp.).

63. Norihiko Shirouzu, "Snapple in Japan: How a Splash Dried Up," *Wall Street Journal* (April 15 1996): B1 (2 pp.).

64 . Glenn Collins, "Chinese to Get a Taste of Cheese-Less Cheetos," *New York Times* (September 2, 1994): D4.

65. Hugh Filman, "Happy Meals for a McDonald's Rival," *Business Week* (July 29, 1996): 77.

66. Julie Skur Hill and Joseph M. Winski, "Goodby Global Ads: Global Village is Fantasy Land for Marketers," *Advertising Age* (November 16, 1987): 22.

67. Matthias D. Kindler, Ellen Day, and Mary R. Zimmer, "A Cross-Cultural Comparison of Magazine Advertising in West Germany and the U.S." (unpublished manuscript, The University of Georgia, Athens, 1990).

68. Marc G. Weinberger and Harlan E. Spotts, "A Situational View of Information Content in TV Advertising in the U.S. and U.K.," *Journal of Marketing* 53 (January 1989): 89–94; see also Abhilasha Mehta, "Global Markets and Standardized Advertising: Is It Happening? An Analysis of Common Brands in USA and UK," in *Proceedings of the 1992 Conference of the American Academy of Advertising* (1992): 170.

69. Jae W. Hong, Aydin Muderrisoglu, and George M. Zinkhan, "Cultural Differences and Advertising Expression: A Comparative Content Analysis of Japanese and U.S. Magazine Advertising," *Journal of Advertising* 16 (1987): 68.

70. Kevin Cote, "The New Shape of Europe," *Advertising Age* (November 9, 1988): 98.

71. Steven Prokesch, "Selling in Europe: Borders Fade," *New York Times* (May 31, 1990): D1.

72. Gary Levin, "Ads Going Global," *Advertising Age* (July 22, 1991):4; Dagmar Mussey and Anika Michalowska, "Wella Unifies Image," *Advertising Age* (March 11, 1991): 22.

73. Yumiko Ono, "Tambrands Ads Try to Scale Cultural, Religious Obstacles," *Wall Street Journal Interactive Edition* (March 17, 1997), interactive4.wsj.com/archive.

74. Clyde H. Farnsworth, "Yoked in Twin Solitudes: Canada's Two Cultures," *New York Times* (September 18, 1994): E4.

75. Hill and Winski, "Goodbye Global Ads."

76. See, for example, Russell W. Belk and Güliz Ger, "Problems of Marketization in Romania and Turkey," *Research in Consumer Behavior* 7 (Greenwich, CT: JAI Press, 1994): 123–155.

77. MTV Europe, (personal communication, 1994); see also Teresa J. Domzal and Jerome B. Kernan, "Mirror, Mirror: Some Postmodern Reflections on Global Advertising," *Journal of Advertising* 22, 4 (December 1993): 1–20; Douglas P. Holt, "Consumers' Cultural Differences as Local Systems of Tastes: A Critique of the Personality-Values Approach and an Alternative Framework," *Asia Pacific Advances in Consumer Research* 1 (1994): 1–7.

78. Roberto Grandi, "Benetton's Advertising: A Case History of Postmodern Communication," (unpublished manuscript, Center for Modern Culture & Media, University of Bologna, 1994).

79. Eric J. Arnould and Richard R. Wilk, "Why Do the Natives Wear Adidas: Anthropological Approaches to Consumer Research," in *Advances in Consumer Research 12* (Provo, UT: Association for Consumer Research, 1985), pp. 748–52.

80. David A. Ricks, "Products That Crashed Into the Language Barrier," *Business and Society Review* (spring 1983): 46–50.

81. Suman Dubey, "Kellogg Invites India's Middle Class to Breakfast of Ready-to-Eat Cereal," *Wall Street Journal* (August 19, 1994): B3.

82. Tara Parker-Pope, "Will the British Warm Up to Iced Tea? Some Big Marketers are Counting on It," *Wall Street Journal* (August 22, 1994): B1 (2 pp.).

83. John Tagliabue, "Proud Palaces of Italian Cuisine Await Pizza Hut," *New York Times* (September 1, 1994): A4.

84. David K. Tse, Russell W. Belk and Nan Zhou, "Becoming a Consumer Society: A Longitudinal and Cross-Cultural Content Analysis of Print Ads from Hong Kong, the People's Republic of China, and Taiwan," *Journal of Consumer Research* 15 (March 1989): 457–72. See also Annamma Joy, "Marketing in Modern China: an Evolutionary Perspective," *CJAS* (June 1990): 55–67, for a review of changes in Chinese marketing practices since the economic reforms of 1978.

85. Quoted in Sheryl WuDunn, "Cosmetics from the West Help to Change the Face of China," *New York Times* (May 6, 1990): 16.

86. Michael Williams and Miho Inada, "Japanese Families Learn to Play House the American Way," *Wall Street Journal* (January 16, 1995): A1 (2 pp.).

87. Steve Glain, "Japan's Big Fish Tale: It's Hip to Emulate American Anglers," *Wall Street Journal Europe* (March 27,1997): 1–2.

88. John F. Sherry, Jr., and Eduardo G. Camargo, "'May Your Life be Marvelous': English Language Labeling and the Semiotics of Japanese Promotion," Journal of Consumer Research 14 (September 1987): 174–88.

89. Bill Bryson, "A Taste for Scrambled English," New York Times (July 22, 1990): 10; Rose A. Horowitz, "California Beach Culture Rides Wave of Popularity in Japan," Journal of Commerce (August 3, 1989): 17; Elaine Lafferty, "American Casual Seizes Japan: Teenagers Go for N.F.L. Hats, Batman, and the California Look," Time (November 13, 1989): 106.

90. Lucy Howard and Gregory Cerio, "Goofy Goods," Newsweek (August 15, 1994): 8.

91. Prof. Russell Belk, University of Utah, personal communication (July 25, 1997).

92. Material in this section adapted from Güliz Ger and Russell W. Belk, "I'd Like to Buy the World a Coke: Consumptionscapes of the 'Less Affluent World,'" Journal of Consumer Policy 19, 3 (1996): 271–304; Russell W. Belk, "Romanian Consumer Desires and Feelings of Deservingness," in Romania in Transition, ed. Lavinia Stan (Hanover, NH: Dartmouth Press, 1997), pp. 191–208. Cf. also Güliz Ger, "Human Development and Humane Consumption: Well Being Beyond the Good Life," Journal of Public Policy and Marketing 16, 1 (1997): 110–25.

93. Prof. Güliz Ger, Bilkent University, Turkey, personal communication (July 25, 1997).

94. Erazim Kohák, "Ashes, Ashes ... Central Europe After Forty Years," Daedalus 121 (Spring 1992): 219,

quoted in Belk, "Romanian Consumer Desires and Feelings of Deservingness."

95 . This example courtesy of Prof. Russell Belk, University of Utah, personal communication (July 25, 1997).

96. Jennifer Cody, "Now Marketers in Japan Stress the Local Angle," Wall Street Journal (February 23, 1994): B1 (2 pp.).

97. Ger and Belk, "I'd Like to Buy the World a Coke."

98. Steven Greenhouse, "The Television Europeans Love, and Love to Hate," New York Times (August 13, 1989): 24.

99. Charles Goldsmith and Charles Fleming, "Film Industry in Europe Seeks Wider Audience," Wall Street Journal (December 6, 1993): B1 (2 pp.).

100. Clyde H. Farnsworth, "The Border War Over Country Music," New York Times (October 23, 1994): F7.

101. John Sherry, Jr., and Eduardo G. Camargo, "French Council Eases Language Ban," New York Times (July 31, 1994): 12.

102. Mike Levin, "U.S. Tobacco Firms Push Eagerly into Asian Market," Marketing News (January 21, 1991): 2.

103. Quoted in Alan Riding, "Only the French Elite Scorn Mickey's Debut," New York Times (1992): A1.

104. Solomon and Englis, "Reality Engineering."

Cases

CASE	MAIN CHAPTER(S)	OTHER RELEVANT CHAPTERS
Jake and the Bear: The Efforts of a Volunteer Organization	2, 4	6
Tomasino's Restaurant Ltd.	7, 8	3, 11, 15
The Train Trip	9, 10	12, 14
Will That Be Kodak or Konica?	10	3, 9
Family Stove Purchase	12	5, 6
The Summer Project	13, 16, 17	8, 12

JAKE AND THE BEAR: THE EFFORTS OF A VOLUNTEER ORGANIZATION

Jake Yule had joined the Sierra Club of British Columbia two months ago and was now being asked to head up a task force of volunteers to develop an action plan for a "Spirit Bear Wilderness Park." He had gathered information about other Sierra Club activities, as well as some limited information about forestry issues in BC, but he was very concerned about his lack of information regarding what it takes to get people and organizations actively involved in environmental issues. He was scheduled to meet in a week with others on the task force, and he knew that he would need the intervening time to come up with an effective approach for developing the action plan.

Jake had graduated two years earlier with a Bachelor of Engineering from the University of Saskatchewan, and he was pleased to find a job with a major engineering firm in Vancouver. He had been to the west coast on holidays and welcomed the chance to live in a different part of the country, away from Saskatchewan winters. Since moving to BC he had been spending more and more of his recreational time in the wilderness parts of the province, and at the same time becoming more and more confused by his friends' conflicting views about logging and environmental issues.

He had always viewed the forests as a renewable resource, and logging as a critical source of employment on the west coast. His "green" friends, on the other hand, always talked about the detrimen-

The Spirit Bear of British Columbia.
Courtesy of Charlie Russell.

tal impact of forestry practices on salmon spawning rivers, threats to endangered species, bio-diversity and the rights of First Nations peoples. Due to these many conflicts Jake had been reading *Balancing Act* by Hamish Kimmins and attending meetings of the Sierra Club (an organization that Jake considered somewhat more balanced in perspective than some other environmental groups).

The Sierra Club of BC

The Sierra Club was founded by naturalist and writer John Muir in 1892 to protect the wilderness of the Sierra Nevada. Over the years, the activities of the Sierra Club expanded to include issues ranging from climate change and ozone depletion to toxic chemical contamination and loss of biological diversity. The Sierra Club had been active in Canada since 1969, working to influence public policy and environmental awareness. There were local chapters and working groups in every region of the country.

Literature provided by the Sierra Club of BC positioned the forestry issue as follows:

> Ancient temperate rainforests are scarce, covering less than 0.2% of the Earth's land mass, Over 20% of the planet's remaining temperate rainforests are found in British Columbia. This highly productive, severely threatened forest supports one of the most abundant fisheries on earth.

> Coastal temperate rainforests once stretched in a thin, continuous band from northern California to southeastern Alaska. Today, almost all of the original ancient forest south of the Canada–U.S. border is gone, and very little remains intact in southern British Columbia and Vancouver Island. The few remaining large fragments in the south, such as the forest of Clayquot Sound, are still threatened with logging.

> The intact low- and mid-elevation forests on British Columbia's central coast contain some of the oldest and largest trees on earth. These forests provide a critical refuge for grizzly bears, salmon, and a rare white variation of the black bear called Kermokde or Spirit Bear.

> Protecting these species requires the preservation of large areas of contiguous ancient forest. Small areas of forest surrounded by clearcuts or parks which protect only mountain tops, meadows, and scrub cannot and will not prevent the extinction of these globally significant forests.

The Spirit Bear

The white bear mentioned above has been described by enthusiasts as ...

> Powerful, yet gentle, an extraordinary wild creature. To scientists it is *Ursus americanus kermodei*. To the Tsimshian people of the Pacific Coast, it is moksgm'ol. [It is] not albino, rather a subspecies with one in ten white and the rest black.

The only remaining habitat of the Spirit Bear is on BC's remote mid-coast, the location of the proposed Spirit Bear Wilderness Park.

Resource Materials

During his initial searching Jake identified several sources that he wanted to bring to the attention of his task force. The Sierra Club's Web site was of obvious interest (***www.sierraclub.ca***). Because he believed that two-sided arguments were more persuasive than one-sided ones, he decided to provide an extract from *The Balancing Act* (*Exhibit 1-1*). His search of the Club archives uncovered a number of issues regarding the proposed Spirit Bear Wilderness park. He thought these issues were important background for his task force (*Exhibit 1-2*).

The Action Plan

As Jake started to think about the task force, he identified several interrelated questions:

1. Should we focus our energy on individuals, interest groups (such as tourism interests) or corporations?

2. What can we hope to accomplish with each target group (i.e., donations, public support, political pressure)?

3. How will we convince each target group to participate (what messages, what media)?

EXHIBIT 1-1 • Extracts from Balancing Act

> Both environmentalist and experienced field foresters should be members of a multidisciplinary team that contributes to the development of policies to guide the sustainable use and development of forests. For such a partnership to be effective, there must be agreement at the outset concerning the meaning of words used in discussions. Loaded terms such as "never" and "forever" would be best "checked at the door." ... The environment is too important for us to go on arguing about it. All sides in the forestry–environment debate must enter a partnership to ensure sustainable development. We must base this partnership on social and environmental realities and our current scientific knowledge. We must use pictures and images that accurately portray the problems we face, and ensure that in our verbal and written communications we use our language in a way that accurately communicates our knowledge and goals.
>
> Source: Hamish Kimmins, Balancing Act: Environmental Issues in Forestry, 2nd ed. (Vancouver: UBC Press, 1997) p. 287.

EXHIBIT 1–2 • Issues Identified in Preliminary Search of the Sierra Club Archives

- 10 parts of the province have been identified as "endangered rainforest areas soon to be lost to clearcut logging." The proposed Spirit Bear Wilderness Park was one of the 10 areas.

- concern that the BC government may soon issue a permit to log the heart of the Spirit Bear's home range

- concern that forest industry interests dominate government actions

- importance of the proposed park in providing shoreline and mid-elevation habitat, and in providing an important ecological link to a nearby inland mountain park

- importance of the park as the ancestral home of the Kitasoo people, who live within the proposed park in the small sea-village of Klemtu

QUESTIONS

1. Why do people become involved in organizations like the Sierra Club?
2. Provide answers to Jake's three questions.

TOMASINO'S RESTAURANT LTD.

As saturated as the Halifax market area was with pizzerias, Thomas Vacon (owner and manager) and Leo Arkelian (business partner) felt they had found a niche for gourmet pizza pies. Unfortunately, another local entrepreneur also identified this niche; and while Tomasino's was still in the planning stage, Salvatore's opened on South Street with a very high quality gourmet pizza.

However, this did not stop Mr. Vacon and Mr. Arkelian, who went ahead with their plans anyway. In November 1994 the partners decided to expand and move Tomasino's to a new location on South Street.

Strategy

Tomasino's Pizzeria opened for business in November 1989, initially as a take-out and delivery operation to test the market for gourmet pizza in downtown Halifax. They were located on McCully Street during their first five years, where the business developed a reputation as "one of Metro's best." This position was won by Tomasino's in a local newspaper's annual pizza contest. However, Tomasino's had plans from the start to expand into a full-service licensed restaurant.

The move and expansion were financed with $10 000 from Tomasino's and a $25 000 small-business bank loan. An expansion budget was prepared but did not include costs associated with the actual move (*Exhibit 2-1*). The main reason for the move was to facilitate the addition of a restaurant to Tomasino's existing business. The eat-in service specialized in Italian pizza and Mediterranean foods, with a broader menu including pastas, soups, salads and desserts.

Location

The new location on South Street was across from the Hotel Nova Scotia in a historical restaurant site. The previous occupant, Citadel Café, had sales exceeding $70 000 per month. Ironically, Tomasino's former closest competitor, Salvatore's, had been in the building adjacent to this new location. In 1993 they had gone bankrupt, blaming the recession and the Goods and Services Tax (GST) for their demise.

In comparison to Tomasino's McCully Street address, this new location was more visible and closer to the downtown core of Halifax. The proximity to office towers, hotels, hospitals, universities and a dense residential area offered the potential for an eat-in restaurant, as well as expanded delivery sales in Halifax's south end.

Promotional Efforts

The owner believed in the old adage that "a good product will sell itself" and relied heavily on word-of-mouth advertising. Tomasino's tried television and newspaper advertising with little success. The primary promotional tool used was direct mail flyers. These efforts had been more effective, more convenient, less expensive and easier to measure.

Tomasino's Restaurant was scheduled to open in April 1995. Coupon flyers (*Exhibit 2-3*) and other advertising methods were budgeted for the grand opening, which coincided with the G7 Conference in June and the return of the student population in September (*Exhibit 2-4*).

Cost Data

The projected cash flow statement (*Exhibit 2-5*) shows conservative growth in 1995 based on the following assumptions:

1. Restaurant income is calculated on seating for 70, with customer turnover of 1.25 per day and an average customer spending $6.50.
2. Take-out sales were projected from monthly historical variations, with eat-in sales varying in the same cycle.
3. Eat-in sales were factored downward for the initial start-up months.
4. Liquor sales were calculated as 35 percent of eat-in sales.
5 Variable costs were based on historical data and industrial averages.
6. The loan is assumed to be amortized over 60 months at 10.5 percent.

Personnel Data

Thomas Vacon is an Acadian from Yarmouth County, Nova Scotia. He holds a Bachelor of Arts degree in Economics and has been working directly in the food and beverage industry for more than 10 years. Most of the employees working at Tomasino's also have a university degree or are pursuing their studies.

The staff at Tomasino's are not only well-educated but also very professional and well-trained. They are more courteous, more polite and more efficient than the industry standards—virtues noticed and liked by the customers. Both the owner and employees of Tomasino's take great artistic pride in their work. "Making or creating a Tomasino pie is not a mechanical process but one that stems from the heart. Our dough is the canvas we use to create a culinary work of art," says Mr. Vacon.

EXHIBIT 2–1 • Restaurant Expansion Budget

Kitchen Equipment (stove, oven)	$ 12 600.00
Tableware (dishes, silverware)	600.00
Furniture (tables, chairs)	3 200.00
Leaseholds (renovations, flooring, lighting)	8 600.00
Total budget	$ 25 000.00

Note: The above prices are based upon cost estimates of work, quoted prices for new items and projected costs of used goods where available.

Source: Company Records

EXHIBIT 2–2 • Map of Halifax

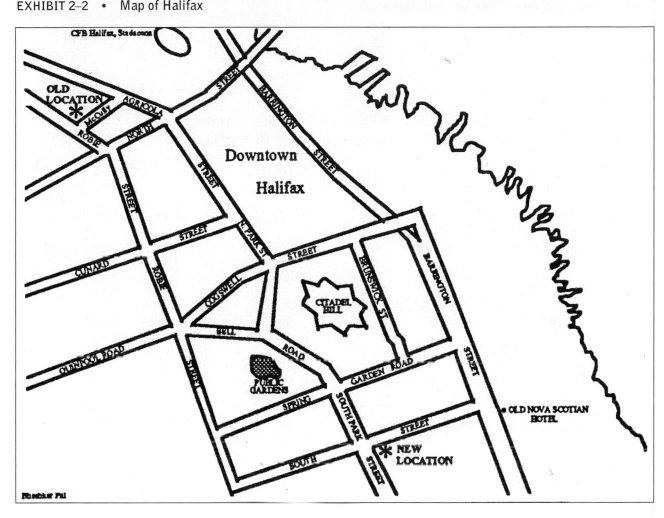

EXHIBIT 2–3 • Coupon Flyer for Grand Opening

TOMASINO'S CELLAR RISTORANTE

5173 South Street–Halifax–Tel: 425-7111

GRAND OPENING LUNCH SPECIALS

Buy One 7" Luncheon Pizza–Get One Free (11am–4pm)

SAMPLES FROM OUR MENU

FOCCACIA BREAD
(asiago, mozzarella, and parmesan with fresh
basil and a light brushing of olive oil. Serves four)

ACADIAN SEAFOOD CHOWDER

CAESAR SALAD (TOMASINO'S FAMOUS)

SPINACH SALAD
(with our delicious poppyseed dressing)

GREEK SALAD
(tomato, Spanish onion, and karama olives on a
bed of romaine, sprinkled with feta)

PENNE PUTINESCA
(penne, sundried tomatoes, black karam olives
and capers in an olive oil herb mixture)

FETTUCCINI ALFREDO
(with smoked ham or vegetarian)

CHICKEN PESTO FUSILLI

SMOKED SALMON & PEPPERS ON
ANGEL HAIR

HALF-9" PIZZA WITH CAESAR SALAD

CEASAR SALAD WITH CHICKEN BREAST

PIZZAS

VOGOLE
(baby clams and artichoke hearts, topped
with fresh garlic and parmesan cheese)

NEW YORK
(mozzarella, parmesan, and feta)

AMBROSIA
(sauteed mushrooms, soin and italian
sausage)

EOS
(feta cheese, black kalamara olives, Spanish
onions and tomatoes)

LOS ANGELES
(pesto, sundried tomatoes, and feta cheese)

LIGHT CHOCOLATE GRAND MARNIER

SORBET DAILY CHEESECAKE

EXHIBIT 2–4 • Proposed Advertising Budget

MONTH	Jan.	Feb.	Mar.	Apr.	May	June	July	Aug.	Sept.	Oct.	Nov.	Dec.
AMOUNT IN $	100	3000	100	100	100	1000	100	100	1500	100	100	100

Source: Company Records

EXHIBIT 2–5 • Projected Cash Flow Summarized Statement Jan.–Dec. 1995

CASH INFLOWS		CASH OUTFLOWS	
		Capital costs	$ 25 000
Take-out sales	$ 153 200	Accounting & Legal	1 800
Eat-in sales	197 306	Advertising	6 400
Liquor sales	63 074	Bank charges	2 700
Loan	25 000	Business taxes	2 100
		Delivery costs	27 576
	Total: $ 438 580	Food purchases	94 637
		Insurance	1 800
		Interest	1 725
		Liquor purchases	31 537
		Loan repayment	4 170
		Miscellaneous	1 200
		Office supplies	900
		Rent	34 000
		Repairs & maintenance	1 440
		Telephone	3 900
		Utilities	5 400
		Wages	134 000
		Total	$ 381 076

Source: Company Records

QUESTIONS

1. How would you segment the market for Tomasino's pizza?

2. Suggest appropriate marketing mix strategies for each of Tomasino's potential target markets.

3. If you were responsible for approving the small-business loan, based on the data provided in the case, would you have granted Tomasino's the money? Why or why not?

4. Evaluate the promotional efforts practised by the business. Should more be invested in advertising the move and expansion? Explain your answer.

THE TRAIN TRIP

On July 21, 1993, Marianne and Robert relived their annoyance as they composed a letter to SNCF (the French National Railway) concerning a recent bad experience with the train system. It had been the only blight on a two-week family holiday in Europe in May/June 1993.

Planning the Family Holiday

Marianne Ricci (aged 41 years) and Robert Dupuis (aged 48 years) were a typical professional couple with one son, Michael (10 years). They lived in a small town in Northeastern Nova Scotia. They usually took their family vacation at the same spot on the Gaspé coast of Quebec. The summer of 1993 would be special, however. Marianne had a special leave from work, Robert was flexible in his job as an independent consultant, and Michael was now old enough to go with the flow of a "big trip."

The family initially contemplated going across Canada, going to Europe, or Marianne taking a trip to Japan by herself. However, she had not been to Europe since 1978 and had always wanted to visit France with Robert because he spoke French fluently. At this point Michael would also appreciate a different cultural setting. Robert was less keen on going to Europe; he saw it as an expensive holiday with the risk of not accommodating the whole family in a truly holiday way. (One of his sisters did not have a good time travelling in Europe in the 1970s. It just might turn out to be an expensive two-week nightmare!) Michael was keen and became increasingly enthusiastic as Mom described her trips to Europe and what he might take with him and what he might see and do. After discussion off and on from November 1992 to February 1993, they came to a consensus and decided to take a trip to Europe. One of the deciding factors was that a trip to Europe would cost about $1400 more than going across Canada, the price difference being accounted for by the availability of accommodation with friends or family in various parts of Canada. As usual, they would work within a predetermined budget.

The family narrowed down their range to France and Italy. Since Marianne had taken two holidays in Europe in the late 1970s, she felt that Robert and Michael should have first choice for places to visit. Her only requests were that they spend time in Florence, Italy, and that she visit, however briefly, a friend who had moved to Milan, Italy. Michael wanted to see the Eiffel Tower, the Leaning Tower of Pisa and Venice. Robert wanted to see the heart of Paris, Venice, and Florence. So they decided to visit Paris, Venice, Florence (with a side trip to Pisa) and Milan, spending about four days in each of the first three cities. They worked out in detail what they would like to see and do.

Marianne investigated travel arrangements with the airlines. The travelling was complicated because they lived two and a half hours from the airport (in Halifax) and would have to fly to Montreal or Toronto, where virtually all international flights originated for travellers from Atlantic Canada. The return trip would involve staying overnight at the Airport Hotel in Halifax. They bought their tickets from Canadian Airlines, who could fly them into Paris on May 26 and out of Milan on June 9 for a reasonable price. The rest of the travel would be by train, since they were not interested in driving in Europe. The routes seemed direct and Marianne's experience on the European trains was very positive; she said they were comfortable, ran on time, and had frequent departures and various routes.

Robert was particularly concerned about accommodations and how they might get from one place to another at reasonable times and at reasonable prices. To enjoy the experience everyone would need adequate sleep and time to rest. Thus, Robert spent a lot of time gathering information on where to stay and how to get around. He spoke to friends and family members, collected brochures from tour companies, talked to travel agents, and spent over $100 during April phoning hotels in Europe. Marianne assisted with gathering this information, but Robert took primary responsibility for it. He wanted to be thorough and to have as few surprises as possible. They spent nearly $150 on travel guides, such as *Let's Go Europe* and the Fodor's guides, purchasing most of them in March during a business trip to Halifax by Marianne.

Robert wanted to know more about how the train schedule would work, so a month prior to the trip he called the French Embassy for the train schedule leaving Paris for Italy. The Embassy forwarded his call to a Canadian agency that looked after train passes for Canadians travelling abroad. He determined that the best route to follow would be a stay in Paris followed by a 12-hour daytime train trip to Florence via Lausanne, Switzerland (with a bonus stopover of two hours), and Milan. After a few days in Florence, they could go up to Venice and then have a day in Milan before flying home. He carefully noted the times of arrivals and departures and took this information with him to Europe. Hotel reservations for each city were made and confirmed with deposits.

The Trip

The trip went very well except for the train trip between Paris and Florence on May 31. On the previous day Robert went to the international travel desk at the Gare de Lyon (a major train station in Paris) and presented the schedule he had brought with him. The agent informed him that they had just been computerized and that Robert's schedule was incorrect. The agent had problems getting the tickets from the computerized set-up, but he finally printed them out after numerous attempts and working with various manuals. Robert paid 1754 French francs for the tickets and three reserved seats (optional, unless you want your seats guaranteed).

Although the agent seemed experienced and knowledgeable about what he was doing, Robert left still having doubts about the schedule.

The train arrived in Lausanne on time, giving the family an opportunity to have lunch and walk around Lausanne. Upon returning to the train station in plenty of time to catch their next train, however, they discovered that they had tickets and reservations for a train departure which did not exist! (In fact, the agent told Robert that the schedule obtained while in Canada was correct and that the agent in Paris had been working off the old schedule.) An unsettling chain of events unfolded.

They were able to use their tickets to get another train to Milan, but did not make their original connection to Florence because the Lausanne train arrived five minutes late. In Milan, after spending nearly one and a half hours speaking to personnel at three different desks, Robert finally learned (through a half-French, half-Italian exchange) that the choice was to take a train which would arrive at 00:30 hours in Florence or to buy tickets for the next train out of Milan, which was first-class only, but would get them there at 22:00 hours. They chose to take the first-class train and called the *pension* (hotel) in Florence to say that they would be late. The tickets cost 170 500 lire plus an additional 33 360 lire for the high exchange rate at the train station. The clerk would not refund the tickets bought in Paris because he insisted that there was no error in the system. However, he did stamp the tickets to indicate that they were not used.

The first-class service offered no consolation. The car was filled with fashionably dressed Europeans, many working on laptop computers and doing business. Two attendants served dinner and generally looked after the passengers. Neither the other passengers nor the attendants seemed particularly pleased at the presence of the family dressed very casually, carrying backpacks and duffle bags, and asking for extra water to quench their thirst. They were hot (from August temperatures in May), tired and annoyed. As they approached Florence, they realized that the train stopped only at the other end of the city from their *pension*. They had chosen to stay at that particular *pension* because it was a short walk from the downtown train station where they were originally supposed to arrive. They managed to find a taxi quite easily, however, and the fare they paid the skilful driver was worth it in comic relief. The three passengers found themselves in a very small automobile travelling at what seemed incredible speed through very narrow streets in a strange city late at night. They were impressed and laughing by the time they reached their *pension* where they were greeted as expected guests. After a good night's sleep they were determined to put the train ordeal behind them and enjoy the rest of the trip—which they did.

The Trip Revisited

When they returned home, they were reminded of the train incident each time they shared the news of their trip with friends and family. As well, the extra expense showed up in accounting for the budget for the trip. The amount was significant to Robert in particular, who looked after the family books. Both Marianne and Robert became increasingly annoyed over time. Although Robert was doubtful that anything would be achieved from such a long distance, Marianne convinced him that they should at least try to appeal for some compensation by writing a letter to the French National Railway. They composed a registered letter (*Exhibit 3-1*) on July 21, 1993, in English, since it would be too complicated for them to try to explain the

EXHIBIT 3–1 · Letter to the French National Railway

12 Pinevale Drive
Smalltown, Nova Scotia
Canada B0Z 4X2
July 21, 1993

French National Railway — SNCF
Département Après-Vente
10 Place Budapest
Paris, France

Dear Sir or Madam:

On Saturday, May 29, 1993, my wife, my young son and I made reservations and bought tickets at Gare de Lyon (in Paris) to go from Paris to Florence (Italy) on Monday, May 31. Our trip required that we change trains in Lausanne and Milan.

While waiting for our train in Lausanne, we became alarmed when Train #323 leaving at 12:55 did not appear on the Departure Notice Board. We immediately spoke to a ticket agent and were informed that our train no longer existed, that a new schedule had recently come into effect, and that the train we should have been on had departed Lausanne for Milan at 11:13. The ticket agent told us to take the next train (#327) at 13:32 to arrive in Milan at 17:45. This was a second class train and reservations were not required. The agent doubted that we would be able to catch Train #541, for which we had reservations, which was leaving Milan for Florence at 17:50. We were told to take Train #511 leaving Milan at 19:40 to arrive in Florence at 22:08 if we missed Train #541.

Unfortunately, Train #327 was late, arriving in Milan at 17:50, and although we tried, it was impossible for us to catch Train #541 for Florence. The ticket agent we spoke to in Milan stamped our reservation card (Milan to Florence) as not having been used. However, the agent also informed us that Train #511 from Milan to Florence at 19:40 would cost us an additional 170 500 Lire. Naturally, we protested, but were forced to pay the additional fee to get to our destination.

The ticket agent at Gare de Lyon made a mistake when he issued our tickets and reservations. This mistake resulted in lost time, a great deal of frustration and additional costs to us of 170 500 Lire. We hold the SNCF responsible and hereby request a refund of our additional costs.

You will find enclosed with this letter photocopies of our tickets, reservations, payment receipt, directions we were given in Lausanne, and our ticket from Milan to Florence with the costs indicated. Should you require the original copies I would be happy to forward them to you.

I look forward to hearing from you.

Sincerely,

Robert S. Dupuis

situation in French. They felt good about having documented the events as best they could along the way and about stating their case.

QUESTIONS

1.   What core benefits was the family trying to satisfy?
2.   Analyze the risk reduction strategies used by Marianne and Robert. How did Marianne and Robert conduct their information search and evaluation of choices?
3.   How did family role structure affect the decision-making process?
4.   What were the major events that occurred in this buying process?
5.   Was the train-trip incident preventable? What conclusions can be drawn for SNCF when things go wrong? For a travel agent?

WILL THAT BE KODAK OR KONICA?

"Oh, #@$%@!!!!" exclaimed Peter. He was now exasperated with this last realization in a string of events.

Peter's spouse, Amy, asked him to pick up two rolls of film for her while he was out running other errands. She usually took care of the shopping for these types of things because she took most of the photographs in the family and kept the photo albums organized. She almost always asked for double prints so that she could share photos with friends and family members.

Their camera, a Minolta, wasn't all that sophisticated, but it did have adjustments for the speed of a film. In fact, since it was a "point and shoot" model, the only requirements were to buy high-quality film and to remember to make the speed adjustments. Peter remembered to ask about the brand of film to buy. Because Amy had a special occasion coming up, she emphasized that Kodak was the brand to buy.

Peter went to the local film development store and asked for two rolls of 35 mm Kodak film with 36 exposures. One of the two young women working at the store mentioned that they had Kodak in 24 exposures for $4.79 a roll. She pointed to the film, which was in black plastic containers with "utility" labelling and was displayed in a bulk bin. Film with 36 exposures was available in Konica only. It was priced at $6.49 and was stored in the refrigerator display case. Peter said, "I'll have those," pointing to the bulk bin. The sales clerk quickly put the order together. Peter paid for the film, as well as for some photos he was also picking up, with a credit card. He left the store.

As he was walking along, he took the credit card slip from the bag to put in his jacket pocket. Glancing at it, he noticed that he had been overcharged for the film. Then he looked in the bag and noticed that he had been given Konica film rather than Kodak. He went back to the store and explained the error. The clerk said, "I thought you wanted 36 exposures and that only comes in Konica." Peter was quite sure that Amy stressed that she wanted Kodak film, and so borrowed the phone to call her. She confirmed that she wanted Kodak film and that 24 exposures was OK. Peter passed on the details to the sales clerk, and asked for an exchange and a refund. The sales clerk exchanged the brand of film but realized that she didn't know how to do a refund on a credit card, since she was a new employee being trained. She apologized and explained that the senior clerk would be back very shortly, and asked Peter if he could return later. Peter was annoyed, but since he still had other errands to run in nearby stores, he agreed to come back in about 15 minutes.

When he returned, the senior clerk was back, and she was expecting him. She took the opportunity to "walk the trainee through the process" of doing the refund. Peter signed the slip they passed to him, picked up the two rolls of film and left.

Now that he was back home from running the errands, Peter took another look at all the credit card slips he had accumulated in buying the film. It was at this point that he realized that, rather than having been refunded the difference in price between two rolls of Kodak film and Konica film, he had been *charged* the difference in price! "#@$%@!!!!" he said again and again.

QUESTIONS

1. What were the underlying causes of the chain of events?
2. What could the clerk have done differently to prevent the chain of events?
3. What should the sales clerk do at this point?
4. How can the store owner prevent these kinds of situations from occurring?

FAMILY STOVE PURCHASE

Gerald Smith, age 55, was filling out his June sales report for the manager of the Household Appliances department of the large modern department store where he was employed. This report was farther off the sales forecast (8 percent) than any he had submitted over the last 20 years, although he had to admit that he had been 3 percent and 5 percent below target for the month of June for the previous two years. June sales were important because, in that month, nearly half of the store's major-appliance sales were made.

If only the couples whose business cards he now thumbed through had listened to him or had come back when they were not in such a hurry, he would have met his sales objective. One of those couples was Richard Barrett and Lise Marchand. They were shopping for a stove for their new home in central Ottawa. Gerald had applied his routine sales approach, but to no avail. This couple had so many questions about the exact time of delivery and the availability of the models—they had heard that there was a major reorganization going on in the appliance industry—that he did not have much opportunity to interject with his sales information. In fact, when he did get a chance to say anything, he was usually treated with indifference. The wife, for example, seemed bored and uninterested in how the design of the latest model of the General Electric stove allowed for easier cleaning, although she did seem interested in the fast-heating stove-top elements. She also interrupted Gerald repeatedly while he was discussing financial options with her husband. Mr. Barrett did not seem to mind at all, although Gerald found that nasty habit of interrupting very irritating.

Mrs., or Ms. (as she insisted), Marchand should behave more like Nancy, Martin Stewart's wife, Gerald thought. Nancy was excited about the new GE stove. None of the other stores she had shopped in had received this latest GE model. Fortunately, he was able to arrange a discount on a floor model that had a two-inch scratch on it when it was delivered to the store. Mr. Stewart then promptly arranged the financing, and within 45 minutes they were off to buy some party favours for the birthday party Nancy was hosting for their two-year-old son the next morning.

Gerald was glad that the majority of the customers were like the Stewarts. They made his job rewarding. It was just that those "other couples" seem to be ruining his day more and more frequently. How could he deal with them more effectively?

QUESTIONS

1. Why does Gerald seem to be successful in selling furniture to people like Nancy and Martin, but not to Robert and Lise?

2. How has family buying behaviour changed? Why has it changed?

3. Contrast the decision criteria and shopping habits of at-home-wife families and dual–career families.

4. What are the implications of the changes in family structure for marketers of household products and services?

THE SUMMER PROJECT

Kate Kimery and Earlene Kenderdine were third-year students in the College of Business Administration. For the past two summers both had returned to their home towns, where Katie worked as an accounting clerk in a large consulting firm and Earlene was employed as a veterinary technician at a local animal hospital. This summer, however, both women decided to remain on campus and look for jobs in the community that would provide them with more of an opportunity to apply the skills they had acquired thus far in their degree program.

After a frustrating month of job searching, unsuccessful interviews and unappealing offers, Katie and Earlene decided to take more of a proactive approach in securing summer employment. Both women hoped one day to run their own businesses. Katie pointed out that this summer might just be the opportune time to test their entrepreneurial prowess.

Over the next week both Katie and Earlene discussed a multitude of business ideas and how these ideas related to their individual strengths and weaknesses. In the end they decided that offering some kind of pet care service would take advantage of the strengths each had to offer: Earlene's knowledge of animals and customer service, and Katie's knowledge of the financial side of business. Thus was born the "U-Travel, WE Sit—U Sit, WE Walk" animal sitting and exercise service. The partners agreed that the pet-sitting service would take place in the pet's home, either on a live-in or frequent visit basis. The pet-sitting service would include the exercise program. The walking service would include two walks per day, each 20 minutes in duration. The partners agreed that, depending on size, more than one pet could be walked at once. Owners with pets requiring solitary walking services (due to age or behaviour problems) would be charged a premium to compensate for potential lost revenue.

CASES • 607

The next step for the two entrepreneurs was to define a time frame for operation, as well as to identify the financial goals they wanted their venture to meet. They decided that they would run their business from mid-May (the end of exams) until mid-September (the start of classes). They believed that this time frame included the most common summer vacation period. If the venture was successful, the women would consider running the business year-round. Based on their earnings over previous summers (*Exhibit 4-1*) and anticipated tuition hikes, the partners decided that they would each have to clear $4500 to meet their expenses in the upcoming academic year.

EXHIBIT 4–1 • Average earnings over previous summers

	Katie	Earlene
Hourly wage	$ 8.00	$ 7.50
Hours/week	35	40
Weeks worked	12	13
Total gross income	$3360	$3900

QUESTIONS

1. Is there demand for this type of business in your area?
2. What competition would this venture face in your area?
3. How should this venture be promoted, and what are the costs involved?
4. What are the other costs and potential revenues associated with this venture?
5. What pricing structure should be used?
6. Is this a viable venture for your area?

© 1997, Shelley M. Rinehart and Kevin T. Berry, University of New Brunswick in Saint John.

Appendix I

SOURCES OF SECONDARY CONSUMER DATA

Many organizations in the government and private sector collect information on consumer buying patterns.

A selected list of other secondary data sources and indexes that are particularly useful to consumer researchers follows. Many of these sources are available in the reference section of your library.

Commercial Sources

- *ABI/Inform Ondisc.* Ann Arbor, MI: University Microfilms International. These are abstracts (on compact disc) of articles from business journals.

- *Aging America: Trends and Projections.* Washington, DC, Government Printing Office: US Senate Special Committee on Aging and the American Association of Retired Persons. This gives data on demographic characteristics and growth projections on the elderly over the next 30 years.

- *American Marketing Association International Directory & Marketing Services Guide.* Chicago: American Marketing Association. This complete directory of AMA members includes both individual and corporate listings and a guide to marketing research firms, by area of specialization (published annually).

- *Angus Reid Group Inc.* Many syndicated studies are available for purchase. The cost of the surveys depends on their age. See www.angusreid.com.

- *BAR/LNA Multi-Media Service.* New York: Leading National Advertisers. This is a listing of advertising expenditures for media and specific brands (updated quarterly).

- *Business Information Sources.* Berkeley: University of California Press. Listed are sources of information about market research and statistical data.

- *Business Periodicals Index.* New York: H. W. Wilson Company. This is an index of business periodicals (updated monthly).

- *Communication Abstracts.* Beverly Hills, CA: Sage Publications, Inc. This is an index of articles and books on topics related to advertising and marketing (published quarterly).

- *Directory of Online Databases.* Santa Monica, CA: Cuadra Associates, Inc. The directory lists databases that are accessible by computer.

- *Dissertation Abstracts International.* Ann Arbor, MI: University of Microfilms International. This is an index of doctoral dissertations, including relevant studies in the Humanities and Social Sciences section, from major universities (updated monthly).

- *Encyclopedia of Information Systems and Services.* Detroit: Gale Research Company. The encyclopedia is a source of information about producers of various databases.

- *Financial Post Canadian Markets.* Toronto: Financial Post Corporation services. Contains forecasts for consumer spending along with economic and demographic information.

- *FINDEX: The Directory of Market Research Reports, Studies, and Surveys.* Bethesda, MD: Cambridge Information Group. This international guide to reports is produced by research companies.

- *Guide to Consumer Markets.* New York: The Conference Board. Data on consumer spending and income is published (annually) in this guide.

- *Print Measurement Bureau Production Profile Guide.* This is product data in a two-year database from a sample of over 20 000 respondents (1-800.PMB.0899)

- *Social Sciences Citation Index*. Philadelphia: Institute for Scientific Information. This is an index of articles in social science periodicals (updated three times a year).
- *Standard Directory of Advertisers*. Wilmette, IL: National Register Publishing Company. This directory is a guide to companies whose advertising spending exceeds $75 000 (US) and includes such information as their agencies, types of media used and specific products advertised.

Academic, Industry and Non-profit Sources

Statistics Canada
R.H. Coats Building
Tunney's Pasture,
Ottawa, Ontario K1A OT6
(613) 951-7277

Center for Mature Consumer Studies
College of Business Administration
Georgia State University
University Plaza
Atlanta, GA 30303
(404) 651-4177

The Conference Board
Consumer Research Center
845 Third Avenue
New York, NY 10022
(212) 759-0900

Marketing Science Institute
1000 Massachusetts Avenue
Cambridge, MA 02138-5396
(617) 491-2060

International Sources

The Roper Center for Public Opinion Research
P.O. Box 440
Storrs, CT 06268
(203) 486-4440

Center for International Research
U.S. Bureau of the Census
Washington, DC 20233
(301) 763-4014

Population Institute
East-West Center
1777 East-West Road
Honolulu, HI 96848
(808) 944-7450

European Society for Opinion and Marketing Research (ESOMAR)
Central Secretariat
J.J. Viottastraat 29
1071 JP Amsterdam
Netherlands
31-20-664.21.41

Euromonitor
87-88 Turnmill Street
London ECIM 5QU
England
0171-251-8024

The European Community
2100 M Street, NW
Suite 707
Washington, DC 20037
(202) 862-9500

Latin American Demographic Centre (CELADE)
Casilla 91
Santiago, Chile
011-56-2-485051

The Organization for Economic Cooperation and Development
2001 L Street, NW
Suite 700
Washington, DC 20036-4905

Population Reference Bureau, Inc.
1875 Connecticut Avenue, NW
Suite 520
Washington, DC 20009
(212) 483-1100

United Nations
Public Inquiries Unit
Public Services Section
Department of Public Information
Room GA-057
New York, NY 10017

The World Bank
1818 H Street, NW
Washington, DC 20433
(202) 473-2943

Major Web Sites

- *www.statcan.ca*
  — a comprehensive list of data available from Statistics Canada
- *www.findsvp.com*
  — this commercial service performs regular industry analyses, and provides one-page industry profile summaries online
- *www.nua.ie/surveys*
  — summaries of surveys about the Internet
- *www.fuld.com*
  — a competitive intelligence service with corporate information online
- *scout.cs.wisc.edu/scout/report/bus-econ/current/index.html*
  — a biweekly summary of new information available on the web

- *www.amic.com*
  — advertising media Internet centre
  — information about Internet commerce
  — a link to the Advertising Research Foundation
  — a link to Georgia Tech Web-user survey
  — plus many more links
- *www.acnielsen.ca*
- *www.kpmg.ca*
- *www.angusreid.com/index.html*
  — These are the Web sites for research firms that sell summaries of reports on various topics.

Appendix II

CAREERS IN CONSUMER RESEARCH

An understanding of consumers is of course essential in virtually every aspect of marketing. To prepare for a career in a consumer-related field, consider getting involved in relevant research that one of your professors may be doing. In addition to your Consumer Behaviour course, be sure to take as many courses as possible in other aspects of marketing. Also, try to achieve proficiency in statistics and computer skills. Courses in the social sciences, particularly psychology and sociology, are also helpful.

Career Paths

The following list identifies aspects of marketing where knowledge of consumer behaviour is particularly valuable.

- *Marketing research.* Researchers define problems and collect information needed to resolve them. They typically design projects, analyze data, present findings and make recommendations to management. Researchers may be employed by corporations that maintain their own market research staffs, or they may work for independent market research firms, trade organizations, advertising agencies, the government or non-profit organizations.
- *Brand management.* Managers direct marketing efforts for a specific product or line of products. They oversee all aspects of product strategy, including research, packaging, sales, promotion and forecasting.
- *Customer affairs.* A customer affairs representative acts as a liaison between the firm and its customers. He or she handles complaints and may act as an advocate for the customer within the company.
- *International marketing.* As firms globalize their operations they need managers who understand the importance of cultural differences and who can adapt strategies to foreign markets.
- *Advertising copywriters.* Copywriters translate a brand's positioning strategy into concrete form by creating words and visual images that convey this imagery. They need to understand the target market in order to employ imagery that will create the desired response.
- *Advertising account executives.* An account executive supervises the development of a marketing plan and makes sure that the agency's clients understand and are happy with the plan. This job requires knowledge about all aspects of marketing, including an understanding of target markets.
- *Retail managers and merchandisers.* A department or store manager must make decisions about such factors as the store's sales force and how merchandise is displayed in the store. He or she must understand the factors that add to or subtract from the quality of the customer's experience while in the store.
- *Retail buyers.* A buyer purchases merchandise for a store. A good buyer is always "tuned in" to upcoming trends and fashions and is sensitive to the wants and needs of the store's clientele.
- *Public relations.* A public relations specialist is responsible for maintaining positive public awareness of the firm and minimizing negative reactions to company activities. Knowledge of how people's perceptions are influenced by the media is integral to this job.

The Industry Route

Many entry-level jobs are available to a competent person with a bachelor's degree (though in some fields it is increasingly difficult to get hired without at least a master's degree). A typical starting position for a university graduate in a marketing research firm, for example, would be as an assistant project manager. This person assists in the design and administration of studies and ensures that they are enacted within the prescribed budget. The beginner may also be assigned to supervise field operations, overseeing the actual collection of data and perhaps coding and analyzing it.

Over time the person would move up to a supervisory position with increasing responsibility. Eventually the person might attain the position of vice president of marketing research in a company, where he or she would be responsible for the entire company's marketing research efforts and be part of senior management. Chances of moving up tend to improve greatly if the individual received advanced training in statistics, experimental design and other aspects of consumer psychology.

The Academic Route

Another alternative is to consider training to become a scholar in the field of consumer behaviour. Many major business schools offer doctoral programs in marketing, where it is possible to specialize in consumer behaviour research. In addition, some psychology departments offer doctoral programs in consumer psychology. The typical doctoral program involves from four to seven years of intensive study, where the student is trained in both theoretical and technical aspects of consumer research. Many doctoral students in business have already earned an MBA, though this is not always the case.

Most consumer behaviour PhDs who did not obtain their degrees in marketing were trained in psychology. Other possible fields of study—as the discipline's perspective continues to widen—include sociology, anthropology, economics, history, English, human ecology and others.

These individuals may take faculty positions in a business school, where they conduct research that is published in such academic journals as the Journal of Consumer Research. They may also work as consultants to corporations, advertising agencies, and the government. In addition, those with PhDs are in demand in full-time non-academic positions, such as in consulting firms and "think-tanks" or in advertising agencies, manufacturing companies, trade groups (e.g., the Wool Bureau or the Conference Board), or government agencies (e.g., Statistics Canada).

For further insight on these possibilities, consider asking your professor about his or her educational background and research activities.

Selected Bibliography

The following publications and articles provide information on employment and career opportunities in marketing.

Advertising Career Directory: 1987. New York: Career Publishing, 1986.

American Marketing Association. *The Employment Kit: Your Career Advantage.* Chicago: American Marketing Association, 1992.

American Marketing Association International Directory & Marketing Services Guide. Chicago: American Marketing Association (published annually).

Barron's Guide to Graduate Business Schools, 6th ed. New York: Barron's Educational Series, Inc., 1989.

"Career Opportunities in Marketing Research." *Marketing Review* (October 1990).

Fox, Marica R. *Put Your Degree to Work: The New Professional's Guide to Career Planning and Job Hunting*, 2nd ed. New York: W.W. Norton, 1988.

Fry, Ronald W., ed. *Marketing & Sales Career Directory*, 3rd ed. Hawthorne, NJ: The Career Press, 1990.

Maresca, Carmela C. *Careers in Marketing: A Woman's Guide.* Englewood Cliffs, NJ: Prentice-Hall, 1983.

Glossary

Absolute threshold the minimum amount of stimulation that can be detected on a sensory channel (57)

Accommodative purchase decision the process using bargaining, coercion, compromise and the wielding of power to achieve agreement among a group whose members have different preferences or priorities (402)

Acculturation the process of learning the beliefs and behaviours endorsed by another culture (131)

Acculturation agents friends, family, local businesses and other reference groups that facilitate the learning of cultural norms (481)

Activation models of memory approaches to memory stressing different levels of processing that occur and activate some aspects of memory rather than others, depending upon the nature of the processing task (95)

Actual self a person's realistic appraisal of his or her qualities (146)

Adaptation the process that occurs when a sensation becomes so familiar that it is no longer the focus of attention (63)

Affect the way a consumer feels about an attitude object (219)

Affinitization process where groups organize around special interests (200)

Affinity marketing a strategy that allows a consumer to emphasize his or her identification with some organization, as, for example, when organizations issue credit cards with their names on them (361)

Age cohort a group of consumers of the same approximate age who have undergone similar experiences (500)

Agentic goals goals that favour the advancement of the individual (153)

AIOs (Activities, Interests, and Opinions) the psychographic variables used by researchers in grouping consumers (192)

Androgyny the possession of both masculine and feminine traits (155)

Animism the attribution of conscious life to inanimate objects (185)

Anticonsumption the actions taken by consumers that involve the deliberate defacement or mutilation of products (32)

Archetype a universally shared idea or behaviour pattern, central to Jung's conception of personality; archetypes involve themes, such as birth, death, or the devil, that appear frequently in myths, stories, and dreams (182)

Art product a creation viewed primarily as an object of aesthetic contemplation without any functional value (554)

Atmospherics the use of space and physical features in store design to evoke certain effects in buyers (335)

Attitude a lasting, general evaluation of people (including oneself), objects or issues (217)

Attitude object (A_o) anything towards which one has an attitude (217)

Attitude towards the act of buying (A_{act}) the perceived consequences of a purchase (235)

Attitude towards the advertisement (A_{ad}) a predisposition to respond favorably or unfavorably to a particular advertising stimulus during a particular exposure occasion (224)

Autocratic decisions those purchase decisions that are made almost exclusively by one or the other spouse (405)

Back-translation to ensure accurate translation of research materials or advertising messages, a process whereby a translated message is again translated back into its original language to verify its correctness (580)

Balance theory a theory that considers relations among elements a person might perceive as belonging together, and people's tendency to change relations among elements in order to make them consistent or "balanced" (229)

Behaviour a consumer's actions with regard to an attitude object (219)

Behavioural economics the study of the behavioural determinants of economic decisions (430)

Behavioural influence perspective the view that consumer decisions are learned responses to environmental cues (287)

Behavioural learning theories the perspectives on learning that assume that learning takes place as the result of responses to external events (78)

Binary opposition a defining structural characteristic of many myths, where two opposing ends of some dimension are represented (e.g., good versus evil, nature versus technology) (531)

Body cathexis a person's feelings about aspects of his or her body (160)

Body image a consumer's subjective evaluation of his or her physical self (160)

Boomerang kids grown children who return to their parents' home to live (398)

Brand equity a brand that has strong positive associations in a consumer's memory and commands a lot of loyalty as a result (81, 184)

Brand loyalty a pattern of repeat product purchases, accompanied by an underlying positive attitude toward the brand (309)

Business ethics the rules of conduct that guide actions in the marketplace; the standards against which most people in a culture judge what is right or wrong (24)

Classic a fashion with an extremely long acceptance cycle (571)

Classical conditioning the learning that occurs when a stimulus eliciting a response is paired with another stimulus that initially does not elicit a response on its own but will cause a similar response over time because of its association with the first stimulus (78)

Cognition the beliefs a consumer has about an attitude object (219)

Cognitive development the ability to comprehend concepts of increasing complexity as a person ages (415)

Cognitive learning theory the perspectives on learning that assume that learning takes place as a result of internal mental processes; people actively use information from the world around them to master their environment and solve problems (88)

Cognitive structure the set of factual knowledge, or beliefs about a product, and the way these beliefs are organized (300)

Collective selection the process by which certain symbolic alternatives tend to be jointly chosen over others by members of a society (567)

Collectivist culture a society that encourages people to subordinate their personal goals to those of a stable in-group; values such as self-discipline and group accomplishment are stressed (529)

Communal goals goals that favour the well-being of the group or community as a whole (153)

Communications model a framework specifying that a number of elements are necessary for communication to be achieved, including a source, message, medium, receivers and feedback (249)

Comparative influence the process whereby a reference group influences decisions about specific brands or activities (359)

Compatibility a prerequisite for a product's adoption, in which the product should fit with consumers' lifestyles (370)

Compensatory decision rules a set of rules that allow information about attributes of competing products to be averaged in some way; poor standing on one attribute can potentially be offset by good standing on another (313)

Compulsive consumption the process of repetitive, often excessive, shopping used to relieve tension, anxiety, depression, or boredom (30)

Conformity refers to a change in beliefs or actions as a reaction to real or imagined group pressure (366)

Consensual purchase decision a decision in which the group agrees on the desired purchase and differs only in terms of how it will be achieved (402)

Conspicuous consumption the purchase and prominent display of luxury goods to provide evidence of a consumer's ability to afford them (451)

Consumer acculturation the process of movement and adaptation to one country's cultural environment by a person from another country (479)

Consumer addiction the physiological and/or psychological dependency on products or services (30)

Consumer behaviour the processes involved when individuals or groups select, purchase, use or dispose of products, services, ideas or experiences to satisfy needs and desires (8)

Consumer confidence the state of mind of consumers relative to their optimism or pessimism about economic conditions; people tend to make more discretionary purchases when their confidence in the economy is high (431)

Consumer satisfaction or dissatisfaction (CS/D) the overall attitude a person has about a product after it has been purchased (340)

Consumer socialization the process by which people acquire skills that enable them to function in the marketplace (411)

Continuous innovation a product change or new product that requires relatively little adaptation by the adopter (563)

Conventions norms regarding the conduct of everyday life (530)

Country of origin the country in which a consumer good was produced (488)

Craft product a creation valued because of the beauty with which it performs some function; this type of product tends to follow a formula that permits rapid production, and it is easier to understand than an art product (554)

Creolization the process whereby foreign customs are integrated into a local culture, producing a blend of foreign and local practices (583)

Cultivation hypothesis is a perspective emphasizing media's ability to distort consumers' perceptions of reality (560)

Cultural categories the grouping of ideas and values that reflect the basic ways members of a society characterize the world (566)

Cultural formula a sequence of media events where certain roles and props tend to occur consistently (556)

Cultural gatekeepers individuals who are responsible for determining the types of messages and symbolism to which members of mass culture are exposed (554)

Cultural resistance the process where subcultures of consumers who are alienated from mainstream society single out objects that represent the values of the larger group and modify them as an act of rebellion or self-expression (32)

Cultural selection the process where some alternatives are selected over others by cultural gatekeepers (552)

Culture the values, ethics, rituals, traditions, material objects and services produced or valued by the members of a society (535)

Culture jamming the defacement or alteration of advertising materials as a form of political expression (32)

Culture production system (CPS) the set of individuals and organizations responsible for creating and marketing a cultural product (554)

Custom a norm that is derived from a traditional way of doing things (529)

Database marketing the process of creating a database of consumers and their purchases through tracking programs, and then customizing marketing appeals to suit these different customers (16)

Deethnicitization the process whereby a product formerly associated with a specific ethnic group is detached from its roots and marketed to other subcultures (467)

Decision polarization the process whereby individuals' choices tend to become more extreme (polarized), in either a conservative or risky direction, following group discussion of alternatives (369)

Demographics the observable measurements of a population's characteristics, such as birthrate, age distribution, income (11)

Dependent variables in causal research, the variables that are affected when the independent variables are manipulated (39)

Desacralization the process that occurs when a sacred item or symbol is removed from its special place, or is duplicated in mass quantities, and becomes profane as a result (543)

Differential threshold the ability of a sensory system to detect changes or differences among stimuli (57)

Diffusion of innovation the process whereby a new product, service or idea spreads through a population (561)

Discontinuous innovation a product change or new product that requires a significant amount of adaptation by the adopter (563)

Discretionary income the money available to a household over and above that required for a comfortable standard of living (430)

Drive the desire to satisfy a biological need in order to reduce physiological arousal (114)

Dynamically continuous innovation a product change or new product that requires a moderate amount of adaptation by the adopter (563)

Early Adopters people receptive to new styles because they are involved in the product category and place high value on being in fashion (562)

Ego the system that mediates between the id and superego (178)

Ego involvement the importance of a product to a consumer's self-concept (149)

Elaborated codes the ways of expressing and interpreting meanings that are more complex and depend on a more sophisticated worldview, which tend to be used by the middle and upper classes (444)

Elaboration likelihood model (ELM) the approach that one of two routes to persuasion (central versus peripheral) will be followed, depending upon the personal relevance of a message; the route taken determines the relative importance of message contents versus other characteristics, such as source attractiveness (272)

Emic perspective an approach to studying cultures that stresses the unique aspects of each culture (576)

Encoding the process in which information from short-term memory is entered into long-term memory in a recognizable form (91)

Enculturation the process of learning the beliefs and behaviours endorsed by one's native culture (131)

Erogenous zones areas of the body considered by members of a culture to be foci of sexual attractiveness (567)

Ethnic subculture a self-perpetuating group of consumers held together by common cultural ties (465)

Ethos a set of moral, aesthetic and evaluative principles (529)

Etic perspective an approach to studying cultures that stresses commonalities across cultures (575)

Evaluative criteria the dimensions used by consumers to compare competing product alternatives (303)

Event marketing a promotional technique where an organization creates a promotion, such as a volleyball tournament, that attracts target consumers to a central location, rather than trying to reach them where they live or work (509)

Evoked set those products already in memory plus those prominent in the retail environment that are actively considered during a consumer's choice process (95, 299)

Exchange the process whereby two or more organizations or people give and receive something of value (9)

Exchange theory the perspective that every interaction involves an exchange of value (339)

Expectancy disconfirmation model the perspective that consumers form beliefs about product performance based upon prior experience with the product and/or communications about the product that imply a certain level of quality; their actual satisfaction depends on the degree to which performance is consistent with these expectations (342)

Experiential perspective an approach stressing the gestalt, or totality, of the product or service experience, focusing on consumers' affective responses in the marketplace (287)

Exposure an initial stage of perception where some sensations come within range of consumers' sensory receptors (57)

Extended family traditional family structure where several generations live together (393)

Extended problem solving an elaborate decision-making process, often initiated by a motive that is fairly central to the self-concept and accompanied by perceived risk; the consumer tries to collect as much information as possible, and carefully weighs product alternatives (287)

Extended self the definition of self created by the external objects with which one surrounds oneself (152)

Extinction the process whereby a learned connection between a stimulus and response is eroded so that the response is no longer reinforced (79)

Fad a very short-lived fashion (568)

Family financial officer (FFO) the individual in the family who is in charge of making financial decisions (405)

Family household a housing unit containing at least one family (a husband and a wife, married or living common law, or lone-parent of any marital status with or without children who have never married living at home) (393)

Family life cycle (FLC) a classification scheme that segments consumers in terms of changes in income and family composition and the changes in demands placed upon this income (400)

Fantasy a self-induced shift in consciousness, often focusing on some unattainable or improbable goal; sometimes fantasy is a way of compensating for a lack of external stimulation or for dissatisfaction with the actual self (146)

Fashion the process of social diffusion by which a new style is adopted by some group(s) of consumers (565)

Fashion acceptance cycle the diffusion process of a style through three stages: introduction, acceptance and regression (570)

Fashion life cycle the "career" or stages in the life of a fashion as it progresses from introduction to obsolescence (570)

Fashion system those people and organizations involved in creating symbolic meanings and transferring these meanings to cultural goods (565)

Fear appeal an attempt to change attitudes or behaviour through the use of threats or by the highlighting of negative consequences of noncompliance with the request (268)

Fertility rate a rate determined by the number of births per year per 1000 women of child-bearing age (396)

Figure-ground principle the gestalt principle whereby one part of a stimulus configuration dominates a situation while other aspects recede into the background (68)

Foot-in-the-door technique based on the observation that a consumer is more likely to comply with a request if he or she has first agreed to comply with a smaller request (228)

Frequency marketing a marketing technique that reinforces regular purchasers by giving them prizes with values that increase along with the amount purchased (87)

Functional theory of attitudes a pragmatic approach that focuses on how attitudes facilitate social behaviour; attitudes exist because they serve some function for the person (218)

Geodemography techniques that combine consumer demographic information with geographic consumption patterns to permit precise targeting of consumers with specific characteristics (196)

Gestalt psychology a school of thought that maintains people derive meaning from the totality of a set of stimuli, rather than from any individual stimulus (66)

Gift-giving ritual the events involved in the selection, presentation, acceptance and interpretation of a gift (535)

Goal a consumer's desired end state (114)

Habitual decision making the consumption choices that are made out of habit, without additional information search or deliberation among products (287)

Hedonic consumption the multisensory, fantasy, and emotional aspects of consumers' interactions with products (49)

Heuristics the mental rules of thumb that lead to a speedy decision (304)

Hierarchy of effects a fixed sequence of steps that occurs during attitude formation; this sequence varies depending upon such factors as the consumer's level of involvement with the attitude object (219)

Homeostasis the state of being where the body is in physiological balance; goal-oriented behaviour attempts to reduce or eliminate an unpleasant motivational state and return to a balanced one (115)

Id the system oriented toward immediate gratification (178)

Ideal of beauty a model, or exemplar, of appearance valued by a culture (160)

Ideal self a person's conception of how he or she would like to be (146)

Impulse buying a process that occurs when the consumer experiences a sudden urge to purchase an item that he or she cannot resist (336)

Individualist culture a society that encourages people to attach more importance to personal goals than to group goals; values such as personal enjoyment and freedom are stressed (529)

Inertia the process whereby purchase decisions are made out of habit because the consumer lacks the motivation to consider alternatives (125, 309)

Information search the process whereby a consumer searches for appropriate information to make a reasonable decision (290)

Informational social influence the conformity that occurs because the group's behaviour is taken as evidence about reality (367)

Innovation a product or style that is perceived as new by consumers (561)

Innovators people who are always on the lookout for novel developments and will be the first to try a new offering (562)

Instrumental conditioning the process by which the individual learns to perform behaviours that produce positive outcomes and to avoid those that yield negative outcomes (85)

Instrumental values those goals that are endorsed because they are needed to achieve desired end states, or terminal values (133)

Interference a process whereby additional learned information displaces the earlier information, resulting in memory loss for the item learned previously (100)

Interpretant the meaning derived from a symbol (21)

Interpretation the process whereby meanings are assigned to stimuli (65)

Interpretivism a research perspective that produces a "thick description" of consumers' subjective experiences and stresses the importance of the individual's social construction of reality (36)

Involvement a person's perceived relevance of an object based on inherent needs, values and interests (123)

JND (Just Noticeable Difference) the minimum change in a stimulus that can be detected by a perceiver (57)

Kin-network system the rituals intended to maintain ties among family members both immediate and extended (406)

Knowledge structures organized systems of concepts relating to brands, stores and other concepts (95)

Laddering a technique for uncovering consumers' associations between specific attributes and general consequences (134)

Lateral cycling a process where already-purchased objects are sold to others or exchanged for other items (347)

Latitudes of acceptance and rejection formed around an attitude standard; ideas that fall within a latitude will be favorably received, while those falling outside this zone will not (229)

Learning a relatively permanent change in a behaviour, caused by experience (77)

Lifestyle a set of shared values or tastes exhibited by a group of consumers, especially as these are reflected in consumption patterns (187)

Limited problem solving a problem-solving process in which consumers are not motivated to search for information or to evaluate each alternative rigorously; they instead use simple decision rules to arrive at a purchase decision (287)

Long-term memory the system that allows us to retain information for a long period of time (95)

Looking-glass self the process of imagining the reaction of others toward oneself (149)

Market beliefs the specific beliefs or decision rules pertaining to marketplace phenomena (305)

Market maven a person who often serves as a source of information about marketplace activities (379)

Mass customization a basic product or service is modified to meet the needs of an individual (208)

Match-up hypothesis the theory that the dominant characteristics of a product should match the dominant features of the communications source (255)

Materialism the importance consumers attach to worldly possessions (136)

Memory a process of acquiring information and storing it over time so that it will be available when needed (91)

Metaphor the use of an explicit comparison ("A" is "B") between a product and some other person, place or thing (270)

Monomyth a myth with basic characteristics that are found in many cultures (531)

More a norm with strong moral overtones (530)

Motivation an internal state that activates goal-oriented behaviour (114)

Motivational research a qualitative research approach, based on psychoanalytic interpretations, with a heavy emphasis on unconscious motives for consumption (180)

Multiattribute attitude models those models that assume that a consumer's attitude (evaluation) of an attitude object depends on the beliefs he or she has about several or many attributes of the object; the use of a multiattribute model implies that an attitude toward a product or brand can be predicted by identifying these specific beliefs and combining them to derive a measure of the consumer's overall attitude (231)

Myth a story containing symbolic elements that expresses the shared emotions and ideals of a culture (531)

Negative reinforcement the process whereby the environment weakens responses to stimuli so that inappropriate behaviour is avoided (85)

Noncompensatory decision rules a set of simple rules whereby a brand with a low standing on one attribute can make up for this position by being better on another attribute (312)

Normative influence the process in which a reference group helps to set and enforce fundamental standards of conduct (359)

Normative social influence the conformity that occurs when a person alters his or her behaviour to meet the expectations of a person or group (366)

Norms the informal rules that govern what is right or wrong (366, 529)

Nostalgia a bittersweet emotion where the past is viewed with sadness and longing; many "classic" products appeal to consumers' memories of their younger days (101)

Nuclear family a contemporary living arrangement composed of a married couple and their children (393)

Object in semiotic terms, the product that is the focus of a message (21)

Observability the visibility of a product (370)

Observational learning the process in which people learn by watching the actions of others and noting the reinforcements they receive for their behaviours (89)

Opinion leaders those people who are knowledgeable about products and who are frequently able to influence others' attitudes or behaviours with regard to a product category (376)

Paradigm a widely accepted view or model of phenomena being studied (36)

Parental yielding the process that occurs when a parental decision maker is influenced by a child's product request (411)

Parody display the deliberate avoidance of widely used status symbols, whereby the person seeks status by mocking it (454)

Perceived age how old a person feels rather than his or her true chronological age (514)

Perceived risk the belief that use of a product has potentially negative consequences, either physical or social (297)

Perception the process by which stimuli are selected, organized and interpreted (47)

Perceptual selectivity process in which people attend to only a small portion of the stimuli to which they are exposed (73)

Personality a person's unique psychological makeup, which consistently influences the way the person responds to his or her environment (177)

Persuasion an active attempt to change attitudes (248)

Pleasure principle the belief that behaviour is guided by the desire to maximize pleasure and avoid pain (178)

Point-of-purchase stimuli (POP) the promotional materials that are deployed in stores or other outlets to influence consumers' decisions at the time products are purchased (337)

Popular culture the music, movies, sports, books, celebrities and other forms of entertainment consumed by the mass market (19)

Positioning strategy the place a brand name occupies in the consumer's mind with regard to important attributes (such as functional features) and competitive offerings (69)

Positive reinforcement the process whereby rewards provided by the environment strengthen responses to stimuli (85)

Positivism a research perspective that relies on principles of the "scientific method" and assumes that a single reality exists; events in the world can be objectively measured; and the causes of behaviour can be identified, manipulated, and predicted (36)

Potlatch an Indian feast where the host shows off his wealth and gives extravagant presents to guests (452)

Priming process in which certain properties of a stimulus are more likely to evoke a schema than others (65)

Principle of closure the gestalt principle that consumers tend to perceive an incomplete picture as complete (67)

Principle of cognitive consistency the belief that consumers value harmony among their thoughts, feelings and behaviours and that they are motivated to maintain uniformity among these elements (227)

Principle of similarity the gestalt principle that describes how consumers tend to group objects that share similar physical characteristics (68)

Problem recognition the process that occurs whenever the consumer sees a significant difference between his or her current state of affairs and some desired or ideal state; this recognition initiates the decision-making process (289)

Product complementarity the view that products in different functional categories have symbolic meanings that are related to one another (189)

Product placement the process of obtaining exposure for a product by arranging for it to be inserted into a movie, television show or some other medium (558)

Profane consumption the process of consuming objects and events that are ordinary or of the everyday world (540)

Progressive learning model the perspective that people gradually learn a new culture as they increasingly come in contact with it; consumers assimilate into a new culture, mixing practices from their old and new environments to create a hybrid culture (480)

Psychographics the use of psychological, sociological, and anthropological factors to construct market segments (190)

Psychophysics the science that focuses on how the physical environment is integrated into the consumer's subjective experience (57)

Punishment the learning that occurs when a response is followed by unpleasant events (85)

Rational perspective a view of the consumer as a careful, analytical decision maker who tries to maximize utility in purchase decisions (286)

Reactance a "boomerang effect" that sometimes occurs when consumers are threatened with a loss of freedom of choice; they respond by doing the opposite of the behaviour advocated in a persuasive message (370)

Reality engineering the process whereby elements of popular culture are appropriated by marketers and become integrated into marketing strategies; examples of this phenomenon include infomercials and product placement (557)

Reference group an actual or imaginary individual or group that has a significant effect upon an individual's evaluations, aspirations or behaviour (358)

Relationship marketing the process of creating, maintaining and enhancing strong, value-laden relationships with customers (16)

Relative advantage the belief that a product's use will provide a benefit other products cannot offer (370)

Repositioning the process of changing the place a brand name occupies in the consumer's mind in order to make it more competitive with other brands or to change its image (70)

Resonance a literary device, frequently used in advertising, that uses a play on words (a double meaning) to communicate a product benefit (270)

Response bias a form of contamination in survey research where some factor, such as the desire to make a good impression on the experimenter, leads respondents to modify their true answers (104)

Restricted codes the ways of expressing and interpreting meanings that focus on the content of objects and tend to be used by the working class (444)

Retrieval the process whereby desired information is accessed from long-term memory (92)

Rites of passage sacred times marked by a change in social status (538)

Ritual a set of multiple, symbolic behaviours that occur in a fixed sequence and that tend to be repeated periodically (533)

Ritual artifacts items (consumer goods) used in the performance of rituals (534)

Role theory the perspective that much of consumer behaviour resembles actions in a play (8)

Sacralization a process that occurs when ordinary objects, events or people take on sacred meaning to a culture or to specific groups within a culture (543)

Sacred consumption the process of consuming objects and events that are set apart from normal life and treated with some degree of respect or awe (540)

Savings rate the amount of money saved for later use that is influenced

by consumers' pessimism or optimism about their personal circumstances (431)

Schema an organized collection of beliefs and feelings represented in a cognitive category (65, 97)

Self-concept the attitude a person holds toward him- or herself (144)

Self-image congruence models the approaches based on the prediction that products will be chosen when their attributes match some aspect of the self (151)

Self-perception theory an alternative explanation of dissonance effects; it assumes that people use observations of their own behaviour to infer their attitudes toward some object (228)

Semiotics a field of study that examines the correspondence between a sign and the meaning or meanings it conveys (21)

Sensation the immediate response of sensory receptors (eyes, ears, nose, mouth, fingers) to such basic stimuli as light, color, and sound (47)

Sensory memory the temporary storage of information received from the senses (94)

Sex-typed traits characteristics that are stereotypically associated with one sex or the other (154)

Shopping orientation a consumer's general attitudes and motivations regarding the act of shopping (332)

Short-term memory the system that allows us to retain information for a short period of time (94)

Shrinkage the loss of money or inventory due to shoplifting and/or employee theft (31)

Sign the sensory imagery that represents the intended meanings of the object (21)

Single-source data a compilation of information that includes different aspects of consumption and demographic data for a common consumer segment (198)

Sleeper effect the process whereby differences in attitude change between positive and negative sources seem to diminish over time (258)

Social class the overall rank of people in a society; people who are grouped within the same social class are approximately equal in terms of their social standing, occupations and lifestyles (432)

Social comparison theory the perspective that people compare their outcomes with others' as a way to increase the stability of their own self-evaluation, especially when physical evidence is unavailable (367)

Social judgment theory the perspective that people assimilate new information about attitude objects in light of what they already know or feel; the initial attitude acts as a frame of reference, and new information is categorized in terms of this standard (229)

Social mobility the movement of individuals from one social class to another (437)

Social power the capacity of one person to alter the actions or outcome of another (364)

Social stratification the process in a social system by which scarce and valuable resources are distributed unequally to status positions that become more or less permanently ranked in terms of the share of valuable resources each receives (435)

Sociometric methods the techniques for measuring group dynamics that involve the tracing of communication patterns in and among groups (381)

Source attractiveness refers to the source's perceived social value (254)

Source credibility a communications source's perceived expertise, objectivity or trustworthiness (253)

Status crystallization the extent to which different indicators of a person's status (income, ethnicity, occupation) are consistent with one another (441)

Status hierarchy a ranking of social desirability in terms of consumers' access to such resources as money, education and luxury goods (435)

Status symbols products that are purchased and displayed to signal membership in a desirable social class (451)

Stimulus discrimination the process that occurs when behaviour caused by two stimuli is different, as when consumers learn to differentiate a brand from its competitors (80)

Stimulus generalization the process that occurs when the behaviour caused by a reaction to one stimulus occurs in the presence of other, similar stimuli (80)

Storage the process that occurs when knowledge entered in long-term memory is integrated with what is already in memory and "warehoused" until needed (92)

Store image a store's "personality," composed of such attributes as location, merchandise suitability, and the knowledge and congeniality of the sales staff (334)

Subculture a group whose members share beliefs and common experiences that set them apart from other members of a culture (463)

Subliminal perception the processing of information presented below the level of the consumer's awareness (60)

Superego the system that internalizes society's rules and that works to prevent the id from seeking selfish gratification (178)

Surrogate consumer a professional who is retained to evaluate and/or make purchases on behalf of a consumer (379)

Symbolic innovation an innovation that communicates a new social meaning (563)

Symbolic interactionism a sociological approach stressing that relationships with other people play a large part in forming the self; people live in a symbolic environment, and the meaning attached to any situation or object is determined by a person's interpretation of these symbols (147)

Symbolic self-completion theory the perspective that people who have an incomplete self-definition in some context will compensate by acquiring symbols associated with a desired social identity (150)

Syncratic decisions those purchase decisions that are made jointly by both spouses (405)

Synoptic ideal a model of spousal decision making where the husband and wife take a common view and act as joint decision makers, assigning each other well-defined roles and making mutually beneficial decisions to maximize the couple's joint utility (410)

Taste cultures a group of consumers who share aesthetic and intellectual preferences (444)

Technological innovation an innovation that involves some functional change (563)

Terminal values end states desired by members of a culture (133)

Theory of cognitive dissonance the perspective that cognitive discomfort results from an individual holding logically inconsistent beliefs about an object or event. The consumer is motivated to reduce dissonance through changing his or her beliefs and evaluations about the object or event (117)

Theory of reasoned action an updated version of the Fishbein multiattitude theory that considers such factors as social pressure and A_{act} (the attitude towards the act of buying a product), rather than attitudes towards just the product itself (235)

Traits the identifiable characteristics that define a person (183)

Trickle-down theory of fashion the perspective that fashions spread as the result of status symbols associated with the upper classes "trickling down" to other social classes as these consumers try to emulate those with greater status (568)

20/80 rule a rule-of-thumb in volume segmentation, which says that about 20% of consumers in a product category (the heavy users) account for about 80% of sales (192)

Two-factor theory the perspective that two separate psychological processes are operating when a person is repeatedly exposed to an ad; repetition increases familiarity and thus reduces uncertainty about the product, but over time boredom increases with each exposure, and at some point the amount of boredom incurred begins to exceed the amount of uncertainty reduced, resulting in wear-out (262)

Uses and gratification theory the perspective that the consumer uses the media to meet more than strictly information needs (250)

Value an enduring belief that a specific mode of conduct is personally or socially preferable to an opposite mode of conduct (130)

Values and Lifestyles (VALS) a psychographic segmentation system used to categorize consumers into clusters, or "VALS Types" (194)

Wall media the use of posters and other forms of announcements to promote

products, services and events to hard-
to-reach populations (e.g., university
students) (509)

Want the particular form of consumption chosen to satisfy a need (116)

Weber's Law the principle that the stronger the initial stimulus, the greater its change must be for it to be noticed (58)

Word-of-mouth communication (WOM) the information transmitted by individual consumers on an informal basis (372)

Indexes

PRODUCT, SERVICE, CORPORATE, AND CELEBRITY INDEX

SUBJECT INDEX

decision rules, 288, 310, 313
   compensatory, 310-11, 313
   noncompensatory, 310-312
deep processing, 95
de-ethnicization, 467
demand
   primary, 289
   secondary, 289
demographics, 11
depth interviews, 180
desacralization, 543
determinant attributes, 303
differential threshold, 57
diffusion of innovation, 561
diffusion of responsibility, 369
directed learning, 293
discontinuous innovation, 563
discretionary income, 430
discrimination, stimulus, 80
   marketing applications of, 84
disjunctive rule, 312
disposer, in family decision
   making, 404
dissociative cue hypothesis, 258
distraction, 267
diversity, 468-72
door-in-the-face technique, 368
dosas, 581
"downshifting," 341
downward mobility, 437
drama, 270
dramaturgical perspective, 147
drive, 114
drive theory, 115
dual component model, 260
duration, adaptation and, 63
dynamically continuous
   innovation, 563

early adopters, 562
eating disorders, 165
ecology, culture and, 528
economic behaviour,430
economic time, 328
economics-of-information
   approach, 294
EDLP. *See* everyday low prices
ego, 178
elaborated codes, 444
elaboration, 125

elaboration likelihood model
   (ELM), 272
   persuasion and, 272
elaborative rehearsal, 95
Elders, 488
elimination-by-aspects rule, 312
embeds, 60
emic perspective, 576
emotional message appeals, 265
enacted norms, 529
encoding, 91
enculturation, 131
England, typology of consumers
   in, 198
environmentalism, as decision
   cue, 202
episodic memories, 93
erogenous zones, 567
ethnic stereotypes, 472-3
ethnic subculture, 465
ethnicity
   felt, 324
   marketing and, 14, 466-8
ethos, 529
etic perspective, 575
Eurobrands, 577
"Euroconsumer," 198
evaluative criteria, 303-4
event marketing, 509
everyday low prices (EDLP), 204
evoked set, 95, 299
exchange, 9
   economic, 535
   symbolic, 535
exchange theory, 339
exercise, consumer trends and,
   207
expectancy disconfirmation
   model, 342
expectancy theory, 115
experience, family decision
   making and, 406
experiencers, 194
experiential hierarchy of effects,
   221
experiential perspective, 287
expert power, 364-5
exposure, 57
extended family, 393
extended problem solving, 287

characteristics of, 287-8
extended self, 152
external memory, 92
external search, 291
extinction, 79
extroversion, 183

fabrics, tactile oppositions to, 55
facilitators, 241
fad(s), 202, 572
familiarity, recall and, 98
family
   defining, 392
   extended, 393
   head of, 397
   nuclear, 393
   segments, 408-9
   size of, 396
family branding, 82
family decision making, 392
   gender roles and, 405
family financial officer (FFO), 405
family household, 393
   growth and distribution of, 395
family level, extended self and,
   152
family lifecycle (FLC), 400
   effects on buying, 401
family structure
   alternate, 398-9
   effects on consumption, 399
   marketing and, 12
   measures of social class and,
   441
fanatic consumer, 113
fantasy, 146
fantasy appeals, 146
fashion, 565
   economic models, 568
   psychological models of, 567
   sociological models of, 568-9
fashion acceptance cycle, 570
fashion adoption, cycles of, 570-1
fashion life cycle, 570
fashion opinion leader, 377
fashion system, 565
fatherhood, 158
fattism, 164
fear, attitude change and, 268
fear appeals, 268